PASCAL

AN INTRODUCTION TO THE ART AND SCIENCE OF PROGRAMMING

THIRD EDITION

The Benjamin / Cummings Series in
Structured Programming

G. Booch
Software Engineering with Ada, Second Edition

G. Booch
Object-Oriented Design with Applications

G. Brookshear
Computer Science: An Overview, Third Edition

D. M. Etter
Structured FORTRAN 77 for Engineers and Scientists, Second Edition

D. M. Etter
Problem Solving in Pascal for Engineers and Scientists

C. Fischer and R. Leblanc
Crafting a Compiler with C

D. W. Gonzalez
Ada® Programmer's Handbook

D. W. Gonzalez
Ada® Programmer's Handbook and Language Reference Manual

P. Helman and R. Veroff
Intermediate Problem Solving and Data Structures

P. Helman and R. Veroff
Walls and Mirrors: Modula-2 Edition

J. Kempf
Fundamentals of Object-Oriented Programming

A. Kelley and I. Pohl
A Book on C, Programming in C, Second Edition

A. Kelley and I. Pohl
C by Dissection

I. Pohl
C++ for Pascal Programmers

I. Pohl
C++ for Programmers

W. J. Savitch
Pascal: An Introduction to the Art and Science of Programming, Third Edition

W. J. Savitch
Turbo Pascal 4.0/5.0/5.5

M. Sobell
A Practical Guide to the UNIX System, Second Edition

PASCAL

AN INTRODUCTION TO THE ART AND SCIENCE OF PROGRAMMING

THIRD EDITION

WALTER J. SAVITCH

UNIVERSITY OF CALIFORNIA, SAN DIEGO

THE BENJAMIN/CUMMINGS PUBLISHING COMPANY, INC.
Redwood City, California • Fort Collins, Colorado • Menlo Park, California
Reading, Massachusetts • New York Don Mills, Ontario • Workingham, U.K.
Amsterdam • Bonn • Sydney • Singapore • Tokyo • Madrid • San Juan

Sponsoring Editor: Alan R. Apt
Production Editor: Mary Shields
Copy Editor: Rebecca Pepper/Rene Lynch
Interior Design Modifications: Seventeenth Street Studios
Cover Design: Juan Vargas
Illustrations: Sally Shimizu
Composition: G&S Typesetters, Inc.

Acknowledgements:

Chapter 2, opening quotation from E. W. Dijkstra, *Notes on Structured Programming,* O. J. Dahl, E. W. Dijkstra, and C. A. R. Hoare. Academic Press (1972). Reprinted by permission of the author and publisher.

Chapter 7, ending quotation from F. P. Brooks, Jr., *The Mythical Man-Month, Essays on Software Engineering,* p. 116. Addison-Wesley Publishing Company (1975). Reprinted by permission of the publisher.

Chapter 11, ending quotation from Niklaus Wirth, *Algorithms + Data Structures = Programs,* title. Prentice-Hall (1976). Reprinted by permission of the publisher.

Chapter 14, opening quotation from John R. Ross, *Constraints on Variables in Syntax,* p.i., Ph.D. dissertation, Massachusetts Institute of Technology (1967). Reprinted by permission of the author.

Chapter 14, midchapter quotation from Jorge Luis Borges, "The Garden of Forking Paths," in Jorge Luis Borges, *Selected Stories and Other Writings,* p. 25. New Directions Publishing Company (1964). Reprinted by permission of the publisher.

Chapter 15, ending quotation from B. W. Kernighan and P. J. Plauger, *The Elements of Programming Style,* 2nd ed., p. 117. McGraw-Hill Book Co. (1978). Reprinted by permission of the publisher and Bell Laboratories.

UNIX is a trademark of AT&T Bell Laboratories.

Library of Congress Cataloging-in-Publication Data

Savitch, Walter J., 1943–
   Pascal, an introduction to the art and science of programming.

   Includes bibliographies and index.
   1. PASCAL (Computer program language)   2. Electronic
digital computers—Programming.   I. Title.
QA76.73.P2S28   1991   005.13′3   86-24474
ISBN 0-8053-7450-7

345678910 −DO− 95 94 93 92 91

The Benjamin/Cummings Publishing Company, Inc.
390 Bridge Parkway
Redwood City, California 94065

to morena

PREFACE

This book was designed for use in introductory computer science or programming classes that use the Pascal language. This edition uses standard Pascal. (There is a separate edition designed for Turbo Pascal users.) The book can be used for courses as short as one quarter or as long as one academic year. It includes a thorough introduction to problem solving and programming techniques as well as a complete description of standard Pascal. It assumes no knowledge of computers and no mathematics beyond high school algebra.

This is the sixth in a series of introductory textbooks I have written featuring the Pascal languages. Each of the books is an introduction to computer science and programming. Each new edition was written to accommodate the changing needs of its users, primarily changes in the Pascal language and newly developed methodologies for designing software. This edition was written, in large part, for the second reason. This new version provides a greater emphasis on abstraction techniques in particular and software engineering in general. An equally important reason for producing this latest edition was purely pedagogical. Like its predecessors, this edition assumes no prior programming experience. However, the beginning student of today is much more sophisticated than the corresponding student of a few years ago. Whether the student has programmed before or not, the beginning student now comes to the classroom with more computer sophistication than the student of a few years ago. This edition incorporates a new topic organization to accommodate this changed student population.

Thorough Coverage of Problem Solving Techniques

The text includes complete coverage of problem solving techniques and illustrates these techniques with numerous case studies showing the complete design process in detail from problem definition to final Pascal program.

Software Engineering

This edition includes expanded coverage of software engineering topics. A complete chapter on program design methodologies discusses the software life cycle and summarizes the software development techniques emphasized throughout the book. These include a strong emphasis on abstraction techniques such as procedural abstraction, data abstraction, algorithm abstraction, and abstract data types. Other topics include documentation techniques, pre- and postconditions, loop invariants, and data structuring techniques. More advanced algorithm and data structure topics include sorting and searching, hashing, numeric programming techniques, dynamic data structures, and trees.

Introduces the While Loop Before Procedures

This edition includes a brief, early introduction to the *while* loop and the *if-then-else* statement prior to the introduction of procedures. This was done to accommodate the changing needs of the students using the text. Instructors using the previous edition recently observed a dramatic change in the background of their students. Many students in their introductory programming classes already had some previous exposure to programming, and even those students with absolutely no computer programming experience had assimilated a sophisticated appreciation for algorithms from their day to day experiences in a world permeated with computers. As a result, all students already had some familiarity with the notion of a loop. It was simply impossible to keep the topic of loops out of class discussion until after the introduction of procedures. Students asked "How do you repeat a program action?" or saw their friends using loops and asked the more straightforward "Will you explain the while loop?" To accommodate this new sophistication and to capitalize on it, we decided to face the situation straight on and explain simple loops and branches as part of our quick introduction to "the minimal basics of Pascal." This introduction is brief, however. Procedures are still introduced as early as in previous editions. Moreover, the chapter on loops is complete, including a review of the material covered earlier. This book does not use a spiral approach to teaching Pascal and is essentially an early procedures book.

Early Introduction of Procedures

As with previous texts in this series, this book introduces procedures very early and presents a complete discussion of parameters as soon as procedures are introduced. Both value and variable parameters are introduced immediately after introducing the notion of a procedure.

It had been my experience in teaching introductory programming classes that students found parameters easier to understand when the topic was presented early. Moreover, they developed a better programming style as a result. Users of previous texts in this series have confirmed the results of that experiment. What was experimental in the first of these texts is now widely accepted as sound pedagogy.

Flexibility

The order in which topics can be covered is extremely flexible. The chapter on text files is divided into two parts to allow for two possibilities, either postponing the topic entirely until later in a course or briefly introducing them early and giving more detail later on. Most advanced topics—such as recursion, some software engineering topics, some numeric programming techniques, and a substantial amount on data structures including records, files, and pointers—are packaged into chapters that can be covered in almost any order. Alternatively, a subset of the chapters may be chosen to form a shorter course. To add even more flexibility, sections with optional topics are included throughout the book. The dependency chart at the front of this book shows the possible orders in which the chapters can be covered without losing continuity.

UNIX Appendixes

Appendixes on basic UNIX file manipulation, input/output redirection, and the vi editor are included at the end of the book. This eliminates the need for a separate UNIX manual for those classes that use the UNIX system.

Extensive Array Coverage

Two full chapters are dedicated to arrays. These chapters cover both one-dimensional and multidimensional arrays, with heavy emphasis on programming techniques such as reading data into arrays, manipulating partially filled arrays, and designing data structures using arrays. The array coverage is followed by a chapter with complete coverage of records. This permits covering records immediately after arrays (or later, if that is preferred).

Extensive Coverage of Recursion

An entire chapter is dedicated to recursion. Extensive use of figures and examples makes this difficult topic accessible to beginners. In addition, this edition also includes expanded coverage of more complicated recursive algorithms such as binary search and quicksort.

Thorough Coverage of Debugging and Programming Techniques

Thorough coverage of debugging and programming techniques is presented throughout the text. Boxed sections on common *Pitfalls* highlight important techniques in a compact easy-to-find and easy-to-digest way.

Self-Test and Summary Sections

Self-Test Exercises, with answers in the back of the book, are provided throughout the text. Each chapter contains a complete *Summary of Problem Solving and Program-*

ming Techniques as well as a complete *Summary of Pascal Constructs*. The Pascal summaries include templates and typical examples for quick and easy reference.

Support Material

INSTRUCTOR'S GUIDE
A complete chapter-by-chapter instructor's guide is available from the publisher.

SOFTWARE
All of the programs in this text are available in machine-readable form. Thus, it is possible to have all the programs available for students to run without having to type them in. Additional tutorial programs are included in the software support package.

COMPUTERIZED TEST BANK
Software for automatically generating tests corresponding to each chapter is also available to instructors.

Acknowledgments

I have received much help and encouragement from numerous individuals and groups while preparing this series of Pascal books. Much of the original edition was written while I was visiting at the University of Washington (Seattle) Computer Science Department. Later editions were worked on while I was visiting the Computer Science Department at the University of Cincinnati. The remainder of the work on these books was done in the Computer Science and Engineering Department at the University of California, San Diego (UCSD). I am grateful to these three institutions for providing facilities and a conducive environment for writing these books.

A number of individuals provided detailed critiques of this edition. Their comments played a critically important role in the general design of this edition as well as providing the feedback needed to polish the details of the book. I gratefully acknowledge their contribution. In alphabetical order they are Mohammad B. Dadfar, Chris Dovolis, Roger Ehrich, Robert M. Holloway, William Kraynek, Ronald L. Lancaster, E. M. Lether, Andrea Martin, James M. Ott, and Jo Ellen Perry.

A large number of other reviewers have contributed critiques and suggestions for previous Pascal books in this series. Their suggestions and comments have helped tremendously in shaping this latest edition. I gratefully acknowledge their invaluable help. In alphabetical order these individuals are Guy Almes, Stephen Andrilli, Bill Appelbe, Owen Astrachan, R. W. Barton, Philip Beckman, Beverly Bilshausen, Andrew Black, Jim Bunch, Baldwin van der Byl, Phillip Carrigan, Scott Cormode, Christine Coulter, Molly E. Daniel, Lieutenant Commander Paul Desilets, Mike Denisevich, John Donald, H. Edward Donley, Patrick Dymond, Klaus Eldridge, Eileen Entin, David R. Falconer, Allyn Fratkin, Capt. C. C. Gardner, Jim Gips, Chia Yung Han, Paul Hanna, Bill Hotard, Dale W. Isner, Brian Johnson, Richard Kaufmann, Ken Kellum, Alean Kirnak, Robert M. Knodel, J. Mailen Kootsey, Gregg

Kornfeld, Karl Krummel, N. Lehmkul, K. W. Loach, Moira Mahony, Michael Main, Keith Muller, Rayno Niemi, G. Ozsoyogui, Jerome Paul, J. F. Paris, James Payne, Gary Phillips, Colette Pirie, Howard Pyron, Vijay Rao, Major W. A. Richardson, Ned Rosen, Robert Rother, Arden Ruttan, Gary Sackett, Joe Sandmeyer, Robert Streett, George Stockman, Major Scott C. Teel, Rena Tobias, Martin Tompa, Dennis Volper, Joseph Waters, Larry Weber, Gregory Wetzel, Anne Wilson, Chin Wu, and Guy Zimmerman.

I extend a special thanks to the many students in my programming classes who tested and helped correct preliminary versions of all editions in this series. I also thank all the individuals at Benjamin/Cummings who organized the reviewing and production of this book. In particular, Jean Foltz, Mark McCormick, Mary Shields, and especially my editor Alan Apt contributed much to the finished product. Finally, I offer a special thanks to Virginia for helping with the day-to-day preparation of the manuscript, and even more importantly for cheerfully putting up with me while I worked to meet the deadlines.

W. J. S.

Dependency Chart of Chapters and Location of Key
Pascal Constructs

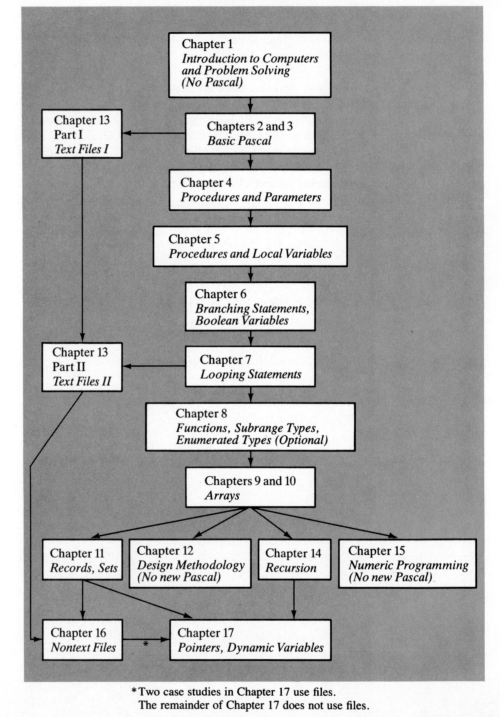

Chapter 1
*Introduction to Computers
and Problem Solving
(No Pascal)*

Chapter 13
Part I
Text Files I

Chapters 2 and 3
Basic Pascal

Chapter 4
Procedures and Parameters

Chapter 5
Procedures and Local Variables

Chapter 6
*Branching Statements,
Boolean Variables*

Chapter 13
Part II
Text Files II

Chapter 7
Looping Statements

Chapter 8
*Functions, Subrange Types,
Enumerated Types (Optional)*

Chapters 9 and 10
Arrays

Chapter 11
Records, Sets

Chapter 12
*Design Methodology
(No new Pascal)*

Chapter 14
Recursion

Chapter 15
*Numeric Programming
(No new Pascal)*

Chapter 16
Nontext Files

Chapter 17
Pointers, Dynamic Variables

*Two case studies in Chapter 17 use files.
The remainder of Chapter 17 does not use files.

BRIEF CONTENTS

CONTENTS

CHAPTER THREE

More Pascal and Programming Techniques

61

CHAPTER FOUR

Designing Procedures for Subtasks   107

CHAPTER FIVE

Procedures for Modular Design   145

CHAPTER EIGHT

Designing Functions and Data Types   261

CHAPTER NINE

Arrays for Problem Solving   309

CHAPTER TEN

Complex Array Structures   349

CHAPTER ELEVEN

Records and Other Data Structures   403

CHAPTER TWELVE

Program Design Methodology 457

CHAPTER THIRTEEN

Text Files and Secondary Storage 483

CHAPTER SEVENTEEN

Dynamic Data Structures   615

A P P E N D I X   O N E
A P P E N D I X   T W O
A P P E N D I X   T H R E E
A P P E N D I X   F O U R
A P P E N D I X   F I V E
A P P E N D I X   S I X
A P P E N D I X   S E V E N
A P P E N D I X   E I G H T
A P P E N D I X   N I N E
A P P E N D I X   T E N

CHAPTER 1

INTRODUCTION TO COMPUTERS AND PROBLEM SOLVING

*The arithmetical machine produces effects which
approach nearer to thought than all the actions of animals.
But it does nothing which would enable us
to attribute will to it, as to the animals.*

BLAISE PASCAL

Chapter Contents

In this chapter we outline some of the basic concepts common to all computer systems and all programming languages. The theme here and throughout this book is that there is a methodology of effective programming that is relatively independent of the particular programming language used or the particular computer used. In fact, this chapter presents no details of the Pascal language.

What a Computer Is

In less than one human lifetime, computers have evolved from a scientific curiosity to an indispensible tool in virtually all areas of our lives. They handle our financial transactions, control manufacturing processes, keep track of airline reservations, forecast weather, control space probes—the list goes on seemingly without end. But just what are these things called *computers?*

The basic nature of computers is surprisingly simple. Computers are machines that perform very simple tasks according to specific instructions. Their ability to perform so many simple tasks at such great speed and with such a high degree of accuracy is what makes computers so useful. One can think of a computer as a clerk who does nothing all day but sit and perform trivial, routine tasks according to given sets of instructions, and who does so with perfect accuracy, infinite patience, a flawless memory, and unimaginable speed.

The Modern Digital Computer

A set of instructions for a computer to follow is called a *program*. The collection of programs used by a computer is referred to as the *software* for that computer. The physical machines that make up a computer installation are referred to as *hardware*. In this book we are concerned almost exclusively with software, but a brief overview of how the hardware is organized will be useful.

software/ hardware

Most computers are organized as shown in Figure 1.1. They can be thought of as having four main components: the input device(s), the output device(s), the central processing unit (CPU), and the memory.

An *input device* is any device that allows a person to communicate information to the computer. For readers of this book, the input device is likely to be a keyboard rather like a typewriter keyboard, but it could instead be some other type of device, or it could consist of a variety of devices.

input keyboard

An *output device* performs the opposite task. It allows the computer to communicate information to the user. One of the most common output devices is a *display screen* that resembles a television screen. This display screen is often referred to as a *CRT screen* or *monitor*. (The initials CRT stand for "cathode ray tube".) Often there is more than one output device. For example, in addition to the display screen there may be a typewriter or typewriterlike device to produce printed output. These devices for producing printed output are called, appropriately enough, *printers*. The keyboard and display screen are frequently thought of as a single unit called a *video display terminal* or simply a *terminal*.

output display screen

In order to store input and to have the equivalent of scratch paper for performing calculations, computers are provided with *memory*. The memory is very simple. It consists of a long list of numbered locations called *words* or, more descriptively, *memory locations*. The number of memory locations varies from one computer to another, ranging from a few thousand to many millions. In fact, memory may be added to a computer almost without limit, although once the memory size exceeds certain thresholds, the computer system must be made a bit more sophisticated. Each memory loca-

memory

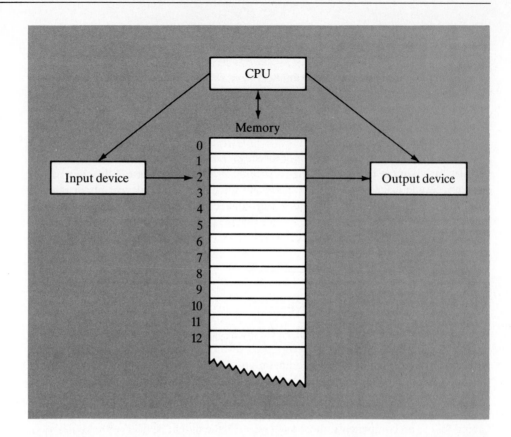

Figure 1.1
Main components
of a computer.

tion or word contains a string of zeros and ones. The contents of these locations can change. Hence, you can think of each memory location as a tiny blackboard that the computer may write on and then erase. In most computers, all locations contain the same number of zero/one digits; some typical sizes are 16, 32, and 64 digits. A digit that assumes only the values zero or one is called a *bit*. Hence, if you are working on a 32-bit machine, it means that each memory location in your computer can hold 32 bits, that is, 32 digits, each either zero or one.

That the information in a computer's memory is represented as zeros and ones need not be of great concern to a person programming in Pascal. The reasons for using only zeros and ones have to do with the physics of hardware design. Computers using larger repertoires of digits can and have been designed. The use of zeros and ones does, however, have a few implications that you should be aware of. First, the computer has to do its arithmetic in what is known as "binary notation." (We will discuss binary arithmetic in Chapter 15.) A more important point is that the computer needs to interpret these strings of zeros and ones as numbers or letters or instructions or other types of information. The computer performs these interpretations automatically according to certain codes. A different code is used for each type of item that can be stored in a location: There is one code for letters, another for whole numbers, another for fractions, another for instructions, and so on. For example, in one commonly used set of codes, 1000001 is the code for both the letter A and the number 65. In order to know what the string 1000001 means in a particular location, the computer must keep track of which code is currently being used for that location. Fortunately for us, the programmer seldom needs to be concerned with such codes and can safely proceed as though the locations actually contained letters, numbers, or whatever type of information is desired.

The memory we just described is called *main memory*. Most computers have additional memory called *secondary memory*, also frequently called *secondary storage* or *auxiliary storage*. Main memory serves as a temporary memory that is used only while the computer is actually following the instructions in a program. Secondary memory is used for keeping a permanent record of information after (and before) the computer is used. On small computers secondary memory is likely to consist of something called a *floppy disk* or *diskette,* and on larger computers it is likely to be something called a *hard disk*. Magnetic tape units are also commonly used for secondary memory. A typical computer installation with different kinds of memory is depicted in Figure 1.2. We will not be concerned with secondary memory until we reach Chapters 13 and 16.

secondary memory

disks

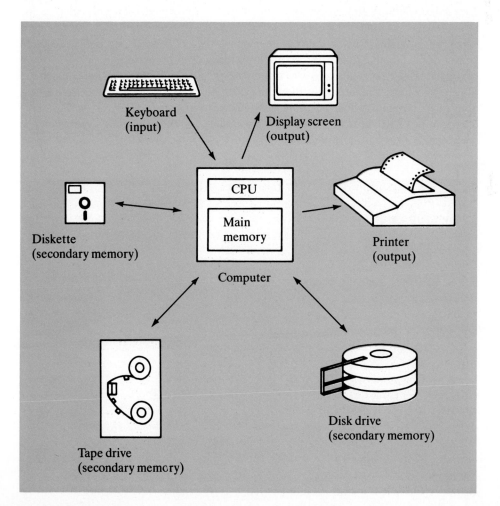

Keyboard
(input)

Display screen
(output)

CPU

Main memory

Diskette
(secondary memory)

Printer
(output)

Computer

Tape drive
(secondary memory)

Disk drive
(secondary memory)

Figure 1.2

A typical computer installation.

CPU

The *central processing unit*, or *CPU* for short, is the "brain" of the computer. It is the CPU that follows the instructions in a program and performs the calculations specified by the program. The CPU is, however, a very simple brain. All that it can do is follow a set of simple instructions provided to it by the programmer.

Typical CPU instructions say things like "interpret the zeros and ones as numbers and then add the number in memory location 37 to the number in memory location 59 and put the answer in location 83" or "read a letter of input, convert it to its code as a string of zeros and ones, and place it in memory location 1298." The CPU can perform subtraction, multiplication, and division as well as addition. It can move things from one memory location to another. It can interpret strings of zeros and ones as letters and send the letters to an output device. The CPU also has some primitive ability to re-arrange the order of instructions. Needless to say, CPU instructions vary somewhat from computer to computer. The CPU of a modern computer can have as many as several hundred available instructions. However, these instructions are typically all about as simple as those just described.

At this point you may be wondering where in the computer the program is kept. The answer is: in the memory. Thus, the memory serves both as a place to store the program and as a kind of "scratch paper" for doing calculations. Usually, we conceptualize the program as being outside of memory, but occasionally we will need to be aware of the fact that it actually resides in memory.

That is it. That is all there is to a computer. Conceptually, it is a simple machine. Its power comes from the size of its memory, its speed, its accuracy, and the sophistication of its programs. Your computer may not be configured exactly as we have portrayed it, but it will be similar and, more important, will behave exactly as if it were the very machine we have just described.

A floppy disk being inserted into a disk drive.

Hard disk pack being inserted into a disk drive.

Hard disk pack.

Tape drives.

The Notion of an Algorithm

When learning your first programming language, it is easy to get the impression that the hardest part of solving a problem on a computer is translating your ideas into the specific language that will be fed into the computer. This definitely is not the case. The most difficult part of solving a problem on a computer is coming up with the method of solution. After you have developed a method of solution, it is routine to translate your method into the required language, be it Pascal or some other programming language. When solving a problem with a computer, it is therefore helpful to temporarily ignore the computer programming language and to concentrate instead on formulating the steps of the solution and writing them down in plain English, as if the instructions were to be given to a human being. A set of instructions expressed in this way is frequently referred to as an "algorithm."

Algorithm   A set of instructions that leads to a solution is called an *algorithm*. Some approximately equivalent words are "recipe," "method," "directions," and "routine." The instructions may be expressed in a programming language or a human language. Our algorithms will be expressed in English and in the programming language Pascal. An *program*   algorithm expressed in a language that a computer can understand is called a *program*, which explains why computer languages are called *programming languages.*

The word "algorithm" has a long history, but its meaning has recently taken on a new character. The word itself derives from the name of the ninth-century Arabic mathematician and astronomer Al-Khowarizmi, who wrote an early and famous textbook on the manipulation of numbers and equations entitled *Kitab al-jabr w' al-muqabala*. The similar-sounding word "algebra" was derived from the Arabic word "al-jabr," which appears in the title of the text and is often translated as "reuniting" or "restoring." The entire title can be translated as "Rules for Reuniting and Reducing." The meanings of the words "algebra" and "algorithm" used to be much more intimately related than they are now. Indeed, until very recently the word "algorithm" usually referred to algebraic rules for solving numeric equations.

Today the word "algorithm" refers to a wide variety of instructions for manipulating symbolic as well as numeric entities. The properties that qualify a set of instructions as an algorithm now are determined by the nature of the instructions and not by the things to which they apply. To qualify as an algorithm, a set of instructions must completely and unambiguously specify the steps to be taken and the order in which they are to be performed. The instructions cannot rely on any intelligence on the part of the person or machine following the instructions. The follower of an algorithm does exactly what the algorithm says, neither more nor less.

sample   An example may help to clarify the concept. Figure 1.3 contains an algorithm ex-
Algorithm   pressed in rather stylized English. The algorithm determines the number of times a specified name occurs on a list of names. If the list contains the winners of each of last season's football games and the name is that of your favorite team, then the algorithm determines how many games your team won. The algorithm is short and simple but is otherwise typical of the algorithms we will be dealing with.

The instructions numbered 1 through 5 in our sample algorithm are meant to be carried out in that order. Unless otherwise specified, we will always assume that the

begin
1. Request the list of names and call it `NameList`;
2. Request the name being sought and it call it `KeyName`;
3. On a blackboard called `Count` write the number zero;
4. repeat the following for each name on `NameList`:
     if the name is the same as `KeyName`
       then add one to the number written on `Count`;
       {the old number is erased, leaving only one number
       on `Count`}
5. Announce the number written on `Count` as the answer.
end.

Figure 1.3
An algorithm.

instructions of an algorithm are carried out in the order in which they are listed. Most interesting algorithms do, however, specify some change of order, usually a repetition of some instruction again and again, as in instruction 4 of our sample algorithm.

This simple example illustrates a number of important points about algorithms. Algorithms are usually given some information. In our example, the algorithm was given a name and a list of names. The information that is given to an algorithm is called *input* or *data*. Algorithms usually give an answer, or answers, back. In the example, the answer was a number. The answers given by an algorithm are called *output*. In addition to being able to remember input and output, algorithms typically need to remember some other information. In the example, a single number was remembered; the number changed as the algorithm proceeded, and only the last value of the number was output.

input or data

output

One final observation about our sample algorithm: It always ends. No matter how long the list is, the algorithm always gets to the end of the list and announces an answer. There are algorithms that never terminate. Common examples are the algorithms used by computerized airline reservation systems. They never terminate; they just keep adding and deleting reservations forever, or until the airline goes bankrupt or changes its computer system. An algorithm that might not end is called a *partial algorithm*. An algorithm that is guaranteed to end is called a *total algorithm*. Some authors, especially in more advanced texts, reserve the word "algorithm" for what we called total algorithms. However, we will use the word to mean any algorithm, whether or not it is guaranteed to terminate.

Programs and Data

As we have already noted, a program is just an algorithm written in a language that can be fed into a computer. As shown in Figure 1.4, the input to a computer can be thought of as consisting of two parts: a program and some data. The data is what we conceptualize as the input to the algorithm that the computer will follow. In other words, the data is the input to the program, and both the program and the data are input to the computer. The word "input" is thus being used in two slightly different ways. This does

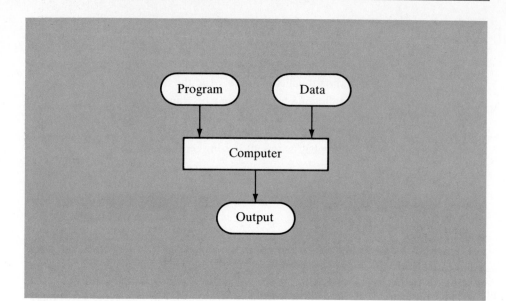

Figure 1.4
Simple view of
running a
program.

require some care to keep from getting confused, but it is standard usage and you may as well get used to it. For the sample algorithm in the previous section, the data was the name sought and the list of names to be searched. In order to get a computer to carry out the algorithm, both the algorithm (translated into a programming language) and the data are given as input to the computer. Whenever we give both a program and some

running
a program

data to a computer, we are said to be *running* the program on the data, and the computer is said to be *executing* the program on the data.

The word *data* also has a much more general meaning than the one we have just given it. In its most general sense, it means any information available to the computer or to some part of the computer. The word is commonly used in both the narrow sense and the more general sense. One must rely on context to decide which meaning is intended.

High Level Languages

high level
language

The language Pascal is a *high level language,* as are most of the other programming languages you are likely to have heard of, such as FORTRAN, BASIC, COBOL, C, Modula, and Ada. High level languages resemble human language in many ways. They are designed to be easy for human beings to write programs in and easy for human beings to read. Like most high level languages, Pascal uses English words combined in ways that resemble English sentences. For example, the following is a line from a Pascal program:

```
if (X = Y) and (Z = W) then
     write('the answer is 42')
```

You can read and understand this instruction almost without any explanation.

A high level language, like Pascal, contains instructions that are much more complicated than the simple instructions a computer's CPU is capable of following. The kind of language a computer can understand is called a *low level language*. A typical low level instruction might be the following:

ADD X Y Z

This instruction might mean "add the number in the memory location called X to the number in the memory location called Y and place the result in the memory location called Z."

The above sample instruction is written in what is called *assembly language*. Although assembly language is almost the same as the language understood by the computer, it must still undergo one simple translation before the computer can understand it. For a computer to follow an assembly language instruction, the words need to be translated into strings of zeros and ones. For example, ADD might translate to 0110, the X might translate to 1001, the Y to 1010, and the Z to 1011. The version of the instruction that the computer ultimately follows would then be

0110100110101011

Programs written in the form of zeros and ones are said to be written in *machine language,* because that is the version of the program that the computer (the "machine") actually reads and follows. Assembly language and machine language are almost the same thing, and the distinction between them will not be important to us. The important distinction is that between machine language and a high level language such as Pascal.

Do not bother to memorize our assembly language instruction to add two numbers, nor its translation into a string of zeros and ones. The exact assembly language instructions and their translation into zeros and ones will differ from machine to machine. The only point to remember is that any high level language must be translated into machine language before the computer can understand and follow the program.

A program that translates a high level language, like Pascal, to a machine language is called a *compiler*. A compiler is thus a somewhat peculiar sort of program in that its input or data is some other program and its output is yet another program. To avoid confusion, the input program is usually called the *source program* and the translated version is called the *object program* or *object code*. The word *code* is frequently used to mean a program or a part of a program, and this usage is particularly common when referring to object programs.

Now, suppose you want to run a Pascal program. In order to get the computer to follow your Pascal instructions, proceed as follows. First, run the compiler, using your Pascal program as data. Notice that in this case the Pascal program is not being treated as a set of instructions. To the compiler your Pascal program is just a long string of characters. The output will be another long string of characters, which is the machine language equivalent of the Pascal program. Next, run this machine language program on what we normally think of as the data for the Pascal program. The output will be what we normally conceptualize as the output of the Pascal program. The process is easier to visualize if you have two computers available, as diagrammed in Figure 1.5.

In reality, the entire process just described is facilitated on one computer by special

low level language

assembly language

machine language

compiler

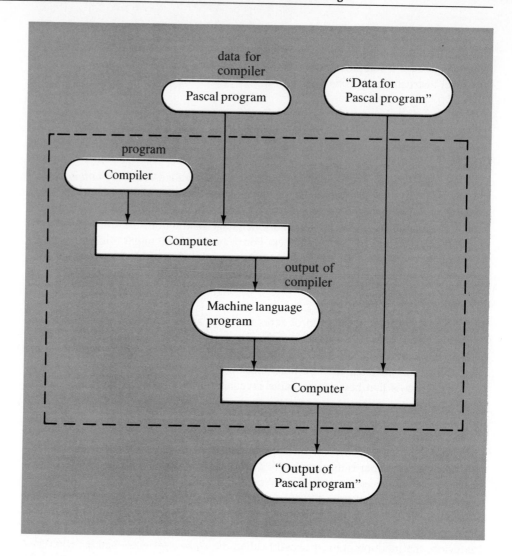

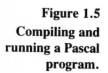

**Figure 1.5
Compiling and
running a Pascal
program.**

programs called *systems programs*. Although there is but one computer, the systems
programs make it appear as though a big box, represented by the dotted line in Figure
1.5, were built around two computers. You simply place your Pascal program and data
in the box and the rest is taken care of automatically. Hence, you can think of the computer as actually running the Pascal program. None of this is peculiar to Pascal. The
translation process is the same with any high level programming language.

The Pascal Language

In this book we will use a programming language called *Pascal*. Pascal is a high level,
general-purpose programming language. When we say Pascal is a *general-purpose language,* we mean that it is suitable for a diverse range of applications. Indeed, it is com-

monly used to write programs for a wide variety of applications, including programs for numeric scientific calculations, for business data processing, and for text editing, as well as to write various systems programs, including compilers.

The Pascal language was developed by Professor Niklaus Wirth and his colleagues at the Eidgenossische Technische Hochschule in Zurich, Switzerland, during the late 1960s and early 1970s. Wirth designed Pascal to be a good first language for people learning to program. As such, Pascal has relatively few concepts to learn and digest. It has a design that facilitates the writing of programs in a style that is now generally accepted as good standard programming practice. Another of Wirth's design goals was ease of implementation. He designed the language so that it is relatively easy to write a Pascal compiler for a new type of computer. This is one of the reasons that Pascal has become available on so many different computers in such a short amount of time. Needless to say, Pascal does have its shortcomings, and they will become apparent as you learn the language. Still, it is one of the best languages to use when learning to program computers. Moreover, it does not lose its usefulness after you learn the rudiments of programming. It is widely available and is frequently used by professional programmers. Also, a number of other popular programming languages are similar to Pascal and are thus easy to learn once you have mastered Pascal.

Programming Environments

operating system

Our description of compiling and running a Pascal program is a correct but over-simplified picture of what actually happens. Systems programs on modern computers include many other programs besides the compiler. The main systems program is called the *operating system*. It is the program in charge of other programs—the "manager," so to speak. It keeps track of which program is running on which piece of data; it brings out the editor program, which allows you to use the computer as a type-writer to write up your programs; it puts the editor program away and brings out the appropriate compiler when needed; and it also runs the machine language program that the compiler produces. On a computer with many simultaneous users, the operating system also keeps the various users from interfering with one another. It does this by moving resources from one user to another at such high speeds that, unless the number of users is very high, each person is given the illusion of being the only one using the computer. The operating system also does whatever accounting and security checking is needed. While all this is going on, the programs that are running usually produce various pieces of information as output. For example, the compiler will look for mistakes in your program and will give one or more output messages should it find any errors.

Computer facilities are now configured in a wide variety of ways. Smaller computers called *microcomputers* or *personal computers* are dedicated to a single user. Larger computers called *mainframes* can serve numerous users simultaneously by means of special operating systems called *time-sharing systems*. Often, the computer facility will consist of a *network* connecting a number of different computers so that they can share certain resources such as printers and secondary storage devices. The particular configuration you are working on will matter little to our study of programming techniques. For our purposes they all serve the same function and behave similarly.

editor

files

We have outlined the basic tasks involved in running a program. They are common to all systems. The details will vary from system to system, however, and you must find out many of these details before you can run a program. Your system will have a program called an *editor* that lets you use the computer as a typewriter. The system will also allow you to store programs and to retrieve them at a later time. The program that controls this storing and retrieving is usually called a *file manager*, or something similar, such as *file system* or *filer*. You will need to learn how to use both the editor and the file manager. Finally, you will have to learn how to get the compiler to translate your program into machine code and how to run the machine language program. (On many systems the processes of compiling and then running the program are combined into a single process.)

Although you will need to find out these details about your computer system, at this point you do not need to know anything about how to write a program in Pascal or in any other programming language. The rest of this book is devoted to teaching you how to go from a problem to a Pascal program to solve that problem.

Designing Programs

Designing a program is frequently a difficult task. There is no complete set of rules, no algorithm to tell you how to write programs. Program design is a creative process. Still, there is the outline of a plan to follow. The outline is given in diagrammatic form in Figure 1.6. As indicated there, the program-design process can be divided into two phases: the problem solving phase and the implementation phase. The result of the *problem solving phase* is an algorithm for solving the problem. The algorithm is expressed in English. To produce a program in a programming language such as Pascal, the algorithm is translated into the programming language. Producing the final program from the algorithm is called the *implementation phase*.

problem definition

The first step, in both the problem solving phase and the entire design process, is to be certain that the task is completely and precisely specified. Do not take this step lightly. If you do not know exactly what you want as the output of your program, you may be surprised at what your program produces. Be certain that you know what the input to the program will be, and exactly what information should be in the output, as well as what form that information should be in. For example, if the program is an accounting program for a bank, you must know not only the interest rate but also whether it is to be compounded annually, monthly, daily, or whatever. If the program is supposed to write poetry, you need to determine whether the poems can be in free verse or must be in iambic pentameter or some other meter.

problem solving phase

Many novice programmers do not understand the need to design an algorithm before writing a program in Pascal and so try to abbreviate the process by omitting the problem solving phase entirely or else reducing it to just the problem definition part. This seems reasonable. Why not "go for the mark" and save time? The answer is that *it does not save time!* Experience has shown that the two-phase process will produce a correctly working program faster. The two-phase process simplifies the algorithm-design phase by isolating it from the detailed rules of a programming language such as Pascal. The result is that the algorithm-design process becomes much less intricate and

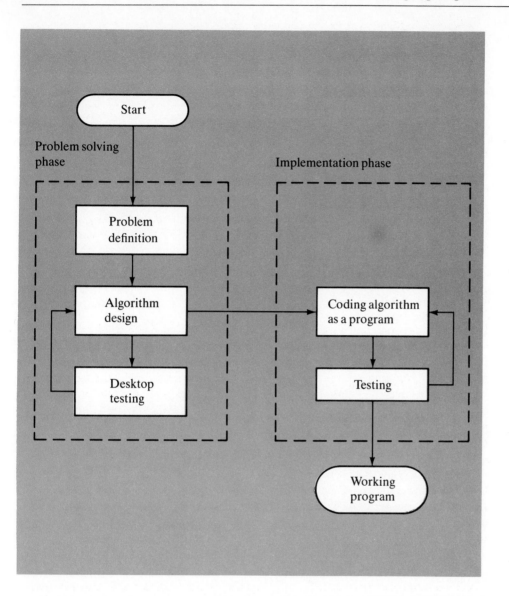

Figure 1.6
Idealized program-design process.

much less prone to error. For a modest-sized program it can represent the difference between a half day of careful work and several frustrating days of looking for mistakes in a poorly understood program.

The implementation phase is not trivial. There are details to worry about, details that occasionally can be quite subtle, but it is much simpler than you might at first think. Once you become familiar with Pascal, or any other programming language, the translation of an algorithm from English into the programming language becomes a routine task.

As indicated in Figure 1.6, testing takes place in both phases. The algorithm is tested and, if it is found to be deficient, it is redesigned. This first phase of testing is

*implementation
phase*

testing

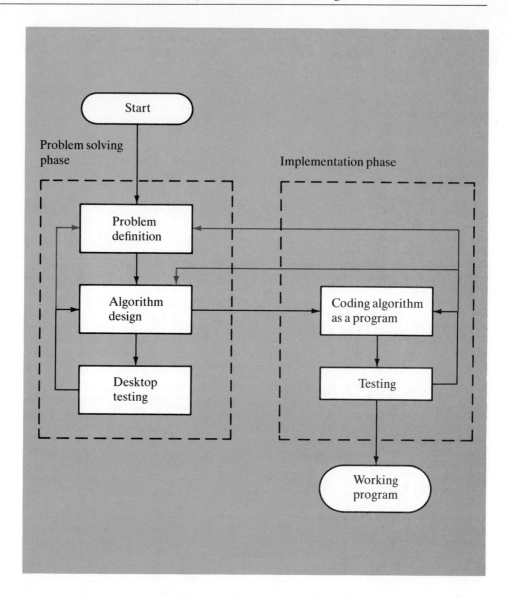

Figure 1.7
Realistic program-
design process.

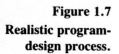

performed by mentally going through the algorithm and executing the steps yourself. With large algorithms this will require the aid of pencil and paper. The Pascal program is tested by compiling it and running it on some sample data. The compiler will give error messages for certain kinds of errors. To find other types of errors, you must somehow check to see whether the output is correct.

The process depicted in Figure 1.6 is an idealized picture of the process. It is the basic picture you should have in mind, but reality is sometimes more complicated. In reality, mistakes and deficiencies are discovered at unexpected times, and you may have to back up, as shown in Figure 1.7. For example, testing the algorithm may reveal that the problem definition was incomplete. In those cases, you must back up and reformulate the definition. Occasionally, deficiencies in the definition or algorithm may not be observed until a program is tested. If this occurs, you must back up and modify the definition or algorithm and all that follows it in the design process.

The next chapter contains an introduction to the Pascal language and some complete examples of this design process.

"And if you take one from three hundred and sixty-five, what remains?"

"Three hundred and sixty-four, of course."

Humpty Dumpty looked doubtful. "I'd rather see that done on paper," he said.

Lewis Carroll, Through the Looking-Glass

Summary of Terms

algorithm Detailed, unambiguous, step-by-step instructions for carrying out a task.

assembly language A low level language that is almost the same thing as machine language. The only difference is that assembly language instructions are expressed in a slightly more readable form, instead of being coded as strings of zeros and ones. See *machine language*.

auxiliary storage Another name for *secondary memory*.

code Sometimes used to mean a program or part of a program.

compiler A program that translates programs from a high level language to machine language.

CPU The *central processing unit* of a computer. It performs the actual calculations and the manipulation of memory according to the instructions in a machine language program.

data This word has two meanings: (1) the input to an algorithm or program; (2) any information that is available to an algorithm or to a computer.

editor A program that allows the computer to be used as a typewriter. An editor also has a number of commands that are more powerful than those of a typewriter, such as ones that move an entire piece of text from one place to another.

execute When an instruction is carried out by a computer, either directly or in some translated form, the computer is said to execute the instruction. When a computer follows the instructions in a complete program, it is said to execute the program.

file manager Also sometimes called a *filer* or *file system*. A program that allows the user to store and retrieve objects called files. Among other things, a file can contain a Pascal program. Hence, a file manager is the program used to store and retrieve Pascal programs.

hardware The physical parts of a computer or computer system.

high level language A programming language that includes instructions that are more powerful than those found in machine language and that typically uses a grammar somewhat like English. Programs in a high level language usually cannot be executed directly by computers. See *machine language*.

machine language A language that can be executed directly by a computer. Programs in machine language consist of very simple instructions, such as to add two numbers. These simple instructions are coded as strings of zeros and ones. See *assembly language*.

main memory The memory that the computer uses as temporary "scratch paper" when carrying out a computation. See *secondary memory*.

object program The translated version of a program produced by a compiler. See *source program*.

operating system The program that controls and manages all other programs. You communicate with the computer through the operating system.

program An algorithm that a computer can either follow directly or translate and then follow the translated version.

running a program The process of giving a program and some data to a computer in such a way that the computer is instructed to carry out the program using the data.

secondary memory The memory a computer uses to store information in a permanent or semipermanent state. (When the computer does not have sufficient main memory for a computation, then secondary memory is also used as an addition to main memory.) See *main memory*.

software Another term for programs.

source program The input program to be translated by a compiler. See *object program*.

Exercises

This book contains three kinds of exercises: Self-Test Exercises, Interactive Exercises, and Programming Exercises. The Self-Test Exercises are designed to provide you with a quick test of your understanding. The answers are relatively short and can be checked against the answers provided in the back of the book. The Interactive Exercises are designed to be done at the terminal. They are typically short programming exercises and are designed to give you a hands-on feel for the material. They may be done quickly; you need not worry too much about style details when working on them. The Programming Exercises are exercises that are suitable to be assigned as homework in a course. In this chapter, they ask you to produce algorithms in English. In subsequent chapters, they ask you to go through the entire design process and produce working Pascal programs.

Self-Test Exercises

1. Write an algorithm to add two whole numbers. The input to the algorithm is to be two strings of digits representing the two numbers. For example, the number 1066 is

thought of as the four symbols 1-0-6-6. The algorithm should be capable of being followed by a child who has not yet learned to do addition.

2. Write an algorithm to tell whether an input word is a palindrome. A *palindrome* is a word that is the same spelled backwards and forwards, such as "radar."

3. Write an algorithm to count the number of occurrences of each letter in an input word. For example, the input word "pop" contains two p's and one o.

Interactive Exercise

4. A good illustration of an algorithm is the instruction set for the U.S. Internal Revenue Service's long form 1040. If you have a copy readily available, read it through, noticing how very explicit the instructions are.

Programming Exercises

5. Write an algorithm to multiply two whole numbers. The rules are the same as in Exercise 1.

6. Write an algorithm to subtract one whole number from another. The rules are the same as in Exercise 1. (This is harder than it sounds.)

7. Write an algorithm to divide one whole number by another whole number. The rules are the same as in Exercise 1.

8. Write an algorithm that takes a page of text as data (input) and corrects the spacing according to the following rules: There should be exactly one space between two adjacent words, except that there are two spaces between adjacent sentences, and paragraphs are indented by exactly three spaces. Define the start of a paragraph as an indentation of one or more spaces at the start of a line. The data may contain any number of spaces, except that you may assume that there are no spaces inside of words and that there is at least one space between any two words on the same line. The output is to be written onto a second sheet of paper.

9. Many banks and savings and loan institutions compute interest on a daily basis. On a balance of $1000 with an interest rate of 6%, the interest earned in one day is 0.06 multiplied by $1000 and then divided by 365, because it is only for one day of a 365-day year. This yields $0.16 in interest, and so the resulting balance is $1000.16. The interest for the second day will be 0.06 multiplied by $1000.16 and then divided by 365. Design an algorithm that takes three inputs: the amount of a deposit, the interest rate, and a duration in weeks. The algorithm then calculates the account balance at the end of the duration specified.

10. Negotiating a consumer loan is not always straightforward. One form of loan is the discount installment loan, which works as follows. Suppose a loan has a face value of $1000, the interest rate is 15%, and the duration is 18 months. The interest is computed by multiplying the face value of $1000 by 0.15 to yield $150. That figure is then multiplied by the loan period of 1.5 years to yield $225 as the total interest owed. That amount is immediately deducted from the face value, leaving the consumer with only $775. Repayment is made in equal monthly installments based on the face value. So the monthly loan payment will be $1000 divided by 18, or $55.56. This method of calcula-

tion may not be too bad if the consumer needs $775, but the calculation is a bit more complicated if the consumer needs $1000. Design an algorithm that takes three inputs: the amount the consumer needs to receive, the interest rate, and the duration of the loan in months. The algorithm should then calculate the face value required in order for the consumer to receive the amount needed and should also calculate the monthly payment.

References for Further Reading

H.L. Capron, *Computers: Tools For an Information Age*, 1987, Benjamin/Cummings, Menlo Park, Ca. A simple introduction to programming systems and modern uses of computers. This book would be good if you are completely bewildered by Chapter 1.

L. Goldschlager and A. Lister, *Computer Science—A Modern Introduction*, 1982, Prentice-Hall International Series in Computer Science, Prentice-Hall, Englewood Cliffs, N.J. Discusses many of the issues in this chapter in greater detail. It is written at the introductory level.

T. Kidder, *The Soul of a New Machine*, 1981, Avon Books, New York. This is a popular description of the engineering effort that went into designing a specific computer. It is entertaining and you do pick up a few technical facts as well.

R.E. Pattis, *Karel the Robot: A Gentle Introduction to the Art of Programming*, 1981, John Wiley, New York. An introduction to algorithms and programming in a very simple setting.

I. Pohl and A. Shaw, *The Nature of Computation, An Introduction to Computer Science*, 1981, Computer Science Press, Rockville, Md. Discusses many of the issues in this chapter in greater detail. It is written at the introductory level.

CHAPTER 2

INTRODUCTION TO PROBLEM SOLVING WITH PASCAL

Once a person has understood the way variables are used in programming, he has understood the quintessence of programming.

E. W. DIJKSTRA, NOTES ON STRUCTURED PROGRAMMING

Chapter Contents

In this chapter we introduce the Pascal programming language. We explain some sample programs and present enough details of the Pascal language to allow you to write simple programs of your own. We continue the discussion of problem solving that we began in Chapter 1 by presenting some fundamental techniques for designing algorithms. Finally, we illustrate these design techniques by developing two Pascal programs from the problem-definition stage through to a final working program.

The Notion of a Program Variable

Programs manipulate data, such as numbers and letters. In order to store the data produced by subcomputations, and in order to have a way to name the data, Pascal and many other common programming languages use objects called *variables*. Variables are the very heart of a programming language like Pascal. These programming variables have some similarity to the variables used in algebra and related branches of mathematics, but they very definitely are not the same. To start with, programming variables traditionally have longer names than the variables used in algebra. In a Pascal program, a variable is written as a string of letters and digits that begins with a letter. Some sample names for Pascal variables are

        X Y Z SUM N1 N2 SALLY Joe rate Time

variables and values

Pascal variables are things that can hold numbers or other types of data. For the moment, we will confine our attention to variables that hold only numbers. These variables are rather like small blackboards on which a number can be written. Just as the number written on a blackboard can be changed, so too can the number held by a Pascal variable be changed. Just like blackboards, variables might contain no number at all, or they might contain the number left there by the last person or thing that used the variable. The words *hold* and *contain* when applied to variables are exact synonyms and, if you think in terms of the blackboard analogy, refer to the item written on the figurative blackboard. The number or other type of data held in a variable is called its *value*.

memory locations and variables

Most compilers translate variables into memory locations. A memory location is assigned to each variable, and the value of the variable, in a coded form consisting of zeros and ones, is kept in that location. For example, Figure 2.1 contains a Pascal program that uses the three variables N1, N2, and SUM. When that program is compiled, the compiler might assign the locations 1001, 1002, and 1003 to the variables N1, N2, and SUM, respectively. When the value of a variable is changed, the coded number in its assigned memory location changes to the new number. Whether or not your particular compiler actually makes this assignment of memory locations to variables is irrelevant, since it will make the program act as if just such an assignment had been made.

To illustrate how program variables can change their value, we will give a step-by-step explanation of the program displayed in Figure 2.1. Unless otherwise noted, we will always assume that input is via a keyboard and that the output is via a display screen.

Stepping Through a Program

statements

In Figure 2.1, the eight lines between *begin* and *end* contain eight instructions to be carried out by the computer. Such instructions are called *statements*. The semicolons at the ends of the statements are used to separate the statements and, strictly speaking, are not part of the statements themselves. That is why the last statement is not followed

Program

```
program Sample(input, output);
var N1, N2, SUM: integer;
begin
  writeln('Enter two numbers');
  readln(N1, N2);
  SUM := N1 + N2;
  writeln(N1, ' Plus ', N2, ' Equals ', SUM);
  writeln('Enter another two numbers');
  readln(N1, N2);
  SUM := N1 + N2;
  writeln(N1, ' Plus ', N2, ' Equals ', SUM)
end.
```

Sample Dialogue

```
Enter two numbers
4 5
     4 Plus        5 Equals       9
Enter another two numbers
8 9
     8 Plus        9 Equals       17
```

Figure 2.1
A Pascal program.

by a semicolon; there is no subsequent statement from which it needs to be separated. Minor points of punctuation like this need not be a serious concern for us yet. For now, simply note that the semicolons must be there. If you prefer, it is perfectly acceptable to add a semicolon after the last statement and thereby make things uniform. The program will perform identically with or without the extra semicolon.

The word `writeln` in the first line is pronounced "write-line." This first statement does not affect any variables. It simply causes the following phrase to appear on the screen:

```
Enter two numbers
```

Suppose that in response to this an obedient user types two numbers on the keyboard, say **4**, followed by a space, followed by a **5**, followed by pressing the return key. (The return key is the one that starts a new line, much like the carriage return on a typewriter.)

The next statement, shown below, tells the computer what to do with these numbers.

```
readln(N1, N2)
```

(We will usually not bother to show the final semicolon when displaying lines out of a program like this.) The word `readln` is pronounced "read-line." This statement instructs the computer to "read" the two numbers into the variables N1 and N2. It causes the value of the variable N1 to become equal to the first number that was typed, namely **4**, and the value of N2 to become equal to the second number, namely **5**. Recall that our hypothetical compiled translation of the Pascal program assigned memory location 1001 to N1 and 1002 to the N2. This means that location 1001 in the computer's memory will contain a coded version of the number 4. Similarly, location 1002 will contain the code for 5. Prior to this time, the variables N1 and N2 had no value.

The next statement in our sample program is

```
SUM := N1 + N2
```

The meaning of the part N1 + N2 is what you might guess. It instructs the computer to add the value of N1 to the value of N2. In other words, add 4 to 5. When the translated version of this statement is executed, the computer (the CPU, to be precise) will retrieve the 4 from location 1001 and the 5 from location 1002 and add them together to obtain 9. This statement also specifies what is to become of the resultant number 9. It becomes the value of the variable SUM and so goes into the location assigned to SUM, namely 1003.

The pair of symbols := is called the *assignment operator*, and statements such as the one under discussion are called *assignment statements*. The assignment operator is composed of two symbols, a colon and an equal sign, but it is considered to be one item and is always treated as a single unit. In particular, there should be no space between the colon and the equal sign. The assignment operator has no standard pronunciation. Many people use the phrase "gets the value," which describes the action; others simply pronounce it "assignment operator." Some people even read it literally as "colon equals," but the meaning of the assignment operator is not derived from the usual meaning of the colon and equal symbols. The := instructs the computer to change the value of the variable on the left-hand side to the value given on the right-hand side. We will say more about the assignment operator shortly, but first let us explain the rest of our sample program.

assignment operator

The next statement is

```
writeln(N1, ' Plus ', N2, ' Equals ', SUM)
```

It shows the result of the assignment statement by causing the following phrase to appear on the screen:

```
4 Plus     5 Equals     9
```

For the moment, do not worry about why the word write is embellished with a funny ending or why words like ' Plus ' are surrounded with blanks and single quotes. We will come back to those details shortly. For now, simply note that the values of the variables and the words in quotes are output to the screen in the order in which they occur in the writeln statement.

The rest of the program is almost a repetition of what we have just discussed. The program requests two more numbers with the statement

changing the value of a variable

```
writeln('Enter another two numbers')
```

This time, let us suppose that the user types in **8** and **9**, again separated by a blank, and terminates the line by pressing the return key. The two numbers are read when the program executes the next statement in the program:

```
readln(N1, N2)
```

This second `readln` statement sets the value of N1 equal to 8 and the value of N2 equal to 9. The old values of 4 and 5 are lost.

Next comes the second assignment statement:

    SUM : = N1 + N2

This changes the value of SUM to the value of N1 plus the value of N2. In other words, the value of SUM is changed to 8 plus 9, or 17. The old value of SUM is lost. The final `writeln` statement outputs the new values of N1, N2, and SUM.

Figure 2.1 also shows the complete dialogue between the computer and the user as it would appear on the screen. The material typed by the user and the output produced by the program are shown in different typefaces, which helps to clarify where the different lines came from. In reality, they would appear in the same typeface.

Assignment Statements

expression

An *assignment statement* always consists of a variable on the left-hand side of the assignment operator and an expression on the right-hand side. The expression may be a variable, a number, or a more complicated expression made up of variables, numbers, and arithmetic operators such as the plus sign and the minus sign. This statement instructs the computer to evaluate the expression on the right-hand side and to set the value of the variable equal to that value of the expression. A few more examples may help to clarify the way these statements work.

In Pascal the traditional multiplication sign is not used and multiplication is represented by an asterisk, as shown in the following assignment statement:

    SUM : = N1 * N2

This statement is just like the assignment statements in our sample program except that it performs multiplication rather than addition. The statement changes the value of SUM to the product of the values of N1 and N2. Of course, that makes SUM a poor choice for the name of our variable, but the program will still run. When the computer sees the identifier SUM, it knows it is a variable capable of storing numbers, but it does not know or care that it spells an English word indicating addition.

The expression on the right-hand side of an assignment statement can simply be another variable. The statement

    N1 : = N2

changes the value of the variable N1 to that of the variable N2. The value of N2 is not affected. This example is illustrated in Figure 2.2.

As yet another example, the following changes the value of N2 to 3:

    N2 : = 3

constants

The number 3 on the right-hand side of the assignment operator is called a *constant* because, unlike a variable, its value cannot change.

Because variables can change value over time, and because the assignment operator is one vehicle for changing their values, an element of time is involved in the

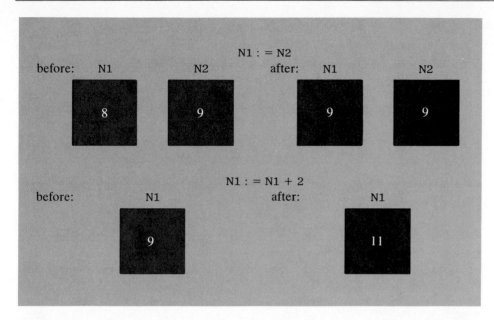

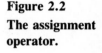

Figure 2.2
The assignment operator.

meaning of an assignment statement. First, the expression on the right-hand side of the assignment operator is evaluated. After that, the value of the variable on the left-hand side of the operator is changed to the value obtained from that expression. This means that a variable can meaningfully occur on both sides of an assignment operator. As an example, consider:

    N1 := N1 + 2

This statement will increase the value of N1 by 2.

Pitfall

Uninitialized Variables

A variable on the right-hand side of an assignment operator must have been given a value before the assignment statement is executed. Until a program gives a value to a variable, that variable has no value. For example, if the variable X has not been given a value, either in an assignment statement or in a read or readln statement (and if it has not been given a value by any of the methods still to be discussed), then the following is an error:

    Y := X + 1

This is because X has no value and so the expression X + 1 has no value. A variable that has not been given a value is said to be *uninitialized*.

    What happens in this situation depends on your particular system. You may get an error message warning you that X has been used without being initialized. In other, less ideal situations, the value of X may simply be set to some random quantity determined by whatever was left in the computer's memory by the previously run program. Hence, it is possible that when the program is run twice with the same input data it may give two different outputs. Whenever a program gives different output on the same data and without any change in the program itself, you should suspect an uninitialized variable.

Some other programming languages automatically initialize all numeric variables to zero. Although this may be true of certain versions of Pascal, you cannot and should not count on it.

Data Types—An Introduction

A *data type* is what the words say it is, namely a type or category of data. Each variable can hold only one type of data. In our sample Pascal program all variables were of type `integer`, which means that their values must be integers. An integer is any whole number, such as

    38   0   1   89   3987   −12   −5

The value of a variable of type `integer` cannot be a fraction. The variables N1, N2, and SUM in the program in Figure 2.1 can never contain fractions like 1/2 or 3.1416. Fractions belong to another data type called `real`, which we will discuss later in this section.

variable declarations

Every variable in a Pascal program must be *declared,* that is, the type of the variable must be stated. This is done at the beginning of the program. In our first sample program the variables were declared by the line

    var N1, N2, SUM: integer;

The declaration consists of the word *var,* followed by one or more blanks, followed by a list of variables separated by commas, followed by a colon, followed by a type name, and finally ended with a semicolon. Extra blanks may be added as long as you do not insert blanks in the middle of words such as *var* and `integer` or in the middle of variable names.

There are two reasons for requiring these declarations: to clarify your thinking by reminding you of the type of data the variable will hold and to provide information to the compiler. Recall that the computer has only strings of zeros and ones in memory. In order to treat these strings as integers, it uses a code to encode each integer as a string of zeros and ones. It uses a different code to encode letters as strings of zeros and ones. The declaration tells the compiler, and ultimately the computer, which code to use.

reals

Numbers that include a fractional part, such as the ones below, are of type `real`:

    2.71828   0.098   −15.8   100053.98

number constants

When such numbers appear in a Pascal program they are called *constants*. All numeric constants have a type, either `integer` or `real`. Conceptually, every whole number is both an integer and a real number. However, the computer makes a distinction between whole numbers of type `integer` and whole numbers of type `real`. In particular, the constant for the `integer` three is written `3`, whereas the constant for the `real` number three is written `3.0`. We will have more to say about this distinction in the next section.

Just as for numeric constants, every numeric variable is either of type `integer` or of type `real`. A variable Z is declared to be of type `real` in the following way:

var Z: real;

Division is one way to obtain values of type `real`. In Pascal division can be expressed using a slash. So N1/N2 means to divide the value of N1 by the value of N2. The result of this operation is always of type `real` no matter what the values or types of the two numbers are. Hence, in the following assignment statement, the variables N1 and N2 might be of type `integer` or of type `real`, but the variable Z can only be of type `real`:

Z : = N1/N2

The type for letters or, more generally, any single symbol is `char`, which is short for "character." Values of this type are frequently called *characters* in books and in conversation, but in Pascal programs this type must always be spelled in the abbreviated fashion `char`. Two variables X and Y of type `char` are declared as follows:

characters (char)

var X, Y: char;

A variable of type `char` can hold any character on the input keyboard. They may each hold only one character; they cannot hold strings containing more than one character. So, for example, X could hold an `'A'` or a `'+'` or an `'a'`. If both upper- and lowercase letters are available, they are considered to be different characters.

The single quotes indicate that we literally mean the letter. Hence, X is used for a variable named X, whereas `'X'` is used for the uppercase version of the third from the last letter of the alphabet. This is an important distinction. For example, the statement

quotes

Y : = X

changes the value of the variable Y to the value of the variable X. If X contained the letter `'A'`, then this statement will change the value of Y to `'A'`. On the other hand, the statement

Y : = 'X'

changes the value of the variable Y to the letter `'X'`, which is quite another thing. The program in Figure 2.3 illustrates this important distinction.

Unlike some printed texts, Pascal has only one kind of single quote; the opening quote and the closing quote are the same symbol.

Expressions consisting of a character in single quotes, such as `'X'`, are also called *constants* and are in fact the same sort of objects as the numeric constants, such as 3 and 5.98, except that they are of a different type, specifically the type `char`. Be sure to note that while `'3'` and 3 are both constants, they are very different constants. The first is a character, a mere symbol. It is of type `char` and may be used on

Program

```
program Tricky(input, output);
var X, Y: char;
begin
  X := 'A';
  Y := X;
  writeln('The first value of Y is:');
  writeln(Y);

  Y := 'X';
  writeln('The second value of Y is:');
  writeln(Y);

  writeln('I hope this helped to explain quotes.')
end.
```

Sample Dialogue

```
The first value of Y is:
A
The second value of Y is:
X
I hope this helped to explain quotes.
```

Figure 2.3
Using single quotes
for characters.

the right-hand side of an assignment statement to give a value to a variable of type
char. The constant 3 is a number. It is of type integer and may be used to give a
value to a variable of type integer. There are constants of other types as well, and
we will discuss them as the opportunities arise.

sample
declarations

It is perfectly acceptable to have variables of more than one type in a program. In
such cases they are all declared at once following the format illustrated below:

```
var N1, N2: integer;
    Time: real;
    Initial: char;
```

Note that the word *var* is only used once, no matter how many variables are declared
and no matter how many variable types are used in the declarations.

The variables need not be declared in any particular order. For instance, the above
declaration is equivalent to the following one:

```
var Initial: char;
    N1: integer;
    Time: real;
    N2: integer;
```

The best order is the one that groups the variables according to their use in the
program.

More about Real Values

Conceptually, a whole number is a special kind of real number, namely one that happens to have only zeros after the decimal point. If that were the only difference between the two types, we would never need to use the type integer. There is another important difference, however. Numbers of type integer are stored as exact values, while numbers of type real are stored only as approximate values. Thus, if we know that a certain variable will always contain a whole number, then it is best to make it of type integer. The precision with which real values are stored varies from one computer to another, but on most systems the extra digits in the following assignment statement are pointless:

reals
versus
integers

    X := 3.14159265358979323846

The program is likely to give exactly the same output if the real value is changed to

    X := 3.14159

Numeric constants of type real are written differently from those of type integer. Constants of type integer must not contain a decimal point. Constants of type real may be written in two different forms. The simple form for real constants is like the everyday way of writing decimal fractions. When written in this form, a real constant must contain a decimal point and there must be at least one digit before and one digit after the decimal point. No number in Pascal may contain a comma. Hence, none of the following are allowed as constants of type real (nor as constants of type integer):

    1,000   .009   -.05   72.

In addition to the simple notation that we have been using for real constants, there is another, more complicated notation for expressing constants of type real. This notation is frequently called *scientific notation* or *floating point notation*. It is particularly handy for writing very large numbers and very small fractions. For instance, the numbers

$3.67 \times 10^{17} = 367000000000000000.0$
and
$5.89 \times 10^{-6} = 0.00000589$

are best expressed in Pascal by the constants 3.67E17 and 5.89E-6, respectively. The E stands for *exponent* and means "multiply by 10 to the power that follows." This *E notation* is used because keyboards normally do not have any way to enter exponents as superscripts.

Another way of understanding E notation is to think of the number after the E as telling you to move the decimal point to the right that many places. For example, to change 3.49E4 to a numeral without an E, you move the decimal point 4 places to the right and obtain 34900.0. If the number after the E is negative, then move the decimal point the indicated number of spaces to the left, inserting extra zeros if need

E
notation
syntax

be. For example, 3.49E−2 and 0.0349 are two ways of writing the same number.

There are rigid rules for writing constants in the E notation. The number before the E can be any decimal number, with or without a plus or minus sign. It need not contain a decimal point, but if it does, there must be at least one digit before and at least one digit after the decimal point. The number after the E is called the *exponent* and must be a whole number, either positive, negative, or zero. It cannot contain a decimal point. Hence, the following are all correctly formed constants of type `real`:

    9.34E13 5E27 5E−27 −8.62713E21
    1.234E−15 −6.783E−12 1.0E+13 +34.78E56

By contrast, none of the following are acceptable constants:

    .5E12 −.7E13 3.5E22.5

The first two are incorrect because they have no digit before the decimal point. The last one is incorrect because it has a decimal point in the exponent.

Type Compatibility

integers
in place of
reals

In Pascal programs, 2 and 2.0 are different kinds of numbers: the first is of type `integer` and is an exact value; the second is of type `real` and represents an approximate value. This is not always an important issue, since the computer will perform an automatic type conversion, converting a number of type `integer` to an approximately equal number of type `real` whenever the situation demands a value of type `real`. Hence, if X is a variable of type `real`, then the following is allowed:

    X := 2

The reverse situation is not allowed, however. If Y is of type `integer`, then the following is illegal in Pascal:

    Y := 2.0

This sort of type conflict is not likely to arise in such a simplistic manner, but the same principle applies in more subtle situations. To take a slightly more likely mistake, note that the following is illegal whenever X is of type `real` and Y is of type `integer`:

    Y := X

Arithmetic Expressions

Constants and variables of the types `integer` and `real` may be combined to form more complex expressions by using the operators +, −, *, and / for addition, subtraction, multiplication, and division, respectively. We have already used simple versions of such arithmetic expressions. By using parentheses, it is possible to build more complicated expressions from these simpler expressions.

As an example, suppose that N, M, and Y are variables and that each one is either of type `real` or type `integer`. The right-hand side of the following assignment statement is then a well-formed arithmetic expression:

```
X := 2*(N +  (M/3)  + 4*Y)
```

The value of the expression is `real` because it contains a division and the result of a division is always of type `real`, Since the expression is of type `real`, the variable X on the left-hand side of the assignment operator must also be of type `real`.

Any combination of the types `real` and `integer` may be used with the operators +, −, *, and /. The type of the value resulting from the arithmetic expression is determined according to the following simple rule: If the operators can ever be used on *any* values of the types being combined so as to produce a number with a nonzero value after the decimal point, then the result is of type `real`; otherwise, it is `integer`. A more detailed statement of the rule is given in Figure 2.4, but this short rule is easier to remember.

mixing reals and integers

Notice that the type of an arithmetic expression is determined by the types of its subexpressions and by the operations it contains, not by the particular value of the expression. Whether an arithmetic expression evaluates to a "whole number" or not is irrelevant to the type of the expression. The quantity $4/2$ is of type `real` despite the fact that the answer "comes out even."

Any reasonable spacing will do in arithmetic expressions. You can insert spaces before and after operations and parentheses, or you can omit them. Do whatever produces a result that is easy to read.

The order of operations can always be determined by parentheses, as illustrated in the following two expressions:

parentheses

```
(X +  Y)  *  Z
 X +  (Y *  Z)
```

To evaluate the first expression, add X and Y and then multiply the result by Z. To evaluate the second expression, multiply Y and Z and then add the result to X.

How to Determine
the Type of an Arithmetic Expression

1. Combining something of type `real` with something either of type `integer` or type `real` always yields something of type `real`.
2. Combining anything with the division sign, /, always yields something of type `real`.
3. Combining two things of type `integer` with either the addition sign, +, the subtraction sign, −, or the multiplication sign, *, yields something of type `integer`.
4. Placing a minus sign, −, in front of an arithmetic expression does not change its type.

Figure 2.4
Type rules for arithmetic expressions.

precedence
rules

If you omit parentheses, the computer will follow precedence rules similar to those used in everyday arithmetic. For example,

X + Y * Z

is evaluated by first performing the multiplication and then the addition. Except for some very standard cases, such as a string of additions or a simple multiplication embedded inside an addition, it is best to use parentheses, even if the intended order of operations is the one dictated by the precedence rules. The parentheses make the expression easier to read and less prone to programmer error. The exact precedence rules for the operations we have seen so far are given in Figure 2.5. A complete set of Pascal precedence rules are given inside the back cover.

Order of Evaluation for Arithmetic Expressions

1. If parentheses are present, they determine the order of operations.
2. If the order is not determined by parentheses, then multiplication and division operations are evaluated before addition and subtraction operations.
3. If there is still a question as to which operation to perform first, the competing operations are performed from left to right.

Figure 2.5
Precedence rules
for arithmetic
expressions.

Unlike written and printed mathematical formulas, which may contain square brackets and various other forms of parentheses, Pascal allows only one kind of parentheses in arithmetic expressions. The other varieties are reserved for other purposes.

While we are on the subject of arithmetic operations, we should point out that Pascal contains no operator for exponentiation. There is no Pascal equivalent of x^y.

exponents

Mathematical Formula	Pascal Expression
$b^2 - 4ac$	B * B − 4 * A * C
$x(y + z)$	X * (Y + Z)
$\dfrac{1}{x^2 + x + 1}$	1 / (X * X + X + 1)
$\dfrac{a + b}{c - d}$	(A + B) / (C − D)

Figure 2.6
Pascal arithmetic
expressions.

Later on we will see how to define expressions that are equivalent to this kind of exponentiation. For now, you will simply have to use repeated products to obtain powers and do without any equivalent of fractional exponents. Thus, X cubed is expressed as

```
X*X*X
```

Figure 2.6 shows some examples of common arithmetic expressions and how they would be expressed in Pascal.

Simple Output

The values of variables as well as strings of text may be output to the screen with `writeln` statements, such as those used in our sample program in Figure 2.1. Any combination of variables of different types as well as strings may be output. The strings of characters are enclosed in single quotes. The items to be output are listed in the order in which they are to appear on the screen.

writeln

The computer will not insert extra space before or after strings or the values of variables of type `char`, which is why the quoted strings in the samples usually start and end with a blank. The blanks keep the various strings and numbers from running together.

blanks

Values of type `real` are often output in E notation. For example, if X is a variable of type `real`, then the statements

outputting reals

```
X := 1234.56;
writeln(X)
```

are likely to produce output that looks something like the following:

```
1.2345600000000E03
```

which means

$$1.2345600000000 \times 10^3$$

and is another way of expressing the number 1234.56.

There are some rules about quoted strings that you must observe when you include them in `writeln` statements, or anywhere else for that matter. Remember that single quotes are used and that both the opening and closing quote are the same symbol. If you want to include a single quote symbol within a quoted string, then you must use two single quotes; otherwise the computer will interpret the single quote as marking the end of a quoted string. For example, the output of

quotes inside of quotes

```
writeln('Surf''s Up')
```

is the following:

```
Surf's Up
```

The suffix `ln` on the word `write` is short for "line." It is usually pronounced "line" but it is always spelled `ln`. Including the `ln` instructs the computer to start a new line *after* writing out the listed items. For example, consider the two statements

write versus writeln

```
writeln('First line');
writeln('Second line')
```

They cause the following to appear on the screen:

```
First line
Second line
```

On the other hand, consider the two statements

```
write('First line');
writeln('Second line')
```

They cause the following to appear on the screen:

```
First lineSecond line
```

The last output statement in a program should always be a `writeln` rather than a `write`. This is because some systems require that the end of all lines, including the last line of output, be explicitly indicated.

While we are on the subject, we should note two minor but useful properties of `writeln`. First, you can use `writeln` without specifying anything to output. This simply causes the computer to skip to the next line, which is handy for skipping lines and for when you do use `write`. Hence, the three statements

```
write('Line one');
writeln;
writeln('Line two')
```

are equivalent to the two statements

```
writeln('Line one');
writeln('Line two')
```

The second property, one that is minor but occasionally useful, is that you can place expressions within a `write` or `writeln` statement. Thus, the following is permitted; its meaning is obvious:

```
writeln(N1, ' Plus ', N2, ' Equals ', N1 + N2)
```

Input

readln   `read` and `readln` are used for input and are analogous to `write` and `writeln`. They are written the same way, namely with a list of items separated by commas and enclosed in parentheses. In this case, all the items must be variables. They instruct the computer to read input values and to set the values of the variables equal to the values read in. We will assume that the input is entered from a keyboard, but the details are similar for input obtained from other sources.

Variables of the types `integer`, `real`, and `char` may be given values with a `read` or `readln` statement. Later we will introduce other data types besides these three. On most systems, however, only values of type `integer`, `real`, and `char` may be read in from the keyboard.

You may mix the types of the variables in a single `read` or `readln` statement, but the types of the values input should match the types of the variables listed in parentheses. If a variable is of type `integer`, then the number entered for that variable should be an integer constant such as `12` or `−7`; it should not be a real such as `12.5`. Even using `12.0` can produce serious problems. If a variable is of type `real`, then the number typed in for that variable may be of type either `real` or `integer`. The computer will automatically convert an `integer` value to an approximately equal `real` value when filling variables of type `real`. Of course, you should never try to fill a variable of type `integer` or `real` with a character such as a letter of the alphabet.

When entering numbers, you must insert one or more blanks between numbers on the same line so that the computer knows where one number ends and the next begins. The situation with characters is different. Anything you type, *including a blank,* is a value of type `char`. Hence, there is no space before an input character that is intended for a variable of type `char`.

blanks in input

The difference between `read` and `readln` is that `readln` instructs the computer to go to the next line *after* reading values for all variables, thus causing the rest of the input on the current line to be discarded. The exact details are different for numbers and for character input.

read versus readln

When reading in numbers with either `read` or `readln`, the computer will automatically go to the next line when it needs more values than are available on the current line. The only difference between the two is that with `read` the computer does not begin reading the next line until the data on the current line is exhausted. On the other hand, after the computer completes a `readln`, it discards anything remaining on the current line, and any subsequent `read` or `readln` will take its first value from the next line.

When reading in characters, `readln` causes a similar discarding of the remainder of the current line; any subsequent `read` or `readln` will take its values from the next line of input. However, with character input, the computer does not automatically go to the next line when the current line is exhausted. For data of type `char`, there should normally be at least as many symbols on a line as the program expects. A `readln` should be used to instruct the computer to go to the next line when the current line is exhausted.

A simple `readln`, without any variables, instructs the computer to disregard the rest of the input on the current line. For example, the two statements

```
read(X, Y);
readln
```

are equivalent to the single statement

```
readln(X, Y)
```

Uses for the unadorned `readln` will occur to you naturally as your programming skills develop.

When writing your first few programs, it is probably best to avoid `read` and `write` in favor of `readln` and `writeln`. Using `writeln` and `readln` to organize the screen display into alternating lines of input and output is usually easier and safer than trying to integrate `read` and `write` instructions.

Designing Input and Output

prompt lines

When the computer executes a `read` or `readln`, it expects data to be entered at the keyboard. If none is typed in, it simply waits for it. The program must tell the user when to type in data; the computer will not automatically ask for the data. That is why the sample programs contain statements like the following:

```
writeln('Enter two numbers')
```

These output statements *prompt* the user to enter input.

echoing input

When the user is entering input from a terminal, the input appears on the screen as it is typed. Nonetheless, the program should always write out the input values at some point before the program ends. This is called *echoing* the input, and it serves as a check to see that the input was read in correctly. Just because the input looks good on the screen does not mean that it was read correctly. There could be an unnoticed typing mistake, or the input could be read in incorrectly because the line breaks are not where the program expects them to be. Echoing input serves as a test of the integrity of the input data.

Pitfall

Input in Wrong Order

A human being given two numbers that represent height and weight will figure out which number is which no matter what order the numbers are given in. Nobody is 180 feet tall and weighs 6 pounds. A computer, however, makes no such test for reasonableness and will happily accept such numbers for height and weight. Therefore, you must always be careful that your programs instruct the user to input values in the correct order, or the program is likely either to terminate abnormally or to produce incorrect results.

Names: Identifiers

In Pascal, variables are written as strings of symbols. The string of symbols serves as the name of the variable. Pascal programs also have names. The name of the program in Figure 2.3 is `Tricky`. As we learn more Pascal, we will encounter other Pascal objects that have names.

A name used in a Pascal program is called an *identifier* and is defined to be any string of letters and digits, provided the string starts with a letter. With the exception of one special class of identifiers that we will discuss later in this section, any Pascal identifier can be used as the name of a variable in a Pascal program. The following are all examples of Pascal identifiers:

names for
variables

```
X  X1  sample  ABC123z7  SUM  Data1  Data2  TEMP
```

The following are not Pascal identifiers:

```
12  3X  DATA.1  FILE.TEXT  DATA-GOOD
```

The first two are not identifiers because they start with a digit rather than a letter. The remaining three are not identifiers because they contain symbols other than letters and digits.

The Pascal standard places no limit on the length of a Pascal identifier. However, many compilers will ignore all characters after some specified number of initial characters. From now on, we will assume that the computer ignores all but the first eight characters. Even under this assumption, the following is a perfectly valid identifier:

long
identifiers

```
TheFinalAnswer
```

In some contexts, this may be the most sensible identifier to use, but if you use such long identifiers, be certain that there is no other identifier with the same first eight letters. On some compilers, the following three identifiers are for all practical purposes equal, because their first eight letters are the same:

```
TheFinalAnswer  TheFinalResult  TheFinal
```

There is nothing special about the number eight, but there often is some limit. The first versions of Pascal used eight as the limit. Many implementations still use this limit, and no system uses a limit of less than eight characters. For these reasons, it is a good idea to pretend that your system uses eight, even if it does not.

To keep from getting confused, do not use two different names for the same variable, even if the names are equivalent on your system. Only one of the three equivalent identifiers displayed above should be used in any one program. There is another compelling reason for having only one identifier per variable. If you move your program to a system that has a limit greater than eight or no limit at all, then your program will still work; otherwise, you might need to rename some of the variables. Many compilers use all the characters in long identifiers.

portability

Unfortunately, there is little uniformity in how systems treat upper- and lowercase letters in identifiers. Lowercase letters, if available, may or may not be treated as distinct from uppercase letters when they occur in identifiers. On some systems, the identifiers SUM, Sum, and sum are all equivalent. On other systems, they are three distinct identifiers. Needless to say, under these circumstances it is not a good idea to rely on the distinction between upper- and lowercase letters when choosing identifiers. Even if your system treats sum and SUM as distinct, there is little reason to think some other system will. Therefore, it is best to use only one of the two variants. These remarks also apply to upper- and lowercase letters in identifiers like *program*, *begin*, integer, and so forth, which have a standard meaning in the Pascal lan-

upper-
and
lowercase

guage. Some systems require that they always be typed in uppercase or always be typed in lowercase. To find out how your compiler treats upper- and lowercase letters, check the documentation or do a bit of experimenting.

Upper- and lowercase letters are always treated as being different when they appear in quoted strings or as the values of variables of type char.

This book uses a convention for upper- and lowercase letters that is designed to emphasize certain concepts: All identifiers whose meaning is defined by the Pascal language are written using all lowercase letters; all identifiers that the programmer must make up are written using at least one uppercase letter, for example, SUM and TheAnswer. We never use two spellings that differ only in the case of some or all of their letters.

reserved words

There is a special class of identifiers, called *reserved words,* that have a predefined meaning in the Pascal language and cannot be used as names for anything else, such as variables. The following is a complete list of all the reserved words we have seen so far:

```
begin  end  program  var
```

In this book all reserved words are written in the special typeface shown here. A complete list of reserved words is given inside the back cover.

standard identifiers

You may wonder why the other words that we defined as part of the Pascal language are not on the list of reserved words. What about words like integer, char, and readln? The answer is that, although they have a predefined meaning, you are allowed to change their meaning. Such identifiers are called *standard identifiers* and, in this book, are written using all lowercase letters, in a slightly different typeface than that used for reserved words. Needless to say, using standard identifiers as names for things other than their standard meaning can be confusing and dangerous and should thus be avoided. The safest and easiest practice is to treat standard identifiers as if they were reserved words.

Putting the Pieces Together

You now know enough details about Pascal to write a program. All you need to do is put the pieces together in the right order and with the correct punctuation.

program heading

Pascal programs start with a line called the *program heading.* This consists of the reserved word *program* followed by an identifier that serves as the name of the program, followed by the standard identifiers input and output, which are separated by a comma and enclosed in parentheses. Finally, the heading is terminated with a semicolon. For example, if the program name is Arthur, the heading would be

```
program Arthur(input, output);
```

body

After the program heading come the variable declarations. Next comes the *body* of the program. The body of the program consists of a list of statements that serve as the instructions to be followed. This is the algorithm part of the program, and it is set off by the reserved words *begin* and *end.* The statements are separated by semicolons. As has already been pointed out, there is no need for a semicolon after the last statement because there is no other statement from which it needs to be separated. However, if you do insert an extra semicolon there, it will not cause a problem. Pascal programs end with a period, placed after the identifier *end*.

In Pascal any two identifiers or numbers must be separated by one or more spaces. Hence, the program heading given above cannot start out *program*Arthur. However, Pascal compilers will accept any number of extra blanks between identifiers. If two identifiers or numbers are separated by a line break or a punctuation symbol (such as a comma, semicolon, or colon), then spaces are allowed but not required.

spacing

Pascal allows programmers wide latitude in deciding when to start a new line. Two or more statements may be placed on the same line. With one exception, a line may be broken anywhere that a blank is allowed. The one exception is that you cannot break a quoted string across two lines. Therefore, the following is not allowed:

line breaks

```
writeln('You may NOT break a quote
across two lines like this.')
```

Almost any pattern of spacing and line breaks will be acceptable to the compiler. However, as we point out in the next section, programs should always be arranged so as to make them easy to read.

Introduction to Programming Style

All the sample programs we have seen were laid out in a particular format. For example, the statements were all indented by the same amount. Similarly, the declarations were aligned. These and other matters of style are of more than aesthetic interest. A program that is written with careful attention to style is easier to read, easier to correct if it contains a mistake, and easier to change should that prove desirable at some later time.

A program should be laid out so that elements that are naturally thought of as a group look like a unit. The standard way of doing this is to indent everything in that group by the same amount. Another way to make a program more readable is to skip a line between pieces that are logically thought of as separate. The important point is to make separations using indentations and line breaks. The exact number of spaces in an indentation is a matter of personal taste. Sometimes there are also natural break indicators, such as the words *begin* and *end,* which can be made to stand out and frame a group.

indenting

blank lines

Variables, constants, and even program names should at least hint at their meaning or use. It is easy just to use X, Y, and Z again and again as variables for numbers. However, it is much easier to understand a program if the variables have meaningful names. Contrast

choosing names

```
X := Y * Z
```

with the more suggestive statement below:

```
Pay := Rate * Hours
```

The two statements accomplish the same thing, but the second is easier to understand.

Blaise Pascal
(Optional)

The language Pascal was named after Blaise Pascal, a mathematician, engineer, scientist, and religious philosopher. Pascal was born in 1623 in Auvergne in central France. At the age of 18, he designed a computing machine capable of performing simple arithmetic calculations. The machine was a type of adding machine and not the sort of programmable machine that would today be called a computer. Nonetheless, the machine received a good deal of attention and served as a prototype for a number of later computing machines. Pascal had a number of models built and attempted to market the machine. Due to its high price, however, the machine was never a financial success.

His calculating machine was only one of Pascal's numerous scientific and engineering contributions. He designed Paris's first public bus system, which used horse-drawn carriages. He made important contributions to geometry, probability theory, and hydrodynamics. Pascal was also a prominent figure in religious philosophy. He belonged to a controversial movement within the Catholic church known as Jansenism. His last and most widely read religious work is now published under the title *Pensées*. The quotations of Pascal in this book were taken from that work. Although the book was intended as a work on religious philosophy, some of the remarks do seem to apply to the philosophy of computer programming.

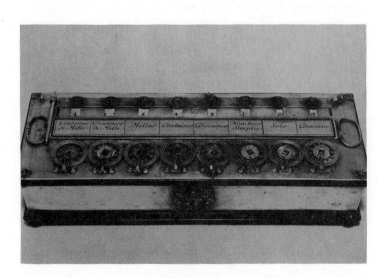

Blaise Pascal and his calculating machine.

Self-Test Exercises

1. What is the output produced by the following three lines (when correctly embedded in a complete program)? The variables are of type `integer`:

```
X := 2; Y := 3;
Y := X;
writeln(X, Y)
```

2. What is the output produced by the following three lines (when correctly embedded in a complete program)? The variables are of type `integer`:

```
X := 2;
X := X + 1;
writeln(X)
```

3. What is the output produced by the following two lines (when correctly embedded in a complete program)? The variables are of type `char`:

```
A := 'B'; B := 'C'; C := A;
writeln(A, B, C, 'C')
```

4. Which of the following are correctly formed constants of type `integer`?

$$3.5 \quad 4.0 \quad 4. \quad 4 \quad 1,295 \quad 9/3 \quad 8/5 \quad '7'$$

5. Which of the following are correctly formed constants of type `real`?

$$98.6 \quad -33.4 \quad .89 \quad -.89 \quad 3,987.85 \quad 4. \quad 4 \quad 4.0$$

6. Which of the following are correctly formed constants of type `real`?

$$.57E12 \quad 57E12 \quad 57E-12 \quad 57E3.7 \quad 57.9E3.7 \quad -9.8E2$$

7. Convert each of the following (non-Pascal) arithmetic expressions into Pascal arithmetic expressions:

$$3x \quad 3x + y \quad \frac{x + y}{7} \quad \frac{3x + y}{z + 2}$$

8. What (if anything) is wrong with the following declarations?

(a) *var* `Count: integer    ;`
     `Answer :    char; AMOUNT: integer;`
(b) *var* `Time: integer;`
     var `Rate: real;`
(c) *var* `Count1; Count2: integer;`
     `Rate: real;`
(d) *var* `N1, N2: integer;`
     `AVE:  real`

9. What are the types of the values of the following expressions? (You need not evaluate them.)

```
2 * 3    5 * (7 + 4/2)     '3'
2.0000    2E9    2/3
```

10. The following program contains errors. What are they?

```
program (input, output)
  begin
    writeln("Hello");
    writeln('This program was written in a hurry);
    writeln('It contains a few mistakes');
    writeln('Can you find them?')
    writeln('The compiler can')
  end
```

Interactive Exercises

11. Type up and run the following program:

```
program DoMeFirst(input, output);
begin
  writeln('Hello.');
  writeln('End of program')
end.
```

12. Write a program that reads in one integer, multiplies it by 2, and then writes the result back to the screen.

"Don't stand chattering to yourself like that," Humpty Dumpty said, looking at her for the first time, "but tell me your name and your business."

"My *name* is Alice, but—"

"It's a stupid name enough!" Humpty Dumpty interrupted impatiently. "What does it mean?"

"*Must* a name mean something?" Alice asked doubtfully.

"Of course it must," Humpty Dumpty said with a short laugh: "*my* name means the shape I am—and a good handsome shape it is, too. With a name like yours you might be any shape, almost."

Lewis Carroll, Through the Looking-Glass

Problem Solving and Program Design

To keep from getting confused when designing a program and to produce a readable, easy-to-change program require patience and a systematic approach to the design process. In the first chapter we outlined one such systematic approach. It consisted of carefully analyzing the problem, designing an algorithm for a hypothetical person to follow, and then translating the algorithm into a Pascal program for the computer to follow. One basic design technique for producing the algorithm is called *top-down design*. We next introduce this technique and illustrate it with a design example.

Top-Down Design

A good plan of attack for designing an algorithm is to break down the task to be accomplished into a few big subtasks, then decompose each big subtask into smaller subtasks, then replace the smaller subtasks by even smaller subtasks, and so forth. Eventually the subtasks become so small that they are trivial to implement in Pascal or whatever language you are using. This method is usually called *stepwise refinement* or *top-down design* or, more graphically, *divide and conquer*.

stepwise refinement

Not only is stepwise refinement an efficient design method, it also produces a good algorithm in the sense that the algorithm is easier to understand and subsequent modifications are relatively easy to make. This is very important as most programs are changed at some time, and some of them are being changed constantly. For example, a simple computerized airline reservation system might be expanded to keep track of seat as well as flight reservations. The top-down design method is illustrated in the two case studies in this chapter.

Case Study

A Guessing Game

Problem Definition

We want to design a program to play a simple game with the user. The rules of the game are as follows: The user chooses two numbers and then tries to guess their average. The user could calculate the average with pencil and paper, but the idea is to choose relatively large, complicated numbers and to really guess rather than compute the average. The program lets the user know whether the guess was correct. This is not much of a game; nonetheless, it can be used to illustrate the program-design process.

Discussion

The task can be broken into three main subtasks:

subtasks

```
begin
  1. Have the user input two numbers and a guess of their average.
  2. Calculate the average.
  3. Output enough information to permit the user to tell whether the guess is correct.
end.
```

ALGORITHM

An algorithm for the first subtask is the following:

1a. Ask the user to type in two numbers;
1b. `readln(N1, N2);`
1c. Ask the user to enter a guess as to their average;
1d. `readln(GUESS)`

Our algorithm for subtask 1 contains a mixture of Pascal and English. This is quite common. When the Pascal way to express a step is obvious, there is little point in writing it in English. When the steps are large or complicated, they are usually first expressed in English. This combination of English and Pascal is sometimes called *pseudocode*.

pseudocode

The algorithm for subtask 1 translates into the following Pascal code:

implementation phase

```
writeln('Enter TWO INTEGERS, separated by a SPACE');
writeln('Then press RETURN');
readln(N1, N2);
writeln('Now GUESS their AVERAGE,');
writeln('Enter your GUESS, then press RETURN');
readln(GUESS)
```

ALGORITHM

The second task is to compute the average of the numbers held in the variables N1 and N2. The definition of average yields our algorithm:

2a. Compute the sum of N1 and N2;
2b. Divide the sum by 2 to get the average

In order to translate this, we use another variable of type `real` to hold the average. If we call the variable AVE, we get the following Pascal code for subtask 2:

```
AVE := (N1 + N2)/2
```

Designing step 3 requires some thought. Since we are not yet experienced programmers, we will settle for a very simpleminded solution. The computer will announce the user's guess and the correct average. The user can then see if the guess matches the true average. This solution is easy enough to translate directly into Pascal:

```
writeln('You guessed ', GUESS);
writeln('The right answer is ', AVE)
```

The complete program is shown in Figure 2.7. A blank line separates the code for each of the three major subtasks from one another.

Integer Division—mod and div

There is a version of division that applies only to values of type `integer` and that returns values of type `integer`. It is essentially the "long division" you learned in grade school. For example, 17 divided by 5 yields 3 with a remainder of 2. The two numbers obtained in this way can be produced with the Pascal operators *div* and *mod*. The *div* operation yields the number of times one number "goes into" another.

Program

```
program Game(input, output);
var N1, N2: integer;
    GUESS, AVE: real;
begin
  writeln('Enter TWO INTEGERS, separated by a SPACE');
  writeln('Then press RETURN');
  readln(N1, N2);
  writeln('Now GUESS their AVERAGE,');
  writeln('Enter your GUESS, then press RETURN');
  readln(GUESS);

  AVE := (N1 + N2)/2;

  writeln('You guessed ', GUESS);
  writeln('The right answer is ', AVE)
end.
```

Sample Dialogue

```
Enter TWO INTEGERS, separated by a SPACE
Then press RETURN
56 99
Now GUESS their AVERAGE,
Enter your GUESS, then press RETURN
76.5
You guessed   76.50
The right answer   is 77.50
```

**Figure 2.7
Game-playing
program.**

The *mod* operation gives the remainder. The operator *mod* is short for "modulo." In both cases, the divisor is given second. For example, the statements

```
writeln('17 Divided by 5 is ', 17 div 5);
writeln('with a Remainder of ', 17 mod 5);
```

yield the following output:

```
17 Divided by 5 is  3
with a Remainder of  2
```

Figure 2.8 shows the relationship between these operations and grade-school long division. Figure 2.9 illustrates the differences between the two kinds of division in Pascal.

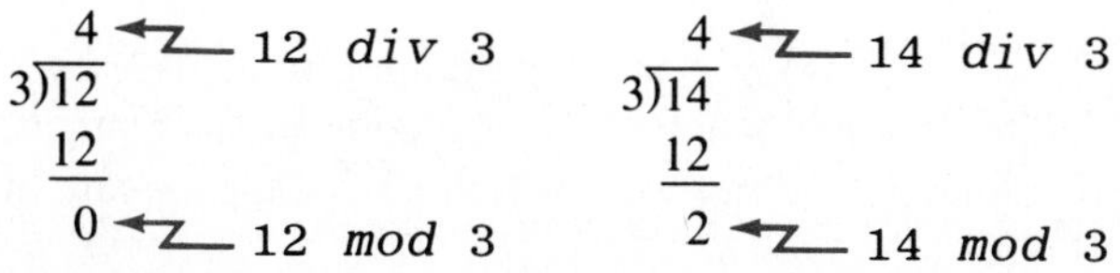

**Figure 2.8
mod and *div*.**

Expression	Value	Expression	Value
16 *div* 5	3	17 *div* 5	3
16 *mod* 5	1	17 *mod* 5	2
16/5	(3 + 1/5 =) 3.2	17 / 5	(3 + 2/5 =) 3.4

Figure 2.9
The different kinds of division.

Desktop Testing

We tend to assume that the person or machine that is following our instructions will not do anything "stupid" and will fill in any "obvious" detail. Both of these assumptions are incorrect when applied to computers. The computer does exactly what the program's instructions say, and in our design strategy, these instructions are simply translations of the instructions in an algorithm expressed in English or pseudocode. Hence, you should test the algorithm before you attempt to translate it into a Pascal program. The testing can be done by mentally stepping through the algorithm and carrying out the instructions. By stepping through an algorithm you can see it in operation and can detect many mistakes in detail as well as find any missing details. When doing this, you will want to use a pencil and paper to write down the values of the variables and to keep track of how the values change.

Case Study

Making Change

In this section we will design a sample program to make change. Given an amount of money, the program will tell how many of each type of coin, such as quarters, dimes and so forth, it takes to equal the given amount.

Problem Definition

The statement of the task to be accomplished by the program seems pretty clear, but before we go on let us make sure that as few details as possible are left unspecified. For example, what is the range of inputs for which the program must work? Does it need to give out dollars as change or not? If yes, what denominations of bills should it use? What should it do with an input of zero? The answers depend on the use to which the program is to be put.

For this example, we will assume that the program is to be used by a cashier who has no trouble with dollars but needs to be told what coins to hand out and who knows that zero cents means no coins. Hence, we can assume that the amount of change will range from one to ninety-nine cents. Are there any other points left unspecified? What if the cashier runs out of a particular coin? After all, this cashier is not too smart. That is why we were asked to write the program. We inquire and discover that the cashier usually has very few if any half-dollar coins and occasionally runs out of nickels but never runs out of any other coin. After consulting with the cashier's boss, we decide to ignore half-dollar coins and nickels. These coins will just be brought to the bank at the end of the day.

Discussion

Now that we understand the problem, we can start to design an algorithm. Our first attempt is the following:

begin
  1. Input the amount;
  2. Compute a combination of quarters, dimes, and pennies whose
     value equals the amount;
  3. Output the list of coins
end.

We have broken our task down into three subtasks. Now we must solve these subtasks and produce some Pascal code for the solutions. (In this context, the word *code* means a part of a program.)

    The first subtask is easy. We simply read the amount into a variable. To make our program easy to read, we choose the name Amount for this variable. Subtask 1 is accomplished by the following:

```
writeln('Enter an amount of change');
writeln('from 1 to 99 cents: ');
readln(Amount)
```

    The second subtask is still quite large and it will help to break it down into still smaller tasks. One sensible breakdown is:

*ALGORITHM
refinement*

  2a. Compute the number of quarters to give out;
  2b. Compute the number of dimes to give out;
  2c. Compute the number of pennies to give out

    These subtasks are not completely independent. For example, the number of dimes given out will depend on the number of quarters given out. In other words, the number of dimes will be computed on the basis of the original amount minus the total value of the quarters given out. When we analyze the information that is being passed between subtasks, we see that there are two different notions of amount. There is the original amount that the cashier input. We decided to save this amount in the variable called Amount. We will also need a variable to store the amount left to be given out as we calculate the number of quarters, dimes, and pennies. We might be tempted to use the variable Amount for this purpose by decreasing it successively by the values of quarters and dimes. However, we would like to output the original amount when we output

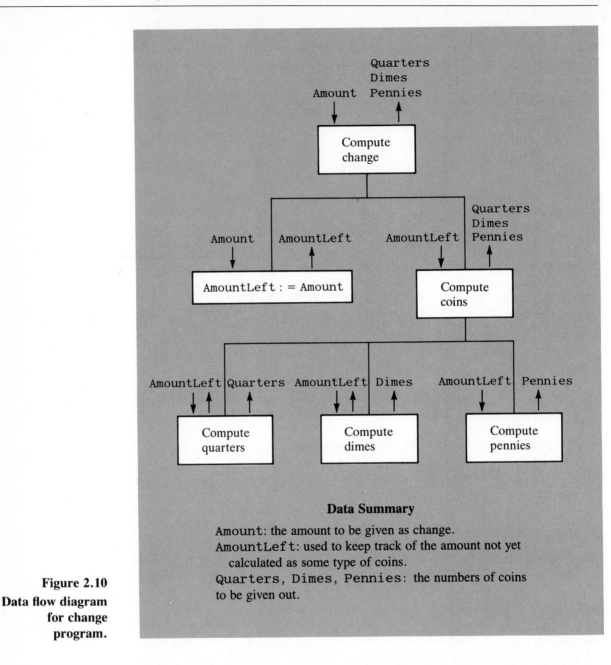

Data Summary

Amount: the amount to be given as change.
AmountLeft: used to keep track of the amount not yet
   calculated as some type of coins.
Quarters, Dimes, Pennies: the numbers of coins
to be given out.

**Figure 2.10
Data flow diagram
for change
program.**

the numbers of coins, and so we wish to preserve the value of Amount unchanged. We therefore introduce a new variable called AmountLeft, which, at various points in the computation, will hold the amount still left to be given as coins. At the start of the computation to calculate coins, the entire amount is the amount left. Hence, we will insert the following assignment before we calculate the number of coins.

    AmountLeft := Amount

After the program calculates the number of quarters to give out, `AmountLeft` will be decreased by the value of the quarters given out. After computing the number of dimes, `AmountLeft` will be further decreased by the value of the dimes. The movement of information such as the value of `AmountLeft` from one subtask to another is often called *data flow*. This interaction of subtasks is depicted in Figure 2.10. Diagrams like this will be called *data flow diagrams*.

data flow

The smaller tasks, into which subtask 2 is subdivided, can now be rewritten into the following more detailed decomposition of subtask 2:

ALGORITHM
second refinement

2a. Compute the maximum number of quarters in `AmountLeft` and decrease `AmountLeft` by the total value of the quarters;

2b. Compute the maximum number of dimes in `AmountLeft` and decrease `AmountLeft` by the total value of the dimes;

2c. Compute the number of pennies in `AmountLeft`

Subtask 2a is already expressed as two smaller subtasks. The first one is to compute the maximum number of quarters in `AmountLeft`. There are a number of ways to do this. We could subtract 25 from `AmountLeft` as many times as is possible (without getting a negative result) and count the number of times we do that. That would work, but before we jump to the keyboard and type it up, we should think about whether there is a simpler solution. There is.

analysis of
possible
solutions

The number of times we can subtract 25 from `AmountLeft` is the number of times 25 "goes into" `AmountLeft`, and we have a standard Pascal operator for that. The number of times 25 goes into `AmountLeft` is:

```
AmountLeft div 25
```

This yields the number of quarters to be given out, and the value will be stored in a variable called `Quarters`. The first part of subtask 2a can therefore be accomplished by the Pascal statement:

```
Quarters := AmountLeft div 25
```

The decrease in the amount left after giving out the quarters can be computed by:

```
AmountLeft := AmountLeft − 25*Quarters
```

Although that formula will work, again there is a simpler expression for the new amount left. The amount left after giving out as many quarters as possible is just the remainder after dividing the old value of `AmountLeft` by 25. In Pascal, this is expressed by

```
AmountLeft := AmountLeft mod 25
```

Hence, subtask 2a can be accomplished by the following Pascal code:

```
Quarters := AmountLeft div 25;
AmountLeft := AmountLeft mod 25
```

Subtask 2b can be accomplished by a similar piece of Pascal code:

```
Dimes := AmountLeft div 10;
AmountLeft := AmountLeft mod 10
```

Program

```
program Change(input, output);
var Amount, AmountLeft,
    Quarters, Dimes, Pennies: integer;
begin
  writeln('Enter an amount of change');
  writeln('from 1 to 99 cents: ');
  readln(Amount);

  AmountLeft := Amount;

  Quarters := AmountLeft div 25;
  AmountLeft := AmountLeft mod 25;

  Dimes := AmountLeft div 10;
  AmountLeft := AmountLeft mod 10;

  Pennies := AmountLeft;

  writeln(Amount, ' cents can be given as:');
  writeln(Quarters, ' quarters');
  writeln(Dimes, ' dimes and');
  writeln(Pennies, ' pennies')
end.
```

Sample Dialogue

```
Enter an amount of change
from 1 to 99 cents:
67
   67 cents can be given as:
    2 quarters
    1 dimes and
    7 pennies
```

Figure 2.11

A program to make change.

The purpose of the variable Dimes above and the variable Pennies mentioned next is obvious.

Subtask 2c is very simple, because the entire amount remaining is given out as pennies. It is accomplished by:

    Pennies := AmountLeft

echoing
input

Subtask 3 can be accomplished by a series of writeln statements that output the values of the variables Quarters, Dimes, and Pennies. As a check to make sure that the original amount was entered correctly, the value of Amount is also output. The complete program is shown in Figure 2.11.

Exploring the Solution Space

The previous discussion about computing the number of quarters illustrates an important lesson about algorithms and their design. There is always more than one algorithm for a given task. Just because you have found one algorithm does not mean you have found the best algorithm. It always pays to look for a simpler or more efficient algorithm.

alternative solutions

The last case study illustrates another technique to help in your search for algorithms. An existing algorithm can often be adapted to fit a new task. In the case study, we used the following to compute the number of quarters and the amount left after giving out that many quarters.

solution by analogy

```
Quarters := AmountLeft div 25;
AmountLeft := AmountLeft mod 25
```

To accomplish a similar task for dimes, all we needed to do was to replace 25 with 10.

We will present other techniques for algorithm design in later chapters, but first we will summarize the tools we have developed thus far for designing algorithms and Pascal programs.

There was a most ingenious Architect who had contrived a
new Method for building Houses, by beginning at the Roof,
and working downwards to the Foundation;
Jonathan Swift, Gulliver's Travels

Summary of Problem Solving Techniques

- Before writing a Pascal program, design the algorithm (method of solution) that the program will use. The algorithm can be expressed in a combination of Pascal and English known as *pseudocode*.
- You should design algorithms using the top-down (divide and conquer) method described in this chapter.
- When designing programs by the top-down method, you should explicitly analyze the flow of information between subtasks.
- You can sometimes produce algorithms by adapting a known algorithm to fit the new task.
- Always look for alternative solutions. Just because you have found one solution to a problem does not mean that you have found the best solution.
- Give an algorithm a "desktop" testing before translating it into a Pascal program.

Summary of Programming Techniques

- Both pseudocode and the final Pascal program should use meaningful names for variables.
- Use an indenting, spacing, and line-break pattern similar to the sample programs.
- All data has a data type. Be sure to check that variables and constants are of the correct data type.
- Use enough parentheses in arithmetic expressions to make the order of operations clear.
- Be sure that variables are initialized before the program attempts to use their value.
- When programming interactively, always include a prompt line in a program whenever the user is expected to enter data.
- Programs should always echo input.

Summary of Pascal Constructs

Each of the following chapters contains a summary similar in form to the following one. The entries in the summary consist of three parts: (1) an outline of the syntax (form) of the construct, (2) one or more typical examples of the construct, and (3) an explanation of the construct. Occasionally, one or two of the parts are omitted.

identifier

Syntax:

Any string of letters and digits that begins with a letter.

Example:

Sum2

Identifiers are used as names for variables and other items in programs.

variable declarations

Syntax:

```
var  <variable list 1>:  <type 1>;
     <variable list 2>:  <type 2>;
                            .
                            .
                            .
     <variable list n>:  <type n>;
```

Example:

```
var N1, N2: integer;
    Rate: real;
```

Each variable list is a list of identifiers separated by commas. All the identifiers on <variable list 1> are declared to name variables of type <type 1>, all the identifiers on <variable list 2> are declared to name variables of type <type 2>, and so forth. The types may be any type names. They may be in any order and may be repeated. The types we have seen so far are `integer` for whole number values, `real` for number values with a fractional part, and `char` for values that are a single character.

the type integer

Syntax:

```
integer
```

The data type whose values are all the whole numbers (positive, negative, or zero) that the computer system can handle. Constants of this type are written as strings of digits optionally preceded by a plus or a minus sign. The values are stored exactly.

the type real

Syntax:

```
real
```

The data type whose values are numbers that, when written in the usual decimal notation, have digits after the decimal point. The values are stored as approximate values. Constants of this type may be in either of the following forms, optionally preceded by a plus or a minus sign:

1. A sequence of digits containing a decimal point that has at least one digit before the decimal point and at least one digit after the decimal point.
2. A number followed by the letter E, followed by a constant of type `integer`. The number before the E must be either an `integer` constant or a `real` constant in form 1.

the type char (characters)

Syntax:

```
char
```

The type consisting of single characters. The constants are formed by placing the character in single quotes. For example, `'A'`, `'$'`, and `'3'`.

assignment statement

Syntax:

```
<variable> := <expression>
```

Example:

```
SUM := N1 + N2
```

The <expression> is evaluated and the value of the <variable> is set to that value. The <variable> and the value of the <expression> must be of the same type.

integer division

Syntax:

<integer expression 1> *div* <integer expression 2>
<integer expression 1> *mod* <integer expression 2>

Examples:

```
X := 14 div 3;
Y := 14 mod 3
```

div returns the quotient obtained from dividing the value of the first expression by the value of the second; *mod* returns the remainder. In the examples, the value of X is changed to 4 and that of Y is changed to 2.

write statement

Syntax:

```
write(<argument list>)
```

Example:

```
write(' Answer is ', SUM)
```

Outputs the values of the items in <argument list> to the primary output device, usually a display screen. <argument list> is a list of variables and quoted strings separated by commas.

quoted strings

Example:

```
'Surf''s up'
```

When used in a `writeln`, the string inside the single quotes is output to the screen. Both the opening and closing quotes are the same symbol. To include a single quote within a quoted string, you must use two single quotes. Quoted strings may not be broken across two lines.

write-line statement

Syntax:

```
writeln(<argument list>)
```

Example:

```
writeln(' Answer is ', SUM)
```

Same as `write` except that any subsequent output will appear on a new line.

read statement

Syntax:

```
read(<variable list>)
```

Example:

```
read(N1, N2)
```

The <variable list> is a list of *n* variables separated by commas. There may be any number *n* of variables. This statement causes the computer to read *n* values from the primary input device, usually the keyboard, and to set the values of the variables in <variable list> to these values. The values read must correspond in type to the variable types.

read-line statement
Syntax:

```
readln(<variable list>)
```

Example:

```
readln(N1, N2)
```

Same as the read statement except that any subsequent input will be taken from the next line of input.

Exercises

Self-Test Exercises

13. Determine the value of each of the following Pascal arithmetic expressions:

15 *div* 12	15 *mod* 12
24 *div* 12	24 *mod* 12
123 *div* 100	123 *mod* 100
200 *div* 100	200 *mod* 100
99 *div* 2	99 *mod* 2
2 *div* 3	2 *mod* 3

Interactive Exercises

14. Write a program that reads two integers into the variables X and Y and then outputs X *div* Y and X *mod* Y. Run the program several times with different pairs of integers as input.

15. Write a program that will convert a number of seconds to the equivalent number of minutes and seconds. Use the *mod* and *div* operators.

16. Type up and run the program given in Figure 2.1. Then modify the program so that it does subtraction instead of addition. Do not forget to change the string ' Plus ' to something appropriate. Run the modified program. Next, modify the program so that it does multiplication instead of addition or subtraction. Run that program.

17. Modify your program from the previous exercise so that it uses data and variables

of type `real` instead of type `integer`. Run the program. Modify the program again so that it does division instead of multiplication.

18. Modify your program from the previous exercise so that it outputs the equal sign instead of the word `'Equals'`.

19. Write a Pascal program that will read in a character typed in on the keyboard and then write it to the screen twice.

20. Write a Pascal program that will read in two characters and then write them both out twice. Remember that the blank is a perfectly good character to the computer, and so things will go wrong if you separate the characters by a blank.

21. Type up and run the program shown in Figure 2.7.

22. Modify the program from the previous exercise so that it also outputs one additional line giving the amount by which the user's guess missed the true average. For this exercise, it is acceptable to output zero or a negative number as the amount by which the guess missed the true average.

Programming Exercises

23. Write a Pascal program that reads in two integers and then outputs their sum, difference, and product.

24. Write a Pascal program that reads in two integers, divides one by the other, places the result in a variable of type `real`, and then outputs both the numbers and their quotient. Be sure to include a `writeln` statement that warns the user not to give input that would cause the computer to try to divide by zero.

25. A class has four exams in one term. Write a program that reads in a student's four exam scores, as integers, and outputs the student's average.

26. A metric ton is 35,273.92 ounces. Write a program that reads in the weight of a package of breakfast cereal in ounces and then outputs the weight in metric tons as well as the number of boxes of cereal needed to yield one metric ton of cereal.

27. A government research lab has concluded that certain chemicals commonly used in foods will cause death in laboratory mice. A friend of yours is desperate to lose weight but cannot give up soda pop. Your friend wants to know how much diet soda pop it is possible to drink without dying as a result. Write a program to supply the answer. The input to the program is the amount of artificial sweetener needed to kill a mouse, the weight of the mouse, and the weight of the dieter. To ensure the safety of your friend, be sure the program requests the weight at which the dieter will stop dieting, rather than the dieter's current weight. Assume that diet soda contains one-tenth of 1% artificial sweetener.

28. A Celsius (centigrade) temperature C can be converted to an equivalent Fahrenheit temperature F according to the following formula:

$$F = (9/5)C + 32$$

Write a Pascal program that reads in a Celsius temperature as a decimal number and then outputs the equivalent Fahrenheit temperature.

29. The straight-line method for computing the yearly depreciation in value D for an item is given by the formula

$$D = \frac{P - S}{Y}$$

where P is the purchase price, S is the salvage value, and Y is the number of years the item is used. Write a program that takes as input the purchase price of an item, its expected number of years of service, and its expected salvage value and then outputs the yearly depreciation for the item.

30. An automobile is used for commuting purposes. Write a program that takes as input the distance of the commute, the automobile's fuel efficiency in miles per gallon, and the price of gasoline and then outputs the cost of gasoline for the commute.

31. Workers at a particular company have won a 7.6% pay increase. Moreover, the increase is retroactive for six months. Write a program that takes an employee's previous annual salary as input and then outputs the amount of retroactive pay due the employee, the new annual salary, and the new monthly salary.

32. The public utilities commission has decided that the electric company overcharged its customers for two months last year. To make up the difference to the customers, the commission orders the company to decrease each of next month's bills by 10%. The city also levies a 3% utility tax, which is to be applied to the bill before it is discounted. Also, the 10% discount does not apply to the utility tax. Assume electricity costs $0.16 per kilowatt-hour. Write a program to compute next month's electricity bill given the number of kilowatt-hours consumed as input.

33. Write a Pascal program for the algorithm about discount installment loans that was given as Exercise 10 in Chapter 1.

MORE PASCAL AND PROGRAMMING TECHNIQUES

". . .—and that shows that there are three hundred and sixty-four days when you might get un-birthday presents—"

"Certainly," said Alice.

"And only one *for birthday presents, you know. There's glory for you!"*

"I don't know what you mean by 'glory,'" Alice said.

Humpty Dumpty smiled contemptuously. "Of course you don't— till I tell you. I meant 'there's a nice knock-down argument for you!'"

"But 'glory' doesn't mean 'a nice knockdown argument,'" Alice objected.

"When I use a word," Humpty Dumpty said, in rather a scornful tone, "it means just what I choose it to mean—neither more nor less."

"The question is," said Alice, "whether you can *make words mean so many different things."*

"The question is," said Humpty Dumpty, "which is to be master—that's all."

LEWIS CARROLL, THROUGH THE LOOKING-GLASS

Chapter Contents

In this chapter we present more features of the Pascal language, including a mechanism that allows Pascal programs to choose between alternative actions and a mechanism that allows a program to repeat an action. We develop two more sample programs, from problem formulation through to Pascal program. In the process we illustrate some new problem solving techniques. We also present some key programming techniques, including techniques for testing programs and correcting programming errors. Since programming style is of more than just aesthetic importance, this chapter both opens and closes with remarks on style. The first topic is a Pascal construct that is used to make programs more readable and easier to modify.

Naming Constants

There are two problems with constants in a computer program. The first is that they carry no mnemonic value. For example, when the number 10 is encountered in a program, the number gives no hint of its significance. If the program is a banking program, it might be the number of branch offices or the number of teller windows at the main office. In order to understand the program, you need to know the significance of each constant. The second problem is that when a program needs to be changed, the process of changing constants tends to introduce errors. Suppose that 10 occurs 12 times in a banking program; four times it represents the number of branch offices, and eight times it represents the number of teller windows at the main office. When the bank opens a new branch and the program needs to be updated, there is a good chance that some of the 10's that should be changed to 11 will not be, or that some that should not be changed to 11 will be changed. Pascal provides a single mechanism to deal with all of these problems.

In Pascal you can assign a name to a constant and then use the name in place of the constant. This is done with a *constant declaration*. Constant declarations are placed between the program heading and the variable declarations.

constant declarations

A constant declaration consists of the reserved word *const* followed by the identifier that is to be the name of the constant, followed by the equal sign and then the constant. The declaration includes sufficient blanks to separate the various pieces and is ended with a semicolon. In this case, an example is clearer than a definition. The following gives the name BranchCount to the number 10:

```
const BranchCount = 10;
```

To declare more than one constant, simply list them all, separated by semicolons, like so:

```
const BranchCount = 10;
      WindowCount = 10;
      InterestRate = 0.06;
      AccountCode = 'S';
```

Any identifier that is not a reserved word can be used as a name. Any type of constant can be named in this way.

Once a constant has been given a name in a constant declaration, the identifier naming the constant can then be used anywhere that the constant is allowed, and it will have exactly the same meaning as the constant it names.

To change a named constant, you need only change the constant declaration. The meaning of all occurrences of BranchCount can be changed from 10 to 11 simply by changing the first 10 in the above declaration.

You can also assign a name to a quoted string with a constant declaration. For example, the following assigns the name Name to a long string:

string constants

```
const Name = 'Mr. E. Z. Victim';
```

The identifier Name can be used anywhere that the string constant can be used and will have the same meaning as the constant. In particular, if the program contains this constant declaration, then the statement

```
writeln('Program designed exclusively for ', Name)
```

will cause the following to appear on the screen:

```
Program designed exclusively for Mr. E. Z. Victim
```

Remember that you do not enclose string constant identifiers like Name in quotes. That will not produce the result you want.

Although unnamed numeric constants are allowed in a program, you should seldom use them. It often makes sense to use unnamed constants for quantities that are well known, easily recognizable, and unchangeable, such as 100 for the number of centimeters in a meter. All other numeric constants should be given names with a constant declaration, and you should use the name, rather than the unnamed constant, in the program. This will make your programs easier to read and easier to change.

Comments

To make a program understandable, you should include explanatory notes at key places in the program. Such notes are called *comments*. In Pascal and most other programming languages, there are provisions for including such comments within the text of a program.

In Pascal a comment may be inserted almost anywhere, as long as it is preceded by the symbol {, sometimes called a "brace" or "curly bracket," and is followed by the matching symbol }. The compiler simply ignores anything between a matching pair of curly bracket symbols { }. Comments cannot appear inside a quoted string. Otherwise, there would be no way to include the symbols '{' and '}' inside a quoted string. Further, comments cannot appear inside other comments; the effect of a comment inside of a comment is unpredictable. Except for these restrictions, a comment can go anywhere that the blank symbol is allowed. It may extend across more than one line, as long as it begins with the curly bracket symbol { and ends with the matching symbol }. Pascal does not demand a pair of the symbols { } on each line of a comment.

If the symbols { } are not available on your keyboard, or if you do not want to use them for some reason, you can use the pair (* and *) instead.

when to comment   Each program unit of any substantial size or complexity should be explained by a comment. In particular, each program should open with a comment that explains what the program does, as in the following sample heading:

```
program PropertyCost(input, output);
{Accepts property assessed value, property tax rate, mortgage rate, and
loan balance as input. Computes the annual after-tax cost of the property.
Assumes full depreciation write-off as a business expense.
Uses 30-year straight line depreciation.}
```

In this book, comments will always be written in italic typeface in order to make them stand out from the program text.

It is difficult to say just how many comments a program should contain. The only correct answer is "just enough," and this answer does not convey a lot to the novice programmer. It will take some experience to get a feel for how and when it is best to generate comments. Whenever something is important and not obvious, it merits a comment. However, too many comments are as bad as too few. A program that has a comment on each line can be so buried in comments that it hides the structure of the program and obscures the critical comments in a sea of obvious observations. Comments like the following contribute nothing to understanding and should not appear in a program:

```
Distance := Speed * Time;  {Computes the distance traveled}
```

Pitfall

Forgetting a Closing Comment Delimiter

If you omit a closing comment delimiter '}', you might expect the compiler to notice this and issue an error message. However, this is not necessarily the case. In many cases, this error may simply cause a portion of the program to become part of one large inadvertent comment. By way of example, consider the following piece of code:

```
{Next adjust pay
Pay := Pay + Bonus;
{Tax includes state and federal tax.}
Pay := Pay - Tax;
```

Because the ending comment delimiter has been omitted from the first line displayed, the compiler will pair the opening delimiter '{' with the next closing delimiter converting the poor employee's bonus into a mere comment. The compiler will give no error message and will appear to run normally, but the following statement will never be executed because it is now inside a comment:

```
Pay := Pay + Bonus
```

What about the extra '{', you might ask. Does it not produce an error message to warn you? Probably not. Most Pascal compilers pair a '{' with the first matching '}' and happily ignore any intervening occurrence of '{', which might hint at a mistake.

Formatted Output

When using write or writeln, you can specify the desired number of spaces used to display each value that is output. To do so, simply add a colon and a number after the expression, variable, or quoted string to be output. The number following the colon is

field widths

called a *field width,* and it specifies the total number of spaces allocated for outputting the number or other type of value. For example,

```
N := 123;
writeln('Start-field', N:5, 'End-field');
```

produces the following output (there are two spaces between the d and the 1:)

```
Start-field  123End-field
```

Any extra spaces are always in front of the value being output. If you allow too few spaces, it is not a disaster; the computer will allocate more space, but the format may not be what you desired.

output as a subtask

In your first few programs it may be best to omit field width specifications and settle for the spacing that the system decides on. It makes sense to omit such detail on your first version of a program. First, get your program to work. Then go back and add the field widths if you want neater output. This is a good example of the divide-and-conquer strategy. The task of designing a program can frequently be subdivided into two main subtasks: computing some quantities, and displaying them in a neat and clear manner. When solving the problem of how to compute the quantities, there is no need to confuse the issue with questions about the number of spaces needed to output the quantities. That is a separate task.

In this book we will frequently omit field width specifications from the write and writeln statements in our sample programs. In many cases, the program presented is only a solution to the task of computing quantities. In order to get a program with neat-looking output, it may be necessary to add some field width specifications.

field specifications for reals

At least one case definitely demands a field width and other related output *field specifications* in order to avoid looking ridiculous. When the output is an amount of dollars and cents, an output without a field specification usually looks absurd.

```
Total cost including tax is $ 1.56347690000000E01
```

The above screen display is a poor way to say that the cost is $15.63. Adding the field width specification :6:2 will convert the output into a reasonable format. The first number, the 6, says to allow a total of six spaces for the output. The second number, the 2, says to allow two digits after the decimal point. This second number is also preceded by a colon. If the second number is present, it tells the computer not to use the E notation. Hence, with the width specification :6:2 the six spaces are allocated as follows: one for the decimal point, two after the decimal point, and three in front of the decimal point. As an example, consider the following two lines from a Pascal program:

```
COST := 15.63;
writeln('Total cost including tax is $', COST:6:2)
```

These two lines produce the following output (there is one space between the $ and the 1):

```
Total cost including tax is $ 15.63
```

Example Using Named Constants and Formatted Output

The program in Figure 3.1 was designed for a new, not yet federally or state chartered, savings institution. This institution is installing an automated 24-hour teller and has a limited amount of capital to spend on hardware and software. The program in Figure 3.1 was designed to handle deposits.

Program

```pascal
program Teller(input, output);
{Accepts deposit amounts as input and writes out the value
of the deposit plus interest after one year.}
const Name = 'FLY BY NIGHT THRIFT';
      Motto = 'We''ll take your money any time.';
      BrCount = 2;
      CountWidth = 2;
      Rate = 7.25;
      RateWidth = 5;  {Field width for outputting the Rate.}
      MoneyWidth = 7; {Field width for outputting the
                          Deposit and the Deposit plus interest.}
var Deposit, Interest, Amount: real;

begin
  writeln('WELCOME TO ', Name);
  writeln(Motto);
  writeln('We currently pay:');
  writeln(Rate :RateWidth:2, '% on deposits,');
  writeln('AND have');
  writeln(BrCount :CountWidth, ' offices to serve YOU!');
  writeln;
  writeln('ENTER the amount of your DEPOSIT at');
  writeln('the keyboard and press the RETURN KEY.');
  writeln('PLEASE, do NOT type in a $ sign.');
  readln(Deposit);
  writeln('Next, put your money in an ENVELOPE,');
  writeln('WRITE your NAME on the envelope,');
  writeln('and slip it UNDER THE DOOR.');
  writeln('Thank you for your deposit of:');
  writeln('$', Deposit :MoneyWidth:2);

  Interest := (Rate/100) * Deposit;
     {The division by 100 changes the percent figure to a fraction.}
  Amount := Deposit + Interest;
```

Figure 3.1

Comments and named constants.

```
    writeln('In just one short year');
    writeln('your deposit will grow to');
    writeln('$', Amount :MoneyWidth:2);
    writeln('Thank you for choosing ', Name, '!')
end.
```

Sample Dialogue

```
WELCOME TO FLY BY NIGHT THRIFT
We'll take your money any time.
We currently pay:
 7.25% on deposits,
AND have
 2 offices to serve YOU!

ENTER the amount of your DEPOSIT at
the keyboard and press the RETURN KEY.
PLEASE, do NOT type in a $ sign.
100.00
Next, put your money in an ENVELOPE,
WRITE your NAME on the envelope,
and slip it UNDER THE DOOR.
Thank you for your deposit of:
$ 100.00
In just one short year
your deposit will grow to
$ 107.25
Thank you for choosing FLY BY NIGHT THRIFT!
```

**Figure 3.1
(continued)**

Since the board of directors is not sure that their current name represents sound marketing practice, the name has been placed in a constant declaration. This makes it easier to change the name if they later decide that they prefer something more dignified, such as Nocturnal Aviators Savings and Thrift Association, Inc. The motto has also been placed in a constant declaration, as have almost all other constants in the program. Even the field widths for formatted output are given names. For example, the fourth writeln is equivalent to

```
    writeln(Rate:5:2, '% on deposits, ')
```

Allowable Range for Numbers

maxint

For each implementation of Pascal, there is a largest allowable positive number of type integer and a smallest allowable negative number of type integer. The language Pascal has a predefined constant called maxint that is equal to the largest value of type integer that can be used on the computer. You do not need to include it in a

constant declaration. It is already defined for you. The smallest value of type integer is not necessarily minus maxint, but it will be close to that value. To discover the largest possible integer value for your machine, simply embed the following
in a complete program:

```
writeln('Largest integer = ', maxint)
```

Like the numbers of type integer, there is also a largest positive and a smallest
negative number of type real that the computer can handle, and these numbers will
vary from one installation to another. There are no predefined constants for these values, and so it is not as easy to discover these limits. However, the largest allowable
number of type real is always much larger than the largest allowable number of type
integer, and the smallest allowable negative number of type real is always much
smaller than the smallest negative number of type integer.

More about Commenting

One way to comment a program is to insert comment statements stating what the programmer expects to be true when the program execution reaches that statement. Such
comments are often called *assertions* because they *assert* something that hopefully is
true. For example, Figure 3.2 shows the change-making program from Figure 2.11
with comment assertions added.

```
program Change(input, output);
{Outputs the coins used to give an amount between 1 and 99 cents.}
var Amount, AmountLeft,
    Quarters, Dimes, Pennies: integer;
begin
  writeln('Enter an amount of change');
  writeln('from 1 to 99 cents: ');
  readln(Amount);

  AmountLeft := Amount;

  Quarters := AmountLeft div 25;
  {Quarters is the maximum number of quarters in AmountLeft cents.}
  AmountLeft := AmountLeft mod 25;
  {AmountLeft has been decreased by the value of
  the number of quarters specified by Quarters.}

  Dimes := AmountLeft div 10;
  {Dimes is the maximum number of dimes in AmountLeft cents.}
  AmountLeft := AmountLeft mod 10;
  {AmountLeft has been decreased by the value of
  the number of dimes specified by Dimes.}
```

Figure 3.2
**Program with
simple comment
assertions.**

```
                    Pennies := AmountLeft;

                    writeln(Amount, ' cents can be given as:');
                    writeln(Quarters, ' quarters');
                    writeln(Dimes, ' dimes and');
                    writeln(Pennies, ' pennies')
                  end.
```

**Figure 3.2
(continued)**

As we proceed with our study of programming techniques, we will introduce some powerful and more sophisticated ways of using assertions.

Testing and Debugging

A mistake in a program is usually called a *bug,* and the process of eliminating bugs is called *debugging.* In this section we will describe the three main kinds of programming mistakes and give some hints on how to correct them.

syntax errors

The compiler will catch certain kinds of mistakes and will write out an error message when it finds one. The compiler will detect what are called *syntax errors.* The *syntax* of a language consists of the grammar and punctuation rules for the language. These rules determine whether or not your program follows the rules for the form of a Pascal program. If your program violates a syntax rule—if, for example, you have omitted a semicolon or failed to declare a variable—the compiler will issue an error statement.

interpreting error messages

If the compiler discovers a syntax error in your program, it will tell you where the error is likely to be and what kind of error it probably is. If the compiler says your program contains a syntax error, you can be confident that it does. However, the compiler may be incorrect about either the location of the error or its nature. It does a better job of determining the location of an error, to within a line or two, than it does of determining the source of the error. As a general rule, the compiler is likely to be right about the location of the first syntax error in your program, but it may not know what the nature of the error is. This is because the compiler is guessing at what you meant to write down and can easily guess wrong. After all, it cannot read your mind.

Error messages after the first one are more likely to be incorrect with respect to either the location or the nature of the error. Again, this is because the compiler must guess your meaning. If the compiler's first guess was incorrect, this will affect its analysis of future mistakes, since the analysis will be based on a false assumption.

Programs tend to contain numerous matching pairs, such as comment delimiters, quotes, parentheses, and other delimiters to be discussed later. A common syntax error is to miss one end of some matching pair. The compiler will always detect such an omission, but the error message it produces may be a little confusing.

As an illustration, consider the statement

```
writeln('Answers are, W, X, Y  Z, 'in miles')
```

The statement has a quote missing in the first quoted string. Yet the compiler will not find a mistake until it reaches the second quoted string. The error message will probably say the error is in the neighborhood of the word ' in ' and may or may not mention a missing quote. The reason for this is that the compiler perceives the quoted string

```
'Answers are,  W,  X,  Y   Z,  '
```

as the first item to be written out. After all, it is a perfectly legitimate quoted string. If you realize that the mistake is in the first constant and you add the quote, you will get

```
writeln('Answers are',  W,  X,  Y   Z,  'in miles')
```

This will, of course, still produce a compiler error message pointing out the missing comma between the Y and the Z. In many cases, of which this is just one example, one mistake can hide another. In this case, the missing quote causes the compiler to ignore the missing comma.

Sooner or later you will find yourself in a situation in which you are absolutely certain that your program is correct, yet the compiler will not accept it and insists that there is a mistake in a particular line. The natural assumption is that there is a mistake in the compiler and that your program is correct. Occasionally, there are mistakes in compilers, but they are rare and it is extremely unlikely that the fault is in the compiler. Frequently it is a mistake that you cannot see for either physical or psychological reasons. You may have typed the letter "Oh" when you meant to type the digit zero. There may be a real and visible mistake that you unconsciously correct in your mind. When you cannot find anything wrong with the line, try retyping it. Amazingly enough, this will sometimes cure the problem.

There are certain kinds of errors that the computer system can detect only when a program is run. Appropriately enough, these are called *run-time errors*. Most computer systems will detect certain run-time errors and output an appropriate error message. The distinction between syntax errors and run-time errors is illustrated in Figure 3.3. *run-time errors*

Many typical run-time errors have to do with numeric calculations. If the program attempts to evaluate an expression that would produce an `integer` value greater than `maxint`, the system should detect this fact when the program is run and should output an error message called an *overflow message*. A similar message should be output when real-valued expressions get to be too large or too small. (Unfortunately, some versions of Pascal do not provide overflow messages.) The system will also provide a run-time error message if the program attempts to divide by zero or to take the square root of a negative number. Other run-time errors have to do with features of Pascal that we have not yet discussed. These errors will be discussed as the relevant Pascal features are introduced. *overflow*

If the compiler approves of your program and the program runs once with no run-time error messages, this does not guarantee that it is correct. Remember, the compiler will only tell you if you wrote a syntactically correct Pascal program. It will not tell you whether the program does what you want it to do. Mistakes in the underlying algorithm or in translating the algorithm into Pascal are called *logical errors*. If the compiler approves of your program and there are no run-time errors but the program does not *logical errors*

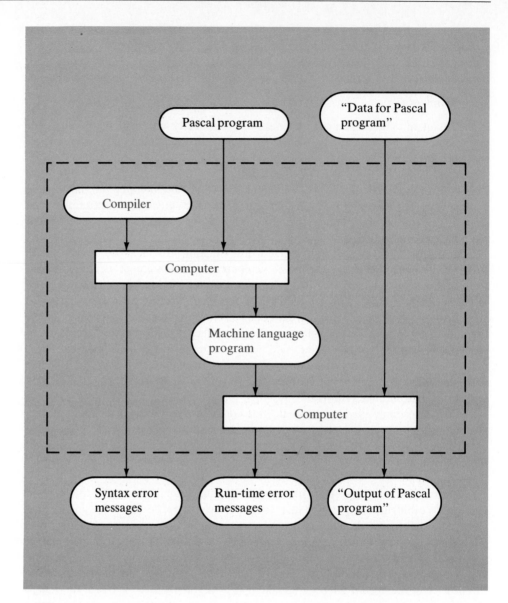

Figure 3.3
Syntax and run-
time errors.

perform properly, then undoubtedly your program contains a logical error. Logical errors are the hardest kind to diagnose. This is because the computer gives you no error
messages to help find the error. It cannot reasonably be expected to give any error messages. For all the computer knows, you may have meant what you wrote. As an example of a simple logical error, suppose that when we wrote the change-making program in Figure 3.2 we were confused about the distinction between *div* and *mod* and
so we mistakenly wrote

```
AmountLeft := AmountLeft div 25
```

instead of

```
AmountLeft := AmountLeft mod 25
```

There would be no way for the computer to know that we made a mistake. As far as the computer is concerned, we did not make a mistake. We wrote a completely legitimate program. Unfortunately, it was not exactly the program we wanted. If you insert this logical error into the program in Figure 3.2, it will compile and run without precipitating an error message. It will give output in the desired format. However, it will usually give an incorrect output for the numbers of dimes and pennies. This would be a logical error. There are no syntax errors and no run-time errors, but the program is incorrect nonetheless.

Other logical errors are more complicated. As another example using the same change-making program, suppose that we forgot to decrease the amount left as we gave out coins. In other words, suppose we calculated quarters, dimes, and pennies in the following incorrect way:

```
Quarters := Amount div 25;
Dimes := Amount div 10;
Pennies := Amount div 1
```

This also would be a logical error. The program would still run, but it would give incorrect output.

These sample errors may seem ridiculously naive. It may seem that they are unlikely to occur and, moreover, that they would be easy to find if you did make one of them. This is not so at all. Remember, all errors are obvious once they are discovered. But at the time that you make an error it is always an undiscovered, hidden error. Otherwise, why would you make it?

A *listing* of a program is a copy of the program printed on paper and is normally produced by a printer. When you are debugging a program, it helps to have a listing. This gives you a view of the entire program and also makes it easy to write notes on the program.

make a listing

In order to test a new program for logical errors, you should run the program on several sets of representative data and check the program's performance on those inputs. If the program passes those tests, you can have more confidence in it, but you still cannot be absolutely sure that the program is correct. It still may not do what you want it to do when it is run on other data.

testing

The only way to justify confidence in a program is to program carefully and so avoid most errors. This approach is far better than trying to fix a program that is riddled with errors. The errors may go undetected, and even if you do detect the presence of an error, it may not be easy to locate its source.

Tracing

Sometimes simply looking at the output of a program does not provide enough information to locate a logical or other type of error. If the program gives incorrect output, you know it is wrong, but you may not know where the mistake is. One way to find out more about a program is to write out the values of variables as they change. For example, again consider the program in Figure 3.2. The value of the variable AmountLeft is never written out. Yet if we had mistakenly written *div* instead of *mod* in the statement

```
AmountLeft := AmountLeft mod 25
```

then the quickest way to notice this would be to notice that the value of AmountLeft is incorrect. To help locate mistakes such as this when testing the program, it is a good idea to insert temporary output statements for variables that change but that are not otherwise output. For example, in the program in Figure 3.2 we might insert

```
writeln('AmountLeft = ', AmountLeft)
```

This is called *tracing*.

Trace statements are temporary statements that will not appear in the final program. Hence, we want them to be easy to find and delete. One way to accomplish this is by labeling each one with a suitable comment, such as

```
{TEMP} writeln('AmountLeft = ', AmountLeft)
```

Use of Assertions in Testing
(Optional)

If your program contains assertions, you can use the assertions as a guide in deciding what variables to trace and where to place the writeln statements. For example, consider the following code from Figure 3.2:

> *{Quarters is the maximum number of quarters in AmountLeft cents.}*
> AmountLeft := AmountLeft mod 25;
> *{AmountLeft has been decreased by the value of*
> *the number of quarters specified by Quarters.}*

It suggests that the value of the variable Quarters as well as both the old and the new values of AmountLeft should be output at this point. To help you interpret the output, it also helps to write out the assertion. The following would therefore be a sensible collection of temporary output statements to insert at the location of these assertions.

```
{TEMP}writeln('Quarters is the maximum number');
{TEMP}writeln('of quarters in AmountLeft cents.');
{TEMP}writeln('Quarters= ', Quarters, 'AmountLeft= ', AmountLeft);
      AmountLeft := AmountLeft mod 25;
{TEMP}writeln('AmountLeft has been decreased by the value of');
{TEMP}writeln('the number of quarters specified by Quarters.');
{TEMP}writeln('AmountLeft= ', AmountLeft)
```

It is possible to place quotes around the actual assertion and then insert it in a writeln. However, if you do that, there is a good chance that you will leave one of the quote marks in the program when you finish your debugging and attempt to restore the assertion to its former state. For this reason it is probably better to just repeat the assertion. Then you can delete entire lines rather than parts of lines when you clean up the final program. Since most editors make it easy to copy and edit lines, this need not be an onerous typing chore.

Self-Test Exercises

1. What is the output produced by the following two lines (when correctly embedded in a complete program)? The variable N is of type `integer`.

```
N := -1234;
writeln('START', N:8, 'END')
```

2. What is the output produced by the following two lines (when correctly embedded in a complete program)? The variable R is of type `real`.

```
R := -12.345678;
writeln('START', R:8:2, 'END')
```

Interactive Exercises

3. Write a program that outputs `maxint` to the screen.

4. Type up and run the program `Teller` given in Figure 3.1. Change the name of the institution, its motto, and the interest rate, and then run it again.

5. Write a program that reads a value of type `real` and then writes it to the screen using the `writeln` statement given below:

```
writeln('START', R:5:2, 'END')
```

Run the program several times trying different numbers. Try some negative numbers as well as positive ones. Try a number that does not fit into the format specified, such as `1234.56`.

> What we anticipate seldom occurs;
> what we least expect generally happens.
> *Benjamin Disraeli*

Syntax Diagrams

The rules of grammar for a programming language are called the *syntax* rules of the language. The syntax rules determine whether or not a string of characters forms a program that the compiler can translate into machine code. There is a standard dia-

syntax

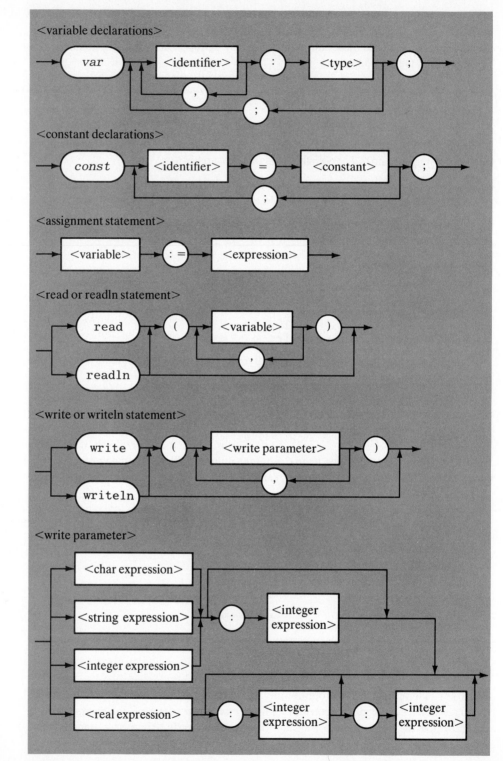

Figure 3.4
Some syntax
diagrams.

grammatic way to represent the syntax of programming languages. These diagrams are called, appropriately enough, *syntax diagrams*. Figure 3.4 contains syntax diagrams for many of the Pascal constructs we have presented thus far.

The procedure for using syntax diagrams is quite intuitive. Each diagram is labeled to indicate what it describes. To test whether a string of symbols satisfies the description, start at the inward pointing arrow on the left edge of the diagram and at the same time place a marker at the beginning of the questionable string; a mental marker usually works, but you can use a real marker such as your finger or a pencil point. Every time you encounter a round or rectangular box in the syntax diagram, check that your marker is at an object of the form described in the box, and then move your pointer to the next element in the string. Objects in round boxes are meant literally. For example, the box containing *var* can only match the word with the three letters v-a-r. Objects in rectangular boxes correspond to defined objects. For example, any Pascal identifier matches the box containing <identifier>. If in this way you can get completely through the syntax diagram and completely through the candidate string, then the candidate string satisfies the syntax diagram. If, for example, the diagram is labeled <constant declarations>, then the string satisfies the description of a constant declaration section.

using syntax diagrams

Since the diagrams can have branches, there is usually more than one path through a syntax diagram. A candidate string satisfies the diagram provided it matches one such path. To check the candidate, you must find the path. It is somewhat like a maze puzzle. If there is some way through the diagram, then the string passes the test. However, the diagram does not tell you how to find a path through the maze of the syntax diagram.

Syntax diagrams do not tell you about spacing, but it is intended that the objects in the boxes be separated in some appropriate way, usually by one or more blanks. Syntax diagrams give an almost complete description of the programming language syntax. Anything that fails the syntax diagram check definitely is not a correctly formed object of the kind described by the syntax diagram. A candidate that passes the syntax diagram test usually must also pass some other simple tests, such as having blanks in the right places.

We will include syntax diagrams as we explore the Pascal language. A complete set of syntax diagrams can be found in Appendix 2, but the simpler ones in the chapters will probably prove more useful.

Simple Branching—If-Then-Else

Sometimes it is necessary to have a program action that chooses one of two alternatives depending on the input to the program. For example, suppose you want to design a program to compute a week's salary for an hourly employee. Assume that the firm pays an overtime rate of 1½ times the regular rate for all hours after the first 40 hours worked. As long as the employee works 40 or more hours, the pay is then equal to

```
Rate * 40 + 1.5 * Rate * (Hours − 40)
```

Program

```
program Payroll(input, output);
{Computes weekly pay for an hourly employee.}
const MaxRegTime = 40; {Max number of hours at the regular rate.}
      OTFactor = 1.5; {Factor for overtime.}
var Hours: integer;
    Rate, GrossPay: real;
begin
  writeln('Enter the hourly rate of pay.');
  readln(Rate);
  writeln('Enter the number of hours worked,');
  writeln('rounded up to a whole number of hours.');
  readln(Hours);

  if Hours > MaxRegTime then
     GrossPay := Rate * MaxRegTime +
             OTFactor * Rate * (Hours - MaxRegTime)
  else
     GrossPay := Rate * Hours;

  writeln('Hours =', Hours);
  writeln('Hourly pay rate = $', Rate);
  writeln('Gross pay = $', GrossPay)
end.
```

Sample Dialogue 1

```
Enter the hourly rate of pay.
20.00
Enter the number of hours worked,
rounded up to a whole number of hours.
30
Hours =    30
Hourly pay rate = $   20.0000
Gross pay = $   600.0000
```

Sample Dialogue 2

```
Enter the hourly rate of pay.
10.00
Enter the number of hours worked,
rounded up to a whole number of hours.
41
Hours =    41
Hourly pay rate = $   10.0000
Gross pay = $   415.0000
```

Figure 3.5
An if-then-else branch.

If, however, there is a possibility that the employee will work less than 40 hours, this formula will unfairly pay a negative amount of overtime. The correct pay formula for an employee who works less than 40 hours is simple:

```
Rate * Hours
```

If both more than and less than 40 hours of work are possible, then the program will need to choose between the two formulas. In order to compute the employee's gross pay (before deductions), the program action should be

Decide whether or not `Hours > 40`.
If it is, execute the following assignment statement:
  `GrossPay := Rate * 40 + 1.5 * Rate * (Hours − 40)`
Otherwise (i.e., if `Hours ≤ 40`), execute the following:
  `GrossPay := Rate * Hours`

There is a Pascal statement that does exactly this kind of branching. The *if-then-else* statement chooses between two alternative actions. For example, the desired action can be accomplished with the following Pascal statement:

```
if Hours > 40 then
    GrossPay := Rate * 40 + 1.5 * Rate * (Hours − 40)
else
    GrossPay := Rate * Hours
```

A complete program that uses this statement is given in Figure 3.5. In the program we have given names to the constants `40` and `1.5`. If the computation had been more complicated, it would have been a good idea to use named constants even in the pseudocode.

The form of an *if-then-else* statement is as follows:

```
if <expression> <comparison operator> <another expression> then
    <first Pascal statement>
else
    <second Pascal statement>
```

The two Pascal statements may be any Pascal statements. When the program reaches the *if-then-else,* exactly one of the two embedded statements is executed. The two expressions are evaluated and compared. If the comparison is true, then the first statement is performed. If the comparison fails, then the second statement is executed.

Any two arithmetic expressions may be compared using the following comparison operators: *greater than, less than, greater than or equal to, less than or equal to, equal to,* and *not equal to.* A list of these *relational operators* is given in Figure 3.6. Some of the operators are formed using two symbols because most keyboards do not have symbols such as ≠ and ≤. For example, the Pascal expression to use in place of ≠ is the symbol pair <>. These symbol pairs are considered to be single items; do not insert any spaces between the two symbols.

relational operators

These comparisons are a special case of a more general class of expressions called "boolean expressions." We will discuss the general case in Chapter 6. For now, we will

Math	Pascal	English	Pascal Sample	Math Equivalent
=	=	equal to	Ans = 'N'	Ans = 'N'
≠	<>	not equal to	X <> Y	X ≠ Y
<	<	less than	X < 2	X < 2
≤	<=	less than or equal to	X <= 1	X ≤ 1
>	>	greater than	Y > 0	Y > 0
≥	>=	greater than or equal to	Y >= 1	Y ≥ 1

Figure 3.6
List of relational operators.

only use arithmetic expressions and operators of the forms just described, plus some simple comparisons of character values.

You can use an *if-then-else* statement to compare two character values to see whether they are equal or unequal. For example, suppose that Ans is a variable of type char and the program is about to execute the following *if-then-else* statement:

```
if Ans = 'Y' then
    writeln('I guess you said Yes.')
else
    writeln('You did not say Yes.')
```

If the value of Ans is 'Y', the first writeln will be executed. If its value is anything other than 'Y', the second writeln statement will be executed.

ordering of characters

When relational operators such as < and <= are applied to items of type char, they check for alphabetic order. Hence, 'A' < 'B' is true and 'Z' < 'H' is false. However, there is no uniformity as to how Pascal treats the interaction of upper- and lowercase letters. On some systems 'a' < 'Z' evaluates to true, and on others it evaluates to false. A check for alphabetical order is guaranteed to be correct only if both letters are uppercase or both letters are lowercase.

Pitfall

The Equality Operator

Upper- and lowercase letters are considered to be different character values. This can sometimes lead to bewildering results when Pascal is comparing characters. For example, the comparison Ans = 'Y' fails if the value of Ans is 'y'. In Chapter 6 we will discuss ways to avoid this problem. For now, you will simply have to keep this problem in mind and program around it.

The approximate nature of real values can cause special problems in comparisons involving equality. Since values of type `real` are approximate quantities, it makes no sense to test them for *exact* equality. In particular, values of type `real` should never be used with the equality operator, since the comparison is, for all practical purposes, meaningless. This rule applies to exact inequality as well. Testing `real` values using the inequality operator <> is equally meaningless and equally dangerous.

Optional Else

It is sometimes the case that we want one of the two alternatives in an *if-then-else* branch to do nothing at all. In Pascal this can be accomplished by omitting the *else* and its accompanying statement. For example, if the value of `Sales` is less than or equal to `Minimum` when the following statement is executed, then nothing will happen, and the program will simply proceed to the `writeln` statement.

```
if Sales > Minimum then
    Salary := Salary + Bonus;
writeln('Salary = ', Salary)
```

A program using *if-then* without the *else* part is shown in Figure 3.7. Figure 3.8 gives a syntax diagram that shows the syntax for both varieties of *if-then* statements.

Program

```
program AgeTalk(input, output);
var Age: integer;
begin
  writeln('Please enter your age.');
  readln(Age);
  if Age >= 18 then
     writeln('You are old enough to join the army.');
  if Age >= 21 then
     writeln('You are old enough to drink.');
  writeln('Good luck!')
end.
```

Sample Dialogue

```
Please enter your age.
19
You are old enough to join the army.
Good luck!
```

Figure 3.7
Program with *if-then* statements.

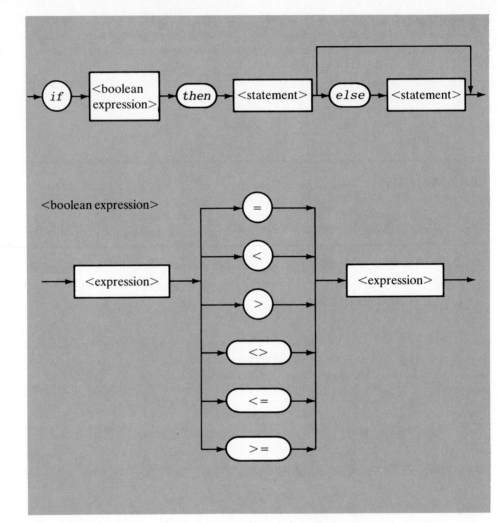

Figure 3.8
Syntax of *if-*
then **and** *if-*
then-else
statements.

```
if X > 0 then
    begin
        writeln(X, ' is positive.');
        writeln('Wow ', X, ' is positive!')
    end
else
    begin
        writeln(X, ' is zero or');
        writeln('it is negative.')
    end
```

Figure 3.9
Compound
statements used
with *if-then-*
else.

Pitfalls

Extra Semicolons

As we have stated before, semicolons are used to separate statements, but a semi-colon is not a part of the statement it follows. This is of particular importance when writing *if-then-else* statements, such as

```
if N > 0 then
    writeln('Positive.')
else
    writeln('Negative or zero.');
writeln('The next statement.')
```

If you place a semicolon after the first `writeln`, your program will produce a compiler error message. The compiler will assume that the semicolon separates two statements and that the next statement starts with the identifier *else*. But that is impossible because there is no statement in Pascal that starts with *else*. If you use an extra semicolon before the *else,* the compiler will misread the statement and will produce an error message.

Now that we have statements inside of statements the terminology can get a bit complicated. Remember that the entire *if-then-else* construct is consid-ered to be a single large statement, even though two smaller statements are em-bedded in it.

Compound Statements

One often wants one or both branches of an *if-then-else* statement to execute more than one Pascal statement. To do this, enclose the statements to be executed be-tween a *begin/end* pair, using semicolons for separators as illustrated in Figure 3.9. (It is permissible to add an extra semicolon after the last statement in the list.)

The statements, together with the *begin/end* pair, are considered to be a single Pascal statement. Statements of this form are called *compound statements*. For ex-ample, the following is a compound statement:

```
begin
  writeln(X, ' is positive.');
  writeln('Wow ', X, ' is positive!')
end
```

Iterative Enhancement

One way to design a program is to simplify the design goals so as to make the programming task easier and to then design the simpler version of the program. After that, features can be added. For example, the program for making change that we designed in the last chapter and reproduced in Figure 3.2 worked acceptably in a variety of situations. We can enhance its performance, however, by adding additional denominations of coins, such as nickels and half-dollars, to use in giving change.

This process of first designing a simple program and then adding features and refinements is sometimes referred to as *iterative enhancement*. Using this technique to develop a program makes each stage relatively easy to design and yet the final program is long, complicated, and powerful. It is not the same technique as top-down design, but it is another way to divide a large programming task into pieces that are smaller and more manageable. This approach has another very important advantage: At each stage of the process, you have a complete working program that does something meaningful and useful. This is a great psychological boost. Moreover, if you fail to achieve the final programming goal by a given deadline, you will at least have a working program and not just a collection of disconnected pieces of code.

Case Study

Payroll Calculation

Problem Definition

We wish to design a program to compute the weekly pay for an hourly employee. The program will take as input the number of hours worked and the hourly pay rate and will output the gross pay as well as the net pay after taxes. To make the problem clear, we need to specify some additional details, namely how the overtime pay and tax is computed. For this problem overtime will be computed as 1½ times the usual rate and will apply to all hours after the first 40 hours worked. The tax will be 10% of all income over $200.

Discussion

To solve this problem, we will apply the iterative enhancement technique described in the previous section. We have already produced a simple program that computes gross pay. It is the program in Figure 3.5. We will enhance it to obtain a version that also computes tax and net pay, and finally we will produce a version with formatted output.

enhancements   Starting with a working program to compute gross pay, we can enhance it by adding code to compute the tax and net pay. The interaction of subtasks for the enhanced program is shown in the data flow diagram in Figure 3.10.

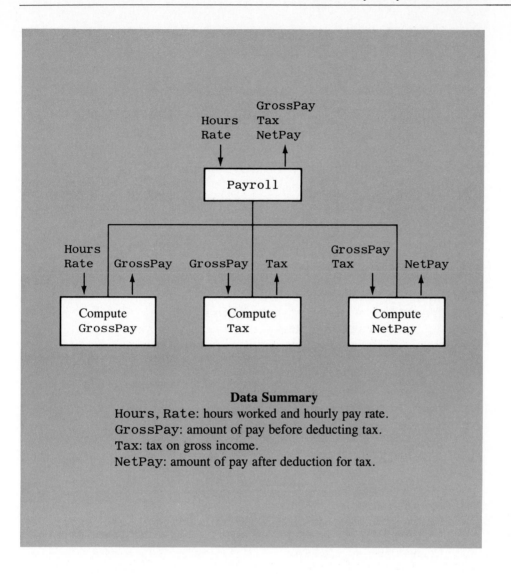

Data Summary
Hours, Rate: hours worked and hourly pay rate.
GrossPay: amount of pay before deducting tax.
Tax: tax on gross income.
NetPay: amount of pay after deduction for tax.

Figure 3.10
Data flow diagram for complete payroll program.

ALGORITHM

The algorithms for computing tax and net pay follow directly from the problem definition.

```
if GrossPay > $200 then
    Tax := 10% of (GrossPay − $200)
else Tax := 0;
NetPay := GrossPay − Tax;
```

Adding this computation to the program produces the version in Figure 3.11. The final enhancement is obtained once that program is fully debugged and working, by improving the output as shown in Figure 3.12.

Program

```
program Payroll(input, output);
{Computes weekly pay for an hourly employee.}
const MaxRegTime = 40; {Max number of hours at the regular rate.}
      OTFactor = 1.5; {Factor for overtime.}
      Exemption = 200; {Free of tax.}
      TaxRate = 0.10; {10%}
var Hours: integer;
    Rate, GrossPay, Tax, NetPay: real;
begin
  writeln('Enter the hourly rate of pay.');
  readln(Rate);
  writeln('Enter the number of hours worked,');
  writeln('rounded up to a whole number of hours.');
  readln(Hours);

  if Hours > MaxRegTime then
     GrossPay := Rate * MaxRegTime +
            OTFactor * Rate * (Hours - MaxRegTime)
  else
     GrossPay := Rate * Hours;

  if GrossPay > Exemption then
     Tax := TaxRate * (GrossPay - Exemption)
  else
     Tax:= 0;

  NetPay := GrossPay - Tax;

  writeln('Hours =', Hours);
  writeln('Hourly pay rate = $', Rate);
  writeln('Gross pay = $', GrossPay);
  writeln('Tax = $', Tax, ' Net pay = $', NetPay)
end.
```

Sample Dialogue

```
Enter the hourly rate of pay.
20.00
Enter the number of hours worked,
rounded up to a whole number of hours.
30
Hours =    30
Hourly pay rate = $    20.0000
Gross pay = $    600.0000
Tax = $ 40.0000 Net pay = $ 560.0000
```

Figure 3.11
**Enhanced version
of program in
Figure 3.5.**

Program

```
program Payroll(input, output);
{Computes weekly pay for an hourly employee.}
const MaxRegTime = 40; {Max number of hours at the regular rate.}
      OTFactor = 1.5; {Factor for overtime.}
      Exemption = 200; {Free of tax.}
      TaxRate = 0.10; {10%}
      Width = 7; {Total field width for money amounts.}
var Hours: integer;
    Rate, GrossPay, Tax, NetPay: real;
begin
  writeln('This program computes');
  writeln('the weekly pay for an hourly employee.');
  writeln('All hours after the first ', MaxRegTime:4);
  writeln('are paid at a rate of');
  writeln(OTFactor:4:2, ' times the basic rate.');

  writeln('Enter the hourly rate of pay.');
  writeln('Do not type a dollar sign.');
  readln(Rate);
  writeln('Enter the number of hours worked,');
  writeln('rounded up to a whole number of hours.');
  readln(Hours);

  if Hours > MaxRegTime then
     GrossPay := Rate * MaxRegTime +
            OTFactor * Rate * (Hours - MaxRegTime)
  else
     GrossPay := Rate * Hours;

  if GrossPay > Exemption then
     Tax := TaxRate * (GrossPay - Exemption)
  else
     Tax := 0;

  NetPay := GrossPay - Tax;

  writeln('Hours =', Hours:4);
  writeln('Hourly pay rate = $', Rate:Width:2);
  writeln('Gross pay = $', GrossPay:Width:2);
  writeln('Tax = $', Tax:Width:2,
    ' Net pay = $', NetPay:Width:2)
end.
```

**Figure 3.12
Further enhanced
version of program
in Figure 3.11.**

Sample Dialogue

```
This program computes
the weekly pay for an hourly employee.
All hours after the first  40
are paid at a rate of
1.50 times the basic rate.
Enter the hourly rate of pay.
Do not type a dollar sign.
20.00
Enter the number of hours worked,
rounded up to a whole number of hours.
30
Hours =   30
Hourly pay rate = $   20.00
Gross pay = $   600.00
Tax = $   40.00 Net pay = $ 560.00
```

Figure 3.12 (continued)

Simple Looping—While Statements

Most programs include some action that is repeated a number of times. For example, the program in Figure 3.12 computes the weekly pay for a single worker. If there are ten workers employed by the company, then a more complete payroll program would repeat this calculation ten times. A portion of a program that repeats a statement or group of statements is called a *loop*. Pascal has a number of ways to create loops; one of these constructions is called a *while statement* or *while loop*. We will first illustrate its use with a short toy example and then do a more realistic example.

Suppose you want your program to execute the following statement three times:

```
writeln('Hello')
```

You could of course repeat that writeln statement three times in your program, but *body of a* we want an example of a loop. Hence, we will do this with a *while* loop. Figure 3.13 *while loop* contains a program with a *while* statement that accomplishes our task.

The action that is repeated in our sample loop is the compound statement

```
begin
  writeln('Hello');
  NumberToDo := NumberToDo - 1
end
```

The action that is repeated in a loop is called the *body* of the loop and so this is the body of our sample *while* loop. The number of times that the body is repeated is controlled by the line

```
while NumberToDo > 0   do
```

The meaning of the *while* statement is suggested by the English words: The body is executed *while* the value of NumberToDo is greater than 0. We will give a precise definition of the *while* statement syntax and action shortly. However, let us first discuss the action of our sample *while* loop using the intuitive description suggested by the English words. That intuition is sufficient to understand our example.

In the program in Figure 3.13 the variable NumberToDo is initialized to 3 before the *while* loop. The value 3 is greater than 0; so the loop body is executed. The first time the loop body is executed the word 'Hello' is written to the screen and the value of NumberToDo is changed to 2. Hence, after executing the loop body once, the condition

```
NumberToDo > 0
```

is still satisfied and so the loop body is executed again. This causes another 'Hello' to be written out and changes the value of NumberToDo from 2 to 1. Since this new number is still greater than 0, the loop body is executed yet one more time. This outputs a third 'Hello' and changes the value of NumberToDo from 1 to 0. After executing the loop body three times, the condition

```
NumberToDo > 0
```

is no longer satisfied and the *while* loop terminates.

The condition NumberToDo > 0 in Figure 3.13 can be replaced by any other comparison and the compound statement can be replaced by any Pascal statement whatsoever. Choosing these two things correctly will produce a *while* loop to perform any looping action that you might wish.

Program

```
program ShowWhile(input, output);
var NumberToDo: integer;

begin{Program}
   NumberToDo := 3;  {Initializing statement}

  {The while loop follows:}
   while NumberToDo > 0  do
       begin
          writeln('Hello');
          NumberToDo := NumberToDo − 1
       end {The while loop ends here.};

   writeln('End of Program.')
end.  {Program}
```

Output

```
Hello
Hello
Hello
End of Program.
```

Figure 3.13
Program with a
while **loop.**

syntax

The syntax of the *while* statement is as follows:

while <expression 1> <comparison operator> <expression 2> *do*
    <body>

The part between the reserved words *while* and *do* is the same sort of comparison as we have been using after the *if* in *if-then-else* statements. In our sample *while* loop the comparison is

    NumberToDo > 0

As we noted when we discussed the *if-then-else* statement, this kind of comparison of two expressions is a special case of a more general class of expressions called "boolean expressions." In Chapter 6 we will describe other boolean expressions, all of which can be used in *while* statements. Until then, we will use only the simple comparisons discussed in this chapter.

The <body> of a *while* loop can be any Pascal statement. In our example, the body of the *while* loop is the compound statement

```
begin
  writeln('Hello');
  NumberToDo := NumberToDo - 1
end
```

As in our example, the body is typically a compound statement. However, a simple statement is allowed if you should have occasion to use such a simple loop. The body of a loop is the part that is repeated. Every execution of the loop body is called an *iteration* of the loop. The expression between the reserved words *while* and *do* controls the number of loop iterations, i.e., the number of times the body of the *while* loop is executed.

*action of
a while
statement*

When the *while* statement is executed, the first thing that happens is that the boolean expression (i.e., the comparison) following the word *while* is checked. If it is not satisfied, then no action is taken and the program proceeds to the next statement after the *while* loop. If the comparison turns out to be true, then the entire body of the loop is executed. At least one of the expressions being compared typically contains something that might change, such as the value of NumberToDo in our example. After the body of the loop is executed, the comparison is again checked. This process is repeated again and again as long as the comparison continues to be satisfied. After each iteration of the loop body the comparison is again checked and if it is satisfied, then the entire loop body is executed again; if it is no longer satisfied, then the *while* statement ends and the program proceeds to the next statement in the program.

While Loop Example—Charge Card Balance

Suppose you have a bank charge card with a balance owed of $50 and suppose the bank charges you 2% per month interest. How many months can you let pass without making any payments before your balance will exceed $100? One way to solve this problem is to simply read each monthly statement and count the number of months that go by until your balance reaches $100 or more. Better still, you can calculate the monthly balances with a program rather than waiting for the statements to arrive. In this way you will obtain an answer without having to wait so long.

After one month the balance would be $50 plus 2% of $50, which happens to be a total of $51. After two months the balance will be $51 plus 2% of $51, which is $52.02. After three months the balance will be $52.02 plus 2% of $52.02, and so on. In general, each month increases the balance by 2%. A program could keep track of the balance by storing it in a variable called `Balance`. The change in the value of `Balance` for one month can be calculated as follows:

```
Balance := Balance + 0.02*Balance
```

If we repeat this action until the value of `Balance` reaches `100` and count the number of times we make this monthly change, then we will know the number of months it takes for our balance to reach `100`. To do this we need another variable to count the number of times we change the balance. Let us call this new variable `Count`. What we want our program to do is given by the pseudocode in Figure 3.14.

The *while* statement corresponding to the loop in Figure 3.14 is the following:

```
while Balance < 100 do
   begin
     Balance := Balance + 0.02*Balance;
     Count := Count + 1
   end
```

A complete program containing this *while* loop is given in Figure 3.15.

```
Balance := 50;
Count := 0;
```

{The loop starts here.}
Do the following provided `Balance` < 100, and continue
to do it again and again as long as `Balance` < 100:
begin{body}
```
   Balance := Balance + 0.02*Balance;
   Count := Count + 1
```
end{body}
{The loop ends here.}

**Figure 3.14
Pseudocode for
a loop.**

Program

program Debt(input, output);
*{This program calculates the number of months it takes for an account balance to
grow from $50 to $100 assuming a monthly interest of 2%.
In a real program, the numbers 50, 100, and 0.02 should be given names by means of
constant declarations. That was not done here so that the code would be very simple.}*

**Figure 3.15
Charge card
program.**

```
var Balance: real;
    Count: integer;  {Counts months}
begin{Program}
  writeln('This program tells you how long it takes');
  writeln('to accumulate a debt of $100, starting with');
  writeln('an initial balance of $50 owed.');
  writeln('The interest charge is 2% per month.');

  Balance := 50;
  Count := 0;
  while Balance < 100 do
    begin{One month's change}
      Balance := Balance + 0.02*Balance;
      Count := Count + 1
    end; {One month's change}

  writeln;
  writeln('After ', Count, ' months');
  writeln('Your balance due will be $', Balance:7:2)
end. {Program}
```

Output

```
This program tells you how long it takes
to accumulate a debt of $100, starting with
an initial balance of $50 owed.
The interest charge is 2% per month.
```

Figure 3.15
(continued)

```
After  36 months
Your balance due will be $ 101.99
```

Pitfall

Infinite Loops

A *while* loop does not terminate as long as the condition after the word *while* is satisfied. This condition normally contains a variable that will change its value so that the condition will eventually become false and therefore terminate the loop. However, if you make a mistake and write your program so that the condition is always satisfied, then the loop will run forever. A loop that runs forever is called an *infinite loop*.

For example, the following will write out the positive even numbers less than 12. That is, it will output the numbers 2, 4, 6, 8 and 10, one per line, and then the loop will end.

```
X := 2; {Initializes X}
while X <> 12 do
   begin
      writeln(X);
      X := X + 2
   end
```

The value of X is increased by 2 on each loop iteration until it reaches the value 12. At that point, the condition between the reserved words *while* and *do* is no longer satisfied, and so the loop ends.

Now suppose we want to write out the odd numbers less than 12, rather than the even numbers. We might, mistakenly, think that all we need to do is change the initializing statement to

```
X := 1; {Initializes X}
```

With this mistake, the loop is an infinite loop. The value of X goes from 11 to 13. The value of X is never equal to 12 and so the loop never terminates.

dangers of = and <>

This sort of problem is common when loops are terminated by checking a numeric quantity for an exact value. When dealing with numbers, it is always safer to test for passing a value. For example, the following will work fine as the first line of our *while* loop:

```
while X < 12 do
```

With this change, X can be initialized to any number and the loop will still terminate.

A program that is in an infinite loop will run forever unless some external force terminates it. Since you can now write programs that contain an infinite loop, it is a good idea to learn how to force a program to terminate. The method for forcing a program to stop varies from system to system. Usually there is a special key that can be pressed to terminate a program whether or not it has reached the final *end*.

Standard Functions

Pascal includes a number of *standard functions* that can appear inside arithmetic expressions. As an example, sqrt is the square root function. It takes a value of type either integer or real and, in either case, yields a value of type real. The value of sqrt(4) is 2.0, for example.

Name	Description	Type of Argument	Type of Result	Example	Value of Example
abs	absolute value	integer real	integer real	abs (−2) abs (−2.4)	+2 +2.4
round	rounding	real	integer	round (2.6)	3
trunc	truncation	real	integer	trunc (2.6)	2
sqr	squaring	integer real	integer real	sqr (2) sqr (1.100)	4 1.2100
sqrt	square root	real or integer	real	sqrt (4)	2.00

Figure 3.16
Some predefined
Pascal functions.

argument

value returned

The value that a function starts out with is called its *argument*. The value it produces is referred to as the *value returned*. In the example, 4 is the argument and 2.0 is the value returned. The argument to a function may be any expression of the appropriate type.

These standard functions can be combined with other arithmetic expressions to obtain new expressions. For example,

```
X :  = 2;
Y := 3 * sqrt(2 * X)
```

sets the value of Y to 6.0.

Figure 3.16 lists some commonly used standard Pascal functions as well as their descriptions and an example of each. The functions round and trunc can be used to obtain an integer value from a value of type real. The former returns the integer nearest to its argument. The latter returns the number you get by discarding the part after the decimal point. Thus, round (4.8) returns 5, while trunc (4.8) returns 4; round (−4.8) returns −5, while trunc (−4.8) returns −4. The function sqr computes the square of its argument. So, sqr (X) means the same as X*X. It is rather redundant, since you can use * to obtain the same effect. Occasionally it makes for neater notation, however, by allowing you to express the square of a long expression without having to write it twice.

The function abs is the absolute value function. It leaves positive numbers unchanged and removes the minus sign from negative numbers. If the argument is real, then abs returns a value of type real; if the argument is of type integer, then abs returns a value of type integer.

Using Known Algorithms

Before you rush off to design a program from scratch, it is a good idea to see if there is a well-known algorithm to solve the task at hand. There are clever, well-known algorithms for many tasks. Often these algorithms are the product of much research and brilliant insights. In such cases, the known algorithm is likely to be better than one designed in a short time, and so you should use the known algorithm and go directly to the implementation phase.

Case Study

Solving Quadratic Equations

Problem Definition

A quadratic equation is one of the form

$$ax^2 + bx + c = 0$$

We will design a program to solve such equations for x. That is, our program will output all real number values that, when substituted for x, will make the left-hand side of the equation equal zero. The input to the program consists of the three coefficients a, b, and c.

Discussion

This is a well-known problem, and there is a standard formula to compute x. The equation has two roots (values of x that satisfy it). They can be computed using the two almost identical formulas

$$x = \frac{-b + \sqrt{b^2 - 4ac}}{2a}$$

and

$$x = \frac{-b - \sqrt{b^2 - 4ac}}{2a}$$

In order for the equation to have a `real` number as a root, the quantity $b^2 - 4ac$, called the *discriminant*, must be positive. Otherwise, the formulas contain the square root of a negative number. A program to solve equations by these formulas naturally breaks down into the following subtasks:

ALGORITHM

1. Input coefficients.
2. Compute discriminant.
3. Evaluate the formulas.
4. Output the roots.

In order to allow the user to solve as many equations as he or she wants, we repeat this series of four subtasks as often as the user wishes.

The final program is given in Figure 3.17. In that program, the user is asked if he or she wishes to repeat the complete calculation for another equation. The variable Ans, which is of type `char`, is used to record the answer. The answer is either "yes" or "no," but the program reads only the first letter and ignores the remaining characters. If the letter is 'y', it repeats the calculations; otherwise it ends the *while* loop. Notice that the program must set the value of the variable Ans before it performs the *while* loop. If it did not do this, then there would be no value of Ans for the first test of

        Ans = 'y'

A *while* loop always checks the controlling boolean expression before it executes the body of the loop. This is true even for the very first time that the *while* loop might execute the body. Therefore, it is critically important that all relevant variables are initialized before the *while* loop begins.

Program

```
program Roots(input, output);
{Solves quadratic equations}
const Width = 6; {Total field width for numbers}
      Digits = 2; {Number of digits after the decimal point}
var A, B, C, Discrim, X1, X2: real;
    Ans: char;
begin{Program}
  Ans := 'y';{To get the while loop started}

  while Ans = 'y' do
    begin{loop body}
      writeln('This program solves equations of the form:');
      writeln('a(x*x) + bx + c = 0');
      writeln('Enter the coefficients a, b, and c.');
      readln(A, B, C);

      Discrim := B * B - 4 * A * C;

      if Discrim >= 0 then
        begin{then}
          X1 := (-B + sqrt(Discrim))/(2*A);
          X2 := (-B - sqrt(Discrim))/(2*A);
          writeln('For the equation ');
          writeln(A:Width:Digits, '(x*x) +', B:Width:Digits, 'x + ',
                                  C:Width:Digits, ' = 0');
          writeln('The roots are ', X1:Width:Digits,
                                  ' and ', X2:Width:Digits)
        end {then}
```

Figure 3.17
Quadratic equation
program.

```
    else
      writeln('No real roots for that equation.');

    writeln;
    writeln('Do you want to solve another equation? (yes/no)');
    readln(Ans)
   end; {loop body}
  writeln('End of program.')
end.  {Program}
```

Sample Dialogue

```
This program solves equations of the form:
a(x*x) + bx + c = 0
Enter the coefficients a, b, and c.
1  -2  -3
For the equation
  1.00(x*x) +  -2.00x +  -3.00 = 0
The roots are   3.00 and   -1.00

Do you want to solve another equation? (yes/no)
yes
This program solves equations of the form:
a(x*x) + bx + c = 0
Enter the coefficients a, b, and c.
2  2  2
No real roots for that equation.

Do you want to solve another equation? (yes/no)
no
End of program.
```

Figure 3.17
(continued)

Defensive Programming

Notice that in the program in Figure 3.17 we tested to see whether the discriminant is negative, since if it is, there are no real-valued roots. If you know that a quadratic equation has a real number solution, then theoretically this need not concern you. In that case, you "know" there will not be a negative square root. However, in programming it is always wise to assume that something will go wrong. It is amazing how often it does. A good idea is to test for possible mistakes such as negative square roots or division by zero. The computer is likely to give an error statement anyway, but it may not be clear, and the error will cause the program to abort. Therefore, it is best to include a test within the Pascal program, as we have done.

*testing for
the "impossible"*

More About Indenting and Commenting

Indenting should display the structure of a program. If there is a statement within a statement, it is best to indicate this by indenting in some way. In particular, *if-then-else* statements and *while* loops should be indented as we have been doing or in some similar manner. The important point is to use some type of indenting that shows the structure. The exact layout is not precisely dictated. However, you should be consistent within any one program.

Because we now can have more than one *begin/end* pair in a program it is a good idea to label each *begin* and *end* with a comment something like the ones in Figure 3.17. This makes it easier to find the matching *end* for each *begin*.

In matters of grave importance,
style, not sincerity, is the vital thing.
Oscar Wilde, The Importance of Being Earnest

Summary of Problem Solving Techniques

- Program errors can be classified into three groups: syntax errors, run-time errors, and logical errors. The computer will usually tell you about errors in the first two categories.
- To test for and locate logical errors, one technique is to trace variables.
- Problems can be solved and programs written in phases. First, a simple version is designed and tested and then enhancements are added in a later version.
- When designing a program, first check to see if there is a well-known algorithm for the task.

Summary of Programming Techniques

- Almost all constants in a program should be given meaningful names with a constant declaration.
- Comments should be inserted to explain major subsections or any unclear part of a program. Inserting assertions is one very effective way to comment a program.
- *begin/end* pairs should be labeled to facilitate matching.
- When you use *if-then-else* statements, they should be indented to clearly display the two alternatives. Even without the *else,* some sort of indenting should be used.
- When you use a *while* loop, indent the body of the loop.
- When solving problems involving numbers of type `real`, do not use a test for exact

equality or exact inequality (= or <>). Since such numbers are only approximately represented in the computer, it makes no sense to test them for equality.
- It is often a good idea to test for errors such as division by zero and negative square roots within a program.

Summary of Pascal Constructs

constant declarations
Syntax:

> *const* <identifier 1> = <constant 1>;
>   <identifier 2> = <constant 2>;
>   .
>   .
>   .
>   <identifier n> = <constant n>;

Example:

> *const* Rate = 7.25;
>   Motto = 'We aim to please';
>   Days = 90;

The constant <constant 1> is given the name <identifier 1>, the constant <constant 2> is given the name <identifier 2>, and so forth. The identifiers can be any Pascal identifiers that are not reserved words. The identifiers can then be used anywhere that the constants can be used and will have the same value as the constants they name.

maxint
Syntax:

> maxint

A predefined constant equal to the largest value of type integer that the computer system can handle.

comments
Syntax:

> {<text>}

Example:

> {*This is a comment*}

The text between the two symbols '{' and '}' is ignored by the compiler and so has no effect on the program. The pair ' (*' and '*) ' may be used as an alternative to '{}'. Hence, the following is also a comment:

> (**This is also a comment**)

The comment delimiters '}' and '*) ' may not be used inside of a comment.

formatted output

Syntax (for arguments to `write` or `writeln`):

   <expression to be output> : <integer expression>

or

   <expression to be output> : <integer expression> : <integer expression>

Example:

```
writeln(X: 6,  R: 6: 2,  'Hi Mom!': 10)
```

The first number indicates the total number of spaces to be used to output the value. The value will appear at the right-hand end of that field, and any extra spaces to the left will be filled with blanks. The version with one field width number can be used with any type of output value, including quoted strings. The second integer expression is optional and can be used only for values of type `real`. The second integer expression, if present, indicates the number of digits to appear after the decimal point. The output is not in the E notation if a second number is specified.

if-then-else statement

Syntax:

```
if <expression 1> <relational operator> <expression 2> then
    <statement 1>
else
    <statement 2>
```

Example:

```
if X > 0 then
    writeln('Value of X is greater than zero')
else
    writeln('Value of X is zero or negative')
```

<statement 1> and <statement 2> may be any Pascal statements. In particular, they may be a compound statement. If the relation between the two expressions is true, then <statement 1> is executed. If the relation does not hold, then <statement 2> is executed.

if-then statement

Syntax:

```
if <expression 1> <relational operator> <expression 2> then
    <statement>
```

Example:

```
if X > 0 then
    writeln('Value of X is greater than zero')
```

<statement> may be any Pascal statement. In particular, it may be a compound statement. If the relation between the two expressions is true, then <statement> is executed. If the relation does not hold, then no action is taken.

while statement (while loop)

Syntax:

```
while <expression 1> <relational operator> <expression 2> do
   <body>
```

Example:

```
while X > 0 do
   begin
      readln(X);
      Sum := Sum + X
   end
```

The <body> can be any Pascal statement. As in the example, the <body> is usually a compound statement. When the *while* loop is executed, the relation between the two expressions is first checked. If it is satisfied, then the entire <body> is executed. If the relation does not hold, then nothing happens. This process is repeated again and again: First the relation between the two expressions is checked. If it is satisfied, the entire <body> is executed. If it is not satisfied, the *while* loop terminates and the program goes on to the next item.

compound statement

A list of statements separated by semicolons and surrounded with a *begin/end* pair. The statements are executed in order. For an example, see the body of the *while* loop example.

Exercises

Self-Test Exercises

6. What is the output produced by the following code when embedded in a complete program?

```
X := 3;
if 2 > X then
    writeln('First writeln')
else
    writeln('Second writeln');
if 2 > X then
    writeln('Third writeln');
writeln('Fourth writeln')
```

7. Classify the following as true or false (when used in a Pascal *if-then-else* statement):

$$(24 \; mod \; 12) \; <> \; 0 \qquad\qquad 'y' \; = \; 'Y'$$
$$'H' \; <= \; 'J' \qquad\qquad -12 \; <= \; maxint$$

8. Determine the value of each of the following Pascal arithmetic expressions:

sqrt(16)   sqrt(4 + 5)

trunc(6.8)   trunc(-6.8)   round(6.8)   round(-6.8)

abs(-6.8)   abs(6.8)   abs(4)   abs(-4)

sqrt(abs(sqr(2) - 20))

9. Convert the following mathematical and English expressions into Pascal boolean expressions:

$\sqrt{x} \leqslant y + 1$

Z is positive, W is not zero, X is evenly divisible by 12

10. What is the output of the following (when embedded in a correct program with X declared to be of type integer)?

```
X := 12;
while X > 0 do
  X := X-5;
writeln(X)
```

Interactive Exercises

11. Write a program that reads in an integer and outputs a statement telling whether or not the number is positive.

12. Write a program that reads in an uppercase letter and outputs a message telling whether or not that letter follows 'M' in the alphabet.

13. Write a program that reads in an integer and outputs a statement telling whether or not the number is evenly divisible by three. If the number is not divisible by three, then the program should also output the remainder obtained when the number is divided by three. Use a compound statement inside of an *if-then-else* statement.

14. Write a program that reads in a number, computes the square root of that number using the standard function sqrt, squares that value using the function sqr, and finally outputs all three values: the input number, the square root, and the square of the square root. Run the program several times using a wide variety of numbers.

15. Write a program that reads in a decimal number, applies the functions trunc and round to the number, and then outputs both values.

16. Determine the smallest real value ϵ such that your computer can distinguish between 1 and $1+\epsilon$. Feel free to use trial-and-error methods.

17. Substitute 20 for 25 in Figure 3.2 (or do something similar) and give the program to a friend to debug. Ask your friend to give you an equally perverse assignment.

18. Modify the program in Fig. 3.15 so that it shows the balance after each month.

19. Embed the *while* loop example from the Summary of Pascal Constructs in a program and run the program. Input the numbers 1, 2, 3, and 0, one per line. Do not forget to initialize the variables X and Sum.

Programming Exercises

20. A liter is 0.264179 gallons. Write a program that reads in the number of liters of gasoline consumed by the user's car and the number of miles traveled by the car, and then outputs the number of miles per gallon the car delivered. Use a constant declaration.

21. The gravitational attractive force between two bodies of mass m_1 and m_2 separated by a distance d is given by the formula

$$F = \frac{G\, m_1 m_2}{d^2}$$

where G is the universal gravitational constant

$$G = 6.673 \times 10^{-8} \text{ cm}^3/\text{g sec}^2$$

Write a program that reads in the mass of two bodies and the distance between them and then outputs the gravitational force between them. The output should be in dynes; one dyne equals a g cm/sec^2. Use a constant declaration for G.

22. According to Einstein's famous equation, the amount of energy E produced when an amount of mass m is completely converted to energy is given by the formula

$$E = mc^2$$

where c is the speed of light. Write a program that reads in a mass in grams and outputs the amount of energy produced when the mass is converted to energy. The speed of light is approximately

$$2.997925 \times 10^{10} \text{ cm/sec}$$

If the mass is given in grams, then the formula yields the energy expressed in ergs. Use a constant declaration to name the speed of light.

23. Write a program to read in a weight in pounds and ounces and output the weight expressed in kilograms and grams. One pound equals 0.453592 kilograms. Use a constant declaration.

24. Write a program to read in a distance expressed in kilometers and output the distance expressed in miles. One kilometer equals 0.62137 miles. Use a constant declaration.

25. Write a program that calculates change for a cashier. The program requests the cost of the item. The user then types in the cost as a decimal numeral. The program then outputs the cost of the item including sales tax. (Use 6% as the sales tax value.) The program next requests and receives the amount tendered by the customer. Finally,

the program outputs a summary of all figures, including the amount of change due to the customer. Use a constant declaration for the tax rate. Be sure to use field width specifications so as to produce reasonable-looking output.

26. Write a program to gauge the amount of inflation over the past year. The program asks for the price of an item (such as a hot dog or a one-carat diamond) both one year ago and today. It estimates the inflation rate as the difference in price divided by the price a year ago.

27. Enhance your program from the previous exercise by having it also print out the estimated price of the item one year from now and two years from now. The increase in cost in one year is estimated as the inflation rate times the current price.

28. The prices of stocks are normally given to the nearest eighth of a dollar; for example, $29\frac{7}{8}$ or $89\frac{1}{2}$. Write a program that computes the value of the user's holding of one stock. The program asks for the number of shares held, the whole dollar portion of the price, and the fraction portion. The fraction portion is to be input as two integer values, one for the numerator and one for the denominator.

29. The relationship between the sides (a, b) of a right triangle and the hypotenuse (h) is given by the Pythagorean formula

$$a^2 + b^2 = h^2$$

Write a program that reads in the lengths of the two sides of a right triangle and computes the hypotenuse of the triangle.

30. The area of a triangle whose sides are a, b, and c can be computed by the formula

$$A = \sqrt{s\,(s-a)\,(s-b)\,(s-c)}$$

where $s = (a+b+c)/2$. Write a program that reads in the lengths of the three sides of a triangle and outputs the area of the triangle.

31. Rewrite the program Change in Figure 3.2 so that it takes as input any amount of dollars and cents (as a number of type `real`) and outputs the correct number of bills as well as coins to give as change. Use bill denominations of $1, $5, and $20 only.

32. An hourly employee is paid at a rate of $9.73 per hour for up to 40 hours worked per week. Any hours over that are paid at the overtime rate of $1\frac{1}{2}$ times that. From the worker's gross pay, 6% is withheld for social security tax, 14% is withheld for federal income tax, 5% is withheld for state income tax, and $6 per week is withheld for union dues. If the worker has three or more covered dependents, an additional $10 is withheld to cover the extra cost of health insurance beyond that paid by the employer. Write a program that takes as input the number of hours worked in a week and the number of dependents and then outputs the worker's gross pay, each withholding, and the net take-home pay for the week.

33. Write a program that computes the cost of postage on a first-class letter according to the following rate scale: 30 cents for the first ounce or fraction of an ounce, 8 cents for each additional half ounce, plus a $5 service charge if the customer desires special delivery.

References for Further Reading

The following are reference manuals. The first is particularly useful if you are changing from one Pascal system to another.

J. Tiberghien, *The Pascal Handbook,* 1981, Sybex, Berkeley, Ca.

The following reference manuals are designed for individuals who already know another programming language besides Pascal:

K. Jensen and N. Wirth, *Pascal Users Manual and Report,* 1974, Springer-Verlag, New York.

D.L. Matuszek, *Quick Pascal,* 1982, John Wiley, New York.

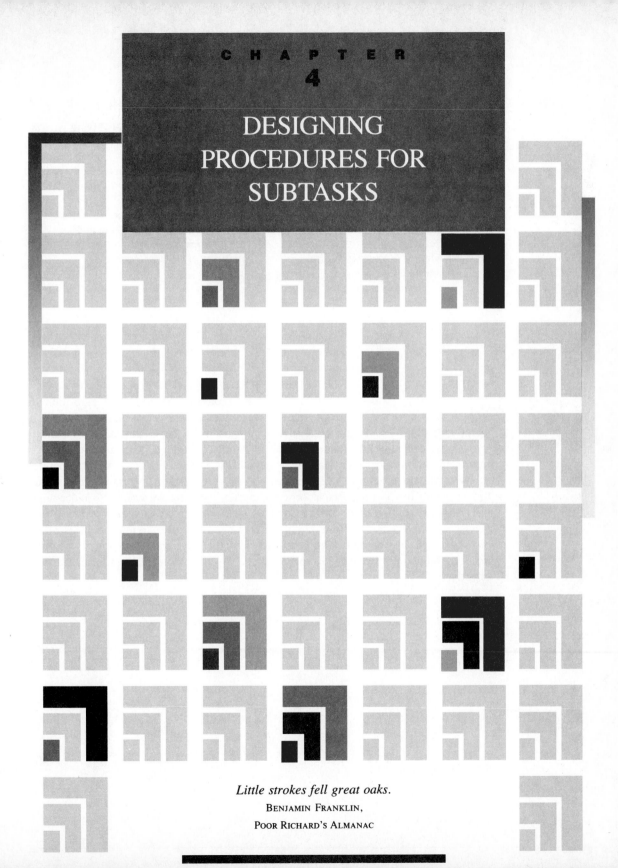

CHAPTER 4

DESIGNING PROCEDURES FOR SUBTASKS

Little strokes fell great oaks.
BENJAMIN FRANKLIN,
POOR RICHARD'S ALMANAC

Chapter Contents

A good way to design an algorithm to solve a task is to break it down into subtasks and solve these subtasks by smaller, simpler algorithms. Ultimately, the subalgorithms to solve these subtasks are translated into Pascal code, and the entire larger algorithm containing these subalgorithms is translated into a Pascal program. Since the subalgorithms are algorithms, it is natural to think of them as smaller programs within a larger program. Moreover, preserving this structure in the final Pascal program makes the program easier to understand, easier to change if need be and, as will become apparent, easier to write, test, and debug. Pascal, like most programming languages, has facilities to include programlike entities inside of programs. The Pascal term for such programlike entities is *procedure*. In this chapter we introduce procedures and give some guidelines for using them effectively.

Simple Pascal Procedures

In Pascal you can assign a name to a sequence of statements by means of something called a *procedure declaration*. Using the procedure name inside the body of the program will then have the same effect as executing the sequence of statements. For example, the following is a sample procedure declaration that assigns the name Compliment to two `writeln` statements:

procedure declaration

```
procedure Compliment;
begin{Compliment}
  writeln('A lovely letter.');
  writeln('One of my favorites.')
end; {Compliment}
```

In a program containing this procedure declaration, the identifier Compliment can be used anyplace a statement can be used, and when it is executed, it will cause the following to appear on the screen:

use of procedures

```
A lovely letter.
One of my favorites.
```

This is illustrated in Figure 4.1.

The syntax for a simple procedure declaration is as follows. The first part of the procedure is called the *heading*. It consists of the word `procedure` followed by a (non-reserved-word) identifier to serve as the procedure name, followed by a semicolon. This is followed by the *body* of the procedure. The body of the procedure is a list of statements separated by semicolons and enclosed between a `begin` / `end` pair; in other words, the body of a procedure is a compound statement. You end a procedure declaration with a semicolon placed after the final `end`. In a Pascal program, procedure declarations are placed after the variable declarations and before the main body of the program. The order of declarations within a program is summarized in Figure 4.2.

procedure declaration syntax

A procedure name occurring inside the body of a program is considered to be a special kind of statement known as a *procedure call* or a *procedure invocation*. These procedure-call statements are treated just like any other kind of statement when it comes to syntactic details such as the placement of semicolons.

procedure call

Variable Parameters

Suppose we want to design a program to help a cashier total the cash on hand at the end of a work day. The cashier counts and enters the number of each coin; the program then computes the dollar value of the coins. To avoid input errors, each input statement is prefaced by a warning of exactly what to enter and how to enter it. The program might start out as follows:

```
writeln('Enter the number of half-dollar coins.');
writeln('Do not total the amount.');
writeln('Just enter the number of coins.');
readln(HalfDollars)
```

The program might next request the number of quarters, as follows:

```
writeln('Enter the number of quarters.');
writeln('Do not total the amount.');
writeln('Just enter the number of coins.');
readln(Quarters)
```

Program

```
program BriefEncounter(input, output);
var FirstI, LastI: char;

procedure Compliment;
begin{Compliment}
  writeln('A lovely letter.');
  writeln('One of my favorites.')
end; {Compliment}

begin{Program}
  writeln('Please enter your first initial.');
  readln(FirstI);
  Compliment;
  writeln('Now enter your last initial.');
  readln(LastI);
  Compliment;
  writeln('Pleased to meet you ', FirstI, '.', LastI, '.')
end. {Program}
```

Sample Dialogue

```
Please enter your first initial.
J
A lovely letter.
One of my favorites.
Now enter your last initial.
R
A lovely letter.
One of my favorites.
Pleased to meet you J.R.
```

Figure 4.1
Program with a procedure.

Figure 4.2
Order of declarations.

1. Constant declarations.
2. Variable declarations.
3. Procedure declarations.

Notice that the last three lines of these two pieces of code perform the same task, namely prompting the user with input instructions and then reading one number. Since this is a repeated subtask, it makes sense to declare these three lines as a procedure. There is, however, one problem with this idea. The last line is slightly different in these two pieces of code. One time we use the variable HalfDollars, and one time we use the variable Quarters. One solution would be to make the procedure only two lines long and omit the last of the three lines from the procedure, just as we are choosing to omit the first of these lines. That will work, but it is not a very good solution. What we really want is a procedure that has a blank that can be filled in with the variable HalfDollars in the first procedure call, filled in with the variable Quarters in the second call, and filled in with the variables Dimes, Nickels, and Pennies later on. Pascal allows us to do just that.

The object which acts as a blank to be filled is called a *formal variable parameter,* and although it looks exactly like a variable, it is not a variable. It is a labeled blank that must be filled in with a variable when the procedure is called. A formal variable parameter may be any identifier other than a reserved word. A procedure called Get-Number, which uses a formal variable parameter called Number and performs the task we desire, is included in the program in Figure 4.3. To use the procedure with the particular variable HalfDollars substituted for the formal variable parameter Number, we use the following procedure call:

formal variable parameters

```
GetNumber (HalfDollars)
```

The variable in the procedure call, in this case HalfDollars, is called an *actual variable parameter.* When the procedure is called, every occurrence of the formal variable parameter within the body of the procedure declaration is replaced by the actual variable parameter, and then the statements in the procedure body are executed. This process is sometimes called *parameter passing.* As the program in Figure 4.3 illustrates, a procedure may be called more than once, using different actual parameters each time.

actual variable parameters

Notice that a formal variable parameter has a type that must be stated in the procedure heading and that the formal and actual parameters must agree in type. The type specification for a formal variable parameter is given in parentheses after the procedure name and looks very much like a variable declaration. Since the type of the parameter is given in the procedure heading, it need not be given anywhere else. In particular, it should not be declared in the variable declarations of the program. After all, it is not a variable.

Parameter Lists

A procedure can have any number of formal variable parameters. They are simply all listed in parentheses after the procedure name in the procedure heading and are separated by semicolons. For example, one procedure heading might be

formal parameter list

```
procedure Total (var P1: integer;
                 var P2: real; var P3: real);
```

Program

```
program TotalChange(input, output);
{Reads in the count of each type of coin and outputs their total value.}
const MoneyLength = 7; {Field length for total amount.}
var HalfDollars, Quarters, Dimes,
    Nickels, Pennies: integer;
    Total: real;

procedure GetNumber(var Number: integer);
{Writes instructions to the user, and then reads a number of
coins from the keyboard and stores that number in Number.}
begin{GetNumber}
  writeln('Do not total the amount.');
  writeln('Just enter the number of coins.');
  readln(Number)
end;  {GetNumber}

begin{Program}
  writeln('Enter the number of half-dollar coins.');
  GetNumber(HalfDollars);

  writeln('Enter the number of quarters.');
  GetNumber(Quarters);

  writeln('Enter the number of dimes.');
  GetNumber(Dimes);

  writeln('Enter the number of nickels.');
  GetNumber(Nickels);

  writeln('Enter the number of pennies.');
  GetNumber(Pennies);

  Total := 0.50*HalfDollars +
           0.25*Quarters +
           0.10*Dimes +
           0.05*Nickels +
           0.01*Pennies;

  writeln(HalfDollars, ' half-dollars, ',
                          Quarters,' quarters,');
  writeln(Dimes, ' dimes,', Nickels,' nickels and');
  writeln(Pennies, ' pennies');
  writeln('total to: $', Total :MoneyLength:2)
end.  {Program}
```

Figure 4.3
Program that uses parameter passing.

Sample Dialogue

```
Enter the number of half-dollar coins.
Do not total the amount.
Just enter the number of coins.
12
Enter the number of quarters.
Do not total the amount.
Just enter the number of coins.
325
Enter the number of dimes.
Do not total the amount.
Just enter the number of coins.
103
Enter the number of nickels.
Do not total the amount.
Just enter the number of coins.
107
Enter the number of pennies.
Do not total the amount.
Just enter the number of coins.
57
    12 half-dollars,   325 quarters,
   103 dimes, 107 nickels and
    57 pennies
total to: $ 103.47
```

Figure 4.3
(continued)

When two or more formal variable parameters are of the same type and occur one after the other in the list of parameters, they may be combined so that their type need only be written once. In that case, the combined parameters are separated by commas. For example, the following procedure heading is equivalent to the one just given:

```
procedure Total(var P1: integer; var P2, P3: real);
```

Notice that there is a *var* for each group of formal variable parameters.

When the procedure is called, the actual variable parameters are given in parentheses after the procedure name. When the procedure call is executed, the actual variable parameters are substituted for all occurrences of formal variable parameters inside the procedure body. The substitution follows the ordering: The first actual parameter listed in the procedure call is substituted for the first formal parameter listed in the procedure heading, the second actual parameter is substituted for the second formal parameter, and so forth. The number of actual parameters in a procedure call must always equal the number of formal parameters in the procedure declaration. Moreover, the type of each actual parameter must be the same as the type of the corresponding formal parameters it replaces. Hence, in the sample procedure call

*actual
parameter
list*

```
Total(Number, Price, Bill)
```

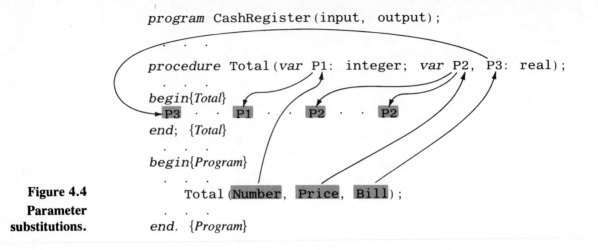

Figure 4.4
Parameter
substitutions.

the actual variable parameter Number must be a variable of type integer; the actual variable parameters Price and Bill must be variables of type real. Number is substituted for *all* occurrences of P1 in the procedure body, Price is substituted for *all* occurrences of P2, and Bill is substituted for *all* occurrences of P3.

As indicated by this example, one minor syntactic difference between formal and actual parameters is that actual parameters are separated by commas rather than by a combination of commas and semicolons. The list of parameters, either formal in the procedure heading or actual in the procedure call, is referred to as a *parameter list*.

procedure call   The order of substituting actual for formal parameters is illustrated in Figure 4.4. Figure 4.5 shows our example embedded in a complete program and illustrates one way to visualize the complete procedure-call process. First, the actual parameters are substituted for the formal parameters. Second, the body of the procedure declaration is substituted for the procedure call. Finally, the actions prescribed by the resulting code are executed. Be sure to notice that the substitution follows the ordering of the formal parameters in the formal parameter list. It does not depend on their order of occurrence inside the body of the procedure.

Implementation of Variable Parameters
(Optional)

Recall that program variables are typically implemented as memory locations. The compiler assigns one memory location to each variable. For example, when the program in Figure 4.5 is compiled, the variable Price might be assigned location 10010, Bill location 10011, and Number location 10012. For all practical purposes, these memory locations are the variables.

As we said in the previous two sections, the formal variable parameters that appear in a procedure heading are formal blanks and the actual variable parameters are vari-

Program

```
program CashRegister(input, output);
const Rate = 0.06; {Sales tax rate.}
      Width = 6; {Field width for money amounts.}
var Price, Bill: real;
    Number: integer;

procedure Total(var P1: integer; var P2, P3: real);
{Sets the value of P3 equal to the total cost of P1 items at a price of P2 each plus sales tax.}
begin{Total}
  P3 := P1 * (P2 + Rate * P2)
end; {Total}

begin{Program}
  writeln('Enter price and number of items:');
  readln(Price, Number);
  Total(Number, Price, Bill);
  writeln(Number, ' items at $', Price :Width:2);
  writeln('Total Bill $', Bill :Width:2)
end. {Program}
```

1. Substitute actual parameters for formal parameters to obtain the meaning of the procedure body:

```
begin{Total}
  Bill := Number * (Price + Rate * Price)
end; {Total}
```

2. Substitute the procedure body for the procedure call:

```
begin{Program}
  writeln('Enter price and number of items:');
  readln(Price, Number);
  begin{Total}
    Bill := Number * (Price + Rate * Price)
  end; {Total}
  writeln(Number, ' items at $', Price :Width:2);
  writeln('Total Bill $', Bill :Width:2)
end. {Program}
```

3. Execute the resulting code:

```
Enter price and number of items:
100.00 2
   2 items at $100.00
Total Bill $212.00
```

Figure 4.5
How variable parameters work.

ables to be substituted for the blanks. For example, consider the following procedure heading from Figure 4.5:

procedure `Total(`*var* `P1: integer;` *var* `P2, P3 :real);`

The formal parameters `P1`, `P2`, and `P3` are not variables and so have no memory locations assigned to them. They are just formal names that name nothing.

Now consider a procedure call like the following call from the same figure:

`Total(Number, Price, Bill)`

When the procedure call is executed, the procedure is not given the actual variable names `Number`, `Price`, and `Bill`. Instead, it is given a list of the memory locations associated with each name. In this example, the list consists of the locations

10012,   10010,   10011

which are the locations assigned to actual variable parameters `Number`, `Price`, and `Bill`, *in that order.* It is these locations that are associated with the formal parameters. The first formal parameter is associated with the first memory location, the second formal parameter is associated with the second location on the list, and so forth. Diagrammatically, in this case the correspondence is

Number	→	10012	→	P1
Price	→	10010	→	P2
Bill	→	10011	→	P3

When the procedure statements are executed, the formal parameters are interpreted as meaning the corresponding memory locations. So when P3 is changed by the assignment statement in the procedure, it is memory location 10011 that is changed. Whatever the procedure instructs the computer to do to P3 is actually done to memory location 10011, which for all practical purposes is the variable `Bill`.

Notice that the order of parameters is critically important. The procedure, when called, receives no variable names at all. It merely receives a list of memory locations, which it associates with formal variable parameters. If the actual variable parameters are not in the right order, the list of memory locations will not be in the right order, and the procedure will use the wrong memory locations and produce undesirable results.

Also notice that by using memory location addresses (numbers) instead of variable names, the compiler can easily handle otherwise confusing substitutions with coincidental collisions of names. An actual parameter may have the same name as some formal parameter, even one other than the one to which it corresponds, and the computer will not be confused.

Procedures Calling Procedures

One procedure may include a call to another procedure. The only restriction is that a procedure call cannot appear before the procedure is declared. An example is given in Figure 4.6. The program in that figure is similar to the one in Figure 4.5 and in fact, the procedure `Total` is identical to the procedure of the same name in Figure 4.5. The

Program

```pascal
program CashRegister2(input, output);

const Rate = 0.06; {Sales tax rate.}
      Width = 6; {Field width for money amounts.}
var Price, Bill: real;
    Number: integer;
    Wholesale: char; {A value of 'y' means "yes, wholesale."}

procedure Total (var P1: integer; var P2, P3: real);
{Sets the value of P3 equal to the total cost of P1 items at a price of P2 each plus sales tax.}
begin{Total}
  P3 := P1 * (P2 + Rate * P2)
end; {Total}

procedure AmountDue(var N1: integer;
                    var N2, N3: real; var C: char);
{Sets the value of N3 equal to the total cost of N1 items at a price of N2 each.
If C = 'y' no tax is added; otherwise sales tax is added.}
begin{AmountDue}
  if C = 'y' then {No sales tax.}
     N3 := N1 * N2
  else {Include sales tax.}
     Total (N1, N2, N3)
end; {AmountDue}

begin{Program}
  writeln('Enter price and number of items: ');
  readln(Price, Number);
  writeln('Is this a wholesale transaction? (y/n)');
  readln(Wholesale);

  AmountDue (Number, Price, Bill, Wholesale);

  writeln(Number, ' items at $', Price :Width:2);
  writeln('Total Bill $', Bill :Width:2);
  if Wholesale = 'y' then
     writeln('no tax')
  else
     writeln('including tax')
end. {Program}
```

Figure 4.6

Procedure calling another procedure.

1. Substitute actual parameters for formal parameters in the procedure body:

```
begin{AmountDue}
   if Wholesale = 'y' then {No sales tax.}
       Bill := Number * Price
   else {Include sales tax.}
       Total(Number, Price, Bill)
end; {AmountDue}
```

2. Substitute the procedure body for the procedure call:

```
begin{Program}
   writeln('Enter price and number of items:');
   readln(Price, Number);
   writeln('Is this a wholesale transaction?(y/n)');
   readln(Wholesale);

   begin{AmountDue}
     if Wholesale = 'y' then {No sales tax.}
         Bill := Number * Price
     else {Include sales tax.}
         Total(Number, Price, Bill)
   end; {AmountDue}

   writeln(Number, ' items at $', Price :Width:2);
   writeln('Total Bill $', Bill :Width:2);
   if Wholesale = 'y' then
       writeln('no tax')
   else
       writeln('including tax')
end. {Program}
```

3. Again substitute actual parameters for formal parameters to obtain the meaning of the other procedure body:

```
begin{Total}
   Bill := Number * (Price + Rate * Price)
end; {Total}
```

4. Substitute the procedure body for the remaining procedure call:

```
begin{Program}
   writeln('Enter price and number of items:');
   readln(Price, Number);
   writeln('Is this a wholesale transaction?(y/n)');
   readln(Wholesale);
```

**Figure 4.6
(continued)**

```
begin{AmountDue}
  if Wholesale = 'y' then {No sales tax.}
      Bill := Number * Price
  else {Include sales tax.}
        begin{Total}
          Bill := Number * (Price + Rate * Price)
        end; {Total}
end; {AmountDue}

writeln(Number, ' items at $', Price :Width:2);
writeln('Total Bill $', Bill :Width:2);
if Wholesale = 'y' then
    writeln('no tax')
else
    writeln('including tax')
end. {Program}
```

5. Execute the code:

```
Enter price and number of items:
100.00  2
Is this a wholesale transaction? (y/n)
n
   2 items at $100.00
Total Bill $212.00
including tax
```

Figure 4.6
(continued)

program in Figure 4.6 allows for two possibilities: the normal retail sale, which includes sales tax, and a sale to a wholesaler, which does not include sales tax (since that will be paid when the item is finally sold retail later). The program contains a call to the procedure AmountDue, which directly calculates the total due for wholesale buyers, but which calls the procedure Total in the case of a retail sale. As shown in the figure, the procedure declaration for Total must precede the declaration of AmountDue.

Multiple levels of procedure calls are handled just like the simple one-level calls we saw earlier. With two levels of procedure calls, we simply apply the substitution mechanism twice, as shown in Figure 4.6. When the procedure call

```
    AmountDue(Number, Price, Bill, Wholesale)
```

is encountered, the actual variable parameters Number, Price, Bill, and Wholesale are substituted for the formal variable parameters N1, N2, N3, and C, in that order. This substitution applies to all occurrences of the formal variable parameters, and so it applies to the procedure call

```
    Total(N1, N2, N3)
```

as shown in Figure 4.6, item 1. After the substitution, this procedure call within the procedure AmountDue reads

```
Total(Number, Price, Bill)
```

As shown in Figure 4.6, item 2, the entire procedure body of AmountDue, including this call to Total, is then substituted into the body of the program. This still leaves one procedure call:

```
Total(Number, Price, Bill)
```

This call is handled by another application of the substitution rules. As shown in items 3 and 4 of Figure 4.6, the actual variable parameters Number, Price, and Bill are substituted for the formal variable parameters P1, P2, and P3, and the resulting code is substituted into the program body. At that point there are no procedure calls left, and the meaning of the code is clear.

The substitution mechanism we have just described correctly mirrors the computer's performance and is easy to understand, but once you become familar with it you may prefer a variant that performs the various substitutions in another order, substituting parameters for parameters. In the example just discussed, you might first take care of the procedure call to Total by substituting N1, N2, and N3 in for P1, P2, and P3 and then substituting the body of the procedure Total into the body of the procedure AmountDue. The result is the same, although it can be a bit more difficult to keep track of.

Procedural Abstraction

One function of procedures is to simplify your reasoning by *abstracting* away irrelevant properties of a program part. When using a procedure, we need only think about what the procedure does; we need not think about how it does it. When we use the procedure Total, which appears in Figures 4.5 and 4.6, we need only know that it computes the total bill for a purchase including sales tax; we need not concern ourselves with how it computes this amount. It happens to perform the computation with the statement

```
P3 := P1 * (P2 + Rate * P2)
```

But it could just as well have been performed with the statement

```
P3 := P1 * (1 + Rate) * P2
```

or even with the slightly less efficient

```
P3 := P1 * P2 + P1 * Rate * P2
```

This detail need not concern us when we use the procedure.

Once a procedure is written, the details of how it works can be ignored. What it does should be expressed in a comment at the start of the procedure declaration. This comment should tell anyone who wants to use the procedure all that he or she needs to know in order to use it. The user of the procedure should not need to even look at the procedure body.

Procedural abstraction is more than a way of summarizing a procedure's actions. It should be the first step in designing and writing a procedure. When you design a program, you should specify what each procedure does before you start to design how the procedure will do it. In particular, the comment that describes a procedure's actions and the list of parameters that shows which items may be affected by the procedure should be designed and written down before you start to design the procedure body. If you later discover that your specification cannot be realized in a reasonable way, you may need to back up and rethink what a procedure should do, but by clearly specifying what you think the procedure should do, you will minimize both design errors and time wasted writing code that does not fit the task at hand.

designing procedures

Procedural abstraction is a way of clarifying your reasoning about your personal programs. It is even more important when programming as a team. In team situations, one programmer often does not know how a procedure written by another programmer works, and need not know. In fact, you have already experienced this. You have used the predefined function sqrt, which calculates square roots. You can use this function effectively even if you know absolutely no algorithm for extracting square roots, and you certainly do not need to know the details of how your particular implementation extracts square roots.

This one thing I do, forgetting those things which are behind,
and reaching forth unto those things which are before,
I press toward the mark.

*The Epistle of Paul the Apostle
to the Philippians 3:13–14*

Self-Test Exercises

1. What is the output of the following program?

```
program Exercise1(input, output);
procedure Friendly;
begin{Friendly}
  writeln('Hello')
end; {Friendly}
procedure Shy;
begin{Shy}
  writeln('Goodbye')
end; {Shy}
begin{Program}
  writeln('Begin Conversation');
  Shy; Friendly;
  writeln('One more time:');
  Friendly; Shy;
  writeln('End Conversation')
end. {Program}
```

2. What is the output of the following program?

```
program Exercise2(input, output);
var A, B: integer;
procedure Arthur(var X, Y: integer);
begin{Arthur}
  X := 2; X := X + 1; Y := 2*X
end;  {Arthur}
begin{Program}
  A := 4; B := 5;
  Arthur(A, B);
  writeln(A, B);
  A := 4; B := 5;
  Arthur(B, A);
  writeln(A, B)
end.  {Program}
```

3. What is the output of the following program?

```
program Exercise3(input, output);
procedure Proced1;
begin  {Proced1}
  write('One ')
end;  {Proced1}
procedure Proced2;
begin  {Proced2}
  Proced1;
  write('Two ')
end;  {Proced2}
procedure Proced3;
begin  {Proced3}
  Proced2;
  writeln('Three ')
end;  {Proced3}
begin  {Program}
  Proced1;  writeln;
  Proced2;  writeln;
  Proced3;  writeln
end.  {Program}
```

4. What is the output of the following program?

```
program Exercise4(input, output);
var X, Y: integer;
procedure Tricky(var Y, X: integer);
begin{Tricky}
  writeln(X, Y)
end;{Tricky}
```

```
begin {Program}
  X := 1; Y := 2;
  Tricky(Y, X);
  Tricky(Y, Y);
  Tricky(X, Y)
end. {Program}
```

5. Write a procedure with one variable parameter of type `integer` that leaves the parameter unchanged if it is positive or zero and changes it to zero if its value is negative.

6. Write a procedure with one formal variable parameter, `Ans`, of type `char`. If the value of Ans is `'Y'`, the procedure changes it to `'y'`; if the value is anything else, it is not changed.

Value Parameters

An actual variable parameter is a variable that the procedure can access or change. Variable parameters can be used to bring information into the procedure and/or pass information out of the procedure to the rest of the program. There is another class of parameter called *value parameters*. Value parameters are "one-way" parameters; they can be used to supply information to a procedure, but they cannot be used to get information out of a procedure. On the positive side, value parameters allow us to use more complicated expressions as the actual parameters in a procedure call. The notion is best introduced by means of an example.

one-way data

Suppose we want to write a procedure that will output the area of a rectangle to the screen. In this case, the procedure will have two parameters, one for the length of the rectangle and one for the width. Our first attempt at writing the procedure might be as follows:

```
procedure OutputArea1(var Length, Width: integer);
begin{OutputArea1}
  writeln('A rectangle of dimensions:');
  writeln(Length, ' by ', Width, ' inches');
  writeln('Has area ', Length * Width, ' square inches.')
end; {OutputArea1}
```

This will work, but in some situations it is inconvenient. If the length and width are stored in variables, say, X and Y, then to output the area of the rectangle, the following procedure call will do nicely:

```
OutputArea1(X, Y)
```

Suppose, however, that we wish to output the area of a rectangle that is 4 inches long by 3 inches wide. Since an actual variable parameter must be a variable, we will first have to set two variables equal to 4 and 3 and then use the variables as the actual parameters. That is unfortunate. It would be easier and cleaner if we could write the following expression and then have the computer substitute 4 for the formal parameter `Length` and 3 for the formal parameter `Width`.

```
OutputArea1(4, 3)
{Will not work with a variable parameter.}
```

As the comment indicates, this simply will not work with variable parameters. To make the above procedure call work, we must change `Length` and `Width` to value parameters.

syntax for formal value parameters

Formal value parameters are listed in the procedure heading just like formal variable parameters are, except that a formal value parameter is not preceded by the word `var`. To make `Length` and `Width` value parameters in our sample procedure, all we need to do is to omit the `var`, resulting in the following procedure heading:

```
procedure OutputArea2(Length, Width: integer);
```

The rest of the procedure is unchanged. The complete procedure using formal value parameters is shown in in Figure 4.7.

actual value parameters

When a procedure with formal value parameters is called, it must be supplied with one *actual value parameter* to correspond to each formal value parameter. The relationship between formal and actual *value* parameters is similar to that between formal and actual *variable* parameters. The formal value parameter serves as a blank to be filled in, and the actual value parameter provides the item that fills in the blank. However, unlike an actual *variable* parameter, an actual *value* parameter is not simply "plugged in" as is. It is first evaluated and its *value* is then plugged in for the formal parameter. For example, if the actual value parameter is a variable X whose value is 5, then it is the 5 that is used rather than the X. After the values of the formal value parameters have been set, the statements in the procedure declaration are executed. In the next chapter, we will give more details about how this substitution is actually carried out, but this simple description is adequate to explain most normal uses of value parameters: The computer evaluates the actual value parameter to obtain a value and then substitutes this value into the formal value parameter.

This substitution mechanism explains why value parameters are one-way parameters. Since an actual value parameter is just a value, it cannot be changed. A procedure can change the value of a variable X, but it cannot change the value of the number 5. To emphasize this point with an example, suppose that X is used as an actual *value* parameter and that X has the value 5. In this case the procedure gets only the 5. It has no access to X and so it cannot possibly change X. Having discussed the largest restriction on value parameters, let us now discuss their biggest advantage.

expressions as parameters

Since only the value of an actual value parameter is used, the actual value parameter can be any expression that evaluates to the specified type. This means that the actual value parameter can be a variable, but it might instead be a constant or an arithmetic expression or anything that evaluates to a value of the correct type. Hence, with `OutputArea2`, all of the following sample procedure calls are allowed (X and Y are variables of type `integer`):

```
OutputArea2(X, Y);
OutputArea2(7, 8);
OutputArea2(X + 7, Y mod X)
```

Program

```
program Value(input, output);
{Sample use of value parameters.}
var X: integer;

procedure OutputArea2(Length, Width: integer);
begin{OutputArea}
  writeln('A rectangle of dimensions:');
  writeln(Length, ' by ', Width, ' inches');
  writeln('has area ', Length * Width, ' square inches.')
end; {OutputArea}

begin{Program}
  OutputArea2(4, 3);
  X := 5;
  OutputArea2(X, X + 1)
end. {Program}
```

Output

```
A rectangle of dimensions:
    4 by        3 inches
has area       12 square inches.
A rectangle of dimensions:
    5 by        6 inches
has area       30 square inches.
```

Figure 4.7
Procedure with
value parameters.

What Kind of Parameter to Use

Deciding whether to use variable or value parameters is fairly easy. If the procedure is supposed to provide information to some other part of the program, then use a variable parameter (or parameters) and have the procedure set the value(s) of the variable parameter(s). If the parameter is being used only to give information to the procedure rather than to get information out of the procedure, then a value parameter can and probably should be used. Some of the differences between the two kinds of parameters are listed in Figure 4.8.

Choosing what parameters as well as what kinds of parameters a procedure will use should be a trivial matter provided you have designed your algorithm with attention to the flow of information between tasks. When you divide the task of your program into subtasks, make two lists for each subtask. One list is the list of all the information that will be needed to accomplish the task; these parameters are sometimes called *in* parameters. The other list should show all the information that must be provided by this subtask to other subtasks or to the calling program; these parameters are sometimes called *out* parameters. The value parameters are easy to derive from the list of *in* parameters. The variable parameters are easy to derive from the list of *out* parameters. If

data flow

	Variable Parameter	Value Parameter
var in formal parameter list	YES	NO
Can be used to pass information to the procedure	YES	YES
Can be used to pass information from the procedure back to the calling program or procedure	YES	NO
Expressions allowed in the actual parameter list	NO (just variables)	YES

Figure 4.8 Differences between variable and value parameters.

a quantity appears on both lists, then it must be a variable that will be changed by the procedure, and so it must be a variable parameter.

summary of the kinds of parameters

There are four kinds of parameters: formal variable parameters, actual variable parameters, formal value parameters, and actual value parameters. The long names convey meaning about how the parameters are used. The way to think of parameters is in a two-step process: First, the parameter is either *formal* or *actual;* second, it is either *variable* or *value.* These two two-way distinctions yield the four possible kinds of parameters. A *formal parameter* appears in a procedure declaration and is changed when the procedure is called. The *actual parameter* governs the change, and that change is always some sort of substitution of the actual parameter for the formal parameter. A formal parameter and its corresponding actual parameter are either both called variable parameters or both called value parameters. The distinction between value and variable parameters refers to the manner in which the substitution is performed. In the case of *variable parameters,* the actual parameter is a variable and is literally substituted for the formal parameter. In the case of *value parameters,* the actual parameter may be a more complicated expression, and it is the value of the expression that is substituted for the formal parameter.

Most programming languages have a distinction similar to the one in Pascal between value and variable parameters. All programming languages with facilities for parameters employ the distinction between formal and actual parameters.

Mixed Parameter Lists

You may use any number of parameters in a procedure, and they may be any combination of variable and value parameters. You simply list them all in the procedure heading. For example, one procedure heading might be

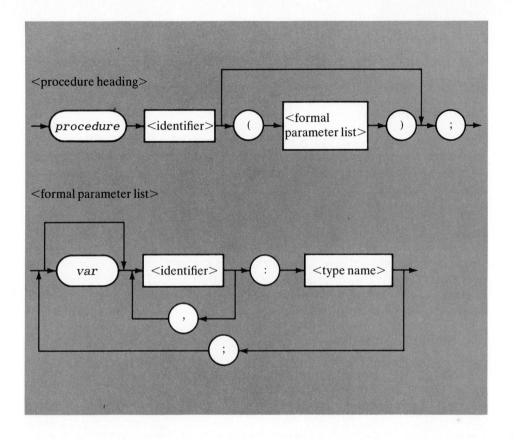

Figure 4.9
Syntax for a
procedure heading.

```
procedure Sample(W: real; var X: real; Y, Z: char);
```

Each formal parameter has a type associated with it. In the parameter list, formal variable parameters are preceded by the word *var*. Formal value parameters are indicated by the absence of the *var*. In the sample heading, X is a variable parameter; W, Y, and Z are value parameters. The various formal parameters are separated by semicolons. When two or more consecutive parameters are of the same type and are either all value or all variable parameters, then you can combine their type specifications in the way illustrated by Y and Z in the sample heading. The details are summarized by the syntax diagram in Figure 4.9.

In the procedure call, the actual parameters are given in parentheses after the procedure name; they must correspond in type to the formal parameters given in the procedure heading. For example, in the procedure call

```
Sample(2.5, A, 'B', C)
```

The variable A must have been declared to be of type real, and the variable C must have been declared to be of type char. All actual variable parameters must be variables, and so in the above example A must be a variable. Since the other parameters in this example are value parameters, they may be variables, constants, or more complicated expressions.

Case Study

Supermarket Pricing

Problem Definition

We have been commissioned by the Super-Duper supermarket chain to write a program that will determine the retail price of an item, given suitable input. Their pricing policy is that any item that is expected to sell in less than one week is marked up 5% and any item that is expected to stay on the shelf for at least one week is marked up 10% over the wholesale price.

Discussion

Like many other programming tasks, this one breaks down into three main subtasks: input the data, perform a computation, and output the results. The decomposition into subtasks, as well as the flow of data and the meaning of the variables to be used are shown in the data flow diagram in Figure 4.10.

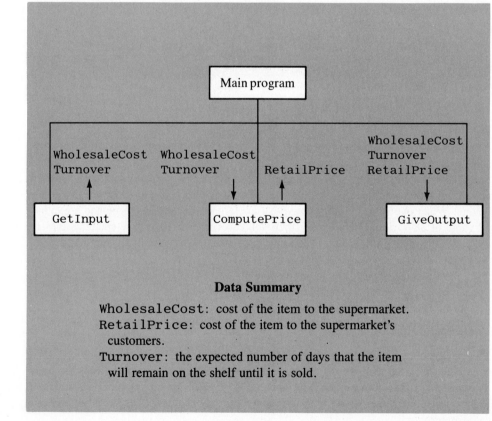

Data Summary

WholesaleCost: cost of the item to the supermarket.
RetailPrice: cost of the item to the supermarket's customers.
Turnover: the expected number of days that the item will remain on the shelf until it is sold.

Figure 4.10
Data flow diagram for supermarket pricing.

The arrows in the data flow diagram indicate the direction of data flow. If an arrow is pointing up out of a box, then the procedure represented by that box will change the quantities associated with that arrow, and so the corresponding procedure parameter will have to be a variable parameter. If a quantity is associated with an arrow pointing down into the box and is not associated with any arrow pointing up out of the box, then we will use a value parameter that takes the value of the quantity. So, for example, the procedure call to the second procedure will read

```
ComputePrice(WholesaleCost, Turnover, RetailPrice)
```

The first two parameters will be value parameters and the last one must be a variable parameter, and so the procedure heading will read as follows:

```
procedure ComputePrice(Cost: real;
                       Time: integer; var Price: real);
```

The algorithm for this procedure is straightforward: *ALGORITHM*

```
if Time < 7 then
   Price := Cost + 5% of Cost
else
   Price := Cost + 10% of Cost
```

The complete program is displayed in Figure 4.11.

Program

```
program Pricing(input, output);
{Determines the retail price of an item according to the
pricing policies of the Super-Duper supermarket chain.}
const LowMarkup = 0.05;  {5%}
      HighMarkup = 0.10;  {10%}
      Threshold = 7;  {Use HighMarkup if do not expect to sell in under 7 days.}
      Width = 5;  {Field width for prices.}
var WholesaleCost, RetailPrice: real;
    Turnover: integer;  {Expected time on shelf, expressed in days.}

procedure GetInput(var Cost: real; var Time: integer);
begin{GetInput}
  writeln('Enter the wholesale cost of the item: ');
  readln(Cost);
  writeln('Enter expected number of days until sold: ');
  readln(Time)
end;  {GetInput}

procedure ComputePrice(Cost: real;
                       Time: integer; var Price: real);
{Determines the retail Price of an item, given the
wholesale Cost and the expected time until it is sold.}
```

Figure 4.11 Supermarket pricing program.

```
begin{Compute}
   if Time < Threshold then
       Price := (1 + LowMarkup) * Cost
   else
       Price := (1 + HighMarkup) * Cost
end;  {Compute}

procedure GiveOutput(Cost: real; Time: integer; Price:real);
begin{GiveOutput}
   writeln('Wholesale cost = $', Cost:Width:2);
   writeln('Expected time until sold = ', Time, ' days');
   writeln('Retail price = $', Price:Width:2)
end;  {GiveOutput}

begin{Program}
   writeln('This program determines');
   writeln('retail prices for stock items.');
   GetInput(WholesaleCost, Turnover);
   ComputePrice(WholesaleCost, Turnover, RetailPrice);
   GiveOutput(WholesaleCost, Turnover, RetailPrice)
end.  {Program}
```

Sample Dialogue

```
This program determines
retail prices for stock items.
Enter the wholesale cost of the item:
1.21
Enter expected number of days until sold:
5
Wholesale cost = $ 1.21
Expected time until sold =    5 days
Retail price = $ 1.27
```

**Figure 4.11
(continued)**

Case Study

Change Program with Procedures

Problem Definition

We will redesign the change program from Chapter 2 so that it uses procedures for subtasks. The program will accept an amount between 1 and 99 and will output a combination of quarters, dimes, and pennies that total to that amount.

Discussion

ALGORITHM

For reference, let us summarize our previous analysis of subtasks and data flow for this problem. We need a variable Amount to hold the total amount of money. We also need variables to hold the number of each coin, as well as a variable AmountLeft to hold the amount left to be given out as we proceed down the list of coins from quarters to dimes to pennies computing the number of each coin to be given out. The breakdown into subtasks is summarized in the following pseudocode:

begin{*Program*}
1. InputAmount: Input the amount and store it in the variable Amount;
2. AmountLeft : = Amount;
3. ComputeChange: Compute a combination of quarters, dimes, and pennies whose value equals AmountLeft;
4. OutputCoins: Output Amount and the number of each coin

end. {*Program*}

All subtasks except subtask 2 will be implemented as procedures. The data flow diagram in Figure 4.12 shows the flow of data and can be used to determine which parameters need to be variable parameters and which may be value parameters. All of the parameters for InputAmount and ComputeChange must be variable parameters. We know this because the variables listed above the InputAmount and ComputeChange boxes all have arrows that point up out of the box, meaning that the parameters may be changed in the procedures. The variables above the procedure OutputCoins have no arrows pointing up out of the box, and so the parameters for this procedure may be value parameters.

Subtask 3 (ComputeChange) is further subdivided as follows; we will implement each of these smaller subtasks as a procedure that uses all variable parameters:

begin{*ComputeChange*}]
2a. ComputeQuarters: Compute the maximum number of quarters in AmountLeft and decrease AmountLeft by the total value of the quarters;
2b. ComputeDimes: Compute the maximum number of dimes in AmountLeft and decrease AmountLeft by the total value of the dimes;
2c. ComputePennies: Compute the number of pennies in AmountLeft

end {*ComputeChange*}

*procedures
for subtasks*

The completed program is given in Figure 4.13. It is equivalent to the program in Figure 2.11. The two programs will carry on exactly the same dialogue with the user, but the version with procedures explicitly shows the breakdown of the program into smaller subalgorithms.

We first wrote this change-making program without procedures and then rewrote it using procedures. We did this because we did not know about procedures when we first wrote the program. Normally, each subtask is translated into a procedure before it is used in a Pascal program. The stepwise refinement of tasks into subtasks and the writing of procedures go hand in hand.

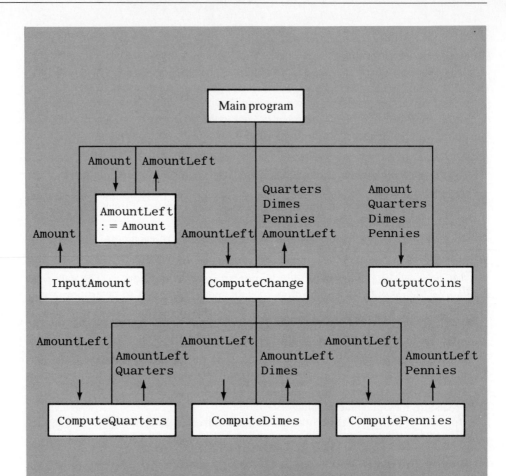

Data Summary

Amount: amount of change to be given out in coins.
AmountLeft: amount left to be given out after calculating each number of coins.
Quarters: number of quarters to be given out.
Dimes: number of dimes to be given out.
Pennies: number of pennies to be given out.

Figure 4.12
Data flow diagram
for change
program.

Program

```
program Change2(input, output);
{Outputs the coins used to give an amount between 1 and 99 cents.}
var Amount, AmountLeft,
    Quarters, Dimes, Pennies: integer;

procedure InputAmount(var A: integer);
{Fills the variable A with a value between 1 and 99 (inclusive).}
begin{InputAmount}
  writeln('Enter an amount of change');
  writeln('from 1 to 99 cents:');
  readln(A)
end; {InputAmount}

procedure ComputeQuarters(var Q, ALeft: integer);
{Sets Q equal to the maximum number of quarters in ALeft cents.
ALeft is decreased by the value of the quarters.}
begin{ComputeQuarters}
  Q := ALeft div 25;
  ALeft := ALeft mod 25
end; {ComputeQuarters}

procedure ComputeDimes(var D, ALeft: integer);
{Sets D equal to the maximum number of dimes in ALeft cents.
ALeft is decreased by the value of the dimes.}
begin{ComputeDimes}
  D := ALeft div 10;
  ALeft := ALeft mod 10
end; {ComputeDimes}

procedure ComputePennies(var P, ALeft: integer);
{Sets P equal to (the number of pennies in) ALeft (cents) and sets ALeft equal to zero.}
begin{ComputePennies}
  P := ALeft;
  ALeft := 0
end; {ComputePennies}

procedure ComputeChange(var ALeft, Q, D, P: integer);
{Sets the value of Q, D, and P to a number of quarters, dimes, and pennies
that total to ALeft cents. (The value of ALeft is changed to zero.)}
begin{ComputeChange}
  ComputeQuarters(Q, ALeft);
  ComputeDimes(D, ALeft);
  ComputePennies(P, ALeft)
end; {ComputeChange}
```

Figure 4.13

Change-making program using procedures.

```
procedure OutputCoins(A, Q, D, P: integer);
{Outputs the values of all parameters. Includes a heading stating that A cents is
equal to the total of Q quarters, plus D dimes, plus P pennies.}
begin{OutputCoins}
  writeln(A, ' cents can be given as:');
  writeln(Q, ' quarters');
  writeln(D, ' dimes and');
  writeln(P, ' pennies')
end;  {OutputCoins}


begin{Program}
  InputAmount(Amount);
  AmountLeft := Amount;
  ComputeChange(AmountLeft, Quarters, Dimes, Pennies);
  OutputCoins(Amount, Quarters, Dimes, Pennies)
end.  {Program}
```

Sample Dialogue

```
Enter an amount of change
from 1 to 99 cents:
96
    96 cents can be given as
    3 quarters
    2 dimes and
    1 pennies
```

**Figure 4.13
(continued)**

Pitfall

Incorrectly Ordered Parameter Lists

If the order of an actual parameter list does not correspond to the desired substitution pattern, the program will not work correctly. The computer substitutes the first actual parameter for the first formal parameter, the second actual parameter for the second formal parameter, and so forth. It does not care about any mnemonic matches such as Quarters for Q or Pennies for P. To see what can happen when parameter lists are ordered incorrectly, let us once again consider the change-making program in Figure 4.13. Suppose we had mistakenly ordered the actual parameters in the procedure call to OutputCoins as follows:

```
    OutputCoins(Amount, Pennies, Dimes, Quarters)
```

If this were the case, the last portion of the output would change to

```
96 cents can be given as
1 quarters
2 dimes and
3 pennies
```

If the formal and actual parameters do not match in type, the computer will give an error message. However, in cases such as this one, in which all the parameters are of the same type, a misordering of the parameter list will simply produce an incorrect result. Parameters "differently arranged have a different meaning, and meanings differently arranged have different effects."

Generalizing Procedures

Once you have broken a problem down into subtasks, it is a good idea to look for general procedures that can solve more than one subtask merely by varying some of their parameters. For example, notice in the change-making program in Figure 4.13 that the procedure for calculating the numbers of quarters and the one for computing the number of dimes are very similar. They each contain one application of *div* to find the number of coins and one application of *mod* to find the amount left after giving out that many coins. For quarters, the calculation is

```
Q := ALeft div 25;
ALeft := ALeft mod 25
```

For computing dimes, it is

```
D := ALeft div 10;
ALeft := ALeft mod 10
```

These two calculations differ in just two places: in one case a Q is used on the left-hand side of the assignment operator, and in the other case a D is used; in one case a 25 is used, and in the other case a 10 is used. By using two formal parameters, we can obtain a single procedure that can perform either of these computations. If we call these parameters Number and CoinValue, the more general calculation reads as follows:

```
Number := ALeft div CoinValue;
ALeft := ALeft mod CoinValue
```

The complete procedure, called ComputeCoins, as well as the procedure ComputeChange that calls it, are shown in Figure 4.14. We have extended the procedure ComputeChange so that it also uses nickels. With the general procedure ComputeCoins at our disposal, this is easy to do. We could just as easily add half-dollar coins; such additions do not significantly complicate the program. If efficiency is

```
procedure ComputeCoins(CoinValue: integer;
                            var Number, ALeft: integer);
```
{Sets Number equal to the maximum number of coins in ALeft cents, where each coin has value CoinValue cents. ALeft is decreased by the value of the coins.}
```
begin{ComputeCoins}
  Number := ALeft div CoinValue;
  ALeft := ALeft mod CoinValue
end;  {ComputeCoins}
```

```
procedure ComputeChange(var ALeft, Q, D, N, P: integer);
```
{Sets the value of Q, D, N, and P to a number of quarters, dimes, nickels, and pennies that total to ALeft cents. (The value of ALeft is changed to zero.)}
```
begin{ComputeChange}
  ComputeCoins(25, Q, ALeft);
  ComputeCoins(10, D, ALeft);
  ComputeCoins(5, N, ALeft);
  ComputeCoins(1, P, ALeft)
end;  {ComputeChange}
```

Figure 4.14
General procedure for number of coins.

a major issue, the last call to `ComputeCoins` can be replaced by the following simpler way of setting the value of `P`.

```
P := AmountLeft
```

Notice that in order to make the general procedure `ComputeCoins` work in a variety of cases, we needed to add one additional parameter beyond those needed by the specialized procedures, such as `ComputeQuarters`. One often needs to add one or more parameters to a procedure design in order to fit it to a particular use.

As was true in this example, it is often the case that the generalization is not apparent until after you have written a few of the specialized procedures that it will replace. If a generalized procedure turns out to be sensible, then do not hesitate to discard the old procedures and replace them with the new one. The work done on the old procedures is not wasted; it helped you to find the better solution.

Choosing Parameter Names

Procedures are self-contained units that are best designed separately from the rest of the program. On large programming projects, a different programmer may be assigned to write each procedure. The programmer should choose the most meaningful names for formal parameters that he or she can find. The actual parameters that will be substituted for the formal parameters should also be given meaningful names, often chosen by someone else. When you are proceeding in this way, it is likely that some or

```
program CashRegister(input, output);
const Rate = 0.06; {Sales tax rate.}
      Width = 6; {Field width for money amounts.}
var Price, Bill: real;
    Number: integer;

procedure Total(var Number: integer; var Price, Bill: real);
{Sets the value of Bill equal to the total cost of Number items at a price of Price each plus sales tax.}
begin{Total}
  Bill := Number * (Price + Rate * Price)
end; {Total}

begin{Program}
  writeln('Enter price and number of items:');
  readln(Price, Number);
  Total(Number, Price, Bill);
  writeln(Number, ' items at $', Price :Width:2);
  writeln('Total Bill $', Bill :Width:2)
end. {Program}
```

actual parameter

formal parameter

Figure 4.15
Procedure call with formal and actual parameters of the same name.

all pairs of formal and actual parameters will have the same name. This is perfectly acceptable. Figure 4.15 shows a rewritten version of the program in Figure 4.5. In the rewritten version, the formal and actual parameters are given identical names. Technically speaking, the formal parameter `Bill` and the actual parameter `Bill` are two different objects that just happen to have the same name. The computer will even substitute the actual parameter `Bill` for the formal parameter `Bill`. The programs in Figures 4.5 and 4.15 are handled in the same way by the compiler and act exactly alike when run.

This unrestricted choice of parameter names is an important part of the top-down, divide-and-conquer method of writing programs. When you are writing a procedure, you should be concentrating on the procedure and what it does. You should not have to think about what names are used for variables in the main program.

After you become comfortable with parameters, you will naturally tend to give formal and actual parameters the same names. For your first few programs, however, parameters may be easier to understand if you use different names for formal and actual parameters.

Words differently arranged have a different meaning, and meanings differently arranged have different effects.
                                                                    Blaise Pascal

---

Summary of Problem Solving and Programming Techniques

- When designing programs by the top-down method, you should normally implement subtasks as procedures.
- Parameters are used to pass information between procedures.
- The first steps in designing a procedure are to decide what task it is supposed to accomplish and what information it needs.
- Analyzing the flow of information into and out of a procedure will make it clear what parameters are needed and whether they should be variable or value parameters.
- Variable parameters can be used to give information to a procedure or to get information out of a procedure. Value parameters can be used to give information to a procedure, but they cannot be used to get information out of a procedure.
- Constants and complicated expressions, as well as variables, can be used as actual value parameters. Only variables can be used as actual variable parameters.
- Once a procedure is written and debugged, a user should not have to know how it works. The procedure heading and accompanying comment should explain what the procedure does, and that should suffice to use the procedure.
- Look for opportunities to combine two or more procedures into one more general procedure.

Summary of Pascal Constructs

procedure declaration
Syntax:

```
procedure <procedure name> (<formal parameter list>) ;
begin
  <statement>;
  <statement>;
       .
       .
       .
  <statement>
end;
```

Example:

```
procedure Check(Hours: integer; var Salary, Tax: real);
begin
  Salary := 12.50 * Hours;
  Tax := 0.25 * Salary
end;
```

The statements may be any Pascal statements and may contain the formal parameters. (See the next two entries in this summary.)

procedure heading
Syntax:

> *procedure* <procedure name> (<formal parameter list>) ;

Examples:

> *procedure* Check(Hours: integer; *var* Salary: real;
> *var* Tax: real);
> *procedure* Check(Hours: integer; *var* Salary, Tax: real);

The procedure heading is the first thing in a procedure declaration. The <procedure name> can be any identifier other than a reserved word. The <formal parameter list> is a list of identifiers that will serve as formal parameters. Each formal parameter is followed by a colon and its type. The formal variable parameters are prefaced by *var;* formal value parameters are not. The parameters are separated by semicolons. Consecutive formal parameters of the same kind (that is, ones that are the same type and that are either all value or all variable parameters) may (optionally) be grouped together and separated by commas. The above two examples are equivalent.

formal parameter
A formal parameter appears in a procedure declaration and is changed when the procedure is called. The change is a substitution of either a variable or a value for the formal parameter. The formal parameters for a procedure are listed in the procedure heading.

procedure call
Syntax:

> <procedure name> (<actual parameter list>)

Example:

> Check(40, PayForJoe, TaxFromJoe)

The <actual parameter list> contains the actual parameters separated by commas. There must be exactly as many actual parameters as there are formal parameters. The first actual parameter corresponds to the first formal parameter, the second actual parameter corresponds to the second formal parameter, and so forth. Corresponding formal and actual parameters must agree in type. If a formal parameter is a variable parameter (that is, one that is prefaced by *var*), then the corresponding actual parameter must be a variable. If a formal parameter is a value parameter (that is, one that is not prefaced by *var*), then the corresponding actual parameter may be anything that evaluates to the type of the formal parameter. When a procedure is called, some kind of substitution of actual parameters for the corresponding formal parameters is made, and then the procedure statements are executed. (See *variable parameter* and *value parameter*.)

actual parameter

The value or variable substituted for a formal parameter when a procedure is called. The actual parameters are listed in a procedure call as shown in the previous entry.

variable parameter

Formal and actual parameters come in pairs. The pair is either a pair of value parameters or a pair of variable parameters. If the pair is a pair of variable parameters, then a *var* is placed in front of the formal parameter in the formal parameter list of the procedure heading. If the pair is a pair of variable parameters, the actual parameter must be a variable; the formal parameter is a labeled blank, and when the procedure is called, the actual parameter is substituted for the corresponding formal parameter. Thus, the actual parameter may be changed.

value parameters

Formal and actual parameters come in pairs. The pair is either a pair of value parameters or a pair of variable parameters. If the formal parameter is not prefaced by *var* in the formal parameter list of the procedure heading, then the pair is a pair of value parameters. If the pair is a pair of value parameters, the actual parameter may be anything that evaluates to the type of the corresponding formal parameter. When the procedure is called, the value of the formal parameter is set equal to the value of the corresponding actual parameter. Thus, the actual parameter cannot be changed.

Exercises

Self-Test Exercises

7. Can a *variable* parameter be used to give information to a procedure? Can a *value* parameter be used to give information to a procedure? Can a *variable* parameter be used to get information out of a procedure? Can a *value* parameter be used to get information out of a procedure?

8. Which of the following are allowed as actual *value* parameters of type `integer`? (X is a variable of type `integer`.)

```
X     X + 1     abs(2*X)    25
```

Which are allowed as actual *variable* parameters of type `integer`?

9. Can an actual *variable* parameter be a variable? Can an actual *value* parameter be a variable? Can an actual *variable* parameter be a constant? Can an actual *value* parameter be a constant?

10. What is the output of the following program?

```
program WatchIt(input, output);
var X, Y: integer;
```

```
procedure Sam(X, Y: integer);
begin{Sam}
  writeln(X, Y)
end; {Sam}
begin{Program}
  X := 1; Y := 2;
  Sam(X, Y);
  Sam(Y, X)
end. {Program}
```

Interactive Exercises

11. Type up and run the program in Figure 4.5. Then interchange the order of the formal parameters P2 and P3 in the procedure heading and run the program again.

12. Write a procedure to find the area of a rectangle and store the answer in a variable parameter called A. This procedure will have two value parameters, as in OutputArea2 (Figure 4.7), plus the variable parameter A, for a total of three formal parameters. Embed this in a program and run the program.

13. Type up and run the program in Figure 4.15. Interchange the parameters Bill and Price in the procedure call (but not in the procedure heading) and run the program again.

Programming Exercises

14. Write a procedure with three parameters, one value parameter of type real and two variable parameters of type integer. One variable parameter is set to the whole number part of the real value; the other is set to the value of the first digit after the decimal point.

15. Write a program that reads in a real number (representing that many inches) and then outputs the area of a square with sides of that length and the area of a circle with a diameter of that length. Use two procedures to compute the two areas.

16. Write a procedure that has two formal parameters, one for the radius of a circle and one for the circumference. Given a radius, the procedure computes the circumference of the circle and stores the answer in the parameter for the circumference. Embed this in a program to compute the circumference of a circle.

17. Write a program that converts dollars to Japanese yen or yen to dollars, depending on the user's desire. The user is asked which conversion he or she wants performed. If the desired conversion is yen to dollars, then the program reads in an amount in yen as well as the yen-to-dollar exchange rate. The program then outputs the equivalent amount in dollars and cents. If the user instead requests a conversion from dollars to yen, the roles of dollars and yen are interchanged. Use at least four procedures: one for input, one for output, one to convert from yen to dollars, and one to convert from dollars to yen. (If you wish, you can write one more general procedure in place of the last two mentioned. You may find it convenient to have two output procedures, one for each type of conversion.)

18. Write a program that writes "HELLO" to the screen, one letter at a time. Use four procedures for the four letters H, E, L, and O. Each letter should be a pattern of asterisks that is at least five times larger than the regular letters on your screen. Each letter of the word should be indented more than the previous letter so that the output looks something like the following, only larger:

To display the next letter, the user presses the return key. (It may not all fit on the screen at once.)

19. Write a procedure that has one value parameter of type char. The procedure writes "YES" to the screen if the parameter value is 'y' and "NO" if it is anything else. Embed it in a test program.

20. Write two parameterless procedures, one to write the word YES and one to write the word NO to the screen in large letters made up of asterisks. The letters should be at least five times the normal size of letters on your screen. Use these procedures to redo the previous exercise to output larger words.

21. Write a procedure that computes the average and standard deviation of four scores. The standard deviation is defined to be the square root of the average of the four values $(s_i - a)^2$, where a is the average of the four scores s_1, s_2, s_3, and s_4. The procedure will have six parameters and will call two other procedures. Embed the procedure in a program to test it.

22. Write a program that asks the user to type in his or her height, weight, and age and then computes clothes sizes according to the following formulas: hat size = weight in pounds divided by height in inches, and all that multiplied by 2.9; sweater size (chest in inches) = height times weight, divided by 301 and then adjusted by adding $\frac{1}{8}$ inch for every 10 years over age 30; waist in inches = weight divided by 5.7 and then adjusted by adding $\frac{1}{10}$ inch for every 2 years over age 28. Use procedures for each calculation.

23. You have a choice of two different auto mechanics with different rate structures. One charges a flat fee of $20 plus $5.00 for each quarter-hour. The other charges $18 for the first quarter-hour and $5.75 for each quarter-hour after that. Any fraction of a quarter-hour counts as a full quarter-hour, and so 1.26 hours counts as six quarter-hours. Write a program that accepts the number of hours as input, displays the two charges, and announces which is cheaper. Use four or more procedures.

24. Redo (or do for the first time) Exercise 26 from Chapter 2. Use three procedures: one for input, one for output, and one to perform the calculation.

25. Redo (or do for the first time) Exercise 27 from Chapter 2. Use three procedures: one for input, one for output, and one to perform the calculation.

26. Redo (or do for the first time) Exercise 29 from Chapter 2. Use three procedures: one for input, one for output, and one to perform the calculation.

27. Redo (or do for the first time) Exercise 30 from Chapter 2. Use three procedures: one for input, one for output, and one to perform the calculation.

28. Redo (or do for the first time) Exercise 31 from Chapter 2. Use three procedures: one for input, one for output, and one to perform the calculation.

29. Redo (or do for the first time) Exercise 32 from Chapter 2. Use three procedures: one for input, one for output, and one to perform the calculation.

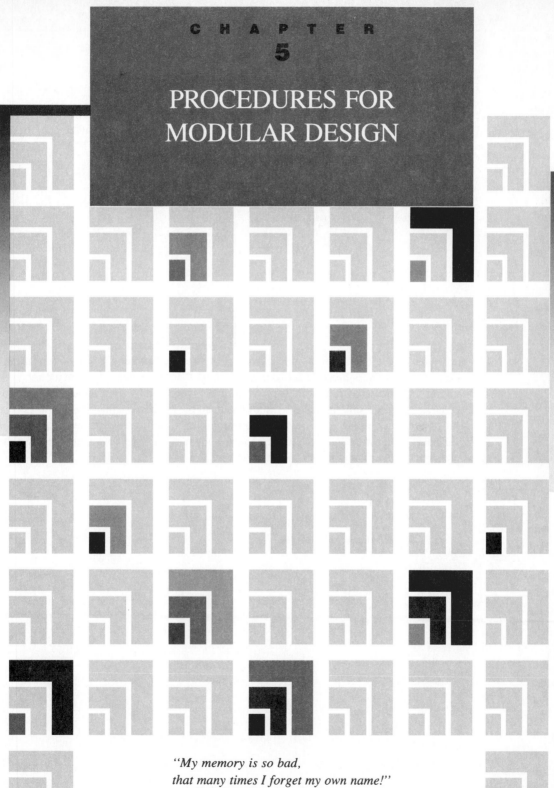

PROCEDURES FOR
MODULAR DESIGN

*"My memory is so bad,
that many times I forget my own name!"*
MIGUEL DE CERVANTES, DON QUIXOTE

Chapter Contents

Procedures separate a program into smaller, and hence more manageable, pieces. In order to get the full benefit of this decomposition, the procedures must be self-contained units that are meaningful outside the context of any particular program. A program that is built out of such self-contained procedures is often said to have a *modular* design. In this chapter we show how a procedure can be made self-contained by providing it with its own independent set of variables. After introducing these variables, known as *local variables,* we then use the construct to give examples of modular design.

Local Variables

In order to introduce the notion of a local variable, we will consider a simple but frequently occurring task and design a procedure to accomplish this task.

Exchange example

Suppose we wish to write a procedure to interchange the values of two variables of type `integer`. The procedure heading will be

```
procedure Exchange(var X, Y: integer);
```

The body of the procedure presents more of a problem. An obvious but incorrect solution to try is

```
X := Y;  Y := X
```

This sets the new value of X to the old value of Y, as desired. But then it sets the new value of Y to the *new* value of X, and so leaves Y unchanged. (If this seems unclear, plug in some values and see what happens.) What we need to do is to save the original value of X before we change the value of X. We can then use that saved value to set the value of Y. What we need is another variable to hold this saved value temporarily. Let us call this extra variable `Temp`. The correct procedure now reads:

```
procedure Exchange(var X, Y: integer);
{Interchanges the values of X and Y.}
begin{Exchange}
  Temp := X;
  X := Y;
  Y := Temp
end;  {Exchange}
```

This procedure will work nicely except for one annoying detail. Because the procedure Exchange changes the value of Temp, we must remember not to use the variable Temp for anything else. This is most unfortunate. The whole idea of top-down design and procedures is to break big tasks into smaller tasks. We make no headway in this direction if, when designing a procedure, we need to remember the details of how all the other procedures work. Once we get a procedure to work, we should only need to remember what it does, not how it does it. The principle of procedural abstraction that we advocated in the last chapter states that the procedure heading and one explanatory comment should suffice to use the procedure. Therefore, the following two lines should be all we need to know in order to use the procedure safely and effectively:

procedural abstraction

```
procedure Exchange(var X, Y: integer);
{Interchanges the values of X and Y.}
```

Clearly, these two lines are not all we need to remember. We must also remember that the procedure changes the value of the variable `Temp`.

Ideally, we should not have to remember anything about Temp, not even that it was used. What we need is a special version of the variable Temp that exists only for the duration of the procedure call. Fortunately, Pascal and many other programming languages allow such variables. They are called "local variables."

local variables

A *local variable* is a variable that is declared within a procedure. Variables that are

*global
variables*

declared for the entire program are called *global variables*. All the variables we have used until now are global variables. Local variables are declared just like global variables except that the declaration is placed inside the procedure declaration, between the procedure heading and the `begin` that marks the start of the procedure body. A local variable is meaningful only inside the procedure. No statement outside of the procedure body may reference a local variable.

The program in Figure 5.1 includes the procedure Exchange with Temp declared as a local variable. A `writeln` has been added to the procedure in order to show the value of the local variable. Although the procedure has numerous useful applications, this particular program does not have any applications. It is just an example to illustrate how global and local variables work.

*interpreting
local
variables*

The program in Figure 5.1 has two variables called Temp: one global variable declared for the entire program and one local variable declared for the procedure Exchange. What is the relationship between these two different variables? They share the same name, but they are two totally different variables. The computer does manage to keep track of these two different variables even though they have but one name be-

Program

```
program Sample(input, output);
var A, B, Temp: integer;

procedure Exchange(var X, Y: integer);
{Interchanges the values of X and Y.}
var Temp: integer;
begin{Exchange}
   Temp := X;
   X := Y;
   Y := Temp;
   writeln(A, B, Temp)
   {This writeln is here to illustrate the concept of a
    local variable. It would not normally be included.}
end; {Exchange}

begin{Program}
   A := 1;
   B := 2;
   Temp := 3;
   writeln(A, B, Temp);
   Exchange(A, B);
   writeln(A, B, Temp)
end. {Program}
```

Output

**Figure 5.1
Procedure with a
local variable.**

```
1   2   3
2   1   1
2   1   3
```

tween them. It is as if the computer acted in the following way: When a procedure is called, the computer checks to see whether there are any local variables, such as `Temp` in the procedure `Exchange`. If there are, it looks to see whether there are also any global program variables of the same name as one of these local variables; in this case, there is one such variable. The computer then saves the value of the global variable. The global variable becomes inactive, and the name is given to the local variable. The computer then executes the procedure call using the Pascal identifier as the name of the local variable. During the execution of the procedure, the shared name always refers to the local variable. When the procedure call is completed, the Pascal name is given back to the global variable, which still has its saved value, and from that point on there is no way to refer to the local variable. All the changes made to the local variable have no effect on the global variable of the same name.

In the procedure declaration in Figure 5.1, the identifier `Temp` on the left-hand side of the assignment operator names the local variable, not the global variable. Hence, the global variable is not changed. This is why the third output line is 2 1 3. If `Temp` had not been declared as a local variable, that is, if the line   *example*

```
var Temp: integer;
```

had been omitted from the procedure declaration, then the output instead would be

```
1   2   3
2   1   1
2   1   1
```

Because the computer handles local variables in this way, we can design procedures using local variables and not even bother to remember which identifiers we used for the local variables. If, outside the procedure, we reuse those identifiers to mean something else, the computer will know we mean something else.

Case Study

Grade Warnings

Problem Definition

We want to design a program that can be used early in the school term to let students know whether they are making satisfactory progress in a class. It is presumed that two tests are sufficient to obtain a meaningful early indication of progress, and so the program will read two test scores and output an answer telling whether or not the average of the two scores is passing. Since there is some danger that a student might use the program at the wrong time, the program will tell the student to see the instructor if the student has not taken exactly two tests.

Discussion

The program will simply ask the student how many tests he or she has taken. If the   *ALGORITHM*
student has taken any number other than two tests, the program tells the student to see the instructor. The main outline of the program is

if the student has not taken exactly two tests *then*
  writeln('See the instructor.')
else
  begin
    Read in the two test scores.
    Compute the average.
    Output a suitable message.
  end

The two test scores will be read in by a procedure called ReadScores. Because the student might make a mistake in entering test scores, the procedure will echo back the test scores and ask the student if they were entered correctly. If they are not cor-

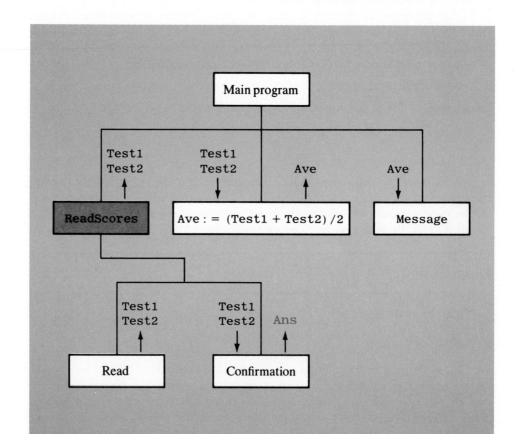

Data Summary

Test1, Test2: two test scores.
Ave: the average of the two test scores.
Ans: answer to indicate that data was or was not entered correctly.

Figure 5.2
Data flow diagram
for the case of
exactly two tests.

Program

```
program Warning(input, output);
{Tells students if their first two tests represent passing work.}
const Passing = 70;
      Width = 7; {Field width for percentages = 5 + Frac.}
      Frac = 2; {Number of digits after the decimal point in average score.}
var Test1, Test2: integer;
    Ave: real;
    Ans: integer;

procedure ReadScores(var Score1, Score2: integer);
var Ans: char;
begin{ReadScores}
  Ans := 'n' ; {To get the while loop started.}
  while Ans <> 'y' do
    begin{loop body}
      writeln('Enter your two test scores:');
      readln(Score1, Score2);
      writeln('The scores are ', Score1, Score2, ' Is that correct? (y/n)');
      readln(Ans);
      if Ans <> 'y' then
          writeln('OK. Try again.')
    end {loop body}
end;    {ReadScores}

procedure Message(Ave: real);
begin{Message}
  writeln('Your average is ', Ave:Width:Frac);
  writeln('To pass you need at least ', Passing);
  if Ave >= Passing then
          writeln('You are passing so far.')
  else
          writeln('Warning: you are failing!')
end; {Message}

begin{Program}
  writeln('Begin assessment of class work:');
  writeln('How many tests have you taken?');
  readln(Ans);
  if Ans <> 2 then
    writeln('See the instructor.')
  else
    begin{2 tests}
      ReadScores(Test1, Test2);
      Ave := (Test1 + Test2)/2;
      Message(Ave)
    end {2 tests}
end. {Program}
```

Figure 5.3
Grade warning program.

Sample Dialogue 1

```
Begin assessment of class work:
How many tests have you taken?
1
See the instructor.
```

Sample Dialogue 2

```
Begin assessment of class work:
How many tests have you taken?
2
Enter your two test scores:
57      90
The scores are    57      90    Is that correct? (y/n)
n
OK. Try again.
Enter your two test scores:
75      90
The scores are    75      90    Is that correct? (y/n)
y
Your average is  82.50
To pass you need at least      70
You are passing so far.
```

**Figure 5.3
(continued)**

rect, the student is given a chance to reenter the scores. A *while* loop will be used to repeat this check until the student says the scores are correct. A complete breakdown of subtasks is shown in the data flow diagram in Figure 5.2. The various variables to be used are also shown there. The arrows indicate the data flow. If an arrow associated with some variable is pointing out of the top of a box and the subtask represented by that box is implemented as a procedure, then we must use a variable parameter for that piece of data. When the procedure is called, the variable will be substituted for the formal variable parameter. If the only arrow associated with a variable on top of a box points into the top of the box and the task represented by that box is implemented as a procedure, then we will use a value parameter, which takes the value of that variable.

Notice that the variable Ans is never used outside of the procedure Read-Scores; no arrows associated with the variable Ans point out of or into the *top* of the box for that procedure. Ans is used to hold an answer from the user that is only needed by that procedure and is never passed out of the procedure. Whenever a variable is used only within a procedure, it should be made a local variable; therefore, we will make Ans a local variable.

The complete program is given in Figure 5.3. Notice that the complete program has both a global and a local variable named Ans. In both cases, this is the most natural name to use. Since one of the two variables is local, this coincidence of names is not a problem.

Other Local Identifiers

Identifiers other than variable names may be local to a procedure. Any kind of declaration allowed in a Pascal program is also allowed in a Pascal procedure. A procedure may have local named constants and local procedures of its own, as well as local variables. The interpretation of these other locally declared identifiers is similar to that of local variables. The local named constant or local procedure exists only while the procedure in which it is declared is executing. Outside of the procedure, you can reuse a local identifier to name something else. The ordering of local declarations within a procedure is the same as the ordering of declarations within a program.

local declarations

Program

```
program Talk2(input, output);
const OpeningLine = 'Hello, my name is Ronald Gollum.';
      Compliment = 'You''re a wonderful person.';
      Farewell = 'I hope we meet again.';

procedure BreakIce;
const OpeningLine = 'Haven''t we met somewhere before?';
var FirstI, LastI: char;
procedure Compliment;
   begin{Compliment}
     writeln('A lovely name.');
     writeln('I really like that name.')
   end;  {Compliment}

begin{BreakIce}
   writeln(OpeningLine);
   readln; {Discards the user's answer.}
   writeln('What is your first name?');
   readln(FirstI);
   Compliment;
   writeln('What is your last name?');
   readln(LastI);
   Compliment;
   writeln('Pleased to meet you ', FirstI, '.',LastI, '.')
end;  {BreakIce}

begin{Program}
   writeln(OpeningLine);
   BreakIce;
   writeln(Compliment);
   writeln(Farewell)
end.  {Program}
```

Figure 5.4
Program using local identifiers.

Sample Dialogue

```
Hello, my name is Ronald Gollum.
Haven't we met somewhere before?
```
I don't think so.
```
What is your first name?
```
Jane
```
A lovely name.
I really like that name.
What is your last name?
```
Doe
```
A lovely name.
I really like that name.
Pleased to meet you J.D.
```
Figure 5.4   You're a wonderful person.
(continued)   I hope we meet again.

local
constants

local
procedures

    The program in Figure 5.4 contains a procedure that has a local constant and a local procedure, in addition to local variables. There are two string constants called OpeningLine, one global and one local to the procedure BreakIce. The identifier Compliment is defined globally to be a string constant. Within the procedure declaration BreakIce, however, it is also declared to be the name of a local procedure. Within the procedure BreakIce, the identifier Compliment names a procedure. Outside of the procedure BreakIce, it names a string constant.

    An advantage of local procedures is that they make the calling procedure a self-contained unit. Hence, if they are short and not used outside of the calling procedure, it makes sense to use local procedures. However, large procedures are seldom made local to other procedures. The inclusion of numerous long local procedures can separate a procedure heading from the main part of the procedure and so make the calling procedure awkward to read.

Pitfall

Use of Global Variables

the problem
with global
variables

Pascal allows procedures to change global variables that are not actual parameters. If X is a global variable of type integer, then the compiler will accept and translate the following procedure:

```
procedure BadForm;
begin{BadForm}
  writeln('Enter a number: ');
  readln(X);
  writeln('I''ll give that number to the program')
end;  {BadForm}
```

However, it is almost always a bad idea to use global variables in this way.

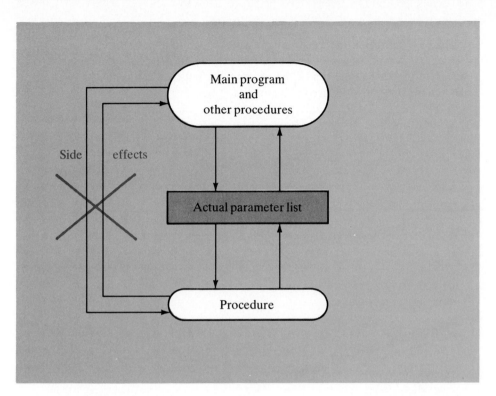

Figure 5.5
Side effects.

Procedures should be self-contained units that are meaningful outside the context of the program. This means that the procedure's interaction with the rest of the program should be entirely through parameters. Any other interaction between the procedure and the rest of the program is referred to as a *side effect*. As indicated in Figure 5.5, side effects are considered undesirable. If a procedure changes a global variable (other than an actual parameter), that is a side effect. Except in very rare circumstances, global variables should not appear anyplace in a procedure declaration. If a temporary variable is needed in a procedure, use a local variable, not a global variable. If you want the program to change the value of a global variable, use a formal variable parameter in the procedure declaration, and then use the global variable as the actual parameter in a procedure call.

The prohibition against global variables is often phrased as "no global variables in procedures," which has led to confusion on the part of some novice programmers. The prohibition does not mean that procedures cannot manipulate global variables. In fact, changing global variables is the common and accepted way for one procedure to pass information to another. However, those global variables should always be passed to the procedure as actual parameters. Global variables should not be used directly in the statements within the body of a procedure declaration; instead, use a formal parameter or local variable.

Although global variables should not appear in a procedure declaration, it is perfectly acceptable to use globally defined named constants in a procedure dec-

global constants

laration (as we did in Figure 5.3). The difference is that constants cannot be changed by the procedure, and so there is no danger of their being changed inadvertently. In fact, it is very convenient to display all the defined constants in a program together at the top of the program so that they can easily be changed should the program ever need to be revised.

He was a local boy,
not known outside his home town.

Common saying

Self-Test Exercises

1. Predict the output of the following program:

```
program Exercise1(input, output);
var N: integer;

procedure Sally;
var N: integer;

begin{Sally}
  N := 7;
  writeln(N)
end;  {Sally}

begin{Program}
  N := 11;
  Sally;
  writeln(N)
end. {Program}
```

2. Predict the output of the following program:

```
program Exercise2(input, output);
var Bozo: integer;

procedure  Test;
const Bozo = 'Hi Folks';
begin{Test}
  writeln(Bozo, ' in procedure')
end; {Test}

begin{Program}
  Bozo := 21;
  Test;
  writeln(Bozo, ' outside of procedure')
end. {Program}
```

3. Predict the output of the following program:

```
program Exercise3(input, output);
var A, B, C: integer;

procedure Funny(var X, Y: integer);
var C: integer;
begin{Funny}
  X := 4; Y := 5; C := 6;
  writeln(X, Y, C)
end; {Funny}

begin {Program}
  A := 1; B := 2; C := 3;
  writeln(A, B, C);
  Funny(A, B);
  writeln(A, B, C)
end. {Program}
```

4. What will be the output of the program in Exercise 3 if the procedure call is changed to

```
Funny(B, A)
```

5. What will be the output of the program in Exercise 3 if the procedure call is changed to

```
Funny(A, A)
```

6. What will be the output of the program in Exercise 3 if the procedure call is changed to

```
Funny(A, C)
```

(This one is tricky. If you do not understand the answer, you may wish to leave it for now and return to it after you have had more practice with local variables.)

Implementation of Value Parameters

Formal *value* parameters are implemented as local variables. A formal value parameter is thus a bit more than a formal blank. It is a special kind of local variable that is used to receive values when the procedure is called. When a procedure with formal value parameters is called, it must be supplied with one actual value parameter to correspond to each formal value parameter. The value of each formal value parameter is then initialized to the value of the corresponding actual parameter.

Since a formal value parameter is a local variable, you can use it just like any other local variable. Figure 5.6 illustrates a value parameter being used as a local variable. The formal value parameter `Minutes` in the procedure `OutputTime` is a local variable that is changed by the procedure. Only the value of the actual parameter `Time-Worked` is used, and so that variable is not changed by the procedure call

formal value parameters used as local variables

```
OutputTime(TimeWorked)
```

Program

```
program Payroll(input, output);
{Input is the number of minutes worked. Output is the time worked in hours
and minutes as well as the pay due at a rate of Rate cents per minute.}
const Rate = 20; {Cents per minute.}
      MoneyLength = 7; {Field width for PayDue.}
var TimeWorked: integer;
    PayDue: real;


procedure OutputTime(Minutes: integer);
{Outputs Minutes number of minutes as hours and minutes. The value
of the actual parameter corresponding to Minutes is unchanged.}
var Hours: integer;
begin {OutputTime}
  Hours := Minutes div 60;
  Minutes := Minutes mod 60;
  writeln(Hours, ' hours and ', Minutes, ' minutes')
end; {OutputTime}


procedure ComputePay(Minutes: integer; var Pay: real);
{Minutes is the time worked in minutes. Rate is a global constant equal to the
pay rate expressed as pennies per minute. Pay is set to the pay due expressed in dollars.}
var PennyPay: integer;
begin{ComputePay}
  PennyPay := Rate * Minutes;
  Pay := PennyPay / 100
end; {ComputePay}


begin{Program}
  writeln('Enter the number of minutes you worked:');
  readln(TimeWorked);
  write('You worked: ');
  OutputTime(TimeWorked);
  ComputePay(TimeWorked, PayDue);
  writeln('At ', Rate, ' cents per minute,');
  writeln('you earned: $', PayDue :MoneyLength:2)
end. {Program}
```

Sample Dialogue

```
Enter the number of minutes you worked:
62
You worked:    1 hours and    2 minutes
At    20 cents per minute,
you earned: $   12.40
```

Figure 5.6
A value parameter used as a local variable.

Pitfall

Inadvertent Local Variables

If you want a procedure to change the value of a variable, then you must use an actual variable parameter. This means that the corresponding formal parameter must be preceded by *var*. If you carelessly omit the *var*, the procedure will have a value parameter where you meant to have a variable parameter. This can be very frustrating because it will undoubtedly result in incorrect output. Yet the program will run with no error messages and is likely to look correct, since the only mistake is typographically very minor. If you make such a mistake and attempt to locate it by tracing variables, you will find that the procedure does not change the value of the actual parameter. This is because a formal value parameter is a local variable—if its value is changed in the procedure, then, as with any local variable, that change will be lost when the procedure call is completed. Any time you find a procedure that does not change a parameter value when it should, check for a missing *var*.

For example, the procedure ReadScores in Figure 5.7 is supposed to use variable parameters. Since the *var* was omitted, the parameters became value parameters, and so the procedure has no effect on the value of the actual parameters.

Scope of an Identifier

A variable that is declared in a procedure is local to that procedure. Its meaning is confined to that procedure and you need not even be aware of its existence at any time other than when you write the procedure. That is the beauty of local declarations. As long as you think of each procedure as a self-contained unit and design each unit separately, you will never even notice that the same identifier names two or more different variables in a program. Life is not as easy for the computer. The computer must decide the meaning of each variable or other identifier in the program. If there is more than one declaration for a single variable name, it must decide which declaration goes with each of the occurrences of that variable name. How it makes this decision is the topic of this section.

A set of declarations, possibly prefaced by a parameter list, together with the body of statements to which they apply, is a program unit called a *block*. This term is used to refer to a procedure and also to an entire program. The syntax for a block is summarized in Figure 5.8. Notice that a procedure is thus divided into two overlapping parts: a procedure heading and a block; the formal parameter list is considered to be both part of the heading and part of the block.

block

A procedure declaration consists of the word *procedure,* followed by the procedure name, followed by a block and a semicolon. All the identifiers described at the

scope

start of a block are said to be *local to that block* or, equivalently, to have that block as their *scope*. The meaning given to an identifier by the parameter list or by a declaration applies only within the block.

> If an identifier is declared or is listed as a formal parameter in each of two blocks, one within the other, then its meaning *within the inner block* is the one *determined by the declaration or parameter list at the start of the inner block.*

Program

```
program Careless(input, output);
{Illustrates the effect of omitting the var from the parameter list of
the procedure ReadScores of Figure 5.3.}
var S1, S2: integer;

procedure ReadScores(Score1, Score2: integer);
var Ans: char;
begin{ReadScores}
   Ans := 'n'; {To get the while loop started.}

   while Ans <> 'y' do
    begin{loop body}
      writeln('Enter your two test scores: ');
      readln(Score1, Score2);
      writeln('The scores are ', Score1, Score2,
                           ' Is that correct? (y/n)');
      readln(Ans);
      if Ans <> 'y' then
          writeln('OK. Try again.')
    end {loop body}
end; {ReadScores}

begin{Program}
   S1 := 1; S2 := 2;
   ReadScores(S1, S2);
   writeln('Procedure call is over.');
   writeln('S1 = ', S1, ' S2 = ', S2)
end. {Program}
```

Sample Dialogue

```
Enter your two test scores:
98 100
The scores are 98 100  Is that correct? (y/n)
y
Procedure call is over.
S1 =   1 S2 =   2
```

Figure 5.7
Effect of forgetting
a *var*.

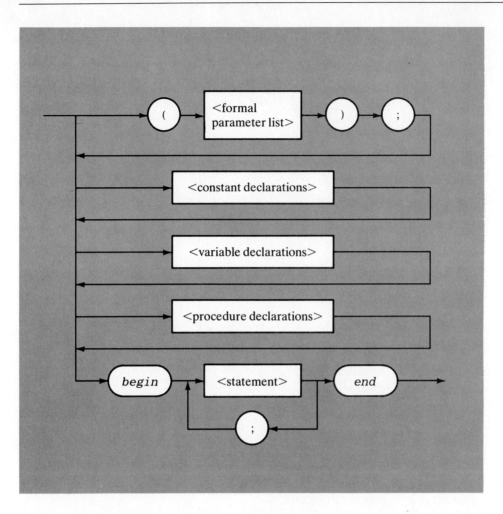

Figure 5.8
Syntax of a block.

If an identifier is given a meaning within the block of a procedure, then when the procedure is called, the identifier takes on that meaning, and when the procedure call is over, it loses that identity. If the same identifier had a meaning before the procedure call, then that meaning is suspended for the duration of the procedure call but returns with all its properties preserved when the procedure call is completed. Figure 5.9 shows a possible arrangement of blocks for a program.

Figure 5.10 contains a program designed to illustrate the notion of scope. The single identifier X appears in three different blocks so that the program contains three different variables named X. Each occurrence of the identifier X names one of these three variables. The three different shadings indicate the three areas of meaning for the identifier X.

When a procedure with a local variable, say X, is called, the computer saves the value of any global variable called X and then executes the procedure call. When the procedure call is completed, the global variable X, with its saved value, is restored. If

```
program MAIN/(input,  output);
    const X = . . .                        Scope
    var . . .                              of X

    procedure A /(var  . . .   Scope
        const Y = . . .            of Y
        var . . .

        procedure B /(var  . . .
            const Z = . . .
            var . . .
            . . .              Scope
            begin {B}          of Z
            . . .
            end;  {B}

        begin {A}
        . . .
        end;  {A}

    procedure C /(var . . .
        const W = . . .
        var . . .
        begin {C}                  Scope
        . . .                      of W
        end;  {C}

    begin{Program}
    . . .
    end. {Program}
```

Figure 5.9
**Scope of
identifiers.**

there is a procedure call within a procedure and both procedures have a local variable called X, then there can be two saved values for the identifier X. This is illustrated in Figure 5.11. The procedure calls in the figure are expanded to show the entire procedure and thereby display all the statements of all the procedures in the order in which they are actually executed. When the procedure ProB is called, the value of the global variable X is saved, and the identifier X then names the local variable in ProB. When the procedure ProA is called, the value of the local variable X in ProB is saved, so that two values are now saved, and the identifier X then names the local variable in the procedure ProA. When the execution of the procedure ProA is completed, the local variable in ProB is restored. When the execution of the procedure ProB is completed, the global variable X is restored. In more complicated programs, even more values may need to be saved.

Program

```pascal
program ShowScope(input, output);
var X: integer;

procedure ProA;
var X: integer;
begin{ProA}
  writeln('****Start ProA');
  X := 3;
  writeln('****In ProA, X = ', X);
  writeln('****End ProA')
end; {ProA}

procedure ProB;
var X: integer;
begin{ProB}
  writeln('*Start ProB');
  X := 2;
  writeln('*In ProB, X = ', X);
  ProA;
  writeln('*In ProB, X = ', X);
  writeln('*End ProB')
end; {ProB}

begin{Program}
  writeln('Start Program');
  X := 1;
  writeln('Global X = ', X);
  ProB;
  writeln('Global X = ', X);
  writeln('End Program')
end. {Program}
```

Output

```
Start Program
Global X =    1
*Start ProB
*In ProB, X =    2
****Start ProA
****In ProA, X =    3
****End ProA
*In ProB, X =    2
*End ProB
Global X =    1
End Program
```

Figure 5.10
One identifier in three scopes.

```
program ShowScope(input, output);
var X: integer;

procedure ProA;
var X: integer;
 . . .

procedure ProB;
var X: integer;
 . . .

begin{Program}
  writeln('Start Program');
  X := 1;                                          X = 1 active
  writeln('Global X = ', X);
          ⎧ procedure ProB;
          ⎪ var X: integer;                        X = 1 saved
          ⎪ begin{ProB}
          ⎪   writeln('*Start ProB');
          ⎪   X := 2;                              X = 2 active
          ⎪   writeln('*In ProB, X = ', X);        X = 1 saved
          ⎪           ⎧ procedure ProA;
          ⎪           ⎪ var X: integer;            X = 2 saved
          ⎪           ⎪ begin{ProA}                X = 1 saved
   ProB; ⎨           ⎪   writeln('****Start ProA');
          ⎪    ProA; ⎨   X := 3;                   X = 3 active
          ⎪           ⎪   writeln('****In ProA, X = ', X);  X = 2 saved
          ⎪           ⎪   writeln('****End ProA')  X = 1 saved
          ⎪           ⎩ end;{ProA}                 X = 2 active
          ⎪   writeln('*In ProB, X = ', X);        X = 1 saved
          ⎪   writeln('*End ProB')
          ⎩ end;{ProB}                             X = 1 active
  writeln('Global X = ', X);
  writeln('End Program')
end. {Program}
```

Figure 5.11 Explanation of Figure 5.10.

Case Study

Automobile Bargaining

Problem Definition

A consumer service organization has commissioned you to write a program that will help people bargain for a low price when purchasing an automobile. The program will

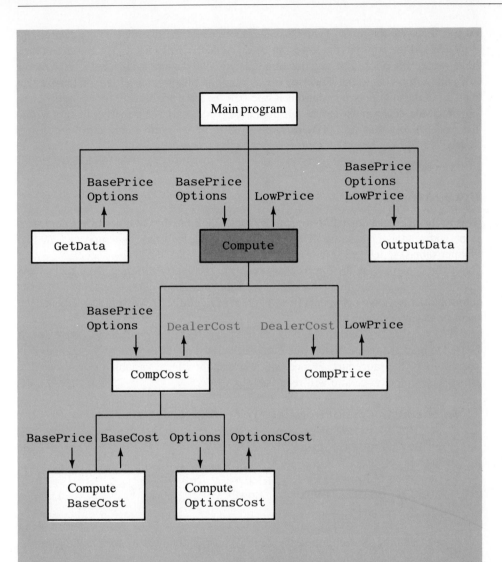

Data Summary

BasePrice: list price of the basic automobile.
Options: list price of desired options.
BaseCost: cost to dealer of basic automobile, including any delivery charge.
OptionsCost: cost to dealer of options.
DealerCost: cost to dealer of the automobile with options.
LowPrice: lowest price acceptable to dealer.

Figure 5.12
Data flow diagram for automobile pricing.

take as input the list price of the basic automobile and the list price of the desired options and will then output the lowest price that a dealer will accept. The buyer can then hold out for this price. The organization tells you that dealers will accept a price that is 10% above the cost to the dealer of the automobile plus options. It also tells you that the cost of the automobile or options is one-half the list price, except for economy cars, on which the dealer must pay an additional delivery charge. Currently, all cars with a list price of less than $12,000 are considered to be economy cars, and the delivery charge is $300.

Discussion

This problem breaks down into three main subtasks: input the data, perform a computation, and output the results. The computation subtask further decomposes into two smaller subtasks: determine the dealer's cost, and calculate the lowest acceptable price. Since the dealer's cost for the basic automobile is slightly different from that of the options, we can subdivide this task into two subcomputations. The breakdown of tasks into subtasks is shown in the data flow diagram in Figure 5.12. We will implement each subtask as a procedure.

local variable The variable DealerCost is never used outside of the procedure Compute. It is used to hold an intermediate value that is calculated by the procedure but that never is passed out of the procedure. Hence, we will make it a local variable in the procedure Compute so the procedure will read

```
procedure Compute(BasePrice, Options: real;
            var LowPrice: real);
var DealerCost: real;
begin{Compute}
  CompCost(BasePrice, Options, DealerCost);
  CompPrice(DealerCost, LowPrice)
end; {Compute}
```

ALGORITHM The algorithm for computing the dealer's cost is obtained by formalizing the description given to us in the problem definition.

```
if the car is an economy car then
  BaseCost := 0.5 * (the base price) + (the delivery charge)
else {it is not an economy car}
  BaseCost := 0.5 * (the base price);
OptionsCost := 0.5 * (the list price of all options);
(the dealer's cost) := BaseCost + OptionsCost
```

The algorithm is implemented as the procedure CompCost. The variables Base-Cost and OptionsCost are not used outside of the procedure CompCost, and they can therefore be local variables. The complete program is given in Figure 5.13.

Testing Procedures

Because they divide big tasks into smaller tasks of more manageable size, procedures make programs easier to write and easier to change. You can solve each subtask separately, write it up as a procedure, and then test it separately.

As a sample case, consider the automobile-pricing program in Figure 5.13. We can test each of the procedures separately. We can check the procedure `GetData` by using a program such as the one in Figure 5.14. Having tested this procedure, we can go on to test the other procedures.

We can test the procedure `CompCost` with a program such as the one in Figure 5.15. The procedure `CompPrice` can be tested by a similar program. Once these two procedures have been tested, we can then test the procedure `Compute`. Testing programs like those shown in Figures 5.14 and 5.15 are often called *driver programs*.

driver programs

Each procedure in a program should be tested separately. The method we outlined for testing the automobile-pricing program is called *bottom-up testing* and is one of two basic methods for testing a program. In the bottom-up testing strategy, each procedure is tested and debugged before any procedure that uses it is tested. One possible order for bottom-up testing of our automobile-pricing program is given in Figure 5.16, on page 171.

bottom-up testing

If you test each procedure separately, you will find most of the mistakes in your program. Moreover, you will find out which procedure contains the mistake. If instead you just test the entire program, and if there is a mistake, then you will probably find out that there is a mistake, but you may have no idea of where it is. Even worse, you may think you know where the error is but be mistaken.

Testing each procedure separately may sound like a very time-consuming process. However, if you follow this strategy, you will find that the time saved by quickly locating bugs will allow you to write the final program faster than if you wrote and tested the program as a single undivided unit.

Top-Down and Bottom-Up Strategies

The bottom-up testing strategy, presented in the last section, is a reasonable approach to testing a small program or small portions of a larger program. However, when testing a large program, the bottom-up strategy does not always make sense. The best way to design a program is top-down. First, break the task into subtasks. Then write procedures for the subtasks. These procedures will contain calls to yet other procedures to perform smaller subtasks. In order to test the basic design strategy, it frequently is a good idea to test each procedure before going on to design the procedures it uses. This method of testing is called *top-down testing*. For example, a possible top-down order for testing the procedures in our automobile-pricing program is given in Figure 5.17.

top-down testing

How can you test a procedure or program, such as `InsideScoop`, before writing the procedures it uses? The answer is to write simple versions of the missing procedures and to use these simplified versions to test the calling program (or procedure).

Program

```
program InsideScoop(input, output);
{Determines a dealer's minimum acceptable price on an automobile.}
const Markup = 0.10; {10% over cost.}
      LuxuryPrice = 12000; {Autos below this price are economy class.}
      Delivery = 300; {Delivery charge on nonluxury models.}
      WholesaleFactor = 0.5;
      {Wholesale is 50% of list price.}
      Width = 8; {Field width for price of auto.}
var BasePrice, Options, LowPrice: real;

procedure GetData(var BasePrice, Options: real);
{Reads list BasePrice (without options) and list price of Options.}
begin{GetData}
  writeln('Enter the base sticker price (without options):');
  readln(BasePrice);
  writeln('Enter the total sticker price for all options:');
  readln(Options)
end;  {GetData}

procedure CompCost(BasePrice, Options: real;
                               var DealerCost: real);
{Calculates DealerCost from list prices for BasePrice and Options.}
var BaseCost, OptionsCost: real;
begin{CompCost}
  if BasePrice < LuxuryPrice then
     BaseCost := WholesaleFactor * BasePrice + Delivery
  else
     BaseCost := WholesaleFactor * BasePrice;
  OptionsCost := WholesaleFactor * Options;
  DealerCost := BaseCost + OptionsCost
end;  {CompCost}

procedure CompPrice(DealerCost: real; var LowPrice: real);
{Is given DealerCost = the total cost of the automobile to the dealer.
Sets LowPrice equal to the lowest price that dealers will accept.}
begin{CompPrice}
  LowPrice := (1 + Markup) * DealerCost
end;  {CompPrice}

procedure Compute(BasePrice, Options: real; var LowPrice: real);
{Is given the list price for BasePrice and Options.
Sets LowPrice equal to the lowest price that dealers will accept.}
var DealerCost: real;
```

Figure 5.13
Automobile-pricing
program.

```
begin{Compute}
  CompCost(BasePrice, Options, DealerCost);
  CompPrice(DealerCost, LowPrice)
end;  {Compute}

procedure OutputData(BasePrice, Options, LowPrice: real);
begin{OutputData}
  writeln('List price for basic model: $', BasePrice :Width:2);
  writeln('List price for options: $', Options :Width:2);
  writeln('Dealer''s lowest total price: $', LowPrice :Width:2);
  writeln('Go for it!')
end;  {OutputData}

begin{Program}
  writeln('I will help you get a bargain on your new car.');
  GetData(BasePrice, Options);
  Compute(BasePrice, Options, LowPrice);
  OutputData(BasePrice, Options, LowPrice)
end.  {Program}
```

Sample Dialogue

```
I will help you get a bargain on your new car.
Enter the base sticker price (without options):
13000
Enter the total sticker price for all options:
4000
List price for basic model: $13000.00
List price for options: $ 4000.00
Dealer's lowest total price: $ 9350.00
Go for it!
```

Figure 5.13 (continued)

```
program Test1(input, output);
const Width = 8;
var BasePrice, Options: real;

procedure GetData(var BasePrice, Options: real);
{Reads list BasePrice (without options) and list price of Options.}
begin{GetData}
  writeln('Enter the base sticker price (without options):');
  readln(BasePrice);
  writeln('Enter the total sticker price for all options:');
  readln(Options)
end;  {GetData}

begin{Program}
  GetData(BasePrice, Options);
  writeln('BasePrice = ', BasePrice :Width:2);
  writeln('Options price = ', Options :Width:2)
end.  {Program}
```

Figure 5.14 Test 1.

Program

```
program Test2(input, output);
const LuxuryPrice = 12000; {Autos below this price are economy class.}
      Delivery = 300; {Delivery charge on nonluxury models.}
      WholesaleFactor = 0.5; {Wholesale is 50% of list price.}
      Width = 8; {Field width for price of auto.}
var BasePrice, Options, DealerCost: real;

procedure CompCost(BasePrice, Options: real;
                              var DealerCost: real);
{Calculates DealerCost from list prices for BasePrice and Options.}
var BaseCost, OptionsCost: real;
begin{CompCost}
  if BasePrice < LuxuryPrice then
     BaseCost := WholesaleFactor * BasePrice + Delivery
  else
     BaseCost := WholesaleFactor * BasePrice;
  OptionsCost := WholesaleFactor * Options;
  DealerCost := BaseCost + OptionsCost
end; {CompCost}

begin{Program}
  writeln('Enter list price for BasePrice and Options:');
  readln(BasePrice, Options);
  CompCost(BasePrice, Options, DealerCost);
  writeln('BasePrice = ', BasePrice :Width:2);
  writeln('Options price = ', Options :Width:2);
  writeln('DealerCost = ', DealerCost :Width:2)
end. {Program}
```

Sample Dialogue

```
Enter list price for BasePrice and Options:
13000 4000
BasePrice =    13000.00
Options price =    4000.00
DealerCost =    8500.00
```

Figure 5.15
Test 2.

The simple version will not do what the final procedure is supposed to do, but it will behave like the procedure is supposed to behave on the test cases for which it is used. For example, a temporary version of Compute is shown in Figure 5.18. Early versions of the program with such simplified versions of some procedures are frequently *stub* called *stub programs*.

programs

The advantages of bottom-up testing are obvious. Each procedure is tested with fully debugged, final versions of the procedures it uses. Hence, any problems discovered can be attributed to the procedure being tested. The advantage of top-down testing

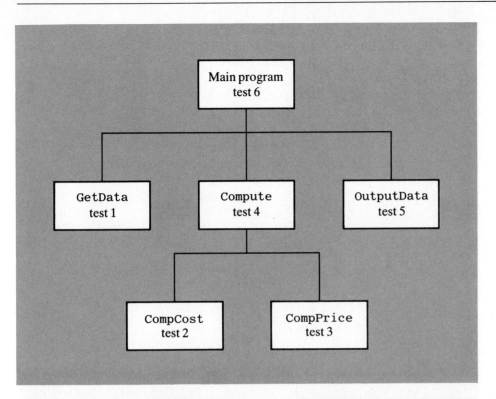

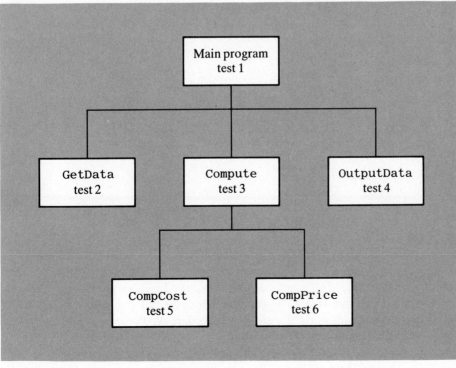

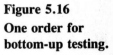

Figure 5.16
One order for
bottom-up testing.

Figure 5.17
One order for top-
down testing.

```
procedure Compute(BasePrice, Options: real; var LowPrice: real);
{Is given the list price for BasePrice and Options.
Sets LowPrice equal to the lowest price that dealers will accept.}
begin{Compute}
   writeln('BasePrice = ', BasePrice :8:2);
   writeln('Options price = ', Options :8:2);
   writeln('Enter LowPrice:');
   readln(LowPrice)
end;  {Compute}
```

Figure 5.18
Temporary version
of procedure
Compute.

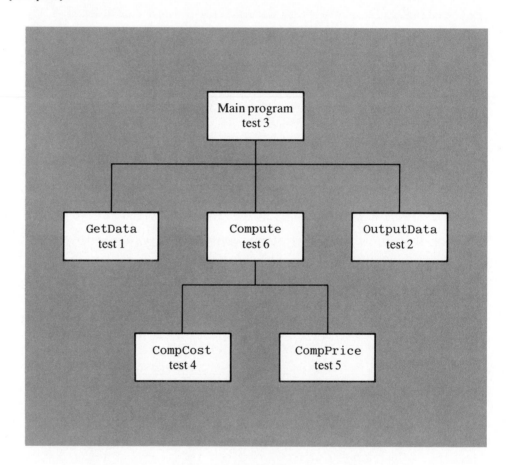

Figure 5.19
One order for a
mixed strategy.

is that it allows you to test your basic design strategy before you get too far along in the design process. It allows you to test whether a particular breakdown of tasks into subtasks will work as desired. If it will not, there is no need to solve the subtasks; instead, you need to back up and rethink the way you divided the task into subtasks. It also lets you test the exact specification of what each procedure should do before you go ahead and design the details of how it will do it.

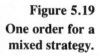

Sometimes it is best to test bottom-up, sometimes it is best to test top-down and sometimes it is best to mix the two strategies, testing some procedures bottom-up and some top-down. Figure 5.19 gives a mixed strategy that we could have used to design and test our automobile-pricing program. If the procedures are designed in the order given there, then the simplified version of Compute from Figure 5.18 can be used until the final version of the procedure is written.

mixed strategies

Preconditions and Postconditions

One way to document what a procedure does is by means of special-purpose assertion comments known as *preconditions* and *postconditions*. A precondition is an assertion that states what is expected to be true whenever the procedure is used. The procedure should not be used and cannot be expected to perform correctly unless the precondition holds. A postcondition states the relevant facts that will be true after the procedure is executed in a situation in which all the preconditions hold. For example, the following are possible pre- and postconditions for the procedure Compute in Figure 5.13:

```
procedure Compute(BasePrice, Options: real; var LowPrice: real);
{Precondition: BasePrice = list price of basic automobile,
         Options = list price of options;
Postcondition: LowPrice = dealer's lowest acceptable price.}
```

The case study in the next section provides an additional illustration of pre- and postconditions.

You should include a comment with each procedure heading. The comment need not follow this exact format of writing preconditions and postconditions, but it should describe any conditions that must hold before the procedure is called and should say what effects will be produced by executing the procedure. The comment should also explain everything else that a programmer using the procedure needs to know, such as what other procedures it calls, what defined constants it uses, and what variables it changes. One popular method for displaying this comment is to frame the comment in a box to make it stand out. For instance, the following would be a good longer comment to add to the procedure Compute discussed in the previous paragraph.

```
procedure Compute(BasePrice, Options: real; var LowPrice: real);
{ **********************************************************************
*Precondition: BasePrice = list price of basic automobile,           *
*         Options = list price of options;                           *
*Postcondition: LowPrice = dealer's lowest acceptable price.         *
*Calls the procedures CompCost and CompPrice.                        *
*Uses the defined constants LuxuryPrice, WholesaleFactor, Delivery, and Markup. *
********************************************************************** }
```

On large programming projects involving more than one programmer, this comment should also contain the author's name and the date written, as well as the date and nature of any modifications to the procedure. In this book we will use a somewhat shorter comment format in order to save space.

Case Study

Calculating Leap Years

Problem Definition

We want to write a program that takes a year as input and provides output that tells whether or not that year is a leap year.

Discussion

SUBALGORITHMS

For most years it is very easy to decide whether the year is a leap year. If the year is divisible by 4, then it is a leap year. So 2004 is a leap year, but 2001 is not. This rule is based on the fact that it takes 365 and one-quarter days for the earth to revolve around the sun. Every fourth year, we add up the four extra quarter-days and insert an extra full day in February to make the calendar consistent with the earth's movement. Unfortunately for calendar makers, the earth actually takes a bit less than 365.25 days to complete its trip around the sun, and so leap years should add a bit less than one full day. This is not practical, however, and so a full day is added and then after a few centuries a leap year day is skipped, which effectively subtracts a day and makes things balance out. The exact rule says that if a year is divisible by 100, then it is not a leap year unless it is also divisible by 400. Therefore, although 2200 is divisible by 4, it will not be a leap year. Our algorithm will include subalgorithms for two separate calculations, one for most years and the other for years divisible by 100.

RegularCalc: {*Precondition: the year is not divisible by 100.*}
if the year is divisible by 4, then it is a leap year; otherwise it is not.
CenturyCalc: {*Precondition: the year is divisible by 100.*}
if the year is divisible by 400, then it is a leap year; otherwise it is not.

We will implement both of these subalgorithms as procedures with a parameter Y for the year. Since the year is not changed, these parameters will be value parameters. The complete program is given in Figure 5.20.

Program

**Figure 5.20
Leap year
program.**

```
program LeapYear(input, output);
{Determines whether the input year is a leap year.}
var Year: integer;
```

```
procedure RegularCalc(Y: integer);
{Precondition: Y is not divisible by 100.
Postcondition: Displays a message saying whether or not Y is a leap year.}
begin{RegularCalc}
   if (Y mod 4) = 0 then
      writeln(Y, ' is a leap year!')
   else
      writeln(Y, ' is not a leap year.')
end; {RegularCalc}


procedure CenturyCalc(Y: integer);
{Precondition: Y is divisible by 100.
Postcondition: Displays a message saying whether or not Y is a leap year.}
begin{CenturyCalc}
   if (Y mod 400) = 0 then
      writeln(Y, ' is a leap year!')
   else
      writeln(Y, ' is not a leap year.')
end; {CenturyCalc}


begin{Program}
   writeln('Enter a year.');
   readln(Year);
   if (Year mod 100) = 0 then
      CenturyCalc(Year)
   else
      RegularCalc(Year)
end. {Program}
```

Sample Dialogue 1

```
Enter a year.
1900
    1900 is not a leap year.
```

Sample Dialogue 2

```
Enter a year.
2000
    2000 is a leap year!
```

Sample Dialogue 3

```
Enter a year.
2004
    2004 is a leap year!
```

Figure 5.20
(continued)

> Good things come in small packages.
>
> *Proverb*

Summary of Problem Solving and Programming Techniques

- Use local variables to hold any temporary information that a procedure may need for its calculations but that is not needed by any other part of the program.
- The interaction of a procedure with the rest of the program should be via parameters. Global variables normally should not appear in a procedure declaration, but they can be passed as actual parameters to the procedure.
- A formal value parameter is a local variable that is initialized to the value of the corresponding actual parameter when the procedure is called. It is possible to use it just like any other local variable.
- If a procedure does not change the value of an actual variable parameter when it should, suspect a missing *var* in the formal parameter list.
- Each procedure should be tested separately in a program that contains no procedures except the one being tested and possibly some other procedures that have already been fully tested and debugged.
- You can test a procedure before all the procedures it uses have been written. To do so, use simplified versions of the missing procedures.
- Preconditions and postconditions are a type of assertion that can be used effectively to document procedures.

Summary of Pascal Constructs

procedure declaration

Syntax:

```
procedure <procedure name> (<formal parameter list>) ;
    <local constant declarations>
    <local variable declarations>
    <local procedure declarations>
begin
    <statement 1>;
    <statement 2>;
            .
            .
            .
    <statement n>
end;
```

The statements may be any Pascal statements. See the following entries for details on declarations.

local variable

A local variable is one that is declared within a procedure declaration. A local variable exists only for the duration of the procedure call. The identifier used to name a local variable can also be used to name another variable (or constant or other object) outside of the procedure declaration.

local identifier

A local identifier is one that is declared within a procedure. The object it names exists only for the duration of the procedure call. A local identifier can also be used outside of the procedure declaration to name something else. Local variable names, local constant names, and local procedure names are examples of local identifiers.

global variable

A variable that is declared for the entire program; that is, one whose scope is the block of the entire program.

block

A block consists of a parameter list followed by a set of declarations, followed by the statements to which they apply, enclosed in a *begin/end* pair. (If there is no parameter list or no set of declarations, it is still a block.) For example, if you remove the procedure name and final semicolon from a procedure declaration, what is left is a block.

scope of an identifier

The block in which an identifier is declared is called its *scope*. If an identifier is declared in two blocks, one inside the other, then its meaning in the inner block is the one declared in the inner block.

Exercises

Self-Test Exercises

7. What will be the output of the program in Exercise 3 if the procedure heading is changed to the following? (The *var* is left out.)

```
procedure Funny(X, Y: integer);
```

8. What is the output of the following program?

```
program Exercise8(input, output);
var X, Y: char;

procedure Mixed(X: char; var Y: char);
begin{Mixed}
  X := 'A'; Y := 'B';
  writeln(X, Y)
end;  {Mixed}
```

```
begin{Program}
  X := 'X'; Y := 'Y';
  writeln(X, Y);
  Mixed(X, Y);
  writeln(X, Y)
end. {Program}
```

Interactive Exercises

9. Run the program in Figure 5.1 twice, once as shown and once omitting the local variable declaration

```
var Temp: integer;
```

10. Write a procedure to interchange the value of two variables of type char.

Programming Exercises

11. Write a procedure with two variable parameters N1 and N2 of type integer that sorts the two values so that after the procedure is called, N1 is less than or equal to N2. The procedure either leaves the values of the variables unchanged or else interchanges the two values. Your procedure will include a call to the procedure Exchange from Figure 5.1. Embed the procedure in a test program.

12. Write a program that computes the annual after-tax cost of a new house for the first year of ownership. The cost is computed as the annual mortgage cost minus the tax savings. The input should be the price of the house and the down payment. The annual mortgage cost can be estimated as 3% of the initial loan balance (credited toward paying off the loan principal) plus 10% of the initial loan balance in interest. The initial loan balance is the price minus the down payment. Assume a 35% marginal tax rate and assume that interest payments are tax deductible. The tax savings is therefore 35% of the interest payment. Use at least three procedures.

13. Write a program for the discount installment loan algorithm described in Exercise 10 of Chapter 1. Implement subtasks as procedures.

14. Write a program that reads in a length in feet and inches and then outputs the equivalent length in meters and centimeters. Use at least three procedures: one for input, one or more for calculating, and one for output. There are 0.3048 meters in a foot, 100 centimeters in a meter, and 12 inches in a foot.

15. Write a program like that of the previous exercise that converts measurements from meters and centimeters into feet and inches.

16. Write a program that reads in a weight in pounds and ounces and then outputs the equivalent weight in kilograms and grams. Use at least three procedures: one for input, one or more for calculating, and one for output. There are 2.2046 pounds in a kilogram, 1000 grams in a kilogram, and 16 ounces in a pound.

17. Write a program like that of the previous exercise that converts weights from kilograms and grams into pounds and ounces.

18. Combine, modify, and extend your programs from the previous four exercises into

a single program that can perform a choice of conversions from the system of weights and measures commonly used in the United States to the metric system and vice versa. It first asks the user whether he or she wants to convert from metric to U.S. measurements or from U.S. measurements to metric. It then asks the user whether he or she wishes to deal with weights or lengths. It then performs the desired calculation. For example, in one case the program asks for a weight in pounds and ounces and outputs the weight expressed in kilograms and grams. Use procedure calls as the substatements in *if-then-else* statements. Some of these procedures will in turn have *if-then-else* statements with other procedure calls for their substatements.

19. Enhance the program in Figure 4.13 so that it accepts as input an amount of dollars and cents as a value of type `real` and then outputs the numbers of the various bills and coins that equal that amount. Use bill denominations of $20, $5, and $1. Also include nickels as a possible coin in this version. Use the procedure `ComputeCoins` from Figure 4.14 and add a similar procedure to compute numbers of bills.

20. Write a program that is a major improvement on the program `CashRegister` in Figure 4.5. This improved version asks for the amount tendered by the customer as well as the price and number of the items. It responds with the price, the number of items, the total bill, the amount tendered, and the change due. It then goes on to tell the cashier exactly what combination of bills and coins will equal the amount of change. Use procedures for subtasks. The program `Change2` in Figure 4.13 can be used as a model for the last task. It would pay to do the previous exercise before doing this one.

21. Write a procedure with two value parameters of type `integer` called `Number` and `Width`. The procedure writes `Number` to the screen in the conventional way, with commas every three digits (beginning from the right). You may assume that the number is seven, eight, or nine digits long. `Width` is used as the field width specification for the total number of spaces *including commas*. Note that you will have to use other field width specifications derived from `Width` inside `write` statements within the procedure body.

22. Redo (or do for the first time) Exercise 20 from Chapter 3. Use three procedures: one for input, one for output, and one to perform the calculation.

23. Redo (or do for the first time) Exercise 26 from Chapter 3. Use three procedures: one for input, one for output, and one to perform the calculation.

24. Redo (or do for the first time) Exercise 27 from Chapter 3. Use three procedures: one for input, one for output, and one to perform the calculation.

25. Redo (or do for the first time) Exercise 29 from Chapter 3. Use three procedures: one for input, one for output, and one to perform the calculation.

26. Redo (or do for the first time) Exercise 30 from Chapter 3. Use three procedures: one for input, one for output, and one to perform the calculation.

27. Redo (or do for the first time) Exercise 32 from Chapter 3. Use three procedures: one for input, one for output, and one to perform the calculation.

28. Redo (or do for the first time) Exercise 33 from Chapter 3. Use three procedures: one for input, one for output, and one to perform the calculation.

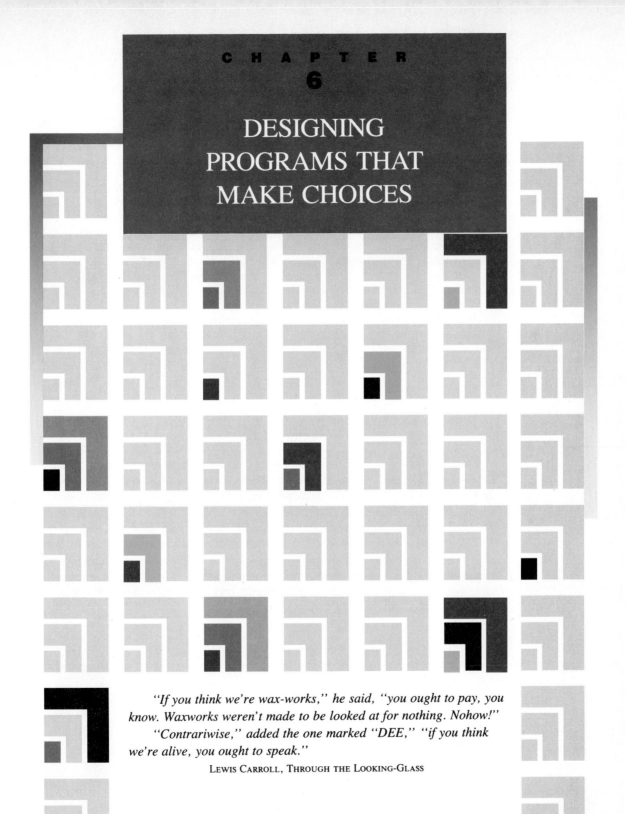

CHAPTER 6

DESIGNING PROGRAMS THAT MAKE CHOICES

"If you think we're wax-works," he said, "you ought to pay, you know. Waxworks weren't made to be looked at for nothing. Nohow!"

"Contrariwise," added the one marked "DEE," "if you think we're alive, you ought to speak."

LEWIS CARROLL, THROUGH THE LOOKING-GLASS

Chapter Contents

Any programming construct that chooses one out of a number of alternative actions is called a *branching mechanism*. The `if-then` and `if-then-else` statements are two examples of branching mechanisms. In this chapter we complete our description of these two types of statements by describing the full class of boolean expressions that can be used to control how they branch. We then go on to describe boolean variables and how they are used as a programming tool. Pascal has one additional branching statement, called the `case` statement, which we introduce in this chapter. We also explore problem solving and programming techniques for designing branches in particular and programs in general. We begin with a discussion of how Pascal branching statements may be nested within other branching statements to produce complex program instructions.

Nested Statements

An *if-then-else* or *if-then* statement contains a smaller statement within it. Thus far we have used compound statements as well as simpler statements such as assignment statements as the substatement. In fact, any statement at all can be used. In particular, we can use an *if-then* statement within a larger *if-then* statement.

This nesting of statements inside of statements points to one peculiarity in the definitions of compound and *if-then* statements. The definitions say that they can contain any sort of statement, including one of the same kind, as illustrated in Figure 6.1. This way of defining statements may seem circular. That is because it is. Circular definitions and even circular program instructions are common in computer science, although in computer science, circular definitions and instructions are usually referred to by the word *recursive* rather than the word *circular.*

recursive (circular) definitions

It is not always wrong or even undesirable to give a circular definition. The same thing happens in defining the rules of English grammar, but there we seldom notice that it is circular. We can make two sentences out of one sentence by joining them with the word "and" or with a semicolon. Hence, if we were to write out the grammatical rules for English sentences, the definition of a sentence would refer to sentences and so would be recursive (that is, circular). For instance, a complete definition of English sentences would begin with something like "A *sentence* is any string of words formed according to the following rules." One of the rules would read "A *sentence* can be formed by taking any *sentence* followed by the word 'and' followed by any other *sentence* (and, for written sentences, adjusting periods and capitalization appropriately)."

Recursive definitions require a bit of care in how they are formulated. In order for such a definition to be meaningful, it should contain some clauses that are not circular. In the case of Pascal statements, this general rule means that some statements may qualify for statementhood because some subpart (or subparts) is itself a statement, and that substatement may similarly contain a subpart that is a statement, and so forth. Eventually, however, this chain of substatement, sub-substatement, and so forth must bottom out with a statement that does not contain any substatements. This bottoming out is what saves these circular or recursive definitions from going on endlessly and meaninglessly when you try to use them. For example, an *if-then* statement can contain another *if-then* statement, and that *if-then* statement can contain yet another *if-then* statement, and so on for any number of times, but eventually this must end, and the innermost *if-then* statement must contain something simple like an assignment statement or a *writeln* statement.

how to formulate recursive definitions

```
if X > 0 then

    if Y > 5 then

        writeln('X > 0 and Y > 5')
```

Figure 6.1
Nesting an *if-then* statement within an *if-then* statement.

*recursive
syntax
diagrams*

The recursive nature of the definition of Pascal statements can be seen in their syntax diagrams. If you look at the syntax diagrams in Appendix 4, you will see that a statement can be formed in a number of ways. Some of these ways, such as <if statement>, refer to the diagram for <statement>. On the other hand, the diagrams for other clauses, such as <assignment statement> and <write or writeln call>, do not refer to the diagram labeled <statement> either directly or indirectly. When using syntax diagrams to verify the correctness of a statement, a successful check must ultimately involve one of these clauses that do not refer to the diagram labeled <statement>.

Nesting If-Then and If-Then-Else Statements

When nesting *if-then* and *if-then-else* statements, the meaning of the nested statement may appear to be ambiguous. To illustrate the problem, consider the following scenario. The variable P contains an integer value representing some number of pennies. We want to design a statement that will output nothing if the value of P is zero and will output the value of P, correctly annotated with the word 'penny' or 'pennies', if the value of P is one or more than one. The following is one way to accomplish this goal:

```
if P > 0 then
    if P = 1 then
        writeln('one penny')
    else
        writeln(P, ' pennies')
```

By properly indenting the statements, we have masked the problem. To see the problem, write it as follows; the spacing is irrelevant to the compiler, and this rewriting should not affect the meaning.

```
if P > 0 then if P = 1
            then writeln('one penny')
            else writeln(P, 'pennies')
```

*rules for
pairing
else
with then*

Written like this, it is not apparent which of the two *then*'s is supposed to be paired with the single *else*.

Pascal clarifies such ambiguities by specifying that an *else* is always paired with the closest preceding, unmatched *then*. So the meaning of our nested statement is what we intended.

Complex Boolean Expressions

A Pascal expression that is either true or false is called a *boolean expression*. For example, we have been using simple boolean expressions such as X > 0 within *if-then-else* statements. You can form more complicated boolean expressions out of these simple boolean expressions by combining them with the operators *and, or,* and *not*. These operators work very much as they do in English, combining simpler boolean expressions to yield a new, complex boolean expression.

A larger boolean expression can be formed from two smaller boolean expressions by joining them with an *and*. The larger expression evaluates to `true` if both subexpressions evaluate to `true`; otherwise, it evaluates to `false`. For example,

and

> (X < Y) *and* (Y < Z)

evaluates to `true` if both the value of X is less than the value of Y and the value of Y is less than the value of Z; otherwise, its value is `false`. In mathematics, pairs of inequalities such as the previous one are usually expressed as follows:

> $x < y < z$

Expressions with such chains of interlocking comparisons are not allowed in Pascal. Instead, you must break them into parts and connect these parts with *and*'s.

These complex boolean expressions are used in the same way as the simple boolean expressions we introduced in Chapter 3. For example, the program in Figure 6.2 uses complex boolean expressions to determine if the user's zodiac sign is Scorpio.

The syntax for expressions involving *or* is similar to that described for *and*. For example

> (X < Y) *or* (Y < Z)

This expression is `true` provided the value of X is less than the value of Y or the value of Y is less than the value of Z *or both*. This is the so-called "inclusive" meaning of "or." This inclusive meaning is always used in mathematics, but it is not always used in ordinary conversation. Ordinary conversational English has trouble coping with situations where two true statements are joined by the word "or." Pascal and mathematical disciplines in general have no such problem. In Pascal, if two things are connected by an *or,* then the resulting expression is `true` provided that one or both subexpressions are `true`; otherwise, its value is `false`.

or

The boolean operator *not* reverses truth values, much as the word "not" does in English. However, the Pascal syntax for *not* is quite different from English. In Pascal the *not* is always placed in front of the expression being negated. As examples, consider the following boolean expressions:

not

> *not*('A' = 'Z')
> *not*(2 < 3)

Since *not* changes `true` to `false` and `false` to `true`, the first of these two boolean expressions evaluates to `true` and the second to `false`.

As the following two examples illustrate, we can repeat this method of combining boolean expressions with *and, or,* and *not* to obtain expressions that are even more complex.

nested expressions

> ((Month = 10) *and* (Day >= 24)) *or* ((Month = 11) *and* (Day <= 22))
> (Time < 60) *and not*((Ans = 'N') *or* (Ans = 'n'))

The first of these sample expressions could be used in a program similar to that in Figure 6.2. It would be true if the values of Month and Day indicate a Scorpio of any kind.

Program

```
program FindScorpios(input, output);
{Determines if user is a Scorpio: birthday between October 24th and November 22nd, inclusive.}
var Month, Day: integer;
begin{Program}
  writeln('Enter your month and day');
  writeln('of birth, as two numbers.');
  readln(Month, Day);

  if (Month = 10) and (Day >= 24) then
      writeln('You''re an October Scorpio.')
  else
      writeln('You''re not an October Scorpio.');

  if (Month = 11) and (Day <= 22) then
      writeln('You''re a November Scorpio.')
  else
      writeln('You''re not a November Scorpio.');

  writeln('I knew it!')
end.  {Program}
```

Sample Dialogue 1

```
Enter your month and day
of birth, as two numbers.
10  25
You're an October Scorpio.
You're not a November Scorpio.
I knew it!
```

Sample Dialogue 2

```
Enter your month and day
of birth, as two numbers.
10  21
You're not an October Scorpio.
You're not a November Scorpio.
I knew it!
```

Figure 6.2
Boolean
expressions using
and.

parentheses

All the examples we have constructed thus far have been fully parenthesized to show exactly what two expressions each *and* or *or* applies to. This is not always required. The default precedence, if you omit parentheses, is as follows: *not* first, *and* second, and *or* third. However, it is good practice to include most parentheses in order to make the expression easier to understand. One place where parentheses can safely be omitted is a simple string of *and*'s or *or*'s, but not a mixture of the two. The following expression is acceptable both to the Pascal compiler and in terms of readability:

$$(X < 100) \ \textit{and} \ (Ans <> \text{'N'}) \ \textit{and} \ (Ans <> \text{'n'})$$

When they are included in more complicated expressions, the parentheses around simple boolean expressions, such as $(X < 100)$, are never optional. If they are omitted, the compiler will either give an error statement or produce unwanted results.

Many high level programming languages have boolean expressions that are formed and used in much the same way as they are in Pascal. Minor details such as the placement of parentheses will vary from language to language, but the general ideas are the same for most programming languages.

George Boole
(Optional)

The word "boolean" is derived from the name of George Boole, a nineteenth-century English mathematician who developed the foundations for a formal calculus of such expressions. Boole was a self-educated scholar with limited formal training. He began his teaching career at the age of 16 as an elementary-school teacher and eventually progressed to a professorship at Queen's College in Cork. He is considered by many to be the father of symbolic logic, and no less a commentator than Bertrand Russell has stated that "Pure mathematics was discovered by Boole, in a work which he called *The Laws of Thought*."

Evaluating Boolean Expressions

Boolean expressions such as

$$(X > 0) \ \textit{and} \ (Y < Z)$$

are evaluated and have a value of either `true` or `false`. The computer obtains values for these boolean expressions in a way analogous to the way in which we (and the computer) normally evaluate arithmetic expressions.

By way of review, consider the following arithmetic expression:

$$(1 + 2) \ * \ (2 + 3)$$

To evaluate this expression, we evaluate the two sums to obtain the numbers 3 and 5. We then multiply the 3 and 5 to obtain 15 as the value of the entire expression. In doing the evaluation, we do not multiply the *expressions* $(1 + 2)$ and $(2 + 3)$. Instead, we multiply the *values* of the expressions. We use 3. We do not use $(1 + 2)$.

The computer evaluates boolean expressions in a similar manner. Subexpressions are evaluated to obtain values each of which is either `true` or `false`. These values of `true` or `false` are then combined according to the rules in the table shown in Figure 6.3. For example, consider the boolean expression

$$\textit{not}(\ (X > 0) \ \textit{or} \ (X < 7) \ )$$

and suppose that the value of X is 5. In this case, $(X > 0)$ and $(X < 7)$ both evaluate to `true`, and so the expression is equivalent to

$$\textit{not} \ (\textit{true} \ \textit{or} \ \textit{true})$$

Expression	Value	Expression	Value
true *and* true	true	true *or* true	true
true *and* false	false	true *or* false	true
false *and* true	false	false *or* true	true
false *and* false	false	false *or* false	false
not (true)	false	*not* (false)	true

Figure 6.3
Truth tables.

Consulting the table for *or,* the computer sees that the expression inside the parentheses evaluates to true and that the entire expression is therefore equivalent to *not*(true). Again consulting the tables, it sees that *not*(true) evaluates to false, and so it concludes that false is the value of the original boolean expression.

Pitfall

Undefined Boolean Expressions

Boolean expressions are evaluated by first evaluating the subexpressions and then combining those values, as we described in the previous section. This method of evaluation gives rise to one subtle problem. In many implementations of Pascal, if two subexpressions are connected by *and* or by *or,* the computer first evaluates *both* of these subexpressions and *then* uses these two values to determine the value of the full expression. This means that the two subexpressions must be well defined and capable of being evaluated. As an example, consider the following reasonable-looking statement:

```
if (Kids <> 0) and (Pieces div Kids >= 2) then
    writeln('Each child may have two pieces!')
```

undefined
subexpressions

If the value of Kids is not zero, this statement performs fine. However, suppose the value of Kids is zero. Then we might expect the boolean expression to evaluate to false. After all, the first subexpression evaluates to false, and using an *and* to combine false with any other value will yield a value of false. Unfortunately, the computer will try to evaluate *both* subexpressions *before* it applies the *and*. This will produce an error, since *div* is being asked to divide by zero, an error that can cause the program to terminate abnormally.

One way to avoid this problem is to use the following:

```
if Kids <> 0 then
    if Pieces div Kids >= 2 then
        writeln('Each child may have two pieces!')
```

In this version, the second boolean expression is not evaluated when the value of Kids is zero.

The compilers for some other programming languages and even some Pascal compilers are smart enough to cope successfully with either of the above two statements. However, the first one should not be used, since it cannot be guaranteed to work.

Self-Test Exercises

1. What output will be produced by the following code when embedded in a complete program?

```
writeln('Start');
if 2 <= 3 then
    if 0 <> 1 then
        writeln('First writeln')
    else
        writeln('Second writeln');
writeln('Next');
if 2 > 3 then
    if 0 = 1 then
        writeln('Third writeln')
    else
        writeln('Fourth writeln');
writeln('Enough')
```

2. Determine the value, `true` or `false`, of each of the following boolean expressions:

```
(0 = 1) and (2 < 3)              (0 = 1) or (2 < 3)
not( 0 = 1)                                'Y' = 'y'
('Y' = 'y') and (maxint = 65535)
not( (4.5 < 12.9) and (6 * 2 <= 13))
not((31 mod 15) <> 1)
```

3. Translate the following English and mathematical expressions into Pascal boolean expressions: two plus two equals four; X plus seven is more than one hundred or else it is less than fifty; the value of the variable Z (of type `char`) is not one of the first three (uppercase) letters of the alphabet; X is not evenly divisible by 3; either X is not evenly divisible by 3 or Y is evenly divisible by 5;

$$x \leqslant y+2 \leqslant z$$

He who would distinguish the true from
the false must have an adequate idea of
what is true and false.

Benedict Spinoza, Ethics

Programming with Boolean Variables

the type boolean

The values `true` and `false` form a complete list of values for the data type called `boolean`. As we have seen, a boolean expression, like an arithmetic expression, yields a value. In the case of an arithmetic expression the value yielded is of type either `integer` or `real`. In the case of a boolean expression, the value is of type `boolean`. This value of type `boolean` can be stored in a variable, just as the value of an arithmetic expression can be stored in a variable, except that a variable that contains a value of `true` or `false` must be of type `boolean`. Hence, if N is a variable of type `integer` and X is a variable of type `boolean`, the following is perfectly meaningful in Pascal and sets the value of X equal to `false`:

```
N := 2;
X := (N > 10) or (N < 0)
```

setting boolean variables

At first, such boolean assignment statements look strange, but you quickly adjust to them. The rules are the same as they are for variables of other types: The expression on the right-hand side of the assignment operator is evaluated (since it is a boolean expression, its value will be either `true` or `false`); after that, the value of the boolean variable is set equal to this value of `true` or `false`. In the preceding example, the value of N is not greater than 10 nor is it less than 0. The boolean expression therefore evaluates to `false`, and the value of X is changed to `false`.

Variables of type `boolean` are declared in the same place and in the same way as other types of variables. A hypothetical program might start out as follows:

```
program Sample(input, output);
var Temperature: real;
    Ans: char;
    Raining, X: boolean;
```

The program might then contain the following statement:

```
Raining := (Ans = 'y') or (Ans = 'Y')
```

If the value of Ans is either `'Y'` or `'y'`, then this statement sets the value of `Raining` equal to `true`; otherwise, it sets it equal to `false`. Hence, this assignment statement is equivalent to the following longer and less efficient statement:

```
if (Ans = 'y') or (Ans = 'Y') then
    Raining := true
else
    Raining := false
```

The longer statement, which was given only to help explain the assignment statement, is poor programming style.

why use boolean variables?

Boolean variables can be used to remember a condition that may change later or that will not be easy to check later on. An equally important use of boolean variables is to make the meaning of a program more apparent. In the program fragment below, the boolean variable `Raining` frees the programmer from having to remember the exact wording of the question 'Is it raining?' The question might have been 'Has it stopped raining?' and the programmer who forgets the exact wording of the question can easily misinterpret the meaning of Ans, even if the value of Ans does not change.

```
writeln('Is it raining?');
readln(Ans);
Raining := (Ans = 'y') or (Ans = 'Y');
if Raining then
    writeln('Too bad.')
else
    writeln('Would you like to go for a walk?')
```

The use of boolean variables is illustrated in the program in Figure 6.4.

Many other common programming languages do not have boolean variables. In these languages, programmers frequently use some trick to simulate boolean variables, such as pretending that the integer value one means true and that zero means false.

Pitfall

Omitting Parentheses in Boolean Expressions

A boolean expression such as the following must include parentheses around simple comparisons like X > Y.

   (X > Y) and (Z > W)

The reason for this has to do with the precedence rules for operations in the Pascal language. Unless parentheses indicate otherwise, the operations *and* and *or* are performed before comparisons such as < and <> are evaluated. Hence, the meaning of

   X > Y *and* Z > W

is the puzzling-looking expression

   X > (Y *and* Z) > W

which does not make sense. Although this boolean expression is incorrectly formed, the subexpression (Y *and* Z) is perfectly legal, provided both Y and Z were declared to be variables of type boolean. If you omit parentheses, the compiler will act as though (Y *and* Z) were a subexpression and will try to evaluate this subexpression. Moreover, it will do this even if the type of the variables is something other than boolean. Depending on details such as the type of the variables, a wide variety of things can then go wrong, but some error will surely be detected.

Program

```
program Talk(input, output);
var Ans: char;
    Raining: boolean;
begin{Program}
  writeln('Good day. My name is Ronald Gollum.');
  writeln('I''m stuck in this box until quitting time.');
  writeln('Please chat with me about the outside.');

  writeln('Is it raining out now?');
  readln(Ans);
  Raining := (Ans = 'Y') or (Ans = 'y');
  if not Raining then
    writeln('Too bad. We need rain.');

  writeln('Do you think it will rain tomorrow?');
  readln(Ans);
  if (Ans = 'Y') or (Ans = 'y') then
    writeln('I''ll worry about that tomorrow.');

  writeln('It''s finally quitting time! Good bye.');
  if Raining then
    writeln('You brightened up this rainy day.')
  else
    writeln('I want to work on my tan.')
end. {Program}
```

Sample Dialogue 1

```
Good day. My name is Ronald Gollum.
I'm stuck in this box until quitting time.
Please chat with me about the outside.
Is it raining out now?
no
Too bad. We need rain.
Do you think it will rain tomorrow?
yes
I'll worry about that tomorrow.
It's finally quitting time! Good bye.
I want to work on my tan.
```

Sample Dialogue 2

```
Good day. My name is Ronald Gollum.
I'm stuck in this box until quitting time.
Please chat with me about the outside.
Is it raining out now?
yes
```

Figure 6.4

Program using a boolean variable.

```
Do you think it will rain tomorrow?
no
It's finally quitting time! Good bye.
You brightened up this rainy day.
```

Figure 6.4
(continued)

Boolean Input and Output

A value of type boolean cannot be read in directly. Instead, some other type of input, such as a character, must be read in and used to set the boolean variable. The following program fragment sets the value of the variable BV of type boolean using the variable Ans of type char:

```
writeln('Type t for True or f for False');
readln(Ans);
BV := (Ans = 't') or (Ans = 'T')
```

In many versions of Pascal, boolean values can be written as output; in others they cannot. In any version of Pascal, the following will serve to output the value of the boolean variable BV:

```
if BV then
    write('true')
else
    write('false')
```

Case Study

Designing Output

Problem Definition

In Chapter 4 we created a program to determine the number of coins needed to give an amount of change from 1 to 99 cents. That program produced output such as the following:

```
       27 cents can be given as:
1 quarters
0 dimes and
2 pennies
```

This sort of output is frequently acceptable, but it would be nicer to have output that is grammatically correct and that does not contain pointless information. Ideally, the output should look like the following:

```
27 cents can be given as:
one quarter and 2 pennies
```

In this section we will design a procedure to produce this sort of output. We will design it for output that includes the possibility of nickels so that it would work for the enhanced version of the program that uses the redesigned procedures given in Figure 4.14. As in the original programming task, we will assume that the total amount of change is between 1 and 99 cents. The procedure will receive the amount and the coin counts as value parameters.

Discussion

When you stop to think of all the grammatical details you take care of automatically when writing phrases such as the desired sample output, you quickly realize that designing output can be a complicated task. The program must somehow ignore coin amounts of zero, it needs to decide between singular and plural forms, it needs to place the 'and' correctly, and it needs to insert commas if three or more types of coins are used, as in

```
32 cents can be given as:
one quarter, one nickel and 2 pennies
```

(There are two accepted ways of inserting commas in such expressions. To simplify the problem, we are using the rule that does not place a comma before the 'and'.)

subtasks   The value parameters for the total amount and for the counts of quarters, dimes, nickels, and pennies will be A, Q, D, N, and P. We will use a very straightforward decomposition of this task into subtasks:

begin
1. Write the heading.
2. If the number of quarters is not zero, then write it out.
3. If the number of dimes is not zero, then write it out preceded by a comma or 'and' if appropriate.
4. If the number of nickels is not zero, then write it out preceded by a comma or 'and', if appropriate.
5. If the number of pennies is not zero, then write it out preceded by a comma or 'and', if appropriate.
end

flags   In order to determine whether it should output a comma or 'and', the program needs some way to test whether any coins were output previously. We will use a boolean variable PreviousCoins. This variable will be initialized to false and will have its value changed to true as soon as a nonzero number of coins is output. The value of PreviousCoins is part of the data that is passed from one subtask to another. A variable such as PreviousCoins that changes its value to indicate that some event has taken place is often called a *flag*. In this sample, when the flag "goes up," it is time to insert a comma or 'and'. The pseudocode for outputting dimes is given below.

{*PreviousCoins is true if some number of quarters has been output.*}
if D > 0 *then*
   begin; {*Dimes > 0*}
     if PreviousCoins *then*
       if there are more coins to follow *then*
          output a comma and appropriate spaces
       else {*Dimes will be the last type of coin.*}
          output the word 'and' and appropriate spaces;
     Write out the number of dimes;
     PreviousCoins : = true
   end {*Dimes > 0*}

The test for more coins to follow can be accomplished with the boolean expression

(N > 0) *or* (P > 0)

The complete procedure, embedded in a test program, is displayed in Figure 6.5. Since it is not used outside of the procedure, we made the boolean variable Previous-Coins a local variable.

Boolean Constants and Debugging Switches

The two values of type boolean can be named using the two predefined constants true and false. These constants can be used anywhere that a boolean expression is allowed. So the following, although pointless, is allowed. It always causes the second writeln to be executed.

true
false

```
if false then
     writeln('I know truth.')
else
     writeln('I know falsehood.')
```

Identifiers that have been given a boolean value in a constant declaration can be used in the same way, and their use is not always pointless. The following declaration makes Debugging a synonym for true.

```
const Debugging = true;
```

A boolean constant such as Debugging can be used as a switch to go between two forms of a program. To switch from one form of the program to the other, the named boolean constant in the constant declaration is changed from true to false or vice versa. This is particularly useful when debugging large programs.

Large programs often have trace statements and other debugging diagnostics written into the program. Often one wants to retain the debugging features even after the program is released for use, either because it will be changed or because you expect the users to discover new bugs. If the program is to be used, or even observed, without these debugging messages being sent to the screen, some method must be found for turning them off. One method is a boolean switch.

If you include a constant declaration such as the sample one displayed for Debugging, then you can use it as a switch to turn on debugging statements like the following, which traces two variables:

```
if Debugging then
     writeln('A = ', A, 'ALeft = ', ALeft)
```

To turn off the debugging features, simply reset the boolean constant by changing the constant declaration to

```
const Debugging = false;
```

Program

```
program Test(input, output);
var TotalAmount, Quarters, Dimes, Nickels, Pennies: integer;

procedure OutputCoins(A, Q, D, N, P: integer);
{Outputs a collection of coins that total to A cents.
Precondition: 0 < A <= 99 and the coins total to A,
that is, 25*Q + 10*D + 5*N + P = A.}
const Comma = ',  ';{Includes  space.}
var PreviousCoins: boolean;
       {Set to true after the first output of a number of coins.}
begin{OutputCoins}
  writeln(A:2, ' cents can be given as:');
  PreviousCoins := false;

  if Q > 0 then
     begin{Quarters > 0}
       if Q = 1 then
         write('one quarter')
       else
         write(Q:1,' quarters');
       PreviousCoins := true
     end;  {Quarters > 0}

  if D > 0 then
     begin{Dimes > 0}
       if PreviousCoins then
         if  (N > 0) or (P > 0) then
               write(Comma)
         else  {Dimes will be the last type of coin.}
               write(' and ');
       if D = 1 then
         write('one dime')
       else
         write(D:1,' dimes');
       PreviousCoins := true
     end; {Dimes > 0}
```

Figure 6.5
Enhanced procedure to output coins.

```
if N > 0 then
   begin{Nickels > 0}
      if PreviousCoins then
         if P > 0 then
            write(Comma)
      else {Nickels will be the last type of coin.}
            write(' and ');
      if N = 1 then
            write('one nickel')
      else
            write(N:1,' nickels');
      PreviousCoins := true
   end;  {Nickels > 0}

  if P > 0 then
     begin{Pennies > 0}
        if PreviousCoins then
           write(' and ');
        if P = 1 then
           write('one penny')
        else
           write(Pennies:1, ' pennies')
     end; {Pennies > 0}
  writeln
end; {OutputCoins}

begin{TestProgram}
  writeln('Enter: Quarters, Dimes, Nickels, Pennies:');
  readln(Quarters, Dimes, Nickels, Pennies);
  TotalAmount := 25 * Quarters
               + 10 * Dimes
               + 5 * Nickels
               + Pennies;
  OutputCoins(TotalAmount, Quarters, Dimes, Nickels, Pennies)
end.  {TestProgram}
```

Sample Dialogue

```
Enter: Quarters, Dimes, Nickels, Pennies:
1 0 1 2
32 cents can be given as:
one quarter, one nickel and 2 pennies
```

Figure 6.5
(continued)

Program

```
program CaseSample(input, output);
var Grade: char;
begin{Program}
   writeln('What grade did you receive?');
   readln(Grade);

   case Grade of
      'A', 'B': writeln('Very good!');
      'C': writeln('Passing.');
      'D', 'F': writeln('Too bad.')
   end; {case}
   writeln('I have to go study. Goodbye.')
end. {Program}
```

Sample Dialogue 1

```
What grade did you receive?
A
Very good!
I have to go study. Goodbye.
```

Sample Dialogue 2

```
What grade did you receive?
F
Too bad.
I have to go study. Goodbye.
```

Figure 6.6

Program with a
***case* statement.**

The Case Statement

An *if-then-else* statement chooses one of two alternative actions. A *case statement* is a different kind of Pascal statement that can choose from a list of any number of actions. A *case* statement is a complex statement made up of any number of simpler statements that serve as the alternative actions. When the *case* statement is executed, one (and only one) of the simpler statements is selected and executed. An example is likely to be more enlightening than an abstract discussion.

example   Consider the program shown above in Figure 6.6. The five lines starting with the identifier *case* and ending with *end* contain a *case* statement (followed by a semicolon and a comment). The *case* statement contains three substatements: one labeled by the pair 'A', 'B'; one labeled by the constant 'C'; and one labeled by the pair 'D', 'F'. When the *case* statement is executed, exactly one of these three substatements will be executed; which one it is depends on the value of the variable Grade. When the *case* statement is executed, the value of Grade is checked and then the substatement labeled with that value is executed. Hence, if the value of Grade is either 'A' or 'B', the writeln following that pair will be executed. If

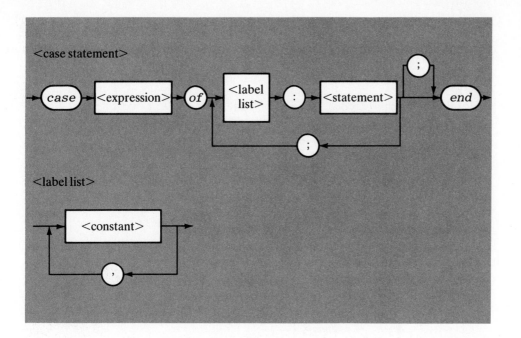

Figure 6.7
Syntax of a *case*
statement.

instead the value of `Grade` is `'C'`, the `writeln` following the `'C'` will be executed. If the value of `Grade` is either `'D'` or `'F'`, the third `writeln` is executed.

The syntax of a *case* statement is given in Figure 6.7. A *case* statement may have any number of alternatives from which to choose. Each alternative consists of exactly one statement. To obtain the effect of executing several statements for one alternative, you can use a compound statement, as shown in the program in Figure 6.8. Each alternative statement must be prefaced by a list of one or more constants, separated by commas and followed by a colon. The list of constants for a given statement is called a *label list*. The same constant may not appear in two label lists, since that would produce an ambiguous instruction. The alternative statements are separated by semicolons. You can add a semicolon after the final statement or not; the *case* statement meaning is the same either way. An *end* is used to terminate the *case* statement. There is no matching *begin* for this final *end*. Instead, it is matched to the reserved word *case*.

The expression that follows the word *case* need not be a variable. You can use any expression of type `integer` or `char` to control a *case* statement. (You can also use an expression of type `boolean`, but that is pointless, since an *if-then-else* statement could be used instead.) You can also use some other types, which are introduced later in this book. However, you cannot use an expression of type `real` to control a *case* statement. (This makes sense, since testing two `real` values for equality yields an unpredictable result.) When the *case* statement is executed, the expression is evaluated, and then the alternative labeled with that value is executed. Hence, the constants that label the alternative substatements must match this expression in type.

syntax

label list

type of controlling expression

Program

```
program GiveDate(input, output);
{Tells registration dates.}
var Class: integer;
begin{Program}
  writeln('Enter your class code');
  writeln('and I will tell you when you can register.');
  writeln('1 for freshman, 2 for sophomore,');
  writeln('3 for junior, 4 for senior.');
  writeln('Enter number (1, 2, 3, or 4):');
  readln(Class);

  if (Class < 1) or (Class > 4) then
    writeln('Error: illegal class code!')
  else
    case Class of
         1: begin{Freshman}
               writeln('Freshman:');
               writeln('Enrollment for next year May 6-12')
            end; {Freshman}
       2,3: begin{Sophomores and Juniors}
               writeln('Sophomores and Juniors:');
               writeln('Enrollment for next year May 1-5')
            end; {Sophomores and Juniors}
         4:writeln('Congratulations!')
    end {case}
end. {Program}
```

Sample Dialogue 1

```
Enter your class code
and I will tell you when you can register.
1 for freshman, 2 for sophomore,
3 for junior, 4 for senior.
Enter number (1, 2, 3, or 4):
0
Error: illegal class code!
```

Sample Dialogue 2

```
Enter your class code
and I will tell you when you can register.
1 for freshman, 2 for sophomore,
3 for junior, 4 for senior.
Enter number (1, 2, 3, or 4):
1
Freshman:
Enrollment for next year May 6-12
```

Figure 6.8
**Use of the *case*
statement.**

Pitfall

Case Expression Value Not on Any Label List

Normally you must ensure that the expression in a *case* statement evaluates to something that labels one of the alternatives. If it does not, then that is considered an error, and almost anything might happen.

Many, but not all, versions of Pascal have been extended to allow one additional clause that is executed when the value of the controlling expression is on none of the label lists. The syntax varies from version to version. Consult an expert or a manual to determine the details for your system.

Another way to defend against such an error in the value of the controlling expression is to embed the *case* statement in an *if-then* or *if-then-else* statement that first checks to see whether the value is on some label list and only executes the *case* statement if it is. This technique is illustrated in Figure 6.8.

The Empty Statement

Pascal has a statement that does absolutely nothing and is written by writing down absolutely nothing. It is called the *empty statement,* and our description makes it sound like a pure joke. Nonetheless, it does have a number of serious purposes. For one thing, it simplifies the syntax diagram for the compound statement.

Since a semicolon is used to separate statements, the last statement in a compound statement or in the body of a procedure or program should not have a semicolon after it. If you look at the syntax diagram for a compound statement in Figure 6.9, you will see that the diagram requires a statement, not a semicolon, just before the final *end*. However, we said earlier that including a final semicolon causes no harm. It seems that

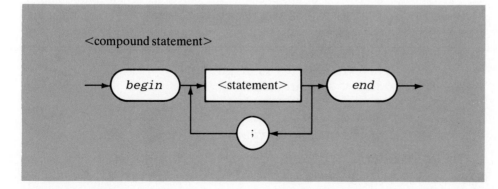

<compound statement>

begin   <statement>   end

;

Figure 6.9
Syntax of the compound statement.

the syntax diagram needs to be complicated by adding another case for the possibility of that extra semicolon, but this complication is not needed. The empty statement is what allows for the extra semicolon. For example, the following compound statement satisfies the syntax diagram for a compound statement because a statement, namely the empty statement, is between the last semicolon and the *end:*

```
begin
   writeln('statement 1');                    ── The empty statement
   writeln('statement 2');                        is here.
end
```

The empty statement is a formal trick that has the effect of sometimes allowing you to add semicolons. However, this trick only works in positions that allow you to insert a statement, such as just before the *end* in a compound statement. It does not allow you to insert semicolons in other places, such as before an *else*.

The empty statement can also be used in a *case* statement to specify that nothing be done in some alternative. In general, it can be used anywhere that you need a statement that causes no action and no changes.

Programming Multiple Alternatives

The *case* statement chooses one of several statements to execute, but it is rather restricted in its use. The choice of which statement to execute must be made on the basis of a single value. Nested *if-then-else* statements are a more versatile way of implementing multiple alternative branches.

By way of example, suppose you are designing a game-playing program in which the user must guess the value of some number. The number can be named Number and the guess can be called Guess. If you wish to give a hint after each guess, you might design the following subalgorithm:

```
writeln('Too high. '), when Guess > Number
writeln('Too low. '), when Guess < Number
writeln('Correct! '), when Guess = Number
```

Any time a branching action is described as a list of mutually exclusive conditions and corresponding actions, as in this example, the branching action can be implemented in Pascal by using a nested *if-then-else* statement. For example, the above pseudocode translates to

```
if Guess > Number then
             writeln('Too high. ')
else if Guess < Number then
             writeln('Too low. ')
else if Guess = Number then
             writeln('Correct! ')
```

The indenting pattern used here is slightly different from what we have advocated previously. If we had followed our indenting rules, we would have produced something like the following:

```
if Guess > Number then
  writeln('Too high.')
else
  if Guess < Number then
      writeln('Too low.')
  else
      writeln('Correct!')
```

The first version, which violates our guidelines for indenting, is the one you should use. This is one of those rare cases in which our general guidelines for indenting nested statements should not be followed. The reason is that by lining up all the *else*'s, we also line up all the condition/action pairs and so make the layout of the program reflect our reasoning.

Since the conditions are mutually exclusive, the last *if* is superfluous and can be omitted, but it is usually best to include it in a comment as follows:

```
if Guess > Number then
                writeln('Too high.')
else if Guess < Number then
                writeln('Too low.')
else {Guess = Number}
                writeln('Correct!')
```

Case Study

State Income Tax

Problem Definition

We will design a procedure to compute state income tax from net income (computed to the nearest dollar) according to the following formula:

1. No tax is paid on the first $15,000 of net income.
2. A tax of 5% is assessed on each dollar of net income from $15,001 to $35,000.
3. A tax of 10% is assessed on each dollar of net income over $35,000.

Discussion

If we let FirstChunk name the amount of income that is taxed at the 5% rate and let SecondChunk name the amount of income taxed at the 10% rate, then our algorithm to compute FirstChunk follows directly from the problem specification:

```
FirstChunk := 0, when NetIncome <= 15000
FirstChunk := NetIncome − 15000,
    when 15000 < NetIncome ≤ 35000
FirstChunk := 20000,
    when NetIncome > 35000;
```

ALGORITHM

```
procedure ComputeTax(NetIncome: integer; var Tax: real);
{Computes tax on NetIncome by rates: first $15000 no tax;
dollars from $15001 to $35000 at 5%; dollars over $35000 at 10%.}
var FirstChunk: integer; {Income to be taxed at 5%.}
    SecondChunk: integer; {Income to be taxed at 10%.}
begin{ComputeTax}
   if NetIncome <= 15000 then
     FirstChunk := 0
   else if (NetIncome > 15000) and (NetIncome <= 35000) then
     FirstChunk := NetIncome - 15000
   else {NetIncome > 35000}
     FirstChunk := 20000;

   if NetIncome <= 35000 then
     SecondChunk := 0
   else
     SecondChunk := NetIncome - 35000;

   Tax := (0.05 * FirstChunk) + (0.10 * SecondChunk)
end; {ComputeTax}
```

**Figure 6.10
Procedure
including
multiple
alternative
actions.**

A similar piece of pseudocode can be written for computing SecondChunk. The total tax is then 5% of the first figure plus 10% of the second figure. Once the pseudocode has been written, it is routine to translate it into a Pascal procedure like the one in Figure 6.10.

Simple Use of Sets
(Optional)

We often want a program to check whether a value is on some list. For example, the program might ask the user to type in the letter 'Y' or 'N' for "yes" or "no" and then read the answer into the variable Ans. The user might get confused and type in something else, such as *OK*. In this situation you want the program to make sure the value of Ans is either 'Y' or 'N' before going on.

in

There is a type of boolean expression that can test to see if the value of an expression is on a specified list of values. As an example, consider the following boolean expression:

    Ans *in* ['Y', 'N']

This boolean expression means just what you naturally expect it to mean. It evaluates to true if the value of Ans is equal to 'Y' or 'N'. In other words it is exactly equivalent to the boolean expression

    (Ans = 'Y') *or* (Ans = 'N')

When the list consists of only two or three values, you can just as well use an expression with *or* like the above, but when the list of values is four or more, this new kind of boolean expression is very handy. For example, the following boolean expressions are completely equivalent, but the first one is easier to write and easier to read:

```
Ans in ['Y', 'y', 'N', 'n']
(Ans = 'Y') or (Ans = 'y') or (Ans = 'N') or (Ans = 'n')
```

The list of values is called a *set*. A set consists of a list of constants, separated by commas and enclosed in square brackets. Only square brackets can be used. In Pascal the different kinds of brackets, ')', '}', and ']', have different uses and you cannot interchange them.

sets

To form a boolean expression involving a set, you write an expression followed by the reserved word *in* followed by a set. For example:

```
(X + Y) in [8, 34, 17]
```

The type of the expression in front of the *in* may be integer or char; it cannot be real. The type can be boolean, but that is seldom of any use. All the constants in the list must be of the same type as the expression. (Some versions of Pascal limit the values of type integer that can be used in a set. For example, some versions do not allow negative integers.) The entire boolean expression evaluates to true if the value of the expression, such as (X + Y), is on the list; otherwise, it evaluates to false.

Because these expressions involving *in* are boolean expressions, they may be used as subparts of other more complex boolean expressions containing *and*, *or*, or *not*. For example, consider the following:

```
(X < 10) and (Ans in ['Y', 'N'])
```

This boolean expression is true provided that the value of X is less than 10 and the value of Ans is one of the letters 'Y' or 'N'.

Figure 6.11 shows an example of a boolean expression involving both *not* and

```
procedure GetAnswer(var Ans: char);
{Instructs the user to type in Y or N for "yes" or "no". Checks
the user's response and asks again if anything else is typed in.
Both upper- and lowercase versions of Y and N are accepted.}
begin{GetAnswer}
   writeln('Type in Y for Yes or N for No: ');
   readln(Ans);
   while not (Ans in ['Y', 'y', 'N', 'n']) do
      begin{loop body}
         writeln('You typed in', Ans);
         writeln('Please type in Y for Yes or N for No: ');
         readln(Ans)
      end {loop body}
end;  {GetAnswer}
```

Figure 6.11
A boolean
expression
using *in*.

in. Be sure to notice the syntax of how *not* and *in* are combined. The following is not allowed as a Pascal boolean expression:

```
Ans not in ['Y', 'y', 'N', 'n']
{NOT ALLOWED IN PASCAL}
```

The correct syntax is

```
not(Ans in ['Y', 'y', 'N', 'n'])
```

> "Contrariwise," continued Tweedledee,
> "if it was so, it might be;
> and if it were so, it would be;
> but as it isn't, it ain't. That's logic."
>
> *Lewis Carroll, Through the Looking-Glass*

Summary of Problem Solving and Programming Techniques

- A boolean variable can be used within a program as a flag to record whether or not some specific action has taken place.
- A boolean constant can be used as a switch to turn program features off and on by changing the constant declaration. One such feature is trace statements for debugging.
- One approach to solving a task or subtask is to write down conditions and the corresponding actions that need to be taken under each condition. This can be implemented in Pascal as a series of nested *if-then-else* statements.

Summary of Pascal Constructs

if-then statements, *if-then-else* statements, and simple boolean expressions are summarized at the end of Chapter 3.

the type boolean

Syntax:

```
boolean
```

Example:

```
var Raining: boolean;
```

A Pascal type. There are exactly two values of this type, namely `true` and `false`. A Pascal program can have variables, constants, and expressions of type `boolean`.

use of and

Syntax:

<boolean expression 1> *and* <boolean expression 2>

Examples:

```
(X < 1)  and  (X <> Y)
(sqrt(X) < 10.7)  and  (Y > 0)
```

One way to make a larger boolean expression out of two smaller boolean expressions. If both <boolean expression 1> and <boolean expression 2> evaluate to `true`, then the entire expression evaluates to `true`. If at least one of <boolean expression 1> and <boolean expression 2> evaluates to `false`, then the entire expression evaluates to `false`. (It is sometimes necessary, and it is usually wise, to place parentheses around the subexpressions.)

use of or

Syntax:

<boolean expression 1> *or* <boolean expression 2>

Example:

```
(Ans = 'Y')  or  (Number = 7)
```

One way to make a larger boolean expression out of two smaller boolean expressions. If at least one of <boolean expression 1> and <boolean expression 2> evaluate to `true`, then the entire expression evaluates to `true`. If both <boolean expression 1> and <boolean expression 2> evaluate to `false`, then the entire expression evaluates to `false`. (It is sometimes necessary, and it is usually wise, to place parentheses around the subexpressions.)

use of not

Syntax:

not(<boolean expression>)

Examples:

```
not(X < 0)
not(  (X < 1)  and  (Y < 0)  )
```

One way to make a larger boolean expression out of a smaller one. *not* reverses boolean values. If <boolean expression> evaluates to `true`, then the expression with the *not* evaluates to `false`. If <boolean expression> evaluates to `false`, then the expression with the *not* evaluates to `true`. If <boolean expression> is a boolean variable (or certain other boolean expressions described later in this book), parentheses are not required around the expression.

case statement

Syntax:

```
case <expression> of
   <label list 1>: <statement 1>;
   <label list 2>: <statement 2>;
                .
                .
                .
   <label list n>: <statement n>
end
```

Example:

```
case N of
   2: writeln('Value of N is 2');
   7,9,4: writeln('Value of N is 7, 9, or 4')
end
```

<expression> must evaluate to a value of type `integer` or type `char`. (Later we will discover other allowable types.) It cannot be of type `real`. The label lists must be lists of values of the same type as that of <expression>, and all these values must be different. The statements may be any Pascal statements. When the `case` statement is executed, <expression> is evaluated and the statement with that value on its label list is executed.

Exercises

Self-Test Exercises

4. The expression A *or* B evaluates to `true` provided that the value of either *or both* of the variables is `true`. Design a boolean expression that evaluates to `true` provided that the value of *exactly one* of the two variables is `true`.

5. What is the output produced by the following code when embedded in a complete program in which X is declared to be a variable of type `boolean`?

```
if true then
   writeln('First writeln')
else
   writeln('Second writeln');
X := (1 < 2) and (4 < 3);
if X then
   writeln('Third writeln')
else
   writeln('Fourth writeln')
```

6. Write a program that reads in three integers and outputs a message telling whether or not they are in numeric order.

7. Write a nested *if-then-else* statement that classifies an integer X into one of the following categories and writes out an appropriate message:

   X < 0 or 0 ≤ X ≤ 100 or X > 100

8. We have seen four types thus far in our discussion of the Pascal language: integer, real, char, and boolean. Which of these types are allowed as the type for the controlling expression in a *case* statement? That is, what can the type of <expression> be in a *case* statement that begins with

   case <expression> of

9. Write a program the input to which is a month entered as a number from 1 to 12 and the output of which is the number of days in that month.

10. The following four boolean expressions divide into two groups with two equivalent expressions in each group. What are the two groups? (Two expressions are equivalent if they evaluate to the same value of true or false for each possible way of setting Footloose and FancyFree to true or false.)

   not (FootLoose) *and not* (FancyFree)
   not (FootLoose) *or not* (FancyFree)
   not (FootLoose *and* FancyFree)
   not (FootLoose *or* FancyFree)

Interactive Exercises

11. Embed the following code in a complete program and run it several times using different input values each time:

```
writeln('Type in three integers: ');
readln(X, Y, Z);

if X > 0 then
   writeln('X is greater than zero')
else if Y > 0 then
   writeln('Y is greater than zero')
else if Z > 0 then
   writeln('Z is greater than zero')
else
   writeln('They are all zero or negative')
```

Predict the outputs before you run the program.

12. Write a program that will read in three integers and output a message telling whether exactly two of them are greater than 10. There is no need to be fancy. It is perfectly all right to use a long boolean expression that tests all possible pairs of variables.

13. Write a program whose input is a one-digit number and whose output is that number written as a word. For example, an input of 5 should produce an output of: f i ve.

Programming Exercises

14. Enhance the program from Exercise 9 so that the month is input as a name, such as "January," and not as a number. If the month is February, the program also asks the year in order to determine whether it is a leap year. The program in Figure 5.20 can be modified into a procedure to determine whether a year is a leap year. The program should allow the month to be spelled with any combination of upper- and lowercase letters. It should accept misspelled months as long as the first three letters are correct.

15. Write a program that computes state income tax according to the following formula: Net income is gross income minus deductions (both given as input); tax is:

   3% on each dollar of net income up to $8,000 plus
   5% on each dollar of net income from $8,001 to 15,000 plus
   8% on each dollar of net income over $15,000

16. Write a program that guesses the user's height. The program makes a first guess and then asks the user if it is too high, too low, or correct. The program continues to guess and ask the user for feedback until the user says the guess is correct or until three tries have been made, whichever comes first.

17. Write a program to determine grades in a course with three quizzes, each scored on a basis of ten points. Grades are determined according to the following rule: A is an average of 9.0 or better; B is an average of 8.0 or better (up to 9.0); C is an average of 7.0 or better; D is an average of 6.0 or better; and less than 6.0 is an F.

18. A bicycle salesperson is offered a choice of wage plans: (1) a straight salary of $300 per week; (2) $3.50 per hour for 40 hours plus a 10% commission on sales; (3) a straight 15% commission on sales with no other salary. Write a program that takes as input the salesperson's expected weekly sales and outputs the wages paid under each plan as well as announcing the best-paying plan.

19. Write a program to compute the interest due, total amount due, and the minimum payment for a revolving credit account. The program accepts the account balance as input and then adds on the interest to get the total amount due. The rate schedules are as follows: The interest is 1.5% on the first $1,000 and 1% on any amount over that. The minimum payment is the total amount due if that amount is $10 or less; otherwise, it is $10 or 10% of the total amount owed, whichever is larger.

20. Write a program to give a student's final grade in a course with the following grading scheme: there are three quizzes worth 10 points each, a midterm worth 100 points, and a final worth 100 points. The grade is based on the following weights: 50% on the final exam, 25% on the midterm, and 25% on the quiz average. (Be sure to normalize the quiz average to 100 by multiplying by 10.) The grade is determined from the weighted average in the traditional way: 90 or over is an A, below 90 down to 80 is a B, below 80 to 70 is a C, below 70 to 60 is a D, and below 60 is an F.

21. Write a program that computes the cost of postage on a first-class letter according to the following rate scale: 30 cents for the first ounce or fraction of an ounce and 7 cents for each additional half-ounce, plus a $5 service charge if the customer desires special delivery.

22. Write a program that reads in a time of day in 24-hour notation and outputs it in 12-hour notation. For example, if the input is 13:45, the output should be

        1:45 PM

The program should instruct the user always to enter exactly five characters. So, for example, nine o'clock should be input as

        09:00

23. Write a program that accepts dates written in the usual way and then outputs them as three numbers. For example, the input

        February 15, 1961

should produce the output

        2   15   61

24. Write a program that accepts a "three-digit" number written in words and then outputs it as a value of type `integer`. The input is terminated with a period. For example, the input

        two hundred thirty-five.

should produce the output

        235

25. Write a program that reads in the radius of a circle and then outputs one of the following depending on what the user requests: circumference of the circle, area of the circle, or diameter of the circle.

26. Write a program to score the "paper-rock-scissors" game. Each of two users types in 'P', 'R' or 'S', and the program announces the winner as well as the basis for determining the winner: "paper covers rock," "rock breaks scissors," "scissors cut paper," or "nobody wins." Be sure to allow the users to use lower- as well as upper-case letters (if they are available on your machine).

27. Write a program that accepts a year written as a four-digit Arabic (ordinary) numeral and outputs the year written in Roman numerals. Important Roman numerals are V for 5, X for 10, L for 50, C for 100, D for 500, and M for 1000. Recall that some numbers are formed by using a kind of subtraction of one Roman "digit"; for example, IV is 4, produced as V minus I; XL is 40; CM is 900, and so forth. Here are a few more sample years: MCM is 1900, MCML is 1950, MCMLX is 1960, MCMXL is 1940, and MCMLXXXIX is 1989. Assume the year is between 1000 and 3000.

28. Write an astrology program. The user types in his or her birthday, and the program responds with the user's sign and horoscope. The month may be entered as a number

from 1 to 12. Use a newspaper horoscope section for the horoscopes and dates of each sign. Then enhance your program so that if the user is only one or two days away from an adjacent sign, the program announces that the user is on a "cusp" and also outputs the horoscope for the nearest adjacent sign. For a nicer but more difficult program, let the user type in the month as a word rather than as a number.

29. Write a program that accepts a number written as a Roman numeral and outputs the equivalent Arabic (ordinary) numeral. Assume that the Roman numeral is 50 or smaller (Roman numeral L or smaller.) See Exercise 27 for a review of Roman numerals.

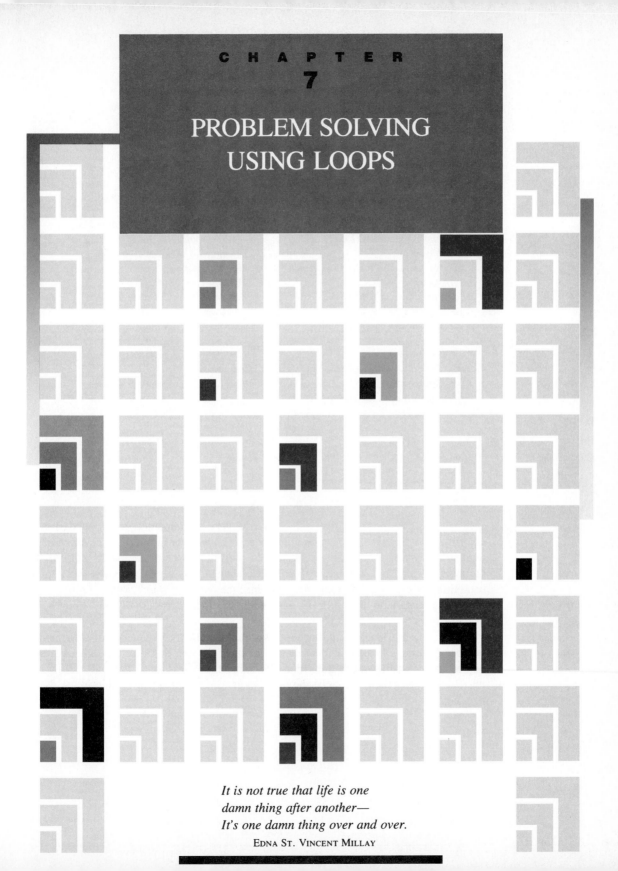

PROBLEM SOLVING
USING LOOPS

*It is not true that life is one
damn thing after another—
It's one damn thing over and over.*

EDNA ST. VINCENT MILLAY

Chapter Contents

A very common sort of instruction in an algorithm is to repeat some action a number of times. A program that reads in a list of numbers may repeat the same sequence of prompt and read statements until all the numbers are read in. A program to calculate change may repeat its entire calculation, computing change for different amounts, until the user is through with the program. A program to update an inventory list may repeat the update process as many times as the user specifies.

Any program instruction that repeats some statement or sequence of statements a number of times is called a *loop*. In this chapter we will describe a number of techniques for designing algorithms and programs that use loops. We will review the *while* loop and then introduce the other looping mechanisms available in the Pascal language.

Basic Loop Considerations

A loop is any program construction that repeats a statement or sequence of statements some number of times. The simple *while* loops that we have already seen are examples of loops. The statement (or group of statements) to be repeated in a loop is called the *body* of the loop and each repetition of the loop body is called an *iteration* of the loop. The two main design questions when constructing loops are: What should the body be? and How many times should the loop be iterated? Another way to phrase the second of these two design questions is: How will the loop stop?

loop body

loop iteration

The While Statement

A simplified form of the *while* statement was introduced in Chapter 3. That form of the *while* statement used only simple comparisons to control the number of loop iterations. However, any boolean expression whatsoever may be used in a *while* statement. For example, the following loop will be iterated until the values of the variables X and Y are both positive:

```
while (X <= 0) or (Y <= 0) do
  begin
    X := X + 1;
    Y := Y + 1
  end
```

(The values of X and Y must, of course, be given some value before the *while* statement is executed.) For the sake of completeness and review, we next give the complete definition of a *while* statement.

The syntax of the *while* statement is shown in Figure 7.1. It consists of the reserved word *while*, followed by a boolean expression, followed by the reserved word *do*, followed by a Pascal statement. This statement is the body of the *while* loop. The statement that forms the body is typically a compound statement. However, any kind of Pascal statement is allowed. When the *while* loop is executed, this statement

syntax

body of a
while loop

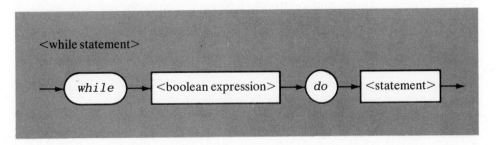

<while statement>

while → <boolean expression> → do → <statement>

Figure 7.1
Syntax of the
***while* statement.**

action of
a while
statement

will be executed some number of times depending on the values of the boolean expression. The boolean expression may be any of the boolean expressions described in Chapter 6.

When a *while* statement is executed, the first thing that happens is that the boolean expression is evaluated. If it evaluates to *false*, then no action is taken and the program proceeds to the next statement after the loop. If the boolean expression evaluates to *true*, then the body of the loop is executed and the boolean expression is again evaluated. This process is iterated again and again as long as the boolean expression remains *true*. After each iteration the boolean expression is again checked and if it is *true*, then the loop is iterated again; if it has changed from *true* to *false*, then the *while* statement ends and the program proceeds to the next statement in the program.

executing
the body
zero times

Notice that the first thing that happens when a *while* loop is executed is that the boolean expression is evaluated. If the boolean expression evaluates to *false* at that point, then the body of the loop is never executed at all. It may seem pointless to execute the body of a loop *zero times*. After all, that has no effect at all on any values or output. However, it is sometimes the desired action. In the next case study, we will design a *while* loop to add a list of numbers. If the numbers are homework scores, it might turn out that some student did absolutely no homework and so the list of scores will be empty. To get the correct sum (and grade) of zero, the loop body must be executed zero times. As another example, suppose the numbers are the values of the checks you have written in a month. You might take a month's vacation in which you write no checks at all. In that case, there are zero numbers to sum and so the loop is iterated zero times.

Case Study

Summing a List of Numbers

loop
body

Suppose we wish to sum a list of numbers typed in at the keyboard. For example, they may be homework scores or sales figures. The obvious way to accomplish this is to read in the numbers and keep a running total of all the numbers seen so far. To hold this running sum we use a variable called Sum. The variable Sum is set equal to zero and then each time that the program reads in a number, Sum is increased by adding in that number. After initializing Sum to zero, the program will repeat the following action for each of the numbers in the list:

```
read(Number);
Sum := Sum + Number
```

This repeated action indicates that we can use a loop. The above two statements will form the body of our loop, or at least part of the body of our loop.

stopping
the loop

When adding a list of numbers with a loop, we need to somehow determine the number of numbers to be added. We need to somehow "stop" the loop. In this example, we will use a very simple strategy: We will first ask the user how many numbers there are and then iterate the loop that number of times. In order to count the number of iterations we will use a variable called `LeftToRead`, which is initialized to the number of numbers to be read in and which is then decreased by one each time the loop is iterated. This adds one more statement to the loop body:

```
LeftToRead := LeftToRead - 1
```

The complete pseudocode for our algorithm that includes this loop is given in Figure 7.2. Figure 7.3 shows how we can realize this algorithm as a complete program using a *while* loop. Be sure to notice that the variables Sum and LeftToRead are initialized before the loop.

Algorithm to Add N Numbers

```
writeln('How many integers will there be in the list?');
```
Read number into variable N;
```
LeftToRead := N;
Sum := 0;
```
{*The loop part of the algorithm starts here.*}
Do the following, provided `LeftToRead` > 0, and continue to
do it again and again as long as `LeftToRead` > 0:
```
  begin{loop}
    read(Number);
    Sum := Sum + Number;
    LeftToRead := LeftToRead - 1
  end;  {loop}
```
{*The loop part of the algorithm ends here.*}
```
writeln('The sum of the ', N, ' numbers is ', Sum)
```

Figure 7.2
Pseudocode for summing a list of numbers.

Program

```
program AddUp(input, output);
```
{*Computes the sum of a list of integers entered as input.*}
```
var N, LeftToRead, Number, Sum: integer;
begin{Program}
  writeln('This program adds a list of integers.');
  writeln('How many integers will there be in the list?');
  readln(N);
  writeln('Now type in the ', N, ' integers.');

  LeftToRead := N;
  Sum := 0;
```

Figure 7.3
Program for summing a list of numbers.

```
while LeftToRead > 0 do
  begin{while}
     read(Number);
     Sum := Sum + Number;
     LeftToRead := LeftToRead - 1
  end;    {while}

  writeln('The sum of the ', N,' numbers is ', Sum)
end. {Program}
```

Sample Dialogue 1

```
This program adds a list of integers.
How many integers will there be in the list?
3
Now type in the   3 integers.
4  6  2
The sum of the   3 numbers is 12
```

Sample Dialogue 2

```
This program adds a list of integers.
How many integers will there be in the list?
0
Now type in the   0 integers.
The sum of the   0 numbers is   0
```

Figure 7.3 (continued)

Pitfall

Uninitialized Variables

The program in Figure 7.3 sums a list of numbers by adding one number to the value of Sum during each loop iteration. Changing one or more variables in some incremental way is a typical action performed in a loop body. When designing such a loop, it is easy to become so concerned with the design of the loop body that you forget to initialize the variables used in the loop. A statement such as the following will produce unpredictable results unless the variable Sum is first given a value:

```
Sum := Sum + Number
```

If this statement is used in a loop to sum a list of numbers, then the variable Sum should be initialized to zero before the loop is executed. To see that zero is the correct initial value, simply note that zero plus the first number produces the correct value for a sum of one number.

Do not assume that zero is always the correct initial value for a variable used in a loop. Different situations require different initial values. For instance, the following computes the product of a list of N numbers:

```
LeftToRead := N;
Product := 1;
while LeftToRead > 0 do
   begin{while}
      read(Number);
      Product := Product * Number;
      LeftToRead := LeftToRead - 1
   end   {while}
```

To see that Product should be initialized to one, note that one multiplied by the first number yields the correct starting value. Any other value would produce problems. In particular, if Product were initialized to zero, its value would remain zero no matter how many times the loop were iterated.

What happens when you fail to initialize a variable varies from system to system, but it almost always produces problems. Even worse, the problem may not be apparent. One common situation is that uninitialized variables simply receive some leftover value stored in memory by a previously run program. This sets the value of the variables to some unpredicable values. The values may even vary from one run of the program to another. Any time that a program is run twice with *absolutely* no changes and with *identical* input and yet produces different outputs, suspect an uninitialized variable of some sort. The problem can even occur if there is no loop. Every variable must be explicitly given a value before it can appear on the right-hand side of an assignment statement or anywhere else that expects it to already have a value.

Pitfall Review

Unintended Infinite Loops

Some loops are not required to end. For example, an airline reservation system might simply repeat a loop that allows the user to add or delete reservations. The program and the loop run forever, or at least until the computer breaks or the airline goes bankrupt. More often, a loop is designed to compute a value or a small list of values and should end after finding the value(s). For example, our sample loop to add up a list of numbers ends after summing all the numbers. A loop that repeats forever is called an *infinite loop*. An unintended infinite loop is a common error that should be guarded against.

Consider the following loop, which displays the interest produced by the value of Amount for some sample interest rates in the range from 10% to 20%:

```
Rate := 10;
while Rate <> 20 do
   begin{while}
      Interest := Rate * 0.01 * Amount;
      {The 0.01 changes percent to a fraction.}
      writeln(Rate, '% yields $', Interest,
                     ' in interest.');
      Rate := Rate + 2
   end   {while}
```

Now suppose that we wish to change the display so that it shows changes of 3% rather than 2%. If we change the last line of the loop body to the following, we will produce an infinite loop:

```
Rate := Rate + 3
```

The problem is that the value of Rate now jumps from 19 to 22 and is never equal to 20. So the value of the boolean expression is never changed to false. The correct boolean expression is

```
Rate < 20
```

It would be safer to use this expression even in the original version of the loop, which increased percentages by 2 and thus happened to terminate correctly. With the change, the loop is robust enough to perform correctly even if we need to alter it slightly.

dangers of equality   As a general rule, it is safer to terminate a loop with a test that involves a greater-than or less-than comparison rather than a test for exact equality or a test using the inequality operator <>. In the case of real values, this is an absolute rule. Since real values are stored as approximate quantities, a test for equality of real values is meaningless. Controlling a loop with a boolean expression that tests two real values for equality is virtually guaranteed to end the loop too soon or not at all. Always arrange to test real values using one of the relations <, <=, >, or >=.

Self-Test Exercises

1. What is the output of the following (when embedded in a correct program with X and Y declared to be of type integer)?

```
X := 10; Y := 3;
while (X > 0) and (Y > 0) do
   X := X - Y;
writeln(X)
```

2. What output would be produced by the code in Exercise 1 if Y were initialized to −3 instead of 3?

3. What is the output of the following (when embedded in a correct program with X declared to be of type `integer`?)

```
X := 10;
while X > 0 do
   X := X + 3;
writeln(X)
```

4. The following is supposed to output all the positive odd numbers less than 10. It contains mistakes. What are they, and how can they be corrected?

```
X := 1;
while X <> 10 do
   begin{while}
      X := X + 2;
      write(X)
   end   {while}
```

Round and round she goes,
and where she stops nobody knows.
Traditional carnival barker's call

Terminating an Input Loop

If your program is reading in a list of values with a *while* loop, it must include some kind of mechanism to terminate the loop. If the program runs out of input, the program will stop, but if no provisions are made for the program to explicitly terminate the loop, the result will be an error condition that terminates the program abnormally. There are four commonly used methods for terminating an input loop:

1. Asking before iterating.
2. Heading the list with its size.
3. Ending the list with a sentinel value.
4. Running out of input.

We will discuss them in order.

The first method is simply to ask the user if there is more input.

asking before iterating

```
Sum := 0;
writeln('Are there any numbers in the list? (y/n)');
readln(Ans);
while (Ans = 'y') or (Ans = 'Y') do
```

```
begin{while}
  writeln('Enter number: ');
  read(Number);
  Sum := Sum + Number;
  writeln('Are there more numbers? (y/n)');
  readln(Ans)
end   {while}
```

This is sometimes acceptable and is very useful in certain situations. However, for a long list this method is very tiresome. Imagine typing in a list of 100 numbers this way. The user is likely to progress from happy to sarcastic to angry and frustrated. When you are reading in long lists, it is preferable to include only one stopping signal.

lists headed by size

On those occasions when the user naturally and easily knows the size of the list beforehand, the program can ask the user for the size of the list. This is the method we used in our sample program in Figure 7.3.

sentinel value

Perhaps the neatest way to terminate a loop that reads in a list of values is with a *sentinel value*. A sentinel value is one that is somehow distinct from all the possible values on the list and so can be used to signal the end of the list. For example, if the loop reads in a list of positive numbers, a negative number can be used as a sentinel value to indicate the end of the list. A loop such as the following can be used to add a list of nonnegative numbers:

```
Sum := 0;
read(Number);
while Number >= 0 do
  begin
    Sum := Sum + Number;
    read(Number)
  end
```

Notice that the last number in the list is read but is not added into Sum. To add up the numbers 1, 2, and 3, the user adds a negative number to the end of the list, like so:

```
1   2   3   −1
```

The final −1 is read in but is not added into the sum.

Also notice that when using a sentinel value, we reversed the order of summing and reading within our *while* loop. With a sentinel value, we want the loop to end as soon as the sentinel value is read, and so the loop needs to have the `read` statement at the end. We also needed to place a `read` statement before the *while* loop so that the boolean expression would be defined and so that the variable Number would have a defined value in the first assignment statement.

In order to use a sentinel value in the way just discussed, the list must be known to exclude at least one value of the data type in question. If the list consists of integers that might be any value whatsoever, then there is no value left to serve as a sentinel value. In this situation, you must resort to some other method to terminate the loop.

running out of input

As already noted, a loop that simply runs out of input will terminate with an error condition. However, if special provisions are made within the program, then in some situations it is possible to test whether there is more input and to end a loop gracefully if there is none. The next section discusses one way to do this.

EOLN

Using the special boolean expression eoln, a Pascal program can detect the end of a line. This expression allows a user to mark the end of a list simply by pressing the return key. It is not very convenient for long lists, but it does work well for lists short enough to fit comfortably on one line. The identifier eoln is a boolean expression that tells the program when it is at the end of a line. When the program still has input available on the line that is currently being read, eoln has the value *false*, but when the end of a line is encountered, the value of eoln changes from *false* to *true*. Less formally, eoln is *true* when the program reaches the end of a line of input and is *false* otherwise.

Figure 7.4 shows a rewritten version of the program in Figure 7.3. This version   *not eoln*

Program

```
program AddUp(input, output);
{Computes the sum of a list of integers entered as input.}
var Number, Sum: integer;
begin{Program}
   writeln('Enter a list of integers all on one line');
   writeln('and then press the return key.');
   writeln('I will compute their sum.');

   Sum := 0;
   while not eoln do
     begin{while}
       read(Number);
       Sum := Sum + Number
     end;    {while}

   writeln('The sum is ', Sum)
end.  {Program}
```

Sample Dialogue 1

```
Enter a list of integers all on one line
and then press the return key.
I will compute their sum.
4 6 2
The sum is    12
```

Sample Dialogue 2

```
Enter a list of integers all on one line
and then press the return key.
I will compute their sum.
4 6 2 −3
The sum is    9
```

Figure 7.4
**Program using
eoln.**

end-of-line character

uses `eoln` to detect the end of a line, rather than asking the user how many numbers there will be. The *not* before `eoln` reverses `true` and `false`, and so *not* `eoln` is `true` when the program is not at the end of the line. As illustrated in Figure 7.4, `eoln` need not be placed in parentheses when it is preceded by *not*.

The exact method for determining the value of `eoln` involves a special character called the *end-of-line character*. When the user presses the return key, that sends a special character to the computer as input. This character is called the end-of-line character. The character does not appear on the screen, but its presence is indicated by the start of a new line. When the program has read all the data on a line, the next character of input is this end-of-line character. When the program executes a `readln`, this end-of-line character is skipped over. The boolean `eoln` has the value `true` whenever the next input character is the end-of-line character; otherwise, its value is `false`. Normally, one can simply think of `eoln` as being `true` when the computer is "at the end of a line," but in some subtle situations you may need to think in terms of the end-of-line character.

It is possible to read the end-of-line character into a variable of type `char`, but the result is neither interesting nor typically useful. The character is converted into a blank when you do so.

Off-Line Data and a Preview of EOF
(Optional)

Data is often prepared ahead of time rather than being entered by the user from the keyboard. This type of input is sometimes called *off-line data*. For example, the input might consist of experimental data collected over a long period of time and given to a program for statistical analysis. Such data is likely to be read by the program directly from some electronic medium. In Chapters 13 and 16 we discuss methods for reading data off-line. Some systems have other methods for entering data that has been prepared ahead of time. In all these cases, there is no need to give prompt lines like the following, since there is nobody to read them:

```
writeln('Enter a list of nonnegative integers');
writeln('and I will compute their sum.');
writeln('Place a negative number after the list');
```

Since the data is known to be ready and waiting, there is no need for any prompt lines at all.

There is also no point in asking the user to reenter the data if the data is not appropriate; there is nobody there to follow the instructions. In the case of off-line data, all the input must be carefully prepared, in order to be certain that it is in the form expected by the program.

With such programs the output is also in a different format. Since the output is not given in a dialogue with the user, it should be carefully annotated to indicate which output is paired with which input. When the output is read by the user, the input will not automatically be at hand, and so the output should include sufficient information about the input to allow the user to interpret the results. For example, the output might write the corresponding inputs and outputs next to each other.

Off-line data is stored in units called *files*. When data is read off-line from one of these files, the end of the file can be detected by a Pascal program in much the same way that the program can detect the end of a line. The predefined boolean expression eof is false as long as there is any input left, and it changes to true as soon as the program has read all the input. The use of eof is similar to that of eoln. For example, the following loop sums a list of numbers that are read off-line. The numbers are stored one per line.

eof

```
Sum : = 0;
while not eof do
  begin{while}
    readln(Number);
    Sum : = Sum + Number
  end   {while}
```

It is safest to use readln, rather than read, when using eof with numeric data. This does, of course, require that the numbers being read are stored one per line in the file.

You must somehow specify that a program is using off-line data. Some systems have special instructions that apply to one specific installation or system. Check your local installation to see if there is a simple way to specify that data is to be read off-line. In Chapter 13 we discuss one method that works for all Pascal systems. If you want to cover some of the material earlier than that, you can read some of Chapter 13, which introduces a form of off-line data called *text files*. It can be read and understood without the material that precedes it. You can then return to this point and continue reading.

text files

Modifying an Algorithm

One way to solve a problem is to modify a solution for a similar problem. Figure 7.4 gives a program to compute the sum of a list of numbers. A simple modification can change it into a program to compute the average of the list of numbers. The modification is to add a variable Count to the loop that will count the number of times the loop is iterated and hence will end with a value equal to the number of numbers read in. To obtain the average, the program simply divides the sum by Count. The modified program is given in Figure 7.5.

The Repeat Statement

A variant of the *while* statement is the *repeat* statement. For example, the following *repeat* statement is almost equivalent to the *while* statement in Figure 7.3. The list of statements between the identifiers *repeat* and *until* form the body of the repeat loop.

```
repeat
   read(Number);
   Sum := Sum + Number;
   LeftToRead := LeftToRead - 1
until LeftToRead <= 0
```

syntax
of repeat

The syntax of the *repeat* statement is given in Figure 7.6. Notice that in a *re-peat* statement the loop body consists of a list of statements and need not be a single

Program

```
program Average(input, output);
{Computes the average of a list of integers entered as input.}
var Number, Sum, Count: integer;
     Average: real;
begin{Program}
   writeln('Enter a list of integers all on one line');
   writeln('and then press the return key.');
   writeln('I will compute their average.');

   Sum := 0;
   Count := 0;  {Counts the number of numbers.}

   while not eoln do
     begin{while}
       read(Number);
       Sum := Sum + Number;
       Count := Count + 1
     end;    {while}

   if Count = 0 then
     writeln('No numbers read in.')
   else
     begin{Count > 0}
       Average := Sum/Count;
       writeln(Count, ' numbers read in.');
       writeln('The average is ', Average)
     end {Count > 0}
end. {Program}
```

Sample Dialogue

```
Enter a list of integers all on one line
and then press the return key.
I will compute their average.
90 88 73 50 100
     5 numbers read in.
The average is 80.2000
```

Figure 7.5
Averaging
program.

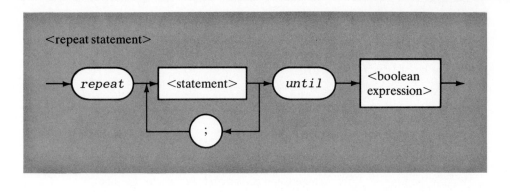

Figure 7.6
Syntax of the
repeat
statement.

statement. The statements are separated by semicolons, as in a compound statement. However, the syntax does not require a *begin/end* pair; the identifiers *repeat* and *until* serve a similar function.

action of
a repeat
statement

With a *repeat* loop, the loop body is always executed at least once. When a *repeat* statement is executed, the first thing that happens is that the loop body is executed. Next, the boolean expression following the *until* is evaluated. If it evaluates to false, the loop body is repeated and the boolean expression is evaluated one more time. After each iteration of the loop body, the boolean expression is evaluated. If the boolean expression evaluates to true, the loop is ended, and the program proceeds to the next statement.

Comparison of the While and Repeat Loops

One syntactic difference between a *repeat* statement and a *while* statement is that the body of a *repeat* statement is a list of statements, whereas the body of a *while* statement is a single statement. However, since the body of the *while* statement can be a compound statement, this is not a significant difference.

A slightly more substantive difference is that a *while* statement terminates when the controlling boolean expression evaluates to false, whereas a *repeat* statement terminates when the value of the boolean expression is true. This is a point to be aware of if you ever translate from one type of loop to the other. Our sample *repeat* loop of the previous section has essentially the same loop body as the *while* statement it mirrors, but the boolean expression is the negation of the one occurring in the *while* statement.

The main difference between the two types of loop statements, however, is that with a *repeat* statement, the body of the loop is always executed at least once; a *while* statement is more general and allows for the possibility that the loop body may not be executed at all. Hence, if we use the sample *repeat* statement of the previous section to replace the *while* statement in Figure 7.3, then the program will no longer be able to cope with empty lists. You cannot use a *repeat* statement unless you are certain that, under all circumstances, the loop body should be repeated at least once.

Self-Test Exercises

5. What is the output of the following (when embedded in a correct program with X declared to be of type `integer`)?

```
X : = 10;
repeat
   X := X - 3
until X <= 0;
writeln(X)
```

6. What is the biggest difference between a *repeat* and a *while* loop?

7. Show that any *while* statement can be replaced by a statement consisting of an *if-then* statement that contains a *repeat* statement as a subpart. Show that any *repeat* statement can be replaced by a compound statement and a *while* statement.

8. Write a program that reads in a line of text and then echoes just the last letter. The characters are read one at a time into a variable of type `char` using a loop, the loop is terminated using `eoln`, and then the last character read in is echoed. So for the input

pineapple pasta

the output is the single letter `a`.

When we see the same effect always recur, we infer a natural necessity in it, as that there will be a tomorrow, etc. But nature often deceives us, and does not subject herself to her own rules.

Blaise Pascal

Case Study

Testing a Procedure

We have advocated testing procedures separately by writing a small test program for each procedure. To add to our confidence in the correctness of the procedure, we need to test it with a number of different parameter values. A *repeat* loop in the test program will allow us to test the procedure as often as we wish without having to rerun the test program.

For example, in Chapter 6 we wrote a program to test a procedure named Out-putCoins. That program tested one set of parameter values and then terminated. If we add a *repeat* loop, as shown in Figure 7.7, then we can test the input on several different sets of parameter values without having to rerun the program.

Program

program Test(input, output);

var TotalAmount, Quarters, Dimes, Nickels, Pennies: integer;
    Ans: char;

procedure OutputCoins(A, Q, D, N, P: integer);
{*Outputs a collection of coins that total to A cents.*
Precondition: 0 < A <= 99 and the coins total to A,
that is 25*Q + 10*D +5*N + P = A.}

      <The rest of the procedure is shown in Figure 6.5.>

begin{*TestProgram*}
  repeat
    writeln('Enter: Quarters, Dimes, Nickels, Pennies:');
    readln(Quarters, Dimes, Nickels, Pennies);
    TotalAmount := 25 * Quarters
               + 10 * Dimes
               + 5 * Nickels
               + Pennies;
    OutputCoins(TotalAmount, Quarters, Dimes, Nickels, Pennies);
    writeln('Do you want to test again?(y/n)');
    readln(Ans)
  until (Ans = 'n') *or* (Ans = 'N');
  writeln('End of testing')
end. {*TestProgram*}

Sample Dialogue

Enter: Quarters, Dimes, Nickels, Pennies:
1 0 1 2
32 cents can be given as:
one quarter, one nickel and 2 pennies
Do you want to test again?(y/n)
yes
Enter: Quarters, Dimes, Nickels, Pennies:
2 0 1 2
57 cents can be given as:
2 quarters, one nickel and 2 pennies
Do you want to test again?(y/n)
no
End of testing

Figure 7.7
Testing a
procedure.

When reading Figure 7.7, there is no need to look back at the previous chapter to see the body of the procedure. The procedure heading and the comment are all you need in order to understand the loop. The sample dialogue is short due to space limitations. This procedure should be tested on many more than the two sets of values shown.

Case Study

Finding the Largest and Smallest Values on a List

One often wants to end a loop partway through the body of the loop. If the loop has three statements, then on the last iteration of the loop body you might want the loop to execute only the first one or the first two statements and then end. Neither the *while* loop nor the *repeat* loop has provisions for doing this directly. However, we can usually rewrite the loop to obtain the same effect. In this case study, we will illustrate a technique for doing exactly that.

Problem Definition

As a sample design problem, consider the task of writing a program to determine the largest and smallest value on a list of positive numbers. We will assume that the list is not empty and that it is followed by a negative number that serves as a sentinel value marking the end of the input list.

Discussion

ALGORITHM first version

One approach is to use two variables, Max and Min, to hold the largest and smallest values read in so far. After each number is read in, it is compared to both Max and Min to see if this new number is a new low or a new high value. The basic operations in the loop body are as follows:

```
begin{loop}
    read(Next);
    if Next > Max then
          Max := Next;
    if Next < Min then
          Min := Next
end   {loop}
```

initializing variables

Since the loop body uses the values of Max and Min, they must be initialized so that they have a value the first time through the loop. After the first number is processed, the values of both Max and Min should be equal to this number, since at that point it is both the largest and the smallest number seen so far. One way to initialize Max and Min is to process one number before starting the loop. The following, placed before the loop, will initialize the values correctly.

```
read(Next);
Max := Next;
Min := Next;
```

*stopping
partway
through the
loop body*

At this point, we are almost through designing the algorithm and even writing the Pascal code. All we need do is design the Pascal code so that the loop stops as soon as a negative number is read in. This does present a problem because, as we have written the loop body, the `read` statement occurs first. We would like the program to not execute the two remaining *if-then* statements after it reads in the negative sentinel value. By coincidence, one of the statements causes no problem, because the test

```
Next > Max
```

will fail when `Next` has a negative value; it still would be neater not to execute this statement, however. Moreover, the other statement would cause the value of `Min` to be set to the negative sentinel value, and that is an incorrect value for `Min`. This is a problem because both the *while* and the *repeat* loops execute the complete loop body on each iteration. Obviously, we must make some kind of change in the loop body. One way to proceed is simply to try random rearrangements of the statements in the loop body. For small loops this trial and error method may work, but it is preferable and faster to proceed instead in a systematic way.

To understand our approach to systematically changing the loop body, you must think of the loop in terms of its action and not just in terms of how the loop body is written in Pascal. On a long list of numbers, the loop body we designed would execute the list of statements displayed in Figure 7.8. If you study that list, you will see that there is more than one way of finding repeated patterns of statements. At the opening of

*possible
loop bodies*

```
read(Next);
if Next > Max then
        Max := Next;
if Next < Min then
        Min := Next;
read(Next);
if Next > Max then
        Max := Next;
if Next < Min then
        Min := Next;
read(Next);
if Next > Max then
        Max := Next;
if Next < Min then
        Min := Next;
read(Next);
```

Figure 7.8
Program actions to be expressed as a loop.

this section, we gave one loop body obtained from the pattern observed starting with the first statement in the list. If we ignore the first read statement, however, we see a different pattern that repeats after three statements, namely

```
if Next > Max then
      Max := Next;
if Next < Min then
      Min := Next;
read(Next);
```

If we ignore the first two statements, we see the following repeated pattern:

```
if Next < Min then
      Min := Next;
read(Next);
if Next > Max then
      Max := Next;
```

This gives us three possible loop bodies to choose from. The second one (the one that ends with the read statement) ends where we want it to. If the loop ends after the read, then that last sentinel value will not be compared to either Min or Max. Hence, if we ignore the first read, we obtain a loop that ends properly:

```
while Next > 0 do
   begin{while}
      if Next > Max then
          Max := Next;
      if Next < Min then
          Min := Next;
      read(Next)
   end   {while}
```

This is the correct loop, but the program design is not yet complete. We obtained this loop by ignoring that first read statement in the list of statements we wanted the program to execute. To make the program work correctly, we must include that one statement by placing it before the loop. The complete program, with the first read statement outside the loop body, is shown in Figure 7.9. The next section summarizes the design technique we used in this case study.

Unrolling a Loop

The technique used in the last section is sometimes called *unrolling the loop*. When designing a loop, we can imagine that the list of statements that form the body are written on a ribbon. The list of statements is repeated a number of times to show the statements that will be executed as the loop is iterated, and the ribbon is coiled around a spool. Each revolution of the spool contains one complete loop body. The loop body starts and ends at the place at which the loose end of the ribbon leaves the spool. To change the order of the statements in the loop body, we unroll the spool of ribbon. This process is depicted in Figure 7.10. When we unroll one or more statements, in this case

Program

```
program MinAndMax(input, output);
{Computes the largest and smallest values on
a list of positive integers entered as input.}
var Next, Min, Max: integer;
begin{Program}
  writeln('This program finds the largest and smallest');
  writeln('values on a list of positive integers.');
  writeln('Enter a list of positive integers.');
  writeln('Place a negative number at the end.');

  read(Next);
  Max := Next;
  Min := Next;

  read(Next);
  while Next > 0 do
    begin{while}
      if Next > Max then
          Max := Next;
      if Next < Min then
          Min := Next;
      read(Next)
    end;  {while}

  writeln('The largest is ', Max);
  writeln('The smallest is ', Min)

end.  {Program}
```

Sample Dialogue

```
This program finds the largest and smallest
values on a list of positive integers.
Enter a list of positive integers.
Place a negative number at the end.
3  2  7  5  −1
The largest is     7
The smallest is    2
```

Figure 7.9

Program to compute largest and smallest numbers.

the read statement, we change the list of statements that represents the loop body, and so the statements in the loop body are then in a different order. The statements that are unrolled from the spool are no longer in the loop, but they are still in the program. In the program, they are placed before the loop.

This technique is one way to design loops that we want to have start and stop at different places. We first design the loop to start where we want. After that, we unroll it until the loop body ends where we want it to. In the program, the extra statements that

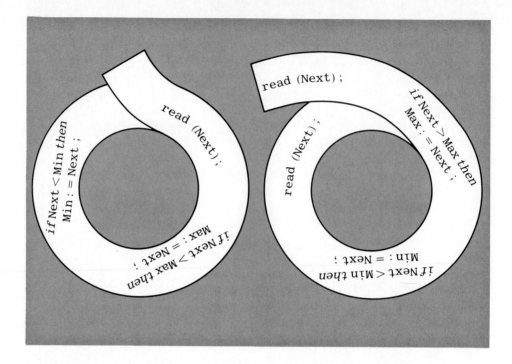

Figure 7.10
Unrolling a loop.

are unrolled are placed before the loop. Hence, the effect of the loop plus these extra statements is equivalent to that of starting and stopping the loop at different places in the loop body.

check the first iteration

There is one problem that can arise when we design a loop by unrolling it. The unrolling technique assumes that the loop statements will be executed at least once. In our example we made the assumption that the list contained at least one number plus the end marker. In this case the assumption was a reasonable one. In other cases it might not be. If it is possible that the loop might not be iterated even once, then you may need to add an additional check, such as embedding a piece of code in an *if-then* statement. With any sort of loop, you should always check to see that the loop body is not repeated one too many times or one too few times.

Designing Robust Programs

A program that aborts or dóes something useless because the user has made a slight typing mistake can be maddening to use. To the extent that it is possible, you should design your programs so that they can cope with minor mistakes on the part of the user. A program should be *robust* enough to perform correctly despite some minor abuse. A program should adapt itself to the user as much as possible, rather than the other way around. Such easy-to-use programs are often referred to as *user friendly,* a pleasant term for a pleasant concept.

For example, if the user is supposed to enter a letter, then the program should

```
procedure ReadCheck(var Amount: integer);
{Reads in a value in the range 0 to 100 from the keyboard.
Allows the user to retry until the value is in the correct range.}
begin{ReadCheck}
  writeln('Enter an amount in the range 0 to 100.');
  readln(Amount);
  while (Amount < 0) or (Amount > 100) do
    begin{Retry}
      writeln('Try again.');
      writeln('Enter an amount in the range 0 to 100.');
      readln(Amount)
    end   {Retry}
end;  {ReadCheck}
```

Figure 7.11
Robust input
procedure.

accept either an uppercase or a lowercase letter. If the letter is used to control a *case* statement, then both upper- and lowercase letters should normally be used on the label lists. If the user is supposed to type in "y" for yes, the program test should read something like the following:

upper- and lower-
case letters
in input

```
if (Ans = 'y') or (Ans = 'Y') then . . .
```

We have already used these techniques in the program in Figure 7.7. If the idea is not clear, you may want to review that program.

Another helpful feature is to echo input and let the user retype the data if it has been entered incorrectly. Sometimes the program can check the data for appropriateness. The procedure in Figure 7.11 reads in an integer and allows the user to retry until it is within the desired range.

retry
input

Invariant Assertions and Variant Expressions
(Optional)

A program with loops can be more complicated and more difficult to understand than the simple programs we examined prior to this chapter. Consequently, you need to document the loops in your programs carefully. In this section we will describe some widely used methods for commenting loops.

Recall that an assertion is a comment that states something that the programmer expects to be true whenever the program execution reaches the assertion. If the program is correct, then the assertion will be true. The only sort of specialized assertions we have had any significant contact with are preconditions and postconditions. As with other programming constructs, loops of any complexity should be documented with preconditions and postconditions. The precondition asserts what is true before the loop is executed, and the postcondition asserts what should be true after the loop is executed.

There is one other kind of assertion that is frequently used to document loops. This type of assertion is called a *loop invariant* or simply an *invariant*. An invariant is an

invariants

assertion that is true before the loop is executed and that remains true after each iteration of the loop. Thus, an invariant is true before the loop is executed, after it is executed, and at certain specific times while the loop is in progress. As a simple example of a loop, consider the following piece of code:

```
N : = 10;
Sum : = 10;
while N > 1 do
   begin{while}
      N : = N − 1;
      Sum : = Sum + N
   end   {while}
```

Since an invariant is an assertion that is true before the loop is executed, it must be true just before the program execution gets to the word *while*. It must also be true after each iteration of the loop; hence, it must be true just before the word *end*. This implies that it is true each time the program reaches the *while* loop. It also implies that it will be true after the *while* loop has ended. One invariant of this loop is the assertion

*$N \geq 1$ and the value of Sum is the sum of
all the integers x such that $N \leq x \leq 10$.*

The assertion is true before the loop is executed, because then the values of Sum and N are both 10. Each iteration of the loop decreases N by one and then increases the value of Sum by the new value of N. Hence, after each iteration the value of Sum is the sum of the integers from the new value of N up to 10. The loop is not iterated unless N has a value greater than one. After each iteration, therefore, we know that $N \geq 1$, as stated in the invariant assertion. The values of N and Sum are changed, but they are changed in such a way that the assertion is true after each loop iteration. This is why it is called an "invariant"; its truth does not vary from one iteration of the loop to the next.

A correct invariant for a loop will be true after each iteration of the loop. However, it may become false at some time during the execution of the loop. In fact, any useful invariant will become false at some time during the execution of the loop. The loop shown in Figure 7.12 has been annotated to indicate when the invariant is true and when it is false. (The comment that starts out "*The variant expression . . .*" will be explained shortly; for the moment you can safely ignore it.)

There is always more than one invariant for a loop. For example, *Sum ≥ 10 and $N \geq 0$* is also an invariant for the loop in Figure 7.12, but a much less informative one. The invariant chosen for documenting the loop should say something informative about what you want the loop to do. A good invariant serves as a bridge between the precondition and the postcondition. It says something about how the precondition is transformed into the postcondition.

As we have described invariants, it sounds as if the precondition must imply the invariant. This is not quite true. Most loops require that certain variables or other items be initialized before the loop is executed. These initialization statements may derive from unrolling the loop or from other considerations. In any event, the initialization statements are conceptually attached to the loop. Hence, the precondition goes before

```
N := 10;
{The value of N is 10.}
Sum := 10;
{N > = 1 and the value of Sum is the sum of
all the integers x such that N < = x < = 10.}
{The variant expression N is decreased until it is
less than or equal to the threshold of one.}
while N > 1 do
    begin{while}                    Invariant
        N := N - 1;                 is false
        Sum := Sum + N
        {N > = 1 and the value of Sum is the sum of      Invariant
        all the integers x such that N < = x < = 10.}    is true
    end {while}
{The value of Sum is the sum of all integers from 1 to 10.}
```

**Figure 7.12
(Optional)
A fully
documented loop.**

the initialization statements. The invariant goes after any initialization statements. For this reason, the invariant need not follow from the precondition alone.

*variant
expression*

One way to see that a loop will eventually end is to find some quantity that is changed in each iteration of the loop until it reaches or passes some given value. An expression for such a quantity that changes each time the loop is executed is called a *variant expression*. The value that the variant expression must reach or pass is called a *threshold*. There are two important properties that the variant expression and threshold must have:

1. There must be some fixed amount such that the value of the variant expression decreases by at least this amount each time the body of the loop is executed.
2. Whenever the value of the variant expression is less than or equal to the threshold, the loop must terminate.

Any loop that has a variant expression and threshold with these properties will eventually terminate. If the value of the expression is below the threshold, the loop terminates right away. In the more typical case, in which the initial value of the variant expression is greater than the threshold, we know that the value will be decreased each time the loop is executed and so will eventually fall below the threshold. We also know that the loop will terminate when that happens. The process is shown diagrammatically in Figure 7.13.

A variant expression for our sample *while* loop is the simple expression N. It is decreased by one on each iteration, and once it is less than or equal to the threshold of one, the loop must terminate.

*increasing to
a threshold*

We chose to define variant expressions and thresholds in terms of a decreasing quantity. It is also possible to think in terms of an increasing quantity. In such cases, the loop terminates when the variant expression is greater than the threshold.

Invariant assertions and variant expressions complement each other very well. One tells what remains constant and the other what changes in a loop. If they are chosen carefully, the postcondition will follow from the invariant assertion and the fact

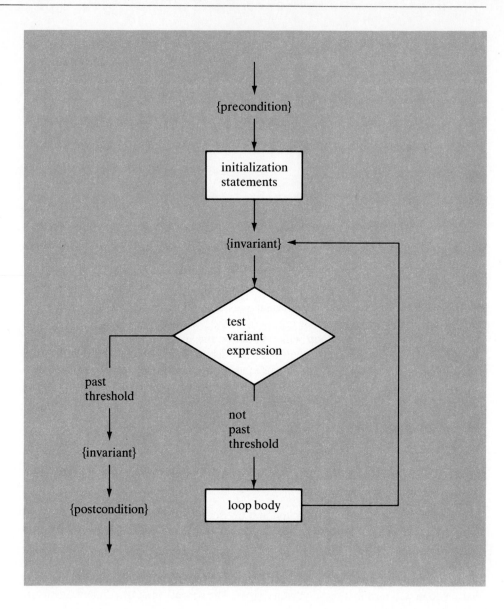

**Figure 7.13
(Optional)
Invariant assertion
and variant
expression.**

that the variant expression has passed the threshold. This means that if these items are chosen carefully, they can be used to demonstrate conclusively that a loop behaves as the programmer claims it does.

*demonstrating
a postcondition*

For example, consider the loop shown in Figure 7.12. The invariant assertion says that the following will be true after each iteration of the loop:

> *{N >= 1 and the value of Sum is the sum of
> all the integers x such that N <= x <= 10.}*

Since it is true after each loop iteration, it must be true when the loop ends, and so N is greater than or equal-to one when the loop ends. Because the *while* statement does not terminate unless N is less than or equal to one, we therefore know that when the loop ends, the variant expression N is both greater than or equal to one and less than or equal to one. This means that the value of N is one. Since N is equal to one and the invariant assertion holds, we see that the postcondition must hold when the loop ends:

The value of Sum is the sum of all integers from 1 to 10.

It may seem that all this documentation is overdoing things a bit. Indeed, the simple loop in Figure 7.12 is buried in comments, some of which can just as well be omitted. Normally, it is sufficient to include the invariant assertion only once, typically at the end of the loop. The precondition stating that the value of N is 10 is obvious and should not be included. We only included it in order to have a complete and simple example. You should have a variant expression and a threshold in mind when writing a loop. However, if they are obvious enough, you need not include them in a comment. For complicated loops all this documentation should be included. For very simple loops, omitting some details can actually aid readability.

For Statements

The *while* and *repeat* statements are the only loop mechanisms that you absolutely need. In fact, the *while* statement alone is enough. However, there is one sort of loop that is so common that Pascal includes a special "tailor-made" loop statement for it. In performing numeric calculations, it is common to perform a calculation with the number 1, then with 2, then with 3, and so forth until some last value is reached. For example, to write out the multiplication table for the number 2, we want the computer to perform the following:

```
writeln('2 times ', I, ' is ', 2*I)
```

first with I equal to 1, then with I equal to 2, and so forth up to, say, 9. One way to do this is with a *while* statement, such as

```
I := 1;
while I <= 9 do
  begin
    writeln('2 times ', I, ' is ', 2*I);
    I := I + 1
  end
```

Although a *while* loop will do here, this sort of situation is just what the *for statement* was designed for. The above piece of code will produce the same output as the following *for* statement:

```
for I := 1 to 9 do
    writeln('2 times ', I, ' is ', 2*I)
```

syntax   *for* statements come in two very similar varieties. The above example is of the first variety whose general form is

> *for* <control variable> : = <initial exp> *to* <final exp> *do*
> <body>

control   The <body> may be any single Pascal statement. In particular, it can be a compound
variable   statement. For now, we will insist that the *control variable* be a variable of type integer. Therefore, the loop control variable must be declared to be of type in-
teger. Eventually we will see how to use other types for the control variable, but the
idea is clearest in the case of integer variables. The expressions <initial exp> and
<final exp> must evaluate to values of type integer. Their values are called the
initial value and *final value,* respectively, of the loop control variable. Typically, we
want the initial value to be less than the final value, but this is not required. Typically,
<body> includes some reference to the <control variable>, but this also is not
required.

behavior   When the *for* loop is executed, the expressions <initial exp> and <final exp>
of for   are evaluated to obtain the initial and final values for the loop control variable. After
loops   that, <body> is executed, first with <control variable> equal to the initial value, then
with <control variable> equal to the initial value plus 1, then with <control vari-
able> equal to the initial value plus 2, and so on, increasing the value of <control
variable> by one each time. The last time through the loop, <body> is executed with
<control variable> equal to the value that was obtained from the expression <final
exp>. This behavior is diagrammed in Figure 7.14.

A *for* loop need not start with the number one. For example, the following will
give the two multiplication table for all values from −9 up to +9:

```
for I := −9 to 9 do
    writeln('2 times ', I, ' is ', 2*I)
```

The loop control variable is automatically increased by one each time through.
There is no need to include anything like the following in the body of the loop:

```
I := I + 1
```

In fact, it is an error to do so. The body of a *for* loop is not allowed to change the loop
control variable in any way. If it does, the effect of the *for* loop is unpredictable. The
body can use the value of the control variable, but it cannot change it.

restrictions   A loop control variable is intended to be used to control the *for* loop and nothing
on loop   else. The value it has before the *for* loop is executed is irrelevant to the *for* loop.
control   When the *for* loop is completed, the value of the loop control variable is undefined,
variables   which means that its value is unpredictable. It should not be reused unless it is first
reinitialized. (Reusing it as a loop control variable requires no extra initialization,
since the *for* loop itself includes an initialization.) For these reasons, it is natural to
make the loop control variable a local variable. Moreover, in Pascal it is required to be
a local variable. If a *for* loop appears in a procedure, then the loop control variable
must be declared in that procedure.

It is natural to wonder what happens when the value of <initial exp> is greater
than that of <final exp>. In Pascal, when this happens the loop body is not executed at

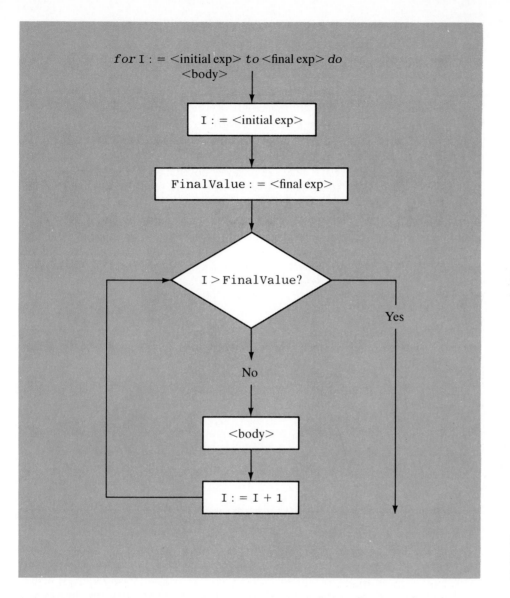

$for\ I := $ <initial exp> to <final exp> do
          <body>

I := <initial exp>

FinalValue := <final exp>

I > FinalValue?

Yes

No

<body>

I := I + 1

Figure 7.14
Behavior of one
type of _for_ loop.

all and the program goes on to the next statement. This means that in Pascal it is impossible to write a _for_ loop that is an infinite loop.

The body of a _for_ statement cannot change the number of times it is iterated by changing the value of <final exp>. The technical explanation of what happens is as follows: Both <initial exp> and <final exp> are evaluated once at the start of the loop, and these two values are used to control the loop.

One cultural point that is of some significance to the design of readable programs has to do with names of _for_ loop control variables. Most of our _for_ loops use I and J as loop control variables. For historical reasons, it has become customary to use I,

J, and K as loop control variables. The letters carry no mnemonic value, but the custom is so well ingrained that it is pointless to fight it. When you see these letters in programs, they will very likely be loop control variables, and this convention can be a slight aid in reading the programs. Of course, if you can come up with good mnemonic names of *for* loop control variables, that is even better.

downto

The second version of the *for* statement is very similar to the first. The only difference in syntax is that *to* is replaced by *downto*. The difference in what happens when it is executed is that with the *downto* version, the loop control variable is decreased by one each time through. In this case, the value of <initial exp> is typically greater than or equal to that of <final exp>; if it is not, the body is not executed at all, and the program proceeds to the next statement. The word *downto* is a single identifier and should not be written as two words.

other
increment
sizes

In Pascal a *for* loop control variable is always changed by either plus one or minus one. Other programming languages allow it to change by any specified amount. At first this looks like a real limitation in Pascal, but it is easy to program around this limitation. To output the even numbers 0, 2, 4, 6, 8, and 10, the following trick works:

```
for I := 0 to 5 do
    write(2*I)
```

This same sort of trick can be used to get the equivalent of increments of fractional size as well. To see the effect of small changes in interest rates, one might use a *for* loop such as the following:

```
for J := 10 to 200 do
    begin{for loop body}
        Rate := 0.001*J;
        Interest := Amount * Rate;
        writeln('a rate of ', Rate*100, ' percent,');
        writeln('yields ', Interest, ' in interest')
    end {for loop body}
```

Example—Summing a Series

Figure 7.15 consists of a complete program that includes a *for* loop. The program computes the average number of times you need to flip a coin in order to get the coin to come up heads. The program uses the following formula to approximate the average:

$$\frac{1}{2} + \frac{2}{2^2} + \frac{3}{2^3} + \cdots \frac{N}{2^N}$$

We need not concern ourselves with how the formula is derived. We will simply assume that it works. Like many such formulas, it yields an approximation to the desired value rather than the exact value. The larger the value of N, the better the approximation of the true value of this average. A value of 100 for N is more than large enough to give as much accuracy as most computers are capable of delivering, and so the program uses the formula with N set equal to 100.

```
program CoinToss(input, output);
{Computes the expected number of coin tosses needed
to obtain a head when flipping a balanced coin.}
const NumberOfTerms = 100;
var I: integer;
    Sum, Power: real;
begin{CoinToss}
  Sum := 0;
  Power := 1;
  for I := 1 to NumberOfTerms do
    begin{for}
      Power := Power * 2;
      Sum := Sum + I/Power
      {Sum is the sum of all numbers of the form:
      x/(2 to the power x) where 1 <= x <= I.
      Power is 2 to the power I.}
    end; {for}
  writeln('On the average it will take ', Sum);
  writeln('tosses of a balanced coin');
  writeln('to get heads the first time.')
end. {CoinToss}
```

Figure 7.15
Summing a series.

Notice that Sum is initialized to zero, whereas Power is initialized to one. This is
because Sum will contain a sum of numbers, while Power will contain a product of
numbers. One way to test that these are the correct initial values is to check to see that
they make the loop assertion true after one iteration of the loop.

*sums
versus
products*

Also notice that Power is declared to be of type `real`, even though its value is
conceptually an integer. The reason for this is that the value of Power becomes extremely large, and on most systems would produce integer overflow, that is, its value
would become larger than `maxint`. Since computers can store much larger `real`
values than they can `integer` values, the change to type `real` overcomes this problem. When performing numeric calculations with `for` loops, you may encounter this
often. We will have more to say about this problem in Chapter 15.

Repeat N Times

One often encounters a section of pseudocode similar to the following:

```
repeat the following loop body N times
  begin{loop body}
    read(Number);
    Sum := Sum + Number
  end {loop body}
```

Some programming languages have a loop construct that corresponds exactly to this type of loop. Pascal does not, but it is easy to construct the equivalent of "repeat the loop body N times." Our first example of a program with a loop, shown in Figure 7.3, illustrates one way to do this with a *while* loop, but the easiest way to implement it is with a *for* loop:

```
for I := 1 to N do
   begin{for}
      read(Number);
      Sum := Sum + Number
   end   {for}
```

At first this may seem strange, since the loop control variable (in this case I) does not appear in the loop body. There is nothing wrong with that. It is perfectly legitimate to use this variable for nothing other than counting the number of loop iterations.

Invariant Assertions and For Loops
(Optional)

for loops do not lend themselves to documentation with invariants as easily as *repeat* and *while* loops do. This is because the natural statement of an invariant for a *for* loop usually includes a reference to the loop control variable. This presents a problem, since the loop control variable of a *for* loop is frequently undefined or irrelevant before the loop is executed and is always undefined after the loop is executed. The problem is more of a notational one than a conceptual one. When you are designing a *for* loop, it makes sense to think in terms of invariants. However, when you are actually writing the *for* loop comments, it is usually easier and clearer to use some close approximation to an invariant. If the *for* loop body is a compound statement, one possible solution is to include an assertion within that compound statement. Since the loop control variable is well defined within the body, that assertion can refer to the loop control variable in a clearly meaningful way.

There is no need to design variant expressions and thresholds for *for* loops, because a *for* loop already has a built-in variant expression and a built-in threshold. The variant expression is the loop control variable, and the threshold is its final value.

What Kind of Loop to Use

When you are designing a loop, the choice of which type of Pascal statement to use is best postponed to the end of the design process. First, design the loop using pseudocode, and then translate the pseudocode into Pascal code. At that point it is easy to decide what type of Pascal loop statement to use.

If the loop involves a numeric calculation that is repeated a fixed number of times using a value that is changed by equal amounts each time through the loop, then use a *for* loop. In fact, any time you have a loop for a numeric calculation, you should consider using a *for* loop. It will not always be possible, but in many cases involving numeric calculations it is the clearest and easiest loop to use. A *for* loop is also the easiest way to construct the equivalent of an instruction that says "repeat the loop body N times."

In all other cases, you must use a *repeat* loop or a *while* loop. It is fairly easy to decide which one to use. If you want to insist that the loop body be executed at least once, then you can use a *repeat* loop. If there are circumstances under which the loop body should not be executed at all, then you cannot use a *repeat* loop and so must use a *while* loop. A common situation that demands a *while* loop is one in which there is a possibility of no data at all. For example, a program that reads in a list of exam scores may run across students who have taken no exams, and hence the input loop may be faced with an empty list. This calls for a *while* loop.

Nested Loops

Figure 7.16 contains a program that writes out the multiplication table. The *for* loop in the main body of the program writes out one line for each value of N from 0 to 9 using the procedure call PrintRow (N). This procedure call writes out the number N to label the row and then writes the table entries for N times the numbers 0 to 9.

The body of a loop may contain any kind of statement, and so it is possible to have loops nested within loops. The program in Figure 7.16 contains a loop within a loop. Normally, we do not think of it as containing a nested loop, because the inner loop is contained within a procedure and it is the procedure call that is contained in the outer loop. There is a lesson to be learned from these unobtrusively nested loops, namely that nested loops are no different from any other loops. The program in Figure 7.17 is rewritten with the nested loop explicitly displayed. The nested loop in Figure 7.17 is iterated once for each value of N from 0 to 9. For each such iteration, there is one complete execution of the inner *for* loop.

The two versions of our multiplication table program are equivalent, but many people find the version in Figure 7.16 easier to understand because the loop body is a procedure. This is an example of procedural abstraction. When considering the outer loop, one thinks of printing a row as a single operation and not as a loop. When writing or reading explicitly displayed nested loops like the one in Figure 7.17, one should think of the loop body as a unit in this way whether or not it is packaged into a procedure.

procedural abstraction

Debugging Loops

No matter how carefully a program is designed, mistakes will still sometimes occur. In the case of loops, there is a pattern to the kinds of mistakes most often made. Most loop errors involve the first or last iteration of the loop. If you find that your loop does not perform as expected, check to see if the loop is iterated one too many or one too few times. Iterating the loop one too many or one too few times is one of the most common loop bugs. Be sure that you are not confusing "less than" with "less than or equal to." Be sure that you have initialized the loop correctly. Check the possibility that

common errors

off-by-one errors

Program

```
program TimesTable(input, output);
{Writes out the multiplication table.}
const Width = 4;{Space to hold one number entry in table.}
var N: integer;

procedure PrintTop;
{Prints a heading for the multiplication table
and a line of digits from 0 to 9.}
var I: integer;
begin{PrintTop}
  writeln('The Multiplication Table' :30);
  write('*': Width);
  for I := 0 to 9 do
      write(I:Width);
  writeln
end; {PrintTop}

procedure PrintRow(N: integer);
{Writes out N followed by N*0, N*1, N*2, . . . , N*9}
var M: integer;
begin{PrintRow}
  write(N:Width);  {Specifies first factor}
  for M := 0 to 9 do
      write(N * M:Width);
  writeln
end; {PrintRow}

begin{Program}
  PrintTop;
  for N := 0 to 9 do
      PrintRow(N)
end. {Program}
```

Output

```
        The Multiplication Table
  *   0   1   2   3   4   5   6   7   8   9
  0   0   0   0   0   0   0   0   0   0   0
  1   0   1   2   3   4   5   6   7   8   9
  2   0   2   4   6   8  10  12  14  16  18
  3   0   3   6   9  12  15  18  21  24  27
  4   0   4   8  12  16  20  24  28  32  36
  5   0   5  10  15  20  25  30  35  40  45
  6   0   6  12  18  24  30  36  42  48  54
  7   0   7  14  21  28  35  42  49  56  63
  8   0   8  16  24  32  40  48  56  64  72
  9   0   9  18  27  36  45  54  63  72  81
```

Figure 7.16
Times table
program, one
version.

```
program TimesTable(input, output);
{Writes out the multiplication table.}
const Width = 4; {Space to hold one number entry in table.}
var N, M: integer;

procedure PrintTop;
{Prints a heading for the multiplication table and a line of digits from 0 to 9.}
var I: integer;
begin{PrintTop}
   writeln('The Multiplication Table' :30);
   write('*': Width);
   for I := 0 to 9 do
       write(I:Width);
   writeln
end; {PrintTop}

begin{Program}
   PrintTop;
   for N := 0 to 9 do
     begin{Row}
     {Writes out N followed by N*0, N*1, N*2, . . . , N*9}
       write(N:Width); {Specifies first factor.}
       for M := 0 to 9 do
           write(N * M :Width);
       writeln
     end {Row}
end. {Program}
```

Figure 7.17
Nested *for* loops.

the loop may sometimes need to be iterated zero times, and make sure that your loop handles that possibility correctly.

Infinite loops usually result from a mistake in the boolean expression of a *repeat* or *while* loop. Check to see that you have not reversed an inequality, confusing "less than" with "greater than." Terminating a loop with a test for equality rather than with one involving a greater than or less than comparison is another common source of infinite loops. *infinite loops*

If you check and recheck your loop and can find no error, but the program still misbehaves, then you will need to do some more sophisticated testing. First of all, make sure that the mistake is indeed in the loop. Just because the program is performing incorrectly does not mean the bug is where you think it is. If your program was designed to be modular and is divided into procedures, then it should be easy to find the approximate location of the bug or bugs. Once you have decided that the bug is in a particular loop, you should trace the key variables in the loop.

Tracing was introduced in Chapter 3. It consists of adding some extra `write` statements to output intermediate results, so that you can watch the program working. For example, consider the following piece of code: *tracing*

```
N := 10;
Sum := 10;
while N > 1 do
    begin{while}
        Sum := Sum + N;
        N := N - 1
        {The value of Sum is the sum of all the integers y such that: N <= y <= 10.}
    end;  {while}
    { The value of Sum is the sum of all integers from 1 to 10.}
```

The last comment explains what the value of Sum is supposed to be. If you run this code, you will find that it does not set Sum to that value. The value of Sum will be larger than it is supposed to be. The loop can be tested by tracing the variable Sum— that is, by writing out its value after each iteration of the loop. Suitable writeln statements to do the job are shown in Figure 7.18.

If you embed the loop containing the trace statement in a program and run it, the source of the error will immediately become apparent. The first two values of Sum will be 10 and 20, but the value of Sum after one iteration of the loop should be 10 + 9 or 19, rather than 20. Thus, we can immediately see that the value of N is the source of the problem. After we discover this, it is easy to see that N should be added into Sum after it is decremented, rather than before. In other words, the correct order for the statements in the loop body is

```
N := N - 1;
Sum := Sum + N
```

Before leaving this example, we should comment on some peculiarities of the trace statements in Figure 7.18. First of all, the trace statements in the figure seem to have semicolons in strange places. This is not necessary, but it is a good idea. If we precede each trace statement with a semicolon, then we know that it will be separated from the previous statement by a semicolon. The writeln that was inserted just before the *end* needs the semicolons. The semicolons preceding the other trace state-

Figure 7.18
Tracing a loop.

```
N := 10;
Sum := 10;
{TEMP}; writeln('N = ', N, ' Sum = ', Sum);
{TEMP}; writeln('Before loop');
    while N > 1 do
        begin{while}
            Sum := Sum + N;
            N := N - 1
            {The value of Sum is the sum of all the integers y such that: N <= y <= 10.}
        {TEMP}; writeln('N = ', N, ' Sum = ', Sum);
        end;  {while}
{TEMP}; writeln('After loop');
{TEMP}; writeln('N = ', N, ' Sum = ', Sum);
    {The value of Sum is the sum of all integers from 1 to 10.}
```

ments do no harm. This saves us from the worry of having to fix up semicolons. It looks strange, but remember that the trace statements are only temporary. They and the extra semicolons will not appear in the final program.

It also may seem that the trace statements that precede and follow the loop are not needed. In this case they were not, but remember that you are using trace statements because you do not know where the error is. It is dangerous to leave any possibility unchecked. A good practice is to place one trace statement before the loop, one after the loop, and one or more inside the body of the loop, even if some of these traces are "clearly" redundant.

The idea of tracing the loop through each iteration will work fine on a loop that is iterated 10 times, but a loop that is iterated 1000 times is likely to produce too much information to digest. For example, the following will produce nothing but a blur of light on a video display screen:

long loops

```
for K := 0 to 1000 do
     begin
        Sum := Sum + K
{TEMP}; writeln(K, Sum);
     end
```

A better approach is to take a smaller sample. One way of doing this is as follows:

```
for K := 0 to 1000 do
     begin
        Sum := Sum + K
{TEMP}; if (K mod 100) = 0 then writeln(K, Sum);
     end
```

This will output a trace statement every time K is a multiple of 100. There is a possibility, however, that such a uniform sampling technique will fail to detect certain kinds of periodic problems. If a trace like the one above yields no insights, try a different sampling technique, such as using

```
(K mod 100) = 1
```

This will also sample every one hundredth iteration, but the value of K will not be a "round" number. If that fails, change 100 to some other number.

Case Study

Calendar Display

Problem Definition

We wish to design a procedure that outputs the traditional calendar display of a month. To simplify the problem, we will assume that the user tells the program how many days there are in the month and on what day of the week the month starts. The day of the week will be input as an integer: 0 for Sunday, 1 for Monday, 2 for Tuesday, and so forth. For example, the input values 30 (for the number of days) and 3 (for Wednesday) should produce the following output:

Sun	Mon	Tue	Wed	Thu	Fri	Sat
			1	2	3	4
5	6	7	8	9	10	11
12	13	14	15	16	17	18
19	20	21	22	23	24	25
26	27	28	29	30		

Discussion

One approach to this problem is the following outline of an algorithm:

Output a heading with the names Sun, Mon, Tues, etc.
Output blanks up to the first day of the month.
Output the rest of the first week.
For each remaining week do the following:
    begin{week}
      write the numbers for the week;
      writeln;
    end {week}

A straightforward refinement of the above algorithm would produce the following pseudocode:

Output a heading with the names Sun, Mon, Tues, etc.
for I := 0 *to* (FirstDay − 1) *do*
  write a blank;
for I := 1 *to* (7 − FirstDay) *do*
    write(I);
writeln;
DayNumber := 7 − FirstDay;
repeat
    for I := 0 *to* 6 *do*
        write(DayNumber + I);
    writeln;
    DayNumber := DayNumber + 7
until DayNumber > (the number of days in the month)

false
starts
Having started to write code for our program, we can observe a number of things wrong with our approach. First of all, the pseudocode does not work. The second 7 should be an 8, or else one number will be output twice. Fixing that will make the code look strange but will eliminate one problem. However, even after that "patch," the output will not be correct. Unless the last week happens to end on a Saturday, that week will be output incorrectly. Another "patch" can make it work, but that will make the code even more complicated and even less understandable. The real problems are that the code is unclear and is too complicated for the task it is accomplishing. In a situation like this, it is best to try starting over.

Let us look at the task in a different way: All we want the program to do is to output the numbers 1 through the number of the last day and to insert writelns at the end of each week. The first of these tasks is trivial:

rethinking the problem

```
for DayCount := 1 to (the number of the last day) do
    write(DayCount)
```

To accomplish the second task, we can add a test for the end of the week inside of the *for* loop:

```
for DayCount := 1 to (the number of the last day) do
    begin{for}
        write(DayCount);
        if "end of a week" then
            writeln
    end {for}
```

To complete our second (and successful) attempt at designing our program, we need only design a test for the end of a week. A first, careless guess might be

```
if DayCount mod 7 = 0 then
    writeln
```

This will work provided the month starts on a Sunday, but again look back at our sample of what we want for output. The first week of that month starts on a Wednesday, and so it should have a writeln after the first four days. If started on a Wednesday, the above test will produce output that begins

Sun	Mon	Tue	Wed	Thu	Fri	Sat			
			1	2	3	4	5	6	7
8	9	10	11	12	13	14			

To determine when the writeln should be executed, the program must count the blanks. To do this we will use another variable called CountAll that starts counting on Sunday even if the month starts on some other day. The correct pseudocode is as follows:

ALGORITHM

```
Output a heading with the names Sun, Mon, Tues, etc.
Output the initial blanks.
CountAll := FirstDay; {for the initial blanks.}
for DayCount := 1 to (the number of the last day) do
    begin{for}
        CountAll := CountAll + 1;
        {If (CountAll mod 7) = 0, then day number DayCount is a Saturday.}
        write(DayCount);
        if (CountAll mod 7) = 0 then
            writeln;
    end; {for}
writeln
```

The complete procedure, embedded in a test program, is shown in Figure 7.19.

Program

```
program Calendar(input, output);
{Displays the calendar layout of any month.}
var FirstDay, NumberOfDays: integer;
    Ans: char;

procedure DisplayMonth(NumberOfDays, FirstDay: integer);
{Displays the usual layout for a month with NumberOfDays days in it.
FirstDay codes the first day of the month: 0 for Sunday, 1 for Monday, etc.}
const Width = 4; {Field width for one day of the calendar.}
      Blank = ' ';
var DayCount, CountAll: integer;
begin{DisplayMonth}
  writeln('Sun':Width, 'Mon':Width, 'Tue':Width,
          'Wed':Width, 'Thu':Width, 'Fri':Width, 'Sat':Width);
  for CountAll := 0 to FirstDay - 1 do
      write(Blank :Width);
  CountAll := FirstDay;{for the initial blanks.}
  for DayCount := 1 to NumberOfDays do
    begin{for}
      CountAll := CountAll + 1;
      {If (CountAll mod 7) = 0, then day number DayCount is a Saturday.}
      write(DayCount :Width);
      if (CountAll mod 7) = 0 then
          writeln;
    end; {for}
  writeln
end; {DisplayMonth}

begin{Program}
  writeln('I will display the calendar of a month.');
  repeat
    writeln('Enter the number of days in the month: ');
    readln(NumberOfDays);
    writeln('Enter the first day of month, 0 for Sunday,');
    writeln('1 for Monday, 2 for Tuesday, and so on.');
    readln(FirstDay);
    DisplayMonth(NumberOfDays, FirstDay);
    writeln('Do you want to see another month?');
    writeln('(yes or no):');
    readln(Ans)
  until (Ans = 'N') or (Ans = 'n');
  writeln('Have a good month!')
end. {Program}
```

Figure 7.19
Calendar program.

Sample Dialogue

```
I will display the calendar of a month.
Enter the number of days in the month:
31
Enter the first day of month, 0 for Sunday,
1 for Monday, 2 for Tuesday, and so on.
2
Sun    Mon    Tue    Wed    Thu    Fri    Sat
                1      2      3      4      5
  6      7      8      9     10     11     12
 13     14     15     16     17     18     19
 20     21     22     23     24     25     26
 27     28     29     30     31
Do you want to see another month?
(yes or no):
no
Have a good month!
```

Figure 7.19

(continued)

Starting Over

The previous case study illustrates an important engineering design principle. If a program or algorithm is very difficult to understand or performs very poorly, do not try to fix it; instead, throw it away and start over. This will result in a program that is clearer to read and that is less likely to contain hidden errors. What may not be so obvious is that by throwing out the poorly designed code and starting over, you will produce a working program faster than if you tried to repair the old code (or old pseudocode). It may seem like wasted effort to throw out the code that you worked so hard on, but that is the most efficient way to proceed. The work that went into the discarded code is not wasted. The lessons you learned by writing it will help you to design a better program and to do so faster than if you started with no experience. The code itself is unlikely to help at all.

> I beheld the wretch—the miserable monster whom I had created.
>> *Mary Wollstonecraft Shelley, Frankenstein*

> Care is no cure, but rather corrosive,
> For things that are not to be remedied.
>> *William Shakespeare, King Henry VI, Part I*

> Plan to throw one away; you will, anyhow.
>> *F. P. Brooks, Jr., The Mythical Man-Month*

Summary of Problem Solving and Programming Techniques

- There are four commonly used methods for terminating an input loop: ask before iterating, list headed by size, list ended with a sentinel value, and running out of input. (The last one can be dangerous if not handled correctly.)
- Using the boolean `eoln` is one good way to end a loop by "running out of input."
- One way to design an algorithm is to modify a known algorithm that solves a related problem.
- It is usually best to design loops using pseudocode that does not specify a choice of Pascal looping mechanism. Once the algorithm has been designed, the choice of which Pascal loop statement to use is usually clear.
- The technique of unrolling a loop can be used to redesign loops to get the effect of ending partway through the loop body.
- A *repeat* loop should not be used unless you are certain that the loop should always be iterated at least once.
- A *for* loop can be used to obtain the equivalent of the instruction "repeat the loop body N times."
- One way to simplify reasoning about nested loops is to make the loop body a procedure.
- Programs should be designed to be robust enough to perform adequately even if the user makes a slight mistake in entering input.
- Always check loops to be sure that the variables used by the loop are properly initialized before the loop begins.
- Never terminate a loop with a test of `real` values for equality. Tests for equality are dangerous with other types as well.
- Always check loops to be certain they are not iterated one too many times or one too few times.
- When debugging loops, always check the first and last iteration of the loop body.
- When you are debugging loops, it helps to trace key variables in the loop body.
- If a program or algorithm is very difficult to understand or performs very poorly, do not try to fix it. Instead, throw it away and start over.

Summary of Pascal Constructs

while statement

Syntax:

```
while <boolean expression> do
      <body>
```

Example:

```
while (X < 0) and (Y < 3) do
  begin
    X := X + 1;
    Y := Y + 1
  end
```

The <body> can be any Pascal statement. When the *while* statement is executed, the <boolean expression> is first evaluated. If it evaluates to true, then the <body> is executed. If the <boolean expression> instead evaluates to false, then nothing more happens. This process is repeated again and again. Each time the <boolean expression> evaluates to true, the <body> is executed. The first time it evaluates to false, the *while* statement terminates and the program goes on to the next item.

repeat statement

Syntax:

```
repeat
  <statement 1>;
  <statement 2>;
         .
         .
         .
  <statement n>
until <boolean expression>
```

Example:

```
repeat
  Sum := Sum + Next;
  read(Next)
until Next <= 0
```

When the *repeat* statement is executed, the statements are executed in order and then the <boolean expression> is evaluated. If it evaluates to true, the *repeat* statement is over, and the program goes on to the next thing. If the <boolean expression> evaluates to false, then the statements are repeated again. The list of statements is repeated again and again until the <boolean expression> evaluates to true. At that point the *repeat* statement is complete, and the program goes on to the next item.

eoln

Syntax:

```
eoln
```

Example:

```
repeat
  read(Next);
  Sum := Sum + Next
until eoln
```

The end-of-line boolean. Its value becomes true after the program reads the last value on a line, using a read statement. Executing a readln statement resets it to false (provided there is some input data on the next line). See the explanation of *end-of-line character* in the chapter text for a more precise description of eoln.

for statement (basic form)

Syntax:

```
for <control variable> := <initial exp> to <final exp> do
                       <body>
```

Example:

```
for J := 20 to 500 do
  begin
    Sum := Sum + J;
    writeln(Sum)
  end
```

<control variable> must be a variable of type integer. (Other types are possible and will be discussed in Chapter 8.) Both <initial exp> and <final exp> must be expressions that evaluate to the same type as the <control variable>. The <body> may be any Pascal statement. When the *for* statement is executed, <initial exp> and <final exp> are first evaluated. If the value of <final exp> is less than that of <initial exp>, then the *for* statement terminates without doing anything else. If the value of <initial exp> is less than or equal to the value of <final exp>, the <body> is executed with the value of <control variable> set equal to the value of <initial exp>, and then executed with the value of <control variable> increased by one, and then by one more, and so forth. The last time <body> is executed, the value of <control variable> is equal to the value obtained when <final exp> was evaluated. The <control variable> may not be changed by the <body>; if it is, the effect is unpredictable.

for statement (downto form)

Syntax:

```
for <control variable> := <initial exp> downto <final exp> do
                       <body>
```

Example:

```
for J := 500 downto 20 do
  begin
    Sum := Sum + J;
    writeln(Sum)
  end
```

Similar to the previous kind of *for* statement, except that in this kind of statement, the <control variable> is decreased by one on each iteration of the loop. If the value of <final exp> is greater than that of <initial exp>, then the *for* statement terminates without doing anything.

Exercises

Self-Test Exercises

9. What is the output of the following program fragment (when embedded in a complete program)?

```
for I := -3 to 11 do
   write(2 * I)
```

10. What is the output of the following program fragment (when embedded in a complete program)?

```
for I := 10 downto 1 do
   write(I)
```

11. Write a program that outputs all the even numbers between 1 and 25.

12. What is the output of the following program fragment (when embedded in a complete program)?

```
Limit := 3;
for I := 1 to Limit do
    begin
       writeln(I, Limit);
       Limit := 2
    end
```

13. Predict the output of the following nested *for* loop:

```
for J := 10 downto 1 do
  for I := 1 to 10 do
     writeln(I, ' times ', J, ' equals ', I * J)
```

14. For each of the following situations, tell which type of loop (*while, repeat,* or *for*) would work best:

a. Summing a series with a specific number of terms.
b. Reading in the list of exam scores for one student in a class.
c. Reading in the number of days of sick leave taken by employees in a department. The input consists of a list of numbers giving the number of days missed by each employee who took sick leave.
d. Testing a procedure with different values of the parameters.

Interactive Exercises

15. Replace the *while* loop in Figure 7.3 with the "almost equivalent" *repeat* loop introduced in the section entitled "The Repeat Statement," and then run the modified program. Since the *repeat* loop is not completely equivalent to the *while* loop, the program will not perform correctly on an empty list. Try running the program on both nonempty and empty lists of numbers. (For the empty list, think of the program as adding the list of sales commissions earned by a lazy salesman for a month in which he only went fishing and never saw a customer.)

16. Embed the nested loop from Exercise 13 in a program and run the program. Try changing the various numbers and running the program again. In each case, predict the output before running the program.

17. Modify any one of the programming exercises you did for Chapter 6 by adding a loop so that the calculation can be repeated again and again with new input as long as the user desires. Do this once with a *repeat* loop. Do it again with a *while* loop, and this time allow the user to change his or her mind and not perform the calculation even once.

Programming Exercises

18. Write a program to read in a list of test scores and output the highest score, the lowest score, and the average score. Most of the solution can be found in Figures 7.5 and 7.9.

19. Write a program to list the numbers from 0 to 25, their squares, square roots, fourth power, and fourth root. The output should be in a neat five-column format.

20. Write a program that reads in a number n and then outputs the sum of the squares of the numbers from 1 to n. If the input is 3, for example, the output should be 14, because

$$1^2 + 2^2 + 3^2 = 1 + 4 + 9 = 14$$

The program should allow the user to repeat this calculation as often as desired.

21. Write a program to determine the largest value of n such that your computer can compute $n!$ without integer overflow. $n!$ is the product of all positive numbers that are less than or equal to n. For example, $3! = 1 \times 2 \times 3 = 6$. By convention, $0!$ is set equal to 1.

22. Write a program that takes one *real* value as input and computes the first integer n such that 2^n is greater than or equal to the input value. The program should output both n and 2^n.

23. Write a program that outputs the balance of an account after each succeeding year. The input is the initial balance, the interest rate, the first year, and the last year. Assume that the deposit is made on January first and that the interest for the past year is calculated and paid once each year on January first. Next, modify the program so that it shows three different balances for three different ways of calculating the interest: simple interest, interest compounded semiannually, and interest compounded quarterly.

24. Modify the program in the previous exercise (or do it from scratch) so that interest is compounded monthly (and not any other way, such as semiannually) and so that the output shows the interest at the end of each month. You should insert a `readln` with no arguments to stop the output at the end of each year. When the user hits the return key, the figures for the following year are displayed. If this were not done, the user would not have time to read the output. After that, enhance the program so that the calculation can be made as often as desired with different inputs.

25. Interest on a loan is paid on a declining balance, and hence a loan with an interest rate of, say, 14% can cost significantly less than 14% of the balance. Write a program that takes a loan amount and interest rate as input and then outputs the monthly payments and balance of the loan until the loan is paid off. Assume that the monthly payments are one-twentieth of the original loan amount and that any amount in excess of the interest is credited toward decreasing the balance due. Thus, on a loan of $20,000, the payments would be $1000 a month. If the interest rate is 10%, then each month the interest is one-twelfth of 10% of the remaining balance. The first month (10% of $20,000)/12 or $166.67 would be paid in interest, and the remaining $833.33 would decrease the balance to $19,166.67. The following month the interest would be (10% of $19,166.67)/12, and so forth. Also have the program output the total interest paid over the life of the loan. Finally, determine what simple annualized percentage of the original loan balance was paid in interest. For example, if $1,000 was paid in interest on a $10,000 loan and it took two years to pay off, then the annualized interest is $500, which is 5% of the $10,000 loan amount.

26. Write a program to reads in a `real` number x and output the integer n closest to the cube root of x. Assume that x is always nonnegative.

27. A *perfect number* is a positive integer that is equal to the sum of all those positive integers (excluding itself) that divide it evenly. The first perfect number is 6, because its divisors (excluding itself) are 1, 2, and 3, and because $6 = 1 + 2 + 3$. Write a program to find the first three perfect numbers (include 6 as one of the three).

28. The Fibonacci numbers F_n are defined as follows: F_1 is 1, F_2 is 1, and $F_{i+2} = F_i + F_{i+1}$, for i = 1, 2, . . . In other words, each number is the sum of the previous two numbers. The first few Fibonacci numbers are 1, 1, 2, 3, 5, 8. One place that these numbers occur is as certain population growth rates. If a population has no deaths, then the series shows the increase in population after each generation. A generation is the time it takes a member to reach reproducing age. The formula applies most straightforwardly to asexual reproduction at a rate of one offspring per parent per generation. In any event, the green crud population grows at that rate and produces one generation every five days. Hence, if a green crud population starts out as 10 pounds of crud, then in 5 days there is still 10 pounds of crud; in 10 days there is 20 pounds of crud, in 15 days there is 30 pounds, in 20 days there is 50 pounds, and so forth. Write a program that takes as input the initial size of a green crud population (in pounds) and a number of days and then outputs the number of pounds of green crud after that many days. Assume that the population size remains the same for four days and then increases on the fifth day.

29. Write a program to find all integer solutions to the equation

$$4x + 3y - 9z = 5$$

for values of x, y, and z between 0 and 100.

30. Write a program that reads in and evaluates expressions such as

$$+15+90-100-7+36\text{end}$$

The expression is a sequence of integers, each preceded by a sign. The expression is terminated with the word *end*. There are no blanks in the expression.

31. The value e^x can be approximated by the sum

$$1 + x + x^2/2! + x^3/3! + \cdots + x^n/n!$$

Write a program that takes a value x as input and outputs this sum for n taken to be each of the values 1 to 100. The program should repeat the calculation for new values of x until the user says he or she is through. Use variables of type `real` to store the factorials, or you are likely to produce integer overflow.

32. Write a procedure that fills one variable parameter of type `integer` with a value read from the keyboard. The procedure will read the input as a string of characters and will check and recover from input typing mistakes as follows: It will skip over all characters other than the ten digits. Thus, it will interpret the input $12**%5 as the number 125. It will then echo the integer value and allow the user to try again if it is not correct. Assume the number is three or fewer digits long.

References for Further Reading

The following books give more detailed discussions of loop invariants (covered in the optional section) and related topics.

S. Alagic and M.A. Arbib, *The Design of Well-Structured and Correct Programs,* 1978, Springer-Verlag, New York.

D. Gries, *The Science of Programming,* 1981, Springer-Verlag, New York.

CHAPTER
8

DESIGNING FUNCTIONS AND DATA TYPES

The White Rabbit put on his spectacles. "Where shall I begin, please your Majesty?" he asked.

"Begin at the beginning," the King said, very gravely, "And go on till you come to the end: then stop."

LEWIS CARROLL, ALICE IN WONDERLAND

Chapter Contents

We have already encountered a number of predefined standard functions, such as sqrt, trunc, and round. They are automatically provided in the Pascal language. You can also define new functions within a Pascal program. In this chapter we describe how these new functions are designed and used. We then describe how some new kinds of data types can be defined within Pascal. In addition to the predefined types, such as integer and char, Pascal allows the programmer to define types. In this chapter we introduce some of the simpler kinds of defined data types and show how they can be helpful in detecting program errors.

Use of Functions

Programmer-defined functions are called in exactly the same way as the standard functions we have been using. To *call* any function in Pascal, the program provides the function with one or more arguments. The function then returns a single value. For example, in the statement

```
X := round(2.9)
```

the function round returns the value 3. A function call is a particular kind of expression and, like all other expressions, it has a value. That value is said to be the *value returned* by the function.

call

value returned

A Pascal function is used differently from a procedure. A procedure call is a statement and, like any statement, it performs some action. A function call is an expression and, like any expression, returns a value. Although it is called in a different way, you declare a function in much the same way that you declare a procedure. The function declarations and procedure declarations appear in the same place in a program, possibly even intermixed. To get a feel for these function declarations, we will start with a simple example.

A Sample Function Declaration

Figure 8.1 shows a program with a function declaration for a function called Cube. This function takes one argument of type integer and returns a value of type integer; more specifically, it returns the cube of its argument. Function declarations have formal parameter lists that have the same syntax as procedure parameter lists. The sample function has one formal value parameter, the value of which is set equal to the value of the function argument when the function is called. Function arguments are nothing more nor less than parameters. Although in functions, they are traditionally called *arguments,* that is simply another word for "parameters."

parameter list

arguments

Although a function declaration greatly resembles a procedure declaration, it does differ in some ways from a procedure declaration. First of all, it starts with the word *function* rather than the word *procedure.* Two more significant differences are concerned with how the value to be returned by the function is specified. The first significant difference is that the function is given a type in the function declaration heading. In the function heading in Figure 8.1, the second instance of integer (the one at the end before the semicolon) tells the compiler that the function Cube is of type integer. This means that the value returned will be of type integer and, hence, that the function can only be used in places where it is appropriate to use a value of type integer. The type of the value returned may be any of the types we have seen thus far: integer, real, char, or boolean, as well as a few additional types that we will discuss later in this book. The complete syntax for a function heading is given in Figure 8.2.

function declaration

The second major difference between a procedure declaration and a function declaration is that somewhere within the body of the function declaration, the function

assignment to function name

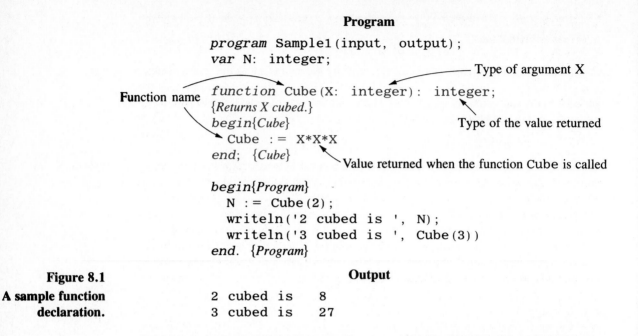

Program

```
program Sample1(input, output);
var N: integer;

function Cube(X: integer): integer;
{Returns X cubed.}
begin{Cube}
  Cube := X*X*X
end;  {Cube}

begin{Program}
  N := Cube(2);
  writeln('2 cubed is ', N);
  writeln('3 cubed is ', Cube(3))
end.  {Program}
```

Function name

Type of argument X

Type of the value returned

Value returned when the function Cube is called

Figure 8.1
A sample function declaration.

Output

```
2 cubed is    8
3 cubed is    27
```

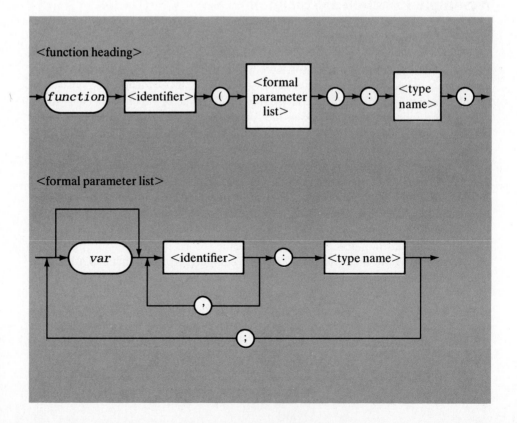

Figure 8.2
Syntax for a function declaration heading.

name must appear on the left-hand side of an assignment statement. This is how the function declaration specifies the value to be returned. Although it looks like a simple assignment of a value to a variable, the statement

```
Cube  : =  X*X*X
```

in Figure 8.1 is something very different. The function name, in this example Cube, is not a variable, and the assignment statement does not mean what an assignment statement usually means. The only reason it is written in this fashion is that this is the traditional way to write it. The purpose of one of these special assignment statements (with the function name on the left-hand side) is to specify the value that is returned by the function call. In this example, the above assignment statement means to return X times X times X as the value of Cube. When the function Cube is called in the program statement

value returned

```
N  : =  Cube (2)
```

the value of the argument, in this case 2, is used to set the value of X, and the expression X*X*X is then evaluated. The statement

```
Cube  : =  X*X*X
```

says to return this value, namely 8, as the value of the function. In the sample program, the value of Cube (2), and hence the new value of N, is 8. There is no variable named Cube that is set to 8 or to any other value. The identifier Cube is not the name of a variable. It is the name of a function.

Case Study

A Function to Compute Powers

Problem Definition

We have a predefined function to compute squares, and we have just written a declaration for a function to compute cubes. Rather than write separate functions for the fourth power, fifth power, and so forth, it makes more sense to have a general-purpose function to compute powers of the form

$$x^n$$

where n as well as x is a parameter. Unlike many other programming languages, Pascal has no predefined function of this form, and so we will need to write a function declaration for it. To make the function even more generally applicable, we will allow the argument x to be of type real, but to simplify the problem, we will assume that the argument n is a nonnegative integer. Hence, if we name the function Power, then the function heading must be the following:

```
function Power (X: real; N: integer): real;
{Precondition: N >= 0.
Returns X to the power N; returns 1 when N equals 0.}
```

Discussion

We wish to compute the value

$$X^N$$

One definition of this quantity is the following:

$$\underbrace{X * X * \quad \ldots \quad * X}_{N \ times}$$

Many problem definitions are already algorithms, sometimes in a disguised form. To obtain an algorithm for translation into Pascal often requires little more than rephrasing the definition. In this case, the definition gives us an algorithm for computing the value we want: Simply multiply X by itself N times. To do this we use a *for* loop and a local variable Product to hold the partial products:

algorithm
from definition

```
for I := 1 to N do
   begin{for}
      Product := Product*X
      {Product is X to the Power I.}
   end {for}
{Product is X to the Power N.}
```

Notice that the *for* loop is used simply to repeat a statement execution N times. The loop control variable I is never referenced inside the loop body. This is an example of the "repeat *n* times" construct we discussed in Chapter 7.

initialize
value

Since the variable Product appears on the right-hand side of the assignment statement inside the *for* loop, it must be given a value before the loop is executed. The correct value is 1. To see that this is true, notice that if Product is initialized with the value 1, then after one loop iteration its value will be X, which satisfies the comment assertion inserted before the *end*.

ALGORITHM

At this stage the algorithm is complete: Initialize Product to 1, and execute the loop. This sets Product equal to the desired value. To return this value as the value of the function, we need only add the statement

```
Power := Product
```

The complete function declaration is given in Figure 8.3.

Pitfall

Thinking the Function Name Is a Variable

In a function declaration the function name can appear on the left-hand side of an assignment operator, as in the following line from the declaration for the function Power shown in Figure 8.3:

Program

```
program Test(input, output);
{Tests the function Power.}
var Arg1: real;
    Arg2: integer;
    Ans: char;
```
— Type of the
  value returned
```
function Power(X: real; N: integer): real;
{Precondition: N >= 0.
Returns X to the power N; returns 1 when N equals 0.}
var I: integer;
    Product: real;
begin{Power}
  Product := 1;
  for I := 1 to N do
    begin{for}
      Product := Product*X
      {Product is X to the Power I.}
    end; {for}
  Power := Product
end; {Power}
```
—— Returns the value of
    Product as the value of
    Power (X, N)
```
begin{Program}
  repeat
    writeln('Enter a real and a nonnegative integer.');
    readln(Arg1, Arg2);
    writeln(Arg1, ' to the power ', Arg2);
    writeln('is ', Power(Arg1, Arg2));
    writeln('Another test? (yes/no)');
    readln(Ans)
  until (Ans = 'N') or (Ans = 'n')
end. {Program}
```

Sample Dialogue

```
Enter a real and a nonnegative integer.
2.0 3
 2.00000000E+00 to the power    3
is    8.00000000000E+00
Another test? (yes/no)
yes
Enter a real and a nonnegative integer.
0.12    2
 1.20000000E-1 to the power    2
is    1.44000000000E-2
Another test? (yes/no)
no
```

Figure 8.3
**Function
declaration in a
test program.**

```
Power  : = Product
```

This leads some programmers to think that the function name can be used as a variable. However, it is not a variable, and it cannot be used as one. For example, the following tempting rewrite for the body of the function declaration in Figure 8.3 is incorrect:

```
begin{Incorrect version of Power}
   Power  : = 1;
   for I : = 1 to N do
       Power  : = Power * X
end;  {Incorrect version of Power}
```

The statement Power : = Power * X will produce an error message. In this situation the compiler is likely to think that the occurrence of Power on the right-hand side is some sort of incorrect function call and will issue an error message to this effect. The message is likely to read something like "Insufficient arguments for a function" or "number of parameters does not agree with declaration."

Pitfall

Special Cases

When designing functions, it is important to pay particular attention to special cases. In the function Power in Figure 8.3, any exponent of zero or less will cause the *for* loop to terminate without performing any iterations at all, and so will cause the function to return a value of 1. As the precondition indicates, we are not using this function for negative exponents, and so we need not be concerned with the value returned in such cases. However, we are allowing it to be used with the exponent zero, and so we should check that special case. Since X to the power zero is traditionally defined to be one, that is the correct value to return. Special cases such as this should always receive a special check to be sure they are handled correctly.

Local Identifiers

Notice that the function in Figure 8.3 has two local variables. Functions may also have local constants. They may even have local procedures and local functions. These local variables, constants, and so forth are declared and used just as they are in procedures. As with procedures, the local declarations plus the parameter list and the list of state-

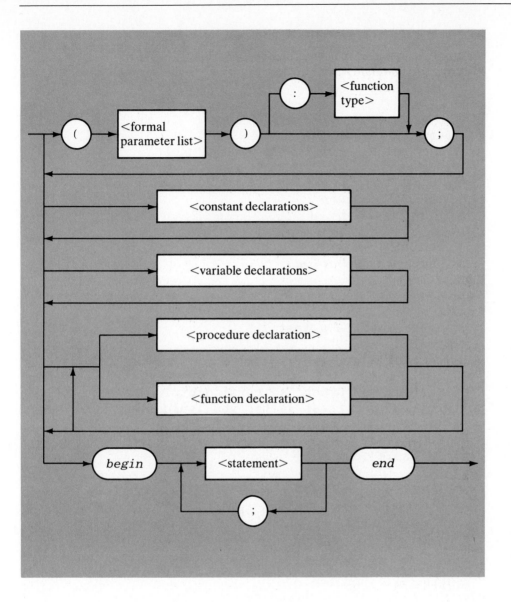

Figure 8.4
Syntax for a block.

ments in a function declaration are referred to as a *block*. Figure 8.4 summarizes the order of declarations within a block. This ordering applies to the main block of a program and the block of a procedure declaration, as well as to the block of a function declaration. Observe that the function and procedure declarations may be intermixed in the declaration section of a program or in the local declaration section of a procedure or function. The only restriction is that the declaration for each function or procedure must appear before the function or procedure is called.

Program

```
program Test(input, output);
{Tests the function CapYN.}
var Ans: char;

function CapYN(Ans: char): char;
{Precondition: Ans has one of the characters 'y', 'Y', 'n',
or 'N' as its value. Returns the uppercase version of Ans.}
begin{CapYN}
   CapYN := Ans;  {tentatively}
   if Ans = 'n' then
       CapYN := 'N'
   else if Ans = 'y' then
       CapYN := 'Y'
   {else the tentative value is used.}
end;  {CapYN}

begin{Program}
   writeln('This is a test.');
   repeat
     writeln('Answer yes or no:');
     readln(Ans);
     writeln('The uppercase version of');
     writeln('the first letter you typed is: ', CapYN(Ans));
     writeln('Test again?  (y/n)');
     readln(Ans)
   until CapYN(Ans) = 'N';
   writeln('End of test.')
end. {Program}
```

Sample Dialogue

```
This is a test.
Answer yes or no:
no
The uppercase version of
the first letter you typed is: N
Test again?  (y/n)
y
Answer yes or no:
No
The uppercase version of
the first letter you typed is: N
Test again?  (y/n)
Yes
Answer yes or no:
yes
```

Figure 8.5
**A function that
changes its mind.**

```
The uppercase version of
the first letter you typed is: Y
Test again? (y/n)
y
Answer yes or no:
YES
The uppercase version of
the first letter you typed is: Y
Test again? (y/n)
n
End of test.
```

Figure 8.5
(continued)

Functions That Change Their Minds

Since a function must always return a value, a function declaration must always contain at least one statement that uses the function name on the left-hand side of an assignment operator. Every call of the function must cause at least one of these assignment statements to be executed. A function can contain more than one such statement, and sometimes a function call may cause two such assignment statements to be executed. If two or more assignments to the function name are made when the function is called, then the value returned by the function is the last value assigned to the function name.

For example, consider the function in Figure 8.5. It assumes that its argument is one of the symbols $'y'$, $'Y'$, $'n'$, or $'N'$. It returns the uppercase version of this argument; if the argument is $'y'$ or $'Y'$, it returns $'Y'$; if the argument is $'n'$ or $'N'$ it returns $'N'$. This function might be used to process yes-or-no answers. For example, to terminate the test loop we used the boolean expression

example

```
CapYN(Ans)  =  'N';
```

instead of

```
(Ans  =  'n')  or  (Ans  =  'N')
```

The function declaration for CapYN first makes the following assignment to the function name:

```
CapYN  : =  Ans
```

This is a tentative choice for the value returned. If the value of Ans were $'N'$, this would cause the value of Ans, namely $'N'$ to be returned. If however, the value of the argument Ans were instead the lowercase letter $'n'$, then the value returned would be recomputed by the following second assignment to the function name:

```
if Ans = 'n' then
   CapYN : = 'N'
```

Side Effects

what a
function
can do

The purpose of a function is to take the values of some arguments and return a *single* value, but a Pascal function can actually do much more. In Pascal a function is a procedure with the added feature of returning a value. Hence, a function can do anything that a procedure can do. All our examples used value parameters as arguments. This is typical, but a function is allowed to have variable parameters as well as value parameters as its arguments. A function can change the value of a global variable, write a message to the screen, read a value from the keyboard, or do anything else that a procedure can do, so long as it also returns a value. However, it is usually a bad idea to use any of these other features when designing functions.

what a
function
should not do

If a function changes the value of a global variable, sets the value of a variable parameter, or causes a `read` or `write` statement to be executed, that extra feature is referred to as a *side effect*. As indicated in Figure 8.6, side effects are usually a bad idea. We think of a function as simply returning a value, and if we want it to do more, it is usually clearer to write a procedure rather than a function and to return the value via a variable parameter.

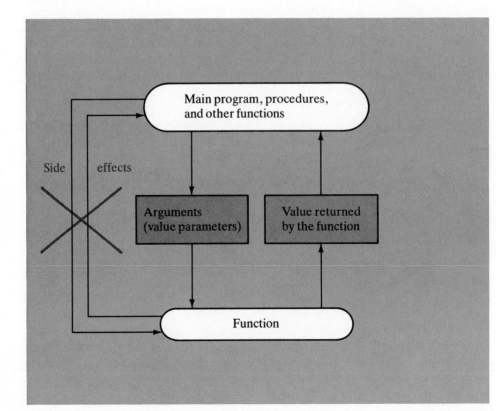

**Figure 8.6
Side effects of a
function.**

> With all appliances and means to boot.
> *William Shakespeare, King Henry IV, Part III*

Self-Test Exercises

1. What is the output of the following program?

```pascal
program Exercise1(input, output);

function Crazy(N: integer): char;
begin{Crazy}
  Crazy := 'X';
  if N = 1 then
     Crazy := 'A';
  if N = 2 then
     Crazy := 'B'
end; {Crazy}

begin{Program}
  writeln(Crazy(1), Crazy(2), Crazy(3))
end. {Program}
```

2. What is wrong with the following function declaration?

```pascal
function TwoPower(N: integer): integer;
{Returns 2 to the power N. Precondition N >= 0.}
var I: integer;
begin{TwoPower}
  TwoPower := 1;
  for I := 1 to N do
     TwoPower := TwoPower * 2
end; {TwoPower}
```

3. Write a function that has two arguments, one for the length and one for the width of a rectangle, and that returns the area of a rectangle with those dimensions.

4. Write a function declaration for a function that has one argument of type integer and that returns the letter 'P' if the number is positive and the letter 'N' if it is zero or negative.

5. For each of the following subtasks, tell whether it is best implemented as a function or as a procedure.

a. Converting a given number of miles to an equivalent number of kilometers.
b. Converting a given number of centimeters to feet and inches.

c. Displaying the output of a program on the screen.

d. Computing the net income and the tax due on an income tax return, given the gross income and the adjustments to income.

e. Computing an automobile's mileage per gallon, given the miles traveled and the number of gallons of gasoline consumed.

Boolean-Valued Functions

A function may return a value of type `boolean`. A call to the function can then be used anywhere that a boolean expression is allowed. This can often help to make a program easier to read. By means of a function declaration, we can associate a complex boolean expression with a meaningful name and use that name as the boolean expression in an *if-then, if-then-else, repeat,* or *while* statement. The result can often make a program read rather like English. For example, the statement

```
if ((Rate >= 10) and (Rate < 20)) or (Rate = 0) then
        begin{then}
            . . .
        end {then}
```

can be made to read as follows:

```
if Appropriate(Rate)  then
        begin{then}
            . . .
        end{then}
```

provided the following boolean function has already been defined:

```
function Appropriate(Rate: integer): boolean;
    begin{Appropriate}
      Appropriate :=
          ((Rate >= 10) and (Rate < 20)) or (Rate = 0)
    end; {Appropriate}
```

Case Study

Testing for Primes
(Optional)

Problem Definition

In this section we will design a function that has one integer argument, which it tests to see whether the integer is a prime number or not. The function will return `true` if it is prime and `false` if it is not. A *prime number* is an integer that is greater than one and that has no divisors other than itself and one. In other words, the prime numbers are the positive integers (other than one) that cannot be factored. For example, 12 can be factored into 2 times 6, and so is not prime. The first few primes are 2, 3, 5, 7, 11, and 13. As is common when discussing prime numbers, we will confine our attention to positive integers.

Discussion

We must first design an algorithm to test a positive integer for primality. A candidate number N is prime provided it has no divisors other than itself and one. Obviously, we cannot check all the positive integers to see if any of them divide N. Fortunately for us, we know that any divisor of N must be less than or equal to N, and so we need only test those integers I which are less than N. This observation yields the heart of our algorithm:

1. For each I such that $1 < I < N$, test whether I is a divisor of N.
2. If *any such* I is a divisor of N, then report that N *is not* a prime. If *no such* I divides N, then report that N *is* a prime.

ALGORITHM
first version

This function, like many functions, has some arguments that are special cases. For example, the definition of prime numbers makes a special case of one. It has no divisor other than one and itself. Yet by definition it is not a prime. (The reason has to do with the theory of numbers and is not a topic for this book.) Although one is not a prime, it technically satisfies the basic test that will become the heart of our algorithm. Substituting 1 for N, we see that there are no numbers I such that

special
cases

$$1 < I < 1$$

and such that I divides 1; in fact, there are no values for I that even satisfy the inequality, and so there are certainly none that both satisfy the inequality and divide 1. Hence, we must add a special case for the argument 1; otherwise, our function will incorrectly claim that it is a prime. Our algorithm will include a special check to see if its argument is 1, and if it is, it will return the value `false`.

This leaves us with the numbers 2 and greater. One should always test the extreme values used by an algorithm to see if they are special cases. The argument 2 is a special case. If we apply the number 2 to the heart of our algorithm, it says to test all integers I such that

$$1 < I < 2$$

Since there is no such I, the test is suspect. The number 2 is a prime, and, if applied rigorously, the heart of our algorithm will say that it is a prime. However, to make our algorithm easier to understand, we will make a special case of 2. The arguments 3 and larger behave normally with no subtleties when we apply the heart of our algorithm to them. Our algorithm now takes shape in more detail:

1. If N is 1, then N is not a prime.
2. If N is 2, then N is a prime.
3. If $N > 2$ then do the following:
   3-1. For each I such that $1 < I < N$, test whether I is a divisor of N.

ALGORITHM
second version

3-2. If *any such* I is a divisor of N, then report that N *is not* a prime. If *no such* I divides N, then report that N *is* a prime.

refining the algorithm

The following boolean expression is true if I is a divisor of N, and is false otherwise:

N *mod* I = 0

So step 3 can be rewritten as follows:

tentatively assume N is a prime;
for I := 2 *to* N − 1 *do*
    if (N *mod* I = 0) *then*
        change your mind and decide that N is not prime.

guilty 'until proven innocent

This is an example of the *guilty-until-proven-innocent* technique. We need to test a list to see if any member of the list is a witness to prove that N is not prime ("not guilty"). If there is no witness to prove that N is not prime, then it is assumed (correctly) to be prime. The guilty-until-proven-innocent technique is naturally implemented using a boolean variable, in this case, one called GuiltyOfPrimality.

ALGORITHM third version

GuiltyOfPrimality := true;
for I := 2 *to* N − 1 *do*
    if (N *mod* I = 0) *then*
            GuiltyOfPrimality := false

changing the value returned

In this case, the answer is the value returned by a boolean-valued function, and since Pascal functions can change their mind about the value ("verdict") returned, we can simply use the function name rather than a boolean variable. If we name our function Prime, then the final Pascal code for this test is

function code

Prime := true;
for I := 2 *to* N − 1 *do*
    if (N *mod* I = 0) *then*
        Prime := false

The value returned is tentatively set equal to true. If a divisor is not found, then the value true is returned. If a divisor is found, then the function changes its mind and returns false. The complete function declaration, embedded in a test program, is displayed in Figure 8.7. The function declaration is now correct but could be made more efficient. Exercise 23, at the end of this chapter, suggests a way of improving the efficiency of the function.

Program

```
program TestPrimes(input, output);
var N: integer;

function Prime(N: integer): boolean;
{Returns true if N is a prime; otherwise returns false. Precondition: N > 0.}
var I: integer;
```

Figure 8.7 (Optional)

A boolean function that tests for prime numbers.

```
begin{Prime}
  if N = 1 then
     Prime := false
  else if N = 2 then
     Prime := true
  else
    begin{N > 2}
      Prime := true; {tentatively}
      for I := 2 to N - 1 do
        if (N mod I = 0) then
           Prime := false
    end   {N > 2}
end; {Prime}

begin{Program}
  writeln('Enter a positive integer and');
  writeln('I will tell you if it is prime.');
  writeln('Enter a zero to quit.');

  writeln('Enter an integer:');
  readln(N);
  while N > 0 do
    begin{while}
      if Prime(N)  then
        writeln(N, ' is a prime.')
      else
        writeln(N, ' is not a prime.');
      writeln('Enter an integer:');
      readln(N)
    end; {while}

  writeln('End of program.')
end. {Program}
```

Sample Dialogue

```
Enter a positive integer and
I will tell you if it is prime.
Enter a zero to quit.
Enter an integer:
15
      15 is not a prime.
Enter an integer:
17
      17 is a prime.
Enter an integer:
0
End of program.
```

Figure 8.7
(continued)

Name	Description	Type of argument	Type of result	Example	Value of example
arctan	arctangent	real or integer	real	arctan(1.0)	0.785 (radians)
cos	cosine	real or integer	real	cos(0.78) (argument in radians)	0.71091
sin	sine	real or integer	real	sin(1.57) (argument in radians)	1.00
exp	exponential	real or integer	real	exp(2)	e^2 (not Pascal notation)
ln	natural logarithm	real or integer	real	ln(2.71828) (e is approx. 2.71828)	1.000
odd	odd/even function	integer	boolean	odd(5) odd(4)	true false

Figure 8.8 (Optional) Some more predefined Pascal functions.

More Standard Functions
(Optional)

Figure 8.8 is a list of some more standard functions. If you have occasion to use trigonometric functions or logarithmic functions, you should use these instead of defining your own versions. Be sure to note that the standard trigonometric functions must have their arguments expressed in radians rather than in degrees. There are 2π radians in a complete circle of 360 degrees. The exponential function exp and the logarithm function ln use the number e as their base. Thus, exp(3) has e cubed as its value. The number e is approximately equal to 2.71828.

Random Number Generators
(Optional)

Suppose you flip a coin, write down zero if it comes up heads, and write down one if it comes up tails. You have just made a *random* choice between zero and one. If you roll a single die and count the number of dots on the top face, you will get a random number between one and six. These are two ways of generating random numbers. There are numerous occasions when a computer program needs, or at least can profitably use, a source of random numbers. Perhaps the most obvious example is that of a game-playing program. Random numbers are also used in simulation programs. A program to model the performance of a proposed new highway interchange would typically use a random number generator to model the arrival times of vehicles. A program to write poetry might use a random number generator to guide the choice of words. These are just a few of the numerous uses for random number generators.

An exact definition of what constitutes a *true random number generator* is a matter of significant philosophical debate. However, the examples of the coin flip and the die provide an adequate feel for the concept. Computer programs typically do not use true random number generators. Instead, they use procedures or functions that generate sequences of numbers that appear to be random. Since these sequences are generated by procedures or functions, they are not "truly" random. Hence, these generators are referred to as *pseudorandom number generators*.

pseudorandom numbers

For most applications, these pseudorandom number generators are a close enough approximation to a true random number generator. In fact, they are usually preferable to a true random number generator. A pseudorandom number generator has one important advantage over a true random number generator: The sequence of numbers it produces is repeatable. If run twice with the same initial conditions, a pseudorandom number generator will always produce exactly the same sequence of numbers. This can be very handy for a number of purposes. It is very useful for debugging. When an error is discovered, the proposed program changes can be tested with the *same* sequence of pseudorandom numbers that exposed the error. Similarly, a particularly interesting run of a simulation program may be reproduced, provided a pseudorandom number generator was used. With a true random number generator, every run of the program is likely to be different.

The most common method of generating pseudorandom numbers is the *linear congruence method*. This method starts out with a number called the *seed*. For each individual run of the program, the seed is usually chosen by the user. It completely determines the sequence of numbers produced. There are three other numbers called the `Multiplier`, the `Increment`, and the `Modulus`, which are fixed constants. The formula for generating what are hopefully random-looking numbers is quite simple:

linear congruence method

seed

The first number is

> (`Multiplier`*(the seed) + `Increment`) *mod* `Modulus`

The *n* + *1st* number is

> (`Multiplier`*(the *n*th number) + `Increment`) *mod* `Modulus`

For example, suppose we take the `Multiplier` to be 2, the `Increment` to be 3, and the `Modulus` to be 5. With a seed value of 1, this produces the following sequence of numbers:

> (2*1 + 3) *mod* 5 or 0,   (2*0 + 3) *mod* 5 or 3,
>   (2*3 + 3) *mod* 5 or 4,   (2*4 + 3) *mod* 5 or 1,
>   (2*1 + 3) *mod* 5 or 0, . . .

```
function Random(var Memory: integer): integer;
{Returns a pseudorandom number between 0 and (Modulus−1);
Memory is changed to a value in this range with each call of the function.
Precondition: The value of Memory is between 0 and (Modulus−1).}
const Modulus = 729;
      Multiplier = 40;
      Increment = 3641;
begin{Random}
  Memory :=
    (Multiplier*Memory + Increment) mod Modulus;
  Random := Memory
end; {Random}
```

**Figure 8.9
(Optional)**

**A pseudorandom
number generator.**

The pattern of numbers produced is thus 0, 3, 4, 1, 0, 3, 4, 1, 0, 3, 4, 1, . . .

Something is not right. This formula should produce a sequence that looks like a sequence of randomly chosen integers between zero and one less than the modulus. In this example, the numbers should range from 0 to 4. But the above pattern is a repeating one and does not contain 2. Hence, the value 2 will never be produced. Changing the seed will not help much. If we use 2 as the seed, we obtain the sequence 2, 2, 2, 2, 2. . . . This certainly produces the value 2, but generates no other numbers. The problem is in the choice of the other constants and not in the choice of the seed.

Any choice of values for the constants in our pseudorandom number generator will produce a sequence that ultimately falls into a repeating pattern. However, if the constants are chosen carefully, the pattern will be large and will appear to be random. The values given in Figure 8.9 should work reasonably well on any implementation with a `maxint` value of 32761 or larger. With the constants used in the figure, the random number generator will produce 729 numbers before repeating a number.

Notice that the function Random has a variable parameter called `Memory`, which it uses to remember one number. The initial value of this variable is the seed. Each time the function is called, this variable parameter is changed, which violates our guideline that functions should not have side effects. This is one of those rare occasions when it is acceptable to violate the guideline. In this case, a variable parameter, or something like it, is necessary. The generator must somehow remember the last value it produced, since that is what determines the next value it will produce.

Using Pseudorandom Numbers
(Optional)

*changing
the range*

Very few programs require an integer chosen at random from the range 0 through 728 (the value of Modulus−1). Usually it is a different and smaller range. For example, a program might need a pseudorandom integer between 0 and 10. One possibility is to use the following formula:

Random(Memory) *mod* 11

The procedure `ZeroToTen` in Figure 8.10 uses this formula. The program shown there uses the pseudorandom numbers to produce random-looking output.

Random numbers can be scaled by additive constants. One way to get a pseudorandom number in the range 1 to 10 is to add one to an expression that yields numbers in the range 0 to 9. The following is one such expression:

`(Random(Memory)` *mod* `10)  +  1`

The function `Random` shown in Figure 8.9 will produce a pseudorandom number in the range 0 to 728. But what if you want a `real` value in the range zero to one? Simply divide by the largest value that our random number generator produces. The function `RandomReal` shown in Figure 8.11 uses this technique to return a pseudorandom value between zero and one. To get a `real` value in any other range, multiply by an appropriate factor and, if need be, add an appropriate constant.

pseudorandom reals

Designing good pseudorandom number generators is not an easy task. They frequently need some sort of "tuning" to keep them from producing a sequence of numbers that looks blatantly nonrandom. The pseudorandom number generators in this section will work reasonably well on virtually any system. However, some systems have been extended to include a predefined generator that has been carefully tuned to run efficiently and to produce the most random-looking sequences possible, given the limitations of the particular computer system. If your system includes such a predefined function, it makes sense to use it rather than the one given in Figure 8.9.

Producing pseudorandom numbers in a specified range requires some scaling of the values produced by the function `Random`. The methods of scaling that we have already seen will work well in most situations. However, they do occasionally produce unsatisfactory sequences, and so we will discuss another slightly more complicated, but preferable, method of scaling that avoids such problems. But before discussing the solution, we will illustrate the problem.

better scaling of random numbers

Sequences of pseudorandom numbers produced by the linear congruence method have a pattern that can become apparent when the numbers are scaled in certain innocent-looking ways. For example, one way to obtain a pseudorandom number chosen from among the three values 0, 1, and 2 is to use the following formula:

`Random(Memory)` *mod* `3`

If this formula is used with `Memory` initialized to the seed value of 100, the resulting sequence will be: 0, 2, 1, 0, 2, 1, 0, 2, 1, . . . The sequence repeats after just three numbers.

Patterns like the one we just saw frequently depend on the last digits of the numbers. One way to break the pattern, therefore, is to discard the last digit. The following formula yields pseudorandom numbers produced by the generator `Random` but with the last digit discarded:

`Random(Memory)` *div* `10`

For example, if `Memory` has a value of 100, then `Random` produces a value of 114, which yields a final value of 11 after applying the *div* operator.

If we combine the two tricks of discarding the last digit and then scaling by applying a *mod* 3, we get the following formula for producing pseudorandom numbers in the range 0 to 2:

Program

```
program RatingGame(input, output);
const Width = 2; {field width for numbers 1 to 10.}
var Memory, Rating: integer;
    Ans: char;

function Random(var Memory: integer): integer;
{Returns a pseudorandom number between 0 and (Modulus−1);
Memory is changed to a value in this range with each call of the function.
Precondition: The value of Memory is between 0 and (Modulus−1).}

<The rest of the declaration is given in Figure 8.9.>


function ZeroToTen(var Memory: integer): integer;
{Returns a pseudorandom number between 0 and 10 (0 and 10 are possible).}
begin{ZeroToTen}
   ZeroToTen := Random(Memory) mod 11
end; {ZeroToTen}

begin{Program}
   writeln('Hi, my name is Gollum.');
   writeln('I''m a perfect 10. What are you?');
   writeln('Answer with a number between 0 and 10.');
   readln(Memory);
   if Memory > 7 then
     writeln('Not bad.')
   else
     writeln('Oh well.');

   writeln('Would you like to rate some other people? (yes/no)');
   readln(Ans);
   while (Ans = 'y') or (Ans = 'Y') do
     begin{while}
       writeln('You name somebody and I''ll give a rating.');
       readln;
       Rating := ZeroToTen(Memory);
       writeln('That individual is a ', Rating :Width);
       writeln('Want to rate somebody else? (yes/no)');
       readln(Ans)
     end; {while}
```

**Figure 8.10
(Optional)**

**Program using a
pseudorandom
number generator.**

```
   writeln('Before I leave, let me rate you.');
   Rating := ZeroToTen(Memory);
   writeln('I''d say you were a ', Rating :Width)
end. {Program}
```

Sample Dialogue

```
Hi, my name is Gollum.
I'm a perfect 10. What are you?
Answer with a number between 0 and 10.
10
Not bad.
Would you like to rate some other people? (yes/no)
yes
You name somebody and I'll give a rating.
Joseph Cool
That individual is a 0
Want to rate somebody else? (yes/no)
yes
You name somebody and I'll give a rating.
Olivia Safran
That individual is a 10
Want to rate somebody else? (yes/no)
yes
You name somebody and I'll give a rating.
Walter Savitch
That individual is a 4
Want to rate somebody else? (yes/no)
no
Before I leave, let me rate you.
I'd say you were a 4
```

Figure 8.10

(continued)

```
function RandomReal(var Memory: integer): real;
{Returns a pseudorandom real value between zero and one.
Calls the function Random given in Figure 8.9.
Precondition: The value of Memory is between 0 and Max (see const declaration).
The function changes the value of Memory to another value in this range.}
const Max = 728; {The largest value returned by Random.}
begin{RandomReal}
   RandomReal := Random(Memory)/Max
end; {RandomReal}
```

**Figure 8.11
(Optional)**

**A random number
generator for
real values
between 0 and 1.**

(Random (Memory) *div* 10) *mod* 3

Again starting with a seed value of 100, this more complicated formula produces a more random-looking sequence that starts out 2, 0, 1, 2, 0, 2, 2, 2, 0, 1, . . .

Chance is a word void of sense;
nothing can exist without a cause.

Voltaire, A Philosophical Dictionary

Self-Test Exercises

6. What is the output produced by the following program?

```
program Exercise6(input, output);
var George: boolean;

function Blaise(N: integer): boolean;
begin{Blaise}
   Blaise := N < 0
end; {Blaise}

begin{Program}
   if Blaise(5) then
      writeln('Hello')
   else
      writeln('Hi');
   George := .Blaise(-8);
   if George then
      writeln('Good-Bye')
   else
      writeln('So long')
end. {Program}
```

7. Write a boolean function of two integer arguments that returns true if the first argument evenly divides the second and returns false otherwise.

8. Write a boolean function declaration for a function InOrder that has three integer arguments and returns true if the three integer arguments are in ascending order. For example, InOrder (1, 2, 3) should return true, and InOrder (1, 3, 2) should return false.

9. (This exercise uses the optional sections "Random Number Generators" and "Using Pseudorandom Numbers.") Write a function that returns a pseudorandom number

chosen from the even numbers between 2 and 20. Use the random number generator developed in this chapter.

Ordinal Types

The most straightforward way to specify the values of a data type is to list them. In the case of the type `boolean`, this is easy to do. There are just two values: `false` and `true`. In the case of the type `char`, the list is much longer: ..., `'A'`, `'B'`, `'C'`, ... In the case of the type `integer`, the list is so long that it would be unrealistic to write it out, but in principle the values could all be listed. In Pascal, a type whose values are specified by a list is called an *ordinal type*. The types `integer`, `boolean`, and `char` are all ordinal types.

Since the items of any list are ordered, the values of an ordinal type have an order *integer* determined by their order in the list. The operation $<$ can be used to test this ordering. It is an operation defined for all Pascal ordinal types, and it always yields a boolean *boolean* value. The most obvious case of this is the ordinal type `integer`. In that case, the order is the usual less than ordering of the integers. For example, $1 < 2$ and $-5 < -3$ both evaluate to `true`. In the case of the type `boolean`, `false` is considered to be less than `true`. There is little intuitive meaning to this ordering. It is completely arbitrary. Nonetheless, it is the prescribed ordering, and so `false` $<$ `true` evaluates to `true`.

The ordering of the type `char` is more or less the obvious one. Letters are ordered *char* alphabetically, and so `'A'` $<$ `'B'` and `'A'` $<$ `'Z'` both evaluate to `true`, whereas `'Z'` $<$ `'X'` evaluates to `false`. The digits are also ordered as you would expect. For example, `'1'` $<$ `'2'` and `'0'` $<$ `'9'` both evaluate to `true`, whereas `'3'` $<$ `'2'` evaluates to `false`. The ordering of the digits reflects the ordering of the numbers they stand for. What about the character pairs that do not have a traditional ordering? Is the semicolon less than the comma or greater than the comma? Is uppercase `'A'` less than or greater than lowercase `'a'`? Pascal does not say. It does specify that the uppercase letters are ordered alphabetically among themselves, the lowercase letters are ordered alphabetically among themselves, and the digits are ordered in the obvious way. Moreover, it says that the digits are contiguous; that is, there is no character between two intuitively adjacent digits such as `'4'` and `'5'`. Within these constraints, the compiler can be implemented in any way the designer finds convenient. So on one system you may find that `'a'` $<$ `'A'` evaluates to `true`, whereas on another system it evaluates to `false`. The moral is clear: Avoid using any ordering properties that can change from system to system.

The type `char` is a good example of a type that is only partially determined by the definition of the language. This is quite common. The usual thing to do is to require a data type to have the properties that programmers normally expect and need but to let the compiler writer do whatever is convenient with the unspecified properties. Although it may be incomplete, the definition of a data type should not be vague. Pascal specifies that the order of the digits is exactly `'0'`, `'1'`, `'2'`, `'3'`, `'4'`, `'5'`, `'6'`, `'7'`, `'8'`, `'9'`. Similarly, the ordering of any two uppercase letters is rigidly specified, and so forth. Whatever is specified is specified precisely.

The ordering properties of ordinal types can be used in a program. For example, it is sometimes useful to test two letters to determine whether they are in alphabetic order. An obvious example of this would be in a program that alphabetizes a list of words. We have already seen that there are numerous reasons why a program might compare two integer values.

When comparing two values of an ordinal type, the variations on the $<$ operation, namely $<=$, $>$, and $>=$, are all available and have the obvious interpretation.

real

Of all the types we have seen thus far, only the type `real` is not an ordinal type. This is a consequence of the abstract model of the real numbers that is used in mathematics. In that model, the real numbers cannot be listed. Computers can represent only a finite number of `real` constants, and so the `real` values for any particular implementation can, in principle, be listed. However, the definition of Pascal does not specify the list; moreover, we do not normally think of the `real` values as being on a list. For these reasons the type `real` is not considered to be an ordinal type. As we have seen, however, the comparison operators, such as $<$, can be applied to values of type `real`, in the same fashion in which they can be applied to values of ordinal types.

simple
types

In many, but not all, ways the type `real` is like an ordinal type. The unifying term *simple type* is used to refer to any type that is either the type `real` or is an ordinal type. The type `real` is both important and troublesome. All of Chapter 15 is devoted to a discussion of this type.

The Functions pred, succ, ord, and chr
(Optional)

pred
succ

Since the values of an ordinal type are ordered in a list, a programmer may find it useful to refer to the value preceding a given value, or to the value following a given value in this list. Pascal provides two functions, `pred` and `succ`, for exactly these purposes. Given a value of some ordinal type as an argument, such as `18`, the function `pred` returns the preceding value of that type and the function `succ` returns the succeeding value in the ordering of that type. For example, `pred(18)` returns `17`, and `succ(18)` returns `19`. Similarly, `succ('B')` usually returns `'C'`, and `pred('B')` usually returns `'A'`. Since the exact ordering of the characters may vary from system to system, the values returned by `pred` and `succ` may vary somewhat from system to system, but we will assume that these are the values returned.

ord

Since the values of an ordinal type are listed in a certain order, we can meaningfully ask where a specific value is located on the list. The Pascal function `ord` provides a way of doing this. However, the ordinal types are usually numbered starting with zero rather than one. So `ord` applied to the first value of an ordinal type returns `0`; when applied to the second value, it returns `1`, and so forth. The type `integer` is the sole exception to this numbering scheme. The function `ord` applied to any value of type `integer` simply returns that value. For example, `ord(-5)` returns `-5`, which makes `ord` an uninteresting function to apply to integers.

chr

Since it is the type `char` that is ultimately used when a program communicates with the outside world, it is a special type in a number of ways. One of its special features is a standard function that is the inverse of `ord`. Given a nonnegative integer value, the function chr returns the character value in that position on the list of values of type char. So chr(0) returns the first value of type char, chr(1) returns the next value, chr(2) returns the next value after that, and so forth. For numbers that do not correspond to any character value, chr is undefined.

These four functions, which depend on the ordering of ordinal types, are occasionally useful but are neither essential nor even very widely used. Only a few specialized uses are very common. One use involves text processing. Although it is not part of the definition of Pascal, most systems order the letters so that the uppercase letters are contiguous (nothing is between 'A' and 'B', for example) and the lowercase letters are contiguous. On these systems, there is some number x such that the uppercase and lowercase versions of a letter are always exactly x places apart. So, for example, chr(ord('A')+x) returns 'a', and chr(ord('P')+x) returns 'p'. Similarly, a program can compute uppercase letters from lowercase letters using minus x. The number x can be computed using the relation

$$x = \text{ord('a')} - \text{ord('A')}$$

Another use for the chr function has to do with nonprintable characters. A computer frequently has the ability to send messages to the video screen that mean things like "clear the screen," "ring the bell," or some other manipulation of the output device other than simply writing a letter on the screen. These signals are usually considered to be values of type char. So, for example, if the "character" that rings the bell happens to be number 29 on a given type of terminal, then the following will ring the bell on that terminal:

nonprintable characters

```
write(chr(29))
```

These sample uses of chr and ord are highly implementation-dependent. Different systems will order the values of type character differently. Even the list of available characters will differ from system to system. Some systems do not have a bell to ring. Some do not have the curly brackets '{' and '}'. Some do not have lowercase letters. Hence, any program written using these techniques will definitely not be portable. These sorts of manipulations should always be isolated into clearly documented procedures, so that they can be easily changed. For example, if the "character" to ring the bell on your system is number 29, the following is a reasonable procedure to ring the bell:

portability

```
procedure Bell;
{Implementation-dependent procedure to ring bell. The "bell"
signal for terminal ABC on system XYZ is character number 29.}
begin{Bell}
   write(chr(29))
end;  {Bell}
```

In Pascal a few tasks, such as the one above, can only be done in implementation-dependent ways. However, if care is taken to isolate the implementation-dependent details, the program can still be quite portable. For example, to change the above procedure to work with another system configuration, all that normally need be done is to change the constant 29 in the procedure Bell.

Subrange Types

The simplest kind of type that can be defined within a Pascal program is a *subrange type*. These types are critically important in constructing other, more complicated and very useful types that we will introduce in the next chapter. They are also useful in their own right as an automatic error-checking facility. But before discussing their uses, we must describe what these types are.

host type

A subrange type is obtained from an ordinal type by specifying two constants of that type. The type from which the two constants are chosen is called the *host type*. The values of the subrange type consist of the two constant values specified plus all the values of the host type that fall between the two specified constants. A subrange type is an ordinal type, and the values are ordered in the same way as they are in the host type. A subrange type definition is a declaration and so is placed in the declaration part of a program. For example, a program might start as follows:

```
program Sample(input, output);
const PI = 3.14159;
type SmallInteger = -10 . . 10;
var Big: integer;
    Little: SmallInteger;
    X, Y: real;
```

type declaration

The third line in this example is called a *type declaration*. The type `SmallInteger` is defined to be all `integer` values between −10 and +10, including the endpoints. The variable `Little` is defined to be of type `SmallInteger`, and so it can take on values from −10 to +10. Hence, the following is a Pascal statement that might legitimately appear in this program:

```
Little := 4
```

However, the following should produce an error message when the program is run:

```
Little := 11{Not allowed.}
```

Subrange type declarations, as well as the other type declarations that we will introduce later, go between the constant and variable declarations. The general layout of the various declarations, is illustrated in Figure 8.12. The general form of a subrange type declaration follows the model of the sample shown in the figure: It consists of the identifier *type* followed by an identifier to serve as the name of the type, followed by an equal sign and then the definition of the type and a semicolon. The definition consists of two constants separated by two periods. The two constants are chosen from an ordinal type, and the first constant must be less than or equal to the second. Notice that defined constant names may be used for the constants in a subrange type definition, as shown in Figure 8.12.

You can define any number of subrange types. Each declaration has its own type name and type definition. The identifier *type* precedes the list of declarations. It is included only once, no matter how many subrange types are declared.

Subrange types and their host types are compatible in the sense that any value of a

```
                    program Example(input, output);

Constant              { const Low  =  0;
declarations          {       High = 100;

Type declarations     { type Score = Low . . High;
                      {      Grade = 'A' . . 'F';

                      { var Exam1, Exam2: Score;
Variable declarations {     Average: real;
                      {     Final: Grade;

Procedure             { procedure ReadScores(var S1, S2: Score);
and                   {  . . .
function              { function Average(S1, S2: Score): real;
declarations          {  . . .
                      { procedure TellAll(. . . .
                      {  . . .


                      begin{Program}
                       . . .
                       . . .
                       . . .
                      end.  {Program}
```

**Figure 8.12
Program layout.**

subrange type is also considered to be of the host type. For example, using the preceding program opening, any value of type SmallInteger is also of type integer. In this program, therefore, the following is a legitimate statement:

*type
compatibility*

```
Big := Little
```

The following program code is also legitimate:

```
readln(Big);
Little := Big
```

However, if the readln statement sets the value of Big to a value outside the range of the subrange type SmallInteger, the assignment statement should precipitate an error message.

The subrange type inherits all the operations of its host type. For example, a program with types declared as above could add or subtract two values of type SmallInteger.

One important use of subrange types is as a device to detect certain programming errors. If you expect a variable to always take on values within a certain range, then that variable should be declared as having a subrange type. That way, if an error does cause it to take on a value outside of the specified range, an error message will be produced. Otherwise, the error might go undetected. For example, if a variable X is

*error
checking*

expected to hold only positive integers, then the following declarations will serve to declare X in such a way that nonpositive values will produce an error message:

```
type PositiveInt = 1 . . maxint;
var X: PositiveInt;
```

As another example, assume that `Final` is supposed to hold a letter grade in a classroom grading program. Furthermore, assume that the possible grades are A, B, C, D, and F. `Final` should then be declared as follows:

```
type Grade = 'A' . . 'F';
var Final: Grade;
```

With the variable `Final` declared to be of a subrange type as shown, the computer should give an error message if for some reason the value of `Final` is set to, say, `'G'`. There is a limit to the amount of checking that can be handled by subrange types. Subrange types consist of *all* the values between the two limits. Hence, the above declaration does not provide for an error message in the event that the value of `Grade` is set to `'E'`.

The For and Case Statements Revisited

Ordinal types are like integers in the sense that they can be listed. Given two bounds, we can proceed from the lower bound to the next value in the ordered list, and then to the next, and so forth until we reach the upper bound. This is the only property of the type `integer` that the `for` statement uses. It thus seems natural to allow the loop control variable in a `for` statement to be of any ordinal type. Pascal does just that. Naturally, the expressions that give the initial and final values of the loop control variable must be of the same ordinal type as the variable. As an example, the following is a perfectly legitimate Pascal statement:

```
for I := 'a' to 'z' do
        write(I)
```

Provided that `I` is declared to be of type `char` or an appropriate subrange type, this will output the alphabet.

Since a loop control variable assumes values between two bounds, it is possible to declare it as a subrange type. Moreover, this is a good idea, since it serves as one additional check on the program.

Now that we have defined the ordinal types, we can define the *case* statement more completely and compactly. The expression that governs a *case* statement may be of any ordinal type. The label lists must, of course, consist of constants of that ordinal type.

Allowable Parameter Types

Procedures and functions may have parameters of any type whatsoever, including all the types we have seen so far and all the defined types we will introduce in succeeding chapters. However, a procedure or function declaration must use type names. It cannot use type definitions. The following is thus an illegal procedure heading:

```
procedure WriteGrades(Quiz1, Quiz2: 0 . . 100);
{NOT ALLOWED}
```

Instead, you must declare a name for the defined type and use the name in the formal parameter list, like so:

```
type Score = 0 . . 100;
procedure WriteGrades(Quiz1, Quiz2: Score);
```

The same rule applies to the type returned by a function. You must use a type name, not a type definition, in the function declaration. Although there are no restrictions as to what types may be used as parameters (arguments) to functions, in the next chapter we will see that there are restrictions on what types may be returned. All the types we have seen thus far are allowed as the type of the value returned by a function.

type returned by a function

Pitfall

Parameter Type Conflicts

Extra care must be taken when you are using a subrange type as the type of a variable parameter in a procedure. The rules for matching parameters state that the formal and actual parameters must be of the same type. This can sometimes cause subtle problems. As an example, recall the procedure Exchange defined in Figure 5.1. All the information we need about the procedure is given in the procedure heading. It as well as some other declarations that might appear in a program are

```
type Rating = 0 . . 10;
var A, B: Rating;
procedure Exchange(var X, Y: integer);
{Interchanges the values of X and Y.}
```

In a program with these declarations, it seems perfectly natural to include a procedure call such as the following:

```
Exchange(A, B)
```

Although it seems natural, it will produce an error message and will prevent the program from running to completion. The reason is that the formal and actual parameter types do not match. The formal parameters are of type integer, whereas the actual parameters are of type Rating. Sometimes this problem can make the use of a subrange type impractical.

Type matching of value parameters is more complicated to explain, but it causes fewer problems because it allows a certain amount of mixing of types. The basic rule that applies for value parameters is the same as that for variable parameters: The formal and actual parameters must be of compatible types. In fact, the value of the actual parameter must be of the same type as the formal parameter, but because of automatic type conversion and the overlapping of type values, this is a fairly forgiving rule.

A value of a subrange type is also considered to be a value of the host type, and so type conflicts with value parameters are not as likely to occur as they are with variable parameters. For example, consider the following procedure:

```
procedure WriteResult(X: integer);
begin
  writeln('The result is ', X)
end;
```

With A declared to be of type Rating, the following procedure call is perfectly valid:

```
WriteResult(A)
```

There is no type conflict in this case because it is the *value* of the actual parameter A that must agree in type with the formal parameter X. Although A is of type Rating, the *value* of A is considered to be of type integer, in addition to being of type Rating.

As has been noted in previous chapters, a value of type integer can be used anywhere that a value of type real can be used. The computer automatically converts the integer value to an approximately equivalent real value. Hence, if a formal value parameter is of type real, the actual parameter is allowed to be of type integer.

Pitfall

Anonymous Types

It is possible to use a subrange type definition directly in a variable declaration, rather than first defining a type name. For example, the following declares the variable I to be of type 1 . . 10:

```
var I: 1 . . 10;
```

These unnamed types are called *anonymous types,* and it is poor programming practice to use them.

type equivalence

To understand the problem with anonymous types, you need to know how the Pascal language determines type equivalence. In Pascal, two types are not the same unless they have the same name. As an absurd but very illustrative example, consider the type declarations below:

```
type SmallInteger = 1 . . 10;
     PetiteInteger = 1 . . 10;
```

In Pascal the two types `SmallInteger` and `PetiteInteger` are considered to be *different types!* Hence, among other things, an actual *variable parameter* of type `SmallInteger` cannot be substituted for a formal *variable parameter* of type `PetiteInteger` in a procedure call.

A more likely instance of this problem involves anonymous types. Consider the following declarations:

```
type SmallInteger = 1 . . 10;
var X: 1 . . 10;
```

With these declarations, the variable X cannot be used as an actual *variable parameter* of type `SmallInteger`. Since the type of the variable X has no name whatsoever, it cannot have the same name as any named type. Hence, it cannot be an actual variable parameter in any procedure whatsoever! (It can be an actual *value parameter,* but that is not much consolation.)

The way to avoid these problems is obvious: Always declare a unique name for every defined type. This lesson applies to all programmer-defined types, including the ones we will introduce in the chapters that follow.

Case Study

Complete Calendar Program

Problem Definition

We want to embed the calendar display procedure from Figure 7.19 in a complete calendar program. The calendar program will accept a month and year which are input as two integers and will then output the calendar display for that particular month and year.

refining the definition

Calendars are now taken for granted, and so we tend to forget that they are a complicated computational task. Historically they have presented society with serious problems, ones that have not always been completely solved. The calendar design has changed more than once. A date like January 1, 1132, has more than one possible interpretation, since a different calendar was used then as opposed to now (which makes one wonder what time the word "then" refers to). As we indicated in Chapter 5, calculating leap years is complicated enough to require a special computation for some century years. Moreover, if we go back far enough in history or go forward far enough into the future, then that algorithm will not work accurately enough, and we will need to complicate the calculation even more. To eliminate all these problems, we will only require that the program apply to years in the relatively near past and the relatively near future. Specifically, we will only require that the program work for the years 1901 through 2999. For those years, a year is a leap year if it is divisible by 4, and no additional corrections are needed. This rule even works correctly for the century year 2000, although it does not work correctly for the years 1900 and 3000.

Discussion

As was indicated in the previous paragraph this task is likely to be computationally complicated and delicate. A hastily constructed solution will undoubtedly give incorrect results as well as the frustration that results from wasted effort. This problem will require more care and more inspiration than the other problems we have seen, and so we will proceed slowly and methodically.

The task of displaying the calendar for a given month can be divided into three main subtasks:

> DayOne: Determine what day of the week (Sunday, Monday, etc.)
> the first day of the month falls on.
> TotalDays: Determine how many days there are in the month.
> DisplayMonth: Call the procedure given in Figure 7.19.

use of functions

The data flow diagram for this decomposition is given in the top portion of Figure 8.13. Since the subtasks DayOne and TotalDays each do nothing other than produce a single value, they will be implemented as functions. To compute the number of days in month 2 (February), the procedure TotalDays will need to determine whether the year is a leap year or not. To find out, it will call a boolean-valued function called LeapYear, as shown in the data flow diagram.

subrange types

The only meaningful values for the variable Month are the numbers 1 through 12. Hence, we can declare it to be of the subrange type 1 . . 12. That way, if we make a mistake and allow the program to set it equal to some other value, we will get an error message that will help us to locate the mistake. We will call this subrange type MonthInteger. Similarly, the variable Year can be declared to be of the subrange type 1901 . . 2999, which we will name YearInteger.

The function TotalDays will return the number of days in a month. We could use the type integer as the type of the value returned, but it would be preferable to use a subrange type as an additional check for mistakes in the function computation. We will therefore define a type MonthDay as 1 . . 31 and use this as the type of the value returned by the function. Thus, our program will include the following declarations (and possibly others as well):

```
type MonthDay = 1 . . 31;
     MonthInteger = 1 . . 12;
     YearInteger = 1901 . . 2999;
var Month: MonthInteger;
    Year: YearInteger;
```

ALGORITHM for TotalDays

The function TotalDays is one part of the program that is easy to construct. The procedure heading shows the subrange type that is returned:

```
function TotalDays(Month: MonthInteger,
                   Year: YearInteger): MonthDay;
```

The computation is carried out by a single *case* statement:

```
case Month of
   4, 6, 9, 11: TotalDays := 30;
```

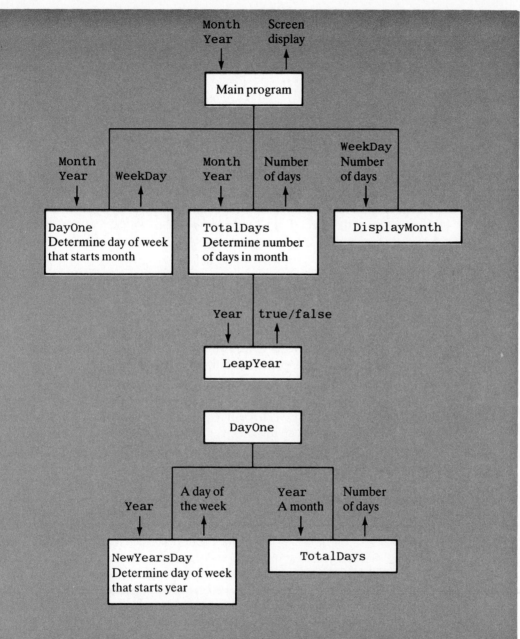

Data Summary

Month: an integer representing the month. (1 for January, 2 for February, etc.)
Year: the year. (Assumed to be in the range 1901 through 2999. 1901 and 2999 are permitted.)
WeekDay: an integer representing the first day of the week for the specified month and year.
(0 for Sunday, 1 for Monday, . . . , 6 for Saturday.)

**Figure 8.13
Data flow
diagram
for calendar
program.**

```
1, 3, 5, 7, 8, 10, 12: TotalDays := 31;
2: if not LeapYear(Year) then
      TotalDays := 28
  else
      TotalDays := 29
end
```

The complete function declaration is trivial to produce by combining these two items.

Discussion of DayOne

The function DayOne is the complicated part of this programming assignment. It takes two arguments, Month and Year, and should return the day of the week (Sunday, Monday, etc.) for the start of the given month of the specified year. The days of the week are coded as the integers of a subrange type called WeekDay, which we define to be 0 . . 6. (Sunday is 0, Monday is 1, etc.) We thus need to add another type declaration:

type WeekDay = 0 . . 6; {*Sunday is 0.*}

January 1, 1901

Our approach to this problem will be to take a fixed date for which we know the day of the week and to calculate days of the week by counting forward from that day. January 1, 1901, was a Tuesday. Since Tuesday is represented by the number 2, we will define a constant called JanFirst1901 to be 2. The calculation for any values of the arguments Month and Year will proceed in two stages:

1. NewYearsDay: Calculate the day of the week for January 1 of Year.
2. DayOne: Use the result of task 1 to calculate the day of the week for the first day of the Month in that Year. (This will require knowing how many days there are in each month from January up to Month.)

The bottom part of the data flow diagram in Figure 8.13 fits this breakdown of subtasks into the overall computation.

Discussion of NewYearsDay

To obtain the algorithm for task 1, note that all years are either 365 days long or, in the case of leap years, 366 days long. If you look at the calendars for two successive years, you will see that if a year has 365 days, then January 1 moves ahead one day of the week the next year. (If you do not have two calendars handy, you can confirm this by the fact that $(365 \bmod 7)$ is equal to 1.) Hence, since January 1, 1901, is a Tuesday (day 2), January 1, 1902, must be a Wednesday (day 3), and January 1, 1903, must be a Thursday (day 4). Although 1904 is a leap year, January 1, 1904, occurs before the extra leap-year day is inserted, and so it is a Friday (day 5). January 1, 1905, falls after the extra day inserted in February 1904, and so January 1, 1905, falls on a Sunday (day 0, obtained as $(5 + 2) \bmod 7$).

To obtain the day of the week for any January first after 1901, we can start with the day JanFirst1901, add one for each 365-day year, and add two for each leap year up to the desired year. All this addition is performed counting by sevens, so that 7 is the same as 0; in other words, we apply the operator *mod* 7 to our calculations.

Hence, our first try at an algorithm for the function NewYearsDay is to return the value

  (JanFirst1901 + (number of non–leap years) + 2 * (the number of leap years)) *mod* 7

An alternative and easier algorithm is to add one for *every* year and then add only 1 instead of 2 for the leap years. This leads to the following code:

```
ElapsedYears := Year - 1901;                    ALGORITHM
LeapYearCount := (ElapsedYears div 4);          for NewYearsDay
   return the value
     (JanFirst1901 + ElapsedYears + LeapYearCount) mod 7
```

Discussion of Dayone, **Concluded**

All that remains is to construct the algorithm for the function DayOne. The function has two arguments, one for the Month and one for the Year. The computation starts with the value

  NewYearsDay(Year)

and then adds in the number of days in every month up to Month to obtain an integer called DayCount. The day of the week for the first day of the specified month is then computed as

  DayCount *mod* 7

The complete program, including this function, is given in Figure 8.14.

Use of Subrange Types for Error Detection

A common mistake when calling a function or procedure is to give the parameters in an incorrect order. For example, if the function DayOne is declared as in Figure 8.14, then the following will evaluate to the first day of February 1950:

  DayOne(2, 1950)

Suppose that we accidentally reverse the arguments:

  DayOne(1950, 2)

Since we used subrange types for the formal parameters, the computer will detect an error and output an error message. The computer will see that the value 1950 is not of the type MonthInteger, which is defined as 1 . . 12, and will alert you to a problem. If the parameters had instead been defined to be of type integer, then the function might simply return an incorrect value. Such a mistake is likely to go unnoticed if you do not use subrange types. (Do you know what day of the week February 1, 1950, fell on?) Even if the computer does catch this mistake in some other way, it is not likely to find the correct location of the mistake unless you use subrange types.

Program

```
program Calendar(input, output);
{Displays a calendar for any month from January 1901 through December 2999.}
type WeekDay = 0 . . 6; {Sunday is 0.}
     MonthDay = 1 . . 31;
     MonthInteger = 1 . . 12;
     YearInteger = 1901 . . 2999; {The simple
     leap-year calculation used does not work for 1900 or 3000.}
var Month: MonthInteger;
    Year: YearInteger;
    Ans: char;

function NewYearsDay(Year: YearInteger): WeekDay;
{Returns a code for the day of the week for January 1 of the specified Year.
The function does not work correctly if you change the type of
Year to integer and use years such as 1900 or 3000.}
const JanFirst1901 = 2; {Tuesday}
var ElapsedYears: integer;
    LeapYearCount: integer;
begin{NewYearsDay}
  ElapsedYears := Year - 1901;
  LeapYearCount := (ElapsedYears div 4);
  NewYearsDay :=
    (JanFirst1901 + ElapsedYears + LeapYearCount) mod 7
end; {NewYearsDay}

function LeapYear(Year: YearInteger): boolean;
{Returns true if Year is a leap year. This function will not work
correctly if the type of Year is changed to the type integer. For example,
1900 and 3000 would both return true, but neither one is a leap year.}
begin{LeapYear}
  LeapYear := (Year mod 4) = 0
end; {LeapYear}

function TotalDays(Month: MonthInteger;
                   Year: YearInteger): MonthDay;
{Returns the number of days in the Month of the given Year.}
begin{TotalDays}
  case Month of
    4, 6, 9, 11: TotalDays := 30;
    1, 3, 5, 7, 8, 10, 12: TotalDays := 31;
    2: if not LeapYear(Year) then
          TotalDays := 28
       else
          TotalDays := 29
  end {case}
end; {TotalDays}
```

Figure 8.14

Complete calendar program.

```
function DayOne(Month: MonthInteger;
                Year: YearInteger): WeekDay;
{Returns a code for the day of the week for the first day of the Month
of the specified Year. Calls the functions NewYearsDay and TotalDays.}
var DayCount: integer;
    PastMonth: MonthInteger;
begin{DayOne}
  DayCount := NewYearsDay(Year);
  for PastMonth := 1 to (Month - 1) do
     DayCount := DayCount + TotalDays(PastMonth, Year);
  DayOne := DayCount mod 7
end; {DayOne}


procedure DisplayMonth(NumberOfDays: MonthDay; FirstDay: WeekDay);
{Displays the usual layout for a month with NumberOfDays days in it.
FirstDay codes the first day of the month: 0 for Sunday, 1 for Monday, etc.
The procedure code is identical to that in Figure 7.19, but the parameter
types have been changed to subrange types in order to provide an additional
check for errors in the program.}
const Width = 4; {Field width for one day of the calendar.}
      Blank = ' ';
var DayCount, CountAll: integer;
begin{DisplayMonth}
  writeln('Sun':Width, 'Mon':Width,
          'Tue':Width, 'Wed':Width,
          'Thu':Width, 'Fri':Width, 'Sat':Width);
  for CountAll := 0 to FirstDay - 1 do
     write(Blank :Width);
  CountAll := FirstDay;
  for DayCount := 1 to NumberOfDays do
    begin{for}
      CountAll := CountAll + 1;
      {If (CountAll mod 7) = 0, then day number DayCount is a Saturday.}
      write(DayCount :Width);
      if (CountAll mod 7) = 0 then
         writeln
    end; {for}
  writeln
end; {DisplayMonth}


begin{Program}
  writeln('This program will display the calendar for');
  writeln('any month from the years 1901 to 2999.');
```

Figure 8.14
(continued)

```
repeat
   writeln('Enter month and year as two integers: ');
   readln(Month, Year);
   writeln('Month ' :12, Month :2, ' Year ', Year :4);
   DisplayMonth(TotalDays(Month, Year), DayOne(Month, Year));
   writeln('Do you want to see another month? (y/n) ');
   readln(Ans)
until (Ans = 'n') or (Ans = 'N');
writeln('Have a good month!')
end. {Program}
```

Sample Dialogue

```
This program will display the calendar for
any month from the years 1901 to 2999.
Enter month and year as two integers:
6 1944
         Month 6 Year 1944
Sun    Mon   Tue   Wed   Thu   Fri   Sat
                           1     2     3
  4      5     6     7     8     9    10
 11     12    13    14    15    16    17
 18     19    20    21    22    23    24
 25     26    27    28    29    30
Do you want to see another month?  (y/n):
no
Have a good month!
```

Figure 8.14
(continued)

Enumerated Types
(Optional)

There is one other kind of ordinal type. Types of this kind are called *enumerated types*. An enumerated type is just a list of values named by identifiers. Enumerated types have some similarity to "society types" who have lost their wealth. The values of an enumerated type have no properties other than their order and their names. Despite their simple nature, enumerated types can be useful. By choosing the identifiers to be meaningful names, you can sometimes use enumerated types to make a program easier to read. For example, the following type declaration declares the names of four kinds of vehicles to be values of an enumerated type:

```
type Vehicle = (Motorcycle, Car, Bus, Truck);
```

This type has four values named by the four identifiers in the list.

declaration   All type declarations are given in the same place in a program, in the same manner that we described for subrange types. Moreover, it is permissible to intermix subrange, enumerated, and other, yet to be introduced, type declarations. The identifier *type* is written once, and then each identifier in the type declaration section is set equal to its definition. For an enumerated type, the type definition follows the above example. The definition consists of a list of identifiers enclosed in parentheses. The list of identifiers are the names of the constants of that type, and they are ordered as in the list.

As with other types, there can be variables of an enumerated type. For example, the following declares `Class` to be of type `Vehicle`:

variables

```
var Class: Vehicle;
```

Variables of an enumerated type and their values behave much like those of any other type. For example, the following makes `Bus` the value of the variable `Class`:

```
Class := Bus
```

One common use of enumerated types is in *case* statements, such as the following:

uses of enumerated types

```
case Class of
   Motorcycle: Toll := 0.25;
   Car: Toll := 0.50;
   Truck, Bus: Toll := 1.00
end
```

The enumerated type serves two purposes here: It makes the program meaning clearer, and it guarantees that the *case* statement is almost always defined. The variable `Class` cannot take on a value that is not on some statement label list. The only way that the *case* statement can be undefined is if the variable `Class` were never initialized. Of course, a subrange type can sometimes serve the same purpose, but an enumerated type allows more flexibility in choosing label names.

It is important to note that the elements of an enumerated type are not strings and can neither be read in nor written out by a program. In a program with the above declarations, the following will produce no output other than an error message:

```
write(Truck)  {Not allowed.}
```

If you wish to output a value of an enumerated type, you must somehow output a string value that indicates the value of the variable. For example, the following will output the value of the variable `Class` of type `Vehicle`:

```
case Class of
   Motorcycle: write('Motorcycle');
   Car: write('Car');
   Bus: write('Bus');
   Truck: write('Truck')
end {case}
```

This may seem like a lot of work just to add two quotes, but it is necessary. The values `Truck` and `'Truck'` are very different; they are not even of the same data type.

Figure 8.15 shows a program that uses an enumerated type for the days of the week. Notice that since an enumerated type is an ordinal type, it can be the type of a *for* loop control variable.

Program

```
program Payroll(input, output);
{Computes an hourly employee's weekly pay.}
const Width = 8; {Field width for total wages.}
      SatAdjustment = 1.5; {Time and a half.}
      SunAdjustment = 2.0; {Double time.}
type WeekDay = (Mon, Tue, Wed, Thur, Fri, Sat, Sun);
var BaseRate, Wages: real;
    Day: WeekDay;
    Hours: integer;

function Rate(BaseRate: real; Day: WeekDay): real;
{Returns the rate of pay for the day of the week.}
begin{Rate}
  case Day of
    Mon, Tue, Wed, Thur, Fri: Rate := BaseRate;
    Sat: Rate := SatAdjustment*BaseRate;
    Sun: Rate := SunAdjustment*BaseRate
  end {case}
end; {Rate}

begin{Program}
  writeln('Enter the basic hourly wage rate: ');
  readln(BaseRate);
  Wages := 0.0;
  writeln('Enter the hours worked');
  writeln('for Monday through Sunday: ');
  for Day := Mon to Sun do
    begin{for}
      read(Hours);
      Wages := Wages + Hours*Rate(BaseRate, Day)
    end; {for}
  readln;

  writeln('Wages for the week total: $', Wages :Width:2)
end. {Program}
```

Sample Dialogue

```
Enter the basic hourly wage rate:
10.00
Enter the hours worked
for Monday through Sunday:
8 8 8 8 8 0 2
Wages for the week total: $ 440.00
```

**Figure 8.15
(Optional)
Program using an
enumerated type.**

It would produce a dreadful mess if
we were to do anything together.
You see, we're different types.

Overheard at a cocktail party

Summary of Problem Solving and Programming Techniques

- When you are designing a program, it is very common for one or more subtasks to be the computation of a single value. In those cases, the subtasks should be implemented as functions.
- A restatement of a problem definition can often yield an algorithm or a hint of an algorithm for the problem.
- When you are designing functions, it is usually a bad idea to allow side effects, such as changing a global variable or using a variable parameter. If such things are needed, it is usually clearer to use a procedure rather than a function.
- A boolean-valued function can simplify an *if-then-else* statement by making a separate task of evaluating the boolean expression.
- When you are designing a function (or any other program part, such as a loop), it is wise to check for special cases and extreme values such as the first or last value in a list.
- Any ordinal type may be used as the type of the control variable of a *for* loop or as the type of the controlling expression of a *case* statement.
- Declaring variables to be of a subrange type is a form of error checking. If your program erroneously produces a value outside the expected range, the computer will detect this and issue an error message.

Summary of Pascal Constructs

function declaration heading

Syntax:

> *function* <function name> (<formal parameter list>) : <type returned>;

Example:

> *function* Area (Length, Width: real): real;

The <formal parameter list> can be anything that is allowed as a procedure formal parameter list. The <type returned> may be the type real or any ordinal type, such as integer, char, boolean, or a subrange type. (Most of the types we will introduce later on are not allowed. In fact, the only other types allowed are the pointer types, a class of types not introduced until Chapter 17.)

function declaration

The syntax for a function declaration is the same as that for a procedure declaration except for two points: The heading of a function declaration is as described above, and the body of the declaration must contain an assignment statement with the function name on the left-hand side of the assignment operator.

function call

Syntax:

<function name> (<argument list>)

Example:

```
X := Area(3.79, 8.9)
```

A function call can appear in exactly the same places that a constant of the type returned by the function can appear. It is an expression and evaluates to a value of the type specified in the function declaration. This value is called the value returned. The value returned is equal to the last value assigned to the function name when the statements given in the function declaration are executed. The <argument list> is the same as an actual parameter list and is handled in exactly the same way as an actual parameter list for a procedure. At the time that the function call is evaluated, all the statements in the body of the function declaration are executed, and so any side effects, such as setting a variable parameter, will take place at that time.

subrange type declarations

Syntax:

type <type name 1> = <lower limit 1> . . <upper limit 1>;
 <type name 2> = <lower limit 2> . . <upper limit 2>;

.
.
.

<type name n> = <lower limit n> . . <upper limit n>;

Example:

```
type Index = 0 . . 100;
     Grades = 'A' . . 'F';
```

The type names are identifiers chosen by the programmer. For each i, <lower limit i> and <upper limit i> must be constants of the same ordinal type. <lower limit i> must be less than or equal to <upper limit i>.

subrange variable declarations

Example:

```
var I: Index;
    Latin, Math, Psych: Grades;
```

Variables of a subrange type are declared just like variables of predefined types such as `integer`. A variable of a subrange type may only take on values in the range specified in the type declaration.

Exercises

Self-Test Exercises

10. Which of the following are legal type definitions?

```
const Max = 1000;
type SmallNegInteger = -100 . . -1;
     SmallNegNumber = -1 . . -100;
     GradePoint = 0.0 . . 4.0;
     Initial = 'A' . . 'Z';
     Range = 0 . . Max;
     SmallRange = 0 . . Max - 100;
```

11. Give suitable type declarations for data of each of the following kinds: exam scores in the range 0 to 100; the nonnegative integers; the integers whose absolute value is at most 100.

12. (This exercise uses the optional section "Enumerated Types.") Can a program read in a value of an enumerated type from the keyboard? Can it write one to the screen?

Interactive Exercises

13. Determine the ordering of the letters on your system. Do lowercase letters come before uppercase letters or after them, or are they intermixed? Are there any special characters mixed in with the letters? For example, is there any character between `'A'` and `'B'`?

14. (This exercise uses the optional section "Random Number Generators.") Write a program that requests a seed value and then outputs 20 random numbers generated by the function Random in Figure 8.9.

15. (This exercise uses the optional sections "Random Number Generators" and "Using Pseudorandom Numbers.") Do the previous exercise, this time using the function RandomReal from Figure 8.11.

16. (This exercise uses the optional section "More Standard Functions.") For positive values of x, the value x^y can be computed as

```
exp( y*ln(x) )
```

The advantage of this formula over the function Power in Figure 8.3 is that this formula allows fractional exponents. Write a program that reads in decimal numbers x and y and outputs x^y.

17. (This exercise uses the optional section "The Functions pred, succ, ord, and chr.") Determine the "ring bell" character number for your system. Feel free to look it up in a manual or to ask a friend.

Programming Exercises

18. Write a function declaration for a function called Grader that takes a numeric score and returns a letter grade. Grader has one argument of type integer and returns a value of type char. Use the rule that 90 to 100 is an A, 80 to 89 is a B, 70 to 79 is a C, and less than 70 is an F. Embed it in a test program.

19. Write a function declaration for a function that computes interest on a credit card account balance. The function has arguments for the initial balance, the monthly interest rate, and the number of months for which interest must be paid. The value returned is the interest due. Do not forget to compound the interest, that is, to charge interest on the interest due. The interest due is added into the balance due, and the interest for the next month is computed using this larger balance. Embed the function in a test program.

20. (This exercise uses the optional section "More Standard Functions.") The perimeter P of an n-sided polygon circumscribing a circle of radius r is given by

$$P = 2nr \times tan(\pi / n)$$

Write a function declaration that will return the perimeter of such a polygon given the values of n and r as arguments. Embed the function in a program as a test of the function declaration. The program should include a test to see if n is less than 3, since the formula, and hence the function, will not work unless n is 3 or more.

21. Write a program that gives the user the choice of computing the area of any of the following: a circle, a square, a rectangle, or a triangle. The program should include a loop to allow the user to perform as many calculations as desired. Use a function for each of the different kinds of calculations.

22. In order to discourage excess consumption, an electric company charges its customers a lower rate, namely $0.11, for each of the first 250 kilowatt hours, and a higher rate of $0.17 for each additional kilowatt hour. In addition, a 10% surtax is added to the final bill. Write a program to calculate electric bills given the number of kilowatt hours consumed as input. Use two function declarations: one to compute the amount due without the surtax and one to compute the total due. The declaration for the second function should include a call to the first function.

23. (This exercise uses the optional case study "Testing for Primes.") The function Prime in Figure 8.7 can be made more efficient in a number of ways. First, there is no reason to continue to loop through more checks once a divisor of N is found. At that point you know that N is not prime. For example, once you know that 1000 is divisible by 2 you know it is not a prime and need not test to see if it is divisible by 3, 4, and so forth. Replace the *for* loop with a *repeat* or *while* loop that will terminate the loop as soon as it is discovered that an argument is not a prime. Also, there is no need to test all numbers up to N−1. Determine and use a smaller limit on the maximum number of loop iterations.

24. The greatest common divisor of two positive integers is the largest integer that divides them both. For example, the greatest common divisor of 9 and 6 is 3. Write a function declaration for a function with two integer arguments that returns their greatest common divisor.

25. (This exercise uses the optional sections "Random Number Generators" and "Using Pseudorandom Numbers.") Write a program that outputs random but grammatically correct sentences. The sentences can be simple sentences that take the following form: a noun followed by a verb, followed by a noun. Use a pseudorandom number generator to choose a noun from a list of 10 nouns and a verb from a list of 10 verbs.

26. (This exercise uses the optional sections "Random Number Generators" and "Using Pseudorandom Numbers.") Write a program that will simulate a roll of two dice to produce a value between 2 and 12. If your system has a predefined pseudorandom number generator, use it; otherwise, use the function Random described in the text.

27. The game of Nim is played as follows. There are three piles of sticks. Two players take turns making moves. A move consists of picking up as many sticks as the player desires, subject to the following constraints: All the sticks must be picked up from the same pile, and a player must pick up at least one stick. The player who picks up the last stick loses. Write a program to play Nim with the user. The piles of sticks should initially contain three, five, and seven sticks each. The computer can use any strategy you wish so long as it obeys the rules. Display the piles as three lists of a symbol of your choice, such as ' ! ', so that the piles are displayed as something like

```
! ! !
! ! ! ! !
! ! ! ! ! ! !
```

28. (This exercise uses the optional sections "Random Number Generators" and "Using Pseudorandom Numbers.") Redo the previous exercise (or do it for the first time), but this time use a pseudorandom number generator to choose the size of the three piles, subject to the constraints that the three piles must be of different sizes and must contain at least 2 and at most 10 sticks. The computer should use a pseudorandom number generator to decide on moves.

29. (This exercise uses the optional sections "Random Number Generators" and "Using Pseudorandom Numbers.") Write a function declaration for a function called Deal that returns a card chosen at random from a standard deck of cards. Code the value of the card as an integer value: 2 through 10 as itself, jack as 11, queen as 12, king as 13, and ace as 14. Your program need not remember what cards are dealt, and so, for example, it might deal five aces. You can ignore suits (diamonds, clubs, etc.).

30. (This exercise uses the optional sections "Random Number Generators" and "Using Pseudorandom Numbers.") Write a program to play blackjack that uses the procedure Deal from the previous exercise. The program deals two cards to the user and two cards to itself (all cards are shown to the user). The user can then request more cards until he or she is busted or wants to stop. The program then deals additional cards to itself until its score exceeds 16. Allow the user to play additional hands until he or she wants to stop.

31. (This exercise uses the optional sections "Random Number Generators" and "Using Pseudorandom Numbers.") One way to estimate the area of a figure is to enclose it in a figure whose area you know and to then choose points at random within the figure of known area. The ratio of the number of points in the figure of unknown area to the number of points in the enclosing figure of known area is the same as the ratio of the unknown area to the known area. (Remember to count the total number of points as the points in the figure of known area. Those that are in the figure of unknown area are also in the larger figure.) Use this technique with a circle enclosed in a square to estimate the area of a circle with a radius of 1. Then use the formula

$$Area = \pi r^2$$

with that estimate of *Area* and solve for π to get an estimate of π. Do this all with a program that uses a pseudorandom number generator to choose points.

32. Write a program to compute the monthly cost of a house based on the following four input values: the purchase price, the annual fuel costs, the tax rate expresses as tax per \$1000, and the down payment. The monthly cost is 1/12th of the annual cost obtained by summing the costs of tax, fuel, and mortgage. The annual tax is obtained by multiplying the tax rate by the purchase price. For example if the rate is \$20.50 per \$1000 and the purchase price is \$100,000, then the annual tax is \$2,050. The annual mortgage cost is 10% of the balance left after deducting the down payment from the purchase price. The program should repeat the calculation for new inputs as often as the user desires.

33. (This exercise uses the optional section "More Standard Functions.") Write a function declaration for a function called `SineDeg`. This function differs from the standard function `sin` in that its argument is in degrees rather than radians. Use a local function that converts from degrees to radians, and use a call to `sin`. Write similar function declarations for `cos` and `tan`. Embed these in a program that takes as input an angular measure in degrees and then outputs the sine, cosine, and tangent of that angle.

References for Further Reading

D.E. Knuth, *The Art of Computer Programming, Volume 2, Seminumerical Algorithms,* second edition, 1981, Addison-Wesley, Reading, Mass. More-advanced material on random number generators. Does not use Pascal, but the text can be read without reading the programs.

*It is a capital mistake
to theorize before one has data.*
SIR ARTHUR CONAN DOYLE (SHERLOCK HOLMES),
SCANDAL IN BOHEMIA

Chapter Contents

In this chapter we introduce a common and extremely useful class of defined data types known as *arrays*. These will be our first examples of *structured types* and will serve to introduce both the idea of a structured type and the importance of these types to problem solving. A structured type can be described briefly as a complex type built up from simpler types. A more detailed discussion of the concept is included in the chapter.

Introduction to Arrays

Suppose we wish to write a program that reads in five test scores and then manipulates the scores in some way. For instance, the program might compute the highest test score and then output the amount by which each score falls short of the highest score. The highest score is not known until all five scores are read in. Hence, all five scores must be retained in storage so that after the highest score is computed each individual score can be compared to it. To retain the five scores, we will need something equivalent to five variables of type `integer`. We could use five individual variables of type `integer`, but five variables are hard to keep track of, so this is not an elegant solution. We could make the program more readable by giving the variables related names, such as `Score1`, `Score2`, and so forth, but this solution becomes absurd if the number of scores is very large. Imagine doing this if there were 100 scores instead of just 5. The solution we will propose is similar to this idea of using a list of variables, but it will handle the details in a much neater fashion.

To solve this dilemma, we introduce a new Pascal construct known as an *array*. An array is rather like a list of variables, each of which has a two-part name. One part of the name is the same for each of the variables that collectively constitute the array. The other part is different for each variable. For example, the five names for the five individual variables we need might be `Score[1]`, `Score[2]`, `Score[3]`, `Score[4]`, and `Score[5]`. The part that does not change, in this case `Score`, is the name of the array. In this example, the part that can change is an integer in the subrange 1 . . 5.

In Pascal the type and variable declarations for an array of the kind just described can be given as follows:

```
type  SmallArray = array[1 . . 5] of integer;
var Score: SmallArray;
```

The type given after the word *of,* such as `integer` in the above declaration, is called the *component type* or *base type*. This declaration is like declaring the following five variables to all be of type `integer`:

component type

```
Score[1], Score[2], Score[3], Score[4], Score[5]
```

Variables like the above five that are derived from an array name are called *indexed variables* in order to distinguish them from the sort of variables we have seen up to now. These five indexed variable names are not valid Pascal identifiers since they contain the square bracket symbols [ ], and so they may not look like variables. However, they have all the properties of variables. An indexed variable like `Score[1]` can be used *anyplace* that an ordinary variable of type `integer` can be used. For example, with `Score` declared in this way all of the following are possible:

indexed variables

```
readln(Score[1], X, Score[5]);
writeln(Score[1], Score[2], X);
X := Score[3];
Score[4] := X;
{X is a variable of type integer.}
```

In addition to having all the properties of simple variables, these indexed variables have other properties that simple variables do not have. The most important such property is that a variable or more complicated expression can be used inside the square brackets.

index

The expression inside the square brackets is called the *index expression* or, more simply, the *index*. These indexes have some similarity to the subscripts on the subscripted variables used in mathematics, like the i in x_i, and hence some programmers use the term *subscript* as a synonym for "index." Array indexes are truly `integer` values. For our sample array `Score`, any integer expression that evaluates to a value of the·subrange type 1 . . 5 can be placed inside the square brackets. This provides the program with a way of manipulating the names of the indexed variables. For example, the following code sets the value of `Score[2]` to 99 and outputs it to the screen twice:

```
X := 2;
Score[X] := 99;
writeln(Score[X]);
writeln(Score[2])
```

The variable X may be of type 1 . . 5 or of type `integer`. Figure 9.1 presents a summary of the terms used in discussing indexed variables.

elements

Two things should be observed in the preceding piece of code. First, the array index can be a variable. This allows the program to say things equivalent to "do the following to the Xth indexed variable." Second, the identity of an indexed variable, such as `Score[X]`, is determined by the value of its index (and, of course, by the array name, like `Score`). In the example of the previous paragraph, `Score[2]` and `Score[X]` are the exact same indexed variable, because the value of X is 2. Similarly, if the value of X is 2, the indexed variable `Score[X + 3]` is the exact same variable as `Score[5]`.

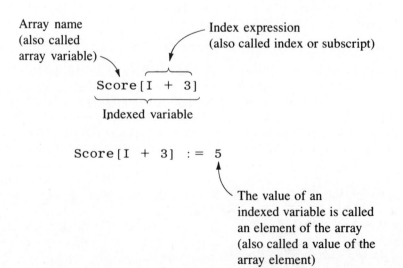

Array name
(also called
array variable)

Index expression
(also called index or subscript)

Score[I + 3]

Indexed variable

Score[I + 3] := 5

The value of an
indexed variable is called
an element of the array
(also called a value of the
array element)

Figure 9.1
Indexed variable.

Score [1]	Score [2]	Score [3]	Score [4]	Score [5]
9	6	2	10	7

Values of array elements before code is executed

Sample Code

```
writeln(Score[2]);  {Display the value of Score[2] = 6 on the screen.}
Score[2] := 9;      {Change the value of Score[2] from 6 to 9.}
I := 2;
Score[I + 3] := 8;  {Change the value of Score[5] from 7 to 8.}
Score[1] := Score[4] - 6;  {Change the value of Score[1] from 9 to
                                   10 - 6 = 4.}
```

Score [1]	Score [2]	Score [3]	Score [4]	Score [5]
4	9	2	10	8

Values of array elements after code is executed

**Figure 9.2
Manipulating
array elements.**

Figure 9.2 provides an explanation of how a sample piece of Pascal code manipulates the indexes and elements of the array Score.

For another example, suppose that the value of X is 2 and that Pro is a procedure with one variable parameter of type integer. Then the procedure call

```
Pro(Score[X])
```

is equivalent to

```
Pro(Score[2])
```

Hence, when an indexed variable serves as an actual variable parameter, the index expression is always evaluated before the indexed variable is substituted for the formal parameter. *indexed variables as parameters*

An array type is declared in the same place and in the same general manner as a subrange type. As with any type declaration, the declaration for an array type consists of the type name followed by an equal sign, the type definition, and a semicolon. The form of an array type definition is given by the syntax diagram in Figure 9.3. For example, consider the declaration for the array Score given earlier in this section. The identifier SmallArray is declared to be an array type. In that declaration we used 1 . . 5 as a <subrange type definition>. Any subrange type definition or any previously declared name of a subrange type can be used instead. As the component type we used the type integer. Any Pascal type, including the types we will introduce in later chapters, may be used as the component type. *type declaration* *component type*

The syntax diagram in Figure 9.3 indicates that you can use any ordinal type name to specify the index type of an array. Hence, you can use the types boolean and char as index types. However, it is not practical to use the full type integer *index type*

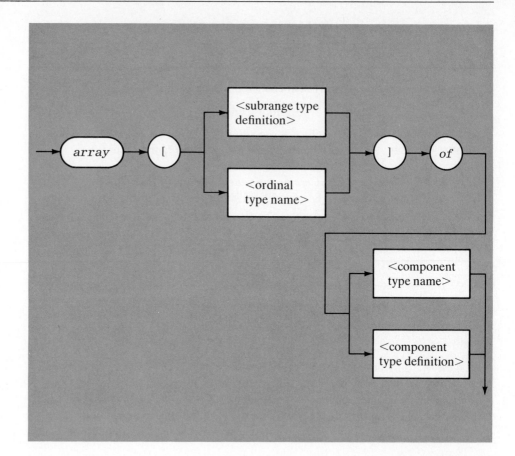

Figure 9.3
Syntax diagram for
an array type
definition.

as the index type of an array, even though it is an ordinal type. Definitions of the form
array [integer] *of* . . . will *not* work because the index type is too large.

Whatever the index type is, an array with that index type has one indexed variable
for each value of the index type. For example, consider the following declarations:

```
type Name1 = array[boolean] of integer;
     Name2 = array[0 . . 2] of char;
     Name3 = array['a' . . 'c'] of real;
var A: Name1;
    B: Name2;
    C: Name3;
```

The array A has two indexed variables: A[false] and A[true], each capable of
holding one integer. The array B has three indexed variables: B[0], B[1], and
B[2], each capable of holding one character value. The array C also has three indexed variables: C['a'], C['b'], and C['c'], each capable of holding one
value of type real.

Program

```
program ShowScores(input, output);
{Reads in 5 scores and shows how much each score differs from the highest score.}
type  SmallArray = array[1 . . 5] of integer;
var Score: SmallArray;
    I, Max: integer;
begin{Program}
  writeln('Enter five scores: ');
  read(Score[1]);
  Max := Score[1]; {Largest so far.}
  for I := 2 to 5 do
    begin{for}
      read(Score[I]);
      if Score[I] > Max then
          Max := Score[I]
      {Max is the largest of the values of Score[1], . . . ,Score[I].}
    end; {for}
  writeln('The highest is ', Max);
  writeln('The scores and');
  writeln('their difference from the highest are: ');
  for I := 1 to 5 do
      writeln(Score[I], ' off by ', Max − Score[I])
end. {Program}
```

Sample Dialogue

```
Enter five scores:
5 9 2 10 6
The highest is    10
The scores and
their differences from the highest are:
    5   off by   5
    9   off by   1
    2   off by   8
   10   off by   0
    6   off by   4
```

Figure 9.4
Program using an array.

Notice that once an array type name has been declared, a particular array is declared just like a variable. Neither the square brackets nor the index expression is included in the declaration of the array.

array
declaration

A complete program that uses an array to display scores in the manner described in the opening discussion of this section can be found in Figure 9.4. The algorithm for finding the highest score is essentially the same as that used for the program in Figure 7.9.

Pitfall

Use of Plurals in Array Definitions

An array of reals contains more than one number. Hence, the following type declaration seems natural:

```
type List = array[1 . . 25] of reals;
```

As innocent as it may look, it will produce an error message. There is no type named reals. The "s" that seems so natural to speakers of English is incomprehensible to the compiler. If you delete the "s," the declaration is correct. In array type definitions, the component type name is used unchanged, even though that may violate your sense of English grammar.

Type Declarations—A Summary

All type definitions are given together. Types may be defined in terms of named constants and in terms of other types. In fact, doing so can aid readability. For example, a program might open as follows:

```
program Sample(input, output);
const Start = 0;
      Stop = 100;
type Subscript = Start . . Stop;
     List = array[Subscript] of real;
var X, Y: real;
    I: Subscript;
    A, B: List;
```

Notice that no type name is used before it is defined.

local types   As with the other kinds of declarations, type declarations may be local to a procedure, although the need for local type declarations is rare. Like constants, types are usually best declared globally. The syntax for the declaration section of a program or procedure is summarized in Figure 9.5.

It is possible to use a type definition directly instead of first defining a type name. Hence, the following is a legal program opening:

```
program Sample(input, output);
var A, B: array[1 . . 100] of real;
```

parameter types   However, it is better to declare names for defined types and to refer to the types by name. When you are specifying a type for a procedure or function parameter, it is absolutely necessary to use a type name. A formal parameter list cannot contain any type definitions, only type names.

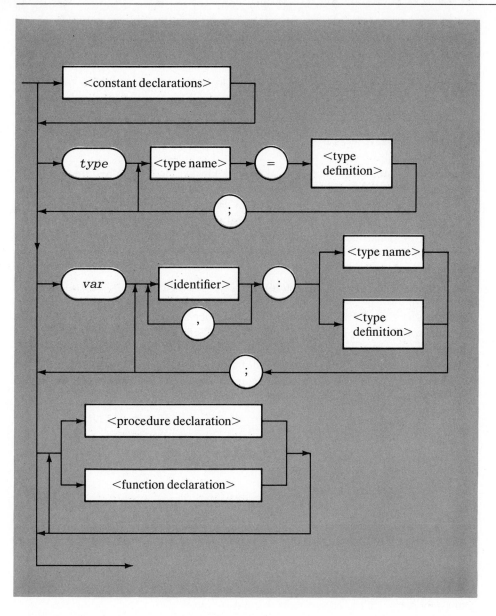

Figure 9.5
Declaration section
of a block.

Input and Output with Arrays

You cannot use an entire array as a parameter to a `read` or `readln` statement. For instance, if the array `Score` is declared as in Figure 9.4, then the following is not allowed:

`read(Score)`   *{NOT ALLOWED if Score is an array type.}*

Similarly, it is not possible to output an array with a statement like

> `write(Score)`   {*NOT ALLOWED if Score is an array type.*}

Typically, input and output of arrays is done with *for* loops, as in Figure 9.4.

Partially Filled Arrays

Often the exact size needed for an array is not known at the time a program is written. Sometimes the required size will differ from one run of the program to another. Some programming languages allow the size of an array to be determined by some sort of input at the time that the program is run; Pascal does not. Thus, if we do not know how large an array is needed, we must declare the array to be of the largest size that the program could possibly need. The program is then free to use as much or as little of the array as it needs.

Partially filled arrays require some special care. The program must keep track of how much of the array is used and must not reference any indexed variable that has not been given a value. To illustrate the point, consider the program in Figure 9.4. That program works fine provided that there are exactly five scores, but suppose that the number of scores varies from one run of the program to another. Perhaps different students who have taken different numbers of exams will be using the program. If we know the maximum possible number of scores, then we can declare the array to be that large. If the maximum number is 10, the following declarations will do:

```
const MaxIndex = 10;
type  Index = 1 . . MaxIndex;
      SmallArray = array[Index] of integer;
var Score: SmallArray;
    Last, I: Index;
```

Since there may be less than the maximum number of scores, the program needs to keep track of which indexed variables have been used. This can be accomplished with a variable `Last` to record the last index used, as illustrated in Figure 9.6. The scores are read into the array `Score`, and every time another number is entered into the array, the value of `Last` is increased by one. A complete program that illustrates this technique is displayed in Figure 9.7. Notice that when writing out the array, the program only outputs those components that have a value.

empty arrays   The sample program in Figure 9.7 had no need to allow for an empty list of scores. However, in other situations a program may have to cope with an empty list of data items. For example, a list of sales figures might be empty if no sales were made. In these cases, a program may need to record the fact that no array elements have been used. If the index type is 1 . . `MaxIndex` and the variable `Last` records the last index used, then an empty list can be indicated by setting `Last` equal to 0. If this is done, then the type of `Last` cannot be the index type of the array, since `Last` may assume a value outside that range. In this situation `Last` would have to be declared to be of type `integer` or of type 0 . . `MaxIndex`.

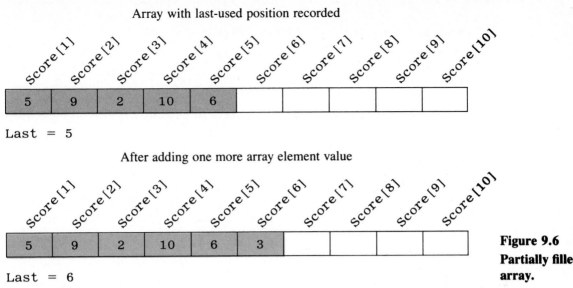

Figure 9.6
Partially filled
array.

Although we cannot write our programs so that the size of an array can be determined by the user, we can write our programs so that the array sizes can be increased or decreased by making only minor changes in the program. If we declare one or both bounds of the index type to be defined constants, like MaxIndex in our sample, we can then write the program in such a way that simply changing these defined constants will produce a correct program for different-sized arrays.

providing
for array
expansion

Pitfall

Array Index Out of Range

The most common programming error made when using arrays is attempting to reference a nonexistent index. If the index type is 1 . . MaxIndex for the array Score, then a reference to Score [I] when the value of I is either less than 1 or greater than MaxIndex is meaningless and will precipitate an error message that is likely to read "value range error" or "value out of bounds" or something similar. This is particularly likely to happen as the first or last step of a loop that processes the entire array.

A related, more subtle problem has to do with variables of the index type of an array. If the program attempts to set the value of such a variable to a value outside the index range, then the error message is likely to read the same, or almost the same, as if the program attempted to reference a nonexistent array index variable. For example, if Last is of type 1 . . 10 and the program sets Last equal to 0, then the error message can easily be mistaken for a reference to an array with index type 1 . . 10. Whenever you receive an error message

Program

```
program ShowScores2(input, output);
{Reads up to 10 scores and shows how much each score differs from
the highest score. Assumes there is at least one score.}
const MaxIndex = 10;
type  Index = 1 . . MaxIndex;
      SmallArray = array[Index] of integer;
var Score: SmallArray;
    Last, I: Index;
    Max: integer;
begin{Program}
  writeln('Enter up to ', MaxIndex, ' scores');
  writeln('and then press return: ');
  read(Score[1]);
  Max := Score[1]; {Largest so far.}
  Last := 1;
  while not eoln do
    begin{while}
      Last := Last + 1;
      read(Score[Last]);
      if Score[Last] > Max then
        Max := Score[Last]
      {Max is the largest of the values of Score[1], . . . ,Score[Last].}
    end; {while}
  writeln('The highest is ', Max);
  writeln('The scores and');
  writeln('their difference from the highest are: ');
  for I := 1 to Last do
    writeln(Score[I], ' off by ', Max - Score[I])
end. {Program}
```

Sample Dialogue

```
Enter up to    10 scores
and then press return:
5 9 2 10 6 3
The highest is    10
The scores and
their differences from the highest are:
   5  off by   5
   9  off by   1
   2  off by   8
  10  off by   0
   6  off by   4
   3  off by   7
```

Figure 9.7

Program using a partially filled array.

that reads "value range error," or whatever message your system gives when an array index is out of range, always check variables of subrange types as well as all arrays. The problem might involve a simple variable rather than an array.

> When reading input into an array with a loop, one way to guard against an illegal array index value is to test to see if the array is full and to terminate the loop if the array is filled. In Figure 9.8 we have rewritten the loop from the program in Figure 9.7 so that it does just that. Be sure to notice that we have inserted code to output a warning if the array is too small. Without such a warning message, we would avoid a value range error, but we are likely to end up with something even worse: an undetected error. If we omit the warning message and there is too much input for the array, the user might not notice that something is wrong.

exceeding array capacity

```
{Last must be initialized before here.}
while (not eoln) and (Last < MaxIndex) do
  begin{while}
    Last := Last + 1;
    read(Score[Last]);
    if Score[Last] > Max then
      Max := Score[Last]
    {Max is the largest of the values of Score[1], . . . ,Score[Last].}
  end; {while}
if not eoln {and hence Last >= MaxIndex} then
  writeln('Warning: Some numbers were not read in. ');
```

Figure 9.8
Checking for exceeding array capacity.

Self-Test Exercises

1. Which of the following are legal type definitions?

```
type AnsList = array[0 . . 10] of boolean;
     Index = −100 . . −50;
     List = array[Index] of real;
     Count = array[char] of integer;
     NonNeg = 0 . .maxint;
     Tally = array['a' . . 'z'] of NonNeg;
     AnswerCount = array[boolean] of NonNeg;
     TempCount = array[real] of integer;
     GradeTally = array[0.0 . . 4.0] of integer;
```

2. Write suitable type declarations for each of the following:
a. An array to hold 100 scores, each between 0 and 10.
b. An array of reals indexed by the type 'a' . . 'z'.
c. An array of characters whose smallest index is −5 and whose largest index is 19.

3. Give suitable type and variable declarations for data of each of the following kinds:
a. A list of 100 or fewer scores, each a whole number in the range 0 to 10.

b. An array to record for each letter of the alphabet the number of students in a class whose last name starts with that letter.

c. An array to record which students have completed graduation requirements. The students are numbered 1 through 100. The array records whether or not they can graduate and nothing else.

4. The following piece of code is supposed to add all the elements in an array A, which has 100 elements. It does not work. What is wrong with it, and how should it be fixed?

```
Sum := 0;
for Element := A[1] to A[100] do
    Sum := Sum + Element
```

5. Write code to initialize an array C, declared as follows, so that each element has a value of zero.

```
type RealList = array[0 . . 100] of real;
var C: RealList;
```

6. If C is declared as in the previous exercise, is the following legal?

```
C := 0
```

7. The following piece of code is supposed to test an array of elements to see whether they are in order. It contains a bug. What is it?

```
var InOrder: boolean;
    I: integer;
    A: array[First . . Last] of integer;
    . . .
        . . .
InOrder := true;
for I := First to Last do
    if A[I] > A[I + 1] then
        InOrder := false
```

8. Write code that reads exactly six letters into an array and then outputs them in reverse order. The array is declared as follows:

```
type Word = array[1 . . 6] of char;
var A: Word;
```

9. Write code that reads a list of up to 10 positive integers into the array A, declared as shown below, and then writes the integers back to the screen. The input list is terminated with either a negative number or zero. The terminating number is not written back out.

```
type PositiveInt = 1 . . maxint;
     List = array[1 . . 10] of PositiveInt;
var A: List;
```

> "But it's always interesting when one doesn't see," she added.
> "If you don't see what a thing means, you must be looking
> at it wrong way round."
>
> *Agatha Christie*

The Notion of a Data Type

The word "data" in its most general sense refers to anything that can be manipulated by a computer program. A *data type* is a particular type or kind of data together with some rules for how these data items can be manipulated. The data types `integer`, `real`, `char`, and `boolean` are provided automatically in the Pascal language. Additionally, we have seen how subrange types and array types can be defined within a Pascal program.

One way to think of a data type is as a description of the values that a variable of that type can have. A data type is specified by specifying the values of that type and by specifying the operations that are allowed on those values. For example, the values of the Pascal type `integer` are all the positive integers that are less than or equal to `maxint`, all the negative integers that are greater than or equal to the smallest negative integer the computer can handle (approximately $-\text{maxint}$), and the integer zero. The operations that are allowed include addition, subtraction, multiplication, *div, mod,* and the comparison operators, such as $=$ and $<$. The subrange type `1 . . 5` has the same operations but a different set of values, namely `1`, `2`, `3`, `4`, and `5`. The type `boolean` consists of the two values `true` and `false`, and the operations allowed consist of *and, or, not,* and a few comparison operations, such as $=$ and $<>$.

The discussion in the previous paragraph is easy to apply to simple data types such as `integer` and `boolean`. However, at first reading it may not be apparent that it also applies to array types. In the next section, we will see that, when viewed properly, it does.

Arrays as a Structured Type

One can consider an array to be a collection of (indexed) variables that are named in a convenient and uniform way. For instance, the array A, declared as follows, can be thought of as five indexed variables, `A[0]`, `A[1]`, and so forth, each capable of holding one value of type `real`.

```
type RealList = array[0 . . 4] of real;
var A, B: RealList;
```

This point of view is often adequate. However, to understand the complete nature of arrays, you must also take another view.

An array can also be viewed as a single variable of a complex type. Our array A

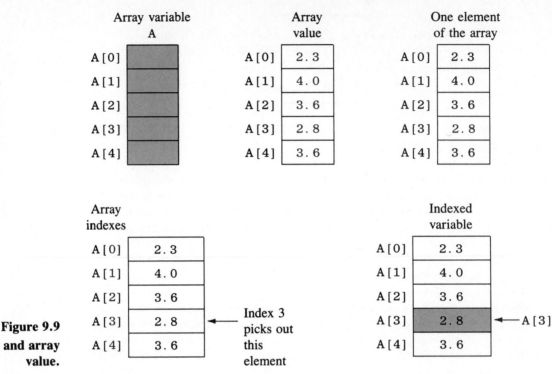

Figure 9.9
Array and array
value.

can be thought of as a single variable whose value is a list of five `real` numbers, for example

>   2.3,   4.0,   3.6,   2.8,   3.6

To emphasize this point of view, variables like A are called *array variables*. Do not confuse the terms "array variable" and "indexed variable:" A is an array variable; A[3] is an indexed variable. Figure 9.9 illustrates the terminology and presents one way of visualizing arrays and array values.

Since an array variable can be viewed as a single variable with a single (compound) value, you can often treat it just like any other variable. For example, with the array variables A and B declared as above, the following assignment statement is perfectly valid:

>   B := A

This statement sets the value of B equal to the value of A. After this statement is executed, the value of B[0] will be the same as that of A[0], the value of B[1] will be the same as that of A[1], and so forth for each component of the array B.

array
parameters

We have already noted that an indexed variable, such as A[1], can be used as a parameter in a procedure call. It is also possible to use an entire array, such as A, as a single parameter to a procedure or function. In such cases, the array is treated as a single variable with a single (compound) value. In this situation, the formal parameter in the procedure heading and the actual parameter in the procedure call are specified by giving the array name without square brackets or indexes. For example, if the array type `RealList` is declared as above, then the following is a legitimate procedure heading:

    procedure `Sample(X: RealList;` *var* `Y: RealList);`

If A and B are declared to be of type `RealList,` the following is a legitimate procedure call:

    `Sample(A, B)`

A complete example of the use of array parameters is given in the next case study.

Be sure to note the difference between using an array variable as a parameter and using an indexed variable as a parameter. To illustrate this difference, let us continue to assume that A is an array of type `RealList,` as in the previous discussion. When the entire array is passed as a parameter, then the parameter type must be `RealList` and the actual parameter is A, written without any square brackets or indexes. When only one indexed variable is passed, such as A[3], then the parameter type must be `real` and both square brackets and an index are used when giving the actual parameter. For example, consider the following procedure heading:

    procedure `SecondSample(X: real;` *var* `Y: real);`

A possible procedure call is

    `SecondSample(A[3], A[1])`

In this case, we want only indexed variables, not entire arrays, as actual parameters. In the previous case, we wanted entire arrays as actual parameters.

Array types are a good illustration of the notion of a *structured type*. All the types introduced in previous chapters are simple types. Simple types, whether provided by Pascal or defined by the programmer, have values that intuitively are indivisible units. The character `'A'` cannot be meaningfully decomposed into parts. The real number `2.34` could intuitively be decomposed in a few different ways, but we usually think of it as a single item, and the Pascal language treats it as such. The same holds true for the other simple types. In addition to these simple types, Pascal and most other programming languages allow the programmer to define more-complicated types whose values are compound items composed of a number of values of some simpler type or types. These sorts of compound types are called "structured types" because, unlike the simple types, they have a structure that can be meaningfully decomposed by operations provided within the programming language. For example, to reference one element, as opposed to an entire array, we can combine an index and an array variable to obtain an indexed variable, such as A[2].

*structured
types*

Allowable Function Types

Viewing an array as a single value naturally leads to the conclusion that a function can return an array as a value. This conclusion is, however, wrong for the Pascal language.

In Pascal the value returned by a function cannot be an array type. The value returned by a function may be any simple type and, with one exception, which we will see in Chapter 17, these are the only possible types for the value returned by a function. There is no compelling conceptual reason for this. It is done solely in order to make the compiler's job easier.

Case Study

Searching an Array

As an example of the use of array parameters, we will construct an algorithm to search a partially filled array for a particular value and then implement it as a boolean-valued Pascal function with an array parameter.

Problem Definition

The array type is as follows:

```
type Index = Low . . High;
     IntegerArray = array[Index] of integer;
```

Low and High are integer constants, such as 1 and 20. Our function will be given three pieces of data: an array A of type IntegerArray, an index value Last, and one integer N. The function is supposed to tell us whether or not the integer N is one of the following elements:

```
A[Low],  A[Low + 1],  A[Low + 2],..., A[Last]
```

For example, the list of numbers might be a list of invalid credit card numbers, and so the function could be used to find out if a given credit card should or should not be accepted by a merchant. Since there are exactly two possible outcomes, we will design the function to return a boolean value. If N is equal to one of the array elements, our function will return true; otherwise, it will return false.

Discussion

brute force method

To accomplish this task, our algorithm will simply try all possible values for the index. The strategy of trying all possibilities is called the *brute force approach*. It is not always efficient, but it is straightforward and effective.

If the possibilities are stored in an array, then the natural way to try all possibilities is to proceed through the array serially from the first index to the last. This *serial search* algorithm proceeds as follows:

ALGORITHM serial search

```
for I := <first index> to <last index> do
    test whether N = A[I]
```

If we name our boolean function Found, then the heart of the code for our function declaration will be the following realization of our serial search algorithm:

```
Found := false; {tentatively}
for I := Low to Last do
  if N = A[I] then
    Found := true
```

This is an example of the *innocent-until-proven-guilty* technique. We need to test a list to see if it is "guilty" of containing the element N. The program starts out assuming that the list is innocent and only changes its mind to "guilty" (i.e., returns true) if it discovers the element N.

innocent until proven guilty

The complete function embedded in a demonstration program, is shown in Figure 9.10. Notice that the variable Last is declared to be of type ExtendedIndex in order to allow it to be initialized to the constant LowMinus1, which is defined to be zero. If we had declared it to be of type Index, that would have precipitated an error message when Last is set equal to zero. This also allows us to represent the empty list with a value of zero. By using ExtendedIndex as the type of the function parameter, we can accommodate an empty list. If you check the code, you will see that for an empty list the function correctly returns the value false.

In the program in Figure 9.10, the entire array List is passed as the actual parameter in the function call

array parameters

```
Found(Number, List, Last)
```

When this function call is executed in the first sample run of the program, the formal parameter N is set equal to the value of the actual parameter Number, and so it is set equal to 9. In exactly the same manner, the formal parameter A is set equal to the value of the actual parameter List and so it is set equal to

```
11, 1, 2, 3, 4, 5, 6, 7, 8, 10
```

The entire array value is passed as a single unit.

Note that in the second dialogue the array is allowed as a parameter even though it is not completely filled. This is permitted, but the function should not attempt to access any of the undefined elements. In this case it does not, and so there are no problems.

Pitfall

Type Mismatches with Array Parameters

As we noted in the last chapter, two Pascal types are not the same unless they have the same name. This can cause problems if you use anonymous types when declaring arrays. Consider the following:

```
type FirstName = array[1 . . 10] of integer;
var A: array[1 . . 10] of integer;
```

With these declarations, the array A cannot be used as an actual parameter of type FirstName. To avoid this problem, always declare a unique name for each array type, and always refer to it by that name.

Program

```
program Search(input, output);
{Searches a partially filled array to see if a value is present.}
const Low = 1;
      LowMinus1 = 0; {Low − 1}
      High = 10;
type Index = Low . . High;
     ExtendedIndex = LowMinus1 . . High;
     IntegerArray = array[Index] of integer;
var Number: integer;
    List: IntegerArray;
    Last: ExtendedIndex;

function Found(N: integer; A: IntegerArray;
                    Last: ExtendedIndex): boolean;
{Returns true if N = A[I] for some I <= Last; returns false otherwise.}
var I: Index;
begin{Found}
  Found := false; {so far}
  for I := Low to Last do
    if N = A[I] then
        Found := true
end; {Found}

begin{Program}
  writeln('Enter a list of at most');
  writeln( (High − Low) + 1, ' integers,');
  writeln('and then press return: ');
  Last := LowMinus1;
  while not eoln do
    begin{while}
      Last := Last + 1;
      read(List[Last])
    end; {while}
  readln;
  writeln('Enter a number to be searched for: ');
  readln(Number);
  if Found(Number, List, Last) then
      writeln('Yep, it''s on the list.')
  else
      writeln('Nope, it''s not on the list.')
end. {Program}
```

Figure 9.10
Searching a
partially filled
array.

Sample Dialogue 1

```
Enter a list of at most
    10 integers,
and then press return:
11 1 2 3 4 5 6 7 8 10
Enter a number to be searched for:
9
Nope, it's not on the list.
```

Sample Dialogue 2

```
Enter a list of at most
    10 integers,
and then press return:
8 7 6 5 4 3 2 1
Enter a number to be searched for:
3
Yep, it's on the list.
```

Sample Dialogue 3

```
Enter a list of at most
    10 integers,
and then press return:

Enter a number to be searched for:
3
Nope, it's not on the list.
```

**Figure 9.10
(continued)**

Efficiency of Variable Parameters

An array uses large amounts of storage compared to that used by a simple variable. The compiler typically allows one storage location for each indexed variable. For example, the array List in Figure 9.10 would normally consume ten times as much storage as a simple variable of type integer. There is no need to be obsessive about saving storage, but excessive use of storage can cause a program to run more slowly, or even to run out of storage and terminate abnormally. There are several things you can do to avoid excessive use of storage with arrays. The most obvious technique is to not declare arrays to be any larger than necessary. Another technique for saving storage has to do with procedure parameters.

Variable parameters typically consume less storage than do value parameters. The reason is that a value parameter is a local variable that is set to the value of the actual parameter. So if A is a formal value parameter of an array type and List is the corresponding actual parameter, then when the procedure is called, two arrays are in stor-

Program

```
program CountLetters(input, output);
{Counts the number of occurrences of each letter in a sentence.
Assumes the lowercase letters are contiguous.}
type Letter = 'a' . . 'z';
     LetterCounter = array[Letter] of integer;
var Count: LetterCounter;

procedure ReadSentence(var Count: LetterCounter);
{Sets Count['a'] equal to the number of 'a'-s in an input sentence;
Count['b'] equal to the number of 'b'-s, and so forth down to Count['z'].}
var Symbol: char;
begin{ReadSentence}
  for Symbol := 'a' to 'z' do
    Count[Symbol] := 0;

  while not eoln do
    begin{reading line}
      read(Symbol);
      if ('a' <= Symbol) and (Symbol <= 'z') then
        Count[Symbol] := Count[Symbol] + 1
    end; {reading line}
  readln
end; {ReadSentence}

procedure DisplayCount(var Count: LetterCounter);
{Outputs the nonzero elements of the array Count.}
const Blank = ' ';
var Symbol: Letter;
begin{DisplayCount}
  for Symbol := 'a' to 'z' do
    if Count[Symbol] <> 0 then
        writeln(Count[Symbol], Blank, Symbol)
end; {DisplayCount}

begin{Program}
  writeln('Enter a sentence and press return.');
  writeln('all lowercase letters, please.');
  ReadSentence(Count);
  writeln('Your sentence contains: ');
  DisplayCount(Count)
end. {Program}
```

Figure 9.11
Program using
'a' . . 'z' as
an index type.

Sample Dialogue

```
Enter a sentence and press return.
all lowercase letters, please.
```
may the hair on your toes grow long and curly.
```
Your sentence contains:
    3 a
    1 c
    1 d
    2 e
    2 g
    2 h
    1 i
    2 l
    1 m
    3 n
    5 o
    4 r
    1 s
    2 t
    2 u
    1 w
    3 y
```

Figure 9.11
(continued)

age: the global array List and the local array A. If, on the other hand, A is a variable parameter, then it is just a formal blank, which is filled in with List. In that case, there is only one array in storage. Hence, even if a procedure does not change an array, it makes sense to declare it as a variable parameter in order to save storage. For example, if the declaration heading for the function Found in Figure 9.10 is changed to the following, then the array parameter A will be a variable parameter, and so the program will use less storage.

```
function Found(N: integer; var A: IntegerArray;
                Last: ExtendedIndex): boolean;
```

Array Example with Noninteger Indexes

As we have already noted, the index type of an array need not be a subrange of the integers; it can be a subrange of any ordinal type. The program in Figure 9.11 illustrates the use of the subrange type 'a' . . 'z', both as an array index type and as the type of a *for* loop control variable. That program reads in a sentence and then uses an array indexed by 'a' . . 'z' to count the number of occurrences of 'a', 'b', and so forth in the sentence. The program assumes that the lowercase letters are contiguous (there are no symbols between any two alphabetically consecutive lowercase letters). This assumption holds for most, though not all, systems.

Random versus Sequential Array Access

The letter-counting program in Figure 9.11 illustrates the two principal methods for accessing array elements. In the procedure ReadSentence, the array elements of the array Count are initialized to zero by stepping through the array indexes in order. This method is called *sequential access.*

The other method of array access is used when the letters of the sentence are read in and counted. If the letter 'a' is read in, then the first array element is changed; if the letter 'z' is accessed, then the last array element is changed; if the letter 'd' is read, then the fourth element is changed. This is referred to as *random access,* since the order of the elements accessed cannot be determined beforehand.

Array Indexes with Semantic Content

The indexes of an array allow us to access individual elements in an organized fashion. Often they serve no purpose other than that of an arbitrary numbering of the array elements, as in our first sample program with a list of five scores (Figure 9.4). Not infrequently, however, the array indexes can carry some meaning. For example, in our letter-counting program, the index 'a' is not arbitrary. It stands for the letter 'a', and the indexed variable Count['a'] has a value equal to the number of times the letter 'a' has been seen. Choosing array indexes with semantic content can often simplify a program. In our letter-counting program, this allowed for random access to the array. The program did not have to search a list of letters to find the location for, say, 'm'; it went directly to Count['m'] by using the index 'm'.

Integers are typically used when we need arbitrary indexes without any particular meaning. Often, they can also have meaning. In a list of students, they might serve as the students' numbers. In a list of checks, they may serve as the check numbers.

Enumerated Types as Array Index Types
(Optional)

Since they are ordinal types, enumerated types and subranges of enumerated types may be used as the index types of arrays. For example, the following declares Sales to be an array of integers indexed by an enumerated type for the days of the week:

```
type WeekDay = (Mon, Tue, Wed, Thur, Fri, Sat, Sun);
     SalesList = array[WeekDay] of integer;
var Sales: SalesList;
```

The array might be used to keep track of the number of automobiles sold by an auto dealer's sales force. Once the array has been filled, the weekly sales can be totaled as follows:

```
Total := 0;
for Day := Mon to Sun do
   Total := Total + Sales[Day]
```

The variable Day is of type WeekDay, and Total is of type integer.

Figure 9.12 shows these details embedded in a complete program that reads in daily sales and then echoes them back with each day marked as above average (+), below average (−), or average (0).

Case Study

Production Graph

Problem Definition

The Apex Plastic Spoon Manufacturing Company has commissioned you to write a program that will display a bar graph showing the productivity of each of their four manufacturing plants for any given week. Each plant keeps separate production figures for each department, such as the teaspoon department, soup spoon department, plain cocktail spoon department, colored cocktail spoon department, and so forth. Moreover, each plant has a different number of departments. For example, only one plant manufactures colored cocktail spoons. The input is entered plant by plant and consists of a list of numbers giving the production for each department in that plant. The output will give the total production for each plant in the form of a bar graph like the following:

```
Plant # 1 * * * * * * * * *
Plant # 2 * * * * * * * * * * * *
Plant # 3 * * * * * * * * * * * * * * * * * * * *
Plant # 4 * * * * *
```

Each asterisk represents 1000 units of output.

Notice that the output is in thousands of units, and hence the program must scale the output by dividing it by 1000. This presents a problem, since the computer must display some whole number of asterisks. It cannot display 1.6 asterisks for 1600 units. We will thus round to the nearest thousand, and so 1600 will be the same as 2000 and will produce two asterisks.

refining the problem definition

Discussion

We will use an array called Units that is indexed by plant numbers 1 . . 4 and that will hold the total output of each plant. For example, Units[3] will be set equal to the total output of plant number three. Since the output is in thousands of units, the program will scale the values of the array elements. If the value of Units[3] is 2040, for example, it will be scaled to 2, and eventually two asterisks will be output. The task can be divided into the following subtasks:

1. GetData: For each plant I, read input and set Units[I] equal to the total production for plant number I.

Program

```
program ShowSales(input, output);
{Displays a week's sales day by day and classifies
each day as above or below average.}
const Width = 6;
type WeekDay = (Mon, Tue, Wed, Thur, Fri, Sat, Sun);
     SalesList = array[WeekDay] of integer;
var Sales: SalesList;
    Day: WeekDay;
    Total: integer;
    Average: real;
begin{Program}
  writeln('Welcome to the sales meeting.');
  writeln('Enter units sold for Monday through Sunday:');
  for Day := Mon to Sun do
     read(Sales[Day]);

  Total := 0;
  for Day := Mon to Sun do
     Total := Total + Sales[Day];
  Average := Total/7;

  writeln('Daily sales compared to average:');
  writeln('Mon':Width, 'Tue':Width, 'Wed':Width,
     'Thu':Width, 'Fri':Width, 'Sat':Width, 'Sun':Width);
  for Day := Mon to Sun do
    write(Sales[Day]: Width);
  writeln;
  for Day := Mon to Sun do
    if Sales[Day] > Average then
       write('+': Width)
    else if Sales[Day] < Average then
       write('-': Width)
    else {Sales[Day] = Average}
       write('0': Width);
  writeln;
  writeln('Go get ''em!')
end. {Program}
```

Sample Dialogue

```
Welcome to the sales meeting.
Enter units sold for Monday through Sunday:
6   7   10   9   8   5   11
Daily sales compared to average:
   Mon     Tue     Wed     Thu     Fri     Sat     Sun
    6       7      10       9       8       5      11
    -       -       +       +       0       -       +
Go get 'em!
```

Figure 9.12
(Optional)
Enumerated type
as an index type.

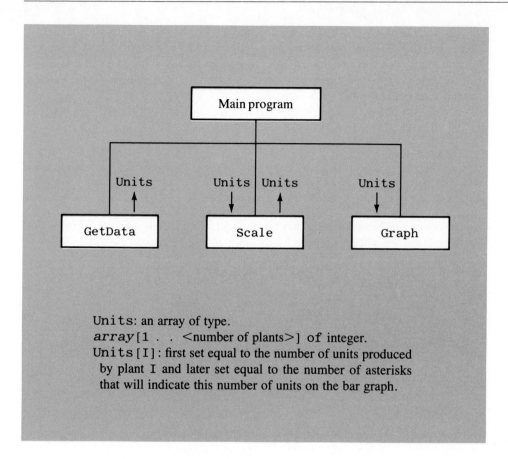

Units: an array of type.
array[1 . . <number of plants>] of integer.
Units[I]: first set equal to the number of units produced
   by plant I and later set equal to the number of asterisks
   that will indicate this number of units on the bar graph.

Figure 9.13
Data flow diagram
for production
graph.

2. Scale: For each I change the value of Units[I] to the correct number of
   asterisks for plant number I.
3. Graph: Output the bar graph.

The interaction of the subtasks is shown in the data flow diagram in Figure 9.13.

GetData

The program receives separate input figures for each department within a plant,
but the output is in terms of the total output for a plant. Hence, the program must total
the output of all departments in a plant in order to get the appropriate figure for that
plant. These observations lead us to the following basic outline of the algorithm for
GetData:

ALGORITHM

```
for I := 1 to <last plant number> do
   begin{for}
      read in all the data for plant number I,
      total the numbers, and
      set Units[I] equal to that total.
   end {for}
```

The *body* of the *for* loop sums a list of numbers and leaves the value of Units[I] equal to this sum. In other contexts we have designed code for just this task. If we wanted the sum stored in a variable called Total instead of being stored in Units[I], then we would know how to proceed. To store a sum of input numbers in the variable Total, we would use the following:

adapting
another
ALGORITHM

```
Total := 0;
while not eoln do
    begin{while}
        read(Next);
        Total := Total + Next
    end   {while}
```

If we instead want the total to be in Units[I], all we need do is substitute Units[I] for Total and we will obtain code for the body of our *for* loop:

```
for I := 1 to <last plant number> do
    begin{for}
        Units[I] := 0;
        while not eoln do
            begin{while}
                read(Next);
                Units[I] := Units[I] + Next
            end;  {while}
        readln
    end {for}
```

The final readln is needed in order to advance to the next input line so that the next iteration of the *for* loop starts at the beginning of a line.

Scale

In order to scale the numbers to an integral number of thousands, we want to divide by 1000 and then round to the nearest integer. Fortunately, both of these are built-in Pascal operations. To scale Units[I], the following works:

```
Units[I] := round(Units[I]/1000)
```

To scale the entire array, we can use a *for* loop to do this to each element of the array. The final procedure declaration is given as part of Figure 9.14.

The algorithm for the procedure Graph is straightforward:

Graph
ALGORITHM

```
for I := 1 to <last plant number> do
    begin
        write('Plant #', I);
        repeat the following Units[I] number of times
                write('*');
        writeln
    end
```

The "repeat *n* number of times" loop can be implemented in the standard fashion using a *for* loop. The complete procedure, included in the complete final program, is given in Figure 9.14.

Off-Line Data
(Optional)

Arrays are often used to process large amounts of data. If the data set is very large, then it is impractical to enter the data interactively from the keyboard. For example, suppose that in the previous case study each plant had hundreds of departments instead of just a few. In that case, it would make sense to read the data off-line in the manner discussed in the optional section of Chapter 7 entitled "Off-Line Data and a Preview of EOF." The general method of reading in the data would be the same, except that there is no point in outputting instructions to the user. The data set is prepared before the program is run and must be in a format that matches what the program expects. If it does not match, then either the data must be reformatted or the program must be changed to accommodate the data.

Case Study

Sorting

Problem Definition

One of the most commonly encountered programming tasks, and certainly the one most thoroughly studied, is that of sorting a list of values. For example, the list might be a list of exam scores, and we may want to see them sorted from lowest to highest or from highest to lowest; the list might be a list of words that we have misspelled, and we may want to see them in alphabetical order. In this section we will consider lists of integers and design a procedure that sorts a list into the order smallest to largest. The list will be stored in an array of the following type, where Low and High are defined constants.

```
type Index = Low . . High;
     List = array[Index] of integer;
var A: List;
```

Since we want to accommodate partially filled arrays, we will use a variable called Last to record the last array index used, and we will write our procedure to sort the elements A[Low] through A[Last] and ignore array locations with indexes greater than Last.

Discussion

One way to design an algorithm is to rely on the definition of the problem. In this case, the problem is to sort an array, such as A, from smallest to largest. This means re-arranging the values so that A[1] is the smallest, A[2] is the next smallest, and so forth. The definition yields an outline for a straightforward algorithm:

first
design idea

(Text continued on page 340.)

Program

```
program ShowProduction(input, output);
{Reads data for each plant in the company and displays a
bar graph showing productivity of each plant.}
const NumPlants = 4;
type Index = 1 . . NumPlants;
     List = array[Index] of integer;
var Units: List;

procedure GetData(var Units: List);
{Postcondition: Units[I] contains the number of units produced by plant I.}
var I: Index;
    Next: integer;
begin{GetData}
  for I := 1 to NumPlants do
     begin{for}
       writeln;
       writeln('Enter number of units produced for');
       writeln('each department in plant number', I);
       writeln('End by pressing return.');
       Units[I] := 0;
       while not eoln do
          begin{while}
            read(Next);
            Units[I] := Units[I] + Next
          end; {while}
       readln
     end  {for}
end; {GetData}

procedure Scale(var Units: List);
{Changes the values of Units[I] so that
it records 1000s of units. Rounds to the nearest
1000, e.g., 5020 is changed to 5, but 5900 is changed to 6.}
var I: Index;
begin{Scale}
  for I := 1 to NumPlants do
     Units[I] := round(Units[I]/1000)
end; {Scale}

procedure Graph(Units: List);
{Displays a bar graph showing production of each plant.
Precondition: Units[I]*1000 is productivity of plant I to the nearest 1000.}
var I: Index;
    J: integer;
```

**Figure 9.14
Production graph
program.**

```
begin{Graph}
  writeln;
  writeln('Units produced in thousands of units:');
  for I := 1 to NumPlants do
    begin{Outer loop}
      write('Plant #', I:2);
      for J := 1 to Units[I] do
        write('*');
      writeln
    end  {Outer loop}
end; {Graph}

begin{Program}
  writeln('This program displays a graph showing');
  writeln('production for each plant in the company.');
  GetData(Units);
  Scale(Units);
  Graph(Units)
end. {Program}
```

Sample Dialogue

```
This program displays a graph showing
production for each plant in the company.

Enter number of units produced for
each department in plant number  1
End by pressing return.
2000    3000    1000

Enter number of units produced for
each department in plant number  2
End by pressing return.
2050    3002    1300

Enter number of units produced for
each department in plant number  3
End by pressing return.
5000    4020    500    4348

Enter number of units produced for
each department in plant number  4
End by pressing return.
2507    6050    1809

Units produced in thousands of units:
Plant# 1******
Plant# 2******
Plant# 3*************
Plant# 4**********
```

Figure 9.14

(continued)

(Text continued from page 337.)

> *for* I := Low *to* Last *do*
>   put the Ith smallest element into A[I]

exploring the problem

There are many ways to realize this general approach. The details can be developed using two arrays and copying the elements from one array to the other in sorted order. However, one array should be both adequate and economical, and so we decide to develop the algorithm using only one array. To help in exploring the problem, we will use the example given in Figure 9.15 as the original array value, and we will try sorting that array using pencil and eraser. (In Figure 9.15, the array is full, and so Last = High = 10.) When we search the array to find the smallest element, we discover that it is the value of A[4], which is 2. We next want to set A[1] equal to this value of 2. However, in doing so we must be careful to not lose the original value of A[1], which is 8. A simple assignment statement like the following would destroy the 8.

> A[1] := A[4]   {*No good; destroys the original value of A[1].*}

Now that we understand some of the problems involved in this example, we can begin to formulate a strategy for handling them.

interchange sorting

We wish to set the value of A[1] equal to the value of the index variable with the smallest value; in the example, that is the value of A[4]. When we do this we must preserve the old value of A[1] so that it can be inserted into the array at some later time. This is illustrated in the second "snapshot" of the array shown in Figure 9.15. The algorithm must do something with the displaced value 8 that was the original value of A[1]. Fortunately we have a vacant array location in which to store it. Since the value 2 has "left" A[4], the algorithm can place the 8 there. In other words, the values of A[1] and A[4] are simply interchanged. A similar thing is done with A[2], as shown in the figure. The entire array can be sorted by a series of interchanges such as these two. Any sorting algorithm that is based on interchanging elements is referred to as an *interchange sort*.

ALGORITHM selection sort

The simplest interchange sorting algorithm is called *selection sort* and is the one we obtain by proceeding as we did with our sample array values. In outline form it is as follows:

> *for* I := Low *to* Last − 1 *do*
>   Exchange (A[I], A[<suitable index>])

(A[Last] will automatically be in place once the previous elements are sorted.)

All that remains is to calculate the expression <suitable index>. When the loop considers A[I] and looks for a suitable interchange, the indexed variables with indexes smaller than I already contain the correct values for a sorted array. So the sought-after index is the index of the smallest of the remaining elements A[I], A[I + 1], . . . A[Last]. Since this index is a single value, we can define a function to return the index. The value of <suitable index> will be Imin(A, I, Last), where Imin is as declared in Figure 9.16. The complete sorting algorithm is implemented by the procedure Sort, which is also declared in Figure 9.16.

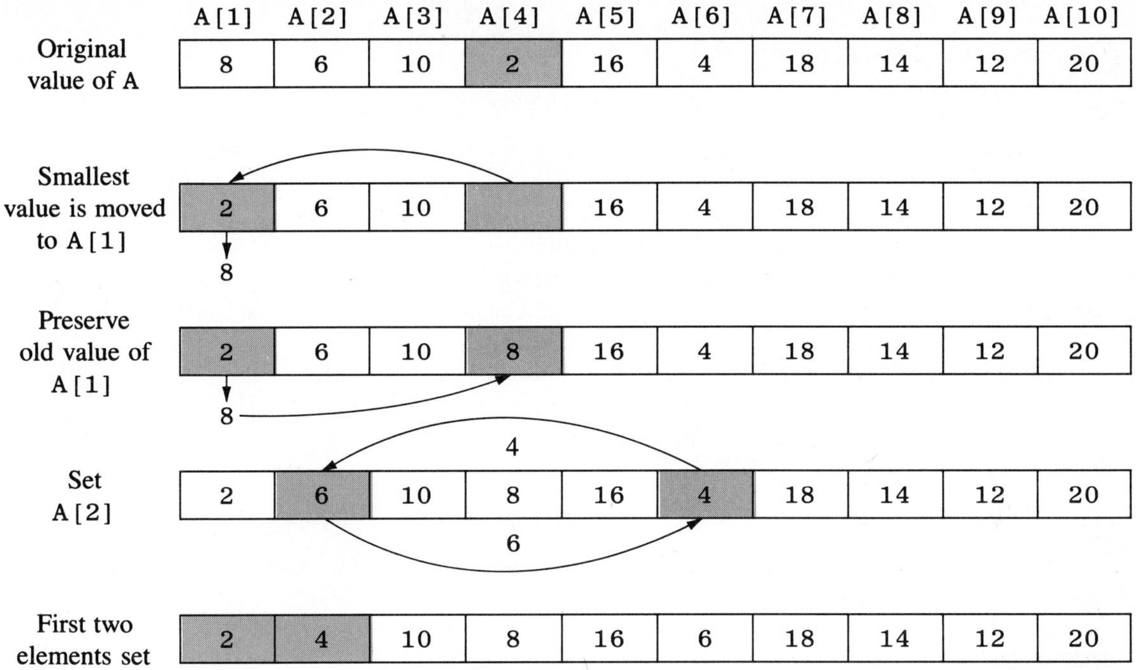

	A[1]	A[2]	A[3]	A[4]	A[5]	A[6]	A[7]	A[8]	A[9]	A[10]
Original value of A	8	6	10	2	16	4	18	14	12	20
Smallest value is moved to A[1]	2	6	10		16	4	18	14	12	20
	8									
Preserve old value of A[1]	2	6	10	8	16	4	18	14	12	20
	8									
Set A[2]	2	6	10	8	16	4	18	14	12	20
First two elements set	2	4	10	8	16	6	18	14	12	20

Figure 9.15 Interchange sorting.

Never trust to general impressions, my boy,
but concentrate yourself upon details.
*Sir Arthur Conan Doyle (Sherlock Holmes),
A Case of Identity*

Summary of Problem Solving and Programming Techniques

- An array type can be used to produce a unified naming scheme for a collection of related values.
- A big advantage of array types is that by manipulating the array index a program can actually compute a name for an (indexed) variable.
- An array indexed variable can be used anywhere that a simple variable of the array's component type can be used.
- In Pascal the size of an array must be declared at the time the program is written. Hence, if the desired size will vary from one run of the program to another, the array must be declared to be of the largest size possible. In such cases, the program must keep track of which indexed variables are actually used.

(Summary continued, page 343.)

Program

```pascal
program SortTest(input, output);
{Tests the procedure Sort.}
const Low = 1;
      High = 10;
      LowMinus1 = 0; {Low - 1}
type Index = Low . . High;
     List = array[Index] of integer;
     ExtendedIndex = LowMinus1 . . High;
var A: List;
    I: Index;
    Last: ExtendedIndex;

procedure Exchange(var X, Y: integer);
{Interchanges the values of X and Y.}
var Temp: integer;
begin{Exchange}
  Temp := X;
  X := Y;
  Y := Temp
end;  {Exchange}

function Imin(var A: List; Start, Last: Index): Index;
{Returns the index I such that A[I] is the smallest of the values: A[Start], A[Start + 1],. . . . A[Last].}
var Min, I: integer;
begin{Imin}
  Imin := Start;  {tentatively}
  Min := A[Start];  {Minimum so far.}
  for I := Start + 1 to Last do
    if A[I] < Min then
       begin{then}
         Min := A[I];
         Imin := I
         {Min is the smallest of the values A[Start], . . . ,A[I];
          the tentative value of Imin is x such that A[x] = Min.}
       end   {then}
end;  {Imin}

procedure Sort(var A: List; Last: ExtendedIndex);
{Sorts the partially filled array A into increasing order using the
selection sort algorithm. Postcondition: The array elements have been
rearranged so that A[Low] <= A[Low + 1] <= . . . <= A[Last]}
var I: Index;
```

Figure 9.16

Selection sort.

```
begin{Sort}
  for I := Low to Last - 1 do
    begin{Place correct value in A[I]}
      Exchange(A[I], A[Imin(A, I, Last)])
      {A[Low]<=A[Low + 1]<= . . . <=A[I] are the smallest of the original array
        elements; the remaining elements are in the remaining positions.}
    end    {Place correct value in A[I]}
end;  {Sort}

begin{Program}
  writeln('Enter a list of numbers.');
  writeln('I will take up to ', High - Low + 1, ' numbers.');
  Last := LowMinus1;
  while not eoln do
    begin{while}
      Last := Last + 1;
      read(A[Last])
    end;  {while}

  Sort(A, Last);

  writeln('In sorted order the numbers are:');
  for I := Low to Last do
    write(A[I]);
  writeln
end.  {Program}
```

Sample Dialogue

```
Enter a list of numbers.
I will take up to   10 numbers.
80 10 50 70 60 90 20 30 40
In sorted order the numbers are:
10 20 30 40 50 60 70 80 90
```

Figure 9.16
(continued)

(Summary, continued from page 341.)

- It is a good idea to use defined constants for one or both bounds of an array index type. That way the array size can be changed simply by changing the constant declarations.
- A common bug in programs that use arrays is attempting to use an index value outside the defined range for an array's indexes.
- One often needs a variable that takes on values one step beyond the index range of an array. In such cases, do not declare the variable to be of the index type. Instead declare it to be of a larger subrange type or of the host type (such as `integer.`)
- A *for* loop is a natural way of proceeding sequentially through an array.
- The "brute force" method of looking at every element of an array can be used to

search an array for almost any property. It can be inefficient, but it is simple and effective.

- The "innocent until proven guilty" technique can be used to check whether some element of an array has a given property (is "guilty.") An example of this technique was seen in the case study on searching an array. Either a boolean variable or a function that potentially changes its mind can be used to implement this technique in a Pascal program.

- One way to design an algorithm is to think about how you would solve the problem using pencil and paper, and then design the algorithm to do that or some variation of it.

- Array indexes can carry information that serves to identify the corresponding elements of the array. For example, the indexes might be student numbers or check numbers or the letters of the alphabet.

- Array elements may be accessed either sequentially, as with a *for* loop, or in a "random" order by computing the desired index.

- There are two different ways of viewing an array: as a collection of (indexed) variables of the component type, and as a single variable with a single (compound) value consisting of a list of values of the component type. Sometimes it is more productive to take one view; other times the alternative view is more productive.

- An array variable without subscripts may be used in an assignment statement, like so: A : = B.

- Either a single array element or an entire array can be passed as a parameter to a procedure. In the first case, the formal parameter type must be the component type of the array; in the second case, it must be the array type.

- If an indexed variable is used as an actual parameter to a procedure, the index expression is evaluated before the actual parameter is substituted for the formal parameter.

- It is good practice to declare a name for each array type definition (or any other type definition) and to use the type name, rather than the type definition, when declaring array variables. Both formal and actual parameters of an array type must always be specified by a type name.

- Arrays consume large quantities of storage, and some care should therefore be taken not to use excessive storage when dealing with arrays. One storage-conserving technique is to use variable rather than value parameters for array type parameters.

Summary of Pascal Constructs

type declaration

Syntax:

> *type* <type name 1> = <type definition 1>;
>   <type name 2> = <type definition 2>;
>
> .
> .
> .
>
> <type name *n*> = <type definition *n*>;

Example:

```
type Index = 0 . . 100;
     List = array[Index] of char;
```

The type names are identifiers chosen by the programmer. The type definitions can be any of the type definitions described in this book. The type declaration section of a block comes after the constant declarations and before the variable declarations. The identifier *type* is used only once, even if there is more than one type definition.

array types

Syntax:

```
array[<index type>] of <component type>
```

Examples:

```
array[0 . . 100] of integer
array[Index] of char
```

Form of an array type definition. <index type> must be either the definition of a subrange type or the name of an ordinal type, such as the name of a defined subrange type or a predefined ordinal type like char. The type integer cannot be used as an <index type>. The <component type> can be any Pascal type.

array declaration

Syntax:

```
var <array variable name> : <array type name>;
```

Example:

```
var A: List;
```

The way to declare an array variable. The declaration for an array variable is just like the declaration for any other type of variable. Note that the array variable is declared without any square brackets or indexes. An array type definition may be used in place of an array type name, but it is usually preferable to use a defined type name. (The sample array type List is defined in the first entry of this summary.)

indexed variable

Syntax:

```
<array name>[<index expression>]
```

Example:

```
A[I + 1]
```

An indexed variable of the array <array name>. The <index expression> can be any expression that evaluates to a value whose type is the index type of the array. An indexed variable can be used anyplace that a variable of the component type of the array can be used.

Exercises

Self-Test Exercises

10. Write suitable array type declarations for each of the following:

a. An array to record the number of students who received a grade of 1 on a quiz, the number who received a grade of 2, and so forth, up to the maximum grade of 10.

b. An array to record the number of children in a school for each age from 5 to 13.

c. An array to hold the amount of each check you write this month, recorded so that you can deduce the amount given the number of the check. Check numbers range from 661 to 753.

11. (This exercise uses the optional section "Enumerated Types as Array Indexes.") Write two suitable enumerated type definitions, one for all the days of the week and one for the days Monday through Friday. Also write two array type declarations, one for an array to record the hours worked on each day from Monday through Friday and one for the number of hours reserved for play on each day of the week, including Saturday and Sunday.

12. Give a simpler way of accomplishing the following:

```
for I := 0 to 10 do
   A[I] := B[I]
```

A, B are of type *array* [0 . . 10] *of* integer.

13. The following is an alternative to the loop used in the function declaration in Figure 9.10. It does not work correctly. What is wrong?

```
Found := false;  {tentatively}
for I := Low to Last do
   if N = A[I] then
      Found := true
   else
      Found := false
```

14. Write a procedure that reverses the order of the elements in an array of the following type:

```
type Word = array [0 . . 100] of char;
```

15. What changes do you need to make to the procedure Sort in Figure 9.16 so that it sorts numbers in the order largest to smallest rather than smallest to largest?

16. What changes do you need to make to the procedure Sort in Figure 9.16 so that it sorts a list of numbers of type real rather than a list of numbers of type integer?

17. What changes do you need to make to the procedure Sort in Figure 9.16 so that it sorts a list of lowercase letters into alphabetical order instead of sorting a list of numbers into numeric order?

Interactive Exercises

18. Run the following two programs to see what error messages your system gives:

```
program IndexProblem(input, output);
var A: array[1 . . 10] of integer;
begin
   A[0] := 1   {Array index is too small.}
end.

program VariableProblem(input, output);
var X: 1 . . 10;
begin
   X := 0   {Subrange variable assigned too small a value.}
end.
```

19. Write a program that allows the user to type in up to 10 positive numbers and then echoes back the numbers typed in but in reverse order. Have the user terminate the list with a negative number. The answers to Exercises 9 and 14 might be of some help.

Programming Exercises

20. Write a program that reads 10 integers into an array, computes the average, largest, and smallest numbers in the array, and finally outputs the numbers plus the amount by which each one differs from the smallest, the largest, and the average.

21. Write a program to keep a budget. There are five numbered budget categories: 1 for food, 2 for housing, 3 for clothing, 4 for utilities, and 5 for entertainment. The program will display the categories, showing the number of each category, and then the user and the program will refer to categories by number rather than by name. The user may name any category by number and then enter an amount. The program records the amount spent and keeps track of the total amount spent in each category. When the user indicates that he or she wants to see the totals, the program prints out the amount spent in each category and the total amount spent in all categories combined. The user may enter more amounts after seeing the total and may ask for a new total later on.

22. Write a program that computes grades for a class of up to 50 students. The program reads in a score in the range 0 . . 100 for each student and then outputs the grades, identifying each student by number. The first student read in is student number 1, the next is student number 2, and so forth. Grades are to be determined as follows. Any student who receives 10 points below the average receives an F. Any student who receives a score above that and at most 10 points above the average receives a C. Any student who receives a score above that receives an A. There are no D's or B's. To use your program for larger classes, you should not need to change anything except the constant declaration section.

23. Write a program to read in four letters and then output all 24 permutations of these letters. Use an array to hold the four letters. Do not cut corners in designing this one; it can be confusing.

24. Write a program to play Nim using five piles of sticks. Use an array to store the sizes of the piles. The game is explained in Exercise 27 of Chapter 8.

25. (This exercise uses the optional sections "Random Number Generators" and "Using Pseudorandom Numbers," both in Chapter 8.) Write a procedure declaration for a procedure called `Deal` that sets the value of a variable parameter to a value that represents a card chosen at random from a standard 52-card deck. The function should also keep track of the cards already dealt out, so that it does not deal a card twice. For example, after dealing out four aces, it should not deal out a fifth ace at any later time. Use an array parameter to keep track of the cards already dealt out. There is no need to keep track of suits (clubs, hearts, etc.).

26. Write a program that reads in two lists of 10 or fewer numbers, each into one of two arrays. The input is assumed to be in numeric order. The program will then output a list of all the (up to twenty) numbers in numeric order. This is called *merging* the lists.

27. Make the unrealistic assumption that your computer has `maxint` equal to 18 and write procedures to read in two numbers of 10 or fewer digits and output their sum. The numbers are to be read as character values one digit at a time, using a variable of type `char`, and then converted into numbers and stored in two arrays of 10 integer values each. If the number is less than 10 digits long, leading zeros should be added to the array. An addition procedure is then called to calculate the sum and store it in a third array. If the sum would be more than 10 digits long, the program issues an "integer overflow" message. If the sum is less than 10 digits long, the two numbers read in and their sum are output.

References for Further Reading

The following books contain more information on sorting:

P. Helman and R. Veroff, *Intermediate Problem Solving and Data Structures—Walls and Mirrors,* 1986, Benjamin/Cummings, Menlo Park, Ca.

B.W. Kernighan and P.J. Plauger, *Software Tools in Pascal,* 1981, Addison-Wesley, Reading, Mass.

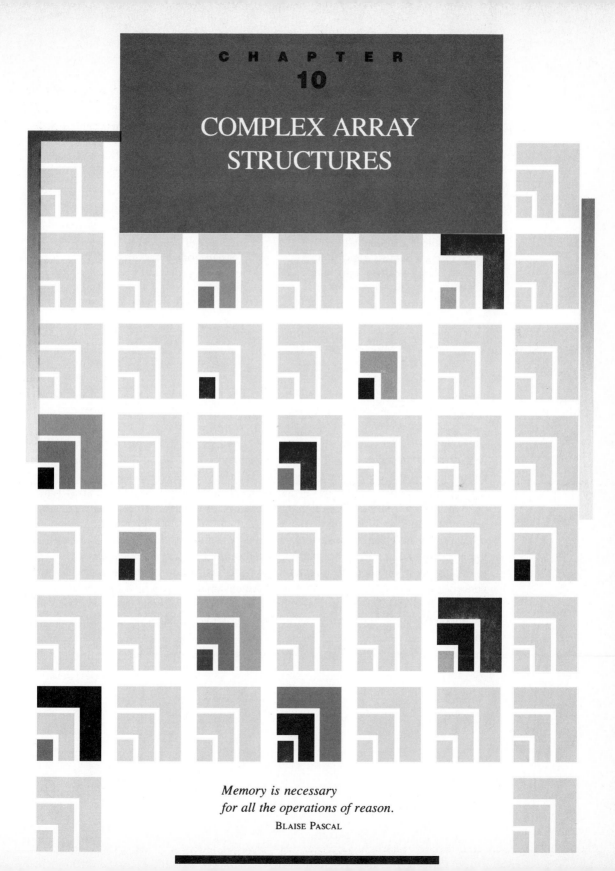

COMPLEX ARRAY
STRUCTURES

*Memory is necessary
for all the operations of reason.*
BLAISE PASCAL

Chapter Contents

Like other structured types, which we will introduce in succeeding chapters, arrays may be declared so that they form a hierarchy. In this case, the hierarchy consists of an array of arrays. Other ways of structuring data involve the way we use arrays rather than the way in which the array type is defined. Two or more arrays, or an array and one or more variables, may form a conceptual unit for handling a particular kind of data. These data types and combinations of data types are called *data structures* and are the topic of this chapter. Most of these topics require no new Pascal constructs, but they do represent significantly new ways of reasoning about the tools we already have available. We do introduce one new Pascal concept in this chapter, namely the multidimensional array, which is an array whose indexed variables have two or more indexes instead of just a single index. We open with an important application using one of the simple array types introduced in the last chapter.

Strings of Characters

One way to represent a string of characters, such as a word or a name or a line of text, is as an array of characters, such as the array variable Line declared as follows:

```
const MaxLength = 20;
type CharString = array[1 . . MaxLength] of char;
     var Line: CharString;
          I: 1 . . MaxLength;
```

To read in a name typed at the key board, you can use:

```
for I := 1 to MaxLength do
   read(Line[I])
```

The name can be written out with the following similar statement

```
for I := 1 to MaxLength do
   write(Line[I])
```

There is one annoying feature of processing strings in this way: The string input must be exactly as long as the array. There must be one character for each indexed variable. For our sample declarations, the string of characters must always be exactly 20 characters long. If it is not, the user must type in extra blanks to fill the extra indexed variables. Filling the extra array positions with blanks is called *padding with blanks*. Typing in the extra blanks is burdensome to the user. A better alternative is to have the program fill the extra position with blanks. In Figure 10.1 we present a procedure to do just that, and we also present a procedure to write out an array of characters.

padding with blanks

Arrays of Arrays

The component type of an array may be any Pascal type whatsoever. In particular, it can be an array type. Thus, we can have an array of arrays. A common situation that requires an array of arrays is an array of strings. The array variable Name when declared as follows, can be used to keep a list of names:

```
type CharString = array[1 . . MaxLength] of char;
     Index = 1 . . MaxI;
     StringList = array[Index] of CharString;
var Name: StringList;
```

MaxLength and MaxI are defined constants. Figure 10.2 illustrates a list of names stored in the array Name. In that figure MaxLength is set equal to 20.

With arrays of arrays, such as these arrays of strings, the notation can get a bit complicated, but there are no new rules involved. Just read or write the expressions

nested indexes

Program

```pascal
program TestProcedures(input, output);
{Tests the procedures StringReadln and StringWriteln.}
const MaxLength = 20;
type CharString = array[1 . . MaxLength] of char;
var Line: CharString;
    I: 1 . . MaxLength;
    Ans: char;

procedure StringReadln(var A: CharString);
{Fills the array A with one line of input characters and fills any extra positions with blanks.
If there are too many characters it discards all characters after the first MaxLength characters.}
const Blank = ' ';
var I, J: integer;
begin{StringReadln}
  I := 0;
  while (not eoln) and (I < MaxLength) do
    begin{while}
      I := I + 1;
      read(A[I])
    end; {while}
  if not eoln {and hence I >= MaxLength}  then
    writeln('Only ', MaxLength, ' characters read in.');
  readln;

  {The entire string has been read in (discarding any characters beyond the
  first MaxLength characters.) The value of I is the last index used.
  If I = MaxLength then, the array A is full.}

  for J := I + 1 to MaxLength do
    A[J] := Blank
end; {StringReadln}

procedure StringWriteln(var A: CharString);
{Writes the string A to the screen and advances to next line.}
var I: 1 . . MaxLength;
begin{StringWriteln}
  for I := 1 to MaxLength do
    write(A[I]);
  writeln
end; {StringWriteln}
```

Figure 10.1
**Reading and
writing strings of
characters.**

```
begin{Program}
  repeat
    writeln('Enter a string and press return.');
    for I := 1 to MaxLength do
        write(I mod 10:1);  {To make it easy to count.}
    writeln;
    StringReadln(Line);
    writeln('The string array contains:');
    StringWriteln(Line);
    writeln('More? (y/n)');
    readln(Ans)
  until (Ans = 'n') or (Ans = 'N');
  writeln('End of test.')
end. {Program}
```

Sample Dialogue

```
Enter a string and press return.
12345678901234567890
```
Do Be Do
```
The string array contains:
Do Be Do
More? (y/n)
```
y
```
Enter a string and press return.
12345678901234567890
```
Life is a jelly doughnut. Isn't it?
```
Only        20 characters read in.
The string array contains:
Life is a jelly doug
More? (y/n)
```
n
```
End of test.
```

Figure 10.1
(continued)

from left to right carefully and with courage. For example, consider the following expression:

    Name[6][3]

Name[6] is an indexed variable of type CharString and in our example would contain the sixth name on our list of names. The type CharString is an array of characters, and so it makes sense to add an index to it. By adding [3] we obtain the third indexed variable of this array of characters. If we put this all together, we see that the above expression designates the location of the third letter in the sixth name on our list.

Expressions such as the one we just discussed usually need not be used at all. Instead it is preferable to think of Name[6] as a unit and to manipulate it as a unit using

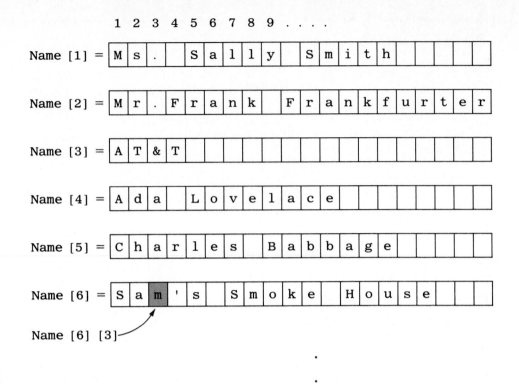

Figure 10.2
An array of
strings.

procedures. For example, the following procedure call reads a string from the keyboard and stores it in the array Name[6]. (The procedure declaration is in Figure 10.1.)

```
StringReadln(Name[6])
```

It is true that when Name[6] is substituted for the formal parameter A in the procedure declaration it will produce expressions such as

```
Name[6][I]
```

However, you need never think about this expression. The procedure StringReadln reads a string into an array of type CharString, and Name[6] is an array of that type. The procedure takes Name[6] as a single unit, gives it a value consisting of a string of characters, and then returns it to the calling program or procedure as a single unit. Once the procedure is written, you need not be aware of the details of how it accomplishes its task. You need not even be aware of the existence of that index I. That is the beauty of procedural abstraction.

Parallel Arrays

Oftentimes one wants the equivalent of two different component values for each indexed variable of an array. There is more than one way to accomplish this in Pascal. We will discuss other ways to do this later, but for now we will describe one standard and easy way to do it: Simply use two arrays with the same index type.

For example, if we need to record both a numeric score and a letter grade for each student in a class, then we can use the following declarations:

```
type ScoreList = array[1 . . Max] of integer;
     GradeList = array[1 . . Max] of char;
var S: ScoreList;
    G: GradeList;
```

The indexes serve as the link between the two types of grades. S[4] is the numeric score for student number four and G[4] is the letter grade for student number four. This is depicted in Figure 10.3. If Last is the number of the last student, then the following will output the list of students along with their scores and grades:

```
for I := 1 to Last do
  writeln('Student #', I, ' Score = ', S[I], ' Grade = ', G[I])
```

The two techniques of using parallel arrays and arrays of arrays can be combined. For example, if we are writing a program to act as a checkbook record keeper, we might use one array to keep track of the amount of each check and another array to keep track of whom each check was made out to. If we let the array indexes be the check numbers, then we can use the following declarations:

```
type Index = 1 . . MaxI;
     AmountList = array[Index] of real;
     CharString = array[1 . . MaxLength] of char;
     StringList = array[Index] of CharString;
var Amount: AmountList;
    Name: StringList;
```

Here again, the indexes serve as the link between names and amounts. Name[7] and Amount[7] are joined by the index 7; they tell us to whom check number seven was made out and for what amount.

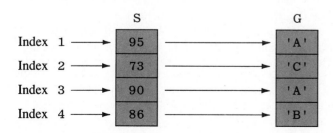

Figure 10.3
Parallel arrays.

Case Study

Making a History Table

Problem Definition

Your music history text continually names composers and dates but has no table of composers and dates so that you can get a feel for the historical progression in one quick glance. We will design a program to solve this problem. Our program will accept input consisting of composer's names followed by their years of birth. The program will output the same list sorted by birth date from the earliest to the most recent composer.

Discussion

data representation

The first step is to decide on a data representation. Now that we have array structures such as arrays of arrays and parallel arrays to choose from, this is no longer a straightforward task of naming a few simple variables. In this case the data will be a list in which each entry consists of a composer's name represented as a string of characters and the composer's year of birth represented as an integer. It sounds like an array would be suitable, except that the data is of two different types: a string of characters and an integer. In such cases, one natural solution is to use parallel arrays. That leads us to the following choice of data types:

```
type CharString = array[1 . . MaxLength] of char;
     Index = 1 . . MaxI;
     StringList = array[Index] of CharString;
     DateList = array[Index] of integer;
var Name: StringList;
    Date: DateList;
```

For each index I, Name[I] will contain the name of a composer and Date[I] will contain his or her year of birth. We do not know the exact size of the list, so we will use a variable Last to record the last index used.

As shown in the data flow diagram in Figure 10.4, the task breaks down in a typical way into the three subtasks: input the data, sort the arrays, and give the output. The input can be handled in a straightforward manner using a loop that contains the procedure StringReadln, which we designed earlier in this chapter. The output can be handled by another loop containing the companion procedure StringWriteln. The task of sorting the arrays is more complicated, and we now turn our attention to it.

false subtasks

It is easy to find natural-sounding subtasks for a problem, but these natural-sounding decompositions can sometimes be fruitless. Our sorting task has two arrays to sort. A natural-sounding breakdown into subtasks is

1. Sort the array of dates.
2. Sort the array of names.

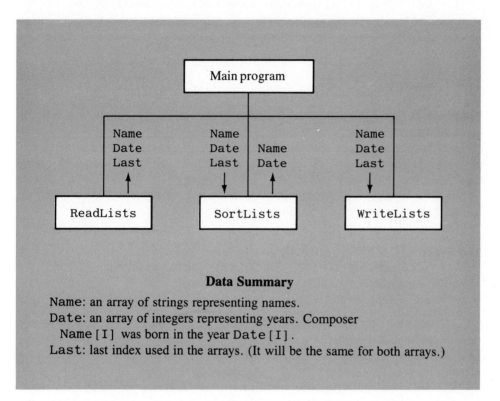

Data Summary

Name: an array of strings representing names.
Date: an array of integers representing years. Composer
  Name[I] was born in the year Date[I].
Last: last index used in the arrays. (It will be the same for both arrays.)

Figure 10.4
Data flow diagram for history table algorithm.

There is a serious problem with this approach. The dates can be sorted with little trouble, but the names present a problem. We have no way to sort them unless we sort them along with the dates. We want the names sorted by date of birth, and these dates are in the other array. These two subtasks are not separable. We must sort the two arrays together, sorting by date and moving the names to follow the dates. We must abandon the idea of solving two separate sorting subtasks, and instead we must treat the sorting of the two arrays as a single task.

In the previous chapter, we designed an algorithm to sort an array of integers. The procedure is in Figure 9.16. We will adapt that procedure to our present task. The procedure heading for our present sorting problem is

```
procedure SortLists(var Name: StringList;
                    var Date: DateList; Last: Index);
{Sorts the array Date into increasing order and moves the names to follow the dates.
Postcondition: The array elements in positions 1 . . Last of Date have been
rearranged so that Date[1] <= Date[2] <= . . . <= Date[Last];
if Date[I] was moved to Date[J], then Name[I] was moved to Name[J].}
```

The procedure Sort in Figure 9.16 can be used to sort the array Date. We will need to adapt the algorithm used by that procedure so that it sorts both the array Date and the array Name. The algorithm applied to a single array such as Date is the following:

> *for* I := 1 *to* Last − 1 *do*
>   Exchange(Date[I], Date[<suitable index>])

For I = 1 the <suitable index> is the index of the earliest date, for I = 2 it is the index of the next earliest, and so forth. The function Imin, which is also given in Figure 9.16, can be used to compute the <suitable index>, just as it was used in that program. (In this version of Imin, the array type is named DateList rather than List as it was in Figure 9.16.)

In order to adapt this sorting algorithm to the two parallel arrays in our problem, we need only move the names to follow the dates:

> *for* I := 1 *to* Last − 1 *do*
>   *begin*{*Set Ith entries*}
>   Exchange(Date[I], Date[<suitable index>]);
>   interchange Name[I] and Name[<suitable index>]
>   *end*   {*Set Ith entries*}

The procedure Exchange is well known to us by now. We need another procedure to accomplish a similar task for Name[I] and Name[<suitable index>]. Let us call this new procedure StringExchange. By way of summary, Figure 10.5 contains the data flow diagram for the procedure SortLists.

The procedure StringExchange must interchange the values of two arrays, Name[I] and Name[<suitable index>]. Since Name is an array of strings, the indexed variables, such as Name[I], are themselves arrays. Therefore, we need an algorithm that will interchange the values of two arrays. Recall that arrays can be treated like single variables with a single (compound) value each. If we take this view, then the procedure StringExchange can be identical to the procedure Exchange except that the type of the variables must be CharString rather than integer. To interchange our two string arrays, the following algorithm works:

> Temp := <array 1>;
> <array 1> := <array 2>;
> <array 2> := Temp

The variable Temp must be of type CharString. The detailed code for the procedure StringExchange is given in Figure 10.6, along with the rest of the program. Using the procedure StringExchange, it is routine to generate the code for the procedure SortLists as well as for the rest of the program.

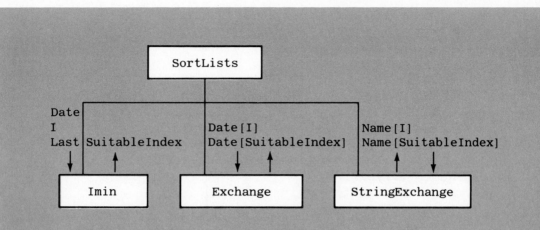

Data Summary

Name: an array of strings representing names.
Date: an array of integers representing years. Composer Name[I] was born in the year Date[I].
Last: last index used in the arrays. (It will be the same for both arrays.)
I: array index.
SuitableIndex: index of the element that belongs in position I of array Date after the array is sorted.

Figure 10.5
Data flow diagram for SortLists.

Self-Test Exercises

1. What is the output of the following program?

```
program Exercise1(input, output);
const MaxLength = 5;
var A: array[1 . . MaxLength] of char;
    I: integer;
begin{Program}
  A[1] := 'a';
  for I := 2 to MaxLength do
      A[I] := 'b';
  writeln(A)
end. {Program}
```

(Self-Test Exercises continued on page 363)

Program

```
program HistoryTable(input, output);
{Reads in a list of composers and their years of birth.
Outputs the list sorted by birth date.}
const MaxLength = 20;
      MaxI = 10;
type CharString = array[1 . . MaxLength] of char;
     Index = 1 . . MaxI;
     StringList = array[Index] of CharString;
     DateList = array[Index] of integer;
var Name: StringList;
    Date: DateList;
    Last: Index;

procedure StringReadln(var A: CharString);
{Fills the array A with one line of input characters and fills any extra positions with blanks.
If there are too many characters it discards all characters after the first MaxLength characters.}
```

. . .

<The rest of the declaration is given in Figure 10.1>

. . .

```
procedure StringWriteln(var A: CharString);
{Writes the string A to the screen and advances to next line.}
```

. . .

<The rest of the declaration is given in Figure 10.1>

. . .

```
procedure ReadLists(var Name: StringList;
              var Date: DateList; var Last: Index);
{Reads in a list of composers and their birth dates.
Postcondition: Date[I] is the year of birth of Name[I],
for all I <= Last; Last is the last index used.}
var I: integer;
    Ans: char;
begin{ReadLists}
   I := 0;
```

**Figure 10.6
History table
program.**

```
  repeat
    I := I + 1;
    writeln('Name?');
    StringReadln(Name[I]);
    writeln('Year of birth?');
    readln(Date[I]);
    writeln('More? (y/n)');
    readln(Ans)
  until (Ans = 'n') or (Ans = 'N');
  Last := I
end; {ReadLists}
```

```
procedure WriteLists(var Name: StringList;
                var Date: DateList; Last: Index);
```
{*Outputs the names and dates in the two arrays with*
Name[I] and Date[I] paired. Uses indexes up through Last.
Precondition: array elements 1 through Last are defined.}
```
const Blank = ' ';
var I: integer;
begin{WriteLists}
  for I := 1 to Last do
    begin{One Composer}
      write(Date[I]:4, Blank);
      StringWriteln(Name[I])
    end   {One Composer}
end; {WriteLists}
```

```
function Imin(var A: DateList; Start, Last: Index): Index;
```
{*Returns the index I such that A[I] is the smallest of the values: A[Start], A[Start + 1],. . . . A[Last].*}

$\bullet$ $\bullet$ $\bullet$

<The rest of the declaration is given in Figure 9.16>

$\bullet$ $\bullet$ $\bullet$

```
procedure Exchange(var X, Y: integer);
```
{*Interchanges the values of X and Y.*}
```
var Temp: integer;
begin{Exchange}
  Temp := X;
  X := Y;
  Y := Temp
end; {Exchange}
```

Figure 10.6

(continued)

```
procedure StringExchange(var X, Y: CharString);
{Interchanges the values of X and Y.}
var Temp: CharString;
begin{StringExchange}
  Temp := X;
  X := Y;
  Y := Temp
end;  {StringExchange}


procedure SortLists(var Name: StringList;
                var Date: DateList; Last: Index);
{Sorts the array Date into increasing order and moves the names to
follow the dates. Postcondition: The array elements of Date have been
rearranged so that Date[1] <= Date[2] <= . . . <= Date[Last];
if Date[I] was moved to Date[J], then Name[I] was moved to Name[J].}
var I, SuitableIndex: Index;
begin{SortLists}
  for I := 1 to Last − 1 do
    begin{Set Ith entries}
      SuitableIndex := Imin(Date, I, Last);
      Exchange(Date[I], Date[SuitableIndex]);
      StringExchange(Name[I], Name[SuitableIndex])
      {Date[1]<=Date[2]<= . . . <=Date[I] are the I smallest of the original
        array elements; the remaining elements are in the remaining positions.}
    end   {Set Ith entries}
end;  {SortLists}


begin{Program}
  writeln('Enter the composers and years of birth:');
  ReadLists(Name, Date, Last);
  SortLists(Name, Date, Last);
  writeln('The Composers in order of birth date:');
  WriteLists(Name, Date, Last)
end. {Program}
```

Sample Dialogue

```
Enter the composers and years of birth:
Name?
Beethoven
Year of birth?
1770
More? (y/n)
yes
Name?
J. S. Bach
Year of birth?
1685
```

**Figure 10.6
(continued)**

```
More? (y/n)
y
Name?
Mozart
Year of birth?
1756
More? (y/n)
y
Name?
Bloch
Year of birth?
1880
More? (y/n)
no
The Composers in order of birth date:
1685 J. S. Bach
1756 Mozart
1770 Beethoven
1880 Bloch
```

Figure 10.6
(continued)

(Self-Test Exercises continued from page 359)

2. The procedure `StringWriteln` in Figure 10.1 always ends by going to the next line. Hence, it cannot be used to write a string followed by a number all on one line. Write a procedure called `StringWrite` (no "ln") that writes but does not advance to the next line. Thus, the output of the following will all appear on one line:

```
StringWrite(Name[I]);
write(' is numbered ', I)
```

3. Give suitable type declarations for the following data: the family records for the children in a large family. The family is so large that the children are numbered 1 through 17. The records are made up of each child's name, his or her year of birth, and whether or not the child has been vaccinated against the flu.

> A man should keep his little brain attic stocked
> with all the furniture that he is likely to use,
> and the rest he can put away in the lumber-room of
> his library, where he can get it if he wants it.
> *Sir Arthur Conan Doyle*
> *(Sherlock Holmes), The Five Orange Pips*

The Notion of a Data Structure

The notion of a data structure and the notion of a data type are intimately intertwined, and so we will preface our discussion of data structures with a review of the notion of a data type. Recall that a data type is a collection of values together with the operations that are provided for those values. For example, the values of the type integer are 0, 1, −1, 2, and so forth. The operations include addition, subtraction, multiplication, *mod, div,* and the comparison relations, such as < and =. The data type real has a different set of values and a different set of operations, although some operations, like addition, can apply to both of these data types. Certain operations relate two or more data types. For example, the function sqrt, when applied to a value of type integer, produces a value of type real. The function round, when applied to a value of type real, produces a value of type integer.

Yet another data type is the array type:

type List = *array*[0 . . 4] *of* real;

The values of this data type are lists of five numbers indexed by the numbers zero through four. The operations for this data type do not combine two values of this type but instead combine a value of this array type with a value of the subrange type 0 . . 4 to produce a value of type real. If A is of type List, for example, then A combined with 0 yields the indexed variable A[0]. In this case, the operation is [ ]. The syntax is a bit unorthodox for an operation, and the result, strictly speaking, is not a value but a variable. However, it is an operation, and it does produce a value of type real, namely the value of the indexed variable A[0].

Like the data types integer, real, and char, the type List is a data type with values and operations. However, it clearly is a different sort of type. It is what we call a *structured data type.* It is called "structured" because it has a structure, namely a list of numbers, that can be decomposed into parts, namely the individual real numbers, by means of operations, namely using [ ] to produce indexed variables like A[0].

A data structure is almost the same thing as a structured data type. Every structured data type is a data structure, and given any data structure, we could redesign the Pascal language to include it as a data type. A *data structure* is a way of structuring data. It organizes the data into composite items and provides operations for manipulating the items. A data structure is like a structured data type in all ways but one: It need not be a declared data type that is named in the type declaration part of the program. For example, consider the parallel arrays that we used in the history table case study. Each separate array type is a data type, but the data structure consists of those two arrays taken together as a unit. There is no data type called "parallel arrays," but there is a data structure called "parallel arrays." Data types are in the declaration section of the program. Data structures are in the mind of the programmer, and might or might not also occur in the declaration section of the program.

Data Abstraction

We have already discussed the concept of procedural abstraction. It consists of forgetting the inessential details of a procedure. Wise use of procedural abstraction means that once we have finished writing and testing a procedure, we can forget how the procedure works and concern ourselves only with what it does. Once we have written (or someone else has written) the procedure `StringReadln` in Figure 10.1, we need not constantly return to the code to see how it works. We need only remember that it fills an array of type `CharString` with characters read from the keyboard and that it pads the string with blanks to make it 20 characters long. There is no need to remember whether it uses a *for* loop or a *while* loop or even whether it uses any loop at all. This forgetting frees our minds of inessential details and so frees our mental energy for the larger details of program writing.

Data abstraction is a similar kind of judicious forgetfulness, but in this case it is applied to data structures rather than to procedures. In order to realize a data structure within Pascal or any other programming language, we may need to specify some details which, while necessary in the particular language, are not a necessary part of our intuitive thinking about the data structure. For example, the type `CharString` discussed in the first few sections of this chapter was designed to hold strings of 20 or fewer characters. A natural way to do this is with an array. This required that we specify an index type. We chose to specify 1 . . 20. We might just as well have chosen 0 . . 19. Some authorities would argue vigorously that that would have been a better choice for an index type. Nobody is likely to argue for 100 . . 119 as the index type, but it would have been adequate. Since the index type matters so little, it would seem safe to just forget about it. This is exactly what data abstraction is all about: forgetting the inessential details of a data structure. The productive way to view the type `CharString` is as strings of 20 or fewer characters and not as an array type with some arbitrary index type. You should think about designing algorithms that manipulate strings. Do not waste mental energy memorizing the particular numbers used to index the characters.

Data abstraction and procedural abstraction go hand in hand. Once a data structure like the type `CharString` has been designed, and once the procedures for the basic operations like `StringReadln` and `StringWriteln` have been written, we can forget the inessential details of both the data structure and the procedures. At that point we are reading and writing strings of characters, not arrays of characters, and we are doing it with procedures, not with *for* loops. Of course, you must remember the details long enough to write the basic procedures, but after that you can forget them. It is no sin, of course, to remember the index type or other details if you happen to be able to fit them comfortably into your memory, but there comes a time when you should not emphasize them in your thinking.

Case Study

Automated Drill

Problem Definition

Earlier in this chapter, we designed a program to produce a history table listing composers and their years of birth. We want now to produce a related automated drill program. The program will accept the same input and build the same parallel arrays, but instead of outputting a table, it will drill the user to see whether the user knows the birth dates of the composers. After receiving the input, the program clears the screen. After that it will ask the user to input a composer and year of birth and will check to see whether or not the birth date is correct. It will repeat this drill as often as the user desires.

Discussion

An outline for the program is the following:

1. Input data and fill the parallel arrays.
2. Clear the screen.
3. Do the following as often as the user wants:
    3a. Read a composer's name and candidate year for birth date.
    3b. Search the list of names to find the composer.
    3c. Output an appropriate response.

This program can be written by adapting procedures that we have already designed for other tasks. The input and filling of the parallel arrays is identical to that in the history table program. The clear screen procedure will simply consist of a series of `writeln`'s to produce enough blanks lines to fill the screen. The input of the composer's name and candidate birth year are standard, as is the output message. Only the search algorithm seems to present anything new, but even that can be adapted from previous algorithms.

ALGORITHM

serial search

The search algorithm will search an array of names. We will again use the array type `StringList`. The type definition is reproduced below:

```
type CharString = array[1 . . MaxLength] of char;
     Index = 1 . . MaxI;
     ExtendedIndex = 0 . . MaxI;
     StringList = array[Index] of CharString;
```

The search will need to return the index of the name if the name is found and will need to indicate when the name is not on the list. Thus we are led to the following function heading:

```
function Search(var Pattern: CharString;
        var Name: StringList; Last: Index): ExtendedIndex;
```
{Returns the index I such that Name[I] = Pattern provided there is such an I in the range 1 through Last; otherwise returns 0.}

In Figure 9.10 we used a serial search algorithm to search an array of integers. That algorithm used no special properties of integers, and so it can be adapted to search any list, including a list of arrays. Although Name [I] and Pattern are entire arrays, we can view them as variables with complex values and compare them with the usual equality operator:

Name[I] = Pattern

The serial search algorithm tests each element of the array to see if Pattern is present:

```
Search := 0;  {not found so far}
for I := 1 to Last do
   if Pattern = Name[I]  then
      Search := I
```

The complete program is given in Figure 10.7.

Adapting a Known Algorithm

The previous case study illustrates one very important programming technique. Problems are very often variations on previously solved problems. Before trying to construct an algorithm from scratch, it always pays to see if the problem is similar to one that you solved previously. If the previously written program is well documented, this will be easy to do. It may even be possible to use entire procedures from previously written, well-documented programs.

Program

```
program DrillDates(input, output);
{Reads a list of composers and their years of birth, then drills the user on years of birth.}
const MaxLength = 20;
      MaxI = 10;
      ScreenSize = 30;  {Number of lines on the screen (or larger).}
type CharString = array[1 . . MaxLength] of char;
     Index = 1 . . MaxI;
     ExtendedIndex = 0 . . MaxI;
     StringList = array[Index] of CharString;
     DateList = array[Index] of integer;
var Pattern: CharString;
    Name: StringList;
    Date: DateList;
    Last: Index;
    Ans: char;
    Year: integer;
    Outcome: ExtendedIndex;
```

Figure 10.7
**Automated drill
program.**

```
procedure StringReadln(var A: CharString);
```
{*Fills the array A with one line of input characters and fills any extra positions with blanks.
If there are too many characters, it discards all characters after the first MaxLength characters.*}

. . .

<The rest of the declaration is given in Figure 10.1>

. . .

```
procedure StringWriteln(var A: CharString);
```
{*Writes the string A to the screen and advances to next line.*}

. . .

<The rest of the declaration is given in Figure 10.1>

. . .

```
procedure ReadLists(var Name: StringList;
            var Date: DateList; var Last: Index);
```
{*Reads in a list of composers and their birth dates.
Postcondition: Date[I] is the year of birth of Name[I],
for all I <= Last; Last is the last index used.*}

. . .

<The rest of the declaration is given in Figure 10.6>

. . .

```
procedure ClearScreen;
var I: integer;
begin{ClearScreen}
  for I := 1 to ScreenSize do
    writeln
end;  {ClearScreen}

function Search(var Pattern: CharString;
          var Name: StringList; Last: Index): ExtendedIndex;
```
{*Returns the index I such that Name[I] = Pattern provided there is
such an I in the range 1 through Last; otherwise, returns 0.*}
```
var I: Index;
begin{Search}
  Search := 0;  {not found so far.}
  for I := 1 to Last do
    if Pattern = Name[I] then
      Search := I
end;  {Search}

begin{Program}
  writeln('Enter the composers and years of birth:');
  ReadLists(Name, Date, Last);
```

**Figure 10.7
(continued)**

```
    ClearScreen;
    writeln('Do you want to test your memory of dates? (y/n)');
    readln(Ans);
    while (Ans = 'y') or (Ans = 'Y') do
      begin{while}
        writeln('Enter composer''s name: ');
        StringReadln(Pattern);
        writeln('Year of birth?');
        readln(Year);
        Outcome := Search(Pattern, Name, Last);
        {Outcome is index of composer; Outcome = 0 if not on the list.}
        if Outcome <= 0 then
          writeln('Sorry, no record of that composer.')
        else if Year = Date[Outcome] then
          writeln('You''re right!')
        else {Year is wrong and composer was found.}
          begin{give correct year}
            writeln('Sorry, you are wrong.');
            StringWriteln(Name[Outcome]);
            writeln('was born in ', Date[Outcome])
          end; {give correct year}
        writeln('Again? (y/n) ');
        readln(Ans)
      end; {while}
    writeln('End of drill.')
end. {Program}
```

Sample Dialogue

```
Enter the composers and years of birth:
Name?
Bloch
Year of birth?
1880
More? (y/n)
y
Name?
J. S. Bach
Year of birth?
1685
More? (y/n)
y
Name?
Beethoven
Year of birth?
1770
More? (y/n)
no
```

Figure 10.7
(continued)

Screen is cleared.

```
Do you want to test your memory of dates? (y/n)
yes
Enter composer's name:
Beethoven
Year of birth?
1776
Sorry, you are wrong.
Beethoven
was born in    1770
Again? (y/n)
y
Enter composer's name:
Bach
Year of birth?
1685
Sorry, no record of that composer.
Again? (y/n)
y
Enter composer's name:
J. S. Bach
Year of birth?
1685
You're right!
Again? (y/n)
n
End of drill.
```

**Figure 10.7
(continued)**

Case Study

Pattern Matching

The sample dialogue for the program in Figure 10.7 points out one shortcoming of that program. The name must be spelled exactly the same as the name in the array or the program will consider it a mismatch. To that program, "Bach," "Johann Sebastian Bach," and "J. S. Bach" are three different composers. In this section we will design a pattern-matching algorithm that will check for the occurrence of one string within another string. Using this algorithm, we can check for "Bach," and it will match any variation on Bach's name. (Those who are concerned about accommodating the other composers in the Bach family are encouraged to do Exercise 14 after reading this section.)

Problem Definition

Both the pattern, like "Bach," and the string it is compared to, like "J. S. Bach," will be stored in arrays of characters of the type `CharString`, which we used in the last case study. We want to design a boolean-valued function that will return `true` if the pattern occurs as a substring in the typically larger target string. However, there is a problem with trailing blanks. The string "Bach," if read in by the procedure `StringReadln`, will be stored as "Bach" followed by 16 blanks. Our pattern-matching function will need to somehow disregard any trailing blanks. The function we want can be described by the following heading:

> *function* Subpattern(*var* Pattern, Target: CharString): boolean;
> {*Returns true if the string in Pattern occurs as a substring of the string in Target; otherwise returns false. Disregards trailing blanks in Pattern.*}

Discussion

Suppose the array `Pattern` contains the string "Bach" in the indexed variables `Pattern[1]` through `Pattern[4]`, followed by trailing blanks. We want to know if "Bach" occurs anywhere in the array `Target`. One way to approach the problem is to assume that the arrays are strips of paper containing the strings and to visualize how we might compare the two strings using the strips of paper. This approach to the problem is diagrammed in Figure 10.8. For each position in the target array, we compare the pattern to the substring beginning at that position. Our approach is nothing but a more involved version of the serial search algorithm we used earlier, and it translates to the following algorithm outline:

> *for* I := 1 *to* <last possible I> *do*
>   *begin*{*Testing at Target[I]*}
>   compare
>   Pattern[1] through Pattern[<length of the pattern>] to
>   Target[I], Target[I + 1], Target[I + 2], etc.
>   if they match, then the pattern is found.
>   *end*; {*Testing at Target[I]*}
> if no match is found, then Target does not contain the pattern.

ALGORITHM

If the pattern string is "Bach," our algorithm needs to know that there are four letters in "Bach." It also needs to be able to compare "Bach" to any four successive elements of the target array. We will need to design a function or procedure for each of these two subtasks: one to find the length of the pattern and another to match the pattern array to a portion of the target array.

The length of the pattern will be computed by the function described in the following heading:

Length function

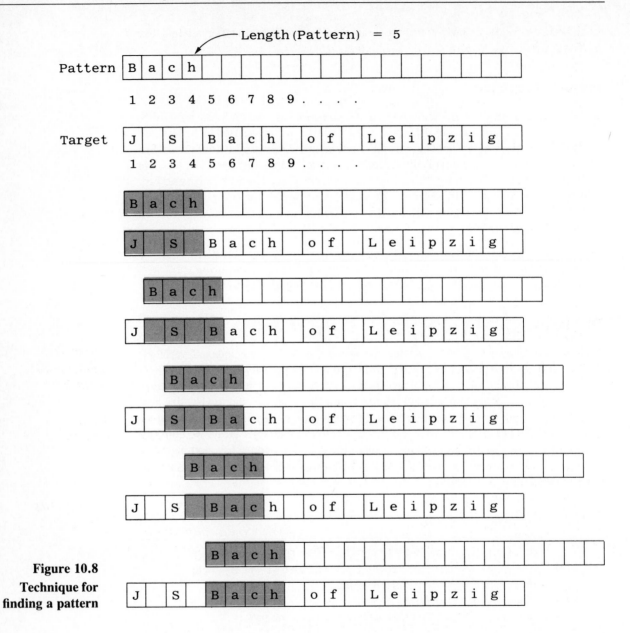

Figure 10.8
Technique for finding a pattern

```
function Length(var A: CharString): integer;
{Returns the length of the string in A, not counting blanks at the end.
Precondition: All indexed variables of A have a value; A is not all blanks.}
```

The most obvious approach is to count the characters starting at the beginning of the string and stopping when we encounter a blank. However, this approach will not work for strings that contain blanks, such as "Vaughan Williams." To accommodate such strings, we will instead count backward from the end of the array until we find a nonblank character. We count by decrementing a variable Count as follows:

```
Count := MaxLength;
while A[Count] = Blank do
  Count := Count - 1;
Length := Count
```

The complete function declaration for Length can be found in Figure 10.9.

```
const MaxLength = 20;
type CharString = array[1 . . MaxLength] of char;
```

```
function Length(var A: CharString): integer;
{Returns the length of the string in A not counting blanks at the end.
Precondition: All indexed variables of A have a value; A is not all blanks.}
const Blank = ' ';
var Count: integer;
begin{Length}
  Count := MaxLength;
  while A[Count] = Blank do
    Count := Count - 1;
  Length := Count
end; {Length}
```

**Figure 10.9
The function
Length.**

We now turn to the task of comparing the pattern to one portion of the array Target. In other words, we want to design a module with some parameters that can perform any one of the various comparisons illustrated in Figure 10.8. For our parameters we will want names that are more meaningful than I but shorter than Length(Pattern). Figure 10.10(a) illustrates our task and presents our naming conventions. EndP is the value Length(Pattern). StartT is the index of Target at which the comparison begins. If StartT has a value of 3, as in Figure 10.10(a), the comparison will fail. If it has a value of 5, and the other values are as shown in Figure 10.10(a), the comparison will succeed. Our module will compare the following two lists of characters:

*Match
function*

```
Pattern[1], Pattern[2], Pattern[3],..., Pattern[EndP]
Target[StartT], Target[StartT + 1], Target[StartT + 2], etc.
```

A natural way to do this is with a boolean-valued function that behaves as indicated below:

```
function Match(var Pattern, Target: CharString;
                        EndP, StartT: integer): boolean;
{Returns true if Pattern[1] through Pattern[EndP] matches the
characters in Target starting with Target[StartT]; otherwise, returns false.}
```

We will be applying the function Match only when the index position StartT is small enough to allow a match. For example, we will not try to compare a pattern of length four to the last three or fewer symbols in the target array. To ensure that we do not lose track of this assumption, we will make it an explicitly stated precondition:

precondition

Precondition: The array Target contains at least EndP elements in index positions StartT through the end of the array.

The "guilty until proven innocent" technique works here. We assume that the pattern is present unless we can find two corresponding characters that do not match. The technique is illustrated in Figure 10.10(b) and can be implemented with the following code to compute the value returned by `Match`:

ALGORITHM for Match

```
Match := true; {tentatively}
for I := 1 to EndP do
    if Pattern[I] <> Target[<corresponding index> ] then
        Match := false
```

To find the correct expression for the corresponding index, try some concrete examples. If I is equal to 1, then the corresponding index is StartT. If I is equal to 2, the corresponding index is StartT + 1. This reveals the pattern. The correct expression is StartT + I − 1. So the pseudocode rewrites to:

```
Match := true; {tentatively}
for I := 1 to EndP do
    if Pattern[I] <> Target[StartT + I − 1] then
        Match := false
```

efficiency

The above code will correctly compute the value we want for the function `Match`, but it is very inefficient. Once a mismatch is found, there is no need to perform any more checking. Look at Figure 10.10(b). The second comparison reveals a mismatch: "Bach" cannot match any pattern that starts with the letter "B" followed by the letter "l." There is no need to look at the entire word "Bach" to see that it does not match "Bloch." To make the algorithm more efficient, we use a local boolean variable `MatchSoFar` as a flag to end the loop as soon as a mismatch is discovered. Using this boolean variable, we rewrite the *for* loop as the following *while* loop (`MatchSoFar` is initialized to `true`):

```
while MatchSoFar and (I <=  EndP) do
    begin{Check one corresponding pair}
        if Pattern[I] <> Target[StartT + I − 1] then
            MatchSoFar := false;
        I := I + 1
        {MatchSoFar is true unless there is a mismatch before position I of Pattern.}
    end; {Check one corresponding pair}
```

After the loop terminates, the value of `MatchSoFar` is returned as the value of the function `Match`. The complete function declaration can be found in Figure 10.11.

first version of Subpattern

We are now ready to piece together the complete pattern-matching algorithm for the function `Subpattern`. The basic algorithm is an example of the "innocent until proven guilty" technique and can be realized as follows:

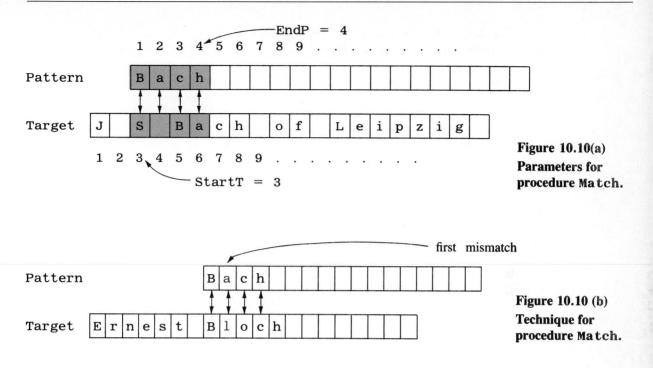

Figure 10.10(a) Parameters for procedure Match.

Figure 10.10 (b) Technique for procedure Match.

```
Subpattern := false; {tentatively}
for I := 1 to MaxLength - Length(Pattern) + 1 do
   if Match(Pattern, Target, Length(Pattern), I) then
           Subpattern := true
```

You should always check that a loop is not executed one too few or one too many times. In designing the above code, you might be tempted to use the following as the final value of the loop control variable:

check boundary values

```
MaxLength - Length(Pattern)
```

However, a careful check will reveal that this would stop the loop one iteration too early. This is easiest to see if you consider some concrete values. Recall that MaxLength is 20, and suppose that the length of the pattern is 4. The value of the above expression (without the +1) would then be 16. Yet if we try 17, we will see that it is possible to fit in a pattern of four letters starting with index variable 17:

```
Target[17] = 'B' Target[18] = 'a'
                     Target[19] = 'c' Target[20] = 'h'
```

Hence, we can see that in fact we need to include the +1 as shown in our *for* loop; otherwise, we will miss one possible location for the pattern.

The algorithm described in our pseudocode will work for the function Subpattern, but it is not very efficient. Once the pattern is found, there is no need to

efficiency

Program

```pascal
program TestMatch(input, output);
{Tests the function Match.}
const MaxLength = 20;
type CharString = array[1 . . MaxLength] of char;
var Pattern, Target: CharString;
    StartT, I: 1 . . MaxLength;
    Ans: char;

procedure StringReadln(var A: CharString);
{Fills the array A with one line of input characters and fills any extra positions with blanks.
If there are too many characters it discards all characters after the first MaxLength characters.}
                        . . .

          <The rest of the declaration is given in Figure 10.1>
                        . . .


function Length(var A: CharString): integer;
{Returns the length of the string in A not counting blanks at the end.
Precondition: All indexed variables of A have a value; A is not all blanks.}
                        . . .

          <The rest of the declaration is given in Figure 10.9>
                        . . .


function Match(var Pattern, Target: CharString;
                        EndP, StartT: integer): boolean;
{Returns true if Pattern[1] through Pattern[EndP] matches the
characters in Target starting with Target[StartT]; otherwise, returns false.
Precondition: The array Target contains at least EndP elements in
index positions StartT through the end of the array.}
var I: integer;
    MatchSoFar: boolean;
begin{Match}
  MatchSoFar := true;
  I := 1;
  while MatchSoFar and (I <= EndP) do
    begin{Check one corresponding pair}
      if Pattern[I] <> Target[StartT + I − 1] then
        MatchSoFar := false;
      I := I + 1
      {MatchSoFar is true unless there is a mismatch before position I of Pattern.}
    end; {Check one corresponding pair}
  Match := MatchSoFar
end; {Match}
```

**Figure 10.11
Program
containing the
function Match.**

```
begin{Program}
  repeat
    writeln('Enter a target string and press return.');
    for I := 1 to MaxLength do
        write(I mod 10:1); {To make it easy to count.}
    writeln;
    StringReadln(Target);
    writeln('Enter a pattern string and press return.');
    StringReadln(Pattern);
    writeln('Enter the index of where you want');
    writeln('to try matching the target.');
    readln(StartT);
    if Match(Pattern, Target, Length(Pattern), StartT) then
        writeln('The pattern was FOUND at index ', StartT)
    else
        writeln('The pattern was NOT FOUND at index ', StartT);
    writeln('More? (y/n)');
    readln(Ans)
  until (Ans = 'n') or (Ans = 'N');
  writeln('End of test.')
end. {Program}
```

Sample Dialogue

```
Enter a target string and press return.
12345678901234567890
J S Bach of Leipzig
Enter a pattern string and press return.
Bach
Enter the index of where you want
to try matching the target.
3
The pattern was NOT FOUND at index   3
More? (y/n)
y
Enter a target string and press return.
12345678901234567890
J S Bach of Leipzig
Enter a pattern string and press return.
Bach
Enter the index of where you want
to try matching the target.
5
The pattern was FOUND at index   5
More? (y/n)
n
End of test.
```

Figure 10.11
(continued)

perform any more checking. Hence, in the final version of the function declaration, given in Figure 10.12, we have replaced the *for* loop with a *while* loop that ends as soon as a match is found. For the sake of additional efficiency, we use a local variable called EndP to hold the value Length(Pattern) so that the program need only compute that value once.

use of
Subpattern

Using the function Subpattern, we can rewrite the function Search used in the drill program in Figure 10.7. The rewritten version of Search is given in Figure 10.13. If this rewritten version is used in the program in Figure 10.7, the user can enter "Bach" during the automated drill and the composer will be recognized as being on the list, even if the composer's name was originally entered as "J S Bach." (Of course, the function declaration for Subpattern must also be added to the program.)

Design by Concrete Example

When you are designing a program or procedure, it is often more fruitful to think in terms of a concrete example rather than an abstract characterization. In the previous example, it helped to think of locating the pattern "Bach" in the target string "J S Bach of Leipzig." This allowed us to visualize the problem and to try out our ideas imme-

Program

```
program TestSubpattern(input, output);
{Tests the procedure Subpattern.}
const MaxLength = 20;
type CharString = array[1 . . MaxLength] of char;
var Pattern, Target: CharString;
    Ans: char;


procedure StringReadln(var A: CharString);
{Fills the array A with one line of input characters and fills any extra positions with blanks.
If there are too many characters it discards all characters after the first MaxLength characters.}
                        ·   ·   ·
```

<The rest of the declaration is given in Figure 10.1>
·   ·   ·

```
function Length(var A: CharString): integer;
{Returns the length of the string in A not counting blanks at the end.
Precondition: All indexed variables of A have a value; A is not all blanks.}
                        ·   ·   ·
```

Figure 10.12
Finding a pattern.

<The rest of the declaration is given in Figure 10.9>
·   ·   ·

```
function Match(var Pattern, Target: CharString;
                         EndP, StartT: integer): boolean;
```
{*Returns true if Pattern[1] through Pattern[EndP] matches the
characters in Target starting with Target[StartT]; otherwise, returns false.
Precondition: The array Target contains at least EndP elements in
index positions StartT through the end of the array.*}

. . .

<The rest of the declaration is given in Figure 10.11>

. . .

```
function Subpattern(var Pattern, Target: CharString): boolean;
```
{*Returns true if the string in Pattern occurs as a substring of the string
in Target; otherwise, it returns false. Disregards trailing blanks in Pattern.
Calls the functions Length and Match. Precondition: Pattern is not all blanks.*}
```
var EndP: integer;
    Found: boolean;
    I: integer;
begin{Subpattern}
  EndP := Length(Pattern);
  Found := false; {so far}
  I := 1;
  while (not Found) and (I <= MaxLength - EndP + 1) do
    begin{Test starting at Target[I]}
       if Match(Pattern, Target, EndP, I) then
                Found := true;
       I := I + 1
    end;   {Test starting at Target[I]}
  Subpattern := Found
end; {Subpattern}

begin{Program}
  repeat
    writeln('Enter a target string and press return.');
    StringReadln(Target);
    writeln('Enter a pattern string and press return.');
    StringReadln(Pattern);
    if Subpattern(Pattern, Target) then
          writeln('The pattern was FOUND.')
    else
          writeln('The pattern was NOT FOUND.');
    writeln('More? (y/n)');
    readln(Ans)
  until (Ans = 'n') or (Ans = 'N');
  writeln('End of test.')
end. {Program}
```

Figure 10.12
(continued)

Sample Dialogue

```
Enter a target string and press return.
Ernest Bloch
Enter a pattern string and press return.
Bach
The pattern was NOT FOUND.
More? (y/n)
y
Enter a target string and press return.
J S Bach of Leipzig
Enter a pattern string and press return.
Bach
The pattern was FOUND.
More? (y/n)
n
End of test.
```

Figure 10.12 (continued)

Figure 10.13 Function Search rewritten to use the function Subpattern.

```
function Search(var Pattern: CharString;
            var Name: StringList; Last: Index): ExtendedIndex;
{Returns the index I such that Name[I] contains the string in Pattern,
if there is such an I; otherwise, returns 0. Disregards trailing
blanks in Pattern. Precondition: Pattern is not all blanks. Calls the function Subpattern.}
var I: Index;
begin{Search}
   Search := 0;  {Not found so far.}
   for I := 1 to Last do
      if Subpattern(Pattern, Name[I]) then
         Search := I
end; {Search}
```

diately. Once we knew how to find "Bach" in "J S Bach of Leipzig," we could then replace "Bach" with an arbitrary array Pattern and "J S Bach of Leipzig" with another arbitrary array Target.

When using this technique, you should consider one concrete case to represent each of the major possibilities. In this case, either the pattern is found or it is not. Hence, we also needed to look at a value for Target that does not contain the pattern "Bach." For this we used the target string "Ernest Bloch." Once you have an algorithm that works for a few special cases, it is not guaranteed that you have the correct algorithm, but you do have some inspiration. Once you have some inspiration and a candidate algorithm, you must determine whether the algorithm works for all cases, and if it does not, you must modify it so that it does.

The technique of using concrete data is particularly fruitful when you are determining the exact form of an arithmetic expression. In designing the algorithm for the procedure `Subpattern,` we needed to know the last index of `Target` that allowed sufficient room to hold a pattern of size `Length(Pattern)`. Clearly, the number is approximately

```
MaxLength - Length(Pattern)
```

but such expressions can often be off by one in either direction. When we considered the concrete examples of 4 for the pattern length and 20 for the `MaxLength`, we immediately saw that we needed to add one to obtain the correct expression. When deciding the exact form of an arithmetic expression, you will find that nothing clarifies your thinking as well as a concrete example.

Time Efficiency

Computers work amazingly fast. For all the programs we have seen to date, the time to run the program is negligible. However, now that we are considering arrays, processing time becomes more significant. We are now writing programs that may take many seconds to run on some machines. As they get more complicated, they will take longer to run. There is no need to be obsessive about making your programs run more quickly, but take care to avoid cases of extreme inefficiency. Seconds add up, and 30 seconds can seem like an endless amount of time when you are waiting for the computer to respond. Moreover, many computer installations charge for time and storage just as the electricity company charges for electricity.

As an illustration of some sources of inefficiency, consider the pattern-matching example discussed previously. The procedure `Match,` when called, will usually find a mismatch within the first few symbols. Hence, we terminate the loop as soon as a mismatch is found. If we did not terminate the loop as soon as a mismatch was found, then the procedure would go on to make many useless comparisons. This waste of time is compounded by the fact that `Match` is called numerous times by the function `Subpattern.` With a pattern of length 4 and an array size of 20, `Match` will be called 17 times if the pattern does not occur in the target array. Hence, any inefficiency might be multiplied seventeen-fold. The fact that array processing can include repeated computations for all (or many) elements of an array can make small inefficiencies multiply and produce noticeably slow programs.

Making a program efficient can often complicate the program. On two occasions in our last case study, we replaced a simple *for* loop with a *while* loop containing a complex boolean expression. This complication increases the chance of introducing program bugs. Whenever you tune a program to make it more efficient, be certain that the program is still correct. Reject any changes that are not certain to produce a correct program. Incorrect output is useless, no matter how rapidly it is produced.

Packed Arrays
(Optional)

There is a special class of arrays in Pascal that are supposed to be implemented so as to save storage. These are the *packed* arrays. They are not absolutely necessary, but on some systems they do save storage.

The Pascal language does not specify exactly how an array must be implemented. However, the language does specify that there will be two different implementations of arrays. One implementation is supposed to make the program run faster but may use more storage. That form consists of the basic array types we have been discussing. The other implementation is supposed to save storage but may make the program run slower.

These storage-efficient arrays are called "packed arrays" and are declared just like ordinary arrays except that the identifier *packed* is inserted before the word *array*. For example,

```
type SqueezeNumbers = packed array[0 . . 100] of integer;
```

The word *packed* instructs the compiler to use memory more efficiently. A typical scenario is as follows. Without the word *packed,* the compiler will reserve one memory location for each indexed variable. When the word *packed* is included, the compiler will instruct the computer to place ("pack") as many array elements as possible into one memory location.

Packed arrays are used in basically the same way as ordinary arrays. For example, if a packed array A is declared by

```
var A: SqueezeNumbers;
```

then it can be used in the same way as an ordinary array of integers, except in the few special cases discussed below.

Packed arrays save storage and so, all other things being equal, it should be preferable to use packed arrays rather than ordinary arrays. However, "all other things" are usually far from equal. Packed arrays have a number of disadvantages. Hence, they are usually used only when storage efficiency is a major issue. One disadvantage of packed arrays is that they tend to make the program run slower.

restrictions on packed arrays

One of the biggest disadvantages of packed arrays has to do with using them as parameters to procedures. On some systems an indexed variable of a packed array cannot be passed as a variable parameter to a procedure. Given a procedure heading of

```
procedure Exchange(var X, Y: integer);
```

and a variable A, declared as above, some systems will not allow the following procedure call:

```
Exchange(A[1], A[2])
```

This may have repercussions beyond user-defined procedures. On some systems the same prohibition applies to the standard procedures read and readln. On those systems data must be read into some other type of variable and then transferred to the packed array.

Other problems with packed arrays arise from the fact that packed arrays are considered to be a different type than the corresponding ordinary array type. Given the declarations

```
var L:  array[1 . . 80] of char;
    PL:  packed array[1 . . 80] of char;
```

the assignment L : = PL produces a type conflict and is not allowed. Similarly, if a packed array is to be the actual parameter to a procedure, the formal parameter must also be a packed type.

Packed Arrays of Characters
(Optional)

There are occasions when storage efficiency is very important. Hence, despite all their disadvantages, packed arrays can sometimes be very useful. The storage savings resulting from using packed arrays may be particularly large in the case of arrays of characters. Usually several characters can be packed into one memory location. Hence, if storage is a major consideration, the type CharString, discussed earlier in this chapter, could be redefined to be a packed array of characters:

```
const MaxLength = 20;
type CharString = packed array[1 . . MaxLength] of char;
var Line: CharString;
```

Although we are using the same identifier CharString to name this type, it is a different type from the previously defined type CharString, and it has certain special properties.

Unlike ordinary arrays, it is possible to fill a packed array of characters by using an assignment operator and a string constant. Packed arrays of characters are also allowed as arguments to the write and writeln statements. For example, with Line declared as in the previous paragraph, the following code is allowed:

assignment of strings

```
Line : = 'It is tight in here.';
writeln(Line)
```

The output produced by these two lines is

```
It is tight in here.
```

Some systems allow the use of a packed array of characters in a read or readln statement, as a way of reading a string constant into the array. However, many other systems do not allow the read and readln statements to be used in this way.

When filling a packed array with a string constant, remember that the length of the array is important: Any constant assigned to it must have exactly the same number of characters as the array has elements. To place the constant `'Loose fit'` into the array `Line` declared above, you must pad it with 11 spaces, like so:

```
Line := 'Loose fit            '
```

Packed arrays of characters can be compared using the less-than relation $<$. The ordering is approximately alphabetical. However, the exact result of a comparison will vary from one implementation to another.

Packed Arrays of Characters and Data Abstraction
(Optional)

The type `CharString`, whether defined as an ordinary array of characters or as a packed array of characters, produces the same abstract data type. Whichever definition we use, a value of type `CharString` is conceptualized as a string of 20 or fewer characters, and when we use the type we need not even be aware of which type definition is at the top of the program. Once the type definition and the basic procedures for manipulating strings have been designed, we can forget about whether we implemented the notion of a string as a packed array or as an ordinary array.

Before we engage in this forgetting process, we must first design the basic procedures for manipulating strings, and, in the case of the packed array version, we must make some minor changes in the basic procedures. These rewritten procedures, along with the new definition of the type `CharString`, are given in Figure 10.14. Since on some systems an indexed variable of a packed array may not serve as a variable parameter to the procedure `read`, the procedure `StringReadln` uses the following two-step sequence:

```
read(Next);
A[I] := Next;
```

in place of the following single statement, which may not work:

```
read(A[I])
```

Program

```
program TestPackedArrays(input, output);
{Tests the procedures StringReadln and StringWriteln rewritten for
the redefined type CharString, which here uses packed arrays of characters.}
const MaxLength = 20;
type CharString = packed array[1 .. MaxLength] of char;
var Line: CharString;
    I: 1 .. MaxLength;
    Ans: char;
```

**Figure 10.14
(Optional)
Strings
reimplemented as
packed arrays.**

```
procedure StringReadln(var A: CharString);
{Fills the array A with one line of input characters and fills any extra positions with blanks.
If there are too many characters it discards all characters after the first MaxLength characters.}
const Blank = ' ';
var Next: char;
    I, J: integer;
begin{StringReadln}
  I := 1;
  while (not eoln) and (I <= MaxLength) do
    begin{while}
      read(Next);
      A[I] := Next;
      I := I + 1
    end; {while}
  if (not eoln) {and hence (I > MaxLength)}  then
      writeln('Only ', MaxLength, ' characters read in.');
  readln;

  {The entire string has been read in (discarding any characters beyond the
  first MaxLength characters.) The value of I is the first available index.
  If I = MaxLength + 1, then the array A is full.}
  for J := I to MaxLength do
      A[J] := Blank
end; {StringReadln}

procedure StringWriteln(var A: CharString);
{Writes the string A to the screen and advances to next line.}
begin{StringWriteln}
  writeln(A)
end; {StringWriteln}

begin{Program}
  repeat
    writeln('Enter a string and press return.');
    for I := 1 to MaxLength do
        write(I mod 10:1); {To make it easy to count.}
    writeln;
    StringReadln(Line);
    writeln('The string array contains:');
    StringWriteln(Line);
    writeln('More? (y/n)');
    readln(Ans)
  until (Ans = 'n') or (Ans = 'N');
  writeln('End of test.')
end. {Program}
```

Figure 10.14

(continued)

Sample Dialogue

```
Enter a string and press return.
12345678901234567890
Do Be Do
The string array contains:
Do Be Do
More? (y/n)
y
Enter a string and press return.
12345678901234567890
Life is a jelly doughnut. Isn't it?
Only       20 characters read in.
The string array contains:
Life is a jelly doug
More? (y/n)
n
End of test.
```

**Figure 10.14
(continued)**

*anticipate
changes*

With packed arrays, the procedure StringWriteln is trivial and almost super-fluous, but we retain it so that if the occasion should arise in the future, we can easily change the implementation of the type CharString and how it is output.

Once these two basic procedures are changed, no other changes need be made to programs that manipulate strings. In particular, the history table program (Figure 10.6) and the automated drill program (Figure 10.7) will work perfectly if the type declaration for CharString and the two basic procedures are changed to those given in Figure 10.14. The rest of the program need not know the details of the type definition. Even the functions Length, Match, and Subpattern of Figures 10.9, 10.11, and 10.12 require absolutely no changes when we redefine the type CharString to be a packed array.

A penny saved is a penny earned.
Proverb

Penny wise, pound foolish.
Robert Burton, Anatomy of Melancholy

Self-Test Exercises

4. How must the data type `CharString` and the procedures `StringReadln` and `StringWriteln` of Figure 10.1 be modified to accommodate strings of up to 40 characters?

5. (This exercise uses the optional material on packed arrays of characters.) Given the declaration

```
type Words = packed array[1 . . 5] of char;
var A: Words;
```

which of the following are allowed?

```
A := 'Stuff';
write(A);
writeln(A);
read(A);
A := 'Hi!'
```

Multidimensional Arrays

An index often contains some sort of information about how the array elements are most naturally organized. For some situations, one index is not sufficient to organize the elements in an ideal fashion. As an example, suppose that we wish to hold a page of text in an array. We could number the characters of the text consecutively and use a larger array index range. If there are 100 characters per line and 30 lines per page, we could make it an array of characters indexed by the type 1 . . 3000. However, it would be much more convenient to use two different indexes, one for the line and one for the character on that line. In Pascal and most other high level programming languages, this is possible. It is possible, for example, to have an array called P that has two indexes, one for the line and one for the character in that line. Although Pascal does not insist on it, it is traditional to make the first index count the lines and the second index count the position in the line. The array declaration in this case would be written as follows:

multiple indexes

```
type OnePage = array[1 . . 30, 1 . . 100] of char;
var P: OnePage;
```

With P declared in this way, the first character of the first line can be stored as the value of P[1, 1]; the second character on the first line can be stored as the value of P[1, 2], and so forth. As another sample, the value of

```
P[5, 38]
```

is the thirty-eighth character on the fifth line. To write out the entire fifth line to the screen, the following will do:

```
for I := 1   to 100 do
          write(P[5, I]);
   writeln
```

two-dimensional example

An array with more than one index is called a *multidimensional* array. The diagram in Figure 10.15 may help to explain this choice of terminology. The array A depicted there contains a list of average grades for a small class with four students numbered 1 through 4. The array can be thought of as a simple list. Such lists are one-dimensional objects. The array G shows more details of the class grading. It gives three quiz scores for each of the four students. This can be visualized as a two-dimensional arrangement, with one row for each student and one column for each quiz.

sample declarations

Multidimensional arrays are declared in the same way as the one-dimensional arrays we have been studying until now. The syntax for a multidimensional type definition is described in Figure 10.16. As is the case with one-dimensional arrays, the index types for multidimensional arrays must be ordinal or subrange types. The various index types need not be subranges of the same type. There may be any number of indexes, so

```
var A: array[1 . . 4] of real;
```

Layout		Sample Values	
	Average		Average
Student 1	A[1]	Student 1	10.0
Student 2	A[2]	Student 2	1.0
Student 3	A[3]	Student 3	7.7
Student 4	A[4]	Student 4	7.7

```
var G: array[1 . . 4, 1 . . 3] of 0 . . 10;
```

Layout				Sample Values		
	Quiz 1	Quiz 2	Quiz 3		Quiz 1	Quiz 2	Quiz 3
Student 1	G[1, 1]	G[1, 2]	G[1, 3]	Student 1	10	10	10
Student 2	G[2, 1]	G[2, 2]	G[2, 3]	Student 2	2	0	1
Student 3	G[3, 1]	G[3, 2]	G[3, 3]	Student 3	8	6	9
Student 4	G[4, 1]	G[4, 2]	G[4, 3]	Student 4	8	5	10

Figure 10.15
One- and two-dimensional arrays.

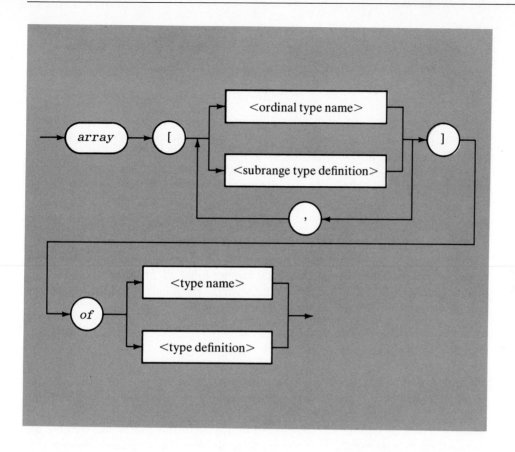

**Figure 10.16
Syntax of array
type definitions.**

long as there is at least one. (If there is just one, then it is a one-dimensional array.) As with one-dimensional arrays, the component type can be any Pascal type. Some sample type declarations for multidimensional arrays are

```
type Matrix = array[1 . . 10, 1 . . 5] of real;
     Count  = array[1 . . 100, 'A' . . 'Z'] of integer;
     Picture = array[0 . . 4, 0 . . 9] of char;
```

Arrays of the first type might hold real numbers for some scientific or engineering calculation. The type Count can be used in text processing. Suppose C is declared as

*sample
applications*

```
var C: Count;
```

The array C might then be used to count occurrences of each letter in a text of 100 lines. With the two-dimensional array, the program can easily keep a separate count for each line. The number of occurrences of, say, 'M' on, say, line 20 would be the value of C[20, 'M']. Arrays of type Picture might be used to hold patterns consisting of 5 lines of 10 characters each, which, when displayed on the screen, form a geometric pattern.

Aside from the fact that they may have more than one index, indexed variables of multidimensional arrays have the same properties as those of one-dimensional arrays.

Case Study

Grading Program

To illustrate the use of multidimensional arrays, we will solve a simple class grading problem. The program we design will compute student averages and display the individual quiz grades and the averages for each student in the class. The program could be used by an instructor to obtain an overview of class grades. To give a perspective on how difficult each individual quiz was, the program will also display the class average for each quiz.

Problem Definition

The quiz scores are to be read into the computer. The program will then display on the screen output consisting of each student's number followed by the student's average grade and a list of all the quiz scores for that student. The program will also display the average score of all the students for each individual quiz.

Discussion

data structure   We need to devise some method for keeping track of each student's score. A natural way to do this is with a two-dimensional array, such as the array G illustrated in Figure 10.15. One index can be the student number; the other can be the quiz number. If the array is called G, then G[SNum, QNum] will contain the grade that student number SNum received on quiz number QNum. If NumStudents and NumQuizzes are constants equal to the number of students and the number of quizzes, and if each quiz is scored on a basis of 0 to 10 points, then the declaration for the two-dimensional array G can be as follows:

```
type Score = 0 . . 10;
     StudentIndex = 1 . . NumStudents;
     QuizIndex = 1 . . NumQuizzes;
     GradeArray =
       array[StudentIndex, QuizIndex] of Score;
     StuAveArray = array[StudentIndex] of real;
     QuizAveArray = array[QuizIndex] of real;
var G: GradeArray;
    SA: StuAveArray;
    QA: QuizAveArray;
```

Figure 10.15 illustrates one possible set of values for G. There and in our program, NumStudents is set to 4 and NumQuizzes is set to 3.

We will use two one-dimensional arrays to hold the averages. The array SA will hold the averages of each student, and the array QA will hold the class average for each quiz. The relation between these two arrays and the array G is illustrated in Figure 10.17. The arrays SA and QA are not absolutely necessary for this simple problem, but they would be needed if we expanded the program to do more complicated tasks, such as displaying the student averages in sorted order or showing how much each score differs from the class average.

The task to be solved by this program can be decomposed into four subtasks: *ALGORITHM*

1. Read in the quiz grades.
2. Compute the average for each quiz.
3. Compute the average for each student.
4. Display the grades and the averages.

Each task is accomplished by a separate procedure. The complete program is shown in Figure 10.18.

As illustrated in the procedure Display, the usual and natural way to step   *nested* through all the elements of a multidimensional array is to use *for* loops nested one   *for loops* inside another. Each *for* loop steps through one of the array indexes.

Pitfall

Exceeding Storage Capacity

It is very easy to use unreasonably large amounts of storage when programming with multidimensional arrays. Even a modest-looking multidimensional array declaration can sometimes cause the computer to use a huge amount of storage. For example, consider the following reasonable-looking array declaration:

> *var* A: *array*[0 . . 50, 0 . . 50, 0 . . 50] of integer;

The compiler must allocate storage for $51 \times 51 \times 51 = 132{,}651$ integers. Many computer installations simply will not have enough storage available to accommodate such a program.

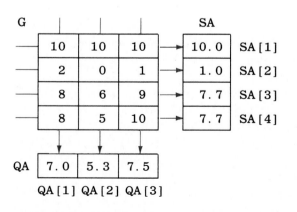

Figure 10.17 Relationship of arrays for grading program.

The more abstract the truth is
that you would teach, the more
you have to seduce the senses
to it.

Nietzsche

Program

```
program ShowGrades(input, output);
{Reads quiz scores for each student into a two-dimensional array G.
Computes the average score for each student and the average score for each quiz.
Displays the quiz scores and the averages.}
const NumStudents = 4;
      NumQuizzes = 3;
type Score = 0 . . 10;
      StudentIndex = 1 . . NumStudents;
      QuizIndex = 1 . . NumQuizzes;
      GradeArray =
         array[StudentIndex, QuizIndex] of Score;
      StuAveArray = array[StudentIndex] of real;
      QuizAveArray = array[QuizIndex] of real;
var G: GradeArray;
    SA: StuAveArray;
    QA: QuizAveArray;

procedure ReadQuizzes(var G: GradeArray);
{Postcondition: G[SNum, QNum] contains the score that
student number SNum received on quiz number QNum.}
var SNum: StudentIndex;
    QNum: QuizIndex;
begin{ReadQuizzes}
   for SNum := 1 to NumStudents do
      begin{Student number SNum}
         writeln('Enter the ', NumQuizzes:3, ' quiz scores');
         writeln('for student number ', SNum:3);
         for QNum := 1 to NumQuizzes do
               read(G[SNum, QNum]);
         readln
      end {Student number SNum}
   end; {ReadQuizzes}
```

Figure 10.18

Program using two-dimensional arrays.

```
procedure QuizAves(var G: GradeArray; var QA: QuizAveArray);
{Precondition: G[SNum, QNum] contains the score that
student number SNum received on quiz number QNum.
Postcondition: QA[QNum] contains the average score for quiz QNum.}
var SNum: StudentIndex;
    QNum: QuizIndex;
    Sum: integer;
begin{QuizAves}
   for QNum := 1 to NumQuizzes do
      begin{Quiz number QNum}
         Sum := 0;
         for SNum := 1 to NumStudents do
               Sum := Sum+G[SNum, QNum];
         {Sum contains the sum of the student scores for quiz QNum.}
         QA[QNum] := Sum/NumStudents
      end {Quiz number QNum}
end;  {QuizAves}


procedure StudentAves(G: GradeArray; var SA: StuAveArray);
{Precondition: G[SNum, QNum] contains the score that
student number SNum received on quiz number QNum.
Postcondition: SA[SNum] contains the average score for student SNum.}
var SNum: StudentIndex;
    QNum: QuizIndex;
    Sum: integer;
begin{StudentAves}
   for SNum := 1 to NumStudents do
      begin{Student number SNum}
         Sum := 0;
         for QNum := 1 to NumQuizzes do
               Sum := Sum+G[SNum, QNum];
         {Sum contains the sum of the quiz scores for student SNum.}
         SA[SNum] := Sum/NumQuizzes
      end {Student number SNum}
end;  {StudentAves}


procedure Display(var G: GradeArray; var SA: StuAveArray;
                                     var QA: QuizAveArray);
{Precondition: G[SNum, QNum] contains the score that
student number SNum received on quiz number QNum.
QA[QNum] contains the average score for quiz QNum.
SA[SNum] contains the average score for student SNum.
Postcondition: The scores and averages are displayed on the screen.}
const Space = ' ';
var SNum: StudentIndex;
    QNum: QuizIndex;
```

Figure 10.18
(continued)

```
begin{Display}
  {First display the student scores and student averages.}
  writeln('Student':10, 'Ave':5, Space:10,'Quizzes');
  for SNum := 1 to NumStudents do
    begin{outer for loop}
      write(SNum:10, SA[SNum]:5:1, Space:4);
      for QNum := 1 to NumQuizzes do
        write(G[SNum, QNum]:5);
      writeln
    end; {outer for loop}

  {Next display the averages of the quizzes.}
  write('Quiz Averages =':15, Space:4);
  for QNum := 1 to NumQuizzes do
    write(QA[QNum]: 5:1);
  writeln
end; {Display}

begin{Program}
  ReadQuizzes(G);
  QuizAves(G, QA);
  StudentAves(G, SA);
  Display(G, SA, QA);
  writeln('Now you know the scores!')
end. {Program}
```

Sample Dialogue

```
Enter the   3 quiz scores
for student number   1
10   10   10
Enter the   3 quiz scores
for student number   2
2   0   1
Enter the   3 quiz scores
for student number   3
8   6   9
Enter the   3 quiz scores
for student number   4
8   5   10
   Student    Ave              Quizzes
         1   10.0        10    10    10
         2    1.0         2     0     1
         3    7.7         8     6     9
         4    7.7         8     5    10
Quiz Averages =            7.0   5.3   7.5
Now you know the scores!
```

Figure 10.18
(continued)

Summary of Problem Solving and Programming Techniques

- When you are designing an algorithm, working with some specific sample data often helps clarify your thinking.
- Drawing a picture can often reveal the structure of a problem and lead to an algorithmic solution.
- You can often adapt a previously designed algorithm to solve a new, but similar, problem.
- One of the first tasks in designing an algorithm is to decide on a data structure to represent the data that will be manipulated by the algorithm.
- Data abstraction allows us to forget the inessential details of a data structure and concentrate on the substantive issues of algorithm design. In this way it is like, and in fact goes hand in hand with, procedural abstraction.
- If you need more than one value for each array index, you can use two or more parallel arrays.
- If you need a list of arrays, you can use an array of arrays.
- If you desire more than one index for each array element, you can use a multidimensional array type.
- Arrays are often processed sequentially. If the array is large, this can be time consuming. You can save time by terminating array processing as soon as the relevant information has been obtained. For example, when looking for something in an array, the processing can stop when the item or condition is found.
- One way to help find the correct index expression for array processing is to try specific numbers in place of the variables and see if the expression yields the correct value.

Summary of Pascal Constructs

array type declaration
Syntax:

```
type <name> =
    array[<type 1>, <type 2>, . . . , <type n>]  of  <component type>;
```

Example:

```
type ArrayName =
         array[0 . . 5, 'A' . . 'F'] of real;
```

The *n* index types must be ordinal types or subrange types. They may be either type names or type definitions. There may be any number of index types as long as there is at least one. The component type may be any Pascal type, including the defined types to be introduced in later chapters.

packed arrays of characters (optional)

Syntax:

```
type <name> =
   packed array[<type>] of char;
```

Example:

```
type CharString =
        packed array[1 . . 20] of char;
var A: CharString;
```

A packed array of characters is like an ordinary array of characters but with some additional properties: The compiler is instructed to use storage more efficiently; the entire array may be an argument to a write or writeln statement, as shown below. A string may be assigned to the array using a string constant and an assignment statement as shown below, provided the string has exactly the same number of characters as the array has indexes.

```
A := 'do be do to you      ';
writeln(A)
```

Exercises

Self-Test Exercises

6. The variable S declared below can be used to hold a page or screen of text consisting of 20 lines with 50 characters per line. Give code to perform each of the tasks listed after the declarations.

```
type OneScreen = array[1 . . 20, 1 . . 50] of char;
var S: OneScreen;
```

a. Write the first character of each line to the screen.
b. Write the last line to the screen.
c. Write the entire page of text to the screen.

Interactive Exercises

7. Write a program to read in a list of 10 numbers and letters that are typed in one letter and one number per line. The program should then echo the input back in the same format. Use two parallel arrays to hold the data.

8. Write a program to fill a two-dimensional array A of the type shown below, display it to the screen in the natural way, and then allow the user to type in any pair of indexes I, J and have the program write out the value of A[I, J].

```
array[1 . . 3, 1 . . 2] of integer
```

Include a loop to let the user enter different values of I and J for as long as the user wishes. The procedures ReadQuizzes and Display from Figure 10.18 can be used as models for the general method of reading in the array and displaying the array. They will not work without changes, but they do give the general idea of what is to be done.

Programming Exercises

9. Write a program that reads in a person's name in the format

    <first name> <middle name or initial or nothing> <last name>

The program should then output the name in the format

    <last name>, <first name> <middle initial>.

If the person inputs no middle name or initial, then the output should of course omit the middle initial. The program should work the same whether or not the user places a period after the middle initial. You may find it helpful to use more than one array. The program should work as long as each name is at most 10 characters long. If a name is over 10 characters long, then the program should use the first 10 letters of the name and should also issue an output statement saying that it did not use all of the letters in a certain name. (There is no "<" or ">" in the input. They are just to make the instructions easier to read.)

10. Write a program that reads in a sentence of up to 50 characters and then outputs the sentence with letters corrected for capitalization. In other words, the output sentence should start with an uppercase letter but should contain no other uppercase letters. Do not worry about proper names. For example, the input

    the Answer IS 42.

should produce the output

    The answer is 42.

(This program can be written more cleanly using material in the optional section of Chapter 8 entitled "The Functions pred, succ, ord, and chr.")

11. Write a program that reads a line of text and then outputs a list of all the letters that occur in the text, together with the number of times each letter occurs in the line. The letters should be listed with the most frequently occurring letter given first, the next most frequently occurring letter given second, and so forth. Use two parallel arrays with the index type 1 . . 26. One array will hold letters, and the other will record the number of times that the corresponding letter occurs. Your program should consider upper- and lowercase versions of a letter to be equal, and so the input line

    DO be do

should produce output similar to the following:

```
letter:     number of occurrences:
   d                 2
   o                 2
   b                 1
   e                 1
```

12. Modify the history table program in Figure 10.6 so that it records the year of death as well as the year of birth for each composer. The output should show both years for each composer, and the list should be sorted by year of death. Composers who died in the same year should be ordered by year of birth. Composers who are still alive should be placed at the end of the list, ordered by year of birth.

13. Write a checkbook balancing program. The program will read in the following for all checks that were not cashed as of the last time you balanced your checkbook: the number of each check, the amount of the check, and whether or not it has been cashed yet. (Use three parallel arrays, one for the numbers, one for the amounts, and one to record whether the check was cashed.) The program also reads in the deposits, as well as the old and the new account balance. The new account balance should be the old balance, plus all deposits, minus all checks that have been cashed. The program outputs what the total of the checks cashed is, the total of the deposits, what the new balance should be and how much this figure differs from what the bank says the new balance is. It also outputs two lists of checks: the checks cashed since the last time you balanced your checkbook and the checks still not cashed. Both lists are sorted by check number.

14. Modify the automated drill program in Figure 10.7 so that it can account for families in which there is more than one composer. The most notable example is the Bach family. The very well known Johann Sebastian Bach had four sons who were composers: Wilhelm Friedemann Bach, Karl Philipp Emanuel Bach, Johann Christoph Freidrich Bach, and Johann Christian Bach. Your modified program looks for multiple matches, and if it finds more than one match for, say "Bach," it tests to see whether the date matches any one of them. If a date does match, the program considers it a correct answer. If no dates match, it outputs all composers whose name contained the sub-pattern, along with the date for each composer.

15. A queue is a list that is used in a restricted way. Items are always added to the end of the list. For example, when X is added to A, B, C, the result is A, B, C, X. Items can only be removed from the front of the list. In order to remove C from the list, A and B must first be removed. Write a set of procedures for treating an array of characters as a queue. It should include procedures for insertion and deletion. The limits of the array index should be defined constants of type `integer`. Allow for the possibility that the number of elements in the queue is less than the size of the array.

16. Use parallel arrays in a program that reads in five playing cards and then displays the hand sorted for poker; that is, cards of the same value are grouped together (all twos are together, all three are together, all kings are together), and the groups are then sorted by value (all twos first, then all threes, then all fours, etc.). Each card has a value (2 to 10, ace, king, etc.) and a suit (clubs, diamonds, spades, or hearts). Count aces as the highest card in the sorted list. A sample display is

```
2 of diamonds
2 of clubs
king of spades
king of hearts
ace of diamonds
```

17. Telephone dials and push-buttons have letters as well as numbers. Hence, some phone numbers spell words. For example 452-4357 is also 452-HELP. Write a program to help people find words for phone numbers. The program should read in the last four digits of a phone number and then output all possible letter versions of that number. For example, 4357 can be HELP. It can also be GDJP, as well as other letter combinations. Use three arrays indexed by 0 . . 9 to hold the three letters that correspond to each number. There are no letters for 0 or 1. Do something graceful with those digits. If you prefer, you can use 1 . . 9 or 2 . . 9 as the array index type.

18. Write a program that does the following: asks the user to type in nine numbers in three rows of three numbers each, reads the numbers into a two-dimensional array, computes the sum of each row and each column, and then outputs the array as well as the row and column sums in the following format:

```
          ARRAY:      ROW  SUMS:
          1   2   3        6
          3   3   3        9
          3   2   1        6
COLUMN  SUMS:
          7   7   7
```

19. Write a program to assign passenger seats in an airplane. Assume a small airplane with seats numbered as follows:

```
1  A  B     C  D
2  A  B     C  D
3  A  B     C  D
4  A  B     C  D
5  A  B     C  D
6  A  B     C  D
7  A  B     C  D
```

The program should display the seat pattern, marking with an 'X' the seats already assigned. For example, after seats 1A, 2B, and 4C are taken, the display should look like

```
1  X  B     C  D
2  A  X     C  D
3  A  B     C  D
4  A  B     X  D
5  A  B     C  D
6  A  B     C  D
7  A  B     C  D
```

After displaying the seats available, the program prompts for the seat desired, the user types in a seat, and then the display of available seats is updated. This continues until all seats are filled or until the user signals that the program should end. If the user types in a seat that is already assigned, the program should say that the seat is occupied and ask for another choice.

20. Write a program that accepts input like that accepted by the program in Figure 9.14 and then outputs a bar graph like the one in that figure with the exception that your program outputs the bars vertically rather than horizontally. A two-dimensional array may be useful.

21. A graph with NumVert vertices can be represented by an array of the type

$$var \; G: \; array[1 \; . \; . \; NumVert, \; 1 \; . \; . \; NumVert] \; of \; boolean;$$

If G[I, J] has value true, it means that there is an arc from node I to node J. Write a program that takes as input the array representation of a graph and two nodes in the graph, and that outputs a path from the first node to the second or else announces that no path exists. Assume that the arcs are "one-way" arrows, so that if there is an arc from I to J, then the path can go from I to J but not necessarily in the other direction.

22. The game of Life, invented by J. H. Conway, is played by choosing an arrangement of marks on a rectangular grid and watching them change according to the following rules: If two or three of the four immediately adjacent positions are marked, then the mark is left; otherwise, it disappears. An unmarked cell becomes marked if exactly three of its immediately adjacent positions are marked. Write a program that accepts a pattern and then shows the series of patterns it produces. Have the program stop after the pattern stabilizes or after 10 iterations if it does not stabilize by then. Use a grid size of at least 10 by 10. All changes occur simultaneously, and so the program will need two copies of the configuration, one for the old pattern and one for the new one.

23. Write a program that reads in a screen display consisting of 20 lines of 20 characters each and then rotates it in stages, displaying each stage as follows: First it is rotated onto its side, then it is rotated more until it is upside down, then it is rotated to three-quarters of the way around, and finally it is rotated back to its original orientation.

24. An n by m matrix is a rectangular array of numbers. For example, the following is a 4 by 3 matrix:

$$\begin{pmatrix} 1 & 2 & 3 \\ 0 & 5 & 9 \\ 1 & 3 & 9 \\ 6 & -3 & 5 \end{pmatrix}$$

The entries of a matrix are normally numbered by two subscripts, one for the row and one for the column. The following illustrates the numbering of a 4 by 3 and a 3 by 2 matrix:

$$\begin{pmatrix} a_{11} & a_{12} & a_{13} \\ a_{21} & a_{22} & a_{23} \\ a_{31} & a_{32} & a_{33} \\ a_{41} & a_{42} & a_{43} \end{pmatrix} \qquad \begin{pmatrix} a_{11} & a_{12} \\ a_{21} & a_{22} \\ a_{31} & a_{32} \end{pmatrix}$$

The product of an m by n matrix with entries a_{ij} and an n by p matrix with entries b_{ij} is an m by p matrix whose entries c_{ij} are defined as follows:

$$c_{ij} = a_{i1}b_{1j} + a_{i2}b_{2j} + \cdots + a_{in}b_{nj}$$

Write a program that reads in an *m* by *n* matrix row by row, then reads in an *n* by *p* matrix row by row, and then computes the product matrix and displays the two matrices as well as their product matrix on the screen. Use integer values for the matrix entries. Use 3, 4, and 5 for the values of *m*, *n* and *p*, but declare constant names for them so that they can easily be changed.

25. Write a program that reads an *n* by *n* matrix into a two-dimensional array A and then determines which, if any, of the following special classes the matrix falls into:

> Symmetric: A[I,J] = A[J,I] for all indexes I and J.
> Diagonal: A[I,J] = 0 whenever I and J are different.
> Upper triangular: A[I,J] = 0 whenever I < J.
> Lower triangular: A[I,J] = 0 whenever I > J.

Use 6 as the value of *n*.

26. Write a program that allows two users to play tic-tac-toe. The program should ask for moves alternately from player X and player O. The program displays the game positions as follows:

```
1   2   3
4   5   6
7   8   9
```

The players enter their moves by entering the position number. After each move, the program displays the changed board. A sample board configuration is

```
X   X   O
4   5   6
O   8   9
```

27. Redo the previous exercise, but this time have the computer be one of the two players.

28. Write a program that allows the user to make a pattern on the screen using the keyboard and then stores the pattern in a two-dimensional array and echoes it back to the user. It continues to do this until the user indicates that the program should end. Use any array dimensions that are convenient, but allow at least a four by four pattern of characters.

References for Further Reading

D.F. Stubbs and N.W. Webre, *Data Structures with Abstract Data Types and Pascal,* 1985, Brooks/Cole. See Chapter 1 and the sections of Chapter 2 that cover arrays.

CHAPTER 11

RECORDS
AND OTHER
DATA STRUCTURES

'The time has come' the Walrus said,
'To talk of many things:
Of shoes—and ships—and sealing wax—
Of cabbages—and kings. . . .'
LEWIS CARROLL, THROUGH THE LOOKING-GLASS

Chapter Contents

In Chapters 9 and 10, we discussed the notion of a structured data type and introduced arrays as our first example of a structured type. In this chapter we introduce two other classes of structured data types, one called *record types* and another called *set types*. Record data types allow us to combine data of different types to obtain a single complex type that packages diverse subelements into a single (compound) value. Set data types let us combine items of the same type, but, unlike arrays, they do not order the items in any way. We also discuss techniques for using these data types as well as ways of deciding which of all the data types we have seen is best suited to a particular application.

Introduction to Records

Sometimes it is useful to have a single name for a collection of values that may be of diverse types. For example, an inventory for a mail-order house might contain the following entry:

> atomic can opener
> item #2001
> price $1,999.99

In this example, each inventory record consists of a name, a stock number, and a price. Although the record is conceptually a unit, the components are items of different data types. In Pascal, it is possible to define a structured data type consisting of a number of components, each of a possibly different type. These kinds of structured types are called *records*.

The individual components of a record are commonly referred to as *fields* or *components* or *component fields*. Each field has a name called a *field identifier,* which is some identifier chosen by the programmer when the record type is declared. Each field also has a type, which is specified when the record type is declared. A possible record declaration for the inventory record mentioned in the previous paragraph is the type StockItem defined below:

component field

```
type StockItem =
        record
           Name: array[1 . . 20] of char;
           Number: integer;
           Price: real
        end;
```

Name, Number, and Price are the field identifiers. StockItem is the name of the type. In a program with this type declaration, variables of type StockItem are declared in the usual way:

```
var Item1, Item2: StockItem;
```

A value of a record type is a collection of values that are each of some simpler type. The record has one value in the collection for each field identifier in the type declaration. The type of each of these values is the type specified for that field in the record type declaration. For example, a value of type StockItem is composed of three simpler values: One is an array of characters, one is of type integer, and one is of type real. These individual values are called the *component values* of the record. A sample record of type StockItem is illustrated in Figure 11.1.

component value

The field identifiers of a record are similar to the indexes of an array. They provide a way to name each individual value in the collection of values that make up the record. By adding the field name to a record variable, we can specialize the variable to one of its components. A component of a record variable is, as you might expect, called a *component variable*. To specify a component variable, we append a period and the field identifier to the record variable. (The period is usually pronounced "dot.") For

component variable

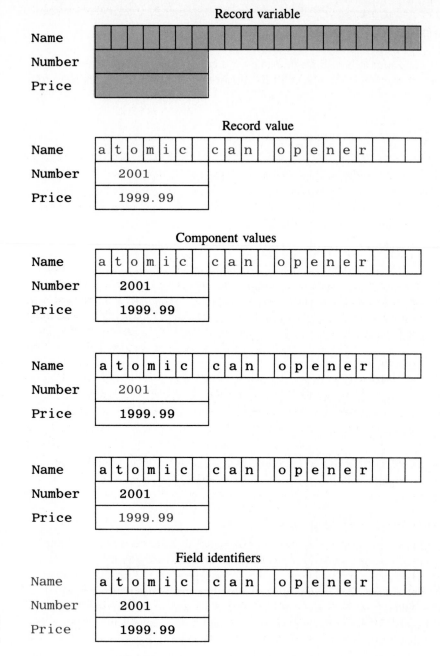

Figure 11.1
A record variable.

instance, the component variable of Item1 named by the field identifier Price is written as follows:

    Item1.Price

It is a variable of type real and can be used just like any other variable of type real. For example, the following will write the real value 9.95 on the screen:

    Item1.Price := 9.95;
    writeln(Item1.Price);

Similarly, the component variable Item1.Number is a variable of type integer, and the component variable Item1.Name is an array of characters. These component variables are illustrated in Figure 11.2.

When reading expressions involving records and arrays, always proceed from left to right. For instance, consider the expression

    Item1.Name[4]

The identifier Item1 names a record variable of type StockItem. By adding the field identifier, we specify a particular component variable. So Item1.Name denotes the component variable called Name. As specified in the type declaration, that is an array, and so we can add an array index to it. The complete expression thus refers to the fourth indexed variable of this array. To be very concrete, it refers to the fourth letter in the name of the item in this inventory record. This notation is pictured in the last illustration of Figure 11.2.

Figure 11.3 presents a Pascal procedure that fills a record variable of type StockItem and illustrates the basic technique for manipulating record variables.

records as single values

A value of a record type is composed of a group of values of the component types specified in the declaration of that record type. This group can sometimes be treated as a single (structured) value. For example, a procedure parameter of a record type is written without any field identifiers. The situation is similar to that of arrays. Also, the value of an entire record variable can be set by a single assignment statement.

For example, suppose that Item1 and Item2 are record variables of the type StockItem, declared in Figure 11.3. The following two statements consist of a procedure call followed by an assignment:

    ReadRecord(Item1);
    Item2 := Item1

If the declarations are as we gave them in Figure 11.3, then the first statement is a procedure call that sets the value of the record variable Item1 by having the user enter the value of each component variable. The second statement sets the value of each component variable of Item2 equal to the value of the corresponding component of Item1.

operations on records

A data type is specified by describing both the values that can be held by the variables of that type and the operations that are allowed on those values. In the case of records, the values are collections of simpler values, each indexed by a field identifier. The "dot" operation combines a value and a field identifier to obtain a component value. For example, the value of the record variable Item1 and the field identifier

```
type StockItem =
        record
          Name: array[1 . . 20] of char;
          Number: integer;
          Price: real
        end;
var Item1: StockItem;
```

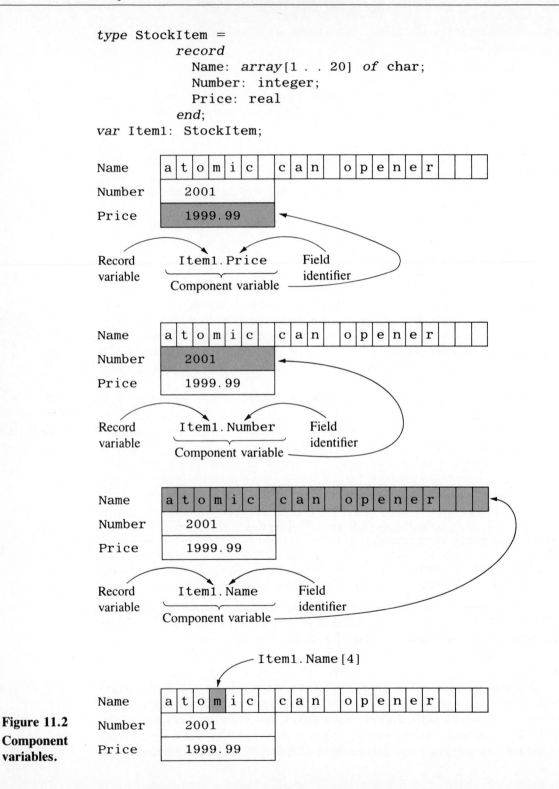

Figure 11.2
Component variables.

```
type StockItem =
        record
          Name: array[1 . . 20] of char;
          Number: integer;
          Price: real
        end;

procedure ReadRecord(var Item: StockItem);
{Sets the value of each component variable of Item
to a value read from the keyboard.}
var I: integer;
begin{ReadRecord}
  writeln('Enter name of item. Add blanks');
  writeln('to make it 20 characters long.');
  writeln('Extra blanks are OK.');
  for I := 1 to 20 do
      read(Item.Name[I]);
  readln;

  writeln('Enter stock number.');
  readln(Item.Number);

  writeln('Enter price.');
  writeln('Do not include a dollar sign.');
  readln(Item.Price)
end;  {ReadRecord}
```

Figure 11.3
Procedure to fill a record variable.

Price can be combined to obtain the component variable Item1.Price, which contains the component value specified by the name Price. Additionally, the usual operations allowed on variables may be used with record variables, such as Item1, and with component variables, such as Item1.Price. Either may be used with the assignment statement, and either may be used as a parameter to a procedure. All this makes a record sound very much like an array. As we will see in the next section, arrays and records are very similar, but they also have important differences.

Comparison of Arrays and Records

Records and arrays are similar in many ways. They both provide a way to give a single name to a collection of values. They both refer to elements of the collection by means of some sort of name. In the case of an array, the name is an index. In the case of a record, the name is a field identifier. A variable of either type can be thought of as a collection of variables of the component types.

On the other hand, arrays and records do have some important differences. The elements in an array list must all be of the same type. The component values of a record may be of different types. The index of an array may be computed by the program. If the index type is 1 . . 50, then a variable of this type may be used as the index. So the name of an array index variable (such as A[I]) may be computed by the program (by computing the value of I). The name of a component variable of a record (such as Item1.Price) must include a field identifier (such as Price), and there is no way for the program to compute a field identifier. The programmer must write it into the program.

The Syntax of Simple Records

Type definitions of records follow the pattern of the inventory record in the opening section of this chapter. The list of field identifiers is enclosed within the two identifiers *record* and *end*. Each field identifier is followed by a colon and the type of that field. A component type may be any Pascal type. In particular, it can be a structured type such as an array or even another record type. The various field identifier parts are separated by semicolons. If two successive field identifiers are of the same type, their declarations may be combined by separating them with commas and only listing the component type once. For instance, the following two type declarations are equivalent:

```
type Employee =
       record
         Number: integer;
         BaseRate: real;
         OvertimeRate: real
       end;

type Employee =
       record
         Number: integer;
         BaseRate, OvertimeRate: real
       end;
```

Of course, you may not use the same field identifier to name two different fields within the same record type. However, field names from two different record types may be the same. Thus, the following is allowed:

```
type Item =
       record
         Number: integer;
         Price: real
       end;
     Temperature =
       record
         Number: real;
         Scale: char
       end;
```

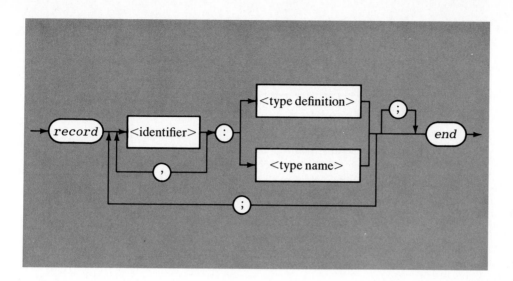

**Figure 11.4
Syntax for simple
record type
definitions.**

The syntax for type definitions is summarized in Figure 11.4. (As indicated there, you may, as usual, insert an extra semicolon after the last component, or you can omit it, as we have been doing in our examples.)

Self-Test Exercises

1. Consider the following type declarations:

```
type Sample = record
                   F1: integer;
                   F2: char
              end;
var X1, X2: Sample;
```

What will the output of the following piece of code be (provided that it is embedded in a complete Pascal program that includes the preceding type declarations)?

```
X1.F1 := 5; X1.F2 := 'A';
writeln(X1.F1, X1.F2);
X2 := X1;
X2.F1 := 6;
writeln(X2.F1, X2.F2)
```

2. Write a type declaration for a record type called Sam with one field of type integer, one of type real, and one of type char.

3. Write a program to fill (with data read from the keyboard) one record of the type described in the previous exercise and then display the record to the screen.

4. Write a type declaration for a student record that contains one field for the name; room for 10 quiz scores between 0 and 10; a midterm, a final exam score, and a final numeric grade, all in the range 0 to 100; and also a final letter grade.

Records within Records

Sometimes it makes sense to structure a record in a hierarchical way by making some component or components themselves records. For example, a record to hold the name and birth date of an individual might be of the following type:

```
type Date = record
                Month: 1 . . 12;
                Day: 1 . . 31;
                Year: integer
            end;
     Info  = record
                Name: array[1 . . 20] of char;
                Birthday: Date
             end;
```

A record variable might then be declared as follows:

```
var Person: Info;
```

If this record variable Person has its value set to record a person's birth date, then the year he or she was born is

```
Person.Birthday.Year
```

As always, the way to read these expressions is very carefully and from left to right. Person is a record variable. The component with field name Birthday is

```
Person.Birthday
```

This component variable is itself a record of type Date. Hence, it has three components, one of which is called Year.

Unfortunately, such complicated expressions are confusing. Fortunately, they can frequently be avoided by the use of procedure calls that manipulate entire records.

Arrays of Records

Simple record types are seldom used by themselves. More often, records are grouped into larger units, such as arrays of records. For example, if StockItem is the record type defined in our introduction to records, then we are likely to use the records in an array of records. If there are 100 items in the inventory, a likely additional declaration would be the following:

```
type List  = array[1 . . 100] of StockItem;
var Inventory: List;
```

The complete list of the inventory could then be read into the array by the following code:

```
for I := 1 to 100 do
        begin
         writeln('Next item: ');
         ReadRecord(Inventory[I])
        end
```

The procedure `ReadRecord` is given in Figure 11.3.

When you are programming with these nested structures, such as arrays of records, expressions can sometimes get quite complicated. To interpret them correctly, you must patiently work your way through them from left to right. As an example, review the declaration of the type `StockItem` and then try to figure out the following expression before reading on: *syntax for nested structures*

```
Inventory[2].Name[3]
```

The expression is interpreted as follows: `Inventory` is an array of records of type `StockItem`. Hence, each indexed variable of that array is a record of that type. `Inventory[2]` is the second indexed variable of this array and hence is a record variable of type `StockItem`. Since it is of this record type, it makes sense to refer to the component called `Name`. The way to specify a component variable of any record variable is to append a period followed by the field name. In this case, the following is the component variable of the record variable `Inventory[2]` that has the field name `Name`:

```
Inventory[2].Name
```

The component named `Name` is an array of characters. Hence, the above is an array of characters whose third indexed variable is

```
Inventory[2].Name[3]
```

This expression is an indexed variable of type `char`. Its value is therefore the third letter in the name of the second item on the inventory list.

In order to truly master records and data structures, you must be able to unravel and understand expressions such as the one we just discussed. However, once you have mastered the notation, it is often best to avoid such complicated expressions. By treating a record as a unit and by using procedures that manipulate these units, we can simplify both our reasoning and our notation. The loop code given earlier in this section filled an array of records but did not need to mention any details about record fields. It filled record number `I` of the array with the single simple procedure call *records as a unit*

```
ReadRecord(Inventory[I])
```

Sample Program Using Records

As a simple example of how arrays of records are used, Figure 11.5 presents a simplified version of the grading program in Figure 10.18. This time we use an array of records rather than parallel arrays. To simplify the example, this version does not compute class averages for the quizzes.

Program

```
program QuizAve2(input, output);
{Reads quiz scores for each student into an array of records;
computes each student's average and stores it in the record; displays each
student number followed by the student average followed by a list of quiz scores.}
const NumStudents = 4;
      NumQuizzes = 3;
type Score = 0 . . 10;
     StudentIndex = 1 . . NumStudents;
     QuizIndex = 1 . . NumQuizzes;
     Student =
       record
         Quiz: array[QuizIndex] of Score;
         Ave: real
       end;
     GradeBook = array[StudentIndex] of Student;
var B: GradeBook;

procedure ReadQuizzes(var B: GradeBook);
{Postcondition: For each student number SNum, B[SNum].Quiz contains the quiz
scores for student SNum in indexed variables B[SNum].Quiz[1], B[SNum].Quiz[2], . . . }
var SNum: StudentIndex;
    I: QuizIndex;
begin{ReadQuizzes}
  for SNum := 1 to NumStudents do
    begin{Student number SNum}
      writeln('Enter the ', NumQuizzes:3, ' quiz scores');
      writeln('for student number ', SNum:3);
      for I := 1 to NumQuizzes do
            read(B[SNum].Quiz[I]);
      readln
    end {Student number SNum}
end; {ReadQuizzes}
```

Figure 11.5
**Grading program
using records.**

```
procedure CompAverage(var B: GradeBook);
{Precondition: B contains the quiz scores for student SNum in
indexed variables B[SNum].Quiz[1], B[SNum].Quiz[2], . . .
Postcondition: B contains the average quiz score for student SNum in B[SNum].Ave.}
var SNum: StudentIndex;
    Sum, I: integer;
begin{CompAverage}
  for SNum := 1 to NumStudents do
    begin{Student number SNum}
      Sum := 0;
      for I := 1 to NumQuizzes do
            Sum := Sum + B[SNum].Quiz[I];
      {Sum contains the sum of the quiz scores for student SNum.}
      B[SNum].Ave := Sum/NumQuizzes
    end {Student number SNum}
end;  {CompAverage}


procedure Display(var B: GradeBook);
{Precondition: Scores and average for student SNum are in B[SNum].
Postcondition: The scores and average are displayed on the screen.}
const Space = ' ';
var SNum: StudentIndex;
    I: QuizIndex;
begin{Display}
  writeln( 'Student':8, 'Ave':5, Space:4,'Quizzes');
  for SNum := 1 to NumStudents do
    begin{outer for loop}
      write(SNum:8, B[SNum].Ave:5:1, Space:4);
      for I := 1 to NumQuizzes do
        write(B[SNum].Quiz[I]:3);
      writeln
    end {outer for loop}
end;  {Display}


begin{Program}
  ReadQuizzes(B);
  CompAverage(B);
  Display(B);
  writeln('Now you know the scores!')
end.  {Program}
```

Sample Dialogue

```
Enter the  3 quiz scores
for student number  1
10   10   10
```

Figure 11.5
(continued)

```
Enter the  3 quiz scores
for student number  2
1   0   0
Enter the  3 quiz scores
for student number  3
7   8   5
Enter the  3 quiz scores
for student number  4
9   7   9
Student    Ave       Quizzes
      1   10.0       10 10 10
      2    0.3        1  0  0
      3    6.7        7  8  5
      4    8.3        9  7  9
Now you know the scores!
```

**Figure 11.5
(continued)**

Choosing a Data Structure

*data
structures*

A *data structure* is a way of organizing data values. The various structured types that we have seen, such as arrays and records, are all data structures. Even simple variables of types such as `integer` or `char` could be considered data structures, although of a particularly simple kind. We now have a number of data structures available. We will eventually learn how to create other data structures within a Pascal program. When you are designing a program, the choice of an appropriate data structure is a critically important part of the design process.

*parallel
arrays versus
arrays of records*

Not infrequently, we have a choice of structures. As an example, we presented two versions of a grading program. The one in Figure 10.18 uses parallel arrays as the data structure. The one in Figure 11.5 uses an array of records as the data structure. The array-of-records data structure is closer to our intuition of how grade information is naturally kept and organized, and so it is often preferable to the two parallel arrays G and SA, which we used for the same data in Figure 10.18. This is a general phenomenon. Whenever parallel arrays are appropriate, an array of records is often also appropriate and usually is a preferable data structure.

In some situations, other array structures are more appropriate than an array of records. The program in Figure 10.18 uses a two-dimensional array and computes two kinds of averages: student averages and quiz averages. The program in Figure 11.5 uses an array of records but computes only student averages. With the two-dimensional array, we have a symmetry between students and quizzes. With the array of records, it is very easy to do calculations for each student, but calculations for one particular quiz are awkward. Which data structure we choose depends on the problem. For the output in Figure 10.18, a two-dimensional array and two one-dimensional arrays served best. For the simpler task in Figure 11.5, an array of records is more natural.

When you are designing a program, the choice of a data structure can be just as important as the designing of an algorithm for the program. The efficiency and clarity of a program can depend heavily on what data structures are used. Unfortunately, there is no algorithm for choosing a data structure. There are, however, a few useful guidelines.

Always consider the possibility of alternative data structures. Just because you find one that works does not mean that you have found the best one. All other things being equal, choose the one that is easiest to understand and manipulate.

Hierarchical data structures, like hierarchical control structures, make a program easier to understand. It pays to combine the basic data-structuring techniques to obtain hierarchical structures such as arrays of records, records of arrays, arrays of records of arrays, and so forth.

hierarchical data structures

There are some rules that apply to choosing between the various options for array types and/or record types. If all the items to be stored are of the same simple type, then a single array with that simple type as its base type can be used. If the items are of different types, then an array-of-records type can be used. An alternative to the array-of-records data structure is to use parallel arrays, that is, a collection of arrays with the same indexes. Some other programming languages do not have record types. When one is programming in these languages, parallel arrays are an even more important data structure.

The With Statement

Look back at the procedure CompAverage given in Figure 11.5. The entire procedure deals with the single record named B[SNum]. Every field identifier refers to B[SNum]. It would be convenient to have a way to say that all references to a record of type Student are references to the record B[SNum]. Then we could simply write the field identifiers and not have to write B[SNum] each time. The *with* statement lets us do just that. But before dealing with arrays of records, as in the procedure CompAverage, let us look at the *with* statement within a simpler context.

Consider the following declarations:

```
type Sample = record
                  F1: integer;
                  F2: char
              end;
var X: Sample;
```

The following code uses a *with* statement:

```
with X do
  begin
    F1 := 5;  F2 := 'A'
  end;
writeln(X.F1,  X.F2)
```

In the statement following *with* X *do,* all references to component field names F1 and F2 refer to X.F1 and X.F2, respectively. Hence, if the preceding code is embedded in a complete program, it will produce the following output:

5   A

Having mastered a simple example, we can now use a *with* statement to rewrite the procedure CompAverage so that the record name B[SNum] needs to be written only once. The procedure in Figure 11.6 does this and is equivalent to the one in Figure 11.5.

Pitfall

Problems with the With Statement

The syntax for the *with* statement is summarized in Figure 11.7. As indicated there, it is possible to have more than one record variable on the record variable list of a *with* statement. However, you must be careful to avoid any ambiguities when doing so. In particular, you cannot have two record variables of the same record type on the record variable list. This is because there would be no way to tell which record variable a field identifier referred to.

Even if you use only one record name in a *with* statement, there can still be a serious style problem. When a field identifier is seen in a *with* statement, it may not be immediately clear that it is a record field and not a simple variable. Although a *with* statement can make program code shorter and less complex, it can sometimes make it more difficult to read. To ensure readability, the *with* statement should be used sparingly.

Case Study

Sales Report

Problem Definition

The program we wrote for the Apex Plastic Spoon Manufacturing Company (in Chapter 9) has helped them to organize and optimize production. However, their annual company report shows that profits are falling despite increases in plant efficiency. The company decides that the problem is with their sales force and commissions us to write another, totally different program that will evaluate the performance of their sales force. For each salesperson, the program reads in the salesperson's total sales for the month and also the total value of goods that were sold by that person but were returned for credit during the month. The program outputs the net yield (sales minus returns) for

```
procedure CompAverage(var B: GradeBook);
{Precondition: B contains the quiz scores for student SNum in
indexed variables B[SNum].Quiz[1], B[SNum].Quiz[2], . . .
Postcondition: B contains the average quiz score for student SNum in B[SNum].Ave.}
var SNum: StudentIndex;
    Sum, I: integer;
begin{CompAverage}
  for SNum := 1 to NumStudents do
    with B[SNum] do
      begin{Student number SNum}
        Sum := 0;
        for I := 1 to NumQuizzes do
              Sum := Sum + Quiz[I];
        {Sum contains the sum of the quiz scores for student SNum.}
        Ave := Sum/NumQuizzes
      end {Student number SNum}
end; {CompAverage}
```

Figure 11.6
Procedure CompAverage rewritten using with.

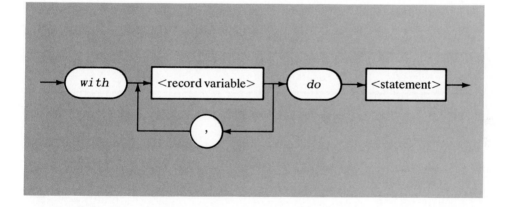

Figure 11.7
Syntax of a with statement.

each member of the sales force as well as the differences between each person's net yield and the average net yield.

Discussion

The first step is to decide on a data structure for the task. The information for each salesperson is most naturally kept in a record:

data structure

```
type  CharString = array[1 . . MaxLength] of char;
      PersonInfo =
          record
            Name: CharString;
            Sales, Return, Net, Comparison: integer
          end;
```

The data consists of a list of records, and so it is most naturally represented as an array of records:

```
type Index = 1 . . NumPeople;
     InfoList = array[Index] of PersonInfo;
```

ALGORITHM   The problem breaks down in a standard way into three main subtasks:

1. `GetData`: Input the data.
2. Compute the results.
3. `WriteTable`: Output the results.

The data flow diagram is given in Figure 11.8, and, as indicated there, the task of computing the results breaks down into three smaller tasks:

2a. Compute the net yield for each person.
2b. Compute the average net yield.
2c. Compute the difference between each person's net yield and the average net yield.

The complete program is given in Figure 11.9. Since subtasks 2a and 2b can each be performed by a loop that processes each record, and since they are each very simple, we have combined the two subtasks and used a single *for* loop to perform both calculations. Subtask 2c requires a separate loop.

Case Study

Strings Implemented as Records

We have already seen how to represent a string of characters as an array of characters. In the last chapter and in the previous case study, a string of up to 20 characters was represented as an array of the type

```
type CharString = array[1 . . MaxLength] of char;
```

where MaxLength is a constant equal to 20. Typically, the strings we encountered were less than the full 20 characters. So, when using arrays of type CharString, we filled the remaining array positions with the blank symbol. When computing the length of the string in tasks such as pattern matching, we discarded these trailing blanks. (See Figure 10.9 for a detailed example of this.) There is a blatant inefficiency in this practice of adding blanks only to remove them later. It would often make more sense to treat the array as being partially filled and to have one variable to record the last array position used, that is, to record the length of the string.

Using a record, we can combine into one unit both the array to hold the string and a variable to record the length of the string. This will have the added advantage of letting us more easily store and manipulate strings that end with a blank. With CharString declared as in the last chapter and in Figure 11.9, the strings 'Bach' and 'Bach ' (the latter has one blank before the final quote) would be stored in the

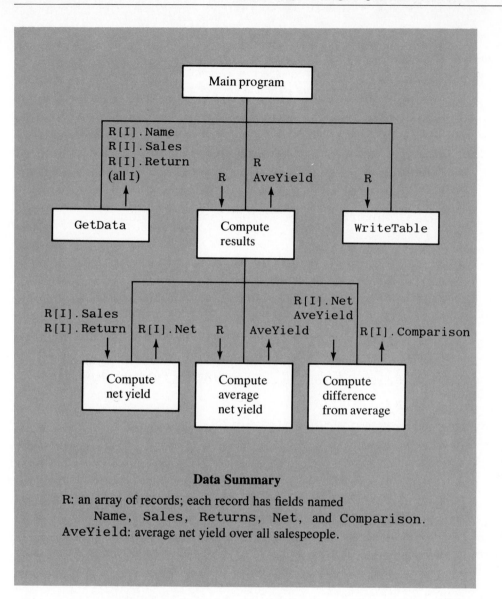

Data Summary

R: an array of records; each record has fields named
        Name, Sales, Returns, Net, and Comparison.
AveYield: average net yield over all salespeople.

**Figure 11.8
Data flow diagram
for sales report
generation.**

same way and so would be indistinguishable. Trailing blanks like that are not often relevant, but occasionally they can be useful. For example, they can be a convenient way to ensure that there will be a space between any two words that we might later join together.

Our new definition of the type CharString is a record with two fields. One field is an array of characters that normally will be only partially filled. The other field is an integer variable that records the last array position used and so records the length of the string. The type declaration is as shown on page 425.

*CharString
redefined*

Program

```
program SalesReport(input, output);
{Reads in sales and return figures for each salesperson. Outputs a table showing,
for each salesperson: the input data plus net yield and comparisons to average net yield.}
const MaxLength = 20;
      NumPeople = 3;
      Width = 12; {Field width}
type  CharString = array[1 . . MaxLength] of char;
      PersonInfo =
          record
            Name: CharString;
            Sales, Returns, Net, Comparison: integer
          end;
      Index = 1 . . NumPeople;
      InfoList = array[Index] of PersonInfo;
var R: InfoList;
    I: Index;
    Total, AveYield: integer; {AveYield is rounded to an integer.}


procedure StringReadln(var A: CharString);
{Fills the array A with one line of input characters and fills any extra positions with blanks.
If there are too many characters it discards all characters after the first MaxLength characters.}
const Blank = ' ';
var I, J: integer;
begin{StringReadln}
  I := 0;
  while (not eoln) and (I < MaxLength) do
    begin{while}
      I := I + 1;
      read(A[I])
    end; {while}
  if not eoln {and hence I >= MaxLength}  then
     writeln('Only ', MaxLength, ' characters read in.');
  readln;

  {The entire string has been read in (discarding any characters beyond the
  first MaxLength characters.) The value of I is the last index used.
  If I = MaxLength, then the array A is full.}

  for J := I + 1 to MaxLength do
      A[J] := Blank
  end; {StringReadln}
```

Figure 11.9
Sales report
program.

```
procedure StringWriteln(var A: CharString);
{Writes the string A to the screen and advances to next line.}
var I:1 . . MaxLength;
begin{StringWriteln}
  for I := 1 to MaxLength do
    write(A[I]);
  writeln
end;  {StringWriteln}

procedure GetData(var R: InfoList);
{Sets the fields Name, Sales, and Return for each record.
Assumes that there are NumPeople records to enter.}
var I: Index;
begin{GetData}
  writeln('Enter names, sales, and returns,');
  writeln('one person at a time:');
  for I := 1 to NumPeople do
    with R[I] do
      begin{Fill R[I]}
        writeln('Enter name of salesperson:');
        StringReadln(Name);
        writeln('Enter Sales and Returns:');
        readln(Sales, Returns)
      end  {Fill R[I]}
end;  {GetData}

procedure WriteTable(var R: InfoList; AveYield: integer);
{Outputs a table showing each record in the array R.
Also outputs the value AveYield labeled as the average net yield.}
var I: Index;
begin{WriteTable}
  writeln('                    Sales Summary:');
  writeln('Name');
  writeln('Sales' :Width, 'Returns' :Width,
                        'Net' :Width, '+/-Average' :Width);
  for I := 1 to NumPeople do
    with R[I] do
      begin{Display R[I]}
        StringWriteln(Name);
        writeln(Sales :Width, Returns :Width,
                        Net :Width, Comparison :Width);
      end;  {Display R[I]}
  writeln('Average net yield of all personnel =',
                                AveYield:Width)
end;  {WriteTable}
```

**Figure 11.9
(continued)**

```
begin{Program}
  GetData(R);

  {Compute net yields and average net yield (rounded to an integer).}
  Total := 0;
  for I := 1 to NumPeople do
    with R[I] do
      begin{Process R[I]}
        Net := Sales - Returns;
        Total := Total + Net
      end;  {Process R[I]}
  AveYield := round(Total/NumPeople);

  {Compute amount above or below average.}
  for I := 1 to NumPeople do
    R[I].Comparison := R[I].Net - AveYield;

  WriteTable(R, AveYield)
end.  {Program}
```

Sample Dialogue

```
Enter names, sales, and returns,
one person at a time:
Enter name of salesperson:
Charles Steak
Enter Sales and Returns:
2000   100
Enter name of salesperson:
Dusty Rhodes
Enter Sales and Returns:
3000   200
Enter name of salesperson:
Rock Garden
Enter Sales and Returns:
1000   500
                 Sales Summary:
Name
          Sales        Returns           Net    +/-Average
Charles Steak
             2000           100          1900           167
Dusty Rhodes
             3000           200          2800          1067
Rock Garden
             1000           500           500         -1233
Average net yield of all personnel =            1733
```

**Figure 11.9
(continued)**

(Text continued from page 421.)

```
type CharString =
        record
           Symbols: array[1 . . MaxLength] of char;
           Length: integer
        end;
```

This is a new type, even though we are using the same type name, CharString. However, although it is a new type, it serves the same purpose as our old type CharString and so can be used to replace it. It is "the new improved CharString type!" Some sample string values of this redefined type are diagrammed in Figure 11.10.

To use this new type CharString, we must rewrite the basic string-manipulating procedures. These rewritten procedures are given in Figure 11.11. Notice that since we now keep a record of the length of a string, we need not fill unused symbol positions with blanks. Also notice that the Length function is now trivial to declare. However, in order to think of the abstract notion of a string and not have to worry about details of field specifications, we still include a length function. The new type CharString and the new basic procedures StringWriteln, StringReadln, and Length can be used anywhere that we used the ones defined in Chapter 10. In particular, these new type, procedure, and function declarations can be used in place of the ones we used in Figure 11.9 with no other changes necessary in the program.

Case Study

Sorting Records

In Chapter 9 we developed a method for sorting an array of integers. In Chapter 10 we adapted that algorithm to a sorting algorithm for parallel arrays. In this section we will adapt the original sorting algorithm from Chapter 9 again. This time we will derive an

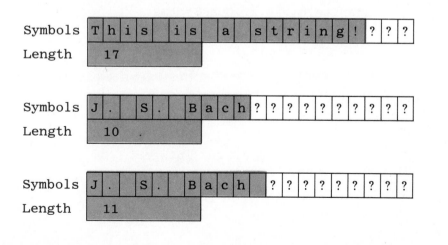

Figure 11.10
Strings as records.

Program

```pascal
program TestProcedures(input, output);
{Tests the procedures StringReadln, StringWriteln, and Length
rewritten to work for the record version of the type CharString.}
const MaxLength = 20;
type CharString =
        record
            Symbols: array[1 . . MaxLength] of char;
            Length: integer
        end;
var Line: CharString;
    I: 1 . . MaxLength;
    Ans: char;

procedure StringReadln(var A: CharString);
{Fills the array A with one line of input characters. If there are
too many characters it discards all characters after the first MaxLength characters.}
var I: integer;
begin{StringReadln}
  I := 1;
  while (not eoln) and (I <= MaxLength) do
    begin{while}
      read(A.Symbols[I]);
      I := I + 1
    end; {while}
  if (not eoln) {and hence (I > MaxLength)}   then
      writeln('Only ', MaxLength, ' characters read in.');
  readln;

  A.Length := I - 1
end; {StringReadln}

procedure StringWriteln(var A: CharString);
{Writes the string A to the screen and advances to next line.}
var I: 1 . . MaxLength;
begin{StringWriteln}
  for I := 1 to A.Length do
    write(A.Symbols[I]);
  writeln
end; {StringWriteln}

function Length(var A: CharString): integer;
{Returns the length of the string in A.}
begin{Length}
  Length := A.Length
end; {Length}
```

Figure 11.11
Strings reimplemented as records.

```
begin{Program}
  repeat
    writeln('Enter a string and press return.');
    for I := 1 to MaxLength do
        write(I mod 10:1);  {To make it easy to count.}
    writeln;
    StringReadln(Line);
    writeln('Array contains the ', Length(Line), ' symbols:');
    StringWriteln(Line);
    writeln('More? (y/n)');
    readln(Ans)
  until (Ans = 'n') or (Ans = 'N');
  writeln('End of test.')
end.  {Program}
```

Sample Dialogue

```
Enter a string and press return.
12345678901234567890
```
Do Be Do
```
Array contains the    8 symbols:
Do Be Do
More? (y/n)
```
y
```
Enter a string and press return.
12345678901234567890
```
Life is a jelly doughnut. Isn't it?
```
Only      20 characters read in.
Array contains the   20 symbols:
Life is a jelly doug
More? (y/n)
```
n
```
End of test.
```

**Figure 11.11
(continued)**

algorithm to sort records according to the values in one particular field. For example, you may want to sort inventory records by price from the least expensive to the most expensive. We will adapt the sorting procedure from Figure 9.16 so that it sorts inventory records according to price.

Problem Definition

Before we begin to adapt our sorting procedure, let us be sure that we understand exactly what kind of records our procedure will need to sort. Rather than using the inventory type that opened this chapter, we will use the following new type definition, in order to have yet another sample type:

```
type Entry =
        record
            Name: CharString;
            Quantity: integer;
            Price: real
        end;
    EntryList  = array[Index] of Entry;
```

The type CharString is defined in the previous Case Study.

Suppose that the array B is of type EntryList. We wish to sort the records in B so that the price fields of the records are in increasing order. If the first array index is 1, then we want the following to hold:

B[1].Price ≤ B[2].Price ≤ B[3].Price . . . .

```
const MaxLength = 20;
      High  = 10;
type CharString =
        record
            Symbols: array[1 . . MaxLength] of char;
            Length: integer
        end;
    Index = 1 . . High;
    ExtendedIndex = 0 . . High;
    {To be consistent with earlier work, we are using 0 to indicate
    the empty list. This is not important to the issues in this figure.}
    Entry =
        record
            Name: CharString;
            Quantity: integer;
            Price: real
        end;
    EntryList  = array[Index] of Entry;

procedure RecordExchange(var X, Y: Entry);
{Interchanges the values of X and Y.}
var Temp: Entry;
begin{RecordExchange}
    Temp := X;
    X := Y;
    Y := Temp
end;  {RecordExchange}

function Imin(var B: EntryList; Start: Index; Last: Index): Index;
{Returns the index I such that B[I].Price is the smallest of the values:
B[Start].Price, B[Start + 1].Price, . . . . B[Last].Price.}
var I: integer;
    Min: real;
```

Figure 11.12
Procedure for sorting an array of records.

```
begin{Imin}
   Imin := Start;  {tentatively}
   Min := B[Start].Price;  {minimum so far}
   for I := Start + 1 to Last do
      if B[I].Price < Min {Test only the Price} then
         begin{then}
            Min := B[I].Price;
            Imin := I
            {Min is the smallest of the values B[Start].Price, . . . ,B[I].Price;
               the tentative value of Imin is x such that B[x].Price = Min.}
         end   {then}
end;  {Imin}
```

```
procedure RecordSort(var B: EntryList; Last: ExtendedIndex);
{Sorts the partially filled array B into increasing order of prices using
the selection sort algorithm. Postcondition: The array elements have been
rearranged so that B[1].Price <= B[2].Price <= . . . <= B[Last].Price.}
var I: Index;
begin{RecordSort}
   for I := 1 to Last − 1 do
      begin{Place correct value in B[I]}
         RecordExchange(B[I], B[Imin(B, I, Last)])  {Interchanges entire records}
         {B[1].Price<=B[2 ].Price<= . . . <=B[I].Price
         are the I smallest of the original array elements;
         the remaining elements are in the remaining positions.}
      end   {Place correct value in B[I]}
end;  {RecordSort}
```

Figure 11.12
(continued)

Discussion

In Chapter 9 we used the following algorithm to sort a simple array of integers A.

```
for I := <first index> to Last − 1 do
      Exchange(A[I], A[<suitable index>])
```

where `Last` records the last array index used.

To adapt this code to an array of records B, we need to do the following:

1. Replace the simple array A with an array of records B.
2. Write a procedure like Exchange that applies to records of type Entry.
3. Design an algorithm to compute the <suitable index>.

Tasks 1 and 2 are trivial. The version of Exchange that applies to records is called RecordExchange. It is shown in Figure 11.12, and it is exactly the same as the procedure Exchange except that the type integer is replaced by the type Entry.

Task 3 will be accomplished by adapting the procedure Imin from Figure 9.16. The version shown there worked for an array of integers A, and so it compared array values A[I]. This version will apply to entire records B[I] in our array of records,

Imin

but only the `Price` field will be used to determine the ordering. Hence, comparisons involving the record `B[I]` are made using `B[I].Price`. However, once the function `Imin` determines the <suitable index>, procedure `RecordExchange` interchanges the entire record `B[I]` with the entire record indexed by <suitable index>. The sorting procedure is given in Figure 11.12.

Algorithm Abstraction

In Chapter 9 we developed an algorithm for sorting an array of integers. In the previous section we adapted that algorithm to obtain an algorithm for sorting an array of records. There is a sense in which those two algorithms are the same algorithm. There is a level of abstraction that captures them both. Instead of writing those two algorithms, we could have written a single algorithm to sort an array of some unspecified type according to some unspecified operator for "less than." The algorithm would step through the array and place the smallest element in the first array location, such as `B[1]` in the procedure `RecordSort` of Figure 11.12, the next smallest in the next array location, such as `B[2]` in that procedure, and so forth. To understand the algorithm we do not need to know the component type of the array. We also do not need to know the exact details of the "less than" relation. We can formulate an algorithm with these details left unspecified. If we then specify that the component type of the array is the type `integer` and that "less than" is to be the normal less than operator on the integers, we obtain the algorithm we presented in Chapter 9. If we instead specify that the component type of the array is the record type `Entry` given in Figure 11.12 and that "less than" is defined by considering only the `Price` fields of the records compared, then we obtain the algorithm we derived in the previous section. This is what is meant by *algorithm abstraction*. If we design our algorithms at a more abstract level, then we can reuse them in a variety of situations. If we think in terms of the more abstract algorithm, then we need not rederive the algorithm every time we want to sort an array of some different type.

The idea of changing the component type of the array and using the same abstract algorithm may seem quite obvious. A less obvious but equally useful change is to change the meaning of "less than." If we define "less than" to mean *greater than,* we still get a sorting algorithm, but now it sorts the entries from the largest to the smallest, rather than from the smallest to the largest. By thinking in terms of a single more abstract algorithm, we do not need to derive separate algorithms to sort into increasing order and to sort into decreasing order. They are the same algorithm but with different relations for what we have been calling "less than." If it helps to eliminate confusion, you might call the unspecified relation in your abstract algorithm something other than "less than," such as "goes-before" or "relation-X," and you might use some phrase other than "the smallest element" to designate the element that belongs in the first array position. For example, you might use the phrase "first with respect to the relation" instead of "smallest element." This will eliminate any prejudice against "greater than" relations. The important point is to think of the relation as being unspecified so that it can later be specialized to any relation that defines an ordering, such as less than on integers, greater than on integers, alphabetical on words, reverse alphabetical on words, and so on. Once we have the abstract algorithm, we can write programs to sort any kind of array into almost any kind of order by making only routine adaptations to our basic abstract algorithm.

ADT's—Abstract Data Types

In this book we have discussed procedural abstraction, data abstraction, and now algorithm abstraction. If you experience a bit of trouble distinguishing between these three techniques, do not be too concerned. They are not totally distinct concepts. They overlap and interrelate with each other. The key idea in all three of these programming techniques is abstraction. Abstraction means the hiding of certain details so as to allow more general thinking and to allow the separation of tasks into independent subtasks. For example, we have seen that an abstract treatment of sorting an array might hide the component type of the array elements and the definition of when one element is "less than" another. Abstract data types, which we will introduce in this section, provide us with a systematic technique for hiding information and so help us with all the forms of abstraction that we have discussed. Many newer programming languages, including some extensions of Pascal, have facilities to implement abstract data types directly. Standard Pascal does not provide for the direct implementation of abstract data types. However, you can still use the technique of abstract data types when programming in standard Pascal.

An *abstract data type* (abbreviated *ADT*) is a data structure (or data structures) and a collection of operations on the data structure defined in a particular way. In an abstract data type the specification of what effects the operations have on the data structure must be separated from the details of how the data structure and the operations are implemented. Moreover, any details of a data structure or operation that are left unspecified in an abstract data type must be clearly noted so that they can easily be filled in when the abstract data type is used in a program. An example is likely to be more informative than this wordy definition so let us go directly to an example.

Figure 11.13 shows a specification for the abstract data type CharString. The values of this type consist of strings of characters. The operations on this type are reading a value from the keyboard and writing a value to the screen. One other operation that is not explicitly mentioned since it comes automatically with all types is that of placing a value in a variable. In practice we might want to add a number of other operations, but these few will suffice to illustrate the concept of an ADT.

The specification of our ADT for CharString is divided into two subparts. One subpart, which we labeled the *Interface Section,* gives all the information that a programmer needs to know in order to use the ADT. The other section, which we labeled the *Implementation Section,* contains the complete code to implement the data type CharString and the operations StringReadln and StringWriteln as Pascal type and procedure declarations. In Figure 11.13 we have merely indicated what should appear in the implementation section, but you should imagine that the declarations from Figure 11.11 are actually written out in their entirety. Let us look at each of these two subparts in more detail.

interface section   The *Interface Section* contains the name of the type `CharString`, a description of the type, and the headings for the procedures that manipulate values of that type. However, it does not contain any type declaration for `CharString`, nor does it contain complete procedure declarations for the procedures that manipulate values of this type. The user of this ADT does not need to know those details in order to use the ADT. The interface section also contains a list of items labeled as *Imported* and a list of items labeled as *Exported*. The exported items are the things that a programmer who uses the ADT has available for use. The imported items are things that must be defined by Pascal declarations before the ADT can be used.

exported   In this example, the exported items are `CharString`, `StringReadln`, and `StringWriteln`. A programmer who uses this ADT can use the type `CharString` and the procedures `StringReadln` and `StringWriteln`, but he or she should not use any of the details about these items that are given in the implementation section. For example, a user of the ADT should not use the details of the type definition in order to access individual characters of a string. If accessing individual characters is a desired operation, then the ADT should have a procedure or function for doing so added to the ADT and listed as an exported item. Like the other exported procedures, this one would be described in the interface section, but the complete Pascal declaration would only be given in the implementation section.

imported   In this example, the only item imported is the constant `MaxLength`. Imported items must be defined before the ADT can be used. However, a user of the ADT does not need to know how they are defined. In this example, `MaxLength` needs to be

```
{
Interface Section:

    Abstract Data Type: CharString
    A data type for strings of characters with operations for reading and writing.
    Import: constant: MaxLength,  Maximum number of characters in a string
    Export: type: CharString
      procedures: StringReadln, StringWriteln


    Operations:
    procedure StringReadln(var A: CharString);
    Fills the array A with one line of input characters. If there are too many
    characters it discards all characters after the first MaxLength characters.

    procedure StringWriteln(var A: CharString);
    Writes the string A to the screen and advances to next line.


    Implementation Section:
}
                              • • •
        <The full type and procedure declarations for CharString,
        StringReadln and StringWriteln from Figure 11.11 go here.>
                              • • •
```

Figure 11.13
Abstract data type for strings of characters.

defined, but the user of the ADT should program as if he or she did not know what integer value it is declared to be.

The implementation section contains the full Pascal declarations for all the items, other than the imported items, that are described in the interface section. In order to use the ADT, a Pascal program would need to contain the implementation section as well as declarations for all the imported items.

implementation section

Some versions of Pascal have been extended to allow ADT's to be written and compiled separately and then stored in a library of ADT's that any program can use. The syntax for writing such ADT's varies from one version of Pascal to another, but is typically something similar to what we have used in Figure 11.13. Standard Pascal does not have facilities for handling ADT's in this way and so, in this book, ADT's are presented as a technique for designing programs rather than as a construct within the Pascal language. This technique can be used in any version of Pascal, whether or not that version has any extra features to accommodate ADT's. Since, for us, ADT's are a technique for thinking about programs rather than a formal Pascal construction, there is no fixed syntax for an ADT. The syntax shown in Figure 11.13 is typical of what programmers use, but other syntax would be equally good.

Although the ADT in Figure 11.13 cannot be compiled separately, we have set up the ADT so that it can be copied directly into any Pascal program that uses it. We have enclosed everything that is not actual Pascal code between two comment delimiters, and we have taken care to omit the comment delimiters around the procedure comments, since nested comments are not allowed in Pascal. A Pascal program that uses this ADT could copy the declaration for the only imported item as well as the ADT shown in Figure 11.13 into its declarations section and then use the ADT. (Depending on the particular ADT and the version of Pascal you are using, you might also have to rearrange the order of the declarations so that, for example, the type declarations precede the procedure declarations.) By setting up ADT's in this way, you can keep a library of ADT's and easily integrate an ADT into any program that uses it.

Figure 11.13 contains a lot of detail, but a substantial part of it is simply comments. What do we get for all this effort of dividing things into sections and giving such detailed documentation? We have gained generality and modularity. We can have several programs that use this ADT and we needed to write it only once. We can design algorithms that depend only on what is defined in the interface section and apply them in a number of different settings. This generality comes from the hiding of information. This hiding of information also produces modularity.

why use ADT's?

If this were part of a group project, we might first write only the interface section. After that, one programmer could be assigned to write the main part of the program and another programmer could be assigned to write the implementation section of the ADT. We have separated these two tasks by putting a wall between them so that each programmer need only see what is on his or her side of the wall. There are advantages to be gained from this separation of interface from implementation, even if all the programming is done by only one programmer. For one thing, you are free to change the implementation section if you later want to. If you discover a more efficient way to write the procedures in the implementation section, then you can change that section and you need not worry about changing the rest of the program. As long as you make your declarations consistent with what it says in the interface section, you need not worry about changing the program that uses your ADT. In this book, we have given three possible ways to fill in the implementation section. They are shown in Figure 10.1, Figure 11.11, and the optional Figure 10.14. You may use any one of them. You may later change from one to another or else write a completely new implementation section, and you need not change anything in the rest of the program.

Searching by Hashing
(Optional)

Suppose we want to store inventory records so that we can later retrieve any particular record by specifying its stock number. To be specific suppose the records are of the following form, with the stock number stored in the Number field:

```
type Item =
      record
        Number: integer;
        Price: real;
        Rating: char
      end;
```

If the records have Number fields with the values 1 through 50, then we could store them in an array of the following type, placing record number N in indexed variable A[N]:

```
var A: array[1 . . 50] of Item;
```

The record numbered N can be retrieved immediately since we know it will be in A[N].

But suppose the numbers do not form a neat range like 1 . . 50. Suppose that we know there will be 50 or fewer numbers but that they will be distributed in the range 1 through 5000. We could use an array with index type 1 . . 5000, but that would be extremely wasteful of storage since only a very small fraction of the indexed variables would be used. Hence, it appears that we have no alternative but to store the records in an array with 50 elements and to use a serial search through the array whenever we wish to find a particular record. Things are not that bad. If we are clever we can store the records in an array with relatively few (well under 200) indexed variables and yet retrieve records much faster than we would by serial search. In fact, there is more than one way to achieve this goal. In Chapter 14, we will present one method that depends on the array being sorted. In this section we will present a method that does not require sorting the array.

To illustrate the trick involved, suppose that somebody tells us that the 50 numbers will turn out to be the following:

```
100, 200, 300, 400,...,4900, 5000
```

In that case, we can store the records in an array A with index type 1 . . 50. The record with number field equal to N is stored in indexed variable

```
A[N div 100]
```

With the aid of the *div* operation, we can make do with the index type 1 . . 50 even though the numbers become as large as 5000. If we want record number 700, we compute 700 *div* 100 and obtain the index 7. The record is stored in indexed variable A[7].

This general technique is called *hashing*. One field of the record type, called the *key,* is singled out to serve as the name of the record. In our example, this was the Number field. A function F, called the *hash function,* maps key values to array indexes. In our example, if N is the value of the Number field of a record, then that record is stored in array position A[F(N)]. The function F must be chosen so that F(N) is always within the index range of the array. The hash function F can be either a declared Pascal function or an arithmetic expression. In our example F(N) was N *div* 100.

key

hash function

In our example, every N produced a different value of F(N). That is perfect, but one can not always find a perfect hash function. Suppose that we change the example by substituting 399 for 400. Then record number 300 will be placed in A[3], as before. Record number 399 is supposed to be placed in A[399 *div* 100]; in other words, record number 399 is also supposed to be placed in A[3]. There are now two different records that belong in A[3]. This situation is known as a *collision*. In this case we could redefine the hash function to avoid the collision. In practice, you usually do not know the exact numbers that will occur as record keys, so you cannot design a hash function that is guaranteed to be free of collisions. Something must be done to cope with collisions.

collisions

Typically you do not know what numbers will be used as the key values, but you do know an upper bound on how many there will be. The usual approach is to use an array size that is larger than is needed, typically two to three times as large as the number of records to be stored. The extra array positions make collisions less likely. A good hash function will distribute the key values uniformly through the index range of the array. If the array index type is 1 . . 100, then you might use the following hash function to produce an array index for the record whose Number field is equal to N:

(N *mod* 100) + 1

(The likelihood of collisions can be reduced by using the pseudorandom number generator discussed in the optional section of Chapter 8 entitled "Random Number Generators." For example, the following might be used as a hash function to obtain an index in the range 1 . . 100:

(Random(N) *mod* 100) + 1

The function Random is defined in Figure 8.9.)

One way to deal with a collision is with the following algorithm:

coping with collisions

Given the key N,

1. Compute the index F(N).
2. If A[F(N)] does not already contain a record, then store the record in A[F(N)] and end the algorithm.
3. If A[F(N)] already contains a record, then use A[F(N) + 1]; if that contains a record, use A[F(N) + 2], etc. until a vacant position is found. (When the highest

numbered array position is reached simply go to the start of the array. For example, if the index type is 1 . . 100, and 99 is full, try 100, 1, 2, etc., in that order.)

This requires that the array be initialized so that the program can test to see if an array position already contains a record. For example, if the key will always be a positive integer, then the key field of each array element can be initialized to 0. As long as it has a value of 0, the program knows that it does not contain a record. The procedure Initialize in Figure 11.14 initializes an array in this way. Figure 11.14 also contains procedures to store and retrieve records using this technique. The next few paragraphs explain the details of how these procedures work.

Insert

The procedure Insert will insert record R into array A by hashing the key value R. Number and handling collisions as in the above algorithm. The heart of the procedure is the following. (the hash function is called Hash)

```
I := Hash(R.Number);
while (A[I].Number <> 0) {position occupied}   do
    begin{Go to next array position.}
        I := (I mod MaxI) + 1
        {I := I + 1, but with wrap around at the end so MaxI + 1 is 1.}
    end;  {Go to the next array position.}
{I is the first vacant position >=Hash(R.Number).}
A[I] := R
```

If everything went smoothly this could be used as the body of the procedure. However, you should always plan on things not going smoothly. Therefore, the procedure in Figure 11.14 includes a number of checks. It checks to see if the array already contains a record with the specified item number; if it does, then it tells this to the user. It also counts the loop iterations to see if it has inspected the entire array. If it inspects the entire array without finding a vacant position it announces that the array is full.

The procedure Find searches an array A to see if it contains a record whose Number field is equal to Key. It assumes that the array has been initialized with the procedure Initialize and then changed only by the procedure Insert. The heart of this procedure is

```
I := Hash(Key);
Count := 1; {Counts up to MaxI to detect if the entire array has been inspected.}
while (A[I].Number <> Key) {Key not found} and
        (Count < MaxI) {entire array not yet checked} do
    begin{Go to next array position.}
        I := (I mod MaxI) + 1;
        {I := I + 1, but with wrap around at the end so MaxI + 1 is 1.}
        Count := Count + 1
    end;  {Go to next array position.}
{Either A[I].Number = Key or no record in the array has its Number field equal to Key.}
```

If the record is in the array then, at the end of the *while* loop, I will be set so that A[I] contains the record. If the record is not in the array, then the above code would search the entire array before it stops looking for the record. That is more work than is needed.

If the record is not in the array, then the loop can usually terminate much sooner. Recall that if there is a record with its Number field equal to Key, then it should be in position Hash(Key) or else in the first available position after that. The loop starts searching at array index Hash(Key). Should it ever encounter a vacant position, it knows that: if the record were inserted, then it would have been inserted there or before there. Hence, it knows it has looked every place that the record could possibly be. The final version of the procedure Search tests for a vacant position and terminates the loop if it finds one.

```
const MaxI = 100;
type Item =
        record
          Number: integer;
          Price: real;
          Rating: char
        end;
      List = array[1 . . MaxI] of Item;

procedure ShowRecord(R: Item);
begin{ShowRecord}
  writeln('The record contains:');
  writeln('Item number: ', R.Number);
  writeln('Price: $', R.Price: 6:2);
  writeln('Rating: ', R.Rating)
end; {ShowRecord}

procedure Initialize(var A: List);
{Sets the Number field of each array element equal to 0,
indicating that no record has yet been stored in the position.}
var I: 1 . . MaxI;
begin{Initialize}
  for I := 1 to MaxI do
      A[I].Number := 0
end; {Initialize}

function Hash(N: integer): integer;
{Returns an integer in the range 1 . . MaxI.}
begin{Hash}
  Hash := (N mod MaxI) + 1
end; {Hash}

procedure Insert(var A: List; R: Item);
{Inserts record R into the array A. Precondition: A has been initialized with
the procedure Initialize and after that has been changed only by this procedure.}
var I, Count: 1 . . MaxI;
```

Figure 11.14 (Optional)

Insert and Find procedures using hashing.

```
begin{Insert}
   I := Hash(R.Number);
   {Look for first available position starting at I.}
   Count := 1; {Counts up to MaxI to detect if the entire array has been inspected.}
   while (A[I].Number <> 0) {position occupied} and
           (A[I].Number <> R.Number) {key not found} and
           (Count < MaxI) {entire array not yet checked} do
      begin{Go to next array position.}
         I := (I mod MaxI) + 1;
         {I := I + 1, but with wrap around at the end so MaxI + 1 is 1.}
         Count := Count + 1
      end; {Go to next array position.}
   {Either A[I].Number = 0, or A[I].Number = R.Number, or the array is full.}

   if A[I].Number = R.Number then
      writeln('Already have an entry for item number ', R.Number)
   else if A[I].Number = 0 then
      A[I] := R
   else
      writeln('Array is full!')
end; {Insert}

procedure Find(var A: List; Key: integer);
{Searches the array A looking for an index I such that A[I].Number = Key.
Displays the record if it is found; otherwise, announces that it is not in the array.
Precondition: The array A has been initialized with the procedure Initialize
and then changed only by the procedure Insert.}
var I, Count: 1 .. MaxI;
begin{Find}
   I := Hash(Key);
   Count := 1; {Counts up to MaxI to detect if the entire array has been inspected.}
   while (A[I].Number <> Key) {Key not found} and
           (A[I].Number <> 0) {vacant record not found} and
           (Count < MaxI) {entire array not yet checked} do
      begin{Go to next array position.}
         I := (I mod MaxI) + 1;
         {I := I + 1, but with wrap around at the end so MaxI + 1 is 1.}
         Count := Count + 1
      end; {Go to next array position.}
   {Either A[I].Number = Key or no record in the array has its Number field equal to Key.}

   if A[I].Number = Key then
      ShowRecord(A[I])
   else
      writeln('Record is not in the array.')
end; {Find}
```

Figure 11.14
(continued)

Another technique for coping with collisions is to use two different hash functions. If a collision occurs, the program uses the second hash function to compute a number *n*, and then, rather than going to the next location, it goes to the location *n* places after the location given by the first hash function. This is called *double hashing*.

We have been discussing hashing for the case where the key is an integer. The same techniques apply if the key is of some other type. For example, the key might be a name. One approach to designing a hash function for such a key would be to assign a number to each letter of the alphabet. (One such function is the function `ord` discussed in the optional section "The Functions `pred`, `succ`, `ord`, and `chr`" of Chapter 8.) The hash function can then add up the numbers associated with each letter of the name to obtain a number and then proceed as if it had a numeric key.

Variant Records
(Optional)

It is frequently convenient and natural to have records in which the field identifiers and component types vary from record to record. For example, a list of publications might naturally be thought of as an array of records. Normally the records would contain slightly different entries for articles and for books. Both articles and books would have an author, a title, and a date. Books normally also have a publisher and city listed, while articles normally list a journal name, volume number, and range of pages. Pascal allows records which have some fields that vary from record to record. These sorts of records are called *variant records*. They are most often used in conjunction with enumerated types. (If you have not read the section on enumerated types, you should go back and read it before continuing with the rest of this section. Enumerated types are covered in Chapter 8.)

The syntax of a variant record type declaration uses something analogous to a `case` statement in order to specify the fields that vary from record to record. For example, Figure 11.15 defines two types. The type `Form` is an enumerated type. The type `Publication` is a variant record type for records, each of which is an entry for either a book or an article. The part before the identifier `case` is called the *fixed part*.

```
type Form = (Book, Article);
     Publication =
       record
         Author, Title: array[1 . . 20] of char;
         Date: 1900 . . 2000;
         case Kind: Form of
           Book:
             (Pub, City: array[1 . . 10] of char);
           Article:
             (Journal: array[1 . . 20] of char;
                       Vol, FirstP, LastP: integer)
       end;
```

Figure 11.15 (Optional)

A variant record type.

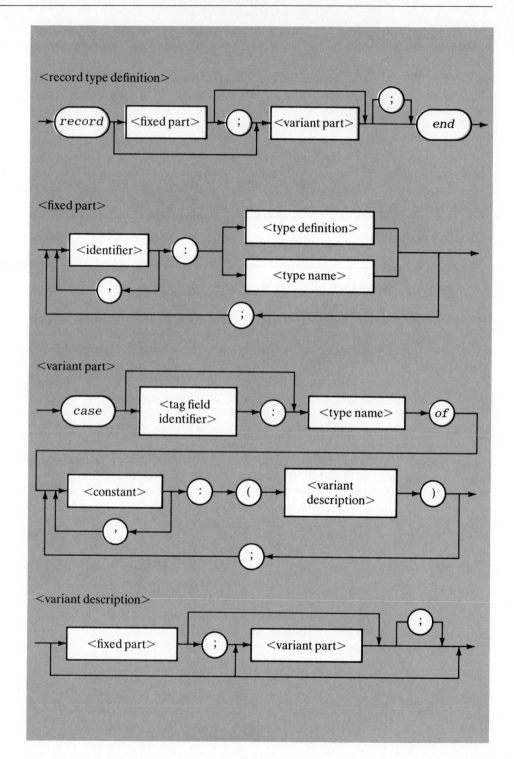

Figure 11.16 (Optional) Complete syntax diagram for record type definitions.

It is just like the other record types we have seen. By way of illustration, suppose that we have the following variable declaration:

   var PubRec: Publication;

The following component variables are then exactly like the ones we have seen for the ordinary records discussed in previous sections:

   PubRec.Author   PubRec.Title   PubRec.Date

The part of the type declaration that starts with the identifier *case* is called the *variant part*. The identifier Kind is called the *tag field identifier*. It is a component of type Form. Every record has this component. Hence, PubRec.Kind can be used as an ordinary component variable. However, this component has an additional property. The value of the component Kind determines the form of the rest of the record. If the value of Kind is Book, then the record will have the following two additional components:

   PubRec.Pub
   PubRec.City

*variant
part*

*tag
field*

If the value of Kind is Article, then these two fields will not exist; instead, the following four fields will be present:

   PubRec.Journal
   PubRec.Vol
   PubRec.FirstP
   PubRec.LastP

In all cases, the types of the components are the ones specified in the declaration.

A complete syntax diagram for record type definitions that can include a variant part is given in Figure 11.16. Notice that there is only one *case* type structure, and it always comes last. (There can be a *case* within the *case,* but such nesting is rare.) All the various field identifiers must be distinct. The <tag field identifier> is a normal field identifier. The <type name> associated with the <tag field identifier> may name any subrange or other ordinal type. It must be a type name; it cannot be a type definition, such as 1 . . 4.

It is possible to omit the tag field identifier. In Figure 11.15, this would be done by replacing

   case Kind: Form *of*

with

   case Form *of*

*omitting the
tag field
identifier*

If this is done, there will be no component called Kind. The programmer must somehow ensure that the various cases are used consistently. If a record has its value set using Pub, it cannot later try to read the component FirstP. If it does, the result is unpredictable. Notice that the tag type must be included even if there is no tag field. The syntax diagram in Figure 11.16 describes all the possible variations.

Variant records are not absolutely necessary. For example, we could have defined the type Publication to have all 10 possible fields and could then write the pro-

*storage
efficiency*

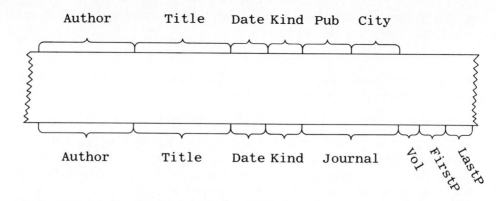

Figure 11.17
(Optional)
Memory allocation
for a variant
record.

gram so that it uses whatever fields are needed. However, on most systems the variant record form will use less storage, because the same storage is used for the Book fields as is used for the Article fields. Hence, the storage needed is the maximum of the two cases rather than the sum of the two. This kind of storage allocation is illustrated in Figure 11.17.

example

Figure 11.18 contains a sample program using a variant record type. In that program the tag field Shape is set to either Rectangle or Circle. In the first case, there will be two additional fields called Height and Width. In the second case, there will be just one additional field, called Radius.

Program

```
program AreaComp(input, output);
{Illustrates the use of variant records by computing
the area of either a rectangle or a circle.}
const Pi = 3.14159;
type Kind = (Rectangle, Circle);
     Figure =
        record
           Area: real;
           case Shape: Kind of
              Rectangle: (Height, Width: real);
              Circle:  (Radius: real)
        end;
var F: Figure;
    Ans: char;

function Convert(Letter: char): Kind;
{Converts a letter code into a value of type Kind.
Upper- or lowercase 'R' for Rectangle, 'C' for Circle.}
begin{Convert}
   case Letter of
      'C', 'c': Convert := Circle;
      'R', 'r': Convert := Rectangle
   end {case}
end; {Convert}
```

Figure 11.18
(Optional)
Use of variant
records.

```
begin{Program}
  {Determine the kind of figure.}
  writeln('Enter type of figure: ');
  writeln('(R for Rectangle, C for Circle)');
  readln(Ans);
  F.Shape := Convert(Ans);

  {Obtain the necessary data and compute the Area.}
  case F.Shape of
    Circle:  begin{Circle}
                writeln('Enter radius: ');
                readln (F.Radius);
                F.Area := Pi * sqr(F.Radius)
             end; {Circle}
    Rectangle:  begin{Rectangle}
                   writeln('Enter height and width: ');
                   readln(F.Height, F.Width);
                   F.Area := F.Height * F.Width
                end   {Rectangle}
  end; {case}

  writeln('Area = ', F.Area);
  case F.Shape of
    Circle: writeln('For radius = ', F.Radius);
    Rectangle: writeln('For dimensions ',
                          F.Height, ' by ', F.Width)
  end   {case}
end. {Program}
```

Sample Dialogue 1

```
Enter type of figure:
(R for Rectangle, C for Circle)
R
Enter height and width:
1   2
Area =   2.0
For dimensions   1.0 by   2.0
```

Sample Dialogue 2

```
Enter type of figure:
(R for Rectangle, C for Circle)
C
Enter radius:
2
Area =   12.5663
For radius =        2.0
```

Figure 11.18

(continued)

Sets in Boolean Expressions

In Pascal, there is a kind of boolean expression that can be used to check if a value is on a specified list of values. For example, the following boolean expression evaluates to `true` provided the value of the variable `Grade` is one of the letters `'A'`, `'B'`, `'C'`, `'D'`, or `'F'`:

```
Grade in ['A', 'B', 'C', 'D', 'F']
```

If you have already read the optional section of Chapter 6 entitled "Simple Use of Sets," this section will serve as a review and elaboration on how to use boolean expressions like the one we just saw involving `Grade`. If you have not read that section, this section will introduce you to such boolean expressions.

sets   A list of values like the one in the above example is called a *set*. A set consists of a list of values, separated by commas and enclosed in square brackets.

in   Pascal allows you to form boolean expressions that test a value for membership in a set. The basic form for one of these boolean expressions is an expression for the value to be checked followed by the reserved word *in* followed by one of these sets. The type of the expression in front of *in* may be any ordinal type such as `integer` or `char`. Notice that this means the expression cannot be of type `real`, since `real` is not an ordinal type. All the constants in the list must be of the same type as the expression. The entire boolean expression evaluates to `true` if the value of the expression, such as `Grade`, is on the list; otherwise, it evaluates to `false`.

The list of values in a set expression may contain variables as well as constants. For example, the following is true provided that the value of N is either 1, 3, or the same as the value of X:

```
N in [1, 3, X]
```

Because these expressions involving *in* are boolean expressions, they may be used as subparts of other more complex boolean expressions containing *and*, *or*, or *not*. For example, consider the following boolean expression:

```
((X + Y) in [1, 2, 4]) and (Z < 90)
```

This complex boolean expression will evaluate to `true` provided the value of (X + Y) is one of the numbers 1, 2, or 4, and the value of Z is less than 90.

not   The syntax of how *not* and *in* are combined does not mirror English usage and this sometimes causes confusion. Note that the following is not allowed as a Pascal boolean expression:

```
X not in [2, 5, 9]
{NOT ALLOWED IN PASCAL}
```

The correct syntax is:

```
not (X in [2, 5, 9])
```

More about Sets
(Optional)

A *set* is almost identical to what most people call a "list." However, there are some differences. The elements of a list have an order, and that order is part of the identity of the list. Thus, the following two lists are different:

```
1,  3,  5
1,  5,  3
```

*sets
versus
lists*

A set is like a list except that the order in which the elements are named is unimportant. For example, the following two Pascal sets are equal:

```
[1,  3,  5]
[1,  5,  3]
```

One other difference between sets and lists is that unlike a list, a set cannot have any repetitions.

In the previous section, we used set constants like `['Y', 'N']`. Pascal also allows variables whose values are sets. These set variables are declared to be of one of the defined types known as *set types*. Set types are structured types like arrays and records. The values of a set type are built up from a group of values of some ordinal type. In the case of sets, these simple values which together form the set are called the *elements* of the set. For example, the set `['Y', 'N']` has two elements, `'Y'` and `'N'`. In Pascal, the elements of a set must all be of the same type, and that type must be an ordinal type. Thus, a set can contain integers only or characters only, but not a combination of integers and characters. A set type definition takes the following form:

set

types

elements

```
set of <base type>
```

The <base type> is an ordinal type, such as `char` or a subrange type. Set types are declared along with all the other defined types, such as arrays and records. Once a set type has been declared, a program can declare variables to be of a set type in the usual ways. For example,

```
type SmallSet = set of 0 . . 10;
var Scores, CheckOn: SmallSet;
    Symbols: set of char;
```

Once a variable is declared, it can have its value changed by an assignment statement, such as

```
Scores := [1,  3,  5]
```

Expressions such as `[1, 3, 5]` are constants of a set type. As we have already seen, a *set constant* can be written by giving a list of elements of the base type separated by commas and enclosed in square brackets. If some of the elements of a set constant form a subrange, then it is possible to abbreviate the list of elements by listing a subrange type. For example,

*set
constants*

```
CheckOn := [0 . . 5,  10]
```

This statement sets the value of CheckOn equal to

```
[0, 1, 2, 3, 4, 5, 10]
```

set operators

Sets can be manipulated with the operators given in Figure 11.19 and can be compared using the relational operators given in Figure 11.20. For example, the following boolean expressions all evaluate to true:

```
['A', 'B', 'C'] = ['B', 'C', 'A']
['A', 'B'] <> ['A', 'B', 'C']
[1, 2] <> [5, 7, 22]
[1, 2] <= [1, 2, 3]
[1, 2] <= [1, 2]
[1, 2, 3] >= [1, 2]
[1, 3] + [3, 5, 7] = [1, 3, 5, 7]
[1, 3] * [3, 5, 7] = [3]
[1, 2, 3, 4] - [4, 2, 5] = [1, 3]
```

Pascal Form	Definition of Value Returned
<set 1> + <set 2>	Union: the set containing all the elements that are in <set 1> or <set 2> or both
<set 1> * <set 2>	Intersection: the set containing those elements that are in both <set 1> and <set 2>
<set 1> − <set 2>	Set difference: the set containing those elements that are in <set 1> but not in <set 2>

Figure 11.19 (Optional) Set operators.

Pascal Form	Definition of Value Returned
<set 1> = <set 2>	Equality: evaluates to true if <set 1> and <set 2> contain exactly the same elements; otherwise, it evaluates to false
<set 1> <> <set 2>	Inequality: evaluates to true if <set 1> and <set 2> are not equal; otherwise, it evaluates to false
<set 1> <= <set 2>	Subset: evaluates to true if every element of <set 1> is also an element of <set 2>; otherwise, it evaluates to false
<set 1> >= <set 2>	Superset: evaluates to <set 2> <= <set 1>

Figure 11.20 (Optional) Set relational operators.

The operator *in,* as well as the operators in Figures 11.19 and 11.20, can be applied
to set variables as well as to set constants.

Figure 11.21 contains a sample program using set variables. Notice that [ ] is   *empty*
used to denote the set with no elements in it. As you might easily guess, that set is   *set*
called the *empty set.* Also notice that a variable (or other expression) of the base type
can be used within a set expression, as in the following line, which appears in the procedure ReadSentence:

```
ChSet := ChSet + [Character];
```

Finally, notice that defined set constants are not allowed in Pascal. It would be nice to
define Terminators to be a constant rather than a variable. Unfortunately, that is
not allowed in Pascal.

Program

```
program Letters(input, output);
{Requests a sentence from the keyboard, forms a set consisting of all symbols
in the sentence, writes out a list of all the uppercase letters used in the sentence.}
type SetOfChar = set of char; {Procedure declarations
                require named types. Hence, this silly-looking type definition.}
var ChSet: SetOfChar;


procedure ReadSentence(var ChSet: SetOfChar);
{Requests a sentence from the keyboard, then reads the sentence
and sets the value of ChSet equal to the set of all characters in the
sentence. Sentence must terminate with a period, question mark,
or exclamation point. The terminator is not put in the set ChSet.}
var Character: char;
    Terminators: SetOfChar;
begin{ReadSentence}
  writeln('Enter a sentence.  End it with');
  writeln('a ''?'', ''!'', or a period.');

  Terminators := [ '.', '?', '!' ];

  ChSet := [];
  read(Character);
  while not (Character in Terminators) do
    begin{while}
      ChSet := ChSet + [Character];
      {ChSet contains the characters read so far.}
      read(Character)
    end   {while}
end; {ReadSentence}
```

**Figure 11.21
(Optional)
Program using set
variables.**

```
procedure WriteLetters(ChSet: SetOfChar);
{Writes out all the uppercase letters that are in the set CharSet.
Each letter is written out only once. (On systems that have characters other
than uppercase letters in the range 'A' . . 'Z', those symbols will also be
written out if they are in the set CharSet.)}
const Blank = ' ';
var Character: char;
begin{WriteLetters}
   for Character := 'A' to 'Z' do
       if Character in ChSet then
                write(Character, Blank);
   writeln
end; {WriteLetters}


begin{Program}
   ReadSentence(ChSet);
   writeln('Your sentence contains the');
   writeln('following uppercase letters:');
   WriteLetters(ChSet)
end. {Program}
```

Sample Dialogue

```
Enter a sentence.   End it with
a '?', '!', or a period.
```
Buy Low and Sell HIGH!
```
Your sentence contains the
following uppercase letters:
B G H I L S
```

Figure 11.21
(continued)

Pitfall

Limitations of Sets
(Optional)

There are some shortcomings in the way Pascal handles sets. First of all, the size
of the base type of a set type is limited. The exact limit varies from system to
system, but you can expect the limit to be relatively small. In virtually all implementations, the type *set of* integer is not allowed because the number of
integers exceeds this limit. Most, but not all, implementations make this limit
large enough to allow the type *set of* char. However, the only way to be sure
that your programs will run on almost all systems is to use small subrange types
as the base type. Also, in most versions of Pascal, there is no efficient way to step
through all the elements in a set. For example, in the procedure WriteLet-
ters (Figure 11.21) we had to test every letter to see if it was in the set ChSet.
This is inefficient, but we have no other alternative in Pascal.

Algorithms + Data Structures = Programs
Niklaus Wirth (book title)

Summary of Problem Solving and Programming Techniques

- Records can be used to combine data of different types into a single compound value of a record type.
- A component variable of a record variable can be used anyplace that a simple variable of the component type can be used.
- A record variable without a field identifier can be used in an assignment statement, like so: `Item1 := Item2`.
- Either a record component or an entire record may be passed as a parameter to a procedure. In the first case, the formal parameter type must be a component type of the record; in the second case, it must be the record type.
- Hierarchical data structures, like hierarchical control structures, make a program easier to understand. It pays to combine the basic data structure types to obtain hierarchical structures such as arrays of records, records of arrays, arrays of records of arrays, and so forth.
- When you are manipulating arrays of records (and other hierarchical data structures), it simplifies notation and reasoning to use procedures that have a record value (or variable) as a parameter or parameters, and to manipulate the records with procedures. This is a form of data and procedural abstraction that eliminates notational detail from the body of the program.
- Always consider the possibility of alternative data structures. Just because you find one that works does not mean that you have found the best one.
- Parallel arrays and arrays of records are data structures that serve the same function. Which one you choose for a particular application will depend on the details of that application.

Summary of Pascal Constructs

simple record type declaration

Syntax:

```
type <type name> =
          record
              <field identifier 1> : <component type 1>;
              <field identifier 2> : <component type 2>;
                              .
                              .
                              .
              <field identifier n> : <component type n>
          end;
```

Examples:

```
type Person =
      record
        Name: array[1 . . 20] of char;
        Age: 1 . . 100;
        Height: real;
        Weight: real
      end;
    Sample =
      record
        A: integer;
        B: char
      end;
```

The <type name> is an identifier that will name the record type. The field identifiers <field identifier 1>, <field identifier 2>, . . . ,<field identifier *n*> can be any non-reserved-word identifiers. All these identifiers must be different. The component types may be any Pascal types and may be different from one another. If two field identifiers are of the same type, then their declaration may be combined by separating them with commas and only listing the component type once, like so:

```
type Person =
      record
        Name: array[1 . . 20] of char;
        Age: 1 . . 100;
        Height, Weight: real
      end;
```

The above type declaration is equivalent to the first type declaration given in the examples.

record variable declaration

Syntax:

```
var <variable name>: <type name>;
```

Example:

```
var MsX, MrY: Person;
    Sam: Sample;
```

This form is the same as any other variable declaration. Note that no field identifiers are used.

component variable of a record variable

Syntax:

```
<record variable> . <field identifier>
```

Example:

```
MsX.Height
```

This is a variable of the type given after <field identifier> in the type definition for the type of the <record variable>.

variant record (optional)
Syntax:

```
type <type name> =
        record
           <field identifier 1> : <component type 1>;
           <field identifier 2> : <component type 2>;
                          .
                          .
                          .
           <field identifier n> : <component type n>
           case <tag field identifier> : <type name> of
           <label 1> : (<variant description 1>) ;
           <label 2> : (<variant description 2>) ;
                          .
                          .
                          .
           <label n> : (<variant description n>)
        end;
```

Fixed
part

Variant
part

Example:

```
type Kind = (Rectangle, Circle);
     Figure =
      record
        Count: integer;
        case Shape: Kind of
          Rectangle: (Height, Width: real);
          Circle: (Radius: real)
      end;
```

The fixed part is the same as in a simple record type definition, which is described in the first entry of this summary. The <tag field identifier> is any non-reserved-word identifier. The <type name> that follows is the type name of a subrange or ordinal type. It is the type for the field named <tag field identifier>. The <label i> are each labels, or a list of labels, of this type. Each <variant description i> is a list of field identifiers followed by their types, with colons and semicolons inserted as in the fixed part. (A <variant description i> can also contain a variant part of its own, although this sort of nesting is rare.) All the field identifiers must be different.

with statement

Syntax:

> *with* <record variable list> *do*
>> <statement>

Example:

> *with* MsX, Sam *do*
>> *begin*
>>> Height := 5.2;
>>> A := 8
>> *end*

The <record variable list> is a list of record variables with no field names in common. Within the <statement>, the component variables of the record variables on the list may be referred to by using only the field identifier. For example, given the declarations in the above entries, the preceding *with* statement is equivalent to the following compound statement:

> *begin*
>> MsX.Height := 5.2;
>> Sam.A := 8
> *end*

use of in

Syntax:

> <expression> *in* <set>

Examples:

> X + Y *in* [3, 4, 7]
> Grade *in* ['A', 'B', 'C']

A kind of boolean expression. The <expression> before the *in* is an expression of an ordinal or subrange type. <set> is a list of constants separated by commas and enclosed in square brackets. The constants must all be of the same type as <expression>. This boolean expression evaluates to true if the value of <expression> is equal to the value of one of the constants on the list.

type declaration for set types (optional)

Syntax:

> *type* <type name> = *set of* <base type>;

Examples:

> *type* SymbolSet = *set of* char;
>> GradeSet = *set of* 0 . . 10;

The way to declare a set type. The <base type> may be any ordinal or subrange type. However, most implementations require that the size of the <base type> be relatively small. The type integer is too large. The type char is allowed on most, but not all, systems. There may be variables of a set type, and the values may be combined using the operations given in Figures 11.19 and 11.20.

Exercises

Self-Test Exercises

5. Suppose that B is declared as follows, where the type is as declared in Figure 11.12.

    var B: EntryList;

Write Pascal expressions for each of the following: the third item on the list B; the price of the third item on the list B; the sixth letter of the name of the tenth item on the list; the length of the name of the second item on the list.

6. The inventory of a shoe store lists shoes by a stock number. With each stock number there is associated a style number in the range 0 to 50, the number of pairs in each size (sizes range from 3 to 14), and a price. A program is to be written to keep track of the inventory. Give type declarations for two different ways to structure the inventory data: as parallel arrays and as an array of records.

7. (This exercise uses the optional section "More about Sets.") Determine the value returned by each of the following expressions:

```
[7, 8, 9] + [8, 1, 3]
[7, 8, 9] + []
[7, 8, 9] * [8, 1, 3]
[7, 8, 9] * [31, 19]
[7, 8, 9] - [8, 9, 15]
[7, 8, 9] = [8, 9, 7]
[7, 8, 9] = [1, 2, 3]
[7, 8, 9] <> [1, 2, 3]
[9, 8, 5] >= [8, 9]
['A', 'C', 'D'] <= ['A', 'C']
['A', 'B', 'C'] >= ['B', 'A']
```

Interactive Exercises

8. Write a program to read data from the keyboard into a record of the type given below and to then echo the data back to the screen.

    type Sample = *record*
                    A: char;
                    B: integer
                end;

9. Redo the previous exercise, but this time replace the type char with the type CharString declared in Figure 11.11.

10. Write a program to fill (with data read from the keyboard) one record of the type Entry declared in Figure 11.12. Use a *with* statement.

Programming Exercises

11. Write a program that records the inventory for a shoe store in an array of records. Use the type declaration from Exercise 6. (See "Answers to Self-Test Exercises" in the back of the book.) The user is given the following choices: enter a new record, display a record, change the price of a stock item, or change the number on hand. When specifying a record, the user may give either the stock number or the style number. The array index can be used as a stock number. If the user decides to change the stock on hand, the program should ask which sizes will have their stock on hand changed. The program should be designed to run indefinitely, keeping track of changes in stock.

12. Write an inventory program for items whose record descriptions are of type Entry, given in Figure 11.12. The program reads in a list of records entered at the keyboard and stores them in an array of records. The program then allows the user to inquire about records. The user can ask to see all records with a given field name; all records in a given price range, such as $5.00 to $9.99; or all records of a given quantity range, such as over 100, or under 2, or between 10 and 20.

13. Write a grading program for a class with the following grading policies:

a. There are three quizzes, each graded on the basis of 10 points.
b. There is one midterm exam and one final exam, each graded on the basis of 100 points.
c. The final exam counts for 50% of the grade, the midterm counts for 25%, and the quizzes count for 25%. (Do not forget to normalize the quiz scores. They should be converted to a percentage before they are averaged in.) Grades are determined by the following rule: 90 . . 100 is an A, 80 . . 89 is a B, 70 . . 79 is a C, 60 . . 69 is a D, and below 60 is an F.

The program reads in the student's name and various scores and outputs a table of students showing the student's name, all scores, average numeric score, and final letter grade. The program also outputs the class average for the final numeric score.

14. Modify the previous exercise in the following ways:

a. The table of students also shows the difference between each student's final numeric score and the class average.
b. The program also calculates the median value of the final numeric scores. (The median score is the score such that there are as many above it as below it, that is, the "midpoint" score. If there is an even number of scores, there are two scores in the middle. In that case, the median is the average of those two scores.)
c. The table of students also shows the difference between each student's final numeric score and the median score.

15. Write a program that reads a line of text into an array of records of type CharString, as defined in Figure 11.11. Each word is read into one record of the array. Each punctuation symbol, such as a comma, colon, and so forth, is also read into

a single record. (You may assume that the only punctuation symbols are commas, colons, periods, exclamation points, and question marks.) The sentence is corrected for spaces and capitalization and then output. For example, the input

```
hi  ,  How  are  yOU?
```

should produce the output

```
Hi,  how  are  you?
```

You need not be concerned about capitalizing proper names. If "John" is changed to "john," that will be acceptable. You will want to write a procedure `StringWrite` that is like `StringWriteln` except that it does not advance to the next line. (The code is the same except that the final `writeln` is omitted.) You will probably want to design a special procedure for reading single words, rather than using the procedure `StringReadln`.

16. Write string-manipulating procedures for strings of the type `CharString`, as declared in Figure 11.11. There should be a concatenation function; for example, the concatenation of "do be" and "do" is "do bedo". There should be a pattern-searching function like the function `Subpattern` in Figure 10.12 but applicable to this new definition of the type `CharString`. There should also be a procedure to delete a substring specified by symbol positions; for example, the procedure should be capable of deleting symbols number two through four from "abcdefg" to obtain "aefg". The string being manipulated should be a variable parameter that is changed by the procedure. Further, there should be a procedure to insert a string at a given position; for example, the procedure should be capable of accepting instructions equivalent to *insert "sam" after location 2 in "dobedo"* to deliver the string "dosambedo". The string like "dobedo" is a variable parameter whose value is changed to the new value like "dosambedo". Embed these procedures in a test program.

17. (You should know about random number generators to do this exercise. They are covered in Chapter 8.) Write a procedure declaration for a procedure called `Deal` that sets the values of a variable parameter of a record type to values that represent a card chosen at random from a standard 52-card deck. The function should also keep track of the cards already dealt out, so that it does not deal a card twice. A card will be represented as two component values, one for the "value"—ace, two, and so forth—and one for the suit—diamonds, clubs, and so forth. Use an array-of-records parameter to keep track of the cards already dealt out.

18. (You should know about random numbers to do this exercise. They are covered in Chapter 8.) Write a program to play "clock patience," displaying the game configurations on the screen. *Clock patience* is a solitaire card game played as follows: The cards in a 52-card deck are dealt into 12 piles of 4 each in a "clock" circle, with the remaining 4 cards in the middle. A move consists of taking a card from a pile and placing it under the pile where it belongs, and this pile provides the card for the next move. (Cards are ordered clockwise: ace for one, then two, three, and so forth, up to queen.) The center pile is for the kings. The game terminates when the four kings have been placed on the center pile. The game is considered successful if all the other cards are correctly placed.

19. Write a program to score five-card poker hands into one of the following categories: nothing, one pair, two pairs, three of a kind, straight (in order), flush (all the same suit), full house (one pair and three of a kind), four of a kind, and straight-flush (both straight and flush). Use an array of records to store the hand. The array index type is 1 . . 5, and the records have one field for the value and one for the suit of a card.

20. (You should know about random number generators to do this exercise. They are covered in Chapter 8. Exercises 17 and 19 should be done before you do this one.) Write a program to play five-card draw poker with the user. The user and the program each get five cards. They may discard and receive replacements for up to three cards. The hands are then scored according to the order given in the previous exercise. Do not forget to keep track of the cards already dealt so that no card is dealt twice. In the easy version, only the above ordering is used, and so any two hands with three of a kind, for example, are equal. In the more difficult version, the hands are compared further; for example, three aces beats three jacks.

References for Further Reading

A. Aho, J. Hopcroft, and J. Ullman, *Data Structures and Algorithms,* 1983, Addison-Wesley, Reading, Mass.

C.A.R. Hoare, "Notes on Data Structuring," in O.J. Dahl, E.W. Dijkstra, and C.A.R. Hoare, *Structured Programming,* 1972, Academic Press, New York.

D.F. Stubbs and N.W. Webre, *Data Structures with Abstract Data Types and Pascal,* 1985, Brooks/Cole Publishing, Monterey, Ca.

A.M. Tenenbaum and M.J. Augenstein, *Data Structures Using Pascal* 2nd Edition, 1986, Prentice-Hall, Englewood Cliffs, N. J.

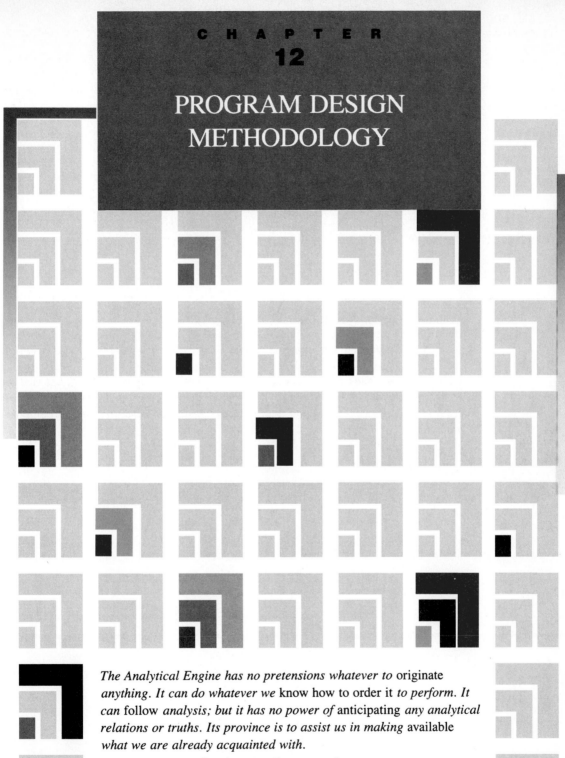

PROGRAM DESIGN METHODOLOGY

The Analytical Engine has no pretensions whatever to originate *anything. It can do whatever we* know how to order it *to perform. It can* follow *analysis; but it has no power of* anticipating *any analytical relations or truths. Its province is to assist us in making* available *what we are already acquainted with.*

ADA AUGUSTA, COUNTESS OF LOVELACE

Chapter Contents

T he production of a program can be divided into two phases: the problem solving phase, including problem definition and algorithm design; and the implementation phase, during which the actual program code is produced. Testing and debugging take place during both of these phases. Throughout this book we have described a number of techniques to apply at various points in this process. In this chapter we summarize these techniques and then go on to discuss a few other issues connected with the design and maintenance of computer programs.

Some Guidelines for Designing Algorithms

The first computer that was similar in character to today's machines was designed by Charles Babbage, an English mathematician and physical scientist. The project began sometime before 1822, consumed the rest of his life, and, although he never completed the construction of the machine, the design was a conceptual milestone in the history of computing. His colleague, Ada Augusta, was an interesting figure in a number of ways. She was the daughter of the poet Byron. Later she became Countess of Lovelace. It is primarily through her writings that the work of Babbage has been made available to the world. Indeed, she is frequently given the title of the first computer programmer. Her comments, quoted in the chapter opening, still apply to the process of solving problems on a computer. Computers are not magic and do not, at least as yet, have the ability to formulate sophisticated solutions to all the problems we encounter. Computers simply do what the programmer *orders* them to do. The solutions to problems are carried out by the computer, but the solutions are formulated by the programmer. Hence, in order to solve problems on a computer, you must know how to design algorithms.

Ada Augusta, Countess of Lovelace and the first computer programmer, left.

Charles Babbage, right.

A model of Babbage's computer

If we could provide you with a method that was guaranteed to lead you to a correct algorithm for any problem you might encounter, then programming would be a very simple task. However, neither this nor any other book can provide such a method. There is no algorithm for writing algorithms. Designing algorithms is a creative process. There are, however, some guidelines that can sometimes help in your search for algorithms. These guidelines have some similarity to an algorithm for writing algorithms. They do, however, fall short of being an algorithm for producing algorithms in two ways: The steps are not precisely defined, and they are not guaranteed to produce a correct algorithm. The guidelines are listed in Figure 12.1.

defining
the problem

The original formulation of a problem is typically imprecise, incomplete, or both. Before attempting to formulate an algorithm for a problem, be sure that the problem definition has been made complete and precise. In particular, be certain that

- You have complete and precise specifications for the inputs that will be needed.
- You have complete and precise specifications for the output.
- You know how the program must react to incorrect data: Is it required to issue an error message? Must it be able to continue computing, or may it end when it encounters input of the wrong type or in the wrong format?
- You know when the program should end and how the program will know when it is time to end.

Some Guidelines for Algorithm Design

1. Formulate a precise statement of the problem to be solved by the algorithm.

2. See if somebody has already formulated an algorithm to solve the problem.

3. See if any standard techniques ("tricks") can be used to solve the problem.

4. See if the problem is a slight variation of a problem for which somebody has already formulated an algorithm. If so, try to adapt that known algorithm to the new problem.

5. Design a data structure to organize the data involved.

6. Break the problem into subproblems and apply this method to each of the subproblems.

7. If all else fails, simplify the problem, and apply this method to the simplified problem. When you obtain a solution to the simplified problem, try to adapt the algorithm to fit the real problem. If that fails, or if the algorithm produced is unclear, incorrect, or inappropriate to the real problem, then discard this first attempt and start the process all over again at step 1. (You should then have a better feel for the problem and a better chance of success.)

Figure 12.1
Guidelines.

The algorithm may be produced at any point after step 1. The earlier the better. For example, if you are asked to write a program for computing the square root of a number, you could design an algorithm from scratch. However, if you simply take an existing algorithm that has stood the test of time, it is likely to be more efficient, and it is less likely to contain any subtle errors. In this extreme case, there is even a predefined Pascal function to do the task. In other cases, such as sorting a list, there is no predefined Pascal procedure for the task, but there are a number of well-known algorithms for the problem, such as the sorting algorithm discussed in Chapter 9. You may wish to solve these problems on your own as a training exercise, but in a "real world" situation, where it is the performance of the program that counts, you should always see what algorithms others have produced. *using known algorithms*

Step 3 requires that you cultivate a "bag of tricks," or do a search of the literature, or both. A number of tricks are well known to experienced programmers. In Chapter 7 we gave a number of well-known techniques for terminating a loop that reads in input data. An example of one of the tricks we presented there was the use of a sentinel value to mark the end of a list of input numbers. Other, more complicated tricks are discussed throughout this book. Frequently, these so-called "tricks" are rare and brilliant insights that are easy to understand and use but difficult to discover on your own. *standard tricks*

As a simple example of step 4, consider the following code for computing the sum of the numbers stored in an array A: *adapting another algorithm*

```
Sum : = 0;
for I : = First to Last do
        Sum : = Sum + A[I]
```

If we instead wish to compute the product of all the numbers in the array, we can adapt the algorithm by substituting multiplication for addition and by substituting 1 for 0. If we also rename the variable Sum to Product, that yields:

```
Product : = 1;
for I : = First to Last do
        Product : = Product * A[I]
```

A more complicated example is given in Chapter 11, where we take an algorithm for sorting arrays of numbers and adapt it to obtain a procedure to sort arrays of records.

If there is no existing algorithm or standard technique that can be applied to the problem, then you must design an algorithm from scratch. But before going on to design the algorithm, first design a suitable data structure. Steps 5 and 6 are not unrelated. The choice of a data structure will influence the algorithm you design and vice versa. As you design an algorithm, it may prove convenient to go back and change the data structure. Do not feel that you are irrevocably committed to a data structure, and do not feel that all the details of the data structure must be determined before you begin the algorithm design, but you should have some data structure in mind when you are designing your algorithm. Chapters 9, 10, and 11 discuss the design of data structures composed of arrays and/or records. Other data structures are discussed in Chapters 13, 16, and 17. *choosing a data structure*

Step 6 is the top-down design strategy that we have been using and advocating throughout this book. The subproblems are attacked by these same guidelines, starting *top-down design* with step 1. Eventually the subproblems become so small that their solution is obvious or one of the other steps applies, such as when there is a well-known solution to the subproblem.

when
all else
fails

Sometimes step 7 can be a variation on step 6. First design an algorithm with some features missing, and then design embellishments for the missing features. The change-making program we designed earlier in this book is an example of this technique. In Chapter 4 we designed a basic program for calculating change. In Chapter 6 we enhanced it to have much neater and clearer output.

Step 7 is also the step to use when you are completely stumped by a problem and need a way to overcome a mental block. If you cannot solve the problem at hand, solve a related and simpler problem as a practice exercise. That should give you some new insights. Then throw out the practice algorithm and start over. Do not be reluctant to throw out an algorithm or program. It is usually faster and easier to design an algorithm from scratch than to salvage a poor design.

These are all just guidelines. You should always consider them, but you need not adhere to them rigidly. In particular, the order of steps (especially the order of steps 3 through 6) is certainly not rigid. Moreover, they are certainly not a complete list of known techniques. They are merely a general plan of attack that can and should be augmented with other design techniques. In Chapter 7 (particularly in the optional sections), we discussed some additional techniques that apply to the design of loops. Those techniques can be used in conjunction with the plan of attack given in Figure 12.1.

Writing Code

When a program is divided into subtasks, the algorithms for the subtasks can and should be coded and tested separately. Even when you are simply coding somebody else's algorithm, divide the algorithm into subparts and code the subparts separately. That way they can be tested and debugged separately. It is relatively easy to find a mistake in a small procedure. It is nearly impossible to find all the mistakes in a large, untested program that was coded and tested as a single large unit rather than as a collection of well-defined modules. The rules we have been advocating for indenting and documentation all apply to the task of writing code. In fact, they apply even earlier. Pseudocode should have an indenting pattern and a collection of comments that will carry over with only minor changes to the final Pascal code.

Abstraction and ADT's

Programs should have a conspicuously modular design. A program should be divided into self-contained subpieces. These subpieces, which are usually implemented as procedures, are a natural consequence of top-down design. Each procedure should include a header comment explaining what the procedure does. This comment should be all you need to know in order to use the procedure. If the procedure is designed with this in mind, then the details of how the procedure performs its task can safely be forgotten. This form of selective forgetting is called *procedural abstraction*. Using procedural abstraction you can build up a library of procedures whose internal structure may be very complicated but which are, nonetheless, straightforward to use. For example, in order to use the procedure Sort in Figure 9.16, you do not need to read the code. All you need to know is that it does somehow sort an array of integers.

This same method of *abstraction* may be applied to data structures and algorithms as well as procedures. When thinking about a data structure, such as an array, it is often productive to ignore certain details, such as the exact bounds on the index type. This is often referred to as *data abstraction*. When designing an algorithm, such as a sorting algorithm, you can obtain a more general algorithm by leaving some details, such as the type of the elements being sorted, unspecified. This is often referred to as *algorithm abstraction*.

One tool that can aid in all these abstraction techniques is the use of *abstract data types (ADT's)*. An *ADT* is a data structure and a collection of operations on the data structure defined so as to separate the details that a programmer using the data structure needs to know from the details of how the data structure and operations are implemented. A more detailed discussion of ADT's can be found in Chapter 11.

Testing and Debugging

When you are producing a program, a natural sequence of events is algorithm design, coding, and then testing and debugging. However, the divisions are not, or at least should not be, very rigid. Some coding and debugging for certain tasks can be done before the complete algorithm is derived. When a task is broken into subtasks, some simple testing can and usually should be done immediately. If the tasks are well defined and fit together simply enough, then a pencil-and-paper simulation of the algorithm can be used to test this formulation of the problem. If the test cannot be carried out with pencil and paper, then a skeleton of a program can be written to see whether the pieces will fit together. If the pieces do not fit together, then there is no point in proceeding to derive algorithms for the subtasks.

For example, consider the following task: Suppose we wish to gather statistics on how much time student programmers spend at the terminal during any one session. Perhaps this will be used to help redesign the chairs so that students will be more comfortable while coding their homework assignments. To get a good profile of usage, we want a program that will compute the average time per session for each individual student, as well as the average session length averaged over all sessions by all students. The input is to consist of a list of students, with each student's name followed by a list of the times that student spent in each individual session. Dividing this task into subtasks might produce the following pseudocode:

example of early testing

1. Compute each student's average time per session.
2. Output the averages.
3. Compute the average of the student averages obtained in 1 and output that as the overall average.

The presence of a logical flaw in this algorithm can be discovered by testing, even before algorithms for the subtasks are designed. Consider the following sample data:

Joseph Cool:
  10 min., 10 min.
Sally Workhard:
  60 min., 60 min., 60 min., 60 min.,
  60 min., 60 min., 60 min., 60 min.

We do not need a computer to simulate the pseudocode on this simple data. The two student averages are trivially seen to be 10 and 60 min. Now step 3 of the pseudocode says to average these two numbers, which yields

$$(10 + 60)/2 = 35 \text{ min.}$$

The algorithm's computation of the average session length is wrong. A little bit of pencil and paper, or mental arithmetic or a hand calculator, will show that the average length of a session is really

$$(2 * 10 + 8 * 60)/10 = 50 \text{ min.}$$

As it turns out, the average length of a session is not the average of the individual student averages.

All programs should be divided into procedures, and the procedures, as well as the interaction between procedures, should be tested separately. This general technique was described in more detail in the section of Chapter 5 entitled "Testing Procedures." Below, we give some hints on how to test and debug the individual procedures.

syntax errors   Programming errors can be divided into three classes: syntax errors, run-time errors, and logical errors. A *syntax error* occurs when a portion of the program violates the syntax rules of the programming language, for example, when it is missing a required semicolon or an *end*. These are usually easy to find. The compiler will discover them and produce an error message. The error message may not accurately describe the nature or location of the error, but it definitely does indicate an error, and the location given is very likely to be the approximate location of the error.

run-time errors   *Run-time errors* also result from the program violating the rules of the language, in our case Pascal. However, they are not syntax errors and so are not discovered by the compiler. As illustrated in Figure 12.2, the two types of errors are discovered at different stages of program processing. A run-time error is detected only when the program is run. For example, the statement below will produce a run-time error if the value of N is 0:

X := 1/N

To find out whether or not it is an error, it is necessary to run the program to see if N does receive the value 0. Run-time errors also produce an error message that gives some hint of the location and nature of the error. They are harder to find than syntax errors but still have the advantage that they are likely to produce an error message, although they are not guaranteed to do so. This is because they may only occur for certain inputs and not for others. For example, the above line of code will not produce a run-time error on those inputs that cause N to take on any value other than 0. (Addi-

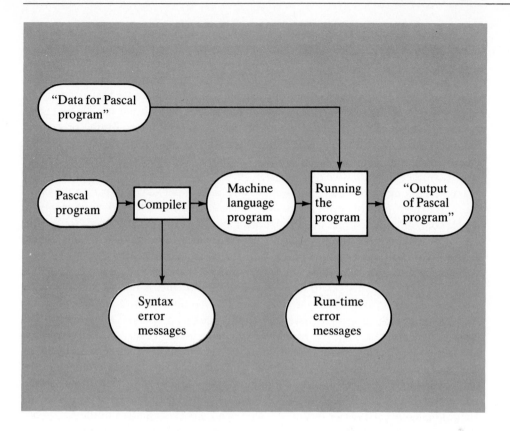

**Figure 12.2
Syntax and run-
time errors.**

tional discussion of these two types of errors can be found in the section of Chapter 3 entitled "Testing and Debugging.")

The third type of error is the hardest to locate. *Logical errors* are errors in the algorithm or in the translation of the algorithm from pseudocode to Pascal. They are difficult to find because the computer does not give any error message. They occur when the program is a perfectly valid Pascal program that performs a perfectly valid computation and gives out an answer. The only problem is that the answer is sometimes wrong. For example, the following piece of code is supposed to output the average of the elements in the array A of type *array* [0 . . 10] *of* integer:

*logical
errors*

```
Sum : = 0;
for I : = 0 to 10 do
      Sum : = Sum + A[I];
writeln(Sum/10)
```

This is a perfectly valid piece of Pascal code and will run with no problems or error messages. For most values of the array elements, the answers will even look "about right." However, there is a logical error. Since the array bounds go from 0 to 10, there are 11 elements, not 10. Hence, the last line should be

```
writeln(Sum/11)
```

When a logical error is discovered, it is usually not too difficult to fix. The problem is finding such errors. Since the computer produces no error messages for logical errors, it is difficult to be certain that a program contains no errors of this nature.

Correcting run-time and logical errors is a three-stage process. The first stage is error avoidance. If a program is carefully designed along the lines we have suggested in this book, then the number of such errors should be few. The second stage is testing. In the testing stage, each procedure should be given a separate test. Testing procedures separately serves to tell which procedure or procedures contain the mistakes. The last stage is debugging. In that stage, the exact nature of the error is determined and the error is corrected.

choosing test data

When testing a procedure, you want to find some input values or parameter values that will expose possible errors. One way to catch an error is to find input values for which you know the correct output—perhaps by doing the calculation in some other way or by looking the answer up. Then you can run the procedure or program on those values. If the procedure's answer differs from the correct answer, then you know there is a mistake in the procedure. However, always remember that just because a procedure or program works correctly on 10 or even 100 test cases, this is not a guarantee that it does not contain an error. It might make a mistake on the next new input that is tried.

boundary values

One other technique to increase your confidence in a program is to use a variety of different types of test data. For example, if the data is an integer, try a large positive number, a small positive number, zero, a small negative number, a large negative number, and any other categories that you can think of. For loops, try data that will cause the loop to be executed zero, one, and more than one times (or as many of those cases as are possible for the loop in question). Be sure to use a representative sample of the possible *boundary values* as test data. There is no precise definition of the notion of a boundary value, but you should develop an intuitive feel for what it means. If a loop will be executed some number of times between 1 and 10, depending on the data, then be sure to have a test run that executes it 1 time and one that executes the loop 10 times. If a procedure does something to only one element of an array, always test the first and last elements of the array. Of course, you should also test a "typical" (nonboundary) value.

fully exercising code

Still another testing technique consists of *fully exercising* the procedure or program. This technique consists of using a collection of test cases that will cause each part of the procedure to be executed. This means executing each statement and substatement, and also making each boolean expression that controls a loop assume the value true at least once and assume the value false at least once. For example, consider the following piece of code:

```
if X > 0 then
    Procedure1
else if Y <= 0 then
    Procedure2
else if Z >= 0 then
    Procedure3
else
    Procedure4
```

```
if <boolean exp> then
        <statement 1>
else
        <statement 2>
```

To test both statements requires at least two test runs, one that makes <boolean exp> `true` and one that makes it `false`.

```
while <boolean exp> do
        <statement>
```

There should be at least two test runs: one that makes <boolean exp> `false` and so skips the loop and one that makes it `true` and so executes at least one iteration of the loop.

Figure 12.3
Fully exercising
code.

The call to `Procedure4` will never take place unless the test data causes X to be less than or equal to zero and at the same time causes Y to be greater than zero and at the same time causes Z to be less than zero. The call to `Procedure3` will never take place unless the test data causes X to be less than or equal to zero and at the same time causes Y to be greater than zero but at the same time causes Z to be greater than or equal to zero. Fully exercising a program is difficult to do. However, if the program is divided into procedures and the procedures are small, then it is possible to fully exercise each procedure separately. Figure 12.3 illustrates some other examples of fully exercising code.

An even better test of a program can be obtained with a technique called *testing all paths*. When you are testing all paths, the tests must not only cause each statement to be executed at least once but must also cause each possible combination of branch and loop behaviors to take place. Some combinations may be impossible to achieve, but the test set should cause all other combinations to occur.

To see the difference between fully exercising a piece of code and testing all paths, consider the following code:

testing
all paths

```
if X > 0 then
    A := B
else
    A := X;
if Y > 0 then
    C := B
else
    C := Y
```

This piece of code can be fully exercised with two inputs, one in which both X and Y are positive, and one in which they are both negative. To test all paths requires four tests, as shown in Figure 12.4. Testing all paths is a good testing strategy. Unfortunately, it is often difficult to find a set of test cases that will test all paths. Frequently you must settle for fully exercising the procedure and then testing as many paths as you reasonably can.

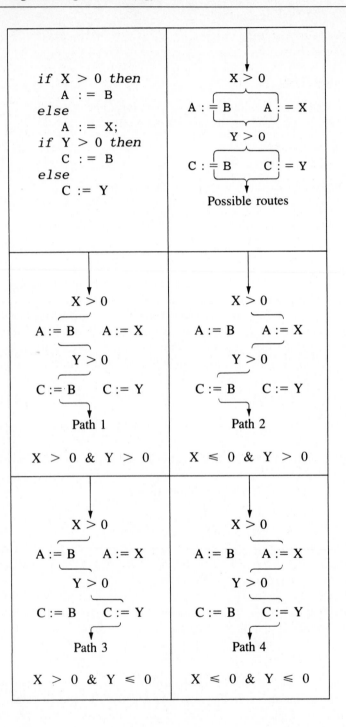

Figure 12.4
Testing all paths.

Testing can tell you that a program or procedure contains an error. Moreover, if it is done correctly, it will tell you which procedure contains the error, but it usually will not tell you what the error is. Once you know that a procedure contains an error, you still must correct the error. This is the debugging stage. At this stage, frustrated programmers are sometimes tempted to make random changes, in the hope that these changes will magically correct the errors. They seldom do, and moreover, they make the program even less understandable. The way to correct an error is to test and analyze until you have located the exact cause of the error. Once the cause is located, the cure is usually easy to find.

debugging

One of the best ways to find the exact location of an error is to watch the procedure while it performs its calculation; that is, to watch the values of the various variables changing. This is called *tracing*. When a variable is traced, its value is written out either every time it is changed or at some other specified times. Some systems provide special debugging facilities for doing this automatically. If your system does not, then you can use temporary `writeln` statements in the manner described in the section of Chapter 7 entitled "Debugging Loops."

tracing

Verification

In the ideal world, there would be no need for testing and debugging, because all programs would be correct. In the ideal world, the programmer would prove the correctness of a program in much the same way that a mathematician proves a theorem. Proving the correctness of a program, that is, proving that it does what the specifications say it is supposed to do, is called program *verification*.

Whether or not it is practical to prove the correctness of large programs is still a hotly debated issue. In practice, testing and debugging will never be completely eliminated, but they may become less necessary, and program verification may become a more common practice than it is today. For small programs, verification is usually a realizable task. The debate arises when the discussion turns to large programs. There certainly is little hope of verifying a large program, such as a compiler, if you are given just the program code (without very extensive comments) and the specifications. On the other hand, if the top-down design strategy is used and each piece is verified separately, then it may be a tractable task. In this scenario, the verification takes place as the program is written, not after it is finished.

The debate over verification is one of degree. How formal should the verification be, and to what extent can it be relied on? Certainly a programmer should always make a serious attempt to somehow demonstrate (at least to himself or herself) that the algorithms are correct and that the code accurately represents the algorithms. Code should never be designed by simply writing down something that "looks like it might work" and then running a few test cases "to see if it works."

We will not discuss verification in any great detail. If you would like to get a feel for what a proof of correctness looks like, read the optional section of Chapter 7 entitled "Invariant Assertions and Variant Expressions."

Portability

A *portable* program is one that can be moved from one computer system to another with little or no change. Since programs represent a large investment in programmer time, it pays to make them portable.

standard language

One way to make a program portable is to adhere closely to a *standard version* of the programming language. There are national and international organizations that set standards for the syntax and other details of programming languages. All the Pascal programs in this book conform to the ANSI/IEEE standard and to the ISO standard. (The initials have the following meanings: ANSI, American National Standards Institute; IEEE, Institute of Electrical and Electronic Engineers; ISO, International Standards Organization.)

As impressive as all those initials may look, it is still not true that all the Pascal programs in this text will run on any system that claims to follow the Pascal standards. There are two reasons for this: The standards leave some details unspecified, such as exactly how many characters the system will have and the value of maxint; also, real systems usually differ at least slightly from the prescribed standard. Despite these shortcomings, standards do serve a purpose. If you adhere to the versions of Pascal described by them, then your program will be more portable. For example, if your system initializes all integer variables to zero, do not use this feature. Instead, always explicitly initialize all variables. That way your programs will also work on systems that do not initialize variables. (None of the standards require that variables be initialized and, in fact, most Pascal systems do not do so.)

Sometimes implementation-dependent details are unavoidable. For example, terminals normally have some sort of bell or beeper on them, yet there is no command in Pascal that will ring the bell. If you want to ring the bell, you must use some implementation-dependent feature. In order to make your program more portable, isolate all such implementation-dependent details into clearly labeled procedures. Then, when the program is moved, the things that need to change are easy to find and easy to modify. Input and output tend to be very implementation-dependent. Hence, input and output should always be isolated into procedures.

Efficiency

time and storage

The *efficiency* of a program is a measure of the amount of resources consumed by the program. Traditionally, the only resources considered have been time and/or storage. The less time it uses, the more time-efficient a program is. The less storage it uses, the more storage-efficient it is.

When you are running small programs of the type you encounter when first learning to program, efficiency is not usually an issue. If the user waits a few extra seconds for an answer, that is insignificant. A small program is also unlikely to use more than a very small fraction of the available storage. Moreover, if the program is run just a few times, then the savings are likely to be minimal at best. However, when you are running large programs repeatedly over a long period of time, the amount of time and storage saved can be significant. Computer time and storage cost money. Hence, if a program can be changed so that it runs faster or uses less storage, then, *all other things being equal,* the change should be made.

In some specialized settings, efficiency is critically important. If the computer is controlling a hospital patient-monitoring system, a fraction of a second delay may mean the patient's life. A very sophisticated storm-predicting program is useless if it takes two hours to predict that a tornado will arrive in one hour. A program to work in a small wrist calculator or a small satellite may have to make do with very little storage.

To illustrate the notion of efficiency, consider the task of searching an array of integers to see whether or not a particular integer is in the array. If the array is called A, and the integer being searched for is called Key, then the following loop will accomplish the task (First . . Last is the array index type):

example—
searching
an array

```
I := First;
while (Key <> A[I]) and (I < Last) do
    I := I + 1;
if Key = A[I] then
    writeln(Key, ' is in the array.')
else
    writeln(Key, ' is not in the array.')
```

The loop checks each element of the array until it either finds the value Key or gets to the end of the array without finding Key.

Now let us suppose that we know the array elements are ordered so that

```
A[First] < A[First + 1] < A[First + 2] < . . . < A[Last]
```

In this case, we can make the loop run more efficiently, in the sense of taking less time. If we know the list is ordered, we can stop looking for the value Key as soon as the following holds:

```
Key <= A[I]
```

This is because if Key equals A[I], we have found the value of Key, and if Key is less than A[I], then we know that Key is smaller than all the array elements that follow and so cannot possibly equal any of them. Hence, assuming that the list is ordered, we can replace the boolean expression in the *while* loop with the following:

```
(Key > A[I]) and (I < Last)
```

With this second boolean expression, the loop will frequently perform fewer iterations. If the value of Key is in the array, then the two loops perform exactly the same number of iterations, but if Key is not in the array, then, "on the average," the second loop will perform a little more than half the number of iterations that the first one does. A precise definition of what we mean by "on the average" is beyond the scope of this book. However, the important thing to observe is that the second version does save a large fraction of time on a large number of inputs. The program in Figure 12.5 illustrates the savings for one particular set of values.

Occasionally, a simple change like the one we just described can improve efficiency significantly. More often, however, the savings due to a minor change are corre-

Program

```
program Compare(input, output);
{Compares two search algorithms.}
const First = 1;
      Last = 10;
type Index = First . . Last;
     List = array[Index] of integer;
var A: List;
    I: Index;
    Key: integer;

procedure Search1(A: List; Key: integer);
{Outputs a message saying whether or not Key is
the value of an array indexed variable A[I], for some I.}
var I: Index;
begin{Search1}
  I := First;
  while (Key <> A[I]) and (I < Last) do
    I := I + 1;
  if Key = A[I] then
      writeln(Key, ' is in the array.')
  else
      writeln(Key, ' is not in the array.');
  writeln('Search 1 executed ', I - First, ' loop iterations.')
end;  {Search1}

procedure Search2(A: List; Key: integer);
{Outputs a message saying whether or not Key is
the value of an array indexed variable A[I], for some I.
Precondition: A[First] < A[First + 1] < . . . < A[Last].}
var I: Index;
begin{Search2}
  I := First;
  while (Key > A[I]) and (I < Last) do
    I := I + 1;
  if Key = A[I] then
      writeln(Key, ' is in the array.')
  else
      writeln(Key, ' is not in the array.');
  writeln('Search 2 executed ', I - First, ' loop iterations.')
end;  {Search2}
```

Figure 12.5
**Comparing two
algorithms.**

```
begin{Program}
   writeln('Enter 10 integers in ascending order:');
   for I := First to Last do
      read(A[I]);
   readln;
   writeln('Enter a Key to search for:');
   readln(Key);
   Search1(A, Key);
   Search2(A, Key)
end. {Program}
```

Sample Dialogue

```
Enter 10 integers in ascending order:
2  4  6  8  10  12  14  16  18  2001
Enter a Key to search for:
11
      11 is not in the array.
Search 1 executed      9 loop iterations.
      11 is not in the array.
Search 2 executed      5 loop iterations.
```

**Figure 12.5
(continued)**

spondingly minor. To make substantial savings, a completely new and more complicated algorithm is usually required. In the next section we discuss the advisability of
using a complicated, efficient algorithm as opposed to a simple, less efficient one.

Efficiency versus Clarity

The current trend is to pay less attention to time and storage efficiency. The reasons for
this switch are that computer time and storage have become less expensive, while programmer time has become more costly. It simply does not make sense to pay thousands
of dollars (or even much less) in programmer salaries in order to realize a few dollars of
savings in computer usage.

Frequently there are also other hidden costs in making a program very "efficient."
A typical way to arrive at an "efficient" program is to start with a simple, easy-to-
understand, correctly running program and then to make changes to the program so
that it runs faster or uses less storage. In the process of doing so, a number of unfortunate things can happen. The changes may introduce an error. That produces the ultimately inefficient program. Getting the wrong answer quickly is never a bargain.
Changing a program to make it run faster may make the program harder to understand.
At some later time, when the program needs to be changed, this will increase the time
needed to change it and will make errors more likely. Large programs typically have a
life span in which they are modified numerous times by a series of different programmers. In that situation, clarity is the critically important consideration. When the
choice is between clarity and efficiency, it usually pays to choose clarity.

A good strategy is the following. First, make sure the program is clear and correct. Within those constraints and the constraints of available programmer time, it pays to make the program more time- and storage-efficient.

Software Engineering

Software engineering is that branch of science and engineering that deals with the production and maintenance of large software systems. Like all engineering endeavors it is concerned with both the quality of its products and the economies of their production and use. It is a "real world" discipline concerned with the production of reliable, economical products for the use of its customers. Since this makes it sound like it is concerned more with the performance of the final product than with the appearance of the product, you might think it is not concerned with niceties of style and technique, such as commenting rules, top-down design, and the use of abstraction. However, one indication of how very useful these techniques are is that they become even more important when designing a large system or any system for a real world application. Software engineering is concerned with all of the design principles that we have advocated throughout this text. It is also concerned with other considerations that only come into play when producing large software systems.

what is "large"?   The programs presented in an introductory programming book are extremely small compared to the programs typically worked on by professional programmers. One widely used Pascal compiler consists of almost 7400 lines of high-level-language code. If written as small as the text of this book, that program would occupy over 130 pages! Programs that large are qualitatively as well as quantitatively different from the sorts of small programs we have seen. Like the servant in the Dickens' story (quoted at the end of this section), the typical reader of this book has only had a "sip" of programming. It is a larger sip than the servant had, and the reader who completes this book will have tasted programming. However, large programs really do have a different flavor from small programs. For one thing they are produced by teams of programmers rather than single programmers working alone or almost alone.

group effort   A program as large as a compiler or a complete operating system is not written by a single person. The effort is too large for any single individual. To take an extreme case, F. P. Brooks reports that the design of the IBM OS/360 operating systems consumed 5000 "man-years." That figure includes support staff and probably would be lower today. However, it is clear that the job is too large for any single programmer. The production of a piece of software of that size requires a major organizational effort. It is a management feat as well as a design feat. The book by Brooks, cited at the end of this chapter, gives a good description of the management problems involved in designing large programs. Most of the book is understandable to anyone who has read the first few chapters of this book.

software life cycle   Development of large software systems is a long-term process. A large amount of planning needs to be done before any code is written down. Moreover, the release of a finished system for customers to use does not end the development process. The system must be continually maintained and updated. This entire development process is often referred to as the *software life cycle*. This life cycle can be divided into the following six phases:

1. Analysis and specification of the task.
2. Design of the software.
3. Implementation (coding).
4. Testing.
5. Maintenance and evolution of the system.
6. Obsolescence.

analysis phase

The first step in the production of a software system is to decide exactly what the system is supposed to do. You might be inclined to think that this analysis phase is the easiest part of the process. After all, the system is supposed to do what the customers want it to do and so all that needs be done is to ask the customers what they want. Unfortunately, it is not that simple. The end user of the system typically has only a vague, high level idea of what the system should do. The user's characterization of the task is likely to be a general statement such as "keep my books," or "produce an automated testing system for my class," or "give me an interactive design environment," or some other equally nonspecific description. The end user typically does not know exactly what he or she wants the system to do. Hence, the software analyst must interact with the user to find out what the user *will* want the system to do. At this stage questions such as the following must all be asked and answered: What should the input and output look like? What should the system do when the user makes errors in input? Who will be using the system, trained specialists or casual users? How fast must the system be? How often and in what ways will it be necessary to change the system after it is delivered?

specifications

The end result of the analysis phase is a specification of the software's requirements. This specification must tell not only what the input and output is to look like, but must also specify exactly what machine environment(s) it must work in, how much data the system must accommodate, how many users it must serve, what specific tests the system must successfully pass, what kind of documentation will accompany the system, what future modifications the system must accommodate, and numerous other details on the capacity of the system. This specification is the definition of the system. It states what the software team is promising to deliver. The final product will be measured against this yardstick.

design phase

The specification for a software systems tells *what* the system should do. The design of the system tells *how* it is to be done. For a very small system the design phase can be as simple as writing an algorithm in pseudocode. For a large system, this phase is still the algorithm design phase, but it includes the design and interaction of a number of different algorithms, often only specified in outline form, as well as a strategy for filling in the details and producing the code. In this phase, the software team formulates its plan of attack. The difficult problems are likely to be organizational. Most software design teams use a collection of known algorithms or variations on known algorithms rather than producing breakthrough discoveries of new clever algorithm techniques. However, the integration and adaptation of a number of known algorithms to a very large task is a formidable challenge. So formidable that many large, well funded, and highly trained teams have failed to perform their tasks successfully. Most of the classic design tools of software engineering, such as top-down design and abstraction, were formulated primarily to facilitate this design phase.

coding

Coding is far from the most difficult of the six phases in the software life cycle. However, the size of the task does present problems that do not arise when coding the short programs encountered in introductory programming classes. Since coding of a large software system is a team effort, questions of style must be made explicit in order to ensure a consistent style. All programmers must know what conventions are being used for choosing identifier names, layout style, commenting style, size of subprograms, parameter passing conventions, and a host of other conventions. The work must be divided among the members of the programming team. This division of labor is not simply a matter of assigning one person to each of the subtasks produced by top-down design. There are overall tasks to be divided. Somebody needs to be in charge. Somebody typically serves as librarian to keep the records on documentation and backup copies of software.

testing

Testing a large software system is a major undertaking. One cannot simply run the entire system, note the error messages, and then look through the code in hopes of finding and fixing bugs. The first testing absolutely must be performed on smaller submodules so as to localize the search for bugs. In addition to the testing that is designed and carried out by the programming team, large software systems must also undergo acceptance testing. After the system is completed and tested by the software production team, it is given to the user for acceptance testing. In acceptance testing the software may be run on a collection of bench mark programs or on a test suite. *Bench mark programs* are programs whose run time and other statistics are known so that the system's efficiency can be compared to that of other systems. A *test suite* is something like a large bench mark program or a collection of bench mark programs that systematically exercise each of the different functions that the system is supposed to satisfy in order to see if the system performs correctly and efficiently. If test suites were reliable enough, that would be the end of the testing process, but no test suite can guarantee that the system will perform well in all situations. The final testing is *site testing* in which the system is placed in service with a small group of users in order to see what unexpected problems arise. This small group of users provides the "field testing" that can only be obtained in a day-to-day real world setting. The problems encountered in the site testing phase are typically severe enough to warrant a second site test after the system has been revised in response to the results of the first site test.

maintenance

When the system has passed its site tests and is released for general use that does not mark the end of the software engineering team's job. The software must be maintained and updated. In fact, the cost of maintenance typically far exceeds the cost of producing the original system. A large system is likely to exhibit bugs for some time after it is released. These bugs must be diagnosed and fixed. As new hardware is introduced, the system may be modified to run in new environments. As users' needs change, it is less expensive and quicker to modify the existing system than to produce a totally new system. The majority of systems programmers' time is spent on maintenance, not on designing completely new systems.

obsolescence

Perhaps the last step in the software life cycle should be called "death." However, while all systems eventually become obsolete, they often do not go away. A large system represents such a huge capital investment that it usually seems less expensive to modify the existing system, rather than build a completely new system. Often this impression is correct. Large systems are designed to be modified. A system may be productively revised many times. However, even large programs eventually become out of date in their basic design. Unless a large program is well written and suitable for the task at hand, then just as in the case of a small program, it is more efficient to write a new program than it is to fix the old one.

"Did you ever taste beer?"
"I had a sip of it once,"
said the small servant.
"Here's a state of things!"
cried Mr. Swiveller. . . .
"She *never* tasted it—
it can't be tasted in a sip!"
Charles Dickens, The Old Curiosity Shop

Summary of Terms

abstract data type (ADT)

A data structure (or data structures) and a collection of operations on the data structure defined so as to separate the details that a programmer using the data structure needs to know from the details of how the data structure and operations are implemented.

algorithm abstraction

Certain details of virtually any algorithm as well as certain details of the data manipulated by the algorithm, while needed to implement the algorithm as Pascal code, are not needed in order to formulate the algorithm. Algorithm abstraction is the disregarding ("forgetting") of some or all of these details.

data abstraction

Disregarding ("forgetting") the features of a data structure that are irrelevant to the problems, algorithms, or programs under consideration.

efficiency

The efficiency of a program is measured by the amount of resources that the program consumes. The less resources it consumes, the more efficient it is. Time and storage are the resources that are usually considered.

fully exercise

A technique for testing a piece of code (such as a program or procedure). It consists of finding a set of test inputs such that running the program on the test inputs will cause each statement and substatement to be executed on at least one of the test runs and will cause each boolean expression that controls a loop to assume the value `true` on at least one run and `false` on at least one run.

logical error

A program error that is due to an error in the algorithm or an error in translating the algorithm into the programming language. Normally, logical errors produce no error messages.

off-line data

Data in any form that can be read by the computer without being entered by the user while the program is running is called off-line data. (For example, data kept in files is off-line data.)

portability

A program is portable if it can be moved from one system to another with little or no change.

procedural abstraction

Disregarding ("forgetting") the features of a procedure that are irrelevant to the problems, algorithms, or programs under consideration.

run-time error

A program error that is discovered by the computer system at the time the program is run. See *syntax error.*

standard version of a programming language

A version of a programming language that is defined by some official standards organization.

syntax error

An error consisting of a violation of the syntax rules of a language. Syntax errors are discovered and reported by the compiler. See *run-time error.*

testing all paths

A technique for testing a piece of code (such as a program or procedure). It consists of finding a set of test inputs such that running the program on the test inputs will cause each possible combination of branch and loop behaviors to occur on at least one of the runs.

tracing

Inserting `write` or `writeln` statements into a program so that the values of the variables will be written out as the program performs its calculations. Some systems have debugging facilities that do this automatically.

verification

Verifying a program means proving that it meets the specifications for the task it is supposed to perform.

Exercises

Self-Test Exercises

1. The following piece of code is supposed to set Sum equal to the sum of the first 100 positive numbers. It contains a bug. What is it?

```
Sum := 0;
I := 1;
repeat
   Sum := Sum + I;
   I := I + 1
until I >= 100
```

If you cannot find the bug, replace 100 with 3 and trace the computation, either with pencil and paper or by embedding the code and a writeln statement in a program.

2. Choose some input values to fully exercise the following piece of code (all the variables are of type integer):

```
readln(X, B, C)
if X >= 5 then
   A := B
else
   A := C;
Sum := 0;
while X > 0 do
   begin
      Sum := Sum + X;
      X := X - 1
   end;
```

3. Choose some input values to test all paths in the code of the previous exercise.

4. What is wrong with the following program? (It correctly computes the average of 10 integers.)

```
program Exercise(input, output);
type Index = 1 .. 10;
     List = array[Index] of integer;
var A: List; I: Index; Sum: integer; Average: real;
begin{Program}
   writeln('Enter 10 integers: ');
   for I:= 1 to 10 do
      read(A[I]);
   Sum := 0;
   for I := 1 to 10 do
      Sum := Sum + A[I];
   Average := Sum/10;
   writeln('The average is: ', Average)
end. {Program}
```

Interactive Exercises

5. Redesign the algorithm for computing average terminal session times that was given in the pseudocode in the section entitled "Testing and Debugging." As noted in the text, the pseudocode contains a logical error.

6. If you have access to more than one computer with Pascal available, run some of your programs from previous exercises on two or more machines. Is it necessary to change the programs in any way?

Programming Exercises

7. Write a program to read in a list of 100 or fewer integers and then do any of the following, as the user requests: display the list in sorted order from largest to smallest; display the list in sorted order from smallest to largest; compute the average; compute the mean; compute percentiles (e.g., the tenth percentile is the 10% of the scores that are highest in value); list the scores in the order largest to smallest or smallest to largest, showing how much each differs from the average and/or median. Do this jointly with two or three other people. Each person should do separate subtasks, and the code should be integrated into a single program.

8. (To do this one, you and another group must have done the previous exercise.) The two groups exchange programs and then each modifies the other's program as follows: The option of computing the standard deviation is added to the program (see Exercise 21 in Chapter 4 for definitions). The user is also given the option of listing the scores in order, either lowest to highest or highest to lowest, with an annotation indicating whether or not the score is within one standard deviation of the average.

9. A polynomial

$$a_n x^n + a_{n-1} x^{n-1} + \cdots + a_0$$

can be evaluated in a straightforward way by performing the indicated operations and using the procedure Power given in Figure 8.3. An alternative method is to factor the polynomial according to the following formula, known as Horner's rule:

$$(\ldots ((a_n x + a_{n-1})x + a_{n-2})x + \cdots + a_1)x + a_0$$

Write two procedures to evaluate polynomials by these two different methods. The procedures will read n as well as the coefficients a_n, a_{n-1}, and so forth from the keyboard. After completely debugging the procedures, insert extra code to count the number of addition and multiplication operations performed. (Do not forget to count addition and multiplication operations performed by all the procedures such as Power.)

References for Further Reading

J.L. Bently, *Writing Efficient Programs*, 1982, Prentice-Hall, Englewood Cliffs, N.J. A good source for more information on writing efficient programs.

F.P. Brooks, *The Mythical Man-Month*, 1975, Addison-Wesley, Reading, Mass. A good collection of essays to give you a feel for the problems involved in writing very large programs.

O.J. Dahl, E.W. Dijkstra, and C.A.R. Hoare, *Structured Programming*, 1972, Academic Press, New York. Good essays on programming techniques, data structures, and programming style.

E.W. Dijkstra, *A Discipline of Programming*, 1976, Prentice-Hall, Englewood Cliffs, N.J. A good series of essays on programming techniques and programming style.

D. Gries, *The Science of Programming*, 1981, Springer-Verlag, New York. A good source for more information on program verification.

John Guttag and Barbara Liskov, *Abstraction and Specification in Program Development*, 1986, MIT Press, Cambridge, Mass; McGraw-Hill, New York.

Gerald M. Weinberg, *The Psychology of Computer Programming*, 1971, Van Nostrand Reinhold, New York. A collection of essays on the subject described by the title.

Edward Yourdon, *Classics in Software Engineering*, 1979, Yourdon Press, New York. A collection of famous essays on programming methodology.

TEXT FILES
AND SECONDARY
STORAGE

Polonius: What do you read, my lord?
Hamlet: Words, words, words.

WILLIAM SHAKESPEARE, HAMLET

Chapter Contents

Part I

Text Files
Writing and Reading Text Files
Opening Files
Pitfall—Mixing Reading and Writing to a Text File
Pitfall—The Silent Program
Self-Test Exercise
Interactive Exercises

Part II

read and write Reexamined
eof and eoln
Using a Buffer
Pitfall—Forgetting the File Variable in eof or eoln

Pitfall—Use of eoln and eof with Numeric Data
Pitfall—Mixing eof and eoln
Text Files as Parameters to Procedures
Pitfall—Portability
Basic Technique for Editing Text Files
Internal Files
Case Study—Editing Out Excess Blanks
Text Editing as a Programming Aid
Summary of Problem Solving and Programming Techniques
Summary of Pascal Constructs
Exercises

PART I

Chapter 1 presented a description of the main components of a computer. That description emphasized what is called *main memory.* Virtually all computers have an additional form of memory called *secondary storage* or *external storage.* On a personal computer, this secondary storage is likely to be a device called a *floppy disk drive.* On a large system, it is likely to be a device called a *hard disk drive.* As the names imply, these storage media are disk shaped. They are similar to phonograph records in that they store information on tracks of a disk and read the information via an arm that rests over the disk. However, their physical properties are closer to those of the magnetic tape commonly used to record music than they are to those of a phonograph record. In any event, it is their characteristics as viewed by the programmer that are important to us. We will not need to know about the physics of how they work.

> *secondary storage*
>
> *disks*

Main memory is often of the type called *volatile,* which means that when you shut off the computer, the data stored in memory goes away. In fact, for all practical purposes, the data goes away as soon as the program ends. Secondary storage is *nonvolatile.* It can be used to store data for as long as is needed. In this chapter we will describe a method whereby a Pascal program can store text data in secondary storage. We will also describe how another program can access that data.

Text Files

In Pascal, a *file* is a named collection of data in secondary storage. The important properties of a file are that a program can write data to it, that it can remain in storage after the program has finished running, that it has a name, and that other programs can read it later on. In a later chapter we will describe all the types of files that are available in Pascal. For now we will only discuss one special kind of file called a "text file."

> *file*

A *text file* is a file that contains the same sort of data as the output screen. More precisely, a text file contains a stream of characters divided into units called *lines.* One way to think of a text file is as if it were a very long sheet of paper that a program can write on and that the same or a different program can later read. These conceptual sheets of paper are divided into lines in the same way that output to the screen is divided into lines. However, unlike screens and sheets of paper, there are no limits to the size of a text file. There is no limit to the number of characters on a line in a text file, and there is no limit to the number of lines (as long as the file does not use all of the computer's available secondary storage).

> *text file*

Inside a Pascal program, a text file is referred to by means of a Pascal identifier that is declared as if it were a variable of a type called `text`. For example, the following declares `Stuff` to be of type `text` and would occur in the variable declaration section of a program:

> *the type text*

```
var Stuff: text;
```

Identifiers such as `Stuff` are called *file variables.* Although a file variable is a kind of variable, it is a very atypical kind of variable. It cannot appear in an assignment statement, nor can it be used in many of the other ways that the usual kinds of variables

> *file variables*

other names
for files

are used. It has special standard procedures and special syntax rules of its own. It is probably better simply to think of it as a name for a file and not think of it as a variable at all.

Text files are used for many purposes that do not involve the Pascal language. Any file that you create or read with the usual editor is a text file. Hence, a text file can exist and have a name before it is used by a Pascal program. On some systems, this name might not even satisfy the Pascal syntax for identifiers. To accommodate such file names, many versions of Pascal provide a mechanism to associate a file variable name with a file and thus rename it for the duration of the Pascal program. The syntax for doing this varies from system to system. On one of these systems a file will have one name outside of the Pascal program, but will be referred to by a possibly different file variable name within the Pascal program. No matter how many names a text file may have, it is always referred to by its file variable name when reading or writing is performed by a Pascal program. In our discussions and examples, we will assume that its file variable name is the same as any other name that a file might have.

Writing and Reading Text Files

write
and
writeln

Data is written to text files in the same way that it is written to the screen—that is, by `write` and `writeln` statements. In order to write to a text file, the `write` statement must contain the file variable associated with the file; otherwise, the output will go to the screen. For example, to write the string `'Hello'` to the file `Stuff`, the following statement will suffice:

```
writeln(Stuff, 'Hello')
```

specifying
the file

Unfortunately, this syntax is confusing. The identifier `Stuff` looks like a variable whose value is to be written out. It is not. It is the file variable name of the file to which the output is being sent. There is no way to determine this by looking only at the `writeln` statement. The only way that you, or the compiler, can figure this out is to look at the variable declaration section. If `Stuff` is declared to be of type `text`, then this first argument names the file that is to receive the output. If, on the other hand, we had declared `Stuff` to be a variable of some type such as `char` or `integer`, then this statement would instead write the value of `Stuff`, as well as the word `'Hello'`, to the screen.

When reading or writing files, a Pascal program handles numbers in the same way it handles numbers entered from the keyboard or written to the screen. The system automatically converts numbers to characters when writing numbers and automatically converts characters to numbers when reading into variables of type `integer` or `real`. A text file can contain nothing but characters divided into lines. It cannot contain numbers, but because of automatic type conversion, the following statement will cause no problems:

```
write(Stuff, 5)
```

Just as with output to the screen, numbers are handled as you would hope. The system changes the number 5 to the character `'5'`, and it is the character `'5'` that is written into the text file.

Text files can be read by means of read and readln statements. There are problems associated with mixing read and write statements to the same text file. Therefore, for now we will assume that different programs are doing the reading and the writing. Suppose another program contains the following declarations:

```
var Stuff: text;
    FirstLetter, SecondLetter: char;
```

This other program can then prepare the same file Stuff for reading. (We will explain how later on.) After that, the program can read from the file by executing a read statement such as the following:

```
read(Stuff, FirstLetter, SecondLetter)
```

Since the first thing in the file is the word 'Hello', this will set the value of First-Letter to 'H' and the value of SecondLetter to 'e'. Reading starts with the first character of the first line of the file and proceeds through the file. The first read statement reads the first so many characters, the next read executed reads the next so many characters, and so forth. There is no way to backspace.

The statements read and readln behave the same for text files as they do for the sort of keyboard-entered data we have used so far. The only difference is that if a text file variable is given as the first argument, then the data is read from the indicated text file rather than from the keyboard. Just as with a write statement, this is confusing syntax. The only way to tell that the first argument of a read or readln refers to a text file is to look at the declaration section to see if it is declared to be of type text.

read and readln (margin note)

Opening Files

The details of naming and opening files differ somewhat from one implementation to another. We have described some of the common variants in Appendixes 10, 13D, and 14. In this section we will present the method prescribed in the official Pascal standards.

The file variable names for the files used by a program are listed in the program heading. We have already been doing that for the files called input and output. The keyboard and the screen are considered to be special kinds of files with the file variable names input and output. A program that reads from the text file Read-Stuff and writes to the text file WriteStuff would start as follows:

program heading (margin note)

```
program Sample(input, output, ReadStuff, WriteStuff);
```

The order of the file variable names is unimportant. (Some Pascal systems have provisions to allow the user to specify the name of a file when the program is run. Those user-specified files are not listed in the program heading. The details for handling those user-specified files vary from system to system.)

Even though the file variables are listed in the program heading, they must be declared in the variable declaration section. Hence the following declaration must appear in the program:

```
var ReadStuff, WriteStuff: text;
```

opening
files

All files must be *opened* before a program can read from the file or write to the file. Opening a file instructs the system to prepare the file for reading or writing. A text file may be opened for reading or for writing but not for both at the same time.

rewrite

A file is opened for writing with the standard procedure `rewrite`. The procedure has one parameter, which is the file variable name of the file to be opened. By way of example, the following opens the file `TestFile` for writing:

```
rewrite(TestFile)
```

After this statement is executed, the program may use `write` or `writeln` statements with the file `TestFile`. The `rewrite` procedure always gives a blank file, a "clean sheet of paper," so to speak. If the file `TestFile` contains any text, it will be completely erased. If there is no file associated with the file variable `TestFile`, the `rewrite` procedure will create one.

A complete example is given in Figure 13.1. That program writes the numbers 3 and 4 to the text file `TestFile`. The numbers will be on two lines. If `TestFile` does not exist before the program is run, the program will create it. If `TestFile` is present before the program is run, then the previous contents of the file will be lost. After the program is run, the file will contain only the two numbers 3 and 4. The first and last `writeln`'s do not contain the identifier `TestFile`, and so their output is sent to the screen. If those two `writeln` statements are omitted, the program will output nothing at all to the screen.

reset

Many of the details for reading from a text file are similar to those we have just described for writing to a text file. The file variable name must be given in the program

Program

```
program Writer(input, output, TestFile);
{Writes the numbers 3 and 4 into the text file TestFile.}
var TestFile: text;
    N: integer;
begin{Program}
  writeln('Start program');
  rewrite(TestFile);
  writeln(TestFile, 3);
  N := 4;
  writeln(TestFile, N);
  writeln('End of program')
end. {Program}
```

Output to Screen

```
Start program
End of program
```

Figure 13.1

Program that writes to a text file.

Output to `TestFile`

```
3
4
```

Program

```
program Reader(input, output, TestFile);
{Reads two numbers from the text file TestFile, places them in variables N1
and N2, and then outputs the contents of N1 and N2 to the screen.}
var TestFile: text;
    N1, N2: integer;
begin{Program}
  reset(TestFile);
  readln(TestFile, N1);
  readln(TestFile. N2);

  writeln(N1);
  writeln(N2);
  writeln('End of program')
end. {Program}
```

Output
(assuming that the program in Figure 13.1 was run first)

```
3
4
End of program
```

Figure 13.2
**Program that
reads from a
text file.**

heading in the same way as in Figure 13.1. The file variable name must be declared to be of type `text`, as shown there. The file must be opened, but the standard procedure that opens a file for reading is called `reset`. For example, suppose the program in Figure 13.1 has been run and so has created the file `TestFile`. Another program can open that same text file for reading with the following statement:

```
reset(TestFile)
```

After this statement is executed, the program may use `read` or `readln` statements with the file `TestFile`. A complete example of reading from a text file is given in Figure 13.2. That program will read from the text file created by the program in Figure 13.1.

Pitfall

Mixing Reading and Writing to a Text File

A program cannot simply intermix reading and writing to the same file. At any one time, a text file that has been opened is available for either reading or writing but not both. To switch from writing to reading, the file must be reopened by a call to `reset`. To switch from reading to writing, the file must be reopened by a call to `rewrite`. This is not a trivial restriction, since opening the file for writing completely erases the file. The typical sequence of actions is to open the file with `rewrite` and write to it, and then to have the same or a different program open the file any number of times with `reset` and read the file contents. The next time it is opened with `rewrite`, the file is erased.

One productive variation on this pattern of writing and reading is as follows: The file can be created or changed by a person using the editor to write to the file instead of having a Pascal program do the writing. Text files are the exact same kind of files as those used to hold Pascal programs, shopping lists, and term papers, and they can be edited with the editor just as a Pascal program can be edited.

Pitfall

The Silent Program

It is quite common to write a program so that all the data that is output is directed to a text file. If you do this, then the program will produce no output to the screen. This can be bewildering. If you write programs that way, the user may not even be able to tell when the program has finished. To let the user know what is going on, there should always be some output to the screen, even if it just says when the program starts and when it ends.

Self-Test Exercise

1. Suppose the text file named by the file variable `Arthur` contains the following:

```
5   63   75
5   63   75
```

Suppose also that variables are declared as follows:

```
var Arthur: text;
    Number: integer;
    Letter1, Letter2: char;
```

What will be the output produced by the following, provided it is embedded in a complete program that opens `Arthur` with `reset` and that declares variables as shown above?

```
read(Arthur, Number);  write(Number);
read(Arthur, Number);  write(Number);
readln(Arthur); writeln;
read(Arthur, Letter1);  write(Letter1);
read(Arthur, Letter1, Letter2);
write(Letter1, Letter2);
```

Interactive Exercises

2. Write a program that writes your name to a text file. Look at the text file after the program is run. On most systems, programs are kept in text files and can be written and read using an editor program. Hence, if your system is typical, you already know how to look at a text file.

3. Create a text file using the editor (as you do when you write a program) and write three numbers in the text file. Write a program to read the three numbers and write them to the screen. After running the program once, go back and change the numbers. Then rerun the program.

4. Using the editor, change the text file from the previous example so that the three numbers are two digits long and have one space between them, and so that there are no spaces at the front of the line. For example, the text file might contain

```
25  36  47
```

Rerun the program from the previous exercise. Next, write a slightly different program that reads three characters from the same text file into three variables of type char and then outputs them to the screen. Run this new program on the same text file.

PART II

The Moving Finger writes; and, having writ,
Moves on: nor all your Piety nor Wit
    Shall lure it back to cancel half a line,
Nor all your Tears wash out a Word of it.
    Omar Khayyam, The Ruba'iyat (Fitzgerald translation)

read and write Reexamined

Before we go further, it will help to have a more precise notion of how the statements `read`, `readln`, `write`, and `writeln` work.

arrow

When a text file is opened, a location marker is placed somewhere in the file. For purposes of explanation, let us call this location marker an *arrow* and think of it as pointing to a file location that contains, or could contain, one character. This arrow tells where the next character to be read is or where the next character to be written will go. In the figures, we will shade the location pointed to by the arrow in order to make it more prominent.

writing

When a file is opened with the `rewrite` statement, the file is erased and the arrow is placed at the first location in the file. Every time the program writes a character, the character is written at the location of the arrow and then the arrow is advanced to the next location. Some sample code and its effect on the text file `TestFile` is shown in Figure 13.3. Notice that a second line is started when the `writeln` statement is executed. This is the only way to initiate a new line. There is no limit to the length of a line in a text file.

Also notice that in the example, the output to the file was written from the beginning of the file and continued on through the file. The arrow did not "back up." When using a text file, the program cannot backspace and change a character. With text files, the moving arrow "writes; and, having writ, moves on," much like the finger of fate described by Omar Khayyam. The only way to get the arrow back to a previous position is to use a `reset` or `rewrite` statement, and these do not allow the program to change a portion of the file. The `rewrite` statement will erase the entire contents of the file. The `reset` statement will move the arrow all the way back to the first character in the file and will only allow the program to read from the file. It will not allow the program to write to the file.

lines

end-of-line marker

In order to fully understand text files, we need to examine the notion of a *line* more carefully. Figure 13.3 is the way we normally think of lines, and text files are implemented so as to reflect this intuition. However, there are no physical lines in a text file. Instead, a text file is just one continuous stream of characters (rather like a ticker tape). The "end of a line" is indicated by inserting a special marker. This marker is a character of sorts, but it is not possible to see it on the screen. The computer can recognize it, though, and it is this character that indicates what we, and the Pascal manuals, call an

The file is `TestFile`.	
Program Action	**File After the Action**
open the file with `rewrite`	▨ ↑
`write(TestFile, 'a')`	a▨ ↑
`write(TestFile, 'b')`	ab▨ ↑
`write(TestFile, 'c')`	abc▨ ↑
`write(TestFile, 'd')`	abcd▨ ↑
`writeln(TestFile)`	abcd ▨ ↑
`write(TestFile, 'e')`	abcd e▨ ↑
`write(TestFile, 'f')`	abcd ef▨ ↑

**Figure 13.3
Writing to a text
file, intuitive
picture.**

end of a line. In Figure 13.4 we have redone Figure 13.3, this time indicating the end of a line with this marker. In the diagram the marker is denoted <eoln>. The only way to insert an <eoln> marker in a text file is with a `writeln` statement.

　　An existing file is opened for reading with the `reset` statement. When a file is opened in this way, the arrow is placed at the first character of the first line of the file. Every time a character is read, the arrow is advanced to the next character. The situation is diagrammed in Figure 13.5. Notice that the `readln` statement moves the arrow to the beginning of the next line, and all the remaining characters on the old line are thus ignored. If the program runs out of characters on one line, there can be problems. Usually, the programmer must ensure that the arrow is explicitly moved to the next line by means of a `readln`. An exception is made for numbers. If the program is reading into a variable of type `integer` or `real` and there is no more data on the current line, it will automatically go to the next line.

　　The <eoln> symbol is a symbol in the file. However, it cannot be read into a variable of type `char` in the same way that other symbols can. If a program reads the

reading

*<eoln> symbol
reads as a blank*

<table>
<tr><td colspan="2" align="center">The file is TestFile.</td></tr>
<tr><td>Program Action</td><td align="right">File After the Action</td></tr>
</table>

Program Action	File After the Action
Open the file with `rewrite`	▮ ↑
`write(TestFile, 'a')`	a▮ ↑
`write(TestFile, 'b')`	ab▮ ↑
`write(TestFile, 'c')`	abc▮ ↑
`write(TestFile, 'd')`	abcd▮ ↑
`writeln(TestFile)`	abcd\<eoln\>▮ ↑
`write(TestFile, 'e')`	abcd\<eoln\>e▮ ↑
`write(TestFile, 'f')`	abcd\<eoln\>ef▮ ↑

Figure 13.4
Writing to a text file, the "real" picture.

<eoln> symbol into a variable, the variable will be filled with a blank; it will not be filled with the <eoln> symbol. It is not possible to read it into a variable and then write it out as the <eoln> symbol. If you wish to insert the <eoln> symbol into a text file, you must do so with a `writeln` statement.

eof and eoln

When a program is reading from a text file, it is often helpful if it can detect the end of the file. Pascal provides a special boolean-valued function that does just that. The function `eof` is officially called the *end-of-file function,* but is usually pronounced by reading the letters "e-o-f". It takes one argument, a file variable, and it returns `true` if the program is at the end of that file. More specifically,

eof

    eof (<file variable>)

evaluates to `true` if the arrow in the file indicated by <file variable> is past the last line in the file; otherwise, it evaluates to `false`.

As an example, the program in Figure 13.6 reads a list of numbers from the file OldFile, multiplies each number by 2, and copies the result into a second (new) file, which it calls NewFile. The function eof is used to detect when all the numbers in the file have been read. Suppose that the file OldFile contains the following when the program is run:

```
1
2
3
```

The body of the while loop in the program will then be executed three times. Each time, one of the following three lines will be written to the file NewFile:

```
2
4
6
```

The file is called TestFile.			

| | **File After the Action** | | **Value of X** |
Program Action	**Intuitive Picture**	**Real Picture**	**After Action**
open the file with reset	abcd ↑ ef	abcd<eoln>ef ↑	?
read(TestFile, X)	abcd ↑ ef	abcd<eoln>ef ↑	'a'
read(TestFile, X)	abcd ↑ ef	abcd<eoln>ef ↑	'b'
readln(TestFile)	abcd ef ↑	abcd<eoln>ef ↑	'b'
read(TestFile, X)	abcd ef ↑	abcd<eoln>ef ↑	'e'

Figure 13.5
Reading from a text file.

```
program Doubler(input, output, OldFile, NewFile);
{Precondition: OldFile contains a list of integers. Postcondition: OldFile is unchanged;
NewFile contains the numbers in OldFile, each multiplied by 2.}
var Buffer: integer;
    OldFile, NewFile: text;
begin{Program}
  writeln('Program started.');
  reset(OldFile);
  rewrite(NewFile);
  while not eof(OldFile) do
    begin{while}
      readln(OldFile, Buffer);
      Buffer := 2 * Buffer;
      writeln(NewFile, Buffer)
    end;  {while}
  writeln('Numbers in OldFile doubled');
  writeln('and results copied to NewFile.')
end.  {Program}
```

Figure 13.6
Program using
eof.

At this point, the arrow in the file OldFile has moved beyond the third and last line. So eof(OldFile) evaluates to true, and the following boolean expression evaluates to false:

> not eof(OldFile)

Since the controlling boolean expression now evaluates to false, the *while* loop is terminated.

eoln   The function eoln is the same eoln that we have already used with input from the keyboard, but we will now see how to use it with other text files as well. It is similar to eof, except that it tests for the end of a line rather than the end of the entire file. In terms of the arrow discussed above, eoln can be explained as follows: When the arrow in the file specified by <file variable> is pointing to the end-of-line marker (what we have been denoting by <eoln> in the diagrams), then

> eoln(<file variable>)

returns true; otherwise, it returns false. (Do not confuse eoln and <eoln>. <eoln> is a symbol in the text file. eoln is a function that tests to see if the arrow in a text file is pointing to <eoln>.)

In order to construct an example using eoln, suppose that a program contains the following declarations:

> var OldFile, NewFile: text;
>   Buffer: char;

If both files are opened properly and the arrow is at the start of a line, then the following loop will copy one line of text from OldFile into NewFile:

```
while not eoln(OldFile) do
  begin
    read(OldFile, Buffer);
    write(NewFile, Buffer)
  end
```

The effect of this loop on some sample file contents is shown in Figure 13.7. After the two characters on the line have been read, the arrow in `OldFile` is at the end-of-line marker, and so `eoln(OldFile)` becomes `true`. That causes the boolean expression for the *while* loop to become `false`, and so the loop terminates after the second iteration of the loop body. Typically, this loop would be followed by

```
readln(OldFile);
writeln(NewFile)
```

OldFile	NewFile	Buffer	eoln(OldFile)
ab\<eoln\>cd\<eoln\> ▓ ↑ ↑		?	false
then program executes read(OldFile, Buffer)			
ab\<eoln\>cd\<eoln\> ▓ ↑ ↑		'a'	false
then program executes write(NewFile, Buffer)			
ab\<eoln\>cd\<eoln\> a▓ ↑ ↑		'a'	false
then program executes read(OldFile, Buffer)			
ab\<eoln\>cd\<eoln\> a▓ ↑ ↑		'b'	true
then program executes write(NewFile, Buffer)			
ab\<eoln\>cd\<eoln\> ab▓ ↑ ↑		'b'	true
then program executes readln(OldFile)			
ab\<eoln\>cd\<eoln\> ab▓ ↑ ↑		'b'	false
then program executes writeln(NewFile)			
ab\<eoln\>cd\<eoln\>	ab\<eoln\>▓ ↑ ↑	'b'	false

Figure 13.7
Copying a line from one text file to another.

This moves the arrow in each file to the beginning of the next line.

Recall that input from the keyboard is considered to be from a special file called `input`. The standard functions `eof` and `eoln` may be applied to this file `input`. Indeed, we have been using `eoln` with the file `input` since Chapter 7. If no argument is given, then the file is assumed to be `input`; that is, `eof` by itself is equivalent to `eof(input)` and, as we saw in previous chapters, `eoln` by itself is equivalent to `eoln(input)`. The end-of-line marker at the keyboard is the return key. The end-of-file marker at the keyboard varies from system to system. Since the exact details vary from system to system, using `eof` with the file `input` is usually more trouble than it is worth.

Using a Buffer

The word "buffer" is frequently used in discussions about files and has a semitechnical meaning. A *buffer* is a location where some data is held on its way from one place to another. This is why we chose `Buffer` as the name of the character variable in the previous loop example. The program reads a character from one file into `Buffer` and then writes it from `Buffer` into the other file. The variable serves as a temporary location for one character. (The phrase "buffer variable" also has a technical meaning in Pascal; it is really a special case of this general notion of a buffer, but that topic comes later.)

Pitfall

Forgetting the File Variable in eof or eoln

There are a number of pitfalls associated with the special boolean functions `eof` and `eoln`. The simplest one of all is forgetting to include the file variable as an argument. For example, if you are testing for the end of the file `OldFile`, you must use `eof(OldFile)`. If you forget and instead use the unadorned `eof`, you are referring to the file `input` and not the file `OldFile`. This can be frustrating, since the program will compile without an error message. After all, the compiler has no way of telling that you did not mean to refer to the file `input`. However, problems will occur when the program is run. The program may stop and do nothing because it is waiting for input from the keyboard. If the program does not stop, then it is likely to produce an error message referring to an unexpected end of file. If your program is reading from the file `OldFile`, and instead of `eof(OldFile)` you mistakenly use `eof` to terminate the reading, then your program is in trouble. It is essentially guaranteed that the unadorned `eof` will not be true when your program reaches the end of the file `OldFile`, and so your program will attempt to read beyond the end of the file.

Pitfall

Use of eoln and eof with Numeric Data

Text files are designed for holding characters. When a program is reading or writing numbers, a type conversion is performed. The exact details of how a system handles numbers in text files will vary slightly from one installation to another. When you are dealing with numeric data, these details can cause the behavior of eoln and eof to vary in an unpredictable way from one system to another. The easiest way to avoid any problems when using eof with numeric data is to always use readln rather than read, and to avoid using eoln completely. When processing data of type char, Pascal has no such problems. However, there are still some other problems in the way that eof and eoln interact.

Pitfall

Mixing eof and eoln

When eof (TextFile) is true, the value of eoln (TextFile) is undefined. Hence, it is not possible to mix these two functions in a single boolean expression. For example, the value, if any, of the following is unpredictable:

```
eof (TextFile)  or  eoln (TextFile)
{This should not be used.}
```

When eof (TextFile) is true, you might expect this expression to evaluate to true. However, the normal way to evaluate a boolean expression using *or* is to first evaluate both arguments and then apply the *or*. In this case, eof (TextFile) evaluates to true, but the attempt to evaluate eoln (TextFile) produces an error condition, since that function has no value. On most systems, this will produce an error message and an abnormal termination of the program.

Text Files as Parameters to Procedures

A text file can be a parameter to a procedure just as things of other data types can. There is, however, one qualification. Text file parameters must be *variable parameters;* they can never be value parameters.

As an example, we will design a procedure that has two text file parameters, one called OldFile and one called NewFile. The procedure will copy the contents of the file OldFile into the file NewFile. A precise definition of the task to be accomplished is

example— copying a file

> *Precondition: OldFile has been opened with reset; NewFile has been*
> *opened with rewrite; but no reading or writing has taken place yet.*
> *Postcondition: The contents of OldFile are unchanged; the contents*
> *of NewFile have been made the same as those of OldFile.*

The basic outline of the procedure is given in Figure 13.8.

In order to convert that piece of pseudocode into Pascal, all we need to do is to design some Pascal code for the informal instruction

Copy a line from `OldFile` to `NewFile`

This is exactly what we did in the section on `eoln`. The Pascal code we developed there is as follows:

```
while not eoln(OldFile) do
  begin
    read(OldFile, Buffer);
    write(NewFile, Buffer)
  end
```

If we now put together all the details, we obtain the procedure Copy, shown in Figure 13.9.

```
while not eof(OldFile) do
  begin{a line}

    {The arrows in OldFile and NewFile are
    both at the start of a line.}

    Copy a line from OldFile to NewFile

    {The arrows in OldFile and NewFile are
    both at the end of a line.}

    readln(OldFile);  {Moves the arrow to the next line.}
    writeln(NewFile) {Inserts an end-of-line marker.}
  end {a line}
```

Figure 13.8
Basic outline of
the procedure in
Figure 13.9.

Pitfall

Portability

The details of file handling vary from one implementation to another. Thus, a program that deals with files cannot be completely portable. Moving it from one implementation to another is likely to require rewriting part of the program. In order to make this rewriting task as easy as possible, all file handling should be isolated into self-contained procedures or at least easy-to-find isolated code. Then, if the program is moved to a new system, only these isolated sections need to be rewritten.

```
procedure Copy(var OldFile, NewFile: text);
{Precondition: OldFile has been opened with reset; NewFile has been
opened with rewrite; but no reading or writing has taken place yet.
Postcondition: The contents of OldFile are unchanged; the contents
of NewFile have been made the same as those of OldFile.}
var Buffer: char;
begin{Copy}
   while not eof(OldFile) do
       begin{a line and outer while}

          while not eoln(OldFile) do
             begin{inner while}
                read(OldFile, Buffer);
                write(NewFile, Buffer)
                {The current lines of NewFile and OldFile
                contain exactly the same thing up to (but not
                including) the positions of their arrows.}
             end; {inner while}
          {The arrow in OldFile is at the end of a line.}

          readln(OldFile);
          writeln(NewFile)
          {The arrows in both files are at
          the beginning of the next line.}
       end {a line and end outer while}
end; {Copy}
```

**Figure 13.9
Procedure with
text file
parameters.**

Basic Technique for Editing Text Files

As we have already noted, there is no way to change part of a text file. The only way to write to a text file is to create a new file or to completely erase an old file. However, there is a way to get the effect of changing a file. In order to change part of a text file, a Pascal program must do something like the following:

1. Copy the entire contents of the given file into some temporary file, making changes as the copying is done.
2. Copy the entire contents of the temporary file back to the original file.

Internal Files

external
versus
internal
files

The files we have been describing so far are called *external text files*. They exist before and/or after the program is run. In many implementations of Pascal, there are also files that exist only for the duration of the program. These are called *internal text files*. The name of an internal file is local to a program. Thus, it is wise to make any temporary file an internal file. In particular, if a program edits a text file in the manner outlined in the previous section, then it will need an extra temporary file. That extra file should be an internal file.

It is very easy to make a file internal to a program. Simply omit it from the program heading. An internal file is manipulated in exactly the same way as an external file, but when the program ends the file disappears. For example, suppose you wish to write a program to edit a file called `DataFile` and your program uses a file called `TempFile` to hold some text temporarily. The program heading should be

```
program Edit(input, output, DataFile);
```

If there coincidentally happens to be a file called `TempFile` in the system, it will not be affected by the program, because `TempFile` is an internal file.

An internal file is like a local variable. It is perfectly correct to think of an internal file variable as one that is local to the program. However, the way to make it internal is to omit it from the program heading. Simply making it a local variable in some procedure will not make it an internal file.

Case Study

Editing Out Excess Blanks

Problem Definition

Suppose that you wish to write a program to edit excess blanks from a text file containing some ordinary English text. To be more precise, let us say that the program is to delete all initial blanks on a line and also is to compress all other strings of two or more blanks down to a single blank. For example, consider the lines below:

```
    The   Answer to the      question of Life,
    the     Universe,                  and Everything is:
```

They should be edited to look like

```
The Answer to the question of Life,
the Universe, and Everything is:
```

Discussion

We will use the basic technique for editing text files that we outlined two sections ago. Let us use `DataFile` as the name of the file to be edited. We will need one temporary file, which we will call `TempFile`. The basic outline of the program is as follows:

1. Open DataFile using reset; open TempFile using rewrite.
2. (CleanBlanks:) Copy DataFile into TempFile, but delete excess blanks as this is done. (That is, copy all characters except the unwanted blanks from DataFile to TempFile.)
3. Reopen TempFile using reset; reopen DataFile using rewrite.
4. (Copy:) Copy the contents of TempFile into DataFile.

We will implement subtasks 2 and 4 as procedures named CleanBlanks and Copy. The Pascal program, with some details still missing, is shown in Figure 13.10. The procedure Copy is the one in Figure 13.9. Thus, all that remains is to design the procedure CleanBlanks that will accomplish subtask 2.

Before designing the code for the procedure CleanBlanks, let us observe a few *mixing* things about the program outline. Notice that the program in Figure 13.10 both reads *reading* from and writes to the same file. This is permitted as long as the reading and writing is *and* not mixed. The program must first read from the file and then reopen it for the purpose *writing*

```
program Edit(input, output, DataFile);
{Edits out excess blanks from the text file DataFile.}

var  DataFile, TempFile: text;

procedure CleanBlanks(var DirtyFile, CleanFile: text);
{Precondition: DirtyFile has been opened with reset; CleanFile has
been opened with rewrite; but no reading or writing has taken place yet.
Postcondition: DirtyFile is unchanged; the contents of CleanFile are made
the same as those of DirtyFile except that superfluous blanks are deleted.}
          .         .        .
       .        .        .

procedure Copy(var OldFile, NewFile: text);
{Precondition: OldFile has been opened with reset; NewFile has been
opened with rewrite; but no reading or writing has taken place yet.
Postcondition: The contents of OldFile are unchanged; the contents
of NewFile have been made the same as those of OldFile.}
          .         .        .
       .        .        .

begin{Program}
  writeln('Program is running');

  reset(DataFile);  rewrite(TempFile);
  CleanBlanks(DataFile, TempFile);

  reset(TempFile);  rewrite(DataFile);
  Copy(TempFile, DataFile);

  writeln('End of program')
end. {Program}
```

Figure 13.10
Program that edits a text file.

CleanBlanks

of writing. It is also possible to write first and then read, but every change from reading to writing and every change from writing to reading requires that the file be reopened.

We next design the algorithm and code for the one unfinished procedure. The procedure heading indicates what the procedure needs to accomplish:

```
procedure CleanBlanks(var DirtyFile, CleanFile: text);
{Precondition: DirtyFile has been opened with reset; CleanFile has
been opened with rewrite; but no reading or writing has taken place yet.
Postcondition: DirtyFile is unchanged; the contents of CleanFile are made
the same as those of DirtyFile except that superfluous blanks are deleted.}
```

ALGORITHM

negative thinking

The procedure CleanBlanks can be very much like the procedure Copy. In fact, the only difference between CleanBlanks and Copy is that CleanBlanks will sometimes read a character and decide not to copy it to the second file. The algorithm is given in Figure 13.11.

We still need some way to tell when a character is an extra blank. For the moment, let us ignore the problem of initial blanks and concentrate only on strings of blanks within a line. We want to compress every string of two or more blanks to a single blank. One solution is to copy only the first blank and to consider the other blanks as extra blanks to be skipped over. In this approach a blank is extra (*not* copied) provided that

1. The character is a blank, and
2. The character that precedes it on the same line is also a blank.

This test requires that the program remember two characters instead of just one. Hence, we will use two variables of type char as buffer variables. One, called Current, serves the same purpose as the variable Symbol did in Figure 13.11. It will

```
while not eof(DirtyFile) do
    begin{a line and outer while}
        while not eoln(DirtyFile) do
            begin{inner while}
                read(DirtyFile, Symbol);
                if Symbol is not an extra blank then
                    write(CleanFile, Symbol);
                {The current lines of CleanFile and DirtyFile
                contain the same thing up to (but not including)
                the positions of their arrows, except that any
                excess blanks do not appear in CleanFile.}
            end;  {inner while}
        {The arrow in DirtyFile is at the end of a line.}

        readln(DirtyFile);
        writeln(CleanFile)
        {The arrows in both files are at
        the beginning of the next line.}
    end {a line and end outer while}
```

Figure 13.11
Basic algorithm for
CleanBlanks.

{Assumes that no line in DirtyFile starts with a blank.}
while not eof(DirtyFile) *do*
  begin{a line and outer while}
    initialize Last to something that will make the first iteration work;
    while not eoln(DirtyFile) *do*
      begin{inner while}
        read(DirtyFile, Current);
        if not((Last = <blank>) *and* (Current = <blank>)) *then*
          write(CleanFile, Current);
        Last := Current
        {The current lines of CleanFile and DirtyFile
        contain the same thing up to (but not including)
        the positions of their arrows, except that any
        excess blanks do not appear in CleanFile. Last
        contains the last character considered and possibly
        copied to CleanFile.}
      end; *{inner while}*
    {The arrow in DirtyFile is at the end of a line.}

    readln(DirtyFile);
    writeln(CleanFile)
    {The arrows in both files are at
    the beginning of the next line.}
  end *{a line and end outer while}*

Figure 13.12
First refinement of
the algorithm for
CleanBlanks.

contain the current symbol, which either does or does not get copied to the second file. The other, called Last, will contain the previous character on the line being copied from. Therefore, the value of Last is just the previous value of Current. The algorithm refinement that uses these two variables is shown in Figure 13.12.

This is not yet a complete solution. It does not make sense for the first symbol of a line. To make it work for the first symbol of a line, recall that we want to copy the first symbol as long as it is not a blank. Hence, if we set Last equal to the blank symbol before we start each line, then this test works for the first symbol of a line as well. The complete, final code is shown in Figure 13.13.

forcing the
special case

Text Editing as a Programming Aid

A Pascal program is a piece of text and is stored in a text file. Hence, it can be edited by another program in the ways we have been describing. This can sometimes be a helpful programming aid. As an example, consider the task of tracing a program, which we discussed in Chapters 3 and 7. Tracing is a technique to aid in debugging programs. Specifically, it consists of inserting temporary writeln statements that output intermediate results. Once the program is debugged, we want to remove these

```
procedure CleanBlanks(var DirtyFile, CleanFile: text);
```
{Precondition: DirtyFile has been opened with reset; CleanFile has been opened with rewrite; but no reading or writing has taken place yet. Postcondition: DirtyFile is unchanged; the contents of CleanFile are made the same as those of DirtyFile except that superfluous blanks are deleted.}
```
const Blank = ' ';
var Current, Last: char;
begin{CleanBlanks}
   while not eof(DirtyFile) do
      begin{a line and outer while}
         Last := Blank;  {This ensures that a blank at the
                          start of a line will be deleted.}

         while not eoln(DirtyFile) do
            begin{inner while}
               read(DirtyFile, Current);
               if not( (Last = Blank) and (Current = Blank) ) then
                  write(CleanFile, Current);
               Last := Current
               {The current lines of CleanFile and DirtyFile
               contain the same thing up to (but not including)
               the positions of their arrows, except that any
               excess blanks do not appear in CleanFile. Last
               contains the last character considered and possibly
               copied to CleanFile.}
            end;  {inner while}
         {The arrow in DirtyFile is at the end of a line.}

         readln(DirtyFile);
         writeln(CleanFile)
         {The arrows in both files are at
         the beginning of the next line.}
      end {a line and end outer while}
end;  {CleanBlanks}
```

Figure 13.13
Procedure to copy text with excess blanks omitted.

extra `writeln` statements used for tracing. To aid us in finding and removing trace statements, or for that matter any other sort of temporary lines, we suggested marking them with a comment, as in the following sample of a temporary `writeln` statement:

{TEMP} `writeln(Sum);`

Suppose all our temporary statements are marked in the way we described. Then, to remove the temporary statements, all we need to do is locate those lines that begin with *{TEMP}* and delete them. This sort of tedious and uninteresting task is best left to the computer. In Exercise 16 you are asked to write a program for the computer to do this editing. After you write the program, it would be a good idea to actually use the program as a programming tool from then on. It is not just a "toy problem."

Summary of Problem Solving and Programming Techniques

- Text files are used for storing data that is to remain in secondary storage after a program terminates. The data is stored as strings of symbols like the data displayed on the output screen.
- The text files that are manipulated by Pascal programs can also be read and changed using the editor.
- Any location, be it a variable or a text file or anything else, that holds data on its way from one place to another is called a *buffer*. Since it is not possible to move data directly from one file to another, a program that moves data between files must use a variable (or variables) as a buffer. The data is read from one file into the buffer and is then written out from the buffer to the other file.
- A text file may not be opened for reading and writing at the same time. Hence, in programs that edit a text file, the usual technique is to use an additional temporary file. The contents of the text file are copied into the temporary file, and the editing changes are made in the process of copying. After that, the edited version of the text is recopied back into the original file.
- One application of text editing is to edit the temporary trace statements out of a debugged Pascal program.
- The exact details of file handling will vary from one installation to another. Hence, file handling should be isolated into procedures in order to make any needed changes easy to carry out.
- When you are designing conditions for some program or algorithm action, it is sometimes clearer to think in terms of when the action should not take place, rather than thinking in terms of when it should take place.
- Once a general solution that applies to most cases has been found, it is often possible to force the solution to fit the remaining cases by setting some initial conditions or by making some other small changes.

> In *theory,*
> there is no difference between *theory* and *practice,*
>   but in *practice,*
> there is.
>   *Remark overheard at a computer science conference*

Summary of Pascal Constructs

program heading

Syntax:

> *program* <program name> (<file list>) ;

Example:

> *program* Sample(input, output, File1, File2);

<file list> is a list of the file variable names for all the external text files used in the program. The file input may be omitted if the program does not read from the keyboard. On most systems, the file output must be listed, because any error messages are written to the file output. All these file variable names, except input and output, must also be declared to be variables of type text.

the type for text files

Syntax:

> text

The Pascal type name for text files.

text file variables

Syntax:

> *var* <file variable>: text;

Example:

> *var* DataFile: text;

Declaration of a file variable of type text. These file variables are used as names for text files within a Pascal program.

reset

Syntax:

> reset(<file variable>)

Example:

> reset(File1)

Opens the text file specified by <file variable> for reading. <file variable> is a variable of type text. Reading starts at the first character of the first line of the text file and proceeds through the file.

rewrite

Syntax:

> rewrite(<file variable>)

Example:

```
rewrite(File2)
```

Opens the text file specified by <file variable> for writing. <file variable> is a variable of type `text`. This always produces a blank file. If no file with <file variable> as its file variable name exists, then a blank one is created. If there already is a file associated with <file variable>, then the contents of that file are erased.

write statement
Syntax:

```
write(<file variable>, <argument list> )
```

Example:

```
write(DataFile, 'Hello', X, Y)
```

Just like using `write` to write to the screen, but when done this way, the items in <argument list> are written to the text file specified by <file variable>. <file variable> is a variable of type `text`. The file specified by <file variable> must have been opened with a call to `rewrite`. <argument list> is a list of variables and quoted strings separated by commas.

writeln statement
Syntax:

```
writeln(<file variable>, <argument list>)
```

Example:

```
writeln(DataFile, 'Hello', X, Y)
```

Same as the previous definition with the addition that it inserts an end-of-line marker in the text file. In other words, it causes any subsequent output to <file variable> to be written on the next line.

read statement
Syntax:

```
read(<file variable>, <variable list>)
```

Example:

```
read(DataFile, X, Y, Z)
```

Just like using `read` to read from the keyboard, but done this way the values are read from the text file specified by <file variable>. <file variable> is a variable of type `text`. The file specified by <file variable> must have been opened with a call to `reset`. The <variable list> is a list of variables separated by commas.

readln statement
Syntax:

```
readln(<file variable>, <variable list>)
```

Example:

```
readln(DataFile, X, Y, Z)
```

Same as the previous definition with the addition that it causes any subsequent read from the file to start at the beginning of the next line.

end-of-file function
Syntax:

```
eof (<file variable>)
```

Example:

```
eof (DataFile)
```

This is a boolean-valued function that returns `true` if all of the text file specified by <file variable> has been read. More precisely, it evaluates to `true` if the arrow (described in the chapter) has moved past the last line in the file. <file variable> is a variable of type `text`.

end-of-line function
Syntax:

```
eoln (<file variable>)
```

Example:

```
eoln(OldFile)
```

This is a boolean-valued function that returns `true` if all of the data on the current line of the file specified by <file variable> has been read. More precisely, it evaluates to `true` if the arrow (described in the chapter) is pointing to the end-of-line marker. <file variable> is a variable of type `text`.

Exercises

Self-Test Exercises

5. What will be the contents of the file Abe after the following program is run with the following input from the keyboard?

Program

```
program Exercise5(input, output, Abe);
var Abe: text;
    S: char;
begin{Program}
  writeln('Start input');
  rewrite(Abe);
```

```
      while not eoln do
        begin
          read(S);
          write(Abe, S)
        end;
      readln;
      writeln(Abe);
      readln(S);
      writeln(Abe, S);
      readln(S);
      writeln(Abe, S);
      writeln(Abe, 'The End.')
    end. {Program}
```

Input

```
Four score and seven years ago,
our fathers brought forth upon
this continent a new nation,
conceived in Liberty and
dedicated to the proposition that
all men are created equal.
```

6. Suppose that the text file named by the file variable Sally contains the following:

   abcdef<eoln>ghijk<eoln>lmnop<eoln>

Suppose variables are declared as follows:

```
var Sally: text;
    L1, L2, Buffer: char;
```

What will be the output produced by the following, provided it is embedded in a complete program that opens Sally with reset and that declares variables as shown above?

```
readln(Sally, L1, L2); writeln(L1, L2);
while not eoln(Sally) do
  begin
    read(Sally, Buffer);
    write(Buffer)
  end;
writeln('Hi')
```

7. Write a program to write the numbers 1 through 10 to a text file, one per line. Run the program and then look at the text file.

8. Write a program that reads the list of numbers from the text file of the previous exercise, computes their sum, and outputs the sum to the screen. The program should use eof to detect the end of the file.

Interactive Exercises

9. It could be handy for a program to read a file name from the keyboard. Many Pascal systems have been extended to allow this. Find out if your system allows programs to read in a file name, and if it does, find out how this is done.

10. Write a program to read a line of text from a text file and display it on the screen. Use `eoln`. Use the editor or another program to create the text file.

Programming Exercises

11. Write a procedure that appends the contents of one text file to the end of another text file. The contents of the first file should be unchanged after the procedure is called.

12. Write a program that creates a table telling how to give change using quarters, dimes, and pennies. It should show the coins for all amounts from 1 to 99 cents. There should be a heading for the table. The program should output the table to a text file.

13. Write a program that outputs a table for converting from Celsius (centigrade) temperatures to Fahrenheit temperatures. Show all temperatures from minus 10 Celsius to 100 Celsius. A Celsius (centigrade) temperature C can be converted to an equivalent Fahrenheit temperature F according to the following formula:

$$F = (9/5)C + 32$$

The program should output the table to a text file.

14. Write a program that gives and takes advice on program writing. The program should open by writing a piece of advice to the screen. It should then ask the user to type in a different piece of advice. The next user of the program receives the advice typed in the last time the program was run. Be sure that the first person to run the program gets some advice.

15. The organization Professional Programmers for Purity in Pascal Programs has declared `'P'` to be a dirty letter and has hired you to write a program to eliminate this letter from text files. Write a program that replaces all occurrences of the letter `'P'` in a text file with the letter `'X'`. The program should replace both upper- and lowercase letters, `'P'` and `'p'`, with `'X'`.

16. Write a program to delete all temporary lines from a text file containing a Pascal program. See the section entitled "Text Editing as a Programming Aid" for a discussion of this problem.

17. (This is an exploratory exercise for those who did the previous exercise.) In writing the program for Exercise 16, you may have added some temporary `write` or `writeln` statements. If you did not, go back now and add some. Now you have a copy of the program with lines that need to be deleted. Run this program on the text file containing the program; that is, "run the program on itself." The program will clean itself, so to speak. (Some systems may require that you have two copies of the program to do this, but most systems will let you do it with just one copy. In any event, you should have an extra copy of the program just in case some mistake causes the program to damage itself.)

18. Write a program that takes two lists of integers, each sorted from smallest to largest, and merges the numbers into a single larger list containing all of the numbers sorted from smallest to largest. The two lists are in two text files, and the merged list is placed in a third text file.

19. Write a program to generate personalized junk mail. The program will work with a text file that contains a letter in which the location of the name of the recipient is indicated by some special string of characters, such as `'#name#'`. The program will ask for the name from the keyboard, read it in, and then make a copy of the letter with the name inserted where indicated. The letter with the name inserted should be written to another text file.

20. Write a program that computes the average number of characters per word and the average number of words per sentence for the text in some text file.

21. Write a program that produces a list of all the words used in a text file as well as the number of times each word is used. The list should be output to the screen as well as to another text file. The list should be in alphabetical order. Do not forget to consider punctuation marks, such as periods and commas, when determining the ends of words. The program should treat upper- and lowercase letters as being the same. For example, `'Word'` and `'word'` should be treated as the same word.

22. Pascal allows either the pair `'{ }'` or the pair `'(**)'` to enclose a comment. The reason for including the pair `'(**)'` is that some systems do not have the symbols `'{'` and `'}'` available. In order to run a Pascal program written using `'{ }'` on a system that does not have these symbols, all occurrences of `'{'` need to be replaced with `'(*'` and all occurrences of `'}'` need to be replaced with `'*)'`. Write a program that changes the text file containing a Pascal program so that this substitution of comment delimiters is made.

23. (This exercise uses the optional sections "Random Number Generators" and "Using Pseudorandom Numbers" in Chapter 8.) Write a program to generate pseudorandom test data for other programs. The data is written to a text file that contains `NumLines` lines of `NumPerL integer` values per line. The values of `NumLines` and `NumPerL`, as well as a range of possible integer values, are to be read from the keyboard. If your system has a predefined pseudorandom number generator, then you may use it; otherwise, use the function `Random` described in Chapter 8.

24. Books and newspapers contain text that is right-justified; that is, all lines are the same length. This is accomplished by copying as many words as possible onto one line and then adding extra blanks between the words so that the line is filled out to the prescribed line length. The line breaks in the original unjustified text are ignored in determining line lengths in the justified text. Write a program that produces right-justified text. The program will read from one file and write the right-justified text to another file. Use 80 characters, or whatever is convenient, as the line length.

25. (This exercise uses the optional sections "Random Number Generators" and "Using Pseudorandom Numbers" in Chapter 8.) Write a program to generate random English sentences. The program will use two text files, one containing a list of nouns and one containing a list of verbs, and will use a random number generator to choose words from these files.

26. Enhance the program of the previous exercise so that it outputs a series of sentences that seem to be related. Do this by repeating the nouns and verbs used. Specifically, once a noun or verb is used, the program remembers it and uses it more often than the other words on the lists. To make the output seem even more reasonable, you might try grouping related words and have the program choose words related to those already chosen. Use your imagination in forming word groupings and in the other details of the algorithm.

27. Since the rules of grammar are not as rigid for poetry as they are for prose, it is usually easier to write a poetry-writing program that produces humanlike output than it is to produce a reasonable prose-writing program. Use the techniques discussed in the previous two exercises to write a program that outputs free verse poetry.

28. Design a version of Pascal in a foreign language of your choice. To do this, choose a fixed translation for each reserved word and standard identifier. Write a program that takes a text file containing a Pascal program and translates it into the foreign language version by replacing each reserved word and standard identifier with its translation. Then enhance your program so that it can also translate a foreign language program into English Pascal.

PROBLEM SOLVING
USING
RECURSION

After a lecture on cosmology and the structure of the solar system, William James was accosted by a little old lady.

"Your theory that the sun is the center of the solar system, and the earth is a ball which rotates around it has a very convincing ring to it, Mr. James, but it's wrong. I've got a better theory," said the little old lady.

"And what is that, madam?" inquired James politely.

"That we live on a crust of earth which is on the back of a giant turtle."

Not wishing to demolish this absurd little theory by bringing to bear the masses of scientific evidence he had at his command, James decided to gently dissuade his opponent by making her see some of the inadequacies of her position.

"If your theory is correct, madam," he asked, "what does this turtle stand on?"

"You're a very clever man, Mr. James, and that's a very good question," replied the little old lady, "but I have an answer to it. And it is this: the first turtle stands on the back of a second, far larger, turtle, who stands directly under him."

"But what does this second turtle stand on?" persisted James patiently.

To this the little old lady crowed triumphantly. "It's no use, Mr. James—it's turtles all the way down."

J. R. ROSS, CONSTRAINTS ON VARIABLES IN SYNTAX

Chapter Contents

recursive
procedures
and
functions

W̲e have encountered a few cases of circular definitions that worked out satisfactorily. The most prominent examples are the definitions of certain Pascal statements. For example, the definition of a *while* statement says that it must contain another (smaller) statement. Since one possibility for this smaller statement is another *while* statement, there is a kind of circularity in that definition. The definition of the "*while* statement," if written out in complete detail, will contain a reference to "*while* statements." In mathematics these kinds of circular definitions are called "recursive definitions." In Pascal, a procedure or function may be defined in terms of itself in the same way. To put it more precisely, a procedure or function declaration may contain a call to itself. In such cases, the procedure or function is said to be *recursive*. In this chapter we will discuss recursion in Pascal, and, more generally, we will discuss recursion as a programming and problem solving technique. We start with an example.

Case Study

A Recursive Function

In Chapter 8 we defined a function called Power, which computed integer powers of the form

$$x^n$$

That function was not recursive, but it will set the stage for a recursive version of the function. The function declaration is reproduced in Figure 14.1.

Problem Definition

Notice that the version of Power given in Figure 14.1 only works for nonnegative values of N. We will define a version of Power that computes powers for negative as well as nonnegative exponents. For a negative exponent $-n$, the value returned is, by definition,

$$x^{-n} = 1/x^n$$

Discussion

Our task is to extend the declaration so that the function also works for negative values of N. To get a feel for what is needed, let us consider a concrete case. Let us say that X is 3.0 and N is -2. We want

    Power(3.0, -2)

to return the value $(3.0)^{-2}$. But that is equal to

    $1/(3.0)^2$

```
function Power(X: real; N: integer): real;
{Returns X to the power N; Returns 1 when N equals 0.
        Precondition: N >= 0.}
var I: integer;
    Product: real;
begin{Power}
  Product := 1;
  for I := 1 to N do
    begin
      Product := Product * X
      {Product is X to the Power I.}
    end;
  Power := Product
end; {Power}
```

Figure 14.1
Nonrecursive function declaration.

Negative powers are the same as positive powers in the denominator. Hence, if we know that the function Power returns the correct answer when N is positive, then we can calculate the correct value for Power (3.0, −2) by the expression

1/Power (3.0, 2)

ALGORITHM   Now let us replace −2 with N. This will produce the clause needed to extend the function declaration to accommodate negative values of N. The correct extra clause for the extended function declaration will be something equivalent to the following:

if N < 0 *then*
    Power := 1/Power (X, −N)

Remember, N is to take on negative values, such as −2. So −N will take on positive values, such as 2. (The negative of a negative number is a positive number.)

recursive   We can now put this all together to get a recursive declaration of Power that works
call   for negative exponents as well as nonnegative ones. The declaration is shown in Figure 14.2. The function call

Power := 1/Power (X, −N)

is called a *recursive call* because it occurs inside of the declaration for Power.

Let us see what happens when this function is called with some sample values. First let us consider the simple expression

Power (3.0, 2)

When the function is called, the value of X is set equal to 3.0, the value of N is set equal to 2, and the code is executed. Since 2 is greater than zero, the *else* part is ignored. In this case, it is easy to see that the value returned is 9.0.

```
function Power (X: real; N: integer): real;
{Returns X to the power N; Returns 1 when N equals 0.
Precondition: If N is negative, then X is not zero.}
var Product: real;
    I: integer;
begin{Power}
  if N >= 0 then
    begin {then}
      Product := 1;
      for I := 1 to N do
          Product := Product * X;
      Power := Product
    end {then}
  else {if N < 0 then }
      Power := 1/Power (X, −N)
end; {Power}
```

Figure 14.2
Recursive function
declaration.

Next let us try a set of parameters that exercise the recursive part of the declaration. Let us determine the value of

*example
of a
recursive
call*

Power (3.0, −2)

We proceed just as before. When the function is called, the value of X is set equal to 3.0, the value of N is set equal to −2, and the code is executed. Since −2 is less than zero, the *else* part is executed. Consequently, the value returned is the following (remember that since the value of N is −2, the value of −N is 2):

1/Power (3.0, 2)

We have already decided that the value of Power (3.0, 2) is 9.0. Hence, the value of Power (3.0, −2) is 1/9.0, which is approximately 0.11111111.

A Closer Look at Recursion

The declaration of the function Power uses recursion. Yet we did nothing new or different in evaluating the function call Power (3.0, −2). We treated it just like any of the function calls we saw in previous chapters. We simply substituted the actual parameters for the formal parameters and then executed the code. When we reached the recursive call Power (3.0, 2), we simply repeated this process one more time.

The computer keeps track of recursive calls in the following way: When a function is called, the computer plugs in the actual parameters for the formal parameters and begins to execute the code. If it should encounter a recursive call, it temporarily stops its computation. This is because it must know the result of the recursive call before it can proceed. It saves all the information it needs in order to continue the computation later on and proceeds to evaluate the recursive call. When the recursive call is completed, the computer returns to and completes the outer computation. Figure 14.3 illustrates this for the example of the previous section. Notice that when a recursive call is encountered, the current computation is temporarily suspended and a second copy of the function declaration is used to evaluate the recursive call. When that is completed, the value returned by the recursive call is used to complete the suspended computation. In the example there are two levels of function calls. There may be several levels of recursive calls. The principle is the same no matter how many levels of recursive calls there are.

*how
recursion
works*

As a further example, let us rewrite the function Power one more time. Observe that for any number *x* and any positive integer *n,* the following relation holds:

*a highly
recursive
example*

$$x^n = x(x^{n-1})$$

This means that an alternative way to define x^n is as follows:

*alternative
ALGORITHM*

The value is 1 when $n = 0$;
the value is *x* times x^{n-1} when $n > 0$;
the value is $1/x^{-n}$ when $n < 0$.

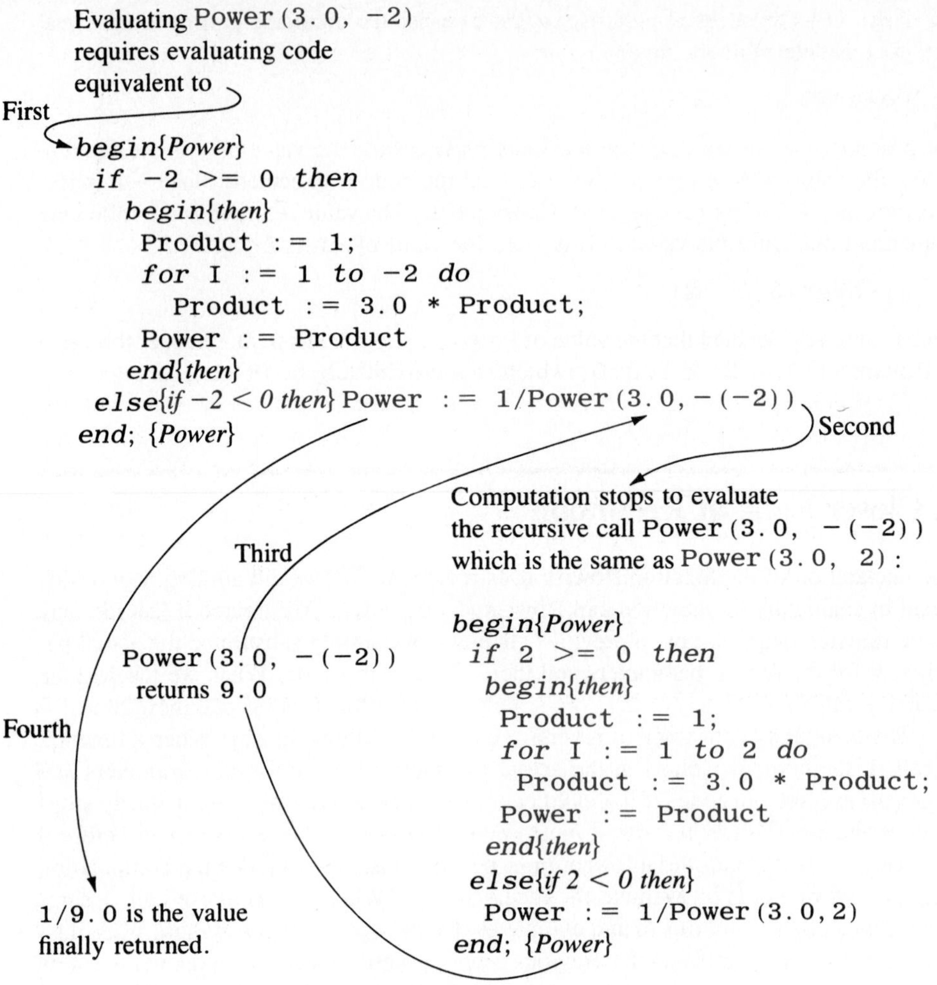

Evaluating Power (3.0, −2)
requires evaluating code
equivalent to

First

```
begin{Power}
  if −2 >= 0 then
    begin{then}
      Product := 1;
      for I := 1 to −2 do
        Product := 3.0 * Product;
      Power := Product
    end{then}
    else{if −2 < 0 then} Power := 1/Power (3.0, − (−2))
  end; {Power}
```

Second

Computation stops to evaluate
the recursive call Power (3.0, − (−2))
which is the same as Power (3.0, 2):

Third

```
begin{Power}
  if 2 >= 0 then
    begin{then}
      Product := 1;
      for I := 1 to 2 do
        Product := 3.0 * Product;
      Power := Product
    end{then}
    else{if 2 < 0 then}
      Power := 1/Power (3.0, 2)
end; {Power}
```

Power (3.0, − (−2))
returns 9.0

Fourth

1/9.0 is the value
finally returned.

Figure 14.3
Evaluation of a
recursive function.

Figure 14.4
A "highly"
recursive function.

```
function POW (X: real; N: integer): real;
{Returns X to the power N; Returns 1 when N equals 0.
Precondition: If N is negative, then X is not zero.}
begin{POW}
  if N = 0 then
    POW := 1
  else if N > 0 then
    POW := X * POW (X, N−1)
  else {if N < 0 then}
    POW := 1/POW (X, −N)
end; {POW}
```

The Pascal version of a recursive function that computes in this way is given in Figure 14.4. To avoid confusion, we have used a slightly different name for this version of the function.

Evaluation of a recursive function such as POW can get fairly involved. Consider what happens when the following statement is executed:

```
Z := POW(2.0, 3)
```

The computer starts to evaluate POW(2.0, 3), but must stop to compute POW(2.0, 2). While computing POW(2.0, 2), it must stop to compute POW(2.0, 1). While computing POW(2.0, 1), it must stop to compute POW(2.0, 0). It can easily compute POW(2.0, 0) to be 1.0. It then returns and completes the computation of POW(2.0, 1) and determines that it is 2.0. It then uses this value to finish the computation of POW(2.0, 2), which it calculates to be 4.0. It then uses that value to complete the computation of POW(2.0, 3). The entire process is diagrammed in Figure 14.5. (To keep the figure uncluttered, we have simplified the code so that it uses the values of the actual parameters. Technically speaking, we should use the formal value parameters X and N as local variables and initialize them to these values. However, the idea is expressed more clearly by showing the values.)

recursion within recursion

Pitfall

Infinite Recursion

Pascal places no restrictions on how recursive calls are used in function and procedure declarations. However, in order for a recursive function declaration to be useful, it must be designed so that any call of the function must ultimately terminate with some piece of code that does not depend on recursion. The function may call itself, and that recursive call may call the function again. The process may be repeated any number of times. However, the process will not terminate unless eventually one of the recursive calls does not depend on recursion in order to return a value. The general outline of a recursive function declaration is as follows:

how recursion terminates

- One or more cases in which the value returned is computed in terms of simpler cases of the same function (i.e., using recursive calls).
- One or more cases in which the value returned is computed without the use of any recursive calls. These cases without any recursion are called *base cases* or *stopping cases.*

Often an *if-then-else* statement or a series of *if-then* statements determine which of the cases will be executed. A typical scenario is for the original function call to execute a case that includes a recursive call. That recursive call may in turn execute a case that requires another recursive call. For some number of times, each recursive call produces another recursive call, but eventually one of the stopping cases should apply. Every call of the function must eventually

Sequence of recursive calls

POW : = 2.0 * POW(2.0, 2)

POW : = 2.0 * POW(2.0, 1)

POW : = 2.0 * POW(2.0, 0)

POW : = 1.0

How the final value returned is computed

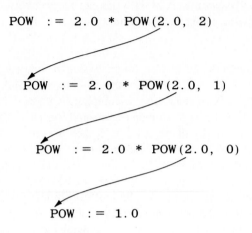

2.0 * 4.0 = 8.0

POW : = 2.0 * POW(2.0, 2)

2.0 * 2.0 = 4.0

POW : = 2.0 * POW(2.0, 1)

2.0 * 1.0 = 2.0

POW : = 2.0 * POW(2.0, 0)

1.0

POW : = 1.0

**Figure 14.5
Evaluating
the recursive
function call
POW(2.0, 3).**

lead to a stopping case, or else the function call will never end because of an infinite string of recursive calls. (In practice, a call that includes infinite recursion will terminate abnormally rather than actually running forever.)

Every call of a recursive function should eventually lead to a stopping case. The most common way to ensure that a stopping case is eventually reached is to write the function so that some numeric quantity is decreased on each recursive call and to provide a stopping case for some "small" value such as zero. This is how we designed the function POW in Figure 14.4. Look back at Figure 14.5. To compute POW(2.0, 3), the function makes the following sequence of recursive calls: POW(2.0, 2), POW(2.0, 1), and POW(2.0, 0). The call to POW(2.0, 0) returns a value by executing the stopping case:

```
if N = 0 then
    POW := 1
```

That piece of code includes no recursive call. Hence, the code does eventually terminate; a value is returned for POW(2.0, 0), and the process works its way back to the original call, which terminates and returns a value for POW(2.0, 3).

In the previous example, the series of recursive calls eventually reached a call of the function that did not involve recursion (i.e., a stopping case). If, on the other hand, every recursive call produces another recursive call, then a call to the function will, in theory, run forever. In practice, such a function will run until the computer runs out of resources and terminates the program abnormally. Phrased another way, a recursive declaration should not be "recursive all the way down." Otherwise, like the lady's explanation of the universe, a call of the function will never end, except perhaps in frustration.

Examples of such infinite recursion are not hard to come by. The following is a syntactically correct Pascal function declaration that might result from an attempt to declare an alternative version of the function Power:

example of infinite recursion

```
function RecPower(X: real; N: integer): real;
begin {RecPower}
    RecPower := 1/RecPower(X, -N)
end; {RecPower}
```

If this declaration is embedded in a program that calls this function, the compiler will translate it to machine code, and the machine code can be executed. Moreover, it even has a certain reasonableness to it. The relation

$$x^n = 1/x^{-n}$$

is true provided x is not zero. However, when called, this function will produce an infinite sequence of recursive calls. An attempt to evaluate RecPower(2.0, 3) will stop to evaluate RecPower(2.0, -3). That evaluation will in turn stop to evaluate an expression equivalent to RecPower(2.0, 3). That in turn will attempt to compute RecPower(2.0, -3). The process will proceed in a circle ad infinitum.

Stacks

To keep track of recursion, and a number of other things, most computer systems make use of a structure called a *stack*. A stack is a very specialized kind of memory structure that is analogous to a stack of paper sheets. In this analogy there is an inexhaustible supply of extra blank sheets. In order to place some information in the stack, it is written on one of these sheets of paper and placed on top of the stack of papers. To place more information in the stack, a clean sheet of paper is taken, the information is written on it, and this new sheet of paper is placed on the stack. In this straightforward way, more and more information can be placed on the stack. (This is a very common memory structure; a large number of office desks are organized in this fashion.)

Getting information out of the stack is also accomplished by a very simple procedure. The top sheet of paper can be read, and when it is no longer needed, it is thrown away. There is one complication: Only the top sheet of paper is accessible. In order to read, say, the third sheet from the top, the top two sheets must be thrown away. For this reason a stack is sometimes called a *last-in/first-out* memory structure.

Let us be a bit more precise about which pieces of paper are available to read and/or write on. In this analogy only the top sheet of paper on the stack is accessible. We will also have one other sheet that is available to work on. That extra sheet is not part of the stack, but it is still available. All sheets of paper in the stack other than the top one are not available. In order to access those sheets, the sheets above them must be thrown away.

stacks
and
recursion
Using a stack, the computer can easily keep track of recursion. Whenever a function is called, a new sheet of paper is taken. The function declaration is copied onto the sheet of paper, and the actual parameters are plugged in for the formal parameters. Then the computer starts to execute the body of the function declaration. When it encounters a recursive call, it stops the computation it is doing on that sheet in order to compute the value returned by the recursive call. But before computing the recursive call, it saves enough information so that, when it does finally determine the value returned by the recursive call, it can continue the stopped computation. This saved information is written on the sheet of paper and placed on the stack. A new sheet of paper is used for the recursive call. It writes a second copy of the function declaration on this new sheet of paper, plugs in the actual parameters, and starts to execute the recursive call. When it gets to a recursive call within the recursively called copy, it repeats the process of saving information on the stack and using a new sheet of paper for the new recursive call.

This process continues until some recursive call is completed and returns a value. When that happens, it takes the top sheet of paper off the stack. This sheet contains the partially completed computation that needs the value just returned. It is now possible to proceed with that computation. The process continues until the computation on the bottom sheet is completed. The value returned by that bottom computation is the value returned by the original function call. Depending on how many recursive calls are made and how the function declaration is written, the stack may grow and shrink in any fashion.

In Figure 14.6 we have redrawn the computation in Figure 14.5 showing how the stack behaves for this particular function call. Notice that the sheets in the stack can only be accessed in a last-in/first-out fashion, but that is exactly what is needed to keep track of recursive calls. The version currently being worked on is the one that was called by the version on top of the stack, and that is the one waiting for it to return a value.

Needless to say, computers do not have stacks of paper of this kind. This is just an analogy. The computer uses portions of memory rather than pieces of paper. The analogy is very exact, though. The contents of one of these portions of memory ("sheets of paper") is called an *activation frame*. These activation frames are handled in this last-in/first-out manner, and the memory dedicated to holding these activation frames is called a *stack*.

activation frames

Stacks are used for a number of things besides recursion. They are also used to keep track of local variables. Whenever any procedure calls another procedure, the computation of the calling procedure is suspended and an activation frame ("sheet of paper") showing where it is in its computation is placed on the stack. Then a new activation frame is started for the procedure just called. If an identifier, say X, is local to the just-called procedure, then there may be values for X in both the new and the old activation frames. These are two different X's: one local to the procedure just called and one local to some procedure with a wider scope. The computer knows they are different because they are in different activation frames. If you look back at Figure 5.11, you will see an illustration of how a stack can be used to keep track of the values of a variable identifier X when it is declared more than once. Although we did not call it a stack in Chapter 5, the illustrative boxes that contain the values of X show how a stack will change as the program is executed. The sequence of boxes shows the changes in stack contents. To simplify the figure, we have assumed that this stack does nothing other than keep track of the values of X. This is the same kind of stack as that used to keep track of recursive function calls. (Pascal does not use this exact mechanism to keep track of local variables, but uses a strategy which combines this stack mechanism with a static approach. However, many programming languages do work in this fashion, and if you do not use global variables in your procedure declarations, then your Pascal program will behave as if the computer worked in this fashion.)

stacks and local variables

Pitfall

Stack Overflow

Many systems limit the size of the stack for various reasons. Suppose the stack is limited to 20 activation frames and that the function POW is declared as shown in Figure 14.4, and then suppose that the following statement is executed:

    X : = POW(2.0, 30)

In that case the system will try to place approximately 30 activation frames on the stack. However, the stack is limited to 20 frames. The system cannot proceed

stack overflow

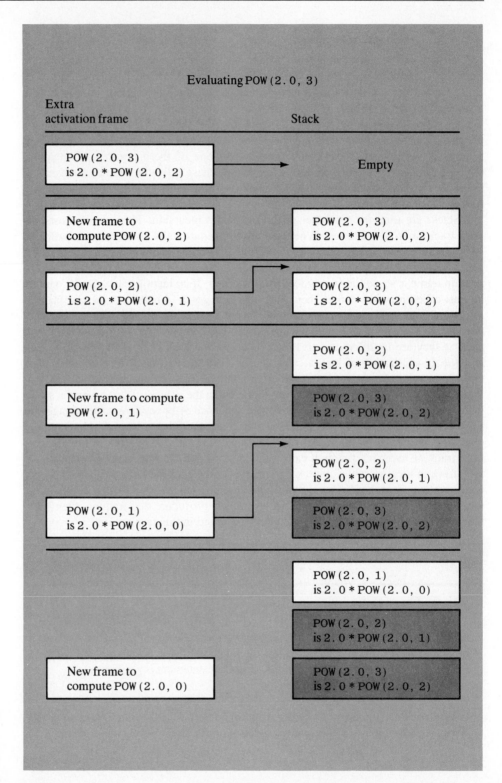

**Figure 14.6
Stack contents
while evaluating a
recursive function.**

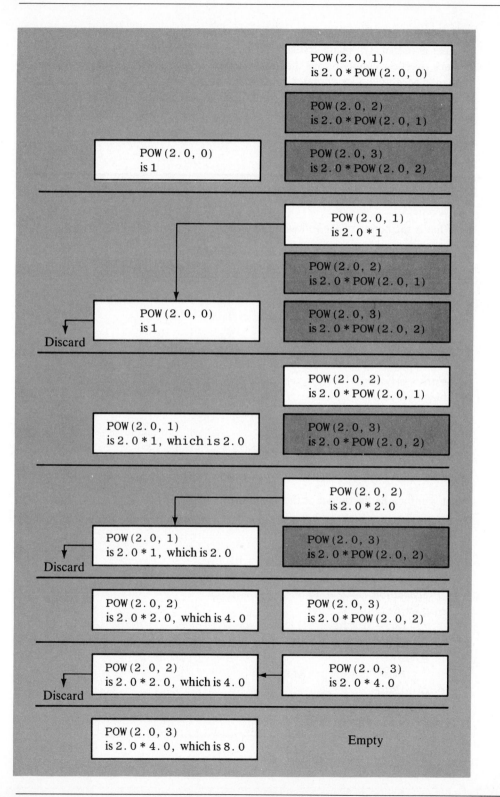

**Figure 14.6
(continued)**

within the constraints imposed, the computation is aborted and an error statement is output. On many systems the error message will say *stack overflow*. A
stack overflow simply means that the system tried to make the stack grow larger
than is permitted. One common cause of stack overflow is infinite recursion. If a
procedure or function is recursing infinitely, it will eventually try to make the
stack exceed any stack size limit.

Self-Test Exercises

1. What is the output of the following program?

```
program Exercise1(input, output);
function Mystery(N: integer): integer;
{Precondition: N >= 1}
begin{Mystery}
   if N = 1 then
      Mystery := 1
   else
      Mystery := N + Mystery(N - 1)
end; {Mystery}
begin{Program}
   writeln(Mystery(3))
end. {Program}
```

2. Suppose that the function call in Exercise 1 is changed to

```
writeln(Mystery(0))
```

What will then be the output of the program?

3. What is the output of the following program? What well-known mathematical function is Rose?

```
program Exercise3(input, output);
function Rose(N: integer): integer;
{Precondition: N >= 0}
begin{Rose}
   if N = 0 then
      Rose := 1
   else
      Rose := N * Rose(N - 1)
end; {Rose}
begin{Program}
   writeln(Rose(4))
end. {Program}
```

4. What is the output of the following program? `Cabin` is a fairly well-known mathematical function. You are likely to know of it or of a similar function.

```
program Exercise4(input, output);
function Cabin(N: integer): integer;
begin{Cabin}
  if N = 1 then
      Cabin := 0
  else
      Cabin := Cabin(N div 2) + 1
end; {Cabin}
begin{Program}
  writeln(Cabin(8))
end. {Program}
```

"I remembered too that night which is at the middle of the Thousand and One Nights when Scheherazade (through a magical oversight of the copyist) begins to relate word for word the story of the Thousand and One Nights, establishing the risk of coming once again to the night when she must repeat it, and thus to infinity."

Jorge Luis Borges, The Garden of Forking Paths

Proving Termination and Correctness for Recursive Functions
(Optional)

Since a recursive function has the potential to go on without stopping, it is similar to a loop. As with a loop, the programmer has a responsibility to make certain that a function with a recursive call will terminate, provided the precondition was satisfied. Fortunately, this can be done by the same technique that we used to demonstrate that loops terminate. To prove that a recursive function terminates, it is enough to find a *variant expression* and *threshold* with the following properties:

variant expression and threshold

0. Whenever the function is called, it will either terminate or make a recursive call.
1. There is some fixed amount such that, between one call of the function and any succeeding recursive call of that function, the value of the variant expression will decrease by at least this amount.
2. If the function is called and the value of the variant expression is less than or equal to the threshold, then the function will terminate without making any recursive calls.

Condition 0 is included to take account of factors other than recursion. For example, if the function declaration consists of a loop followed by a recursive call of the function, then the loop must be shown to terminate by means of the techniques discussed in Chapter 7. That has nothing to do with recursion, but it can affect termination.

Conditions 1 and 2 have to do with recursion. To see that they, together with 0, guarantee termination, reason as follows: Suppose the three conditions hold. Since 0 is true, every call of the function will either terminate or produce a recursive call. Since 1 is true, every recursive call will decrease the variant expression. This means that either the function will terminate, which is fine, or else the variant expression will decrease until it reaches the threshold. But if condition 2 holds, then once the variant expression reaches the threshold, the function will terminate. That covers all the cases.

Interestingly enough, the preceding set of conditions is itself recursive. Conditions 0 and 2 include a test for termination, and it is termination for which we are testing. However, this is not a problem, since the conditions only discuss termination when there are no recursive calls of the function, and that kind of termination can be checked by the techniques we discussed in Chapter 7. A complete list of our conditions would also summarize those tests for termination.

As an example, consider the recursive function POW declared in Figure 14.4. The variant expression can be taken to be

$$\text{abs}(N) + 1 \text{ \textit{for negative values of} } N, \text{ \textit{and}}$$
$$N \text{ \textit{for nonnegative values of} } N.$$

With a threshold of zero, the conditions 0 through 2 hold, and so we know that any call of the function will eventually terminate and return a value.

induction
In addition to checking that a recursive function terminates, you should also check that it always returns the correct value. The usual technique for that is called *induction*. (If you have heard of mathematical induction, it may help to note that this is the same thing.) To show that a recursive function returns the correct value, all you need show is the following:

3. If the function returns without making any recursive calls, then it returns the correct value. (This is sometimes called the *base case*.)
4. If the function is called, and if all subsequent recursive calls return the correct value, then the original call will also return the correct value. (This is sometimes called the *inductive step*.)

By the *correct value* we mean whatever it is you want the function to return. That is part of the specification of the task of the function.

The conditions are numbered 3 and 4 to emphasize that they only ensure correctness if you know that the function calls always terminate. You must also ensure that conditions 0 through 2 hold in order to guarantee that a recursive function declaration performs its task as desired.

To complete our example, let us return to the function POW defined in Figure 14.4. To complete our demonstration that it performs as desired, we must show that 3 and 4 hold.

It is easy to see that condition 3 holds. The only way that the function can terminate without a recursive call is if the value of N is 0. In that case it returns 1, which is the answer we said we wanted. Any number to the power 0 is 1 by definition. (There is a reason for that definition, but that is a topic in algebra, not program verification.)

To see that condition 4 holds, we need only recall the algebraic identities

$$x^n = x(x^{n-1}),$$

and

$$x^n = 1/x^{-n}$$

Case Study

A Simple Example of a Recursive Procedure

Problem Definition

All our remarks about recursive functions apply equally well to recursive procedures. As a first example, consider the task of writing an integer to the screen with its decimal digits reversed. For example, the number 1234 should be output as

    4321

Discussion

It is easy to decide what the first digit output should be, namely, the last digit of the number. If the number is 1234, then the first digit output is 4. Suppose we then delete that last digit from the number being processed. In the example, that would delete 4 from 1234, leaving the smaller number 123. The task remaining is then to output the digits of this smaller number in reverse order. Since this is a smaller version of the original problem, it is natural to use recursion here. We will design a recursive algorithm based on this strategy. The solution outline is as follows:

ALGORITHM

```
if the number is one digit long then
      write that digit
else
   begin
      write the last digit;
      remove the last digit;
      write the rest to the screen backwards
   end
```

In the example, 4 is the last digit and 123 is the rest. This algorithm is recursive because the last step performs the same task as the algorithm as a whole—writing a number backwards. It is routine to implement it as a recursive procedure. The imple-

recursive solution

Program

```pascal
program ReverseTheDigits(input, output);
var Number: integer;

procedure WriteBackwards(Number: integer);
{Writes the decimal digits of Number to the screen
in reverse order. Precondition: Number >= 0.}
var LastDigit, TheRest: integer;
begin {WriteBackwards}
  if Number  < 10 then
    write(Number:1)
  else
    begin {else}
      LastDigit := Number mod 10;
      TheRest := Number div 10;
      write(LastDigit:1);
      WriteBackwards(TheRest)
    end {else}
end; {WriteBackwards}

begin{Program}
  writeln('Enter a nonnegative whole number: ');
  readln(Number);
  writeln(Number, ' written backwards is: ');
  WriteBackwards(Number);
  writeln
end. {Program}
```

Sample Dialogue

Figure 14.7
Program with a
recursive
procedure.

```
Enter a nonnegative whole number:
1066
   1066 written backwards is:
6601
```

mentation is shown in Figure 14.7, and execution for the parameter 1234 is shown in Figure 14.8. The arithmetic is straightforward. The last digit is always the remainder after division by 10; that is,

(the number) *mod* 10

For example, $(1234 \text{ } mod \text{ } 10)$ is 4. "The rest" is just the quotient when the number is divided by 10; that is,

(the number) *div* 10

For example, $(1234 \text{ } div \text{ } 10)$ is 123.

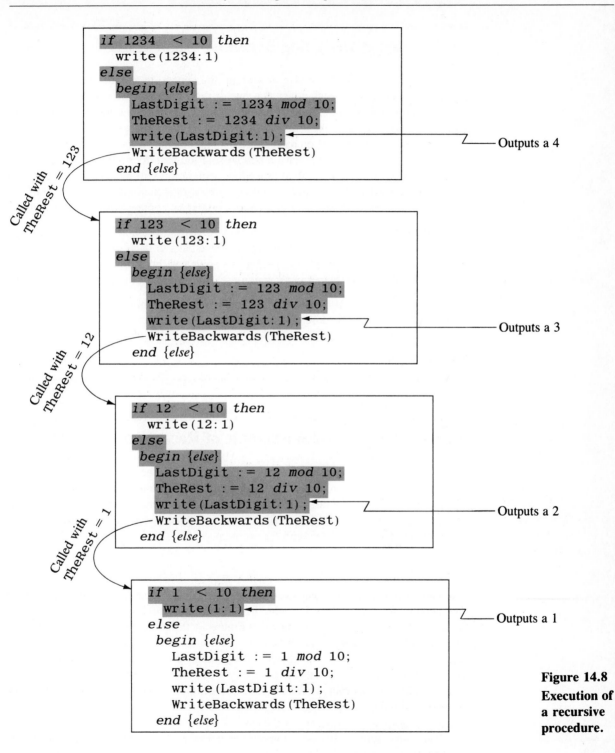

Figure 14.8 Execution of a recursive procedure.

Technique for Designing Recursive Algorithms

When one is designing a recursive procedure, the general technique is to try to divide the task into subtasks in such a way that one or more subtasks are smaller instances of the same problem. These smaller instances of the same problem will be the recursive calls. The sense in which they are smaller is a bit vague and depends on the particular problem, but the idea is that on each successive recursive call the tasks should become smaller and smaller until they have a simple solution that does not involve recursion. Hence, the algorithm and the final procedure declaration will include some cases that involve a recursive call and others that do not. As with recursive function declarations, the general outline of a recursive procedure declaration contains cases of two forms:

- One or more cases in which the procedure solves the problem in terms of simpler cases of the same problem (i.e., using recursive calls to itself).
- One or more cases in which the problem is solved without the use of any recursive calls. These cases without any recursion are called *base cases* or *stopping cases*.

As with recursive functions, every procedure call must ultimately lead to a stopping case; otherwise, the procedure call will produce infinite recursion. In the previous case study of reversing the digits in a number, the stopping case applies when the number is one digit long.

Case Study

Towers of Hanoi—An Example of Recursive Thinking

Recursion can be a very powerful programming tool. Sometimes a problem that appears to be difficult when tackled with any other programming technique can turn out to be very simple when thought of in terms of recursion. One dramatic example of this is provided by a children's game called Towers of Hanoi. As with any programming task, the first step is to understand the problem.

Problem Definition

The game consists of three pegs and a collection of rings that fit over the pegs, rather like phonograph records on a spindle. The rings are of different sizes. The initial configuration for a six-ring game is shown in Figure 14.9. Notice that the rings are stacked in order of decreasing size. A move consists of transferring a single ring from the top of one peg to that of another. The object of the game is to move all the rings from the first peg to the second peg. The difficulty is that you are never allowed to place a ring on top of one with a smaller radius. You do have one extra peg to temporarily hold rings, but the prohibition against placing a larger ring on a smaller ring applies to it as well as to the other two pegs. A solution for the case of three rings is given in Figure 14.9.

This game apparently has an impressive and long history. Legend has it that it was

Initial configuration for a six-ring game

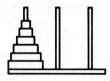

Solution for a three-ring game

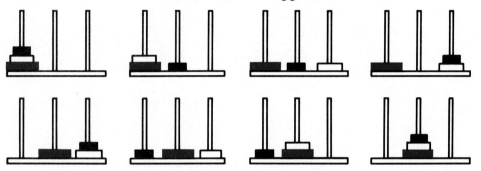

Figure 14.9
Towers of Hanoi.

invented by God at the dawn of time and was given to man as one of the major tasks of humanity. The task of solving it eventually fell to the monks of a certain monastery in what was then an obscure Eastern village called Hanoi. The legend goes on to say that when the game is completed, the last task assigned to humanity will have been accomplished and that will mark the end of the world. The version God presented to mankind had 64 rings. So do not worry about trying it with three or four rings. (Besides, it cannot end the world unless the rings and pegs are made of stone and it is played in Hanoi.)

We want a procedure that solves the problem for any number of rings. Hence, there will be one parameter N that specifies the number of rings. The procedure cannot actually move rings, and so instead it will output instructions of the form "move a ring from peg x to peg y." The list of instructions that is output will be instructions for solving the puzzle.

parameters and output (first try)

Discussion

The game sounds simple enough, but a solution has not been easy to derive, at least not until very recently. It is easy to solve it for the case of three rings, but even four can take some thought. Ten rings boggle the mind. Sixty-four is almost unimaginable. To get the feel of it, try to solve it for the case of four rings. If you do, then try the six-ring case.

Although it is very difficult to solve by other means, the solution is almost trivial if you think recursively. The trick is to reduce the problem to a smaller one of the same

thinking recursively

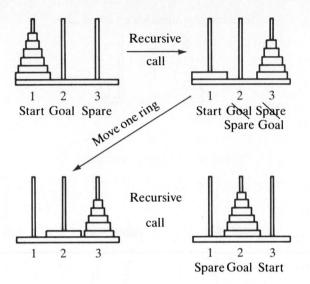

Figure 14.10
Idea of a recursive
solution.

type. The trick is illustrated in Figure 14.10. First we move all but one ring onto the spare peg. We do this by a recursive call that uses peg 3 rather than peg 2 as the goal peg. Then we move the last ring to where it belongs. After that we move the rings from the original spare peg to peg 2 (the ultimate goal peg) by another recursive call.

All the pegs are identical, and so we can mix up their roles like this. Sometimes we make peg 3 the goal peg for a recursive call, even though our ultimate goal is to move the rings to peg 2. Moving the rings from the first peg to the second using the third as a spare is exactly the same problem as moving them from, say, the first to the third using the second as a spare.

parameters
(final form)

Our analysis required that we change the roles of the various pegs. We want to move the rings to peg 2, but for the recursive calls we sometimes want to change the roles of the various pegs, using, for example, peg 3 in the role of the goal peg and thus moving some of the rings to peg 3. To allow this, we will use three more parameters, in addition to the parameter specifying the number of rings. The parameters will tell us which peg is the start peg, which is the goal peg, and which one is left over as a spare. For each call, these three parameters will be given values chosen from the integers 1, 2, and 3. The complete procedure heading will be the following, where the type PegNumber has been defined to be the subrange type 1 . . 3.

```
procedure WriteMoves(N: integer; Start, Goal, Spare: PegNumber);
{Outputs the moves needed to move N rings
from Start peg to Goal peg, using Spare as the extra peg.}
```

For example, if we want to move rings from peg 3 to peg 1 using peg 2 as the spare, then we call the procedure with Start set equal to 3, Goal set equal to 1, and Spare set equal to 2.

Program

```
program Hanoi(input, output);
type PegNumber = 1 . . 3;
var N: integer;

procedure WriteMoves(N: integer; Start, Goal, Spare: PegNumber);
{Outputs the moves needed to move N rings
from Start peg to Goal peg, using Spare as the extra peg.}
begin{WriteMoves}
   if N = 1 then
      writeln('Move a ring from ', Start:1, ' to ', Goal:1)
   else
      begin{else}
         {Spare becomes the goal peg for a recursive call.}
         WriteMoves(N − 1, Start, Spare, Goal);

         writeln('Move a ring from ', Start:1, ' to ', Goal:1);

         {Spare becomes the start peg for a recursive call.}
         WriteMoves(N − 1, Spare, Goal, Start)
      end {else}
end; {WriteMoves}

begin {Program}
   writeln('Enter the number of rings and');
   writeln('I''ll explain how to play Towers of Hanoi.');
   readln(N);
   writeln('To move ', N,' rings');
   writeln('from  peg 1 to peg 2, proceed as follows:');
   WriteMoves(N, 1, 2, 3);
   writeln('That does it.')
end. {Program}
```

Sample Dialogue

```
Enter the number of rings and
I'll explain how to play Towers of Hanoi.
3
To move 3 rings
from peg 1 to peg 2, proceed as follows:
Move a ring from 1 to 2
Move a ring from 1 to 3
Move a ring from 2 to 3
Move a ring from 1 to 2
Move a ring from 3 to 1
Move a ring from 3 to 2
Move a ring from 1 to 2
That does it.
```

Figure 14.11

**Program to play
Towers of Hanoi.**

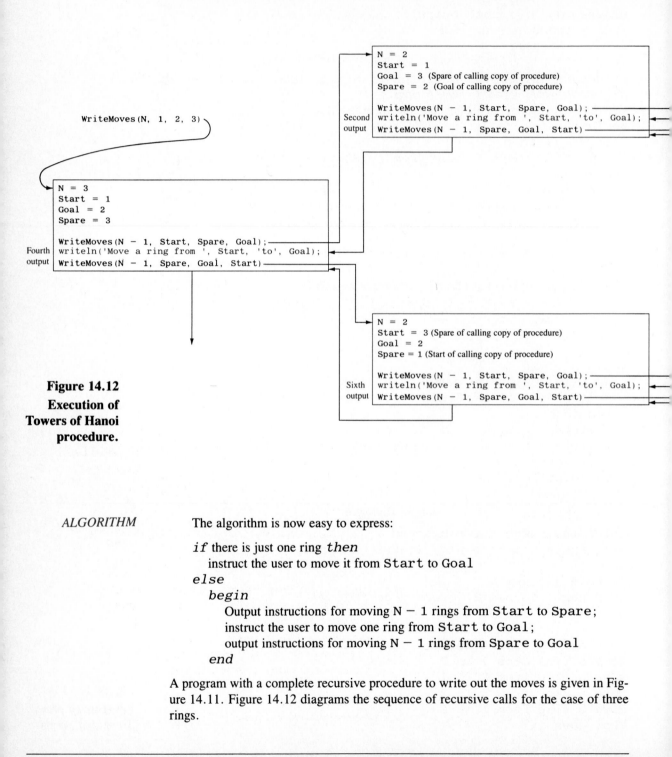

Figure 14.12
Execution of
Towers of Hanoi
procedure.

ALGORITHM

The algorithm is now easy to express:

if there is just one ring *then*
    instruct the user to move it from Start to Goal
else
    begin
        Output instructions for moving N − 1 rings from Start to Spare;
        instruct the user to move one ring from Start to Goal;
        output instructions for moving N − 1 rings from Spare to Goal
    end

A program with a complete recursive procedure to write out the moves is given in Figure 14.11. Figure 14.12 diagrams the sequence of recursive calls for the case of three rings.

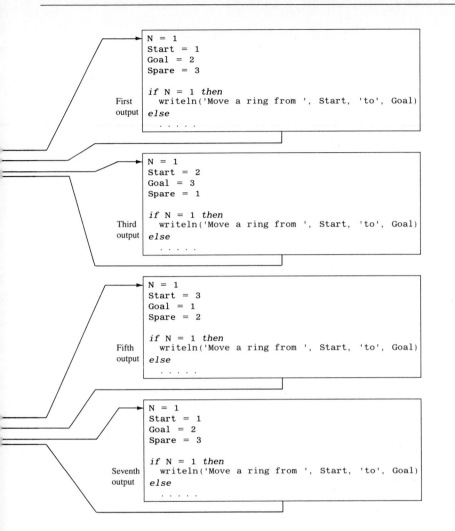

N = 1
Start = 1
Goal = 2
Spare = 3

if N = 1 then
  writeln('Move a ring from ', Start, 'to', Goal)
else
  . . . . .

First output

N = 1
Start = 2
Goal = 3
Spare = 1

if N = 1 then
  writeln('Move a ring from ', Start, 'to', Goal)
else
  . . . . .

Third output

N = 1
Start = 3
Goal = 1
Spare = 2

if N = 1 then
  writeln('Move a ring from ', Start, 'to', Goal)
else
  . . . . .

Fifth output

N = 1
Start = 1
Goal = 2
Spare = 3

if N = 1 then
  writeln('Move a ring from ', Start, 'to', Goal)
else
  . . . . .

Seventh output

**Figure 14.12
(continued)**

Recursive versus Iterative Procedures and Functions

Recursion is not absolutely necessary. In fact, many programming languages do not allow it. Any task that can be accomplished using recursion can also be done in some other way without using recursion. For example, Figure 14.4 contains a recursive function declaration. A nonrecursive version of that function is given in Figure 14.13. In such cases, the nonrecursive version typically uses a loop of some sort in place of recursion. For that reason, the nonrecursive version is usually referred to as an *iterative* version.

iterative version

On many computer systems, the recursive version of POW given in Figure 14.4 will run slower and use more storage than the iterative version given in Figure 14.13. The

```
function POW(X: real; N: integer): real;
{Returns the value of X to the N. Returns 1 whenever N is 0.
Precondition: If N is negative, then X is not zero.}
var  I: integer;
     Product, Factor: real;
begin{POW}
  Product := 1.0;
  if N >= 0 then
    Factor := X
  else
    Factor := 1/X;
  for I := 1 to abs(N) do
     Product := Product*Factor;
  POW := Product
end; {POW}
```

Figure 14.13
**Iterative version of
the function in
Figure 14.4.**

reason is that the recursive version uses a significant amount of time and storage to keep track of the recursive calls. Recall our discussion of how recursion is implemented using a stack. Suppose the recursive version is called to evaluate

POW(3.0, 10)

The computer will create about 10 stack frames in the process of evaluating this function call. This consumes an extra amount of time and memory. On the other hand, the iterative version does not do all this extra manipulating of the stack. It just performs 10 simple multiplications and returns the answer.

The POW example is typical. A recursively written function will usually run slower and use more storage than an equivalent iterative version. The difference in efficiency depends on how large the stack grows when the recursive version is used; that is, it depends on how long the string of recursive calls is. For example, the version of the function Power given in Figure 14.2 returns the same value as POW, is recursive, and yet is about as efficient as the iterative version of POW. This is because no call of Power ever produces a long string of recursive calls.

If efficiency is an important issue, it may make sense to avoid recursion. However, the efficiency issue is a subtle one. First of all, not all recursive declarations are equally inefficient. As discussed in the previous paragraph, the inefficiency introduced by the recursive call in the function Power of Figure 14.2 is negligible. Moreover, the recursion makes the code easier to read, since it reflects our normal manner of thinking about this computation. Also, recursion can sometimes make a procedure or function so much easier to understand that it would be foolish to avoid it. Consider the Towers of Hanoi procedure. If we did not think recursively, we might not have produced a solution at all. If we convert that procedure to an iterative procedure, it will be much more complicated and, as a result, will most likely contain bugs. No procedure can be considered efficient unless it gives the correct answers.

Finally, we should note that this discussion about efficiency assumes that recursive procedures are implemented with a stack using a method like the one we described. They need not be implemented in exactly that way. Some compilers will try to convert a recursive function declaration to an iterative one before they translate the declaration into machine code. On one of these compilers, recursive and iterative versions of a function will probably be equally efficient.

Case Study

Binary Search

In this section we will develop a recursive procedure that searches an array to find out whether a given value is in the array. For example, the array may contain a list of the numbers for credit cards that are no longer valid, perhaps because the card has been stolen. A store clerk will need to search the list to see if a customer's card is still valid. In Chapter 9 (Figure 9.10) we discussed a simple method for searching an array by simply checking every array element. In Chapter 12 (Figure 12.5) we showed how the search could be made more efficient if the array is first sorted. In this section we will develop a method for searching a sorted array that is much faster than either of those two algorithms.

Let us call the array A. The indexes of the array A are the integers First through Last. First and Last are some specified integers, but their values are not relevant to the discussion. In order to make the task of searching the array easier, we will assume that the array is sorted. So if the array is A, then

A[First] ≤ A[First+1] ≤ ... ≤ A[Last]

When searching an array, we are likely to want to know both whether the value is in the list and (if it is) where it is in the list. For example, if we are searching for a credit card number, then the array index may serve as a record number. Another array indexed by these same indexes may hold a phone number or other information to use for reporting the suspicious card.

Problem Definition

We will design the procedure to use two variable parameters to return the outcome of the search. One parameter, called Found, will be of type boolean and will be set to true if the value is found. If it is found, then another parameter, called Location, will be set to the index of the value found. If we use Key to denote the value being searched for, the task to be accomplished can be formulated precisely as follows:

> *Precondition: First ≤ Last; A[First] through A[Last] are sorted into increasing order.*
> *Postcondition: If Key is not one of the values A[First] through A[Last]*
> *then Found = false; otherwise A[Location] = Key and Found = true.*

Discussion

Now let us proceed to produce an algorithm to solve this task. To do so it will help to visualize the problem in very concrete terms. Suppose the list of numbers is so long that it takes a book to list them all. This is, in fact, how invalid credit card numbers are distributed to stores that do not have access to a computer. If you are a clerk and are handed a credit card, you must check to see if it is on the list and hence invalid. How would you proceed? Open the book to the middle and see if it is there; if not, and if it is smaller than the middle number, then work backward toward the beginning of the book; if it is larger than the middle number, work your way toward the back of the book. This idea produces our first draft of an algorithm:

ALGORITHM
(first version)

```
Mid := approximate midpoint between First and Last;
if Key = A[Mid] then
    begin{found Key}
        Found := true;
        Location := Mid
    end   {found Key}
else if Key < A[Mid] then
    search A[First] through A[Mid − 1]
else if Key > A[Mid] then
    search A[Mid + 1] through A[Last]
```

Since the searching of the shorter list is a smaller version of the very task that we are designing the algorithm to perform, it naturally lends itself to the use of recursion. The smaller lists can be searched with a recursive call to the algorithm.

Our pseudocode is a bit too imprecise to be easily translated into Pascal. The problem has to do with the recursive calls. There are two recursive calls shown:

```
search A[First] through A[Mid − 1]
search A[Mid + 1] through A[Last]
```

more
parameters

In order to implement the recursive call, we need two more parameters. The recursive call specifies that a subrange of the array is to be searched. In one case, it is the elements indexed by First through Mid − 1. In the other case, it is the elements Mid + 1 through Last. The two extra parameters will specify the lower and upper bounds of the search. Let us call these two parameters Low and High. Using these parameters instead of First and Last, we can express the pseudocode more precisely as follows:

ALGORITHM
(first refinement)

```
To search A[Low] through A[High], do the following:

Mid := approximate midpoint between Low and High;
if Key = A[Mid] then
    begin{found Key}
        Found := true;
        Location := Mid
    end   {found Key}
else if Key < A[Mid] then
    search A[Low] through A[Mid − 1]
else if Key > A[Mid] then
    search A[Mid + 1] through A[High]
```

To search the entire array, the algorithm would be executed with Low set equal to First and High set equal to Last. The recursive calls will use other values for Low and High. For example, the first recursive call will set Low equal to First and High equal to the calculated value Mid − 1.

As with any recursive algorithm, we must ensure that our algorithm ends rather than producing infinite recursion. If the number is found on the list, then there is no recursive call and the process terminates, but we need some way to detect when the number is not on the list. On each recursive call the value of Low is increased or the value of High is decreased. If they ever pass and Low actually becomes larger than High, then we will know that there are no more indexes left to check and that the number is not in the array. If we add this test to our pseudocode, we obtain a complete solution, as shown in Figure 14.14.

termination

ALGORITHM (final version)

Now we can routinely translate the pseudocode into Pascal. The result is shown in Figure 14.15. The procedure Search is an implementation of the above recursive algorithm. A diagram of how the procedure performs on a sample array is given in Figure 14.16.

Notice that the procedure Search solves a more general problem than the original task. Our goal was to design a procedure to search an entire array of type List. Yet the procedure will let us search any interval of the array by specifying the index bounds Low and High. This is a common phenomenon when designing recursive procedures. Frequently, it is necessary to solve a more general problem in order to be able to express the recursive algorithm. In this case, we only wanted the answer in the case where Low and High are set equal to First and Last. However, the recursive calls will set them to values other than First and Last.

solving a more general problem

The binary search algorithm is extremely fast compared to an algorithm that simply tries all array elements in order. In the binary search, we eliminate about half the array from consideration right at the start. We then eliminate a quarter and then an eighth of the array, and so forth. These savings add up to a dramatically fast algorithm. For an array of 100 elements, the binary search will never need to compare more than

efficiency

```
if Low > High then
   Found := false
else
  begin{Low <= High}
    Mid := approximate midpoint between Low and High;
    if Key = A[Mid] then
        begin{found Key}
           Found := true;
           Location := Mid
        end   {found Key}
      else if Key < A[Mid] then
         search A[Low] through A[Mid − 1]
      else if Key > A[Mid] then
         search A[Mid + 1] through A[High]
  end   {Low <= High}
```

Figure 14.14
Pseudocode for binary search.

```
program BinarySearch(input, output);
const First = 1;
      Last = 10;
type Index = First . . Last;
     List = array[Index] of integer;
var A: List;
    Key: integer;
    Found: boolean;
    Location: Index;

procedure Search(var A: List; Low, High, Key: integer;
                      var Found: boolean; var Location: Index);
{Precondition: A[Low] through A[High] are sorted into increasing order.
Postcondition: Key and A are unchanged; if Key does not equal one of A[Low]
through A[High], then Found = false, else Found = true and A[Location] = Key.}
var Mid: integer;
begin {Search}
   if Low > High then
      Found : = false
   else
     begin{Low <= High}
        Mid : = (Low + High) div 2;
        if Key = A[Mid] then
            begin{found Key}
               Found : = true;
               Location : = Mid
            end   {found Key}
        else if Key < A[Mid] then
            Search(A, Low, Mid − 1, Key, Found, Location)
        else{if Key > A[Mid] then}
            Search(A, Mid + 1, High, Key, Found, Location)
     end   {Low <= High}
end;   {Search}

begin{Program}
   . . .
   This portion of the program contains some
   code to fill the array A. The exact
   details are irrelevant to the example.
   . . .
   writeln('Enter number to be located:');
   readln(Key);
   Search(A, First, Last, Key, Found, Location);
   if Found  then
      writeln(Key, ' is in location  ', Location)
   else
      writeln(Key, ' is not in the array')
end. {Program}
```

**Figure 14.15
Program with
a recursive
procedure for
binary search.**

seven elements to the key. By contrast, either of the two simple search algorithms we have presented—Figures 9.10 and 12.5—could require as many as 100 comparisons, and on the average will require 50 comparisons to locate a key that is in the array. Moreover, the larger the array is, the more dramatic the savings will be. On an array with 1000 elements, the binary search will use at most 11 comparisons, compared to an average of 500 for the simple search algorithms. There are some cases for which the search algorithm in Figure 12.5 is faster in determining that a key is not in the array. However, these cases are not the most commonly occurring ones, and in other cases the binary search algorithm is dramatically faster.

Any recursive procedure can be replaced by an iterative procedure that accomplishes the same task. In some cases, the iterative procedure may be more efficient, and

iterative version

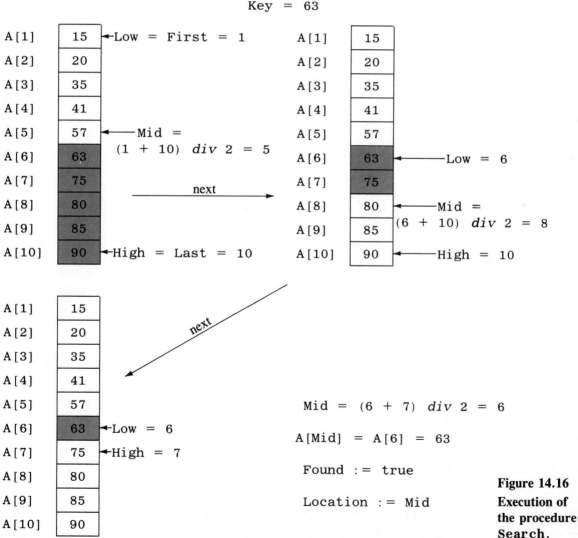

Figure 14.16 Execution of the procedure Search.

```
procedure Search(var A: List; First, Last, Key: integer;
                         var Found: boolean; var Location: Index);
```
{Precondition: A[First] through A[Last] are sorted into increasing order.
Postcondition: Key and A are unchanged; if Key does not equal one of A[First]
through A[Last], then Found = false else Found = true and A[Location] = Key.}
```
var Mid, Low, High: integer;
begin {Search}
  Low := First;
  High := Last;
  Found := false; {so far}
  while (Low <= High) and (not Found) do
    begin{while}
      Mid := (Low + High) div 2;
      if Key = A[Mid] then
          begin{found Key}
              Found := true;
              Location := Mid
          end   {found Key}
      else if Key < A[Mid] then
          High := Mid − 1
      else {if Key > A[Mid] then}
          Low := Mid + 1
    end{while}
end;   {Search}
```

Figure 14.17
Iterative version of
binary search.

if efficiency is a major issue, you may want to convert a recursive procedure to an iterative one. An iterative version of the binary search algorithm is given in Figure 14.17. On some systems it will run more efficiently than the recursive version. The algorithm for the iterative version was derived by mirroring the recursive version. In the iterative version, the local variables Low and High mirror the roles of the parameters of the same names in the recursive version. As this example illustrates, it often makes sense to derive a recursive algorithm even if you expect to later convert it to an iterative algorithm.

Case Study

Quicksort
(Optional)

Problem Definition

In this case study we will describe an efficient method for sorting an array of integers. The algorithm, which is called *quicksort,* has some similarity to the binary search algorithm of the previous case study. We will develop the algorithm into a procedure for sorting an array of integers of the same type as we used in the binary search case study.

Discussion

In the binary search algorithm we divided a sorted array at its midpoint and then compared the sought after value to the midpoint value in order to determine which half of the array could possibly contain the sought after value. We can apply this same general idea of dividing the array in half and comparing values to an approximate midpoint value in order to obtain an efficient algorithm for sorting an array. The basic idea is simple. Suppose you know the value that belongs in the middle of the array, or at least the approximate middle of the array. We will call this value the *splitting value*. When the array is correctly sorted, this splitting value will have some particular index giving its array location. Suppose we somehow put this splitting value into its correct location in the array, somehow put all the values less than or equal to it in array positions before the splitting value, and somehow put all the values greater than the splitting value in array positions after the splitting value. We do not sort the values less than the splitting value; we simply place them, in any order, in array positions before the splitting value. Similarly, we do not sort the values greater than the splitting value; we simply place them, in any order, in array positions after the splitting value. After this initial moving of array elements, we have moved the array closer to being sorted. We know that the splitting value of the array is in the correct position. We also know that all other values are in the correct segment of the array, either the segment before the splitting value or the segment after the splitting value. However, although we know they are in the correct segment, those segments are still not sorted. One way to proceed is to sort the two segments separately. This works because we know that all values in the first segment are less than all values in the second segment and so no value ever needs to move from one segment to the other. How do we sort the two segments? These are smaller versions of the original sorting task and so we can sort the two smaller array portions by recursive calls.

How do we know our recursive procedure will stop? If we continue to divide the array into smaller portions in the way we outlined, we will eventually get down to array segments of size one and we can use that as a stopping case. An array segment with just one element is always sorted. Hence, for array segments of size one, our procedure can return without making any recursive calls.

stopping case

The above idea is sound except for one problem. How do we find a splitting value and its correct final position in the sorted array? There is no obvious way to quickly find the midpoint value until the array is sorted. Our solution will be to take an arbitrary array value and use it as the splitting value. As a result, we may not be dividing the array exactly in half, but as long as we do divide it into smaller pieces our algorithm will still eventually sort the array. We perform the subtask of dividing the array elements with a procedure called `Partition`. The procedure `Partition` chooses some arbitrary splitting value, positions it at the correct index position, and divides the remaining array elements as we have described. The procedure will not necessarily do those three things in that order, but it will do them all. Because the procedure will be used on subportions of the array when we make recursive calls, it will need two pa-

rameters that give the lowest and highest indexes for the array portion being partitioned. The procedure heading is as follows:

procedure Partition(*var* A: List; Low, High: integer;
                                         var SplitIndex: integer);
{*Chooses a splitting value SplitV, rearranges the array elements A[Low] through A[High],
and sets the value of SplitIndex so that A[SplitIndex] = SplitV and the following holds:
A[I] <= SplitV, for all I < SplitIndex, and A[I] > SplitV, for all I > SplitIndex.*}

We will formulate our sorting algorithm as a recursive procedure called Quicksort, which makes a call to the procedure Partition. The procedure Quicksort will need one variable parameter for the array. When it is called recursively, the
procedure will be called on to sort subparts of the array. Hence, it will also need two
parameters to specify the indexes that bound the subarray to be sorted. The complete
procedure Quicksort is given in Figure 14.18. At this point, you need not worry
about the code for the procedure Partition. We will discuss it in the next few paragraphs. For now, simply look at the declarations for the procedure Quicksort
and convince yourself that it works correctly, assuming that the procedure Partition does what it is supposed to do. The code for Quicksort is straightforward.
However, we still need to show how the code for the procedure Partition was
developed.

Since we have no information about the values in the array, any value is equally
likely to be the value that belongs in the middle of the array. Moreover, we know that
the algorithm will work no matter what value we use for the splitting value. Hence, we
arbitrarily choose the first array element to use as the splitting value.

The procedure Partition will move all the values that are less than or equal to
this splitting value toward the beginning of the array and all values that are greater than
this splitting value toward the tail end of the array. Because the splitting value is not
necessarily the value that belongs at the midpoint position of the array, we do not know
where the dividing line between the two array portions belongs. Hence, we do not
know how far forward we need to move elements less than or equal to the splitting

Figure 14.18
Procedure for
quicksort.

```
type Index = First. Last;
     List = array[Index] of integer;

procedure Exchange(var X, Y: integer);
{Interchanges the values of X and Y.}
var Temp: integer;
begin{Exchange}
  Temp := X;
  X := Y;
  Y := Temp
end; {Exchange}
```

```
procedure Partition(var A: List; Low, High: integer;
                                  var SplitIndex: integer);
```
{Chooses a splitting value SplitV, rearranges the array elements A[Low] through A[High], and sets the value of SplitIndex so that A[SplitIndex] = SplitV and the following holds: A[I] <= SplitV, for all I < SplitIndex, and A[I] > SplitV, for all I > SplitIndex.}
```
var SplitV, Up, Down: integer;
begin{Partition}
   SplitV := A[Low];

   Up := Low;
   Down := High;

   repeat
       while (A[Up] <= SplitV) and (Up < High) do
          Up := Up + 1;
       while (A[Down] > SplitV) and (Down > Low) do
          Down := Down - 1;
```
{A[I] <= SplitV, for all I < Up; A[I] > SplitV, for all I > Down; A[Up] > SplitV and A[Down] <= SplitV}
```
       if Up < Down then {there is still room for both portions to grow so}
           Exchange(A[Up], A[Down])  {and iterate the loop}
   until Up >= Down;
```
{A[I] <= SplitV, for all I < Up; A[I] > SplitV, for all I > Down; A[Up] > SplitV and A[Down] <= SplitV}
```
   SplitIndex := Down;
```
{Move the split value SplitV to A[SplitIndex].}
```
   Exchange(A[Low], A[SplitIndex]);
end; {Partition}
```

```
procedure Quicksort(var A: List; Low, High: integer);
```
{Sorts the array positions A[Low] through A[High] using the Quicksort algorithm. If Low < High, the array elements A[Low] through A[High] are rearranged so that A[Low] <= A[Low+1] <=...<= A[High]. If Low >= High, nothing happens.}
```
var SplitIndex: integer;
begin{Quicksort}
    if Low < High then
      begin{A[Low..High] has at least two elements.}
         Partition(A, Low, High, SplitIndex);
         Quicksort(A, Low, SplitIndex - 1);
         Quicksort(A, SplitIndex + 1, High)
      end {A[Low..High] has at least two elements.}
   {else if Low >= High then do nothing}
end; {Quicksort}
```

Figure 14.18
(continued)

value nor do we know how far toward the end of the array we must move elements that are greater than the splitting value. We solve this dilemma by working inward from the two ends of the array. We move smaller elements to the beginning of the array and we move larger elements to the tail end of the array. In this way we obtain two segments, one segment of smaller elements growing inward from the front of the array and one segment of larger elements growing inward from the tail end of the array. When these two segments meet we have correctly partitioned the array. The correct location for the splitting value is at the boundary of these two segments. Starting at the front of the array, the algorithm passes over smaller elements at the front of the array until it encounters a larger element. This larger element is not in the correct segment and must somehow move to the tail segment. Starting at the tail end of the array, the algorithm passes over larger elements at that end of the array until it encounters a smaller element. This smaller element is not in the correct segment and must somehow move to the front segment. At that point we know that the elements in the two segments up to, but not including, these out-of-place elements are in the correct segment of the array. If we switch these two out-of-place elements, then we will know that they also are in the correct portion of the array. Using this technique of locating and switching elements at incorrect ends of the array, our algorithm proceeds to continually expand the segment at the front end of the array and the segment at the tail end of the array until these two segments meet.

For example, suppose the following represents our array value:

| 40 | 20 | 10 | 80 | 60 | 50 | 7 | 30 | 100 | 90 | 70 |

We choose the first value, 40, as our splitting value. Starting at the beginning we look for the first element that is not less than or equal to the splitting value. That is the 80. Starting from the other end we look for the first value that is not greater than the splitting value. That is the 30. We use two variables called Up and Down to hold the indexes of these two array elements. The array can be represented as follows:

| 40 | 20 | 10 | 80 | 60 | 50 | 7 | 30 | 100 | 90 | 70 |

        ↑   ↑
       Up   Down

We have just located two elements in incorrect segments of the array. If we interchange them, the array will be closer to being divided correctly. After the exchange the array will contain

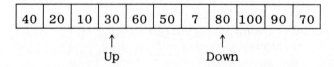

| 40 | 20 | 10 | 30 | 60 | 50 | 7 | 80 | 100 | 90 | 70 |

        ↑   ↑
       Up   Down

We now repeat the process. Continuing from the places we left off, we increment Up until we find an element larger than the splitting value and decrement Down until we find an element less than or equal to the splitting value. That changes the values of Up and Down so that we obtain the following situation:

| 40 | 20 | 10 | 30 | 60 | 50 | 7 | 80 | 100 | 90 | 70 |

                 ↑   ↑
               Up   Down

Exchanging these two elements places them in the correct array portions and yields the following array value:

| 40 | 20 | 10 | 30 | 7 | 50 | 60 | 80 | 100 | 90 | 70 |

                 ↑   ↑
               Up   Down

If we continue to look for elements to exchange, we will increment Up until it reaches the element 50 and we will decrement Down past the element 50 to the index of the element 7. At this point the indexes Up and Down have passed each other so the situation is as follows:

| 40 | 20 | 10 | 30 | 7 | 50 | 60 | 80 | 100 | 90 | 70 |

               ↑ ↑
             Down Up

Once the indexes Up and Down pass each other, we have partitioned the array. All elements less than or equal to the splitting value of 40 are in the first five positions. All elements greater than the splitting value of 40 are in the last six positions. However, the splitting value is not yet at the dividing point between the two parts of the array. To complete the algorithm, we move the splitting value, 40, to the last position in the first of the two array segments. Because we know that the index Down is one beyond (i.e., one less than) the segment of larger elements at the tail end of the array, we know that it is the last index in the segment of smaller elements at the front of the array. Hence, A [Down] is where the splitting value 40 belongs. After moving the splitting value the array configuration is as follows:

| 7 | 20 | 10 | 30 | 40 | 50 | 60 | 80 | 100 | 90 | 70 |

               ↑ ↑
             Down Up

The pseudocode for our algorithm is given below. The splitting value is stored in the variable SplitV. The complete code for the procedure is given in Figure 14.18.

1. Initialize values:

```
SplitV := A[Low];
Up := Low;  Down := High.
```

2. Repeat the following until Up and Down pass each other:
  2a. Increase Up until A[Up] > SplitV.
  2b. Decrease Down until A[Down] <= SplitV.
  2c. If Up < Down, then there is still room for both end portions to grow so interchange the values of A[Up] and A[Down]

3. Set SplitIndex and position the splitting value:
  3a. SplitIndex := Down;
  3b. Interchange A[Low], which still contains the splitting value, and A[SplitIndex].

efficiency

If the two subarrays produced by the procedure Partition are of approximately equal size, then the number of levels of recursion will be relatively small. If we are unlucky and one subarray always contains almost the entire array, then the number of levels of recursion will be relatively large and the procedure will take longer to sort the array. Ironically, this means that our procedure will run slowest when the array is already sorted. If the array elements are in random order, then the splitting value will be close enough to the midpoint value most of the time and the procedure will run much faster than the sorting algorithm we developed in Chapter 9. If there is a likelihood of using this procedure on arrays that are already sorted or almost sorted, then it may pay to use a different splitting value, such as the middle value of the array. However, our procedure, without any changes, will sort any array. Only the efficiency of the procedure is affected by the choice of a splitting value.

Forward Declarations
(Optional)

Normally, you declare a procedure or function before the place where it is first used. However, there is a way around this rule. If you wish to declare a procedure after the declaration of some other procedure that uses it, you can, provided you warn the compiler by including a *forward declaration* before the first location where the procedure is called. A forward declaration consists of the procedure heading followed by the identifier forward and terminated by a semicolon. For example,

```
procedure Reject(var Ans: char); forward;
```

The procedure declaration can then be placed anywhere after the forward declaration. Since the formal parameter list is given in the forward declaration, it is not given again when the procedure is declared. (However, it is a good idea to include the parameter list in a comment.) Functions as well as procedures can be given forward declarations in this way.

mutual recursion

The program in Figure 14.19 requires a forward declaration. In that program the procedures GetAnswer and Reject each include a call to the other. Such a phenomenon is called *mutual recursion*. Forward declarations can also be used for less essential reasons, such as for putting all the most important procedures together in one place.

Program

```
program Test(input, output);
{Tests the mutually recursive procedures GetAnswer and Reject.}
var Ans: char;

procedure Reject(var Ans: char); forward;
{Outputs a message saying Ans is not an acceptable
answer and then calls the procedure GetAnswer(Ans).}

procedure GetAnswer(var Ans: char);
{Sets the value of Ans to 'Y' or 'N' depending on what the user
types in. Repeats the process until the user types in one of these
two characters. Mutually recursive with the procedure Reject.}
begin{GetAnswer}
  writeln('Answer cap Y for Yes or cap N for No.');
  readln(Ans);
  if not (Ans in ['Y', 'N']) then
    Reject(Ans)
end; {GetAnswer}

procedure Reject{(var Ans: char)};
begin{Reject}
  writeln(Ans, ' is not an acceptable response.');
  GetAnswer(Ans)
end; {Reject}

begin{Program}
  writeln('This is a test.');
  GetAnswer(Ans);
  writeln('The value of Ans is ', Ans);
  writeln('That ends the test.')
end. {Program}
```

Sample Dialogue

```
This is a test.
Answer cap Y for Yes or cap N for No.
y
y is not an acceptable response.
Answer cap Y for Yes or cap N for No.
OK
O is not an acceptable response.
Answer cap Y for Yes or cap N for No.
Y
The value of Ans is Y
That ends the test.
```

**Figure 14.19
(Optional)
Example of
a forward
declaration.**

Summary of Problem Solving and Programming Techniques

- If a problem can be reduced to smaller instances of the same problem, then a recursive solution is likely to be easy to find and easy to implement.
- A recursive algorithm for a function or procedure declaration normally contains two kinds of cases: one or more cases that include a recursive call and one or more *stopping* cases in which the problem is solved without the use of any recursive calls.
- When writing recursive procedures or functions, always check to see that the procedure will not produce infinite recursion.
- When you are designing a recursive procedure to solve a task, it is often necessary to solve a more general problem than the given task. This may be required in order to allow for the proper recursive calls, since the smaller problems may not be exactly the same type of problem as the given task. For example, in the binary search problem, the task was to search an entire array, but the recursive solution is an algorithm to search any portion of the array (either all of it or a part of it).

To iterate is human, to recurse divine.

Anonymous

Exercises

Self-Test Exercises

5. What is the output of the following program?

```
program Test2(input, output);
procedure Cheers(N: integer);
begin{Cheers}
  if N = 1 then
    writeln('Hurray')
  else
    begin{else}
      write('Hip ');
      Cheers(N - 1)
    end {else}
end; {Cheers}
begin{Program}
  Cheers(3)
end. {Program}
```

6. Write an iterative version of the function `Mystery` declared in Exercise 1.

7. Write an iterative version of the function `Rose` declared in Exercise 3.

8. Write a recursive procedure that has one parameter which is a positive integer and that writes out that number of asterisks `'*'` to the screen.

Interactive Exercises

9. Take a pad of paper to use as the inexhaustible supply of paper for a stack. Simulate the following procedure call using a stack of real paper. First, use the one-word sentence *Hi*. Next, use a sentence of your own choice that is about 10 characters long. After that, type up the program and run it.

```
program ReverseInput(input, output);
procedure RecReadWrite;
const Period = '.';
var Letter: char;
begin{RecReadWrite}
   read(Letter);
   if Letter <> Period then
      RecReadWrite;
   write(Letter)
end; {RecReadWrite}
begin{Program}
   writeln('Type in a sentence ending with a period.');
   RecReadWrite;
   writeln
end. {Program}
```

10. Get hold of a real Towers of Hanoi game. Run the program in Figure 14.11 and follow its instructions for playing the game. Also simulate the program using a stack of paper, as in the previous exercise. The stack simulation is worth doing even if you do not have the game available.

Programming Exercises

11. Write a recursive function with one argument N of type `integer` that returns the Nth Fibonacci number. See Exercise 28 in Chapter 7 for the definition of Fibonacci numbers.

12. The formula for computing the number of ways of choosing *r* different things from a set of *n* things is the following:

$$C(n,r) = \frac{n!}{r!\,(n-r)!}$$

$n!$ is the factorial function $(n! = n*(n-1)*(n-2)* \ldots *1)$. Discover a recursive version of the above formula and write a recursive Pascal function that computes the value of the formula.

13. Write a recursive procedure that has as arguments an array of characters and two bounds on array indexes. The procedure should reverse the order of those entries in the array whose indexes are between the two bounds. For example, if the array is

A[1] = 'A' A[2] = 'B' A[3] = 'C' A[4] = 'D' A[5] = 'E'

and the bounds are 2 and 5, then after the procedure is run the array elements should be

A[1] = 'A' A[2] = 'E' A[3] = 'D' A[4] = 'C' A[5] = 'B'

Embed the procedure in a program and test it.

14. Write an iterative version of the procedure in the previous exercise. Embed it in a program and test it.

15. Write a recursive procedure to sort an array of integers into ascending order using the following idea: First place the smallest element in the first position, and then sort the rest of the array by a recursive call. (This is a recursive version of the selection sort algorithm discussed in Chapter 9.)

16. Write a procedure that takes two parameters that are arrays of integers of the same size and one parameter that is an array of integers of twice that size. The procedure assumes that the two smaller arrays are sorted and copies their contents into the larger array. It does so in such a way that the integers in the larger array are also sorted. Embed the procedure in a program in order to test it.

17. Use the ideas of the previous exercise to design a recursive sorting procedure that works along the following general lines: The array is divided in half. Each half is sorted by a recursive call and then the two halves are merged into a single sorted array. Embed the procedure in a program and test it.

18. Write an iterative version of the procedure in the previous exercise.

19. Write an iterative version of the procedure `WriteMoves` from the Towers of Hanoi program (Figure 14.11).

20. Write a set of procedures for using an array of characters as a stack. There should be one procedure to add a character to the stack, one to remove a character, and one to read the "top" character on the stack.

21. Write a recursive procedure that takes as input an array of characters and outputs all permutations of the characters in the array. The array can hold a maximum of five characters, but need not be full. One other parameter tells how many array elements are being used.

22. Find a formula for the number of times a ring is transferred from one peg to another in the Towers of Hanoi game with *n* rings. Compute the values for *n* equal to 5, 10, and 20.

23. Rewrite the Towers of Hanoi procedure so that it draws a stylized picture of the game being played. The output should be a series of pictures showing the game configuration after each ring is moved.

24. A *pretty-print* program takes a program, which may not be indented in any particular way, and produces a copy with the same program indented so that *begin/end*

pairs line up, with inner pairs indented more than outer pairs, and so that *if-then-else* statements are indented, with the *if* and *else* lined up and with comments lined up and so forth. Write a program that reads a Pascal program from one text file and produces a pretty-print version of the program in a second text file. To make it easier, simply do this for the body of the program, ignoring the declarations, and assume that all substatements of complex statements (other than compound statements themselves) are compound statements enclosed in *begin/end* pairs. To make it harder, add any or all of the features omitted from the easy version.

References for Further Reading

P. Helman and R. Veroff, *Intermediate Problem Solving and Data Structures,* 1986, Benjamin/Cummings, Menlo Park, Ca., Chapters 4 and 5.

E.S. Roberts, *Thinking Recursively,* 1986, John Wiley & Sons, New York.

J.S. Rohl, *Recursion via Pascal,* 1984, Cambridge Computer Science Texts 19, Cambridge University Press, Cambridge and New York, Chapter 1.

SOLVING
NUMERIC PROBLEMS

I confess that I cannot recall any case within my experience which looked at first glance so simple, and yet which presented such difficulties.

SIR ARTHUR CONAN DOYLE,
(SHERLOCK HOLMES) THE MAN WITH THE TWISTED LIP

Chapter Contents

Most of the computing done by scientists and engineers involves computing with numbers, and more often than not with fractional numbers rather than with integers. The general program-design rules that we have presented throughout this book apply to numeric calculations. There are also some additional considerations that apply specifically to numeric calculations. These considerations arise because of a very important but perhaps not obvious principle. To illustrate the principle, consider the following very simple piece of code, and predict its output:

```
X := 1/3 + 1/3 + 1/3;
writeln(X)
```

The calculation hardly needs a computer. The expected output is 1.0. Yet many computers will give an output such as

```
0.9999
```

One need not be Sherlock Holmes to observe that the computer's performance is either incorrect or more subtle than our simple mental model of arithmetic. As it turns out, the second alternative is the better explanation. The numbers inside a computer are unlike the numbers you learned about in mathematics classes from grade school through calculus. Consequently, you must learn to think quite differently when performing involved numeric calculations on a computer. A detailed treatment of numeric programming techniques is beyond the scope of this book, but in this chapter we will describe some of the basic principles involved.

A Hypothetical Decimal Computer

Most computers work in binary notation, and some of the problems that arise when one is doing numeric calculations are due to the differences between binary and decimal notation. However, the difference between the two ways of writing numerals is small, and the problems caused by this difference are typically small. We will discuss numeric calculations in terms of a fictitious computer that works in decimal (base ten) rather than in binary (base two) notation. Since we normally think in base ten, this will make the entire process easier to understand. Aside from the fact that it works in base ten, our hypothetical computer handles numbers in a very typical way.

word
size

In Chapter 1 we observed that most computers have their main memory divided into a series of locations called *words*. Numeric values are usually stored one value per word. The size of a word will vary from machine to machine, but usually all words in any one machine are of the same size. One word of our hypothetical computer has room for eight symbols, each either a sign or a decimal digit. Hence, a word may be diagrammed as follows:

Each of the small boxes within a word can hold any one of the following 12 symbols: 0, 1, 2, 3, 4, 5, 6, 7, 8, 9, +, −.

storing
integers

In our hypothetical computer, values of type `integer` are stored as their usual base ten numeral preceded by a sign. For example, the number 2957 would be stored as

| + | 0 | 0 | 0 | 2 | 9 | 5 | 7 |

The number −67543 would be stored as

| − | 0 | 0 | 6 | 7 | 5 | 4 | 3 |

The largest integer that can be stored in our computer is thus

| + | 9 | 9 | 9 | 9 | 9 | 9 | 9 |

maxint

which is one less than ten million. With Pascal implemented on our computer in this way, the value of `maxint` is `9999999`. Similarly, the smallest possible negative integer value is minus this amount.

floating point
(real)
numbers

On our computer, values of type `real` are stored in what is called *floating point notation*. This is a variation on the E notation used to write `real` constants in Pascal. The computer word is divided into two parts. On our hypothetical computer, one part consists of five boxes and the other part consists of three boxes. The value of each real number is first converted to a form consisting of a decimal fraction multiplied by a power of ten. For example, the value 123.4 would be converted to the equivalent form

$$+0.1234 \times 10^{+3}$$

fractional part The number with the decimal point in it is called the *fractional part* (or *mantissa*). The fraction part (including the sign) is stored in the first five boxes, and the exponent of 10 (including its sign) is stored in the last three boxes. So 123.4 is stored as

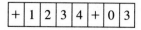

exponent part The position of the decimal point is assumed to be before the first digit. It is not marked in any way in the computer word. The division between the exponent part and the fractional part is also fixed and understood by the computer. It is not marked in any way. (In our hypothetical computer, the boundary can be inferred by the presence of a plus or minus sign. However, in a typical computer, plus and minus would be represented by two digits, such as 0 and 1.)

significant digits Other examples of storing values of type real are given in Figure 15.1. Notice that all numbers are normalized so that the fractional part has the decimal point immediately in front of the first nonzero digit. This is an attempt to preserve the maximum number of significant digits. Consider the number 0.01234. If the computer merely stores the first four digits after the decimal point, then the final digit 4 would be lost. However, because the computer normalizes the position of the decimal point, this number is stored as follows:

$$+0.1234 \times 10^{-1}$$

The normalization has saved that last digit. This moving of the decimal point is the origin of the term "floating point."

equality of reals There is room for only four decimal digits in our computer. For this reason, the value stored is sometimes only an approximation of the value we might expect a Pascal expression to represent. For example, 0.1234123 and 0.12340 have the same representation in our computer. Hence, on our hypothetical computer, the following boolean expression evaluates to true:

$$0.1234123 = 0.12340$$

As this example indicates, testing for equality between two values of type real is pointless and even dangerous.

Our computer rounds numbers when they have too many digits to fit in a word. For example, 765.46 is rounded to 765.5. Some systems truncate the number (i.e., discard the extra digits) instead. If our computer were to truncate instead of round, then the number 765.46 would be stored as 765.4 instead of 765.5.

largest real number On our computer, the largest positive value of type real that we can store would look as follows in memory:

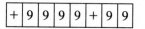

−0.1234E+03

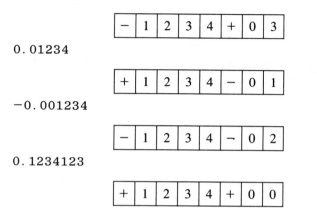

0.01234

−0.001234

0.1234123

**Figure 15.1
Storing real
(floating point)
values.**

Expressed more conventionally, this is the value

0.9999×10^{99}

Hence, the largest possible value of type `real` is about 10^{99}. By contrast, the largest possible value of type `integer` is only 9999999, or about 10^7.

If a program attempts to compute a value of type `real` whose exponent is too large to fit into the space allocated for one exponent, that is called *real overflow* or *floating point overflow*. Similarly, if a program attempts to compute a value of type `integer` that is larger than `maxint` or smaller than the smallest integer that can be held in one word, that is called *integer overflow*. (Remember, small negative numbers are large in absolute value. For example, $-9999999 < -1$. Hence, an equivalent way to describe overflow is to say that it occurs when the computer attempts to produce numbers that are too large in magnitude, that is, too large in absolute value.) Whenever any sort of overflow occurs, an error message should be produced. However, many systems give no such error messages. They simply produce some meaningless value and keep on computing. At that point, the entire computation becomes meaningless.

overflow

In addition to there being a largest magnitude that can be stored as a value of type `real`, there is also a smallest possible magnitude. The smallest positive number of type `real` that can be stored in our machine will be produced by the following word configuration:

*smallest
fraction*

This is the number

0.1000×10^{-99}

which is a decimal point followed by ninety nine zeros and then a one—certainly a very small number. However, calculations involving such small quantities do occur.

underflow

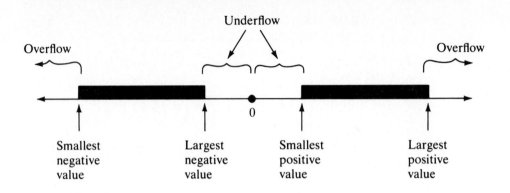

Figure 15.2
Range of available
real values.

When the computer attempts to produce a nonzero number whose absolute value is smaller than this quantity, that is called *real underflow* or *floating point underflow*. On many systems, any such small quantity is simply replaced by zero, which usually is a satisfactory approximation. Some systems give an error message in the case of floating point underflow. Unfortunately, a few other systems produce a meaningless result and continue the computation. The situation is similar to that of overflow but generally produces fewer problems. A diagram showing the ranges of overflow and underflow is given in Figure 15.2.

As you can see from the preceding discussion, the types integer and real are implemented in different ways. As an illustration, consider the difference between the constants 123412 and 123412.0. The first is of type integer and is stored exactly as

+	0	1	2	3	4	1	2

The second is of type real and so is stored only as the approximate value

+	1	2	3	4	+	0	6

Most problems peculiar to numeric calculations arise because of the approximate nature of real values. When studying mathematics, we frequently think in terms of an ideal world where quantities are represented as exact values called "real numbers." These exact numbers are not available on a computer. If the quantity we need requires more than four decimal digits after the decimal point in order to write it down, then it will not be represented exactly in our computer. If it consists of a decimal point followed by five or six nonzero digits, then we could use a computer with a larger word size. However, some quantities, such as the number pi used in geometry, cannot be represented exactly by any finite string of digits. For these "real numbers" even a computer with a word size of one million digits could store only an approximation of the quantities they represent. Many of the "real numbers" of classical mathematics are simply not available on computers. Moreover, the missing numbers are not always very exotic ones. Recall the example that opened this chapter. It performs the calculation

```
X := 1/3 + 1/3 + 1/3
```

The number one-third has no representation as a finite string of decimal digits. Our computer will represent $1/3$ as

$$0.3333 \times 10^0 = 0.33330$$

When three of these are added together, the result is 0.99990, rather than the value 1.0 that is predicted by the usual idealized model of arithmetic.

Binary Numerals
(Optional)

Most computers represent numbers in *binary notation* rather than in the more familiar base ten notation. On occasion, this can have a significant effect on the outcome of a numeric calculation. The basic idea of binary notation is quite simple. It is just like the base ten notation we normally use, except that the role of ten is replaced by the number two. Base ten notation uses the ten digits 0 through 9. Base two notation uses only two digits, 0 and 1. In base ten each change in position, from the rightmost to the leftmost digit, represents multiplying by ten. In base two each change in position, from the rightmost to the leftmost digit, represents multiplying by two.

For example, consider the ordinary base ten numeral 3019. It satisfies the following equality:

$$3019 = 3 \times 10^3 + 0 \times 10^2 + 1 \times 10^1 + 9 \times 10^0$$
$$= 3 \times 1000 + 0 \times 100 + 1 \times 10 + 9 \times 1 = 3000 + 0 + 10 + 9$$

The meaning of any base ten numeral is decomposed in a similar way.

Next, consider an example of a binary (base two) numeral, such as 100101. The situation is the same except that now each digit position represents some power of two. For example,

example

(the base two numeral) $100101 =$
(the base ten expression) $1 \times 2^5 + 0 \times 2^4 + 0 \times 2^3 + 1 \times 2^2 + 0 \times 2^1 + 1 \times 2^0$
$= 1 \times 32 + 0 \times 16 + 0 \times 8 + 1 \times 4 + 0 \times 2 + 1 \times 1$
$= 32 + 4 + 1 = 37$ *(base ten)*

In binary notation the rightmost digit represents that digit multiplied by $2^0 = 1$, the next digit to the left represents that digit multiplied by $2^1 = 2$, the next multiplied by $2^2 = 4$, the next multiplied by $2^3 = 8$, and so forth. Any integer can be represented in this binary notation.

whole numbers

The treatment of fractions in binary notation is similar to that of decimal fractions. In decimal fractions, the digit positions after the decimal point represent smaller and smaller fractions. Each shift to the right represents dividing by ten. For example, in base ten,

fractions

$$0.103 = 1/10 + 0/10^2 + 3/10^3$$
$$= 1/10 + 0/100 + 3/1000$$

Fractions in binary notation follow the same principle, but with 10 replaced by 2. For example,

(the base two numeral) 0.1101
= *(the base ten expression)* $1/2 + 1/2^2 + 0/2^3 + 1/2^4$
= $1/2 + 1/4 + 0/8 + 1/16 = 0.8125$ *(base ten)*

In binary notation the "point" is called a *binary point,* rather than a decimal point. The first digit after the binary point represents that number divided by $2^1 = 2$, the next digit after the binary point represents that digit divided by $2^2 = 4$, the next digit represents the digit divided by $2^3 = 8$, and so forth.

In both decimal and binary notation, any quantity between zero and one can be represented by a point followed by a string of digits. In both binary and decimal notation, this may sometimes require an infinite string of digits. For example, in base ten,

$1/3 = 0.3333333333333333$ . . .

As we add more 3s, we get a better approximation to 1/3, but no finite number of digits after the decimal point will yield a number exactly equal to 1/3.

A similar phenomenon occurs in binary notation. In binary notation, the fraction 1/4, for example, can be expressed as the finite string 0.01, but the exact representation of 1/5 requires an infinite string of binary digits after the binary point.

$1/5 =$ (in binary) $0.001100110011001100110011$ . . .

Any finite string of binary digits can only approximate the value 1/5. In decimal notation 1/5 can be represented exactly as 0.2. As this example indicates, some quantities that we express exactly in decimal notation can become approximate quantities when stored in a binary computer.

In both binary and decimal notation, you can combine the notation for whole numbers and that for fractions. In base ten, 12.34 means 12 plus 0.34. In base two, 10.101 means 10 (base two) plus 0.101 (base two).

binary arithmetic   Arithmetic on binary numerals is very similar to arithmetic on base ten numerals. In particular, shifting the binary point is similar to shifting the decimal point in base ten. In base ten, shifting the point one position to the right is the same as multiplying by ten. In base two it is the same as multiplying by two. For example, in base two, 1.011 multiplied by two is 10.11, and 1.011 multiplied by four is 101.1.

Machine Representation of Numbers in Binary
(Optional)

bits   Like our hypothetical decimal computer, most real computers have a memory that is divided into locations called "words." However, these words usually store strings of zeros and ones rather than strings of decimal digits. Recall that a digit that must always be either zero or one is called a *bit.* Computer word sizes are usually described as being some number of bits. Some typical word sizes are sixteen, thirty-two, and sixty-four bits. When people refer to a "sixteen-bit machine," they mean that each word of the machine holds sixteen binary digits. (They do not mean that the computer costs $2.)

Since computer words usually hold bits, most computers store numbers in binary notation. Aside from the fact that the numbers are expressed in binary notation, the method of representing numbers is the same as we described for our hypothetical decimal machine.

Numbers of type `integer` are stored as binary numerals, either in the exact form described in the previous section or in some variant of that notation. Each value of type `integer` is stored in one word. For example, the number five has the binary representation 101 and, in a sixteen-bit word, it might be stored as

integers

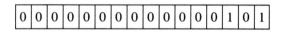

A word holds only zeros and ones. What we have written as the sign + must therefore be represented as a zero or one. If we take 0 to stand for plus and 1 to stand for minus, then in this sixteen-bit computer, the preceding word's contents would really be

0	0	0	0	0	0	0	0	0	0	0	0	0	1	0	1

We will always use the plus and minus sign rather than 0 and 1 to denote the sign of a number in storage. It helps avoid confusion.

Since one bit is occupied by the sign, the largest integer that can be stored in a sixteen-bit computer is the number with binary representation consisting of fifteen 1's. In base ten that number is written 32767. You can compute this base ten numeral by evaluating the sum

largest integer

$$1 \times 2^{14} + 1 \times 2^{13} + 1 \times 2^{12} + 1 \times 2^{11} + 1 \times 2^{10} + 1 \times 2^9 + 1 \times 2^8 +$$
$$1 \times 2^7 + 1 \times 2^6 + 1 \times 2^5 + 1 \times 2^4 + 1 \times 2^3 + 1 \times 2^2 + 1 \times 2^1 + 1 \times 2^0$$

(If you understand a bit of binary arithmetic, you can calculate it more quickly as follows:

111111111111111 *(base two)* = 1000000000000000 − 1 *(base two)* =
(in base ten) $2^{15} - 1 = 32768 - 1 = 32767$

However, if you are uncomfortable with binary arithmetic, simply do it the long way.)

Thus, if you are working on a sixteen-bit machine, you can expect the value of `maxint` to be 32767. The smallest negative number your sixteen-bit machine can hold will probably be about −32767. This is not part of the definition of the Pascal language. The exact way that numbers are represented is left up to the implementers. Hence, the value of `maxint` and the value of the smallest negative integer in your machine might vary somewhat from these figures. However, these values will be approximately correct for most sixteen-bit machines.

Aside from the fact that binary notation is used, numbers of type `real` are stored in the same way as we described for our decimal computer. For example, a sixteen-bit word might be divided to allow four digits to express the exponent and twelve digits to express the fractional part. On a binary machine, the exponent represents a power of two rather than a power of ten. For example, consider the following word configuration for such a machine:

real numbers

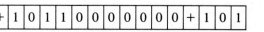

It represents the number

(in binary) $0.1011 \times 2^{101} = $ *(in decimal)* $(1/2 + 0/4 + 1/8 + 1/16) \times (2^5)$

We have taken the liberty of using the digit 2 in our binary expression. This mixed notation is sometimes easier to understand than absolutely pure binary notation.

Although numbers are invariably stored in binary notation, that notation normally has little, if any, effect on the outcome of a numeric computation. Therefore, we will end our discussion of binary arithmetic here and return to using our hypothetical decimal computer.

Extra Precision
(Optional)

Some computer installations have facilities to store numbers in more than one word and so obtain a more accurate representation for values of type `real`. This is not part of the definition of Pascal and is not available on most Pascal systems. However, it is a common feature of other programming languages and does occur in some Pascal implementations.

*double
precision*

One common method for obtaining extra accuracy when storing `real` values is called *double precision*. In double precision, each `real` number is stored in two words. This yields more than double the number of meaningful digits, because all the extra digits of the second word normally go into the fractional part. Our hypothetical decimal computer had an eight-decimal-digit word size. On that computer, a typical double precision implementation would store one `real` value in two words, as illustrated by the example in Figure 15.3. In our hypothetical decimal computer, this accurately represents the decimal number

12.3456789012

With this sort of double precision, the largest possible `real` value that can be stored is about the same as it is for the normal one-word representation. However, a full twelve decimal digits of accuracy can be represented. The ordinary one-word representation allowed for only four decimal digits of accuracy.

The disadvantages of double precision are that it uses more storage and that it usually causes programs to run more slowly.

There is no standard Pascal syntax for double precision numbers. You will have to consult the documentation for your particular system to see if it is available and, if available, to see how to use it in a Pascal program.

**Figure 15.3
(Optional)
Example of a
double-precision
number.**

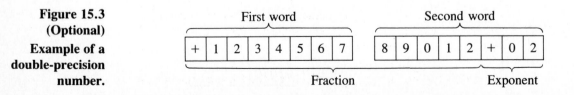

Self-Test Exercises

1. Describe how each of the following `integer` and `real` constants are represented in our hypothetical decimal computer:

```
123456          -123456
123.456         -123.456
0.00123123      -0.00123123
3.14159265358979323846
```

2. Our hypothetical decimal computer had a word size of eight. To store values of type `real`, it used five digit positions for the fractional part and three digit positions for the exponent part. Suppose that we instead used other combinations. At what value would `real` overflow occur if we instead used the following combinations?

a. Fractional part uses four digit positions and exponent part uses four.
b. Fractional part uses three digit positions and exponent part uses five.
c. Fractional part uses six digit positions and exponent part uses two.

3. (This exercise applies to the optional section "Binary Numerals.") Convert the following binary numerals into equivalent decimal numerals: 111, 101, 100, 11011, 010110, 0.1, 0.01, 0.001, 0.101, 1.001, 101.101

4. (This exercise applies to he optional section "Machine Representation of Numbers in Binary.") What would you expect as the value of `maxint` in a thirty-two-bit machine? Assume that numbers are stored as described in this chapter. What about a sixty-four-bit machine?

"So so" is good, very good,
very excellent good; and yet it is not;
it is but so so.

William Shakespeare, As You Like It

Pitfall

Sources of Error in real Arithmetic

In computations with values of type `real`, errors arise because numbers are stored as approximate values. These approximations are sometimes accurate enough and other times very inaccurate. In this and the next section we will discuss some common sources of inaccuracy in programs that compute values of type `real`.

As you will recall, overflow results when the computer tries to compute

overflow

a number larger than it can hold in memory. The problem of integer overflow can sometimes be avoided by using variables of type `real` to do calculations involving large numbers, even if the quantities involved are whole numbers. The computer can store much larger values of type `real` than it can values of type `integer`. There is a certain loss of accuracy in doing this, but often this loss of accuracy is tolerable.

underflow

Recall that real underflow occurs when the computer attempts to produce a nonzero value of type `real` that is too small in absolute value, that is, too close to zero. These values cannot be represented in memory. Most computers, including our hypothetical decimal computer, simply estimate such values as zero and store a zero as the result of the calculation. This is called *rounding to zero*. If your computer rounds to zero on underflow, then underflow will seldom be a problem. If your computer does anything else, then you must be careful to avoid underflow.

multiplication and division

When a multiplication or division is performed, the answer usually has more digits than either of the two numbers being combined. Frequently, these extra digits cannot be represented in memory and so are lost, along with a little bit of accuracy. For example, consider the following code: (Here and in the examples that follow, we will set the values of variables by means of assignment statements. This is to keep the examples small. In practice, these values might be read from the keyboard or might be the results of other calculations.)

```
X := 912.0;
Y := 0.11;
Z := X * Y;
```

The value that should be stored in Z is

$$912.0 \times 0.11 = 100.32$$

However, our hypothetical decimal computer only stores four digits in the fractional part of a `real` value. Hence, it will store the value of Z as

+	1	0	0	3	+	0	3

which represents the value

$$0.1003 \times 10^3$$

This means that the last digit is lost, and the value of Z becomes `100.30`. Even if the values of X and Y were completely accurate, the value of Z has lost one digit of accuracy as the result of a simple multiplication. In all the examples of this section and the next, we will use our hypothetical decimal computer. Hence, we are only allowed four digits of accuracy.

simple addition

Even very simple addition or subtraction can produce a slightly inaccurate result. If the computer adds the number `9.222` to itself, the result should be

$$9.222 + 9.222 = 18.444$$

However, our computer only retains four digits and so will store the answer as

$$0.1844 \times 10^2$$

This means that 18.444 was rounded to 18.440, and one digit of the answer was lost.

Under some circumstances, the loss of accuracy in addition can be dramatic. Consider the following piece of code:

```
X := 2000.0;
Y := 0.4;
X := X + Y
```

The values of X and Y are stored as

$$0.2000 \times 10^4$$
$$0.4000 \times 10^0$$

Like most computers, our hypothetical decimal machine cannot add two numbers unless they have the same exponent part. Hence, it must change one of the two numbers. On our machine the second number is changed to

$$0.00004 \times 10^4$$

Then the following addition is performed

$$
\begin{array}{r}
0.2000 \times 10^4 \\
+0.00004 \times 10^4 \\
\hline
0.20004 \times 10^4
\end{array}
$$

This answer is what we might expect as the value of X, but unfortunately that is not the value stored. Since our computer stores only four digits after the decimal point, it stores the following as the value of X:

$$0.2000 \times 10^4$$

The adding in of Y thus had absolutely no effect on the value of X.

Situations like the one in the preceding example are common. To avoid this sort of problem, you must somehow avoid adding or subtracting two values of very different size. Sometimes this can be done by rearranging the order in which numbers are combined. As an example, consider the following code:

adding large and small numbers

```
X := 2000.0;
Y := 0.4; U := 0.3; V := 0.4;
X := X + Y;
X := X + U;
X := X + V
```

As we have just seen, adding Y has no effect on the value of X. Similarly, adding U and adding V each have no effect. This calculation leaves the value of X unchanged at:

$$0.2000 \times 10^4$$

However, if we first combine Y, U, and V to obtain a larger number and then combine this larger number with X, the resultant value of X will be close to the value we expect.

Consider the following slightly different code for the same computation:

```
X := 2000.0;
Y := 0.4;  U := 0.3;  V := 0.4;
W := Y + U + V;
X := X + W
```

The value of W is obtained by first adding the values of Y and U and then combining that sum with the value of V:

$$\begin{array}{r} 0.4000 \times 10^0 \\ +0.3000 \times 10^0 \\ \hline 0.7000 \times 10^0 \end{array}$$

$$\begin{array}{r} 0.7000 \times 10^0 \\ +0.4000 \times 10^0 \\ \hline 1.1000 \times 10^0 = 0.1100 \times 10^1 \end{array}$$

This value is then added to the value of X, as follows:

$$\begin{array}{r} 0.2000 \ \ \times 10^4 \\ +0.00011 \times 10^4 \\ \hline 0.20011 \times 10^4 \end{array}$$

The final value of X is stored as

$$0.2001 \times 10^4$$

By rearranging the order of the additions, we have added one digit of accuracy to the answer. This is a standard trick. If the small numbers are first added together, then that will produce a somewhat larger value. This larger value can then be combined with other large values. In this way the numbers being combined are more nearly equal, and so the results of their addition will be more accurate.

Pitfall

Error Propagation

Each individual operation on a value of type `real` is likely to introduce only a very small error. However, after a number of operations, these small errors may be compounded to produce a very large inaccuracy. Again, we illustrate the pitfall with a piece of code:

```
  . . .
B := 0.1232;
C := A - B;
D := 10000.0;
X := C * D
```

The three dots represent some computation that sets the value of A. Let us say that A gets set to 0.1234, a value very close to that of B. The value of C gets set by the calculation

$$\begin{array}{r} 0.1234 \times 10^0 \\ -0.1232 \times 10^0 \\ \hline 0.0002 \times 10^0 = 0.2000 \times 10^{-3} \end{array}$$

The value of X is then computed by multiplying that value by 10,000 to obtain the following value of X:

$$0.2000 \times 10^1$$

So far things look fine. The answer appears to be 2. However, as we have already seen, it is easy for a program to calculate a value that is slightly in error. Suppose that the value of A was slightly in error. Specifically, suppose the correct value of A is 0.1233, rather than 0.1234. Then the correct answer is

$$(0.1233 - 0.1232) \times 10,000 = 1$$

The correct answer is 1, but our code computed it as 2. A slight mistake has been compounded, and our answer is now wrong by a factor of two.

The problem is that when subtraction is performed on two nearly equal numbers, the answer is the difference between the end digits of the two numbers. After the subtraction, only the last digits of the two almost-equal numbers have any effect on the rest of the computation. But these are exactly the digits that are likely to be incorrect. Hence, a program should somehow avoid subtracting two almost-equal numbers of type `real`.

All the examples in this and the previous section are unrealistic in the sense that most computers represent `real` values with an accuracy equivalent to more than four decimal digits. In all other respects, they are real pitfalls. Realistic examples can be manufactured simply by adding a few more digits to the initial values and leaving the rest of the code unchanged.

*subtracting
almost equal
numbers*

Case Study

Series Evaluation

Problem Definition

One common numeric task is to sum a series. For example, consider the following series:

$$\frac{1}{2} + \frac{2}{2^2} + \frac{3}{2^3} + \cdots \frac{N}{2^N}$$

Suppose that we have already declared a function called Power such that the value of Power *(x,y)* is

$$x^y$$

Our task is to compute the value of the sum given the value of *N*.

Discussion

For concreteness, suppose that the value of *N* is 100. The most obvious way to calculate the sum is as follows:

```
Sum := 0;
for I := 1 to 100 do
    Sum := Sum + (I/Power(2,I))
```

If the calculation is carried out with complete accuracy, this will set the value of Sum to the desired value. However, the operations are not carried out with complete accuracy. Moreover, the values of the successive terms rapidly become very small, while in comparison, the value of Sum remains moderately large. Hence, after the first few iterations, the loop is adding two numbers of very different size. As we have seen, this can lead to inaccuracies in the answer.

order of summation
We can avoid adding numbers of such greatly differing size by summing the series in the other direction, like so:

```
Sum := 0;
for I := 100 downto 1 do
    Sum := Sum + (I/Power(2,I))
```

The numbers being combined will then be more nearly equal, and hence the results of the additions are likely to be more accurate.

ALGORITHM
The general algorithm is the same but with 100 replaced by N.

```
Sum := 0;
for I := N downto 1 do
    Sum := Sum + (I/Power(2,I))
```

Case Study

Finding a Root of a Function

A common numeric programming task is to solve an equation. For example, consider the equation

$$x^3 + 2x = 33$$

One solution is 3, since,

$$3^3 + 2 \times 3 = 33$$

By rearranging the equation, we can always get it into the form

$$F(x) = 0$$

where $F(x)$ is some expression that can be made into a Pascal function having one argument of type `real` and returning a value of type `real`. For example, the equation

$$x^3 + 2x = 33$$

can be rearranged to the following equivalent equation:

$$x^3 + 2x - 33 = 0$$

The expression on the left-hand side is computed by the Pascal function declared as

```
function F (X: real): real;
   begin
      F := X * X * X + 2 * X - 33
   end;
```

Solving equations of this form is equivalent to finding a value x such that the expression $F(x)$ on the left side of the rearranged equation is made equal to zero. Such a value x is called a *root* of the function $F(x)$.

roots

Problem Definition

In this section we will design a program to find a root of a function F. The function F is given as a Pascal function declaration, which we will incorporate into our final program. The user will provide two values x_1 and x_2 such that there is exactly one root between x_1 and x_2. We will design a program that finds the approximate value of the root of the function F. The method works for a wide range of different functions F. We need only assume that the graph of the function can be drawn on paper as a smooth line. (The technically precise condition is that the function must be *continuous*. However, we will not stop to define that term. The informal notion of "easy to draw as a smooth line" will do here.)

Discussion

Our goal is to find a value M such that $F(M)$ is approximately equal to zero. The method we will use is called the *bisection method*. (The technique is similar to that of the binary search algorithm we discussed in Chapter 14, but you need not have read that section in order to understand this method.) The idea of the bisection method is depicted in Figure 15.4. The graph represents the function F. Two values, Low and High, are chosen so that exactly one root lies between them. We therefore know that the following relation holds:

bisection method

```
Low < root < High
```

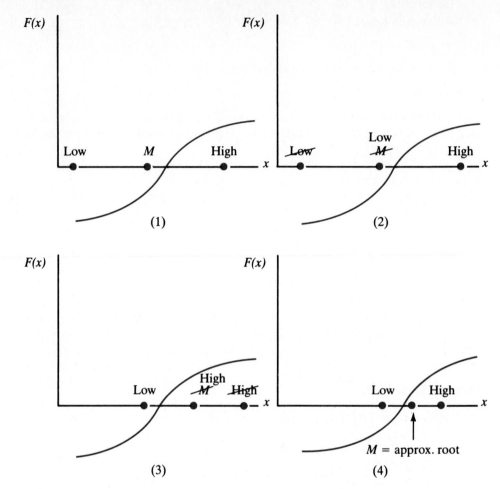

Figure 15.4
One way to find a
root.

The midpoint between these two values Low and High is then computed. In Figure 15.4, this midpoint is denoted by M. The root is either between Low and M or else it is between M and High. For now, assume that we can tell which of these two intervals contains the root; later we will return and figure out a way to do so. In the figure the root is between M and High. This process has managed to narrow down the location of the root. Originally we knew it was between Low and High. Now we know that it is in the smaller interval between M and High (or, in other cases, between Low and M). Next, we change the values Low and High to these new endpoint values; in the figure example, M becomes the new value of Low, and the value of High is unchanged. If we keep repeating this process, we eventually get a very small interval that contains the root. This gives us an approximation to the value of the root. The method is outlined in the following pseudocode:

request values x_1 and x_2 such that

ALGORITHM

    $x_1 < root < x_2$;
Low := x_1; High : =x_2;
M : = (Low + High)/2;
RootFound : = false;
while not(RootFound) *do*
   begin
     if (F(M) is approximately equal to 0.0) *then*
       RootFound : = true
     else if the root is between Low and M *then*
       High : = M
     else if the root is between M and High *then*
       Low : = M;
     M : = (Low + High)/2
   end;
output: "The root is approximately M. "

We still must design a subalgorithm to decide whether the root is between Low and M or between M and High. The interval containing the root can be determined from the signs of the values F(Low), F(M), and F(High). One of the two values F(Low) and F(High) will be positive and one will be negative. If the sign of F(M) matches that of F(High), then High gets its value changed to M. If the match is with Low, then Low gets changed. So the pseudocode for the nested *if-then-else* statement can be refined to the following:

ALGORITHM
refinement

   if (F(M) is approximately equal to 0.0) *then*
     RootFound : = true
   else if SameSign(F(High), F(M)) *then*
     High : = M
   else if SameSign(F(Low), F(M)) *then*
     Low : = M

where SameSign is a boolean-valued function that tests two values to see whether they have the same sign.

The test for approximate zero will depend on a constant called Threshold. As long as a number is less than Threshold in absolute value, it will be considered close enough to zero. The value of Threshold will depend on the accuracy of the computer and the accuracy needed for the particular application. Hence, we will ask the user to supply the value. The test for approximate zero can then be expressed as

*additional
input needed*

   abs(F(M)) <= Threshold

The final program is given in Figure 15.5. The function declaration for F is indicated by three dots. It can be filled in with any function definition that satisfies the assumptions we have made.

If incorrect initial values are used, the algorithm expressed in our pseudocode can go into an infinite loop. Hence, in the final program, we have placed a limit on the

*additional
error checks*

```pascal
program FindRoot(input, output);
{Finds a root of the function F by the bisection method.}
const  MaxIterations = 1000;
var Low, High, M: real;
    Threshold: real;
    RootFound: boolean;
    Count: 0 . . MaxIterations;

function F(X: real): real;
{The function whose root is being sought.}
        . . .


function SameSign(V1, V2: real): boolean;
{Returns true if V1 and V2 have the same sign; otherwise returns false.}
begin {SameSign}
  if (V1 >= 0.0) and (V2 >= 0.0) then
    SameSign := true
  else if (V1 <= 0.0) and (V2 <= 0.0) then
    SameSign := true
  else
    SameSign := false
end; {SameSign}

procedure ReadInterval(var Low, High: real);
{Reads in two values that are supposed to have exactly one root
between them. Makes a test to see if they are plausible values.}
begin {ReadInterval}
  repeat
    writeln('Enter two values,');
    writeln('the first less than the root,');
    writeln('the second greater than the root.');
    writeln('Be sure there is');
    writeln('exactly one root between them.');
    readln(Low, High);
    if SameSign(F(Low), F(High)) then
        begin{then}
          writeln('Those cannot be right.');
          writeln('Try again.')
        end{then}
  until not (SameSign(F(Low), F(High)))
end; {ReadInterval}
```

Figure 15.5
Program to find a root of a function.

```
begin {Program}
  writeln('Enter accuracy desired.');
  readln(Threshold);
  RootFound := false;
  ReadInterval(Low, High);
  M := (Low + High)/2;
  Count := 0;

  while not(RootFound) and (Count < MaxIterations) do
    begin {while}
      {Low < (the root) < High and M = (Low + High)/2}
      if abs(F(M)) <= Threshold then
        RootFound := true
      else if SameSign(F(High), F(M)) then
        High := M
      else if SameSign(F(Low), F(M)) then
        Low := M
      else
        writeln('Something is wrong!');

      M := (Low + High)/2;
      Count := Count + 1
    end; {while}

  if Count = MaxIterations then
    writeln('Exceeded iteration limit.')
  else
    writeln('The root is approximately', M)
end. {Program}
```

Figure 15.5
(continued)

number of loop iterations allowed. When that limit is exceeded, the program halts and reports that something is likely to be amiss. As an additional check on faulty data, we have added a clause with an error message at the end of the nested if-then-else statement within the main program loop. If the data and function are as they should be, then this clause will not be executed. However, incorrect data could cause all of the boolean expressions to be false. The extra clause will catch this situation immediately.

As a wise programmer once said, "Floating point numbers are like sandpiles: every time you move one, you lose a little sand and you pick up a little dirt." And after a few computations, things can get pretty dirty.

B.W. Kernighan and P.J. Plauger,
The Elements of Programming Style

Summary of Problem Solving and Programming Techniques

- The largest value of type `real` that an installation can accommodate is always much larger than the largest value of type `integer` that it can handle. Hence, one way to avoid `integer` overflow is to represent quantities as values of type `real` even though they are whole numbers.
- Values of type `real` are stored as approximate quantities. Hence, computations involving these numbers yield only approximations of the desired results. Unless particular care is taken to minimize errors, these approximations can often be very inaccurate.
- Since `real` values are stored as approximate quantities, any test of two real values for exact equality yields a meaningless result.
- Some common sources of error in programs involving the type `real` are round-off error in any arithmetic operation, such as addition or multiplication, but most especially in certain combinations such as adding two numbers of very different size or subtracting two numbers of almost equal size.

Summary of Terms

floating point numbers
In Pascal, numbers of type `real`.

overflow
The condition that results when a program attempts to compute a numeric value whose magnitude is too large. More precisely, it is the condition that results when a program attempts to compute a numeric value that is larger than the largest value of that type that the computer can represent in memory, or is smaller than the smallest negative value of that type that the computer can represent in memory.

underflow
The condition that results when a program attempts to compute a value of type `real` such that the value is smaller in absolute value than the smallest positive `real` value that the system can represent in memory. In other words, it is the condition that results when a program attempts to compute a nonzero value that is too close to zero to be represented in memory (except possibly by the approximately equal value of zero).

Exercises

Self-Test Exercises

5. Assume that Pascal arithmetic is implemented as we described for our hypothetical decimal computer. What is the output of the following when embedded in a complete program with the variables declared to be of type `real`?

```
X := 300.00;
Y := 0.12345678;
writeln(X + Y)
```

6. Assume that Pascal arithmetic is implemented as we described for our hypothetical decimal computer. What is the output of the following when embedded in a complete program with the variables declared to be of type `real`?

```
X := 1.000E-90;
Y := 1.000E-25;
Z := 1.000E+25;
writeln(X * Y * Z, X * Z * Y)
```

Remember that multiplication is performed in order from left to right and that our hypothetical computer rounds to zero on floating point underflow.

Interactive Exercises

7. Find (approximately) the largest value for the constant `Epsilon` that will cause the following `writeln` to be executed on your system:

```
X := 1.0 + Epsilon;
if X = 1.0
   then writeln('It''s really nothing')
```

8. Type up and run the program in Figure 15.5. Use the following declaration for F:

```
function F(X: real): real;
begin{F}
   F := X * X - 4
end;  {F}
```

The exact root is thus 2.0. The program will approximate that root.

Programming Exercises

9. Write a function declaration for a function called `Digit` that returns the value of the nth digit from the right of an `integer` argument. The value of n should be a second argument. For example, `Digit(9635,1)` returns `5`, and `Digit(9635,3)` returns `6`.

10. If e denotes the base of the natural logarithm then the value e^x can be calculated by the series:

$$e^x = 1 + x + \frac{x^2}{2!} + \frac{x^3}{3!} + \frac{x^4}{4!} + \frac{x^5}{5!} + \ldots$$

Write a program that computes an approximate value of e by summing that series for N terms. Have the program compute the series from left to right and from right to left, and then output both results. The value e^x can also be computed by the standard function $\exp(x)$. Have the program also output the value of e calculated by $\exp(1.0)$. Compare the three results. Embed these three calculations in a loop that repeats the calculation for values of N from 1 to 100. To avoid integer overflow, store the factorials as values of type `real` (or avoid using them altogether).

11. Write a program to sum the following series from left to right until a term whose absolute value is less than 0.00001 is encountered, and to then output the answer:

$$4 - \frac{4}{3} + \frac{4}{5} - \frac{4}{7} + \frac{4}{9} - \cdots$$

(The denominators are the positive odd numbers 1, 3, 5, 7, 9, 11, . . .) Have the program then recalculate the sum from right to left, using the same number of terms and output that value as well. Compare the two results.

12. (This exercise applies to the optional section "Binary Numerals.") Write a program that takes base two numerals (for whole numbers) as input and outputs the equivalent base ten numeral.

13. (This exercise applies to the optional section "Binary Numerals.") Write a program that takes base ten numerals (for whole numbers) as input and outputs the equivalent base two numeral.

14. (This exercise applies to the optional section "Binary Numerals.") A *hexadecimal numeral* is a numeral written in base sixteen. Write a program that takes a hexadecimal numeral (for a whole number) as input and outputs the equivalent base ten numeral. Use the first six letters of the alphabet for the digits "ten" through "fifteen."

15. (This exercise applies to the optional section "Binary Numerals.") Write a program that takes base ten numerals (for whole numbers) as input and outputs the equivalent hexadecimal numeral. (See the previous exercise for a definition of hexadecimal numerals.)

16. One way to obtain extra digits is to store numbers as arrays of digits. Write a program that reads in two whole numbers with up to 20 digits each and stores their digits in arrays of type

```
array[0 . . 19] of integer
```

The program then computes the sum of the two numbers, stores the result in an array of the same type, and outputs the result to the screen. Use the ordinary addition algorithm that you learned in grade school. Be sure to issue an "overflow" message if the result is more than 20 digits long.

17. It is wasteful to store just one digit in an array location that can hold about the number of digits in `maxint`. Redo the previous exercise, but this time store L digits in each array variable, where L is two less than the length of `maxint` written in base ten. You will need to modify the addition algorithm slightly, but the idea is still the same. Use 0 . . 4 as the array index type.

18. Do the previous exercise for multiplication instead of addition.

19. Use the ideas in the previous exercise to design a program that can perform multiplication of "real" numbers that yields at least twice as many significant digits as your system's ordinary Pascal `real` multiplication does.

20. (This exercise assumes that you know what a derivative is.) If x is a maximum or minimum of a function f, and f has a derivative at x, then the derivative of f is zero at x. Use this idea to design a program to find local minima and maxima of polynomials of degree two. Use any input format that is convenient.

21. Redo the previous exercise, but allow polynomials of arbitrary degree, and use the bisection method to find the roots of the derivatives.

References for Further Reading

B.W. Kernighan and P.J. Plauger, *The Elements of Programming Style,* 1978, McGraw-Hill, New York. Includes material on pitfalls in both numeric and nonnumeric programming. The examples are in Fortran and PL/I, not in Pascal.

D.E. Knuth, *The Art of Computer Programming, Volume 2, Seminumerical Algorithms,* 2nd ed. 1981, Addison-Wesley, Reading, Mass. Also does not use Pascal, but the text can be read without reading the programs.

T. Stoer and R. Bulirsch, *Introduction to Numerical Analysis,* 1980, Springer-Verlag, New York. Uses Algol, a language similar to Pascal.

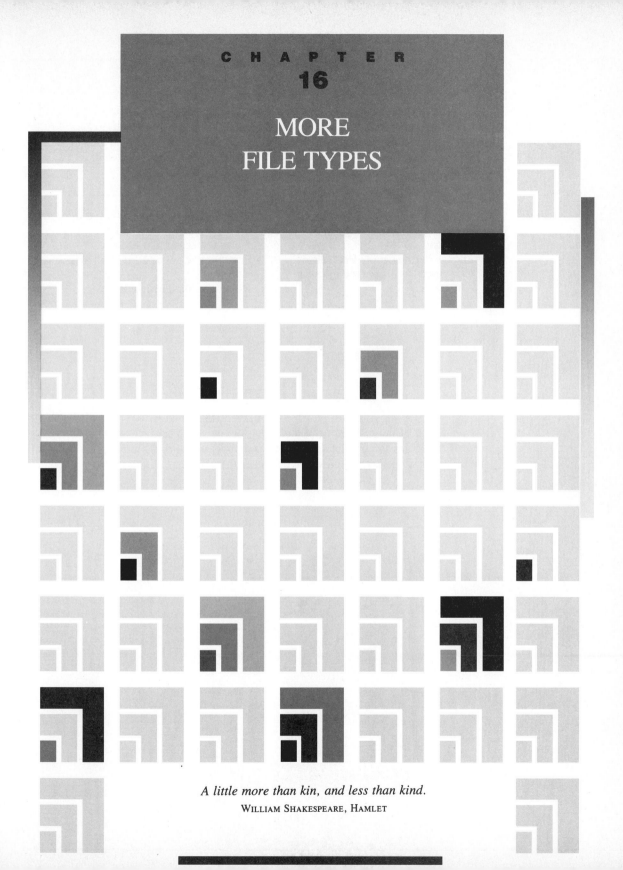

C H A P T E R
16

MORE
FILE TYPES

A little more than kin, and less than kind.
WILLIAM SHAKESPEARE, HAMLET

Chapter Contents

T ext files, which we have already used, are a special case of the more general construct known as "files." In this chapter we describe Pascal files in complete generality and also present programming and problem solving techniques that use files of types other than text.

The General Notion of a File

Files are used for holding data in secondary storage so that the data may remain after the program has run to completion. At some later time the same or another program may access the data in the file. A file is a named collection of data in secondary storage. In any kind of file, all the data must be of the same type. A text file is a special kind of file in which the data is all characters. In general, the data in a file may be of almost any Pascal data type. All types of files are similar in nature, but text files have some additional properties that are not shared by other file types. Files of type `text` can be read by using an editor and so are accessible by means other than a Pascal program. Other types of files cannot normally be accessed by an editor; they can only be used as input and/or output data for Pascal programs. This is because data is represented differently in text files and in nontext files. With text files, all data is converted into characters and so can be read by the editor. In nontext files, data is stored using the same binary encoding that is used in main memory to encode variable values of that data type. Since the data is not converted into characters, these files cannot be read using the editor. Because they use these binary encodings, files of types other than `text` are often referred to as *binary files*. We will simply call them *nontext files*.

A *file* consists of a sequence of items called *components,* all of which are values of some one type know as the *component type*. The component type of a file can be any of the data types we have seen. The component type may be a simple type, such as `integer` or `char`. It might be an array type, such as an array of integers. It very frequently is a record type. The only data types that are not allowed are file types, and structured types that involve files, such as an array of files. In particular, you cannot have a file of files.

component type

This description makes a file sound very much like an array, and indeed, a file is conceptually very much like a one-dimensional array. There are, however, three important conceptual differences between a file and an array. First, the size of an array must be declared in advance and so is bounded by some fixed number. On the other hand, there is no limit to the size of a file. The number of components that are placed in a file is not declared anywhere in the program, and there is no limit to the number of such components. Any particular implementation will impose an upper bound on the size of a file, but this is typically so large that, for most purposes, it can be considered unbounded. Second, files are kept in secondary storage and so can remain in storage after the program has run to completion. Finally, files are accessed sequentially. For example, to get to the tenth component of a file, a program steps through the first nine components before it reaches the tenth component. With an array, a program can go directly to any element of the array by naming an index. No such simple indexing scheme is available for files. (Some versions of Pascal do allow nonsequential access to files, but this is nonstandard. If it is available on your system, you cannot rely on its being available if you later move your programs to another system.)

comparison to arrays

A type definition for a file type consists of the two words *file of* followed by the component type. For example, if you want `FileInt` to be the name of a type consisting of a file of integers, then the type declaration is as follows:

syntax for type definitions

```
type FileInt = file of integer;
```

Below is a sample type declaration section that declares three file types:

```
type List = array[0 . . 10] of integer;
     Item = record
                  Name: array[1 . . 20] of char;
                  Number: integer;
                  Price: real
               end;
     FileType1 =  file of real;
     FileType2 =  file of List;
     FileType3 =  file of Item;
```

text
files
A text file is almost the same thing as a *file of* char. The only difference is that a text file is divided into lines and a *file of* char is not. Despite their similarities, text files and other types of files are usually thought of as two different categories of files. Moreover, text files and other files are treated slightly differently by the standard procedures for reading from and writing to files. Because of these small differences, it is best to treat text files as a special category of files; when compared to other types of files, text files are "more than kin and less than kind." To avoid problems, use the descriptions presented in this chapter for files other than text files, and use the descriptions presented in Chapter 13 for text files.

The details for opening nontext files, declaring file variables, and even much of the use of read and write are the same as, or very similar to, what they are for text files, and so we can be brief in presenting the details.

File Variables

Variables of file types are declared in the same way as other variables. For example,

```
var Y: file of integer;
```

An alternative, and usually preferable, way to declare Y would be to declare the type FileInt as in the previous section and to declare Y by

```
var Y: FileInt;
```

Within a Pascal program, file variable names are used to refer to files when retrieving input from the file or producing output to the file. The situation for other types of file variables is similar to that for file variables of type text.

Opening Files

All types of files must be opened before a program can access the file. The details of naming and opening files differ somewhat from one implementation to another, but within any one system it is the same for all file types. If you have already discovered the idiosyncrasies of how your system treats text files, you can apply the same technique to other files with reasonable confidence that it will apply to them as well. In this chapter we will describe a method that works on virtually all systems with a reasonable claim to being "standard Pascal." (Consult your manual or a local expert to see if other methods also work on your system.)

Any type of file may be either external or internal. If the file is external, then it must be listed in the program heading. For example, if the file `IntData` is the file variable name for a file of `integer` values in secondary storage, then a program that accesses this file would start as follows:

external and internal files

```pascal
program Sample(input, output, IntData);
```

Internal files exist only for the duration of the program and are not listed in the program heading. The details are identical to those of text files.

A file is opened for writing with the standard procedure `rewrite` and is opened for reading with the standard procedure `reset`. The syntax is identical to that of text files.

rewrite reset

A `write` statement may be used with any file that has been opened with the standard procedure `rewrite`. A `read` statement may be used with any file that has been opened with the standard procedure `reset`. In addition, files opened with `rewrite` can have data added to them by means of the standard procedure `put`, described later in this chapter. Files opened with `reset` may have data "read" from them by means of the standard procedure `get`, also described later in this chapter. `writeln` and `readln` cannot be used with files of types other than `text`, since these files are not divided into lines.

(A few versions of Pascal do not allow `read` and `write` to be used with files other than text files. If you are working with one of these versions, you will have to use the techniques described in the optional section entitled "`put and get`." That section provides an alternative method for reading and writing to files.)

Windows

Before we go on to discuss ways of reading from and writing to nontext files, we must first explicate one preliminary concept, namely, the notion of a *window*. As we have already said, a file is a sequence of components all of the same type. Every file has a window that is positioned at exactly one of these components. If these components are integers, then the window is positioned at one integer. If the file is a file of records, then the window is positioned at one record. As the term "window" indicates, the program has access to (can "see") only one component in the file, namely, the component at which the window is positioned. To read things in a file, the program must somehow move the window to the position of the component to be read. Similarly, when writing to a file, the program can only write at the current position of the window. That means that files can only be accessed one component (integer or record or whatever) at a time.

read and write

In most versions of Pascal, the standard procedure write may be used with files of any type, not just with files of type text.[1] For example, suppose that File1 and File2 are declared as follows:

```
type RealArray = array[1 . . 100] of real;
var File1: file of integer;
    File2: file of RealArray;
```

Suppose further that the files File1 and File2 have been opened with calls to rewrite. Now suppose that we wish to write some new components to File1. Specifically, suppose we wish to write the three values 5, 4, and the value of the integer variable N. The following statement will accomplish the writing:

```
write(File1, 5, 4, N)
```

If B and C are array variables of type RealArray, then their values can be written to the file File2 by the one statement

```
write(File2, B, C)
```

As with text files, the first argument to write is the file variable name of the file. The rest of the arguments must be expressions that evaluate to values of the component type. If the component type is integer, then the values written must all be of type integer. If the component type is an array type, then the values written must all be of that array type.

As with write, most versions of Pascal allow the standard procedure read to be used with files of any type. The first argument to read is a file variable name, and the remaining arguments are variables of the component type of the file. The call will set the values of the variables equal to as many of the components of the file as there are variables. After each value is read from the file, the file window is advanced to the next component. Reading is performed sequentially from the first component to the second and so forth. The use is essentially the same as for text files, except that all variables must be of the component type.

The procedures writeln and readln do not work for files of types other than text. In fact, they do not make sense for files of types other than text, since such files are not divided into lines.

---

[1] If your system does not allow read and write with nontext files, then you may skip this section and go directly to the sections entitled "File Buffer Variable" and "put and get".

Case Study

Processing a File of Numeric Data

Problem Definition

As a simple example of the use of files, we will design a program that reads numbers from a file of reals, multiplies each number by 2, and then copies the result to a second file of reals. The file type is declared as follows:

```
type NumberFile = file of real;
```

The file variable name for the file being read is OldFile, and the file variable name for the file being written to is NewFile. Suppose that before the program is run, the file NewFile does not exist and the file OldFile contains the components

1.1   2.2   3.3   4.4   5.5

Then, after the program is run, the file OldFile will be unchanged, the file New-File will have been created, and NewFile will contain the components

2.2   4.4   6.6   8.8   11.0

(Although the above displays might make you think you could read the numbers in the file using the editor, you cannot. The numbers are coded in machine-readable form and can be read only by a Pascal program.)

Discussion

In order to copy a number from one file to another, a Pascal program must first read the number into a variable and then write the value of the variable to another file. Such a variable is usually called a *buffer variable*. If the buffer variable is named Buffer, the basic way to copy a number from OldFile to NewFile is

```
read(OldFile, Buffer);
write(NewFile, Buffer)
```

If we want to double the numbers, we simply double the value in Buffer before we have the program write it to the second file. So the basic outline of our algorithm is

```
open OldFile with reset;
open NewFile with rewrite;
for each number in OldFile do the following:
begin
   Read(OldFile, Buffer);
   Buffer := 2 * Buffer;
   write(NewFile, Buffer)
end
```

ALGORITHM

```
program Double(input, output, OldFile, NewFile);
{Reads reals from the file OldFile, multiplies each by 2 and writes
the result to the file called NewFile. If NewFile does not exist, it is created;
if it already exists, the old contents are lost. OldFile is not changed.}
type NumberFile = file of real;
var OldFile, NewFile: NumberFile;
    Buffer: real;

begin{Program}
  writeln('Doubling program started.');

  reset(OldFile);
  rewrite(NewFile);
  {The window is at the first component of OldFile; NewFile is blank.}

  while not eof(OldFile) do
    begin{while}
      read(OldFile, Buffer);
      Buffer := 2 * Buffer;
      write(NewFile, Buffer)
      {Up to but not including the position of the windows, the
        components of NewFile are those of OldFile multiplied by 2.}
    end;  {while}

  writeln('End of program.')
end.  {Program}
```

Figure 16.1
Program using
nontext files.

eof   Just as we did with text files, we can use the boolean eof to detect the end of the file being read from. So the loop in our algorithm can be implemented with a while loop that uses the boolean eof (OldFile). The complete program is given in Figure 16.1.

Pitfall

Unexpected End of File

If a program is reading from the keyboard, it can ask the user whether there is more data or not. If it is reading from a file, there is no user to ask, and so the program must know when to stop reading data. If your program is not written so that it stops reading when the end of a file is reached, then the program will terminate abnormally when the file has been exhausted. Fortunately, the boolean eof can be used to detect the end of a nontext file. The boolean eof is used in the same way for nontext files as it is for text files. The use is illustrated in Figure 16.1.

Self-Test Exercises

1. Give a suitable type declaration for a file that is to hold student records consisting of a name, a final exam score in the range 0 to 100, and a letter grade.

2. Write a program to create a file of type *file of* integer and to write the numbers one through ten to the file.

3. Write a program that displays to the screen the contents of a file of the type used in the program of the previous exercise.

4. Write a program to search a file of integers to see whether it contains a particular integer. The particular integer should be read in from the keyboard.

Files as Parameters to Procedures

Procedures may have parameters of any file type, but they must be *variable parameters;* they cannot be value parameters. The situation for other types of files is the same as it is for text files. The next case study illustrates the use of file variable parameters.

Case Study

Changing a File of Records

Problem Definition

In this section we will design a program that modifies a file of records so that one field of each record is changed. For this case study, we assume that a file named PayFile contains employee records each consisting of an employee's number, name, and rate of pay. We will design a program that increases the rate of pay field for each record by 10%. In other words, we want to write a program that will give every employee a raise of 10%. The file type PayRecords is declared as follows, where MaxLength is a defined constant:

```
type Spell = array[1 . . MaxLength] of char;
     Employee = record
                   Number: integer;
                   Name: Spell;
                   PayRate: real
                end;
     PayRecords  = file of Employee;
```

Discussion

Some versions of Pascal allow random access to nontext files. However, many other systems do not. The only way to modify a non-text file with a portable Pascal program is to use the same basic technique that we used for modifying a text file: The program copies the file records into a temporary file, making the desired changes as it performs the copying. After that, the contents are copied back to the original file. (A slight variation, which we will not use but that also works, is to first copy to a temporary file without making any changes and to then copy back to the original file, making the changes as part of the second copy operation.)

ALGORITHM   The basic outline of this technique for modifying the file is shown in Figure 16.2. The extra file is called `Temp`. The variable `OneRecord` is used as a buffer variable to hold one record.

The complete program is given in Figure 16.3. The copying, including the reopen-

```
open PayFile with reset;
open Temp with rewrite;

while not eof (PayFile) do
  begin
    read (PayFile, OneRecord);
    change the value of the record variable OneRecord;
    write (Temp, OneRecord)
  end;

open Temp with reset;
open PayFile with rewrite;
Copy the contents of Temp into PayFile
```

Figure 16.2
Technique for modifying the data file PayFile.

```
program GiveRaise (input, output, PayFile);
{The external file PayFile is changed so that each component record has the
PayRate increased by (UpFactor*100) percent. Precondition: The file PayFile exists
in secondary storage and the PayRate record fields of each component have a value.}
const MaxLength = 30; {Maximum length for a name.}
      UpFactor = 0.1; {For a pay raise of 10 percent.}
type Spell = array[1 . . MaxLength] of char;
     Employee = record
                      Number: integer;
                      Name: Spell;
                      PayRate: real
                  end;
     PayRecords  = file of Employee;
var PayFile, Temp: PayRecords;
    {PayFile is an external file name; Temp is an internal file name.}
    OneRecord: Employee;
```

Figure 16.3
Program to modify a file of records.

```
procedure Copy(var Source, Dest: PayRecords);
{Copies the contents of the file Source into the file Dest.
Previous contents of Dest are lost.}
var OneRecord: Employee;
begin{Copy}
  reset(Source);
  rewrite(Dest);
  {The window is at the first component of Source. Dest is blank.}
  while not eof(Source) do
    begin{while}
      read(Source, OneRecord);
      write(Dest, OneRecord)
      {Up to but not including the position of the windows,
      the components of Dest are the same as those of Source.}
    end;  {while}
end;  {Copy}


begin{Program}
  writeln('I''m going to give everyone a raise.');
  {First copy each record to Temp, adjusting the value of PayRate in each record.}
  reset(PayFile);
  rewrite(Temp);
  while not eof(PayFile) do
    begin{while}
      read(PayFile, OneRecord);
      with OneRecord do
        PayRate := PayRate + UpFactor * PayRate;
      write(Temp, OneRecord)
    end;  {while}

  Copy(Temp, PayFile);

  writeln('Everybody is now richer.')
end.  {Program}
```

Figure 16.3
(continued)

ing of the files, is performed by the procedure Copy. Notice that the file Temp is an internal file. Any temporary file like this should be an internal file.

Deciding What Type of File to Use

Since integer and real values can be stored in text files, there may seem to be no need for the file types *file of* integer and *file of* real. This is not quite true. When storing numbers in a file of type text, a type conversion is performed whenever a number is read from or written to the file. With the other file types, no type conversion is needed. Hence, if all the data in a file is of type integer, then a program will run more efficiently if the type of the files used is *file of* integer rather than text. In the case of the type real, accuracy is also an issue. When using a text file, each reading or writing of a value of type real can introduce inaccuracies in the value stored. This loss of accuracy is a result of the type conversion calculation. By using a file of type *file of* real, you avoid these type conversions and the inaccuracies they produce.

When choosing a file type, remember that the components of a file can be of a structured type. If your program needs to place an array of real values in secondary storage, then a *file of* real will work acceptably. However, a much simpler program can be written using a file with an array component type. For example, consider the following declarations:

```
type ArrayType = array[1 . . 100] of real;
var A: ArrayType;
    DiskFile: file of ArrayType;
```

Once the file has been opened, the array can be placed in secondary storage with the one write statement displayed next.

```
write(DiskFile, A)
```

This is much simpler and easier to read than a *for* loop that separately copies each value from the array to a *file of* real.

Case Study

Merging Two Files

Problem Definition

Data is often provided in the form of files that need to be processed at some central location. As a simple example, let us suppose that a company has two plants, which keep employee pay records of the form used in Figure 16.3. The files are sent from the plants to corporate headquarters, where they need to be merged into a single file containing all the records from the two files. In this section we will design a procedure to merge two such files into a third master file. We assume that both files are sorted by employee number from lowest to highest and that each file has a sentinel record that marks the end of the file. This sentinel record is assumed to have an employee number field that is larger than any actual employee number.

Discussion

The procedure that performs the merging must read the records in each file in the order that they occur, which is assumed to be lowest to highest employee number, and it must write them to the master file one at a time in the order lowest number to highest number. Things seem to be ordered in a fortuitous way. If the procedure reads the first record from each of the smaller files into two buffer variables, then we can be certain that one of the two buffer variables contains the lowest numbered record of all the records in the two files. Therefore, the procedure can write this record to the master file and then replace the just-written-out record with the next smallest record from the same

(a)

(b)

Figure 16.4

Merging two files.

(c)

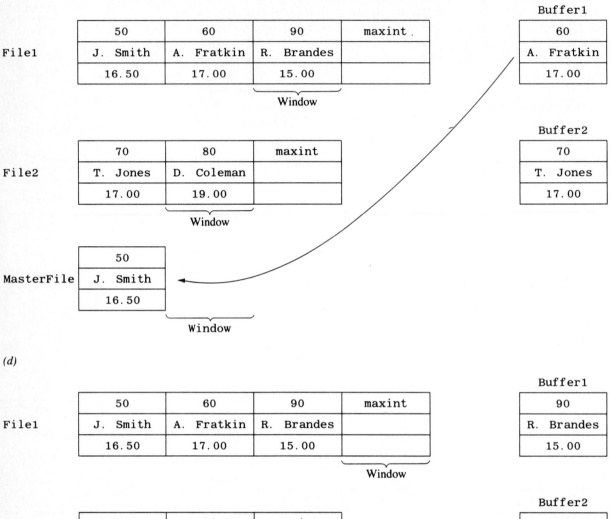

Figure 16.4 (continued)

(e)

Buffer1

90
R. Brandes
15.00

File1

50	60	90	maxint
J. Smith	A. Fratkin	R. Brandes	
16.50	17.00	15.00	

Window

Buffer2

80
D. Coleman
19.00

File2

70	80	maxint
T. Jones	D. Coleman	
17.00	19.00	

Window

MasterFile

50	60	70
J. Smith	A. Fratkin	T. Jones
16.50	17.00	17.00

Window

(f)

Buffer1

90
R. Brandes
15.00

File1

50	60	90	maxint
J. Smith	A. Fratkin	R. Brandes	
16.50	17.00	15.00	

Window

Buffer2

maxint

File2

70	80	maxint	End of file
T. Jones	D. Coleman		
17.00	19.00		

Window

MasterFile

50	60	70	80
J. Smith	A. Fratkin	T. Jones	D. Coleman
16.50	17.00	17.00	19.00

Window

Figure 16.4 (continued)

(g)

Buffer1

50	60	90	maxint
J. Smith	A. Fratkin	R. Brandes	
16.50	17.00	15.00	

File1

End of file

maxint

Window

Buffer2

70	80	maxint
T. Jones	D. Coleman	
17.00	19.00	

File2

End of file

maxint

Window

50	60	70	80	90
J. Smith	A. Fratkin	T. Jones	D. Coleman	R. Brandes
16.50	17.00	17.00	19.00	15.00

MasterFile

Window

(h)

A sentinel record is added to MasterFile.

50	60	70	80	90	maxint
J. Smith	A. Fratkin	T. Jones	D. Coleman	R. Brandes	
16.50	17.00	17.00	19.00	15.00	

MasterFile

Figure 16.4 (continued)

file as the record just disposed of. At this point the two records in buffer variables include the next lowest number, and the process can be repeated. The process is illustrated in Figure 16.4. Since each file is terminated with a sentinel record that contains a very large number, we know that neither file will run out of records until the procedure empties both files and needs to compare the two sentinel values. At that point we can have the procedure end the process and then arbitrarily write either of the sentinel records at the end of the master file.

variables   Let us use File1 and File2 as the file variables for the two files being merged and MasterFile as the file variable for the file to receive the merged list. The two buffer variables to hold one record from each file will be called Buffer1 and Buffer2. The files File1 and File2 are opened with reset, MasterFile is opened with rewrite, and then the following algorithm is executed to perform the merge:

ALGORITHM

```
read(File1, Buffer1);
read(File2, Buffer2);
while (not eof(File1)) or (not eof(File2)) do
   begin
      Find out which of Buffer1 or Buffer2
      has the smaller number and write that record to MasterFile;
      Replace the record written with one from the same file.
   end
write(MasterFile, Buffer1);   {Buffer1 is a sentinel record.}
```

The final procedure is shown in Figure 16.5. The body of the *while* loop is implemented as the procedure CopySmaller.

The procedure Merge can be quite inefficient for some files. If the records in one file are all copied before the other file is emptied, then the procedure will compare all the remaining records to the sentinel record. If the number of records remaining is large, this can be very time-consuming. A more efficient procedure would detect when it had reached the end of one of the files, and at that point would simply copy the records remaining in the other file into the master file. We leave the design and coding of such an efficient procedure as an exercise. (See Exercise 11.)

efficiency

File Buffer Variable
(Optional)

The term "buffer variable" has two related meanings. As we have been using it thus far, it means any variable that is used to hold data on its way from one location to another. Within the specifications of the Pascal language, it also has a very narrow meaning that applies to a very special kind of variable. Whenever a file variable is declared, Pascal automatically provides a special variable called a *buffer variable*, which is used in very specialized ways to move data into or out of the file. In this section we describe this special variable.

Whenever any type of file variable is declared, a variable called the *buffer variable* for the file is automatically declared. In Pascal programs, this file variable is always written as the identifier for the file variable followed by the "up-arrow" symbol ↑. The "up arrow" symbol may look a bit different on some screens. A common variant is ˆ, called a *circumflex* and looking like an arrow without the shaft. Some systems even use

```
type Spell = array[1 . . MaxLength] of char;
     Employee = record
                   Number: integer;
                   Name: Spell;
                   PayRate: real
                end;
        PayRecords  = file of Employee;
```

Figure 16.5
Procedure to merge two files.

```
procedure CopySmaller(var Buffer1, Buffer2: Employee;
                          var File1, File2, MasterFile: PayRecords);
```
{*Precondition: not eof(File1) or not eof(File2); Buffer1 and Buffer2 contain
the last records read from File1 and File2 respectively. Postcondition: The correct
record has been copied to MasterFile and replaced by the next record from the same file.*}
begin{*CopySmaller*}
   if `Buffer1.Number` < `Buffer2.Number` *then*
     begin{*Buffer1.Number < Buffer2.Number*}
       `write(MasterFile, Buffer1);`
       `read(File1, Buffer1)`
     end   {*Buffer1.Number < Buffer2.Number*}
   else
     begin{*Buffer2.Number <= Buffer1.Number*}
       `write(MasterFile, Buffer2);`
       `read(File2, Buffer2)`
     end   {*Buffer2.Number <= Buffer1.Number*}
end; {*CopySmaller*}

```
procedure Merge(var File1, File2, MasterFile: PayRecords);
```
{*Precondition: The files File1 and File2 are sorted by employee number and
each is terminated with a sentinel record whose Number field has the value maxint.
Postcondition: MasterFile contains all the records from File1 and File2, they
are sorted by employee number, and there is a sentinel record at the end.*}
```
var Buffer1, Buffer2: Employee;
```

begin{*Merge*}
  `writeln('Merging started.');`

  `reset(File1);`
  `reset(File2);`
  `rewrite(MasterFile);`

  `read(File1, Buffer1);`
  `read(File2, Buffer2);`
  while (*not* eof(File1)) *or* (*not* eof(File2)) *do*
    `CopySmaller(Buffer1, Buffer2, File1, File2, MasterFile);`
  {*Both eof(File1) and eof(File2) are true.*}

  {*Buffer1 contains a sentinel record.*}
  `write(MasterFile, Buffer1);`

  `writeln('Merging completed.')`
end; {*Merge*}

Figure 16.5
(continued)

the totally different symbol @ in place of ↑.) The type of the buffer variable is the same as the component type of the file variable. The value, if any, of the buffer variable is some item of the component type that typically either is in the file window or can easily be placed in the window.

To illustrate the notion of a buffer variable, suppose that a program contains the declarations:

```
type FileInt = file of integer;
var  File1: FileInt;
```

As a side effect of this file variable declaration, a buffer variable spelled as follows is automatically declared:

```
File1↑
```

This buffer variable is of type `integer`. It need not be explicitly declared. In fact, it is an error to do so. Including the following line in the program will cause a syntax error message:

```
var File1↑: integer;
{THIS LINE IS NOT ALLOWED IN ANY PROGRAM.}
```

Still, `File1↑` is a variable of type `integer` and may be manipulated in many of the same ways that any other `integer` variable is manipulated. Hence, under some but not necessarily all conditions, the following are valid Pascal statements.

```
File1↑ := 5;
X := File1↑;
readln(File1↑);   {This reads from the keyboard.}
writeln(File1↑);   {This writes to the screen.}
Proc4(File1↑)   {Proc4 is a procedure name.}
```

If a file has been opened with `reset`, then the value of the buffer variable is the component currently in the window. (The program can explicitly change the value of the buffer variable by assigning it a new value, but the value always starts out as the value in the window.) Every time the window is moved, the value of the buffer variable is automatically changed to the component that is moved into the window. So the buffer variable is a way to "see into the window." If `File1↑` has been opened with `reset` (and the value of the buffer variable has not been changed), then the following sets the variable X equal to the value currently in the window:

```
X := File1↑
```

The buffer variable is also needed if you are using the standard procedures `put` and `get`, described in the next section.

put and get
(Optional)

put—
"writing"

Entering data into a file is called *writing* even if the procedure write is not used. The standard procedure put can be used to write one component to a file. For example, suppose File1 is the file variable name for a file of integers and that the file has been opened using rewrite. A call to put is of the form

    put (File1)

This command "puts," or "writes," the value of the buffer variable File1↑ into the window of File1 and then moves the window to the next position. For example, writing the number 5 to File1 can be accomplished by the two statements

    File1↑ : = 5;
    put (File1)

Writing the number 6 into the next position in the file can be accomplished by next executing the two statements

    File1↑ : = 6;
    put (File1)

After execution of the procedure put, the value of the buffer variable is undefined. Hence, the buffer variable must be given a value before an additional call to put.

If the program is going to use put with a file, then the file is opened with rewrite. When a file is opened using rewrite, the window is at the location to receive the first component, but since rewrite produces an empty file, there is no value in the window. The value of the buffer variable is undefined at this point and must be given a value before a put is executed. When put is executed, the new component is entered at the window location and the window is moved to the next position. Each execution of put appends another component to the end of the file. After each execution of put, the value of the buffer variable is undefined. The process is diagrammed in Figure 16.6.

get—
"reading"

Retrieving data from a file is called *reading* even if the procedure read is not used. The standard procedure get can be used to read one component from a file. For example, suppose File1 is the file variable name for a file of some type (say *file of* integer to be specific, but the same remarks apply whatever the component type is). Suppose that the file has just been opened with reset. The call to reset positions the window at the first component and causes the value of the buffer variable File1↑ to be set to this first component. So to set the variable X1 equal to the first component in the file, all that is needed is an assignment statement, like so:

    X1 : = File1↑

To "get" the next component in the file, the procedure get can be used. A call to get is of the form

    get (File1)

eof

This moves the window to the next component in the file and sets the value of the buffer variable File1↑ equal to the value of the component that then comes into the win-

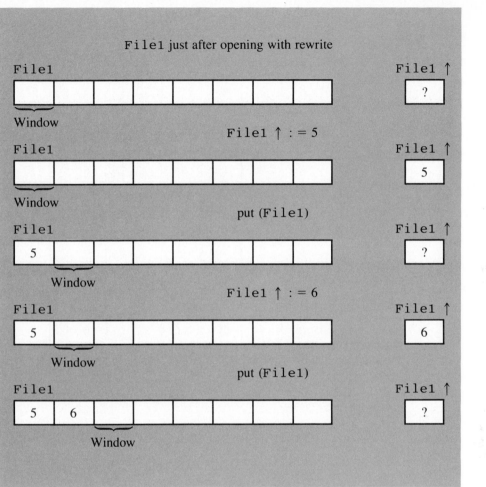

Figure 16.6
(Optional)
Use of put.

dow. If there is a next component so that all this can be carried out, then the call to get also sets the value of eof (File1) to false. If there is no next component, then the location of the window and the value of File1↑ are undefined, and the value of eof (File1) is set to true.

As an example, the following piece of code sets the values of X1 and X2 equal to the first and second components (in that order) of the file File1:

{*The file File1 has been opened with* reset *and has not been manipulated since being opened.*}
```
X1 := File1↑;
get(File1);
X2 := File1↑
```

The process is illustrated in Figure 16.7.

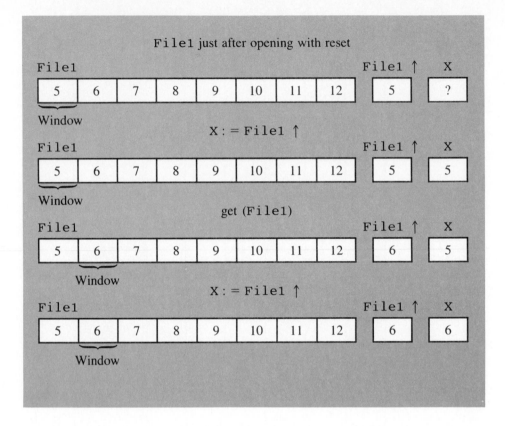

**Figure 16.7
(Optional)
Use of get.**

*write and
read
redefined*

Alternative, and in fact the official, definitions of write and read are expressed in terms of put and get. To illustrate, consider the statement

    write(File1, X)

That statement is equivalent to

    File1↑ := X;
    put(File1)

The statement

    read(File1, Y)

is equivalent to

    Y := File1↑;
    get(File1)

Example Using put and get
(Optional)

Figure 16.8 is a Pascal program that illustrates the use of put and get. The program reads from a file of real values called OldFile, multiplies each number by 2, and then copies the result to a second file of real values called NewFile. The program performs the same task as the one in Figure 16.1 but it uses put and get instead of read and write.

```
program DoubleVersion2(input, output, OldFile, NewFile);
{Reads reals from the file OldFile, multiplies each by 2, and writes the result to the file NewFile.
If NewFile does not exist, it is created; if it already exists,
the old contents are lost. OldFile is not changed.}
type NumberFile = file of real;
var  OldFile, NewFile: NumberFile;

begin{Program}
  writeln('Manipulating files.');

  reset(OldFile);
  rewrite(NewFile);
  {The window is at the first component of OldFile;
  NewFile is blank.}

  while not eof(OldFile) do
    begin{while}
      NewFile↑ := 2 * OldFile↑;
      put(NewFile);
      get(OldFile)
      {Up to but not including the position of the windows, the
      components of NewFile are those of OldFile multiplied by 2.}
    end;  {while}

  writeln('End of program')
end. {Program}
```

**Figure 16.8
(Optional)
Pascal program
using put and
get.**

Summary of Problem Solving
and Programming Techniques

- Data of almost any type, including record types, may be kept in secondary storage by using a file with that particular component type.
- Although numeric data can be stored in a text file, it is usually more efficient and clearer to store it in a file whose component type matches the type of the data.

- Nontext files are opened and named in the same way as text files.
- The procedures writeln and readln and the boolean eoln do not make sense for and so cannot be used with nontext files. The procedures read and write, as well as the boolean eof, can be used with other files in basically the same way that they are used with text files.
- The exact details of file handling will vary from one installation to another. Hence, file handling should be isolated into procedures in order to make any needed changes easy to carry out.
- Data in a file is accessed one component at a time.
- To change a file, a program must use another, temporary file: The data is copied into the temporary file and changed as part of the copying; the contents are then copied back to the original file. The temporary file should be an internal file. (Some versions of Pascal allow random access to files, but you cannot count on that feature being available.)

Summary of Pascal Constructs

file types

Syntax:

> *file of* <component type>

Example:

```
type Item =
        record
          Field1:  integer;
          Field2:  array[1 . . 10] of real
        end;
     DataFile = file of Item;
```

Type of a file to hold components of type <component type>. The <component type> may be any type that does not involve a file type.

file variable declarations

Syntax:

> *var* <file var>: <file type name or definition>;

Examples:

```
var File1:  file of integer;
    File2:  DataFile;
```

Declaration of a file variable. (The sample type DataFile is defined in the previous example.)

reset

Syntax:

```
reset (<file var>)
```

Example:

```
reset (File1)
```

Opens the file named by the file variable <file var> for reading, positions the window at the first component in the file, and sets the value of the buffer variable <file var> ↑ equal to the value of this first component.

rewrite

Syntax:

```
rewrite (<file var>)
```

Example:

```
rewrite (File1)
```

Creates a new file named by the file variable <file var>, opens the file for writing, and positions the window to receive the first component. If there already is a file whose file variable name is <file var>, and <file var> is an external file name (i.e., appears in the program heading), then the contents of the old file are lost.

read

Syntax:

```
read (<file var>, <component type var>)
```

Example:

```
read (File1, X)
```

The standard procedure read used with a file of type other than text. <file var> is the file variable name of the file, and <component type var> is a variable of the component type of the file. There may be any number of variables. The value of <component type var> is set equal to the value of the component in the window and the window is advanced to the next component. If there is more than one variable to receive values, then a value is read into each variable in this way.

write

Syntax:

```
write (<file var>, <expression>)
```

Example:

```
write (File1, X + 9)
```

The standard procedure `write` used with a file of type other than `text`. <file var> is the file variable name of the file, and <expression> is an expression that evaluates to a value of the component type of the file. There may be any number of expressions. The value of the component in the window is set equal to the value of the expression, and the window is advanced to the next component. If there is more than one expression, then this is repeated for each expression.

eof

Syntax:

    eof (<file var>)

Example:

    eof (File1)

A boolean function that returns `true` if the window in the file named by the file variable <file var> is beyond the last component and `false` when a file component is in the window.

Summary of put and get
(Optional)

buffer variable

Syntax:

    <file var>↑

Example:

    File1↑

Buffer variable for the file named by the file variable <file var>. A variable whose type is the component type of the file variable <file var>. The buffer variable is meant to be used in conjunction with the standard procedures `put` and `get`.

put

Syntax:

    put (<file var>)

Example:

    put (File1)

Writes the value of the buffer variable <file var>↑ into the window in the file <file var> and moves the window to the next position. After execution, the value of the buffer variable <file var>↑ is undefined.

get

Syntax:

```
get (<file var>)
```

Example:

```
get (File1)
```

If the window is at some component other than the last component, then this moves the window in <file var> to the next component, sets the value of the buffer variable <file var> ↑ equal to the value of this next component, and sets the value of eof (<file var>) to false. If the window is at the last component, this sets eof (<file var>) to true and leaves both the window position and the value of <file var> ↑ undefined.

Exercises

Self-Test Exercises

5. Write a boolean-valued function with two arguments, F, a file of type PayRecords, and N, an integer. The type PayRecords is defined in Figure 16.3. The function should return true if the file contains a record for employee number N and should return false if the file contains no such record.

Interactive Exercises

6. (This exercise uses the optional section "put and get.") Rewrite the code for the procedure Copy in Figure 16.3 using put and get (rather than read and write.)

7. Write a program that fills an array with 10 integers read from the keyboard and then stores the array value in a file of the type defined as follows:

```
type List = array[1 . . 10] of integer;
     AFile = file of List;
```

8. Write a program that fills an array from the file created by the program of the previous exercise and then displays the array values to the screen.

Programming Exercises

9. Write a program to search an existing file of integers and find both the largest and the smallest integers in the file.

10. Write a program that fills a file of the type used in Figure 16.3 with data read from the keyboard.

11. Rewrite the procedure Merge in Figure 16.5 so that it is more efficient in the manner described in the chapter. The sentinel records are not essential in this approach, and so your program should be designed to work with files that do not contain a sentinel record at the end.

12. Write a program that reads 10 `integer` values from a *file of* integer into an array, sorts the array, and then writes the sorted list back into the same file, so that the effect is to sort the numbers in the file.

13. Write a program that sorts a file of type *file of* integer so that the numbers appear in numeric order from the smallest to the largest. The final sorted list should be in the same file as the one originally containing the integers. The program should work for any size file, and so the program cannot read the numbers into an array as in the previous exercise. (One simple way to do this is to use a second file; the smallest number is copied to the file, then the next smallest, and so forth. Then the sorted file is copied back into the original file. There are also more efficient ways to do the sorting.)

14. A record for describing a person is to consist of the following items: last name, initial of first name, sex, age, height, weight, and telephone number. The records are to be stored in an array indexed by integers in the range 1 to `Limit`. `Limit` is to be declared as a constant. Write a program that reads in up to `Limit` records from the keyboard, stores them in an array, writes them out to the screen, and then writes them to a file. The file should be a file of records, not a text file or a file of arrays. Your program should allow the possibility of fewer than `Limit` records being read in.

15. Write a program that reads the file created in the previous exercise, places the components into an array, sorts the records in the array according to the alphabetical order of the last names, writes the sorted records to the screen, and then copies the records back to the file in alphabetical order.

16. Modify your program from Exercise 14 so that the second and succeeding times that it is run, the contents of the file are copied into an array; the user then has the option of either clearing all records and starting over or adding more records to those already in the array. Modify your program further to allow the user to delete individual records by specifying the last name for the record to be deleted. The user should also have the option of clearing all records without having to specify every name. Modify your program further to allow the user to see all records of a given category (such as all records for individuals between two specified ages) on the screen. All manipulations should be done with the array. When the user is finished, the program should copy the modified collection of records back to the file so that the file then contains the same records as the array.

17. Redo the previous assignment, but this time have your program deal directly with the file and not use an array.

18. Write a program for a computerized dating service. The information on individuals should be kept in a file of records and should include all the information described in Exercise 14, plus other information, such as a hobbies, favorite color, and so forth. A user should be able to request a list of all dates that satisfy the user's specifications. Include a "best match" option that finds the date that is best suited to the user based only on the user's own record. Use a file of records.

19. Write a program to sort a file of records of the type described in Exercise 14. The files are to be arranged into alphabetical order according to last names. (One simple way to do this is to use a second file; the alphabetically first record is copied to the file,

then the alphabetically next, and so forth. There are also more efficient ways to do the sorting.)

20. Write a program to keep track of airline flight reservations and seat reservations. Allow any number of flights. Display seating plans as described in Exercise 19 of Chapter 10. The program should be able to add or delete flights. It should keep track of who is in what seat, as well as which seats are reserved. Keep the information in a file so that the program can be rerun and the information will be as it was left the last time the program was run. Use some file type other than `text`.

21. Write a program that fills a two-dimensional array of characters with a pattern typed in from the keyboard and then echoes back the pattern on the screen. Next write a program that uses a file whose component type is the type of the two-dimensional array. This program should store one array for each letter of the alphabet. When displayed, the array for each letter should display that letter as a large block letter. Finally, write a program that uses this file of arrays to read a word from the keyboard and to echo it back to the screen in block letters, one letter at at time.

22. If you are enrolled in a programming (or other) course, write a program that will serve as a record keeper for grades in your course. The program should allow the entry, display, and changing of any particular grade, such as a particular quiz or exam. If there is a formula for the final numeric grade, the program should calculate it. The program should allow the user to ask the class average for any particular grade, such as a quiz or exam grade. Use a file of records.

References for Further Reading

The reference manuals for your particular system are likely to be your best source of detailed information. The reference by Tiberghen listed in Chapter 3 is also helpful.

DYNAMIC
DATA STRUCTURES

"You are sad," the Knight said in anxious tone: *"let me sing you a song to comfort you."*

"Is it very long?" Alice asked, for she had heard a good deal of poetry that day.

"It's long," said the Knight, *"but it's very,* very *beautiful. Everybody that hears me sing it—either it brings the* tears *into their eyes, or else—"*

"Or else what?" said Alice, for the Knight had made a sudden pause.

"Or else it doesn't, you know. The name of the song is called 'Haddocks' Eyes.'*"*

"Oh, that's the name of the song, is it?" Alice said, trying to feel interested.

"No, you don't understand," the Knight said, looking a little vexed. *"That's what the name is* called. *The name really is* 'The Aged Aged Man.'*"*

"Then I ought to have said 'That's what the song *is called'?"* Alice corrected herself.

"No, you oughtn't: that's quite another thing! The song *is called* 'Ways and Means': *but that's only what it's* called, *you know!"*

"Well, what is *the song, then?"* said Alice, who was by this time completely bewildered.

"I was coming to that," the Knight said. *"The song really is* 'A-sitting On A Gate': *and the tune's my own invention."*

LEWIS CARROLL, THROUGH THE LOOKING-GLASS

Chapter Contents

A *static data structure* is one whose structure is completely specified at the time the program is written and which cannot be changed by the program. Most of the data structures we have seen thus far, such as arrays and simple records, are static data structures. The values of the various components in these structures may change, but the structures themselves do not change. A program cannot change the number of items in an array or the number of indexes for the array. The structure is fixed.

Dynamic data structures may have their structure changed by the program. They may expand and contract in size as the program is executed, and as we will see in this chapter, the program can even change the manner in which the data is organized. In this chapter we will introduce a construct called a *pointer* and show how pointers can be used to construct a wide variety of dynamic data structures including *lists, stacks,* and a new data structure called a *tree*.

The Notion of a Pointer

A *pointer* is, quite plainly and simply, something that points. That definition is very abstract. To make it concrete, we will give it a geometric interpretation in terms of figures drawn on paper. These figures will always be configurations of boxes connected by arrows. In these figures a pointer is represented by an arrow. Each of these arrows, or pointers, usually points to an object called a *node*. In these drawings a node is represented by a box, of any shape, in which things may be written or, more abstractly, in which data may be stored. For example, a list of records might be represented as nodes and pointers in the manner of Figure 17.1. In this case each record contains a number and a letter, and so the records might be student numbers and final course grades.

nodes

Before we present any more discussion of dynamic data structures, we will stop and discuss the Pascal syntax for pointers and nodes. This will allow us to express our algorithms as Pascal programs.

Pascal Pointers and Dynamic Variables

In Pascal there is a special class of variables called *dynamic variables*. These dynamic variables are designed to be used as the nodes in dynamic data structures such as the

dynamic variables

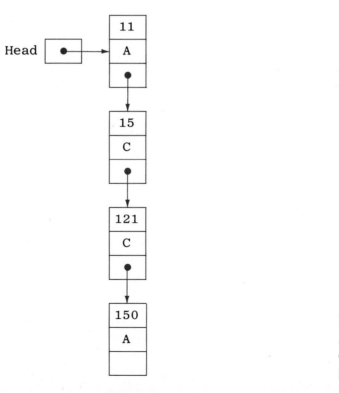

Figure 17.1

A data structure containing pointers.

list in Figure 17.1. In many ways dynamic variables are like the ordinary variables we have been using up until now. Like other variables, dynamic variables have a type. Dynamic variables may be of almost any type. The only exception is that dynamic variables of types involving files are not allowed. Dynamic variables can be assigned a value by means of an assignment operator, or a `read` statement, or by any other means that the value of an ordinary variable can be set. Similarly, the value in a dynamic variable can be accessed in any of the ways that the value of an ordinary variable can be accessed: by a `write` statement, by being an actual parameter to a procedure, or by any other means that the value of an ordinary variable can be accessed.

Dynamic variables differ from ordinary variables in only two ways. First, they may be created and destroyed by the program, and hence the number of such dynamic variables need not—indeed cannot—be determined at the time the program is written. Second, they have no names in Pascal; there are no identifiers that name them in the way that ordinary variables are named by identifiers. For these reasons, dynamic variables are not declared.

pointer variables

In order to refer to a dynamic variable, Pascal uses another type of variable called a *pointer variable*. Pointer variables are declared and do have identifiers associated with them. Pointer variables also have a type associated with them, and this type specifies the type of the dynamic variables with which they can be used. The value of a pointer variable is a pointer, and a pointer may point to a dynamic variable of the appropriate type. In this way, a dynamic variable may be referred to indirectly by giving a pointer that points to the dynamic variable. Typically, this is done by giving a pointer variable whose value points to the dynamic variable.

As an example, suppose we have the following record type declared in a program:

```
type Student = record
                   Number: integer;
                   Grade: char
               end;
```

The program can have dynamic variables of type `Student`. They are not declared, but pointer variables, which can hold pointers that point to them, are declared. The following declares the variable P to be a pointer variable whose values are pointers to dynamic variables of type `Student`:

```
var P:  ↑Student;
```

The symbol ↑ is the "up-arrow" symbol. (It may look a bit different on some screens. A common variant is ˆ, called a *circumflex* and looking like an arrow without the shaft. Some systems even use the totally different symbol @ in place of ↑.)

domain type

The type of the dynamic variables, such as `Student` in this example, is sometimes called the *domain type* of the pointer. The variable P can only contain pointers to dynamic variables of type `Student`. To hold a pointer to a dynamic variable of some other type, for instance `real`, requires a different pointer variable of the type ↑`real`. Dynamic variables and pointer variables both have types and, in order to hold a pointer to a dynamic variable, the type of the pointer variable must match that of the dynamic variable.

```
type Student = record
                    Number: integer;
                    Grade: char
                end;
var P:  ↑Student;
```

new(P)

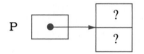

P↑.Number := 5

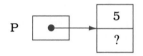

P↑.Grade := 'A'

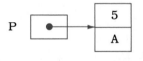

**Figure 17.2
Use of pointer
variables and
dynamic variables.**

Of course, a pointer variable is of no use unless there is something for it to point
to. In order to create a dynamic variable, the standard procedure new is used. For example, suppose that P is as previously declared, and consider the following statement:

new

new(P)

This will create a new dynamic variable of type Student and set the value of P equal
to a pointer that points to this new dynamic variable. This dynamic variable can then be
referred to as "the thing pointed to by P. " In Pascal the phrase "the thing pointed to by
P" is denoted P↑. In order to set the value of the component field Number in this
new dynamic variable, we can use an assignment statement, like so:

P↑.Number := 5

This is illustrated in Figure 17.2. As shown there, the Grade field can be set in a
similar way.

The values of the component fields of this dynamic variable can be written to the
screen in the usual way:

writeln(P↑.Number, P↑.Grade)

Similarly, P↑ can be used anyplace else that it is appropriate to use a record variable of type Student.

Manipulating Pointers

Before going any further, we had best stop and clarify the common English syntax used by programmers when discussing pointers and pointer variables. In the preceding example, P was a pointer variable. Technically speaking, it does not point to anything. It has values that are pointers, and these pointers point to dynamic variables. It may help to think of the pointer as an arrow and the pointer variable as something or somebody that can hold one pointer arrow at a time. This distinction between a pointer and a pointer variable is sometimes important. However, we will follow common usage and will usually blur this distinction. We will usually write, for example, "P points to a dynamic variable" when we really mean "the value of P points to a dynamic variable."

Program

```
program Test(input, output);

type Student = record
                   Number: integer;
                   Grade:  char
               end;
     StuPointer =  ↑Student;
var P1, P2: StuPointer;

begin{Program}
   new (P1);
   P1↑.Number := 1;
   P1↑.Grade := 'A';
   writeln(P1↑.Number, P1↑.Grade);
   new(P2);
   P2↑.Number := 2;
   P2↑.Grade := 'B';
   writeln(P2↑.Number, P2↑.Grade);
   P1 := P2;
   P2↑.Number := 3;
   P2↑.Grade := 'C';
   writeln(P1↑.Number, P1↑.Grade, P2↑.Number, P2↑.Grade)
end.  {Program}
```

Output

Figure 17.3
Program that illustrates pointers.

1A
2B
3C 3C

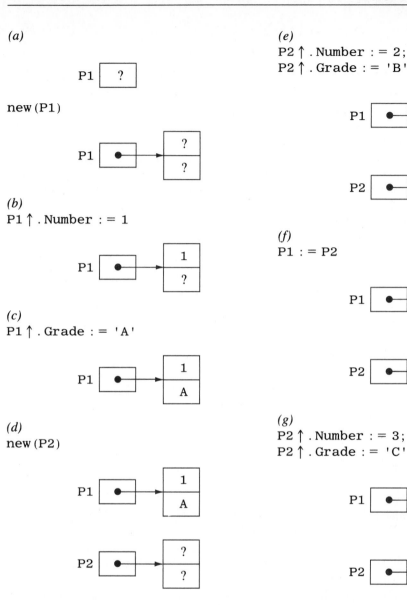

(a)

P1   ?

new (P1)

P1 ● → ? / ?

(b)
P1 ↑ . Number : = 1

P1 ● → 1 / ?

(c)
P1 ↑ . Grade : = 'A'

P1 ● → 1 / A

(d)
new (P2)

P1 ● → 1 / A

P2 ● → ? / ?

(e)
P2 ↑ . Number : = 2;
P2 ↑ . Grade : = 'B'

P1 ● → 1 / A

P2 ● → 2 / B

(f)
P1 : = P2

P1 ● → 1 / A

P2 ● → 2 / B

(g)
P2 ↑ . Number : = 3;
P2 ↑ . Grade : = 'C'

P1 ● → 1 / A

P2 ● → 3 / C

Figure 17.4
Explanation of
Figure 17.3.

Dynamic variables may have more than one pointer that is pointing to them. Also, pointers may be changed so that they point to different dynamic variables at different times. These changes are accomplished with the assignment operator : = . Technically speaking, there is nothing new involved. The assignment operator works with pointer variables in exactly the same way that it does with the other types of variables we have seen. However, interpreting the result can be a bit subtle. A sample program will help to illustrate the concepts. The workings of the program in Figure 17.3 are illustrated in Figure 17.4.

:= and
pointers

P1 : = P2

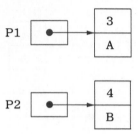
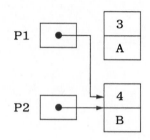

P1 ↑ : = P2 ↑

Figure 17.5
The distinction
between
P1 and P1 ↑.

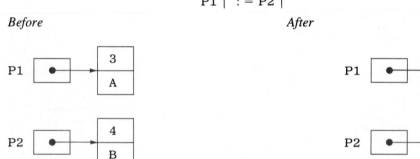

In Figure 17.3 the statement

    P1 : = P2

changes the value of P1 to that of P2. The values of P1 and P2 are pointers, and the only property a pointer has is that it points to something. Hence, the effect of this statement is to give P1 a value that points to the same dynamic variable as the value of P2 does. Stated this way, it makes it sound as though the two pointers in Figure 17.4(f) are the same pointer, and in a sense they are, just as two values of the number 5 stored in two different integer variables are the same integer 5. Those who find this too confusing, or too philosophical for their liking, can instead remember the more prosaic rule that if X and Y are pointer variables, then the statement

    X : = Y

changes X so that it points to the same thing that Y is currently pointing to.

When dealing with pointer variables, the distinction between a pointer variable, P1, for example, and the thing it points to, P1 ↑ , is very important. When using the assignment operator, always be sure you check to see that you are referring to objects of the appropriate type. The distinction is illustrated in Figure 17.5.

Nodes

The program in the previous section is a toy program. Nobody would use it for anything other than a learning aid. In fact, dynamic variables of type Student have almost no uses. Like the type Student, the type of a dynamic variable is invariably
some sort of record type. However, the record type of a dynamic variable normally
contains at least one field that is of a pointer type. By way of example, consider the
data structure in Figure 17.1. The nodes in that data structure would be represented by
records with three fields: two are of the types integer and char, the same as the
type Student, but there is also one more field of a pointer type that can point to such
nodes. The Pascal type declarations, as well as the declaration of the pointer variable
Head, are shown at the end of this paragraph. The identifier Node can be replaced by
any other identifier, but since the record represents a node, there is a tendency to call
the type Node.

type
declaration

```
type NPointer = ↑Node;
     Node = record
                Number: integer;
                Grade: char;
                Link: NPointer
            end;
var Head: NPointer;
```

This declaration is blatantly circular. NPointer is defined in terms of Node,
and Node is defined in terms of NPointer. As it turns out, there is nothing wrong
with this circularity, and it is allowed in Pascal. One indication that this definition is not
logically inconsistent is the fact that we can draw pictures representing such structures.
Figure 17.1 is one such picture. This is fortunate, since we must use some sort of circularity if we are to have data structures of this kind. After all, we want each node to
contain a pointer to other nodes of the same type. If this is to be the situation, then the
straightforward definition of the node type must refer to the pointers, and the straightforward definition of the pointer type must refer to the nodes. (In an attempt to avoid
circularity, one clever programmer suggested defining a "pointer" as an arrow that
points to "anything." But alas, the programmer's definition of "anything" referred to
nodes, and the definition of "nodes" referred to pointers.) This is yet another example
of how circular definitions can be not only meaningful, but also extremely useful in
computer programming.

Pascal does require that the pointer type definition precede the associated node
type definition; hence, the definitions of the types NPointer and Node must be in
the order shown.

We now have pointers inside of records, and have these pointers pointing to
records that contain pointers, and so forth. In these situations the syntax can sometimes
get involved, but in all cases the syntax follows those few rules that we have described
for pointers and records. As an illustration, suppose the declarations are as above, the
situation is as diagrammed in Figure 17.1, and we want to change the value of the

Number field of the second node to 23; in other words, we want to change the 15 to a 23. One way to accomplish this is with the following statement:

```
Head↑.Link↑.Number := 23
```

To understand the expression on the left-hand side of the assignment operator, read it carefully from left to right. Head is a pointer; Head↑ is the thing it points to, namely the node (dynamic variable) containing 11. (This node can be referred to as Head↑, "but that's only what it's called, you know!" What it really is is the first node.) This node, referred to by Head↑, is a record, and the field of this record that contains a pointer is called Link, and so Head↑.Link is the name of a pointer that points to the node containing 15. Since Head↑.Link is the name of a pointer that points to the node containing 15, Head↑.Link↑ is a name for the node itself. Finally, Head↑.Link↑.Number is a name for the Number field of the node containing 15, and the assignment statement changes its value to 23. One can usually avoid such long expressions involving pointers, but occasionally they are useful, and they are a good test of whether or not you understand the syntax and semantics of pointers.

The Pointer nil

There is one last Pascal construct that we need to describe before going on to discuss the applications of pointers. That is the constant *nil*. The constant *nil* is a predefined constant in the same sense that maxint is a predefined constant, although *nil* is of a different type than maxint. The constant *nil* is used to give a value to pointer variables that do not point to anything. As such, it can be used as a kind of end marker. For example, in the data structure shown in Figure 17.1, it would be reasonable to set the pointer field of the last node equal to *nil*. Then the program could test for the end of the list by checking to see if the pointer field equals *nil*. The usage of *nil* as an end marker is illustrated in the next section.

Pitfall

Forgetting That nil Is a Pointer

To avoid syntax errors, remember that *nil* is a pointer and not the thing pointed to. For example, suppose the declarations are as we described previously, and suppose the situation is as diagrammed in Figure 17.6(a); in that figure the pointer Last is of the same type as Head and has been positioned by some other part of the program. In order to set the pointer field of the last node to *nil*, the Pascal statement would be

```
Last↑.Link := nil
```

The effect of this assignment is diagrammed in Figure 17.6. Before this assignment, one pointer field had no value. Afterward it has the value *nil*. Notice that the type of the expression on the left-hand side of the assignment operator is a pointer type, namely the type NPointer. It is not a node type and so does not end with ↑.

    The type of *nil* is a bit unorthodox, since its type can be that of a pointer to a dynamic variable of any type. To make this seem less strange, it should be pointed out (after a while the pun is unavoidable or perhaps just irresistible; anyway, it should be pointed out) that *nil* does not point to anything and, since it is a constant, it cannot be changed so that it does point to something.

type
of nil

Linked Lists—An Example of Pointer Use

Structures like those in Figures 17.1 and 17.6 are called *linked lists*. The pointer Head (in either of these figures) is not part of the linked list, but is inevitably present when a linked list is being manipulated. A linked list consists of nodes, each of which has one

head

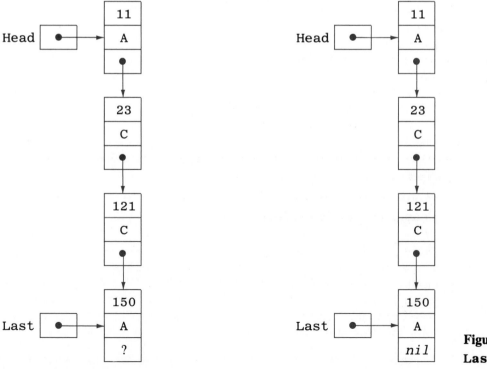

(a) Before   *(b) After*

Figure 17.6
Last ↑.Link : = *nil*.

pointer field. The pointers are set so that they order the nodes into a list. There is always one node called the *head* such that if you follow the arrows starting from that node, you will pass through each node exactly once. To put it less formally, the head is the first node in the list. The pointers called Head in these figures point to the heads of the linked lists given in the figures. (Do not confuse the pointer called Head with the head of the list. The first node in the list is called the head. The pointer variable is named Head, *not* because it *is* the head, but because it *points to* the head.)

Linked lists are used for many of the same things that arrays are used for, namely for storing lists of data. As we will see, a program can change the size of a linked list. Also, it is easy to insert or delete nodes in a linked list. For these reasons, linked lists are preferable to arrays for some applications.

Case Study

Building a Linked List

As a warmup exercise, let us consider how we might construct the start of a linked list—that is, how we might make a short linked list consisting of one node. We will use nodes of the same type as we have been discussing. For reference, we repeat the type declarations.

```
type NPointer = ↑Node;
     Node = record
                  Number: integer;
                  Grade: char;
                  Link: NPointer
            end;
var Head: NPointer;
```

To create a node we use the procedure new, set the two data fields, and then, since this is the last node as well as the first node, we set the Link field equal to *nil* in order to mark the end of the list. The following code will accomplish our goal and produce the short, one-node list displayed:

```
new(Head);
Head↑.Number := 150;
Head↑.Grade := 'A';
Head↑.Link := nil
```

adding
nodes

Our one-node list was built in a purely ad hoc way. In order to have a large linked list, a program must be able to add nodes to the linked list in a systematic way. We next describe one simple way to insert nodes in a link list. It will turn out that the procedure will work even if we start with an empty list. However, the process is clearer if we first assume that the list already has at least one node in it.

Problem Definition

We want a procedure to insert new data in a linked list of the type shown in Figure 17.7(a). The linked list will be given by a pointer Head pointing to the head of the list. The data will be given by a record variable called NewData of the type Data, defined as follows:

```
type Data = record
              Number: integer;
              Grade: char
            end;
```

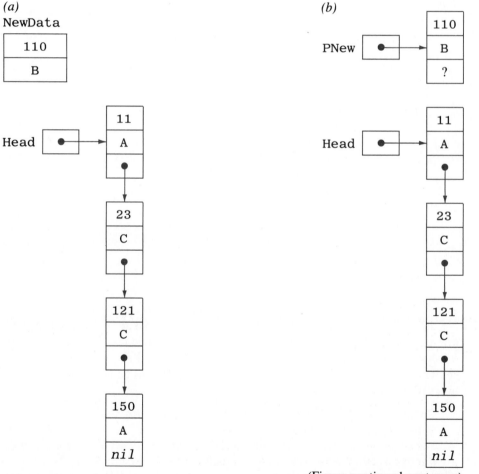

(a)

NewData

(b)

Head

PNew

Head

Figure 17.7

Inserting a node at the head of a list.

(Figure continued next page)

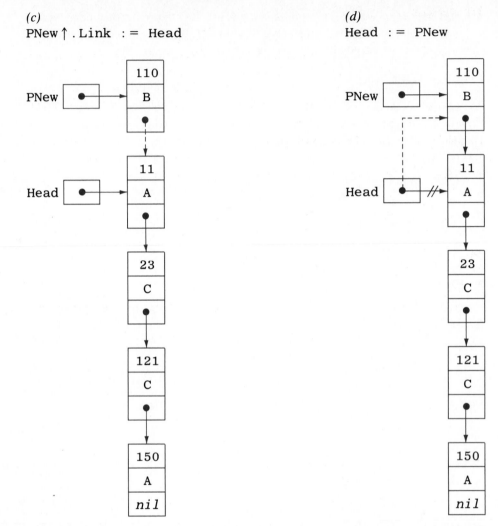

(c)
PNew ↑ . Link : = Head

(d)
Head : = PNew

Figure 17.7
(continued)

The procedure will change the list so that a new node with the given data is inserted and will redirect Head so that it points to the head of the modified list. For this problem we will not require that the list be in any particular order, and so the new node may be inserted anyplace in the list that is convenient. The task to be accomplished can be summarized as follows:

Precondition: Head is pointing to the head of a linked list and
NewData contains data for a new node.
Postcondition: A node, containing the data in NewData, has been added to the
linked list; Head is pointing to the head of this enlarged list.

Discussion

In order to insert the data into the linked list, the procedure will need to use new to create a new node. The data is then copied into the new node, and the new node is inserted at the head of the list. Since dynamic variables have no names, we must use a local pointer variable to point to this node. If we call the local pointer variable PNew, then the new node can be referred to as PNew ↑ . The complete process can be summarized as follows:

1. Create a new dynamic variable pointed to by PNew;
2. Place the data in this dynamic variable (which can be referred to as PNew ↑);
3. Make PNew ↑ point to the head (first node) of the original linked list;
4. Make Head point to PNew ↑ (i.e., the new dynamic variable).

ALGORITHM

   Figure 17.7 gives the algorithm in diagrammatic form. Steps 3 and 4 can be expressed by the two Pascal assignment statements given below. The complete procedure is given in Figure 17.8.

```
PNew ↑ . Link  : =  Head;
Head  : =  PNew
```

```
type NPointer  =  ↑ Node;
     Node  =  record
                 Number:  integer;
                 Grade:  char;
                 Link:  NPointer
              end;
     Data  =  record
                 Number:  integer;
                 Grade:  char
              end;

procedure HeadInsert (NewData:  Data;  var Head:  NPointer) ;
{Inserts a node containing the data in the record NewData
at the head of the linked list headed by Head ↑ .}
var PNew:  NPointer;
begin{HeadInsert}
   new (PNew) ;     {Creates a new node to hold NewData.}
   PNew ↑ . Number  : =  NewData. Number;
   PNew ↑ . Grade  : =  NewData. Grade;
   PNew ↑ . Link  : =  Head;
     {Places the new node at the head of the list.}
   Head  : =  PNew
     {Moves Head so it points to the new head of the list.}
end;  {HeadInsert}
```

Figure 17.8
Procedure to add a node to a linked list.

The Empty List

A linked list is named by naming a pointer that points to the head of the list. To specify an empty list, the normal thing to do is to set this pointer equal to *nil:*

    Head : = *nil*

Whenever you design a procedure for manipulating a linked list, you should always check to see if it works on the empty list. If it does not, then it may be possible to add a special case for the empty list. If you cannot design the procedure to apply to the empty list, then the program must be designed to handle empty lists in some other way or to avoid them completely. One way to avoid empty lists is to add a *dummy node* that contains no real data but marks the end of the list and is never deleted.

Fortunately, the empty list can often be treated just like any other list. For example, the procedure HeadInsert in Figure 17.8 was designed with nonempty lists as the model, but a check will show that it works for the empty list as well.

Pitfall

Losing Nodes

You might be tempted to write the procedure HeadInsert using the pointer variable Head directly, instead of using the local pointer variable PNew to construct a new node. If we were to try, we might start the procedure as follows:

    new (Head) ;   {*Creates a new node to hold NewData.*}
    Head ↑ . Number : = NewData. Number;
    Head ↑ . Grade : = NewData. Grade;

At this point, the new node is constructed, contains the correct data, and is pointed to by the pointer Head, all as it is supposed to be. All that is left to do is to attach the rest of the list to this node by setting the pointer field Head ↑ . Link so that it points to what was formerly the first node of the list. Figure 17.9 shows the situation in the case where the new data values are 110 and 'B'. The diagram reveals the problem. If we proceed in this way, then unfortunately there would be nothing pointing to the node containing 11. Since there is no named pointer that is pointing to it or to any of the nodes below it, all those nodes are lost. There is no way that the program can reference them. It cannot make a pointer point to any of the nodes, nor can it access the data in those nodes, nor can it do anything else to the nodes. It simply has no way of referring to these nodes. To avoid such lost nodes, the program must always keep some pointer pointing to the head of the list, usually the pointer in a pointer variable like Head.

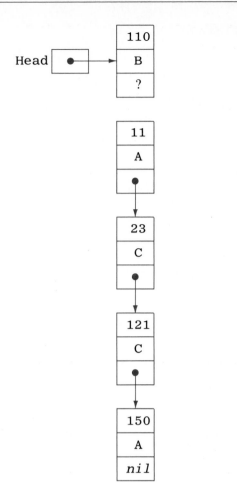

Figure 17.9
Lost nodes.

Case Study

Tools for Manipulating a Linked List

In this section we will design a set of procedures to perform some basic manipulations on linked lists of the type shown in Figure 17.7. Specifically, we want to be able to search the list to find a node that has a particular number. We also want a more versatile procedure for adding a node to the list. The procedure HeadInsert inserted a node at the head of a list. We will design a procedure that can insert a node at any point in the list, rather than just at the head of the list. Finally, we want a way to delete a node from the list. For example, if the linked list contains a list of student numbers and grades, then one procedure will find a student's record given the student's number. Another procedure will allow us to add a student record. We will also give code for deleting a student record. We will use the same type declarations as those in Figure 17.8.

Problem Definition

*searching
a list*

We will first consider the problem of locating a node. We want to design a procedure that will locate a node in a linked list made up of nodes of the type Node. More precisely, the procedure has a value parameter Key of type integer and two variable parameters: Here of type NPointer and Found of type boolean. The procedure sets Found equal to true or false, depending on whether or not the list contains a node whose Number field has the value Key. If there is such a node, then Here is left pointing to it.

We assume that the head (first) node is pointed to by a pointer called Head and that the end of the list is marked with *nil*. If the list is empty, then the value of Head will be *nil*. The pointer Head is another parameter to the procedure. The situation is diagrammed in Figure 17.10(a). Our assumptions can be summarized by the following precondition:

> *Precondition: Head points to a linked list of nodes of type Node; the end of the list is marked by nil; if the list is empty, then Head = nil.*

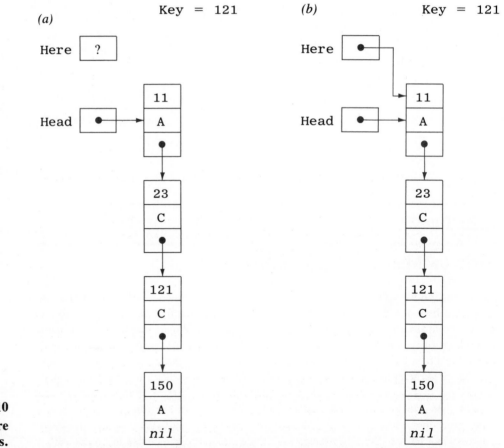

Figure 17.10
**How the procedure
Search works.**

(c)   Key = 121   *(d)*   Key = 121

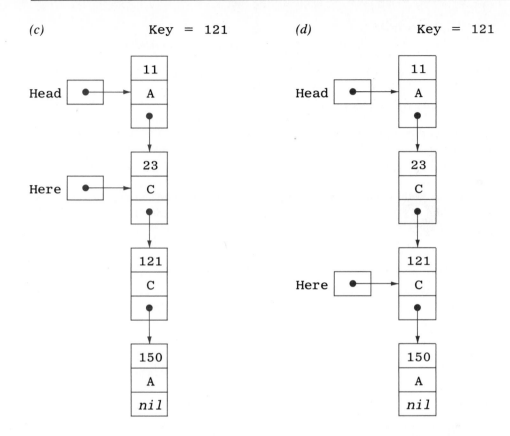

**Figure 17.10
(continued)**

The goal for a sample situation is shown in Figure 17.10(d). The goal can be expressed precisely by the postcondition

> *Postcondition: If there is a node that contains the integer Key, then Here points to the first such node and Found is equal to true. If no node contains Key, then Found is equal to false.*

Discussion

The only way to move around a linked list, or any other data structure made up of nodes and pointers, is to follow the arrows. So we will place the pointer Here at the first node and then move it from node to node, following the pointers until we find a node containing the integer Key or until we encounter the end of the linked list. The technique is diagrammed in Figures 17.10(b) through (d). Since empty lists present some minor problems that would clutter our discussion, we will at first assume that the linked list contains at least one node. Later we will come back and make sure the algorithm works for the empty list as well. This search technique yields the following algorithm:

ALGORITHM
Make `Here` point to the head (first node) in the list;
while (`Here` is not pointing to a node containing `Key`) *and*
    (`Here` is not pointing to the last node) *do*
        make `Here` point to the next node in the list;
    if `Here` ↑ contains `Key`, then the number is in the node
        pointed to by `Here`; otherwise, it is not on the list.

We can now translate this algorithm into Pascal code. Since the pointer `Head` points to the first node, the following will leave `Here` pointing to the first node:

```
Here := Head
```

In order to move the pointer `Here` to the next node, we must think in terms of the named pointers we have available. The next node is the one pointed to by the pointer field of the current node pointed to by `Here`. The node currently pointed to by `Here` is `Here` ↑. The pointer field of that node is

```
Here ↑ . Link
```

In order to move `Here` to the next node, we want to change `Here` so that it points to *the node that is pointed to by the above-named pointer field*. Hence, the following will move the pointer `Here` to the next node in the list:

```
Here := Here ↑ . Link
```

refinement   Putting the pieces together yields the following refinement of the algorithm pseudocode:

```
Here := Head;
while (Here ↑ . Number <> Key) and (Here ↑ . Link <> nil) do
     Here := Here ↑ . Link;
if Here ↑ . Number = Key, then the number is in the node pointed to
   by Here; otherwise, it is not on the list.
```

empty   We still must go back and take care of the empty list. If we check the above al-
list   gorithm, we find that there is a problem with the empty list. If the list is empty, then `Here` is equal to *nil* and hence the following expression is undefined:

```
Here ↑ . Number
```

Hence, we make a special case of the empty string. The complete procedure is given in Figure 17.11.

Problem Definition

inserting   We next design a procedure to insert a node at a specified place in a linked list. Since
nodes   we may want the nodes in some particular order, such as in numeric order, we cannot simply insert the node at the beginning (head) of the list nor at the end of the list. We will therefore design the procedure to insert a node between two specified nodes in a linked list. We assume that some other procedure or program part has placed two point-

```
type NPointer  =  ↑ Node;
     Node = record
                 Number:  integer;
                 Grade:  char;
                 Link:  NPointer
               end;

procedure  Search(Key:  integer;  Head:  NPointer;
                      var Here:  NPointer;  var Found:  boolean);
```
{Precondition: Head points to a linked list of nodes of type Node; the end
of the list is marked by nil; if the list is empty, then Head = nil.
Postcondition: If there is a node that contains the integer Key, then Here
points to the first such node and Found is equal to true. If no node
contains Key, then Found is equal to false.}
```
begin{Search}
   if Head = nil then
      Found  : = false
   else
      begin{nonempty list}
         Here  : = Head;
         while (Here↑.Number <> Key) and (Here↑.Link <> nil) do
              Here  : = Here↑.Link;
         {Here is either pointing to a node containing Key or
            is pointing to the last node in the list (or both).}
         Found  : =  (Here↑.Number  = Key)
      end   {nonempty list}
end;  {Search}
```

Figure 17.11
Procedure to locate a node in a linked list.

ers called Before and After pointing to two nodes in the list, as shown in Figure 17.12(b). We wish to insert a new node with new data as shown in Figure 17.12(c). The data for the new node will be of the type Data as defined in Figure 17.8. The procedure will create a new node, copy the data into the new node, and insert the node into the linked list. (The pointer After is not absolutely necessary, but does simplify our reasoning.)

Discussion

A new node is set up in the same way that we did in the procedure HeadInsert. The difference between this procedure and that one is that we now wish to insert the node not at the head of the list but in some location inside the list. The method of inserting the node is shown in Figure 17.12b. The way to express the indicated resetting of pointers is given below:

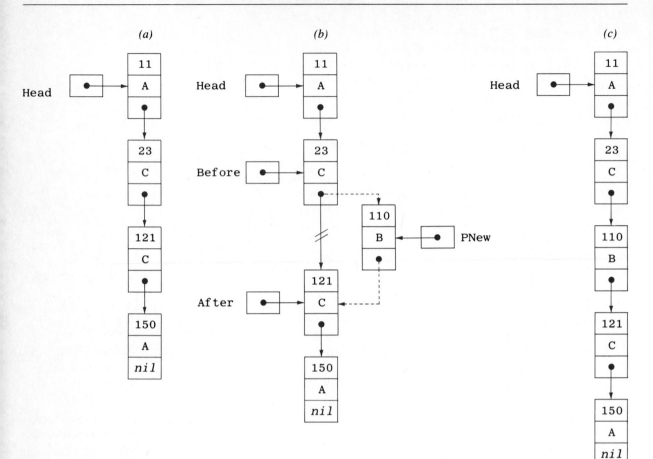

Figure 17.12
**Inserting a node in
the middle of a
linked list.**

ALGORITHM

Before ↑ . Link : = PNew;   {*Redirect a link to the new node*}
PNew ↑ . Link : = After   {*Set a link from the new node back to the list.*}

The complete procedure is given in Figure 17.13.

*insertion
at the ends*
The procedure Insert will not work for inserting a node at the beginning or the end of a linked list. The procedure HeadInsert in Figure 17.8 can be used to insert a node at the head of the list. Exercise 7 in the next section indicates how the procedure Insert can be changed so that it also can insert a node at the end of a list.

```
type NPointer = ↑Node;
     Node = record
                  Number: integer;
                  Grade: char;
                  Link: NPointer
            end;
     Data = record
                  Number: integer;
                  Grade: char
            end;

procedure Insert(NewData: Data;
                 Before, After: NPointer);
{Inserts a node containing NewData between
the two nodes pointed to by Before and After.}
var PNew: NPointer;
begin{Insert}
  new(PNew);
  PNew↑.Number := NewData.Number;
  PNew↑.Grade := NewData.Grade;
  Before↑.Link := PNew;
  PNew↑.Link := After
end; {Insert}
```

Figure 17.13
Procedure to insert a node in a linked list.

By using the procedure `Insert`, we can maintain the linked list in numerical order without rewriting existing nodes. We could "squeeze" a new node into the correct position simply by adjusting two pointers. Furthermore, this is true no matter how long the linked list is or where in the list we want the new record to go. If we had instead used an array of records, then much, and in extreme cases all, of the array would have to be copied over in order to make room for a new record in the correct spot. In spite of the overhead involved in positioning the pointers, inserting into a linked list is frequently more efficient than inserting into an array.

comparison to arrays

Deleting a node from a linked list is also quite easy. Figure 17.14 illustrates the method. Once the pointers `Before` and `Discard` have been positioned, all that is required to delete the node is the following Pascal statement:

deleting nodes

```
Before↑.Link := Discard↑.Link
```

(a)

(b)

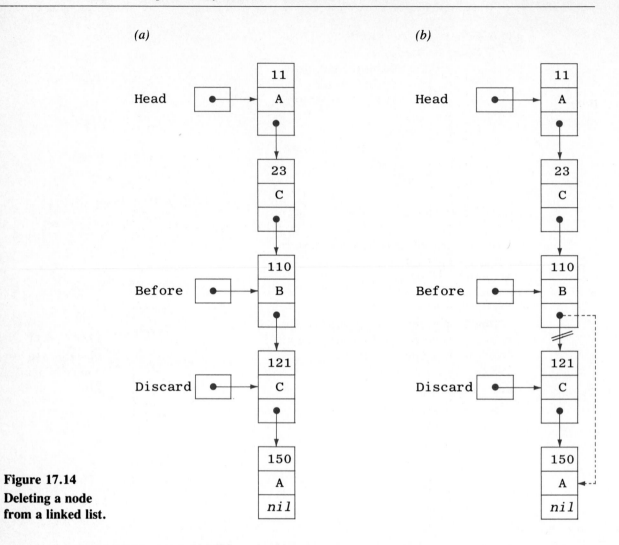

Figure 17.14
Deleting a node
from a linked list.

(c)   *(d)*

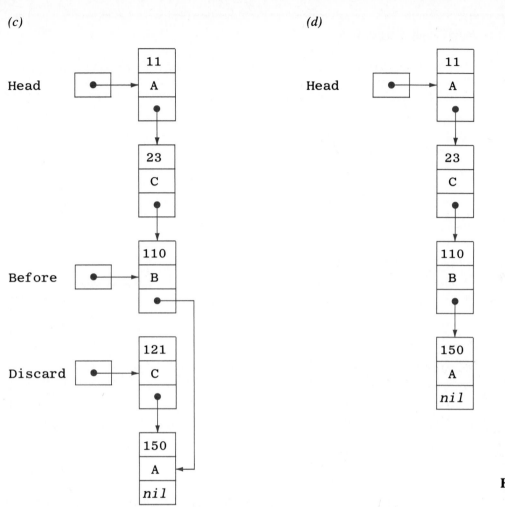

Figure 17.14
(continued)

She was poor but she was honest,
And her parents were the same,
Till she met a city feller,
And she lost her honest name.

Old army song

Self-Test Exercises

1. What is the output produced by the following code? All the pointers are of type ↑integer.

```
new (P1);
new (P2);
P1↑ := 10;
P2↑ := 20;
writeln(P1↑, P2↑);
P1 := P2;
writeln(P1↑, P2↑);
P1↑ := 30;
writeln(P1↑, P2↑);
P2↑ := 40;
writeln(P1↑, P2↑)
```

2. What is the output produced by the following code? All the pointers are of type ↑integer.

```
new (P1);
new (P2);
P1↑ := 10;
P2↑ := 20;
writeln(P1↑, P2↑);
P1↑ := P2↑;
writeln(P1↑, P2↑);
P1↑ := 30;
writeln(P1↑, P2↑);
P2↑ := 40;
writeln(P1↑, P2↑)
```

3. How would the output of the program in Figure 17.3 change if the lines

```
P2↑.Number := 3;
P2↑.Grade := 'C';
```

were replaced by the following lines?

```
P1↑.Number := 3;
P1↑.Grade := 'C';
```

4. Given the situation diagrammed below, what is the effect of the assignment statement shown? The pointers and nodes are of the types given in Figure 17.13.

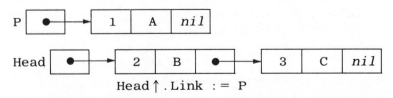

5. Write a procedure to fill a linked list with the integers 1 through N. N should be a parameter.

6. Write a procedure to display to the screen all the integers in a linked list of the same general kind as you used in the previous exercise. (The list may be of a different length and may contain numbers other than the ones that would be placed there by the procedure of the last exercise.)

7. The pointer parameter `After` in the procedure `Insert` in Figure 17.13 is not absolutely necessary. Rewrite the procedure so that it works without this parameter.

Pointer Functions

In Pascal, functions may return pointers. In Figure 17.11 we designed a procedure to search a linked list and to set the value of a variable parameter equal to a pointer that is pointing to the desired record. Alternatively, we could design a function to return the pointer. The function heading might be as follows:

```
function  Find(Key: integer; Head: NPointer): NPointer;
{ Returns a pointer that points to the first node containing Key;
returns nil if Key is not in the list.
Precondition: Head points to a linked list of nodes of type Node; the end
of the list is marked by nil; if the list is empty, then Head = nil.}
```

Since a function can return only one type of value, we have used the pointer *nil* to indicate that the desired node was not found on the list.

We could design the body of the function `Find` to be similar to the body of the procedure `Search` in Figure 17.11. However, we will instead use a recursive algorithm in the design of this function. Linked lists and other data structures made using pointers lend themselves to recursive algorithms because the structure is repeated. The pointer Head points to a linked list. The pointer coming out of the first node (Head ↑ . Link) points to another, shorter linked list, namely the one starting with the second node of the longer list. This repeated structure allows us to state very simple recursive algorithms.

recursion and pointers

```
if Head = nil then
     Key is not on the list
else if Head ↑ .Number = Key then
     Key  is in the node pointed to by Head
else
     Search the linked list pointed to by Head ↑ . Link
```

recursive ALGORITHM

A complete function declaration is displayed in Figure 17.15.

```
type NPointer = ↑Node;
     Node = record
                Number: integer;
                Grade: char;
                Link: NPointer
            end;

function Find(Key: integer; Head: NPointer): NPointer;
{ Returns a pointer pointing to the first node containing Key; returns nil if Key is not in the list.
Precondition: Head points to a linked list of nodes of type Node; the end
of the list is marked by nil; if the list is empty, then Head = nil.}
begin{Find}
   if Head = nil then
      Find := nil
   else if Head↑.Number = Key then
      Find := Head
   else
      Find := Find(Key, Head↑.Link)
end;  {Find}
```

Figure 17.15
Function that
returns a pointer.

Pitfall

Testing for the Empty List

When designing recursive algorithms, the stopping case is typically the empty
list, which is represented by the pointer nil. Hence, even if you know that the
linked list or other structure in your program will not be empty, you may still
need to include a test for the empty list. For example, the function Find in Figure 17.15 can terminate when the value of the parameter Head is equal to nil,
and so a series of recursive calls starting with a nonempty list can end with this
case.

   When dealing with the pointer nil, remember that it does not point to anything, and so any reference to a node that it points to is undefined. For example,
again consider the function Find. The test for nil must be the first case in the
nested if-$then$-$else$ statement. The reason for this is that if the value of
Head is nil, then Head↑.Number is undefined.

Case Study

Using a Linked List to Sort a File

Problem Definition

If we wish to sort a file of records, then we must read the records into some other location as we sort them. A linked list is a convenient intermediate data structure to use for this purpose. As an example, we will design a program to sort a file of records of the type declared below:

```
type Data = record
              Number: integer;
              Grade: char
            end;
```

We assume that the file is called `GradeFile` and that the records might be in any order. We want the program to change the file so that it contains the same records but so that they are sorted from smallest to largest according to the `Number` field.

Discussion

Since we cannot open a file for both reading and writing at the same time, the only way to sort a file is to copy the data into some other location for sorting. One possible way to proceed is to copy the data into a linked list, inserting each piece of data in the correct place so as to keep the list sorted. After that the program can simply copy the sorted list back into the file. (Even in those implementations that allow a Pascal program random access to a file, this might be an easy and relatively efficient way to accomplish the task.)

One breakdown of the task into subtasks yields the following algorithm outline: *ALGORITHM*

I. `BuildList`: for each record in the file:
    1. read the record
    2. `FindSlot`: find the correct place to insert the record data in the list.
    3. `Insert`: insert a new node with the record data in the list.
II. `CopyToFile`: copy the linked list back into the file.

Figure 17.16 contains the data flow diagram for the algorithm. For the procedure `Insert` we can use the procedure by that name in Figure 17.13. The procedure `FindSlot` positions the two pointers `Before` and `After` so that they point to two adjacent nodes such that the new node belongs between these two nodes. Expressed more precisely, this means that the following must hold after the procedure `FindSlot` has completed:

`Before` ↑ . `Number` <= (the number in the node to be inserted) <= `After` ↑ . `Number`

If the list is empty, as it is at the start, or if the node to be inserted belongs at the   *sentinel* start or end of the list, then there will not be two nodes with these properties. Rather   *nodes*

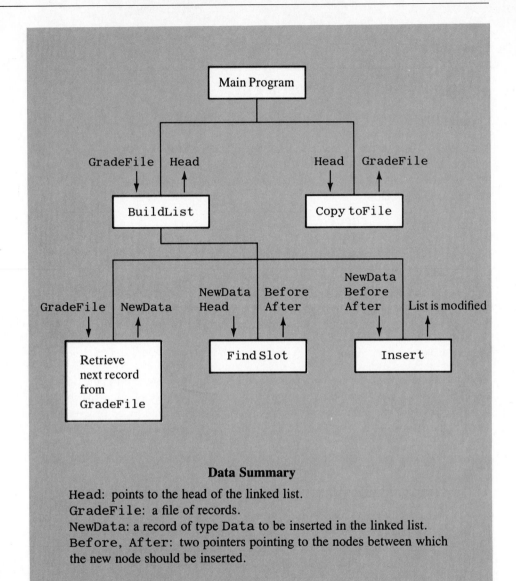

Data Summary

Head: points to the head of the linked list.
GradeFile: a file of records.
NewData: a record of type Data to be inserted in the linked list.
Before, After: two pointers pointing to the nodes between which the new node should be inserted.

Figure 17.16
Data flow diagram
for building a
sorted linked list.

than make special cases for empty lists and insertions at the ends of a list, we will instead add two sentinel nodes to mark the two ends of the list. The first sentinel node will contain a number smaller than all the numbers in the file. The other sentinel node will contain a number larger than all the nodes in the file. Since the list will initially contain these two nodes, the case of the empty list is eliminated. Since these two nodes will have numbers that ensure that they stay on the ends of the list, the case of inserting a node at the end of the list is also eliminated. The procedure FindSlot can thus be written without any special cases. The complete program, including the procedure FindSlot, is given in Figure 17.17.

```
program SortFile(input, output, GradeFile);
{Sorts the records in GradeFile by their Number fields. Works by reading
records into a linked list, sorting them by insertion in the process; the records
are then read back into the file, leaving a sorted file. Assumes that the
constants Small and Large have the properties stated in their comments.}
const Small = −maxint;  {A number smaller than any number in the file.}
      Large = maxint;  {A number larger than any number in the file.}
type NPointer = ↑Node;
     Node = record
                Number: integer;
                Grade: char;
                Link: NPointer
            end;
     Data = record
                Number: integer;
                Grade: char
            end;
     RecordFile = file of Data;
var Head: NPointer;
    GradeFile: RecordFile;

procedure FindSlot(NewData: Data; Head: NPointer;
                        var Before, After: NPointer);
{Precondition: Head points to the head of a linked list; the Number fields
of the nodes are in increasing order starting from the head. The ends of the
list are marked with two sentinel nodes, one containing the number Small
and one containing the number Large.
Postcondition: Before and After point to nodes of the list and
Before↑.Number <= NewData.Number <= After↑.Number.}
begin{FindSlot}
  Before := Head;
  After := Head↑.Link;
  while  (Before↑.Number > NewData.Number) or
         (NewData.Number > After↑.Number) do
     begin{move pointers one node}
        Before := Before↑.Link;
        After := After↑.Link
     end  {move pointers one node}
end;  {FindSlot}
```

Figure 17.17
Sorting with a
linked list.

```
procedure Insert(NewData: Data;
                 Before, After: NPointer);
{Inserts a node containing NewData between
the two nodes pointed to by Before and After.}
var PNew: NPointer;
begin{Insert}
  new(PNew);
  PNew↑.Number := NewData.Number;
  PNew↑.Grade := NewData.Grade;
  Before↑.Link := PNew;
  PNew↑.Link := After
end;  {Insert}
```

```
procedure BuildList(var GradeFile: RecordFile; var Head: NPointer);
{Creates a linked list of records from records in the file GradeFile. The linked
list is sorted by the Number field. Head is left pointing to the head of the list;
An extra node containing the number Small is at the head of the list and
an extra node containing the number Large is at the end of the list.}
var Before, After: NPointer;
    NewData: Data;
begin{BuildList}
  new(Head);
  Head↑.Number := Small;
  new(Head↑.Link);
  Head↑.Link↑.Number := Large;
  {The linked list has two nodes; the first with a number smaller
  than any record; the last with a number larger than any record.}
  reset(GradeFile);

  while not eof(GradeFile) do
    begin{one record}
      read(GradeFile, NewData);
      FindSlot(NewData, Head, Before, After);
      Insert(NewData, Before, After)
    end {one record}
end;  {BuildList}
```

```
procedure CopyToFile(Head: NPointer; var GradeFile: RecordFile);
{Copies the data in all nodes except the first and last nodes of a linked list
into the file GradeFile. Precondition: Head points to the head of the linked list;
the first node contains the number Small; the last node contains the number Large.}
var Finger: NPointer;
    OneRecord: Data;
```

Figure 17.17

(continued)

```
begin{CopyToFile}
  rewrite(GradeFile);
  Finger := Head↑.Link;  {Pass over node with Small.}
  while Finger↑.Number <> Large do
    begin{one record}
      OneRecord.Number := Finger↑.Number;
      OneRecord.Grade := Finger↑.Grade;
      write(GradeFile, OneRecord);
      Finger := Finger↑.Link
    end {one record}
end;  {CopyToFile}

begin{Program}
  writeln('Reading GradeFile into a sorted list.');
  BuildList(GradeFile, Head);
  writeln('Copying sorted list into GradeFile.');
  CopyToFile(Head, GradeFile);
  writeln('GradeFile sorted.')
end.  {Program}
```

Figure 17.17
(continued)

Stacks

We introduced the notion of a stack in Chapter 14 and showed how it could be used to keep track of recursive procedure calls and local variables. One way to implement a stack is by means of a linked list. In this implementation a stack is nothing but a linked list that is used in a restricted way, namely, nodes are only added at the head of the list and are only deleted from the head of the list. When you are dealing with stacks, adding a node is usually called a *push* operation, and deleting a node is called a *pop* operation. These operations and their implementations as operations on linked lists are illustrated in Figure 17.18. This terminology will explain the procedure names used in Figure 17.19. That program uses a stack of characters to read in a line of text and output it in reverse order. The procedure Push is essentially the same as the procedure HeadInsert we designed earlier, except that the nodes have one less data field. The procedure Pop simply moves the pointer at the head of the list in the manner shown in Figure 17.18.

*push
and
pop*

Push

Intuitive picture

Actual structure

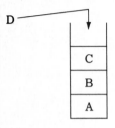

Before

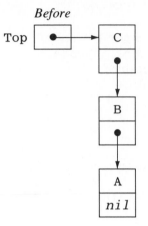

After

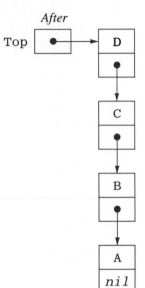

Pop

Intuitive picture

Actual structure

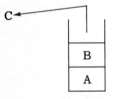

Before

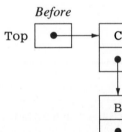

After

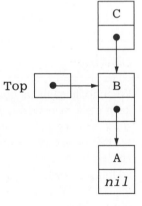

Figure 17.18
Stack operations.

Program

```
program Reverse(input, output);
{Reads a line of text and outputs it written backwards.}

type FPointer = ↑Frame;
     Frame = record
                 Data: char;
                 Link: FPointer
             end;
var Top: FPointer;  {Points to the top of the stack.}
    Symbol: char;

procedure Push(NewData: char; var Top: FPointer);
{Pushes a frame (node) containing the data onto the stack.
Top points to the top frame (head node) on the stack.}
var PNew: FPointer;
begin{Push}
   new(PNew);     {Creates a new node to hold NewData.}
   PNew↑.Data := NewData;
   PNew↑.Link := Top;
     {Places the new node at the head of the list.}
   Top := PNew
     {Moves Top so it points to the new top (head) of the stack (list).}
end;  {Push}

function Empty(Top: FPointer): boolean;
{Returns true if the stack pointed to by Top is empty.}
begin{Empty}
   Empty := (Top = nil)
end;  {Empty}

procedure Pop(var Top: FPointer; var Out: char);
{Pops one frame(node) off the stack pointed to by Top;
Out is set equal to the Data field of the popped frame (node).}
begin{Pop}
   if Empty(Top) then
      writeln('Error: attempted to pop an empty stack.')
   else
      begin{Popping}
        Out := Top↑.Data;
        Top := Top↑.Link
      end   {Popping}
end;  {Pop}
```

Figure 17.19
Program using a stack.

```
begin{Program}
    writeln('Enter a line of text.');

    Top := nil; {Makes an empty stack.}

    while not eoln do
      begin{reading a symbol}
        read(Symbol);
        Push(Symbol, Top)
      end; {reading a symbol}
    readln;

    while not Empty(Top) do
      begin{writing a symbol}
        Pop(Top, Symbol);
        write(Symbol)
      end; {writing a symbol}
    writeln;

    writeln('That''s it, forwards and backwards!')
end. {Program}
```

Sample Dialogue

```
Enter a line of text.
Able was I ere I saw Elba. Cute?
?etuC .ablE was I ere I saw elbA
That's it, forwards and backwards!
```

**Figure 17.19
(continued)**

dispose

Look again at Figure 17.18. The node that is popped off the stack is no longer on the stack (linked list) and cannot be referenced by the program. It is a lost node, but it has not been destroyed. Unless the program explicitly eliminates the node, it will remain in storage and will waste storage. For the program in Figure 17.19 this is not of any significant consequence, since the wasted storage is so small. However, if we were to enclose the body of the program in a loop that repeated the reading and writing a large number of times, then the program will generate extra lost nodes on every iteration of the loop. These lost nodes will remain in storage. If the loop iterates enough times, the lost nodes could even cause the program to terminate because of lack of storage. The standard procedure dispose can be used to avoid this waste of storage.

The procedure dispose can eliminate useless dynamic variables and so make more storage available. For example, the following will eliminate the dynamic variable (node) pointed to by Discard:

```
dispose(Discard)
```

Using the procedure dispose we can rewrite the procedure Pop from Figure 17.19 so that it needs only enough storage to hold one line of text no matter how many times the procedure is called. The following version of Pop uses dispose to eliminate dynamic variables once they are no longer on the stack:

```
procedure Pop(var Top: FPointer; var Out: char);
{Pops one frame(node) off the stack pointed to by Top;
Out is set equal to the Data field of the popped frame (node).}
var Discard: FPointer;
begin{Pop}
  if Empty(Top) then
     writeln('Error: attempted to pop an empty stack.')
  else
     begin{Popping}
        Out := Top↑.Data;
        Discard := Top;  {Discard points to the node being popped.}
        Top := Top↑.Link;
        dispose(Discard)
     end  {Popping}
end;  {Pop}
```

Case Study

Implementing Queues

Problem Definition

A stack is a "first-in/last-out" data structure, that is, if you fill a stack and then empty it, the elements are removed from the stack in the reverse of the order in which they were placed in the stack. In this section we will discuss a data structure known as a "queue." A *queue* is a "first-in/first-out" data structure for storing and retrieving data; that is, if you fill a queue and then empty it, the elements are removed from the queue in the same order in which they were placed in the queue. A queue works on the same principle as a line in a bank. In a bank line, the customers are served in the order in which they enter the line. In a queue, the data are removed from the queue in the same order in which they were stored in the queue. For example, consider a queue for storing integers. If the numbers 8, 9, 2, and 7 are placed in the queue in that order, then they must be retrieved in exactly that order. If your program wants the 2, it must first re-

queue

Adding to the queue

Intuitive picture   *Actual structure*

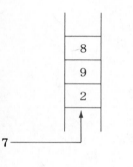

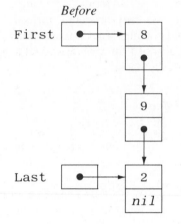

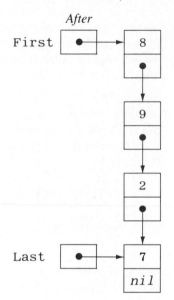

Removing an element

Intuitive picture   *Actual structure*

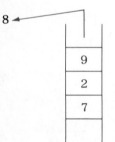

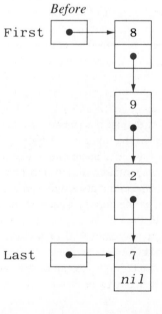

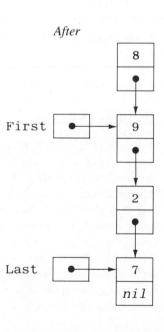

Figure 17.20
Queue operations.

move the 8 and the 9. Those two numbers will then no longer be in the queue. As far as the queue is concerned, they were thrown away. The first column of Figure 17.20 shows a diagrammatic representation of a queue of integers and the basic operations of adding an integer and retrieving the next integer in the queue. A queue such as this might be used to keep track of the students waiting to see an instructor on a day when office hours are particularly crowded. When a student arrives, the student places his or her student number in the queue. When the instructor has finished talking to one student and is ready to talk to another, the instructor takes the next available number from the queue and announces that that student is next.

In this case study, we will leave the data type for the elements in a queue unspecified. We will design a data type for a queue that stores elements of a type called ElementType. If our application requires storing integers, then we can define ElementType to be the type integer. If some other application requires storing data of some other type, we can define ElementType to be that type.

We will need to design a way to represent a queue. We will also need to design operations for adding an element to the queue and for removing an element from the queue. Since we will want to know if the queue contains any elements at all before we try to remove an element, we will also need to design a test to see if the queue is empty.

Discussion

We will implement a queue as a linked list of the kind diagrammed in Figure 17.20. In that figure the elements stored in the queue are integers, but the idea is the same for queues with elements of any other type. Elements will be added at one end of the linked list and removed from the other end. Because we must keep track of both ends of the linked list, we will use two pointers to access this linked list. One pointer will be called First and will point to the element (node) to be removed first. The other pointer will be called Last and will point to the element (node) at the other end of the linked list. To help keep the terminology straight, think of the queue as a line in a bank and think of First and Last as standing for "first in line" and "last in line." The queue itself will be a record with the two pointer fields First and Last. Since the last node in our linked list is pointed to by the pointer Last, we could get by without marking it in any other way. However, it seems neater and will prove to be useful to mark the last node in the list by setting its pointer field equal to *nil*, as is customary with linked lists.

The operations of adding and removing an element from a queue of integers are diagrammed in Figure 17.20. These will be implemented by two procedures called Add and GetFirst. The queue will be passed to the procedures as a record parameter called Q. Q.First will point to the first element in the queue; Q.Last will point to the last element in the queue. However, we will use *with* statements to simplify notation. This will allow us to use the simpler notation First and Last instead of the more cumbersome Q.First and Q.Last.

The empty queue will be indicated by setting the pointer First equal to *nil*. When the queue is empty, the value of Last is irrelevant.

empty
queue

```
type NPointer  =  ↑Node;
     Node  =  record
                    Entry:  ElementType;
                    Next:  NPointer
                end;
     Queue  =  record
                    First:  NPointer;  {Points to the first node in the queue.}
                    Last:Npointer  {Points to the last node in the queue.}
                end;
function  Empty(Q:Queue):boolean;
{Returns true if Q is an empty queue.}
begin  {Empty}
  Empty  :=  (Q.First  =  nil)
end;  {Empty}


procedure  Add(NewEntry:ElementType;  var Q:  Queue);
{Adds an element (node) containing the data NewEntry to the queue Q.}
begin{Add}
   with Q do
      begin{with Q}
         if  Empty(Q)  then
             begin{Start Queue}
                new(First);
                Last  :=  First
             end  {Start Queue}
         else
            begin{Nonempty Queue}
                new(Last↑.Next);  {New node at end}
                Last  :=  Last↑.Next;  {Move Last to new node}
            end;    {Nonempty Queue}
            {A new node with all fields still undefined has been created
             and positioned at the end of the queue.}

         Last↑.Entry  :=  NewEntry;
         Last↑.Next  :=  nil
      end  {with Q}
end;  {Add}


procedure  GetFirst(var Receiver:ElementType;  var Q:  Queue);
```
{Removes the first element (node) from Q and sets Receiver equal to the value of its Entry fie
Precondition: The queue is not empty.
(A warning is written to the screen if the precondition is violated.)}
```
var Temp:  NPointer;
```

Figure 17.21
Implementation of
a queue.

```
begin{GetFirst}
  if Empty(Q) then
    writeln('ERROR: Trying to retrieve from an empty queue.')
  else
    with Q do
      begin{with Q}
        Temp := First;
        Receiver := First↑.Entry;
        First := First↑.Next;
        dispose(Temp)
      end   {with Q}
end;  {GetFirst}
```

**Figure 17.21
(continued)**

The final implementation of our queue, along with operations on the queue, is given in Figure 17.21. Notice that the procedure `GetFirst` works correctly even when removing the last element. This is because we have set the pointer field of the last node in our linked list equal to *nil* and so the assignment

```
First := First↑.Next
```

sets `First` equal to *nil* when `First` is pointing to the only, and hence last, node in a list with only one node.

Doubly Linked Lists—A Variation on Simple Linked Lists

A *doubly linked list* is like a simple linked list, except that in a doubly linked list, there are pointers pointing backward as well as forward. The following is a diagram for the general structure of a doubly linked list:

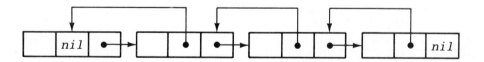

Doubly linked lists illustrate the point that a node may contain more than one pointer. Doubly linked lists are handled very much like ordinary linked lists except that they allow the program to move along the list in either direction, which can sometimes be useful. Our handling of linked lists would have been easier if they were doubly linked. In that case we would usually not need trailer pointers such as the pointer `Before` in Figure 17.14. Doubly linked lists do, however, require more storage than ordinary linked lists, because of the extra pointer in each node.

A possible set of type declarations for a doubly linked list is as follows:

```
type Link = ↑Node;
     Info = record
                 Number: integer;
                 Price: real;
                 Style: 1 . . 8
              end;
     Node = record
                 Data: Info;
                 Back, Forward: Link
              end;
```

Notice that in the preceding type declarations, nodes have three fields, one of which is itself a record. A node can be almost any sort of record. A hierarchical arrangement, such as that shown above, is often convenient.

Implementation
(Optional)

In order to program in a high level language such as Pascal, you do not need to know how the language is implemented, any more than you need to understand the workings of the human larynx or of the human brain in order to use the English language. Pascal programs are implemented as the machine code produced by the Pascal compiler, and all you need to know is that the machine code makes the input and output behave as we have described for the language Pascal. Still, it is sometimes helpful, and invariably interesting, to know some details of the implementation. This is particularly true of pointers and dynamic variables. Since the description of their implementation is very much more concrete than the high level description of Pascal pointers, many people find it easier to understand pointers in terms of their implementation. Additionally, it gives you a good idea of how the notion of pointers can be implemented in other programming languages, including many high level programming languages that do not have pointers as a basic predefined construction.

address In order to describe a typical implementation for Pascal pointers and dynamic variables, we need to recall our discussion of the internal structure of computers. Recall that a computer's main memory consists of a very long sequence of numbered memory locations, and that each memory location can hold one string of binary digits, which we can interpret as a data value of some simple type, such as an integer or a character. The locations are frequently called *words,* and the number of a location is frequently called its *address.* As this discussion indicates, a computer memory is structured much like a very large one-dimensional array.

To be concrete, let us say that we want to implement a linked list of the type shown in Figure 17.12(a). Each node will contain an integer field and a field of type char in addition to the one pointer field. One way to do this is to allocate three adjacent memory locations for each dynamic variable that is to serve as a node in the linked list. One of the three locations will hold the integer in the node, one will hold the character, and the third location will hold some integer that can be interpreted as a pointer to a node.

What can be interpreted as a pointer to one of these dynamic variables? These dynamic variables are implemented as three adjacent memory locations. Hence, one way to name one of these dynamic variables is to name the three addresses of these locations. That is exactly what we will do; however, we will use only the first address, since the other two are trivial to compute from the first one. In our implementation a dynamic variable of the type under discussion is just three adjacent memory locations: the first two hold the integer and character values, and the third holds the pointer. In this implementation the pointer is realized as the address of the first of the three memory locations that represent the dynamic variable that is pointed to.

By way of example, consider Figure 17.22. It shows a possible implementation of the linked list shown in Figure 17.12(a). The *nil* pointer is indicated by the number minus one. Minus one is used for *nil* because we know there is no location with that address. Any other negative number would do as well. The right-hand figure is an abstraction that ignores the particular address numbers used. Since the particular address numbers used are not important to the realization, that right-hand figure is easier to deal with.

As a program proceeds to add and delete nodes from a linked list, the picture of memory becomes a good deal more intricate. Suppose we wish to add a node containing the integer 110 and the character 'B' in a position that will keep the nodes in the

adding nodes

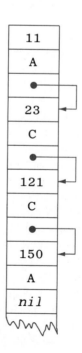

Figure 17.22 (Optional)

Implementation of a linked list.

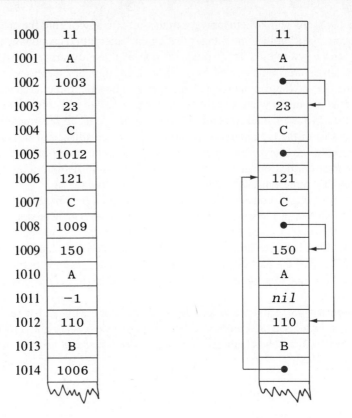

**Figure 17.23
(Optional)**

**Implementation of
a linked list with
added node.**

linked list in numeric order; the result should be as shown in Figure 17.12(c). Figure 17.23 shows the configuration of memory after the dynamic variable has been added. Note that the dynamic variable for this node was implemented with the next three available memory locations. The way to think about a linked list is as if the new node is squeezed in. However, in this implementation all the old nodes stay where they are. Only the values of the pointer fields change.

*deleting
nodes*

Figure 17.24 shows the implementation of the same linked list after adding the node containing 110 and 'B', as just described, and then deleting the node containing 121 and 'C'.

*garbage
collection*

Notice that as we add nodes, the pattern of arrows gets to be rather messy, but that need not concern us. Ordinarily, we need not be concerned with the actual memory addresses when we use pointers and dynamic variables. We need only think in terms of an abstraction of the pointer structure that ignores the actual locations of the dynamic variables. If we have enough memory, we can get away with thinking only on an abstract level, which ignores all the details of the particular memory addresses used. Unfortunately, there is some danger of wasting memory if we think exclusively on this abstract level. Look again at the memory configuration shown in Figure 17.24. Notice

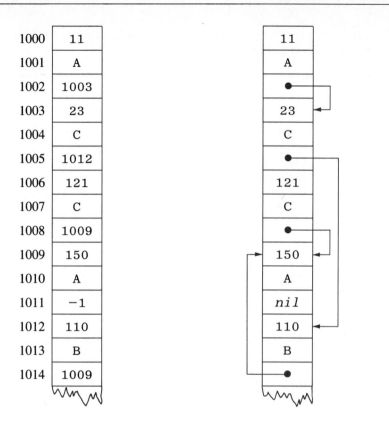

**Figure 17.24
(Optional)
Implementation of
a linked list with
deleted node.**

that the dynamic variable in locations 1006, 1007, and 1008 still has an integer, a letter, and a pointer in it. Yet the node represented by that dynamic variable is no longer on the linked list. The program will never be able to use the dynamic variable stored in locations 1006 through 1008, and so those memory locations should be made available for other uses. Yet if we continue to add dynamic variables at the bottom of memory, then locations 1006 through 1008 will never be reused. Locations like 1006, 1007, and 1008 are frequently referred to by the technical term *garbage*—not a very dignified word, but a descriptive one and the one that is generally used. A good implementation would keep track of these garbage memory locations and reuse them. Locating such garbage memory locations so that they can be reused is called, appropriately enough, *garbage collection*.

Many implementations of Pascal do not have very good garbage collection, and the system must be given some help in order to perform this task. Specifically, the system must be told which dynamic variables are garbage. This is what the dispose command does.

The idea of this implementation can be used in high level languages as well. If Pascal did not have pointers as a built-in feature, we could still implement something like pointers by using an array of records in the same way that we used the computer's main memory in the implementation just described.

Trees

binary
trees

A useful kind of data structure that is significantly different from the linked list structure is the *binary tree*. A sample binary tree, together with possible type declarations for the pointers and nodes of the tree, is shown in Figure 17.25. That tree stores names and hours worked for the employees of a small firm. (Any reasonable type definition for CharString would be acceptable, such as an array of characters or the more complex record type defined in Chapter 11.) To understand why structures such as this are called "trees," turn the page upside down. The resulting branching structure should, with a little bit of help from your imagination, look like the branching structure of a tree.

In order to simplify the notation in our discussion of trees, we will use a simpler node that stores only a single integer plus the two pointers. However, the techniques we

```
type Branch = ↑NodeRecord;
      NodeRecord = record
                     Name: CharString;
                     Hours: real;
                     Left, Right: Branch
                   end;
var Root: Branch;
```

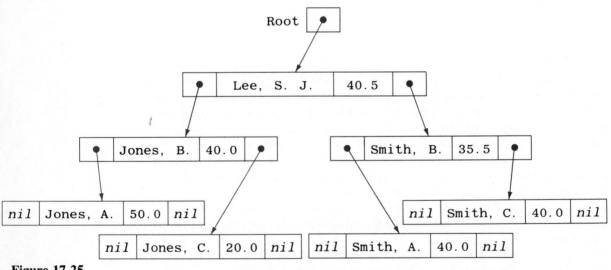

Figure 17.25
A binary tree.

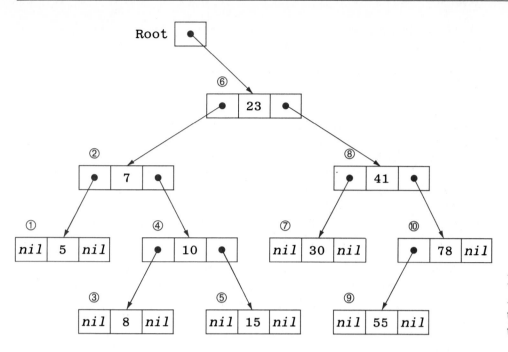

Figure 17.26

A binary tree of the type used in the text examples.

develop will apply to other node types as well. The type declarations we will use are as follows, and a sample tree with nodes of this type is shown in Figure 17.26.

```
type Pointer = ↑TreeNode;
     TreeNode = record
                    Data: integer;
                    Left, Right: Pointer
                end;
var Root: Pointer;
```

The pointers called Root in Figures 17.25 and 17.26 each point to a special node called the *root node*. The name comes from the fact that if you turn the picture upside down, then that node is located where the root of the tree would start. The root node is the only node from which every other node can be reached by following the pointers. It serves a function similar to that of the head node in a linked list.

root node

If we want to list the data in a tree, we must design our program to traverse the nodes in some order and to write out the contents of each node. Algorithms for traversing a tree are expressed most easily in their recursive form.

traversing a tree

Figure 17.27 will help to explain why it is convenient to express tree algorithms recursively. Notice that each pointer emanating from the root node points to a smaller binary tree. In the figure these subtrees are circled and labeled *left subtree* and *right subtree*. Hence, algorithms can be stated very neatly in the form "do something to the root and apply the algorithm recursively once to the left subtree and once to the right subtree." As an example, the following traversal algorithm is called *inorder traversal:*

recursion on trees

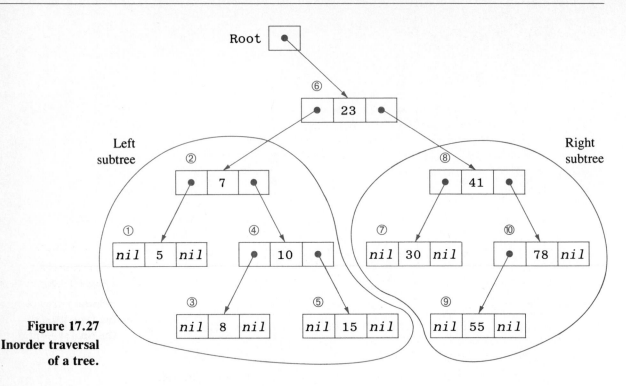

Figure 17.27
Inorder traversal
of a tree.

ALGORITHM—
inorder traversal

1. Traverse the left subtree.
2. Visit the root node (for example, to write out its contents.)
3. Traverse the right subtree.

empty
tree

   The above algorithm assumes that the tree is nonempty and does not specify what should be done with an empty tree. Yet recursively searching left and right subtrees will produce smaller and smaller subtrees until the algorithm is applied recursively to the empty tree, indicated by *nil*. At this point the algorithm should stop; to output the empty tree the instruction is "do nothing." Hence, the complete procedure will execute the above algorithm only if the tree is nonempty. If the tree is empty, then after testing for and finding *nil*, the algorithm literally does nothing. Figure 17.28 shows the complete algorithm implemented as a procedure.

   The circled numbers in Figure 17.27 indicate the order in which the nodes are processed by the inorder traversal procedure. Notice that the numbers are output in numeric order. We will come back to discuss this interesting observation shortly.

   Two other common methods for traversing a tree are similar and correspond to permuting the three instructions in the recursive algorithm. If the root node is visited first, the algorithm is called *preorder traversal*. If the root is visited last, the algorithm is called *postorder traversal*. However, we will not discuss these alternative algorithms here except to note that they would traverse the nodes in a different order from the inorder traversal we coded in Figure 17.28.

binary
search
trees

   Let us return to our inorder procedure for outputting the node contents and analyze why the nodes are output in numeric order. The reason is that we have stored the numbers in the tree in a special way known as the *Binary Search Tree Storage Rule:*

```
type Pointer = ↑TreeNode;
     TreeNode = record
                    Data: integer;
                    Left, Right: Pointer
                end;
```

```
procedure OutputNodes(Root:Pointer);
```
{*Outputs the integers in the nodes of the tree with root node Root↑;*
if the tree contains numbers that satisfy the Binary Search Tree Storage Rule,
then they will be output in numeric order.}
```
begin{OutputNodes}
   if Root <> nil then
     begin{nonempty tree}
        OutputNodes(Root↑.Left);  {Output left subtree.}
        write(Root↑.Data);  {Output root node.}
        OutputNodes(Root↑.Right)  {Output right subtree.}
     end   {nonempty tree}
end;  {OutputNodes}
```

**Figure 17.28
Procedure for
inorder output of a
tree.**

Binary Search Tree Storage Rule

1. All the numbers that are less than the number in the root node are in the left subtree.
2. All the numbers that are greater than the number in the root node are in the right subtree.
3. This rule applies recursively to the right and left subtrees.

As long as the numbers are stored in this way and we use the inorder traversal algorithm, then the root node number will always be output after all smaller numbers and before all larger numbers, and so the root node number is output in its correct location. Moreover, this applies to the root nodes of the subtrees and their subtrees and so on, until all nodes are accounted for and are seen to be output in their correct position. As the heading of the rule indicates, these sorts of trees are called *binary search trees*. The name is not derived from the fact that they can be output in this nice way but from another useful property they have, namely that they lend themselves readily to a binary search algorithm similar to the binary search algorithm we described for arrays in Chapter 14. The version for binary trees is given by the function in Figure 17.29. The algorithm in outline form is

ALGORITHM

```
if Root = nil then
        the tree is empty and the number is not in the tree
else if the number is in the root node then
        the number is found
else if the number sought is less than the number in the root node then
        search the left subtree
else if the number sought is greater than the number in the root node then
        search the right subtree
```

```
type Pointer = ↑ TreeNode;
     TreeNode = record
                     Data: integer;
                     Left, Right: Pointer
                 end;
```

```
function TreeSearch(Query: integer;
                        Root: Pointer): boolean;
```
{*Searches the binary search tree whose root node is pointed to by
Root. Returns true if the number Query is in some node of
the tree. Returns false if Query is not in the tree.*}
```
begin{TreeSearch}
   if Root = nil then
         {empty tree}
         TreeSearch := false
   else if Query = Root↑.Data then
         {found Query}
         TreeSearch := true
   else if Query < Root↑.Data then
         {Search subtree to the left of the root.}
         TreeSearch := TreeSearch(Query, Root↑.Left)
   else {if Query > Root↑.Data then}
         {Search subtree to the right of the root.}
         TreeSearch := TreeSearch(Query, Root↑.Right)
end;  {TreeSearch}
```

Figure 17.29
**Function that
searches a binary
tree looking for
a node.**

This same basic method applies to retrieving data, such as names, that is stored in alphabetical order, or for that matter to any other type of ordered data.

The advantage of the binary search algorithm for trees is the same as it is for the binary search algorithm for an array: it is faster than other methods, such as searching a linked list or serially searching an array. One advantage of using trees rather than arrays is that trees may be of any size and may even change size during program execution, while an array is of a fixed size declared when the program is written.

Case Study

Building a Search Tree

Problem Definition

We wish to design a binary search tree that stores numbers according to the recursive rule we gave in the last section, so that we can later use the function TreeSearch

(Figure 17.29) to search for numbers in the tree. For example, the numbers might be invalid credit card numbers that are read from a file or entered from the keyboard and then placed in a binary tree. For this problem we will assume they are read from a file of integers called `NumberFile`. The function `TreeSearch` can then be used to see if a given credit card is invalid. Since two cancellations of a credit card are the same as one cancellation, we will discard any repetitions and enter each number only once. Our goal can be summarized as follows:

> *Postcondition: Root is pointing to the root node of a tree that:*
> *contains all the numbers in the file NumberFile,*
> *contains no repetitions of numbers, and*
> *satisfies the Binary Search Tree Storage Rule.*

Discussion

Searching a binary search tree is easy. Building one for a given collection of data is slightly more complicated but is still not too difficult. The idea of the algorithm is the same as that of the binary search algorithm implemented in Figure 17.29. Given a number to search for, that algorithm either finds the number or else it finds a *nil* pointer at the point where it expects to find a node that contains the number. Hence, if we already have a binary search tree and want to add a number, we can apply the same algorithm but end it slightly differently. If the number is found, the algorithm does nothing, since the number is already in the tree. If the number is not found, the algorithm replaces the *nil* pointer with a pointer that points to a new node containing the number. The algorithm follows this paragraph. To build a binary tree from a list of numbers, this algorithm can be used to add one node at a time, starting with the empty tree.

ALGORITHM
for inserting a node

Input: A pointer `Root` and a `Number` to be inserted
if `Root` is *nil then*
    insert a new node containing `Number`
else if `Number` is in the node pointed to by `Root` *then*
    `Number` is already in the tree and so do nothing
else if `Number` is less than the number in the node pointed to by `Root` *then*
    insert `Number` in the left subtree by a recursive call
else if `Number` is greater than the number in the node pointed to by `Root` *then*
    insert `Number` in the right subtree by a recursive call

A Pascal procedure for building a binary search tree from a file of numbers is given in Figure 17.30. That procedure includes a call to the recursive procedure `Tree-Insert`, which implements the above algorithm.

empty tree

The empty tree is represented by setting the `Root` equal to *nil,* so the first clause of the algorithm serves to start things off. However, it applies more often as the result of a recursive call when the search finds its way down to a *nil* marking an empty position in which to insert the node. Some people find the algorithm more intuitive if the clauses are read backwards. This is fine for intuition, but in fact is not correct, since if the pointer is *nil,* then it makes no sense to talk of left and right subtrees.

```
type Pointer =  ↑TreeNode;
     TreeNode = record
                     Data: integer;
                     Left, Right: Pointer
                  end;
     IntFile = file of integer;
```

```
procedure TreeInsert(Number: integer; var Root: Pointer);
```
{*Precondition: Root points to the root node of a binary search tree.*
Postcondition: If Number was not in the binary search tree, then a new node containing Number
has been added to the tree so as to preserve the Binary Search Tree Storage Rule.}
```
begin{TreeInsert}
   if Root = nil then
      begin{Insert Number in a new node pointed to by Root}
         new(Root);
         Root↑.Data := Number;
         Root↑.Left := nil;
         Root↑.Right := nil
      end   {Insert Number in a new node pointed to by Root}
   else if Number < Root↑.Data then
      TreeInsert(Number, Root↑.Left)
   else if Number > Root↑.Data then
      TreeInsert(Number, Root↑.Right)
   {else if Number = Root↑.Data then
      do nothing since Number is already in the tree.}
end;  {TreeInsert}
```

```
procedure TreeBuild(var Root: Pointer; var DataFile: IntFile);
```
{*Builds a binary search tree. Reads the integers for the nodes from the*
file DataFile. DataFile has been opened with reset. Numbers in the file
may be in any order.}
```
var Next: integer;
begin{TreeBuild}
   Root := nil;
   while not eof(DataFile) do
      begin{Insert one integer}
         read(DataFile, Next);
         TreeInsert(Next, Root)
      end {Insert one integer}
end;  {TreeBuild}
```

Figure 17.30
**Procedure to build
a binary search
tree.**

The tree-building procedure in Figure 17.30 will always produce a binary search tree and, if the list of numbers is in random order, it will produce a balanced tree. A *balanced tree* is one in which all paths from the root node to the ends (the *nil*s) are of the same or almost the same length. In order to get all of the speed advantage of the binary search algorithm, the tree must be balanced or almost balanced. If the data arrives in an unfortunate sequence, then the tree will not be balanced, and the search will be slower. Techniques for making the tree balanced are quite complicated and are discussed in the references at the end of this chapter. In any event, the only issue is efficiency. The algorithm works for any sequence of integers.

balanced trees

"Would you tell me, please, which way I ought to go from here?"
"That depends a good deal on where you want to get to," said the Cat.
                    Lewis Carroll, Alice in Wonderland

Summary of Problem Solving and Programming Techniques

- Pointers provide a means for designing a wide variety of dynamic data structures, such as linked lists, stacks, and trees.
- As one check to see that you have a pointer expression correct, check the type to see if it is a pointer type or a node type.
- The advantages of a linked list over an array are that the linked list can grow and shrink and that it is easy to insert or delete a value (node) in the middle of a linked list.
- A node (dynamic variable) can only be named by naming a pointer that points to the node. Unless a named pointer points to some key node(s) of a structure, the nodes in that structure can be lost to the program because the program has no way to refer to the nodes.
- The constant *nil* is used to mark endpoints, such as the end of a linked list, and to denote empty structures, such as an empty linked list or empty tree.
- Remember that *nil* is a pointer and not a node.
- Always check to see whether procedures to manipulate dynamic data structures, such as linked lists and trees, work correctly for the empty structure. Recursive procedures often terminate only when a series of recursive calls leads to an empty structure.
- Binary search trees can be used to store ordered data for rapid retrieval. Like a linked list, a binary search tree can grow and shrink in size. Like an array, a binary search algorithm can be used with the tree. Hence, in many situations, the tree combines the advantages of both arrays and linked lists.

- Research on trees in particular and dynamic data structures in general has produced a large number of nonobvious techniques for building and maintaining dynamic data structures. The references that follow include much more material on the subject.

Summary of Pascal Constructs

pointer types
Syntax:

   ↑ <domain type>

Example:

```
type Arrow =  ↑ Node;
      Node = record
                 Data: integer;
                 Link: Arrow
             end;
   var P1: Arrow;
```

The type for pointers that point to dynamic variables (nodes). In the example, the variable P1 is declared so that it can contain pointers to dynamic variables of type Node.

naming the dynamic variable pointed to
Syntax:

   <pointer variable> ↑

Example:

   P1 ↑

One way to name the dynamic variable pointed to by <pointer variable>.

new
Syntax:

   new (<pointer variable>)

Example:

   new (P1)

Creates a new dynamic variable of the domain type of the <pointer variable> and leaves the value of the <pointer variable> pointing to this new dynamic variable.

pointer variables in assignment statements
Syntax:

   <pointer variable1> : = <pointer variable2>

Example:

```
P1 := P2
```

Makes the value of <pointer variable1> point to the same thing as the value of <pointer variable2>.

nil
Syntax:

```
nil
```

Predefined constant of a type that is compatible with pointers to any type of dynamic variable. *nil* does not point to any dynamic variable but is used to give a value to pointer variables that do not point to any dynamic variable (i.e., to give a value to "end points").

dispose
Syntax:

```
dispose(<pointer variable>)
```

Example:

```
dispose(P)
```

Releases the memory occupied by the dynamic variable pointed to by <pointer variable>. The value of <pointer variable> becomes undefined. The statement is undefined if <pointer variable> points to no dynamic variable. In particular, it is undefined if the value of <pointer variable> is *nil*.

Exercises

Self-Test Exercises

8. What is the difference between the kind of node used in a binary tree and the kind used in a doubly linked list?

9. Modify the type declaration in Figure 17.30 so that each node of the tree can have one more pointer that points to the node above it. The node above is often called the *parent node,* so call the new field Parent.

Interactive Exercises

10. Using pencil and paper, simulate the procedure OutputNodes (Figure 17.28) on the tree in Figure 17.27.

Programming Exercises

11. Write a procedure that takes as parameters a linked list of integers (the parameter will literally be a pointer to the head of the list) and two integers L and U such that L is

less than U. The procedure should write to the screen all integers in the list that are between L and U. The list need not be sorted.

12. Write a procedure that takes a (singly) linked list and reverses the order of the nodes in the linked list. For concreteness, make it a linked list of characters.

13. The procedure `GetFirst` in Figure 17.21 both reads and removes the first element in the queue. Separate these tasks by writing declarations for the following: *procedure* `ShowFirst(var Receiver:ElementType; Q:Queue);`
{Sets Receiver equal to the Entry field of the first element in Q. Q is not changed. Precondition: The queue is not empty.}
procedure `RemoveNext(var Q:Queue);`
{Removes the first element from Q, provided Q is not empty.
Does nothing, if Q is empty.}

14. Redo Exercise 16 in Chapter 15, but this time use linked lists rather than arrays. With linked lists there is no limit to the number of digits in the two numbers being added.

15. Redo Exercise 19 in Chapter 15, but this time use linked lists rather than arrays. With linked lists there is no limit to the number of digits after the decimal point. Hence, this gives unlimited accuracy.

16. Write procedures to insert, find, and delete nodes in a doubly linked list. For simplicity, suppose that the nodes store integers.

17. A binary tree can be used to classify items according to a series of yes/no questions. Write a program that builds a tree to classify animals according to yes/no questions. The questions are stored in the nodes, and the answer determines which pointer to follow. Each leaf (end) node of the tree contains the name of an animal for which the yes/no answers are correct. For example, Is it very big? Does it eat meat? Does it have big ears? The answers *yes, no,* and *yes,* respectively, might lead to the name "elephant." The program first constructs a tree with three levels of questions. It asks the user to input seven yes/no questions about animals. It then uses these seven questions as the questions in the tree. Each series will consist of three questions, and there will be eight possible sets of yes/no answers leading to animal names. The program displays each of the eight yes/no question sequences along with their answers, and then asks the user for an appropriate animal to enter. At that point the program offers to guess animals that the user is thinking of. It tells the user to think of an animal, and then asks the questions. The program works its way to an end node and then "guesses" the animal named in that node.

18. Redo the previous exercise, but this time have the program start with a very small tree with just one question—like Is it big?—and with two animals, like a mouse and an elephant. It then plays the game with the user, but whenever it guesses wrong (for example, if it guesses an elephant and the user says he/she was thinking of a dinosaur), it asks for a new question. For the two animals in this example, it would ask, "Please give me a question that will distinguish between an elephant and a dinosaur." The user might give the question "Is it extinct?" The program then adds a new node with that question and adds the two animals below that node. In this way the tree gets larger as the game is played.

19. Write a recursive procedure that takes a linked list of integers, already sorted into ascending order, and produces a binary search tree that contains the same integers, stored according to the Binary Search Tree Storage Rule. The tree should be balanced. A tree is balanced if for each node, the two subtrees led to by its two pointer fields contain the same number of nodes (plus or minus one node).

20. Write a procedure that takes a binary search tree with integers stored according to the Binary Search Tree Storage Rule and copies them to a second tree that also satisfies this rule. The second tree should be as close to balanced as possible. The first tree may not have been balanced, and so this is a way to obtain a balanced search tree. A tree is balanced if for each node, the two subtrees led to by its two pointer fields contain the same number of nodes (plus or minus one node).

References for Further Reading

A.V. Aho, J.E. Hopcroft, and J.D. Ullman, *Data Structures and Algorithms,* 1983, Addison-Wesley, Reading, Mass. Covers more advanced topics.

R.J. Baron and L.G. Shapiro, *Data Structures and Their Implementation,* 1980, Van Nostrand Reinhold, New York.

P. Helman and R. Veroff, *Intermediate Problem Solving and Data Structures,* 1986, Benjamin/Cummings, Menlo Park, Ca.

J.S. Rohl, *Recursion via Pascal,* 1984, Cambridge Computer Science Texts 19, Cambridge University Press, Cambridge and New York.

D.F. Stubbs and N.W. Webre, *Data Structures with Abstract Data Types and Pascal,* 1985, Brooks/Cole, Monterey, Ca.

A.M. Tanenbaum and M.J. Augenstein, *Data Structures Using Pascal,* Second Edition, 1986, Prentice-Hall, Englewood Cliffs, N.J.

APPENDIX 1
THE GOTO STATEMENT

The term *flow of control* refers to the order in which the statements and substatements of a program are executed. There is one Pascal mechanism for flow of control that we have not yet discussed. That mechanism is the *goto statement*. The method of using this statement, in fact the very question of whether or not it should be used at all, is very controversial. In this appendix we briefly explain the $goto$ statement and the controversy surrounding it.

As an example, consider the following program fragment:

```
    writeln('First Statement');
42: writeln('Statement Labeled 42');
    writeln('Third Statement');
    goto 42;
```

The number 42 on the second line is called a *label*. It has no effect on the statement. It is just a way of giving a name to the second writeln statement.

The $goto$ instructs the computer to next execute the statement labeled 42. After executing the statement labeled 42, the computer proceeds to the next statement after that; in other words, the computer forgets whether it arrived at a labeled statement via a $goto$ statement or by some other means.

Thus, the above example is an infinite loop with the output

```
First Statement
Statement Labeled 42
Third Statement
Statement Labeled 42
Third Statement
Statement Labeled 42
Third Statement
```

The last two lines are repeated indefinitely.

In Pascal all labels, such as 42, must be integers in the range 0 to 9999. However, they are used only as names of statements and not as numbers. In particular, a $goto$ statement cannot contain an integer variable. All *labels* must be declared. The label declarations come before all other declarations in a block. The syntax consists of the reserved word $label$ followed by a list of labels; the labels are separated by commas and terminated with a semicolon. For example, the following declares 100 and 42 to be labels:

```
label 100, 42;
```

Once a label is declared, it may be used to label a statement and then used in a *goto* statement. A *goto* statement consists of the identifier *goto* followed by a label. The identifier *goto* is a single word with no spaces. The execution of a *goto* statement is frequently called a *jump* because the execution "jumps" to the labeled statement specified after the *goto.*

There is one important restriction that applies to the use of *goto* statements. It is possible to use a *goto* statement to jump out of a structure such as a loop or procedure. However, a *goto* statement may not be used to jump into a structure. If a *goto* is used to jump into a structure, the effect is undefined and unpredictable.

The *goto* has a long history; at least, it is long when compared to other things in the young field of computer science. Although it was usually spelled differently, the *goto* was an important feature in virtually all early programming languages. Machine languages invariably have *goto* statements. In fact, most flow of control in machine language programs is typically by means of *goto* statements or similar constructs. Most high level languages include *goto* statements. Moreover, until very recently, most high level programming languages depended on the use of *goto* statements for much or even most flow of control.

Around 1960 a class of languages referred to as *structured programming languages* began to appear. A structured language is one that includes constructs for flow of control that allow for a systematic way to structure a program into meaningful subparts. Procedures and *while* statements are examples of such constructs. One of the earliest of these languages was ALGOL. Pascal is also a typical example of a structured language. These structuring constructs provided an alternative to the *goto* statement. Programs written with many *goto*s have a structure that is usually not apparent to the reader. Programs written without the *goto* can more easily exhibit a clear structure for the flow of control.

Although there are varying views on the details of how and when *goto*s should be used, some things about *goto* statements are clear. First of all, there is no absolute need for *goto*s. Any program that is written with *goto*s can be rewritten to do the same thing and to not include any *goto* statements. The question is whether *goto* statements enhance or detract from good programming style. Even in the less exact domain of style, some things are clear. A program that uses very many *goto*s is harder to read than a well-written program that uses very few *goto*s or no *goto* statements at all. A consensus has arisen that *goto* statements should be avoided.

When you are first learning to program, it is best to avoid *goto*s completely. Otherwise, it is difficult to learn that they are never needed and seldom even of any help. After you become proficient at programming, you may want to use an occasional *goto,* or you may agree with the school of thought that says they should never be used.

Situations in which *goto* statements may be reasonable are various sorts of exiting situations. When an error or other terminating condition is encountered, a *goto* can be used to jump directly to the end of a loop, a procedure, or an entire program.

For example, a program can be designed to terminate on detection of an error, by the following scheme:

```
program Sample(input, output);
label 100;
var · · ·
   · · ·
begin {Program}
     · · ·
  if <error condition> then
    goto 100;
     · · ·
100: end.  {Program}
```

In this scheme the label 100 labels the empty statement. This trick produces the equivalent of labeling the *end*.

Additional material on *goto*s can be found in the following references:

E.W. Dijkstra, "Goto Statement Considered Harmful," *Communications of the ACM*, Vol. 11, No. 3, March 1968, 147–148, 538, 541.

D.E. Knuth, "Structured Programming with goto Statements," *Computing Surveys*, Vol. 6, No. 4, Dec. 1974, 261–298.

APPENDIX 2
SYNTAX DIAGRAMS FOR
STANDARD PASCAL

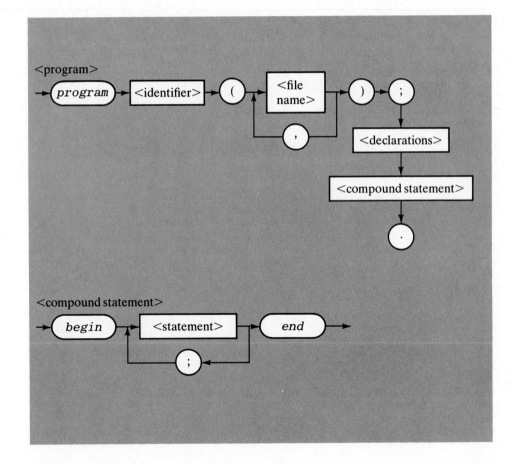

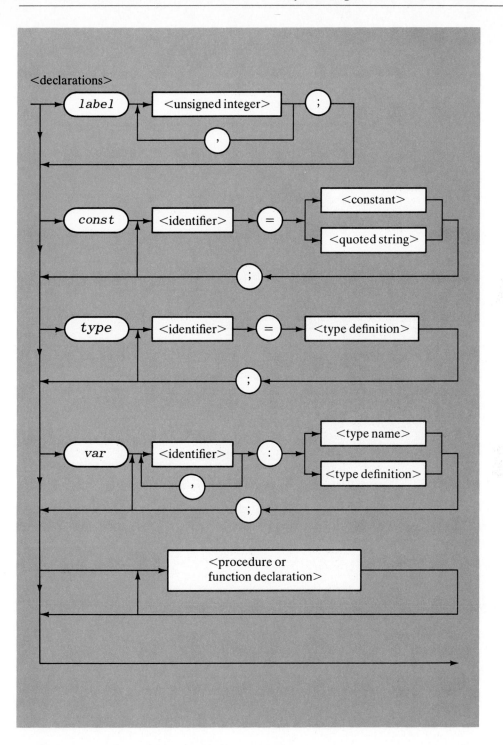

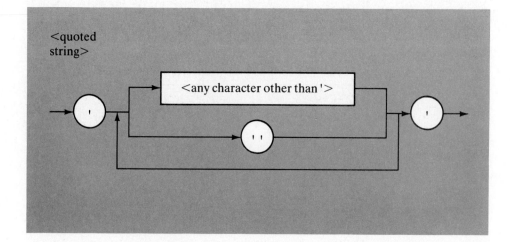

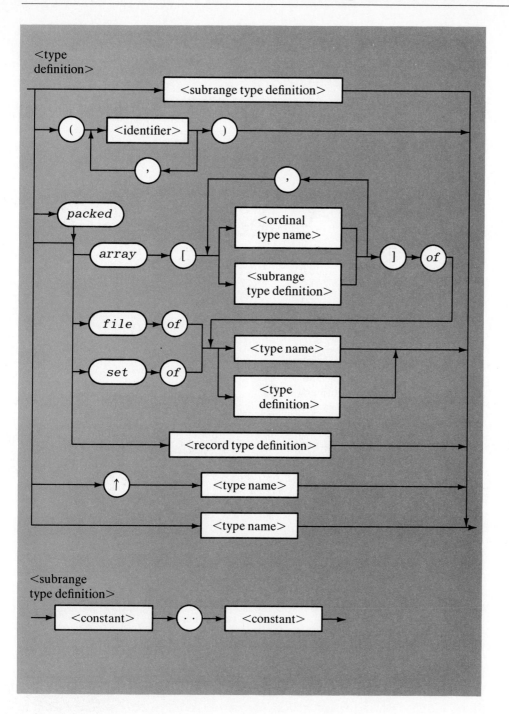

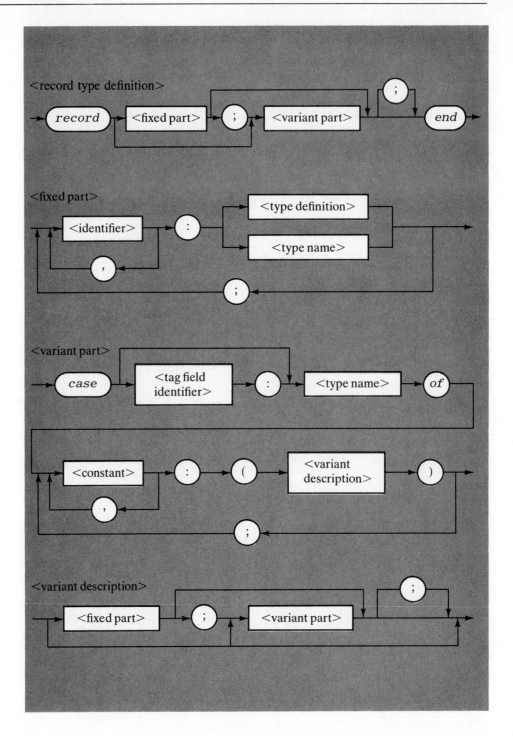

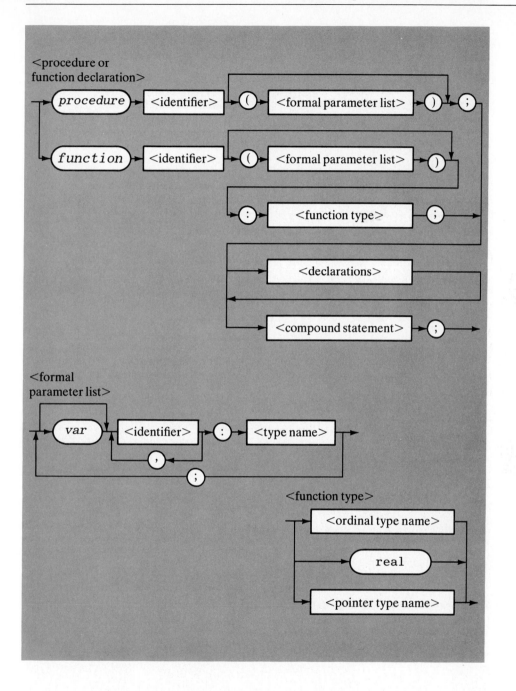

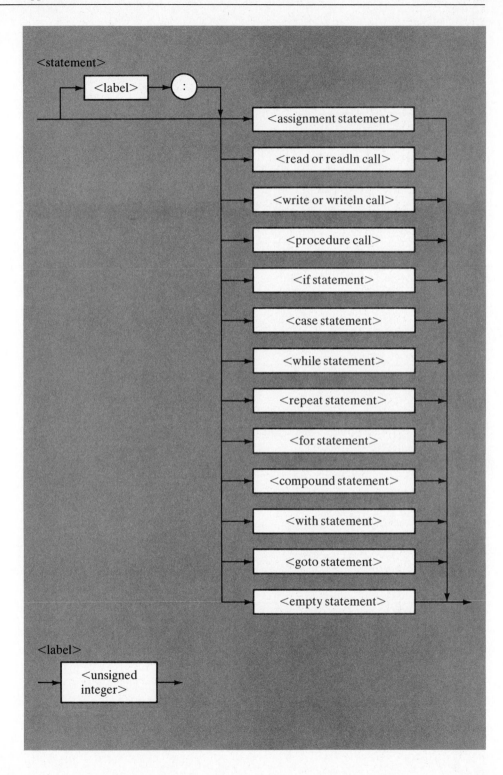

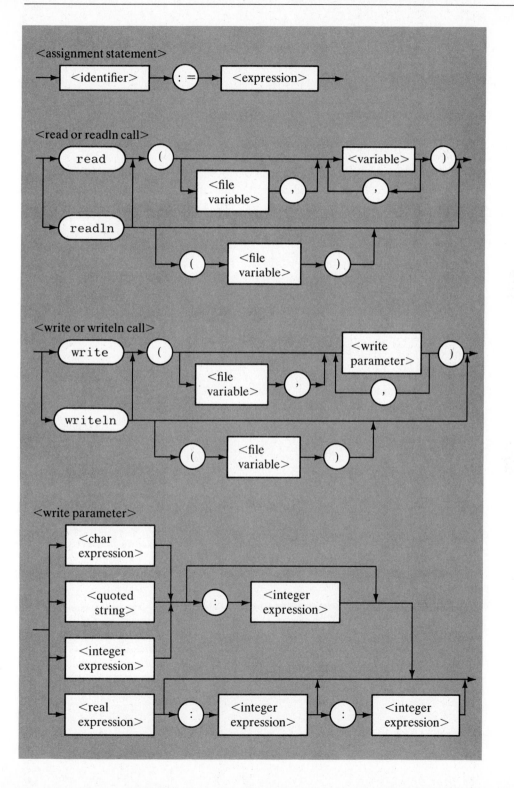

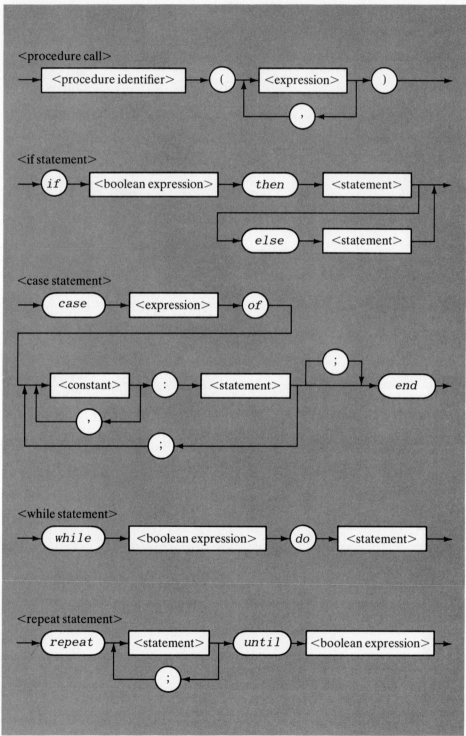

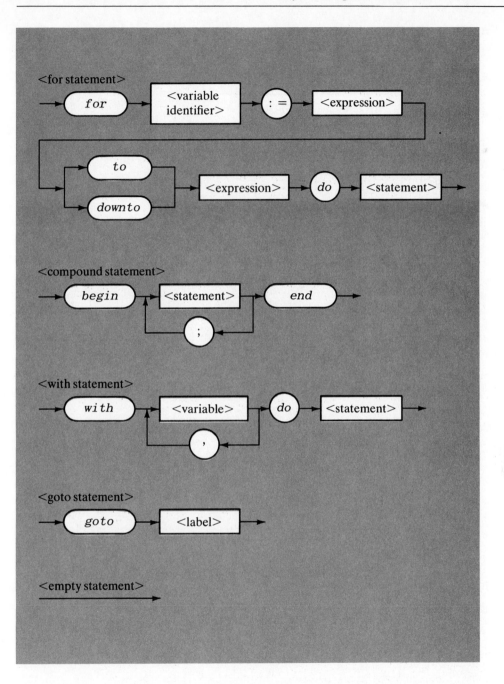

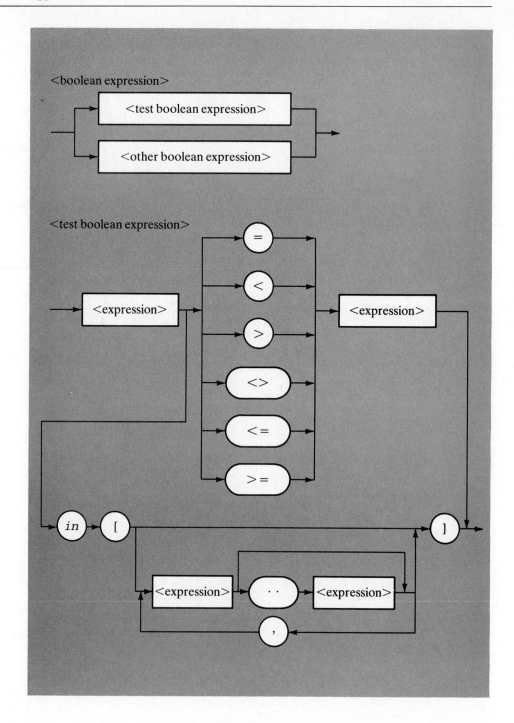

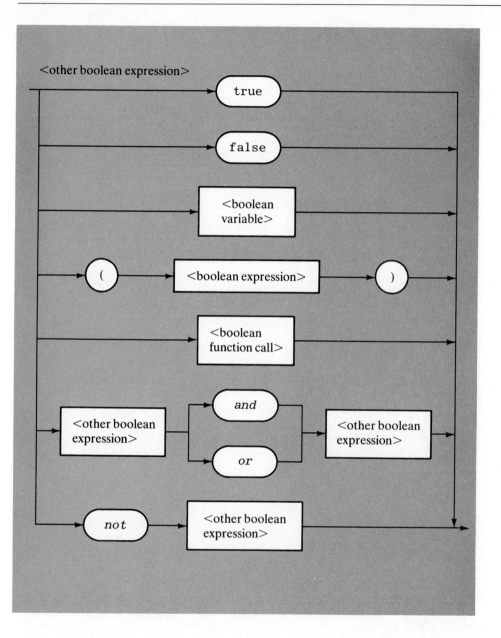

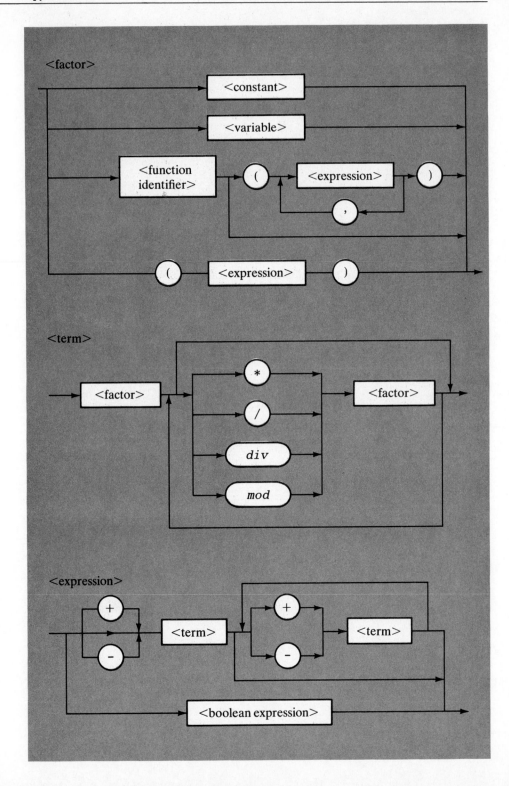

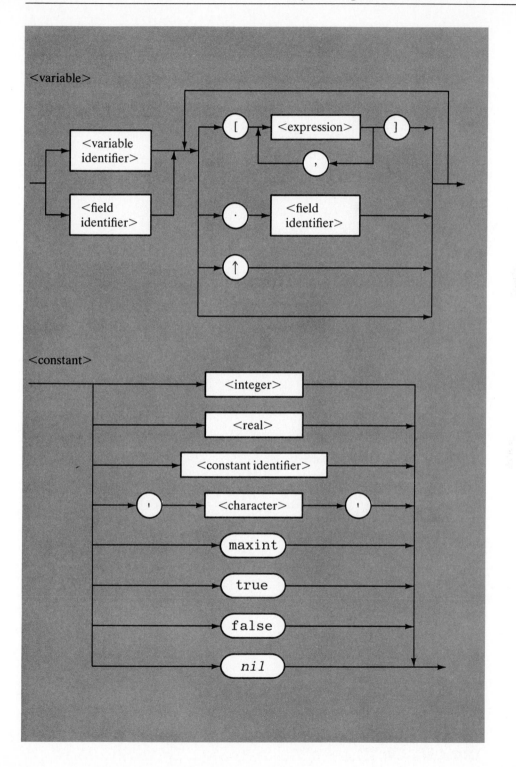

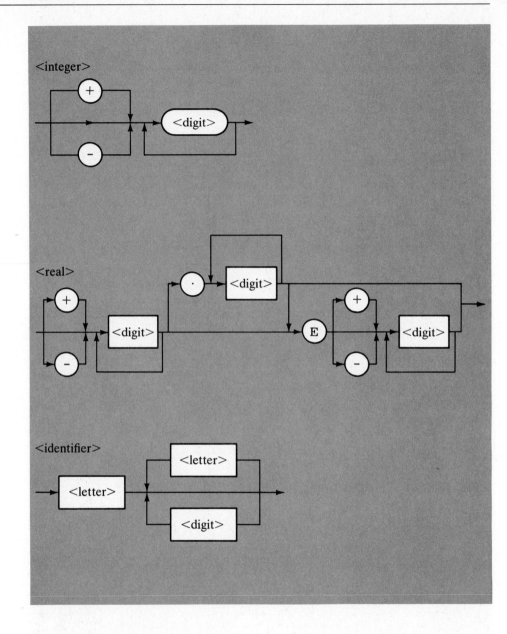

APPENDIX 3
CONFORMANT ARRAY
PARAMETERS

In Pascal formal and actual array parameters for a procedure or function must ordinarily be of the same type. According to the older ANSI/IEEE standard, this rule is absolute. For example, consider the type definitions

```
type List1 = array[1 . . 20] of real;
     List2 = array[0 . . 10] of real;
```

Now suppose we design a procedure to fill arrays of type List1. The procedure heading might be

```
procedure Fill(var A: List1);
{Fills the array A with numbers read from the keyboard.}
```

If we later want a procedure to fill an array of type List2, we must write a new procedure declaration, even though the body of the List1 procedure and the body of the List2 procedure may differ only in the values of two constants.

The ISO standard allows procedure and function declarations for which the upper and lower bounds of the array parameters may vary from one call of the procedure (or function) to another. This type of array parameter is called a *conformant array parameter* and is not available on all implementations that follow the ISO standard. The standard says they may be implemented, but does not require that they be available.

As an example, the following procedure can fill arrays of type List1 or List2 or certain other types:

```
procedure FlexFill(var A: array[Low . . High: integer] of real);
{Fills the array A with numbers read from the keyboard.}
var I: integer;
begin{FlexFill}
   writeln('Enter ', High − Low + 1, ' real values');
   for I := Low to High do
      read(A[I])
end; {FlexFill}
```

The new element in this sample procedure is the following type specification:

```
array[Low . . High: integer] of real
```

This is called a *conformant array scheme*. The corresponding actual parameter can be any array of `real` values whose index type is a subrange of the type `integer`. Any type may be used in place of `real`. Any ordinal type may be used in place of `integer`. Any nonreserved words may be used in place of the identifiers Low and High, and, as illustrated by the example, the two identifiers may be used in the body of the procedure as if they were constant values.

If they can be used at all, conformant array schemes can be used with packed arrays and multidimensional arrays as well as simple one-dimensional arrays.

APPENDIX 4
FUNCTIONS AND
PROCEDURES AS
PARAMETERS

Many versions of Pascal allow function and procedure names to be parameters to other functions and/or procedures. Unfortunately, not all implementations allow this; moreover, the details vary somewhat from system to system. We will describe the most common way of doing this, as well as one common variation in syntax.

A procedure or function parameter is neither a value nor a variable parameter. *Function parameters* and *procedure parameters* are two additional kinds of parameters. In the formal parameter list, function parameters and procedure parameters are listed by giving a function or procedure heading. Since they are formal parameters that will be replaced by other identifiers when the procedure is called, the identifiers may be any non-reserved-word identifiers. For example, the following is a sample procedure heading:

```
procedure Sample(var X:real;
    function F(N:integer):real; procedure Pro(Y:char));
```

This procedure has three formal parameters: X is a variable parameter of type `real`, F is a function parameter, and `Pro` is a procedure parameter. Such long procedure headings seldom fit comfortably on one line. Hence, you should be certain to indent the second line so that the identifiers *procedure* and *function* in the formal parameter lists are not misinterpreted as the start of a new declaration. A sample procedure call corresponding to this heading is

```
Sample(Z, G, ActualPro)
```

The actual parameter Z must be a variable of type `real`. The actual parameter G must be the name of a function that has one argument of type `integer` and that returns a value of type `real`. The actual parameter `ActualPro` must be a procedure with one value parameter of type `char`.

The exact syntax for listing the formal function parameters and procedure parameters varies a little from system to system. On some systems, the formal function and

```
program  Sample(input, output);
{Outputs the sum 1/1 + 1/2 + 1/3 + 1/4 + 1/5.}

function Reciprocal(Int: integer): real;
{Precondition: The value of Int is not zero.}
begin{Reciprocal}
   Reciprocal := 1/Int
end;  {Reciprocal}

function SumValue(function F(X: integer): real;
                                       N: integer): real;
{F is a formal function argument.
SumValue returns the value F(1)+F(2)+ . . . +F(N).}
var I: integer;
    Sum: real;
begin{SumValue}
   Sum  := 0;
   for I := 1 to N do
       Sum := Sum + F(I);
   SumValue := Sum
end;  {SumValue}

begin{Program}
   writeln('The sum of the reciprocals of');
   writeln('1 through 5 is:');
   writeln(SumValue(Reciprocal, 5))
end.  {Program}
```

Figure A.4.1
Function with
another function as
an argument.

procedure parameters are given in a shorter form. On these systems the parameter lists within function and procedure parameters are not listed in the formal parameter specifications. On these systems the sample procedure heading would instead be

```
procedure Sample(var X:real;
            function F:real; procedure Pro);
```

A complete example using a function parameter is given in Figure A.4.1. The function SumValue in that program has a function parameter.

There are restrictions on what kinds of functions and procedures may be used as parameters. Specifically, a function or procedure parameter may itself have only value parameters. Hence, a procedure parameter may not have either variable, function, or procedure parameters.

APPENDIX 5
A QUICK INTRODUCTION
TO THE VI EDITOR

An editor is used to write or change text stored in units called *files*. The text created with an editor and stored in a file can be anything from a shopping list to a major literary work. We are interested in editors because they can be used to write Pascal programs and to store them in files. One of the most commonly used editors available in the UNIX operating system is the vi editor. The name "vi" is pronounced by saying the two letters v-i. The *vi editor* is a "visual" editor, which is why it was named "vi." This means that when you are using the vi editor, you will see the text on the screen just as you would see it on a sheet of paper. You can write, erase, and change text very much as you would with a pencil and eraser. The vi editor has a large number of commands. In this and the following appendix we will introduce you to some of the most common and useful commands. The best way to use this appendix is to sit down at a terminal and try out each of the commands as you read about them. If you have a file that already contains some text, it would be best to use it to practice on (provided you do not mind changing it), but you can also practice by creating a new file.

Before using the vi editor, you need to log in to the UNIX system. You may also need to tell UNIX the type of terminal you are using. You need to find out about those two details from your instructor or some other local expert. Once you have logged in (and if necessary, told UNIX the type of terminal you are using), all you need to do in order to start up the vi editor is to type `vi` followed by the name of the file you want to edit. For example, if you want to write a Pascal program in a file called `first.p`, then you would type the following:

starting vi

```
vi first.p
```

If there already is a file called `first.p`, you will then see the contents of that file on the screen. If the file `first.p` does not already exist, then this will create the file and you will see an essentially blank screen, since this new file is empty.

Once you are in the vi editor, you will see a square (or line) of light. This is called the *cursor* and it serves as your pencil and eraser. Writing takes place at the location of the cursor, and the cursor is used to mark the location of text to be deleted. The cursor can be moved using the group of four arrow keys marked for the four directions

cursor

up, down, left, and right. If you do not have a working set of four arrow keys on your terminal or if you do not wish to use the arrow keys, you can use the h, j, k, and l keys to move the cursor. Those letters do not stand for anything. Those four keys were chosen because they are in a convenient location for your fingers. The outer of the four keys, h and l, move the cursor to the left and right respectively. The middle two keys move the cursor up and down. The k key moves it up and the j key moves it down.

upper- and lowercase

Notice that we used lowercase letters to specify the keys for moving the cursor. Commands can be either lowercase, formed by simply pressing the letter key, or uppercase, formed by holding down the shift key while pressing the letter key. In the vi editor, upper- and lowercase versions of letters usually are different commands so you should be sure to notice whether a command is upper- or lowercase. Most of the commands we will give are lowercase letters or combinations of lowercase letters.

The terminal keyboard is used for two different things: It is used to type text into the file and it is used to give commands to the vi editor. You need to tell the editor which of these two things you mean when you type something. For example, if you want to move the cursor down one line, you press the j key. If you want to type the letter "j" into the file, you also do this by pressing the j key. How does the editor know which of these two things you mean when you press the j key? Obviously, you must somehow tell it. In the vi editor, anytime you press a key it is interpreted as a command to the editor unless you first do something to tell the editor that you want to type text into the file. Hence, if you have just begun an editing session and you press the j key, that will tell the editor to move the cursor down one line (if that is possible).

writing

How do you tell the editor that you want to write something into the file? There are several ways. The most common way is to press the i key. After that, anything you type will be considered text to be inserted in the file and will appear on the screen. That is fine as long as you want to write text into the file, but eventually you will have written all that you want to write and will then want to give commands to the editor, such as the command to leave the editor. To end typing in text you press the *escape* key. This key is likely to be labeled Esc, or something similar, and is likely to be in the upper left-hand corner of the keyboard. After pressing the escape key, anything you type in will again be interpreted as a command. No matter which of the many available commands you use to initiate the typing, you always use the escape key to tell the editor when you are through typing in text. Whenever a command does not work, it usually means that you have inadvertently told the editor that you want to type in text. To correct this situation, simply press the escape key. Whenever things seem wrong, try pressing the escape key. It can cause no harm and may correct the situation.

Pressing the i key tells the editor that you want to "insert" text. Whatever you type in after pressing that key will be placed before the cursor. The old text will move to get out of the way; it will not be written over. If you press the a key instead of the i key, then the text will be inserted *after* the cursor instead of *before* the cursor. The a stands for "append." With the a, as with the i, you press the escape key when you have finished typing in text. If you want to write over the text that is already in the file rather than squeezing in new text, you can press the R key. (Be sure to note that the i and a are lowercase letters while the R is an uppercase letter.) After pressing the R, anything you type will be written to the file and will replace the text that is already there. If you type in ten characters, then the first ten characters starting at the original cursor position will be replaced by the ten you type in. To end this typing of replacement text, you press the escape key just as you do for the i and the a commands.

When you are typing in text, you can back up, using the backspace key, and change any mistakes you might make. Once you press the escape key, backing up will no longer erase what you typed in. However, you can always undo the last command you gave to the editor by simply pressing the u key. For example, if your last command was to insert some text, then you can undo this by pressing the u key. When you press the u key, all the text you inserted will disappear. (What do you think will happen if you press the u key again? Think about it and then try it.) You can only undo the very last command. If you wish to correct any earlier mistake, you must use some other technique. The most obvious technique is to delete the incorrect text and then type in the correct text. There are numerous commands to delete text. We will describe a few.

correcting mistakes

The cursor is used to tell the editor the location of text to be deleted. If you want to delete one character, you move the cursor to that character and then press the x key. This will delete the character under the cursor. To help remember this command, think of the x as standing for "x-ing out" the character. If you want to delete five characters simply press the x key five times. This will not leave a space. The old text will move to close up the space. To delete an entire word you can move the cursor to the first letter in the word and then press the d key followed by the w key. The two-letter sequence dw stands for "delete word." You can delete an entire line by moving the cursor to any position on the line you want to delete and then pressing the d key twice.

deleting text

Although it looks like you are changing the file you are editing when you insert or delete text, the editor does not really change the file you are editing. When you enter the vi editor, the editor makes a copy of the file you are editing. This copy is called the *buffer file* and it is this buffer file that you see on the screen and that you change when you insert or delete text. This is an advantage, because if you do not like the changes you made, you have not really changed the file you are editing and so no harm has been done. However, you do want to eventually change the file you are editing or else there would be no point to editing it. Typing a colon followed by a w tells the editor to "write out" the buffer file. Unlike the other commands we have discussed so far, you must follow the :w by pressing the return key. When you type this command, the editor makes the file you are editing identical to the buffer file. Before you type :w, all your changes are confined to the buffer file and therefore are tentative. After you type :w, the changes are really made to the file you are editing. If you are editing a file called first.p, then first.p is unchanged until you type :w. This makes it sound like you should be very reluctant to write out the buffer file, i.e., reluctant to type the command :w. Unfortunately, things are not that simple. If you wait too long to write out the buffer file, that can also be a problem. You can always retract all the changes you have made since the last time you wrote out the buffer file, but it is an all-or-nothing situation. You cannot undo half of what you have done. Hence, when you are sure you want to keep some changes you should write out the buffer file. If you frequently write out the buffer file this also has the advantage of insuring that you will not lose too much work if the system should stop working for some reason.

buffer file

There are two basic ways to leave the editor: You can write out the buffer file as you leave or you can leave without writing out the buffer file. The normal way to leave the editor is to write out the buffer file as you leave. This way all of the changes that

leaving the editor

you made to the buffer file will also be made to the file you are editing. The command to do this is given by typing a colon followed by the two letters w and q and ending by pressing the return key. The w stands for "write out" the buffer file and the q stands for "quit." This is actually two commands combined: the : w command that we discussed in the last paragraph and the : q command. If you have just written out the buffer file, you could simply type : q followed by return, rather than : wq, but that only saves typing one letter. It is easier to always type : wq when you want to quit in the normal way. (An alternate command that is equivalent to : wq is ZZ. Some find this alternate spelling easier to type than : wq.)

The second basic way to leave the editor is to quit without writing out the buffer file. The command for this is : q!, that is, a colon, followed by a q, followed by an exclamation point, followed by pressing the return key. If you leave the editor in this way, then the file will contain all the changes you made up to the last time you wrote out the buffer file (i.e., up to the last : w), but will contain none of the changes you made since then. If you never wrote out the buffer file, then the file would not be changed at all.

The exclamation point is used as a way of telling the editor that you know that you have not written out the buffer file and that you really want to leave without writing it out. If you simply type : q without the exclamation point, the editor will try to protect you from yourself. If you have made no changes since the last : w, then it will let you leave the editor, since it does not matter whether or not you write out the buffer file again. However, if you have made some changes since the last : w, then it will insist that you leave by one of the two commands : wq or : q!.

There are a few general principles that may help to keep all these editor commands straight. Most of the commands we have discussed apply to a particular location in the file. These commands, like i, x, dw, etc. all perform their action at the location of the cursor. You do not need to end these commands by pressing the return key. Other actions apply to the entire file. The only commands of this sort that we have discussed so far are : w, : wq, : q!, and : q. All of these commands start with a colon and they are all ended by pressing the return key. In addition to giving commands, you can also use the keyboard to type in text. Whenever you want to type in text, you must first give a command telling the editor that you want to do so. Examples of these commands are i to insert text and a to append text. Whenever you want to stop typing in text and use the keyboard to again give commands, you must first press the escape key. Whenever things go wrong, try pressing the escape key. It cannot hurt and might help.

scrolling   As soon as you start to write programs of any significant size, you will find that the screen is too small to hold the entire program. When the amount of text is too large to fit on one screen you will need to move the text so that the portion you wish to work on is visible on the screen. Typing control D will scroll the text, revealing text that is *down* below the end of the screen. Typing control U will scroll the text, revealing text that is *up* above the screen. These commands are formed by holding down the control key (marked Ctrl or something similar) while pressing the appropriate letter key.

automatic   The vi editor can be told to automatically indent for you. When it is in this *auto-*
indenting   *indent* mode and you indent a line, it will automatically indent the next line by the same amount. Pascal programs are normally written with a good deal of indentation and

many find this autoindent feature helpful; others find the autoindent mode to be a nuisance. You can turn this autoindent feature off or on to obtain the environment you like best. To turn on the autoindent feature the command is

> `:set ai`

The command to turn off autoindent is

> `:set noai`

Notice that there is no space between the `no` and `ai`. These commands for turning autoindent on and off are ended by pressing the return key.

Congratulations! You now know enough to use the vi editor. After you practice the commands we have discussed in this appendix, you should go on to the next appendix and learn a few more commands. That will make using the editor even easier.

APPENDIX 6
SUMMARY OF VI
COMMANDS

To enter vi type the following after the system prompt:

    vi *file name*

If any of the following commands do not seem to work, try pressing the escape key and then try the command again. Commands that begin with a colon are ended by pressing the return key; other commands do not require you to press the return key.

Cursor Movements

One character

The h, j, k, and l keys move the cursor; so do the space bar and the backspace-key. (h moves it left one space, j moves it down one line, k moves it up one line, l moves it right one space.) On many terminals there is also a set of four arrow keys that can be used to move the cursor.

One word

w moves it to the next word. b moves it to the previous word.

To ends of line

$ moves the cursor to the end of the line.
^ moves the cursor to the beginning of the line.

To a specified line

*n*G moves it to line number *n*. G moves it to the last line.

Scrolling

All commands are control characters formed by holding down the control key and pressing the letter key. For example, Ctrl-E is typed by holding down the control key while pressing the e key.

One line

Ctrl-Y up one line, Ctrl-E down one line

Several lines

Ctrl-U up, Ctrl-D down

Full screenfull

Ctrl-F forward, Ctrl-B backward

Adding Text

Type in the text after giving one of the following commands. Finish by pressing the escape key.

Inserting text

i inserts before the cursor; I inserts at the beginning of the line;
a appends after the cursor; A appends at the end of the line.

Opening a new line

o opens a new line below the line of the cursor.
O opens a new line above the line of the cursor.

Deleting Text

One character

x deletes ("crosses out") the one letter under the cursor.

One word

dw deletes from the cursor to the end of the word.

Deleting lines

dd deletes one line, *n*dd deletes *n* lines starting with the line containing the cursor.

To end of line

D deletes from the cursor to the end of the line.

Changing Text

One character

r changes the character under the cursor to the character typed next.

One word

cw changes one word to whatever is typed after it. The cursor should be on the first letter of the word to be changed. End the new text by pressing the escape key.

Unlimited length

If you type R, then whatever you type next will replace the text under the cursor. To end the replacement text press the escape key.

Joining text

J joins the line containing the cursor and the line below into one long line.

Correcting Mistakes

Typing u undoes the last thing that you did. Typing : q! quits and disregards all file changes since the last time you typed : w.

Also see the section Recovering Lost Text.

Redrawing the Screen

Sometimes spurious characters may appear on your screen that are not actually in the file you are editing. For example, this may occur if someone sends you mail while you are using vi or if there is a message broadcast to all users; on some terminals, deleting lines may cause the character @ to appear on the screen. You can clean up the screen by typing control L. To type this command you press the L key while holding down the control key. The control key is usually marked Ctrl or something similar. Sometimes you need to use control R instead. Try them both to see which ones work in your situation.

Writing Out the Buffer File and Leaving

: w writes out the buffer file; all the file changes since the last time you gave this command become "permanent."

: q leaves vi, but this is seldom used. Instead one typically uses one of the following commands:

: wq writes out the buffer file and then leaves vi (usual way to end a session)

ZZ equivalent to : wq

: q! quits but disregards any changes since the last : w.

Reading and Writing Files

: r *file name*   reads a file and inserts it at the position of the cursor.

: w *file name*   writes the contents of the buffer file to the named file.

Autoindent

Turn on automatic indentation

: set ai

Turn off automatic indentation

: set noai

Searching for Text

Type / followed by the word (or words) you want to find. For example, if you type /sample followed by pressing the return key, the cursor will move to the first occurrence of the word "sample." To get the next occurrence, type n. To get the previous occurrence, type N.

Marking Text

You can mark a line by moving the cursor to that line and then typing ma. You will see nothing on the screen, but an "invisible" mark called a will be left at that line. Later on, you can move the cursor directly to that line by typing ' a, i.e., by typing the single quote symbol, followed by a. Want more marks? Use mb and ' b, mc and ' c, etc.

Deleting Large Pieces of Text

d'a deletes all of the text between the cursor and mark a. (Use d'b for mark b, etc.)

dG deletes all the text from the cursor to the end of the file.

d1G deletes all the text from the cursor to the beginning of the file.

Copying Text

Vi has a number of places where it can hold a piece of text so that it can be copied to some other file or location. These temporary holding places are called *buffers*. These should not be confused with the buffer file. You cannot see these directly as you can see the buffer file and they are used differently. One of these is an unnamed buffer that is available to hold a piece of text (line, paragraph, or whatever). The contents of this buffer can then be written into the file at any desired location.

yw yanks (copies) the word the cursor is on into the buffer. The cursor should be on the first letter of the word.

yy yanks the entire line containing the cursor into the buffer.

*n*yy yanks *n* lines (starting with the line containing the cursor) into the buffer.

y'a yanks all of the text between the cursor and mark a into the buffer. (y'b yanks up to mark b, y'c yanks to mark c, etc.)

p prints the contents of the buffer at the location of the cursor.

Copying Text into Named Buffers

In addition to the unnamed buffer, there are a number of named buffers that can be used in ways similar to how the unnamed buffer is used. All of the copy commands can be used to copy text into buffers named, a, b, c, etc. This way you can move or copy several different pieces of text. To use a named buffer preface the command with a double quote and the letter name of the buffer. For example, typing the five characters "xy'a means you are giving the y'a command using buffer x. This will yank all of the text between the cursor and marker a into buffer x. Typing the three characters "xp means you are giving the p command using buffer x. That will print the contents of buffer x at the location of the cursor.

Recovering Lost Text

The most recent few deletions are saved in numbered buffers and can be recovered. The command "1p will print the contents of buffer 1 below the line containing the cursor. If that was not what you wanted, type u to undo it. Typing a dot (i.e., period) will repeat the command, but vi is smart enough to know you mean the next buffer and so it will print out the contents of buffer 2. Another dot (i.e., period) gives buffer 3 and so forth. Alternatively, you can type the longer "3p to get the contents of buffer 3. (The limit is 9.)

Repeating a Command

A "dot" (i.e., period) repeats the last command.

Repeat Numbers

Placing a number in front of a command causes that command to be done that number of times. For example,

8dd deletes 8 lines

5yy yanks 5 lines

3w moves the cursor right 3 words

11x crosses out 11 characters

Copying Text to Another File

To copy a portion of text from *source-file* to *destination-file* proceed as follows:

- If you are not already editing *source-file*, then call the vi editor with *source-file*:

vi *source-file*

- Move the cursor to the top line of the text to be copied.

- Type ma which puts mark a (or some other letter if you wish) at the top of the block of text to be copied.

- Move the cursor to the bottom line of the text to be copied.

- Type "xy'a which yanks all of the text from the current cursor position to mark a and puts a copy into buffer x. This does not delete the text from the file. (If you used some marker other than a, then substitute the name of that marker for a. If you want to use some buffer other than x, then substitute the name of that buffer for x.)

- Type : e *destination-file* which will switch the editor from *source-file* to *destination-file*.

- Position the cursor where you want the block of text to go.

- Type "xp which prints the contents of buffer x.

APPENDIX 7
UNIX FILES AND
DIRECTORIES

In UNIX and most other computer environments information is stored in units called *files*. In particular, Pascal programs are stored in files. To make files easier to locate, they are often grouped together into collections called *directories*. In this appendix we will describe the basic techniques for handling files and directories in the UNIX environment.

Part I
Manipulating Files

file
names

Almost any string of characters can be used to name a UNIX file. Names typically consist of strings of letters and numbers, often with a period used as punctuation. For example, your first Pascal program can be written in a file with any name, but a likely choice is first.p. Many Pascal compilers require that the name of a file containing a Pascal program end in .p, as in our example. The period is pronounced "dot" in computer jargon. So, first.p is normally pronounced "first dot p." Upper- and lower-case letters are considered different when used in UNIX file names. Hence, first.p and First.p are considered two distinct names and can name two distinct files.

creating
and removing
files

The most common way to create a file is to use an editor. Appendix 5 describes the vi editor. The command for removing a file is rm. For example, to remove the file first.p, you would give the following command:

```
rm first.p
```

To remove some other file, simply use that file name in place of first.p. This command, as well as all the other UNIX commands we will discuss, is ended by pressing the return key.

copying
files

When you edit a file, or otherwise change it, it is a good policy to first make a copy of the file you are changing. That way, if you make a mistake, you have an unchanged version of the file available so that you can start over again. The command to copy a file is `cp`. For example, suppose you want to make a copy of the file called `goodies` and to name the copy `goodies.spare`. The command to do this is

    cp goodies goodies.spare

In general, you write `cp` followed by the name of the file you want to copy and then the name you want the copy to have. Here, and with all the other UNIX commands we will discuss, the various parts of a command, such as the `cp` and the file names, must be separated by one or more spaces. The exact number of spaces does not matter as long as there is at least one space between each part.

The command to change the name of a file is `mv`. The command is read "move." To make it easy to remember this command, think of it as "moving" the file from one name to another. For example, if you want to change the name of the file `goodies` to `junk`, the command is

changing names

    mv goodies junk

When you use the `cp` or `mv` commands, such as in the following two examples,

warning

    cp oldfile newfile

    mv oldfile newfile

be sure that the new name, `newfile` in the examples, does not name a file that you want to keep. If it does name a file, then the old contents of the file will be destroyed and the file `newfile` will be made identical to what was in the file `oldfile`.

If you wish to see the names of all the files you have, use the `ls` command. Simply type `ls` followed by pressing the return key. This is called "listing" the files.

listing file names

You now know enough about files to begin writing Pascal programs. After you have mastered the editor and become comfortable with the few file manipulating commands we have already discussed, you should return to this point and complete reading this appendix.

Part II
Using Directories

Files are grouped together into larger units called *directories*. There is a hierarchical (upside-down tree-shaped) arrangement of directories. Figure A.7.1 is a diagram of a possible arrangement of directories. The top directory is called the *root* directory and it is always named `/`. To name a directory you give a list of the names of the directories you pass through on a path from the root directory to the directory being named. This is called a *complete path name*. For example, the complete path name of the circled directory is

    /usr/smith/programs

The symbol `/` is being used for two different things. It names the root directory and it is also used as a punctuation to separate directory names. (This double meaning is unfortunate, but this usage is standard.)

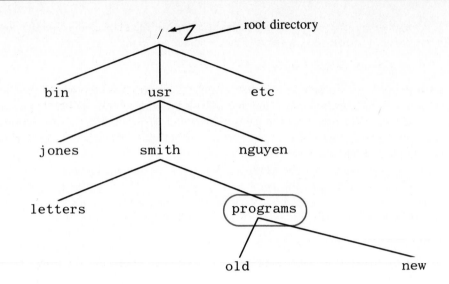

**Figure A.7.1
Hierarchy of
directories.**

Files and directories can be thought of as belonging to the same tree-like structure. Figure A.7.2 shows the same set of directories together with some of their files. The circled directory contains four items: `hints`, `old`, `new`, and `records`; `records` and `hints` are files whereas `old` and `new` are directories. You cannot always tell which are directories and which are files by looking at the diagram, but there always is a distinction.

The complete path name for a file is formed in the same way as the complete path name for a directory. To name a file, you give a complete path name to the directory containing the file followed by a / and the name of the file. For example, the complete path name for the file `hints` in the directory `programs` in Figure A.7.2 is

`/usr/smith/programs/hints`

*relative
names*   Directories and files are seldom referred to by complete path names. Usually they are referred to by relative path names. A *relative path name* is one that does not start with /. Relative path names are relative to a specific directory called your *current working directory*. This is sometimes called the directory you are "in." When you log in, you are automatically *in* a directory that is reserved for your use. This directory is called your *home* directory. (Later on in this appendix we will tell you how to change the directory you are in.) If you are in your home directory and want to name a file in that directory, you simply give the file name without any slashes or directory names. That is the simplest kind of relative path name, but relative path names are more general than that simple case. In a relative path name it is assumed that you start in the directory you are in and follow a path from there. For example, if you are in the circled directory in Figure A.7.2, then

`old/records`

will name the file enclosed in a box in that figure. The complete path name for that same file is

/usr/smith/programs/old/records

which explains why you usually want to use relative path names. Complete path names mean the same thing in any directory, but relative path names are much shorter.

Two different files in two different directories can have the same name. Notice the two files called records in Figure A.7.2. They are distinguished by their path names. Their complete path names are

/usr/smith/programs/records and
/usr/smith/programs/old/records

If you are in the circled directory, their relative path names are

records and old/records.

Two different files or directories may have the same name, but they will always have different path names.

All of the file manipulating commands we have seen so far, such as cp, mv, rm, and so forth, will accept full or relative path names. For example, if you are in the circled directory in Figure A.7.2 and wish to remove the file junk, you can do so using rm and the file's relative path name as follows:

use of
path names

rm old/junk

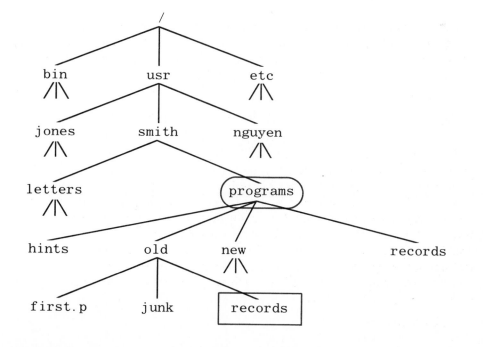

Figure A.7.2
Hierarchy of directories and files.

You can remove that file using rm and its full path name as follows: (This works no matter what directory you are in.)

```
rm  /usr/smith/programs/old/junk
```

home directory

Whenever you log in you are always in the same directory. That directory is called your *home* directory. Your home directory's name is normally the same as your log in name. This directory and all the directories and files below it *belong to you*. All other files and directories belong either to somebody else or to the system as a whole. The root directory belongs to the system as a whole and is someplace above your home directory.

changing directories

The command to change directories is cd. If you type cd followed by the full path name of some directory you will then be *in* that directory. You can also use cd with relative path names. There are also some abbreviated forms of the cd command. The command

```
cd  ..
```

that is, cd followed by two periods, will move you to the directory directly above the one you are in. For example, if you are in the directory smith in Figure A.7.2, then this command will move you to the directory usr. The command cd with nothing after it will move you from wherever you are to your home directory.

what directory am I in?

If you become confused about what directory you are in, simply type the command pwd. That stands for "print working directory" and it will tell you the full path name of the directory you are in.

creating directories

The command mkdir can be used to create a subdirectory of the directory you are in. If you want to create a subdirectory called, for example, homework, the command is

```
mkdir  homework
```

If you later want to remove this directory, the command is

```
rmdir  homework
```

To remove some other subdirectory of the one you are in, use that directory name in place of homework. Most systems require that you remove all files and subdirectories from a directory before you can remove the directory.

APPENDIX 8
SUMMARY OF UNIX
COMMANDS

File Manipulations

vi *file name*
    calls the vi editor with the named file.
cp *file1 file2*
    makes a second copy of *file1* and calls it *file2*.
mv *file1 file2*
    changes the name of *file1* to *file2*.
rm *file name*
    removes the named file. You may use either a complete path name or a relative
    path name.
ls
    lists all the items (files and directories) in your current directory.
ls *path name*
    lists all the items (files and directories) in the named directory. You may use either
    a complete path name or a relative path name.

Directories

cd *path name*
    moves you to the named directory. You may use either a complete path name or a
    relative path name.
cd ..
    moves you to the directory above your current directory.
cd
    moves you to your home directory.
pwd
    prints the full path name of your current directory.

`mkdir` *name*

creates a subdirectory of your current directory and calls it *name*.

`rmdir` *path name*

removes the named directory. You may use either a complete path name or a relative path name.

APPENDIX 9
I/O REDIRECTION
IN UNIX

In the UNIX operating systems a Pascal program (or any other program) may be run so that it takes its standard input from a file rather than from the keyboard. Similarly, it may be run so that it writes its output to a file rather than to the screen. The program is written just as if it were receiving input from the keyboard and giving output to the screen. The difference is in how the program is run.

Different compilers have different commands to compile and run a program, but for concreteness let us suppose you run your Pascal program by typing the following:

```
run program
```

(If you normally compile and run your program with one single command, then proceed as we describe below, but use that single command wherever we use run program. If you normally first compile your program with one command and then run your program by typing another command, compile your program as usual and then do what we describe below using your run command wherever we use run program.)

If you want your program to read data from a file called InData, rather than from the keyboard, then run your program with the command

```
run program < InData
```

input from a file

The standard output will still go to the screen, but your program will read its input from the file InData.

This is a general phenomenon that does not depend on what compiler or program is used. If your program is run by typing

```
mush dogs
```

then substitute mush dogs for run program. In general, to make any execution of any kind of program read its standard input from a file, the command is

command line < *file name*

where *command line* is whatever you would normally type to execute the program reading its input from the keyboard.

output
redirection

Similarly, a program may be run so that it writes its standard output to a file rather than the screen. The syntax is the same as what we described for redirected input except that the symbol > is used instead of <. To execute your program and have it write its standard output to a file called OutData the command is

```
run program > OutData
```

Your program will still take its input from the keyboard, but its output will be written to the file OutData instead of to the screen. If the file OutData did not exist before the program is run, it will be created. If it did exist, its old contents will be lost and it will contain only the output of the program just run.

In general, to make any execution of any kind of program write its standard output to a file, the command is

command line > *file name*

where *command line* is whatever you would normally type to execute the program writing its output to the screen.

combining
> and <

You can combine both < and > to execute a program so that it reads its standard input from one file and writes its standard output to another file. The command to run your program with input taken from the file InData and output sent to the file OutData is

```
run program < InData > OutData
```

In general, the syntax for both reading from one file and writing to another is as follows:

command line < *input file name* > *output file name*

where *command line* is whatever you would normally type to execute the program reading its input from the keyboard and writing its output to the screen. This notation makes the pair < > look like angular parentheses, but do not think of them as such. Think of them as arrowheads redirecting input and output. That makes the notation more suggestive and easier to remember.

APPENDIX 10
CHARACTER SETS

The following charts show the ordering of the characters in the three commonly used character sets. Only printable characters are shown. The blank is indicated by a "□". For example, in the ASCII character set, character number 37 is the percent sign "%".

Left Digit(s)	Right Digit → ASCII									
	0	1	2	3	4	5	6	7	8	9
3			□	!	"	#	$	%	&	'
4	(	)	*	+	,	−	.	/	0	1
5	2	3	4	5	6	7	8	9	:	;
6	<	=	>	?	@	A	B	C	D	E
7	F	G	H	I	J	K	L	M	N	O
8	P	Q	R	S	T	U	V	W	X	Y
9	Z	[	\	]	^	—	`	a	b	c
10	d	e	f	g	h	i	j	k	l	m
11	n	o	p	q	r	s	t	u	v	w
12	x	y	z	{	|	}	~			

Codes 00–31 and 127 are nonprintable control characters.

**Figure A.10.1
The ASCII
character set.**

Left Digit(s)	\	0	1	2	3	4	5	6	7	8	9
	Right Digit					EBCDIC					
6						□					
7						¢	.	<	(	+	|
8		&									
9		!	$	*	)	;	¬	−	/		
10									'	%	—
11		>	?								
12				:	#	@	'	=	"		a
13		b	c	d	e	f	g	h	i		
14							j	k	l	m	n
15		o	p	q	r						
16				s	t	u	v	w	x	y	z
17									\	{	}
18		[	]								
19					A	B	C	D	E	F	G
20		H	I								J
21		K	L	M	N	O	P	Q	R		
22								S	T	U	V
23		W	X	Y	Z						
24		0	1	2	3	4	5	6	7	8	9

Figure A.10.2 The EBCDIC character set.

Codes 00–63 and 250–255 are nonprintable control characters.

Left Digit(s)	\	0	1	2	3	4	5	6	7	8	9
	Right Digit					CDC					
0			:	A	B	C	D	E	F	G	H	I
1			J	K	L	M	N	O	P	Q	R	S
2			T	U	V	W	X	Y	Z	0	1	2
3			3	4	5	6	7	8	9	+	−	*
4			/	(	)	$	=	□	,	.	≡	[
5			]	%	≠	→	∨	∧	↑	↓	<	>
6			≤	≥	¬	;						

Figure A.10.3 The CDC character set.

ANSWERS TO SELF-TEST EXERCISES

Chapter 1

1. Algorithm to add two whole numbers:

begin

1. Write the two numbers down one above the other so that they line up digit by digit with the rightmost digits one above the other; (If the two numbers are not of the same length, then add extra zeros to the front of the shorter number until they are of equal length.)
2. Add the two rightmost digits, obtaining a one- or two-digit number;
3. Write the rightmost of these two digits down as the rightmost digit of the answer and remember the leftmost digit; Call the digit that needs to be remembered by the name Carry; (If the number has only one digit, then the new value of Carry is zero.)
4. Do 4a, 4b and 4c again and again until you run out of digits:
   (If the two numbers are each only one digit long, then you "run out" before you start and so do 4a, 4b and 4c zero times, i.e., not at all.)
   4a. Move to the next pair of digits to the left;
   4b. Add these two digits and the Carry, obtaining a new one- or two-digit number;
   4c. Write the rightmost digit of the number so obtained as the next (reading right to left) digit of the answer and use the leftmost digit of this number as the new (possibly changed) value of Carry; (If the number has only one digit, then the new value of Carry is zero.)
5. If Carry is zero at this point (i.e., at the left end of the two numbers), then you are done;
6. If Carry is not zero, then write down the value of Carry as the leftmost digit of the answer

end.

2. As with virtually all problems, there is more than one algorithm for this problem. One algorithm is:

begin

1. Write the word down on one line;
2. Write it down on the line below, but this time write it backwards; (Align the letters on the two lines.)
3. For each letter in the word:
   compare the letter to the one written just below it;
4. If all letters matched then the word is a palindrome; if at least one mismatch was found, then it is not a palindrome

end.

3. This algorithm assumes that the input word is written on a sheet of paper.

begin

1. Write the letters of the alphabet down on a sheet of paper, one per line;
2. Write zero after each letter;
3. Place your finger on the first letter of the word;
4. Repeat the following until you run out of letters (at the end of the word):
   4a. Read the letter pointed to by your finger;
   4b. Add one to the number written after that letter on the sheet of paper; (The old number is erased or crossed out.)
   4c. Move your finger to the next letter in the word (provided there is one);
5. The number of occurrences of each letter is written on the sheet of paper

end.

Chapter 2

1. 2   2

If your system outputs

22

(i.e., no blanks between the numbers), then on your system you need to explicitly insert a blank between any two consecutive numbers output. One way to do this is the following:

`writeln(X, ' ', Y)`

(The second argument is a blank in single quotes.)

2. The output is the single number:

3

3. BCBC

4. They are all *incorrect* except for the constant 4 (with no decimal point).

5. The following are all *incorrect*. The rest are correctly formed.

`.89    -.89    3,987.85    4.    4`

4, is a correctly formed constant of type `integer`, and so it can be used anyplace that a constant of type `real` can be used; that makes 4 pragmatically as good as correct.

6. The following are all *incorrect*. The rest are correctly formed.

`.57E12    57E3.7    57.9E3.7`

7. `3*X    3*X + Y    (X + Y)/7`
    `(3*X + Y)/(Z + 2)`

8. (a) In a sense it is correct as is. The compiler will accept it and process it properly. However, the style is very poor. The spacing and line breaks are not well designed for readability.
(b) The identifier *var* should only be used once.
(c) The first semicolon should be a comma.
(d) It needs a semicolon at the end.

9. `integer    real    char`
    `real    real    real`

10. Type it up and compile it; the computer will tell you the first mistake as well as a guess of the other mistakes. Correct the first mistake, and compile it again. Continue until you have corrected all the mistakes. (The first mistake is that program name is missing. The second mistake is that the first line needs a semicolon. The third mistake is that the double quotes are used where single quotes should be used. The other mistakes are all missing punctuation marks: a closing single quote, a semicolon and the final period.)

13. 15 *div* 12 is 1   15 *mod* 12 is 3
24 *div* 12 is 2   24 *mod* 12 is 0
123 *div* 100 is 1   123 *mod* 100 is 23
200 *div* 100 is 2   200 *mod* 100 is 0
99 *div* 2 is 49   99 *mod* 2 is 1
2 *div* 3 is 0   2 *mod* is 2

Chapter 3

1. START   −1234END
(There are three spaces between the *T* and the minus sign.)

2. START   −12.34END
(There are two spaces between the *T* and the minus sign.)

6. Second writeln
Fourth writeln

7. false   false
true   true

8. 4;⁰ 3, 6, −6, 7, -7, 6.8,
6.8, 4, 4, 4

9. sqrt(x) <= y + 1
Z > 0   W <> 0   X *mod* 12 = 0

10. −3

Chapter 4

1. Begin Conversation
Goodbye
Hello
One more time:
Hello
Goodbye
End conversation

2. 3   6
6   3

3. One
One Two
One Two Three

4. 1   2
2   2
2   1

5. *procedure* NoNeg(*var* N: integer);
begin{*NoNeg*}
  if N < 0 *then*
    N := 0
end; {*NoNeg*}

6. *procedure* NoCapY(*var* Ans: char);
begin{*NoCapY*}
  if Ans = 'Y' *then*
    Ans := 'y'
end; {*NoCapY*}

7. *Yes*, a *variable* parameter can be used to give information to a procedure. *Yes*, a *value* parameter can be used to give information to a procedure. *Yes*, a *variable* parameter can be used to get information out of a procedure. *No*, a *value* parameter cannot be used to get information out of a procedure.

8. They are all allowed as actual value parameters. Only X is allowed as an actual variable parameter.

9. *Yes*, an actual *variable* parameter can be a variable. *Yes*, an actual *value* parameter can be a variable. *No*, an actual *variable* parameter cannot be a constant. *Yes*, an actual *value* parameter can be a constant.

10. 1   2
2   1

Chapter 5

1. 7
11

2. Hi Folks in procedure
21 outside of procedure

3. 1 2 3
  4 5 6
  4 5 3

4. 1 2 3
  4 5 6
  5 4 3

5. 1 2 3
  5 5 6
  5 2 3

6. 1 2 3
  4 5 6
  4 2 5

Even though there is a local variable named C, the global variable C can be changed *provided it is an actual parameter*. When the procedure is executed there are two distinct variables named C, one global and one local. (If you want a more detailed explanation of how this can be done, you should consult the optional section of Chapter 4, entitled "Implementation of Variable Parameters.")

7. 1 2 3
4 5 6
1 2 3

8. XY
AB
XB

Chapter 6

1. Start
First writeln
Next
Enough

2. false   true
   true   false
        false
        false
        true

3. 2 + 2 = 4
(X + 7 > 100) *or* (X + 7 < 50)
(Z <> 'A') *and* (Z <> 'B') *and* (Z <> 'C')
   –The following is also correct, although a bit harder to read:
   not((Z = 'A') *or* (Z = 'B') *or* (Z = 'C'))
(X *mod* 3) <> 0
   –It is all right to omit the parentheses around X *mod* 3–
(X *mod* 3 <> 0) *or* (Y *mod* 5 = 0)
(X <= Y + 2) *and* (Y + 2 <= Z)

4. (A *or* B) *and not*(A *and* B)
There are other equivalent expressions that would be correct here. For example, the following will also work:

(A *and not* B) *or* (B *and not* A)

5. First writeln
Fourth writeln

6. Program Exercise(input, output);
var N1, N2, N3: integer;
begin{Program}
   writeln('Enter three integers: ');
   readln(N1, N2, N3);
   if (N1 <= N2) *and* (N2 <= N3) *then*
     writeln('In order. ')
   else
     writeln('Not in order. ');
   writeln('End program')
end. {Program}

7. *if* X < 0 *then*
     writeln(X, ' is Negative.')
   else if (0 <= X) *and* (X <= 100)
     then writeln(X, ' is between 0 *and* 100.')
   else { X > 100}
     writeln(X, ' is greater than 100.')

8. The types integer, char, and boolean may be used; the type real may not be used. Use of the type boolean is pointless since an *if-then-else* statement is a preferable way to accomplish the same effect, but the type boolean is legal.

9. *program* ShowCase(input, output);
   var MonthNum: integer;
   begin{*Program*}
     writeln('Enter a month as a number between 1 and 12.');
     writeln('I''ll tell you how many days it has in it.');
     readln(MonthNum);
     case MonthNum *of*
        4, 6, 9, 11: writeln('30 days');
        1, 3, 5, 7, 8, 10, 12: writeln('31 days');
        2: writeln('28 days (29 if leap year)')
     end; {*case*}
     writeln('That''s it !')
   end. {*Program*}

10. *not*(FootLoose) *and not*(FancyFree)
    is equivalent to (always evaluates to the same value) as:
    not(FootLoose *or* FancyFree)
    The other two expressions are equivalent to each other, but not equivalent to the above two.

Chapter 7

1. −2

2. The boolean expression evaluates to false and so the loop body is never executed. The output is thus the number 10.

3. This is an infinite loop. There is no regular output, although most systems will eventually produce an error message after the program consumes too much time or when the program attempts to increase the value of X above maxint.

4. There are two mistakes: (1) The value 1 is never output. (2) The value of X is never exactly 10 and so there is an infinite loop. One way to correct the code is:

   X := 1;
   while X < 10 *do*
     begin{*while*}
       write(X);
       X := X + 2
     end   {*while*}

5. −2

6. The body of a *repeat* loop is always executed at least once; the body of a *while* loop may be executed zero times.

7. *while* <boolean> *do* <statement>
is equivalent to:
if <boolean> *then*
      repeat
         <statement>
      until not (<boolean>)

repeat <body> *until* <boolean>
is equivalent to:
begin
   <body>
end ;
while not (<boolean>) *do*
   begin
      <body>
   end

8. *program* EchoLetter(input, output);
   var Symbol: char;
   begin{*Program*}
      writeln('Enter a line of text.');
      writeln('End by pressing the return key.');
      while not eoln *do*
         read(Symbol);
      writeln('The last symbol you typed in is ', Symbol)
   end. {*Program*}

Alternatively, the *while* loop may be replaced by the following:

repeat
   read(Symbol)
until eoln

9. −6 −4 −2 0 2 4 6 8 10 12 14 16 18 20 22

10. 10 9 8 7 6 5 4 3 2 1

11. *program* Even(input, output);
   var I: integer;
   begin{*Program*}
      for I := 1 *to* 12 *do*
         write(2 * I);
      writeln;
      writeln('That''s all folks!')
   end. {*Program*}

12. 1 3
    2 2
    3 2

13. The output is too long to reproduce here. The pattern is indicated below:

```
1 times 10 equals 10
2 times 10 equals 20
   .
   .
   .
10 times 10 equals 100
1 times 9 equals 9
2 times 9 equals 18
   .
   .
   .
10 times 9 equals 90
1 times 8 equals 8
   .
   .
   .
```

14. a. A *for* loop.
b. and c. Both require a *while* loop since the input lists might be empty.
d. A *repeat* loop can be used since some nonzero number of tests will be performed.

Chapter 8

1. ABX

2. The function name, TwoPower, is not a variable but is being used as a variable. The following is not allowed:

```
TwoPower := TwoPower*2
```

3. *function* Area(Length, Width: real): real;
   {*Returns the area of a rectangle of the given dimensions.*}
   begin{*Area*}
      Area := Length * Width
   end; {*Area*}

4. *function* Pos(I: integer): char;
   begin{*Pos*}
      if I > 0 *then*
         Pos := 'P'
      else
         Pos := 'N'
   end; {*Pos*}

5. a. A function.
b. Since it computes two values, a procedure with one value and two variable parameters should be used. (Two functions could be used, but since the two computations are so interrelated they do not separate neatly into two subtasks, a procedure is preferable.)
c. A procedure.
d. Since it computes two values, it makes sense to use a procedure with two variable parameters (in addition to two value parameters). Alternatively, two functions could be used: one to compute net income from gross income and adjustments and another to compute the tax from the net income.
e. A function.

6. Hi
Good-Bye

7. *function* Divides(A, B: integer): boolean;
{Returns true if A evenly divides B; otherwise, returns false.
Precondition: A is not zero.}
begin{Divides}
   Divides := (B *mod* A = 0)
end; *{Divides}*

The following also works, but is poor style:

function Divides(A, B: integer): boolean;
{Returns true if A evenly divides B; otherwise, returns false.}
begin{Divides}
   if (B *mod* A = 0) *then*
      Divides := true
   else
      Divides := false
end; *{Divides}*

8. *function* InOrder(A1, A2, A3: integer): boolean;
{Returns true if A1 <= A2 <= A3; otherwise returns false.}
begin{InOrder}
   InOrder := (A1 <= A2) *and* (A2 <= A3)
end; *{InOrder}*

9. *function* Ran2to20(var Memory: integer): integer;
{Returns a pseudorandom even number between 2
and 20, inclusive. Uses the function Random in Figure 8.9.}
var OneToTen: integer;
begin{Ran2to20}
   OneToTen := (Random(Memory) *mod* 10) + 1;
   {OneToTen is a pseudorandom number between 1 and 10.}
   Ran2to20 := 2 * OneToTen
end; *{Ran2to20}*

10. SmallNegNumber is illegal because −1 is greater than −100. GradePoint is illegal because you can not have a subrange of the type real. SmallRange is illegal because it contains an expression (other than a constant) in its definition. All the other type definitions are legal.

11. *type* Score = 0 . . 100;
         NonNegInteger = 0 . . maxint;
         Abs100 = −100 . . 100;

12. No. There are no provisions in Pascal to either read in a value of an enumerated type or to write one out. A user defined procedure could be written to do something similar by reading or writing a string which names the value.

Chapter 9

1. TempCount and GradeTally are illegal because the type real is not an ordinal type and because it can not have subrange types. All the others are legal.

2. *type* Score = 0 . . 10;
     ScoreList = *array*[1 . . 100] *of* Score;
     RealList = *array*['a' . . 'z'] *of* real;
     LastType = *array*[-5 . . 19] *of* char;

There are other ways of stating the definitions, for example, the following is also acceptable:

type Score = 0 . . 10;
     Index = 1 . . 100;
     ScoreList = *array*[Index] *of* Score;
     Alphabet = 'a' . . 'z';
     RealList = *array*[Alphabet] *of* real;
     LastType = *array*[-5 . . 19] *of* char;

3. a. *type* Score = 0 . . 10;
        Index = 1 . . 100;
        ExtendedIndex = 0 . . 100;
        ScoreList = *array*[Index] *of* Score;

   var A: ScoreList; {*holds the scores.*}
        Last: ExtendedIndex; {*Tells how many are in the array.*
        If the array is empty it is set equal to 0.}
   b. *type* TallyList = *array*['A' . . 'Z'] *of* 0 . . maxint;
      var Count: TallyList;

For example, Count['M'] will hold the number of students whose last name starts with 'M'. There are other variations that are correct. For example, it would be acceptable to use integer as the component type of the array.

   c. *type* Checkoff = *array*[1 . . 100] *of* boolean;
      var Passed: Checkoff;

For example, if Passed[7] is true, then student number seven can graduate.

4. As written it sums the numbers between A[1] and A[100]. If the value of A[1] is 1 and the value of A[100] is 2, then the final value of Sum will be 1 + 2 or 3. The correct code is:

Sum := 0;
for I := 1 *to* 100 *do*
   Sum := Sum + A[I]

The variable I should be of type integer or better still type 1 . . 100.

5. *for* I := 0 *to* 100 *do*
      C[I] := 0.0

(It is permissible to use 0 in place of 0.0.)

6. C := 0 is not legal (nor is C := 0.0.) You must set the value of each array element separately.

7. The loop ends with the value of I equal to Last. At that point I + 1 evaluates to Last + 1, and so A[I + 1] has an illegal index. To fix it, change the final expression of the *for* loop to Last - 1.

8. *for* I := 1 *to* 6 *do*
      read(A[I]);
   for I := 6 *downto* 1 *do*
      write(A[I]);
   writeln

9.
```
Last := 0;
read(Next);
while (Next > 0) and (Last < 10) do
    begin
      Last := Last + 1;
      A[Last] := Next;
      read(Next)
    end;
if Next > 0 then
    writeln('Warning: some numbers are not in the array.');
for I := 1 to Last do
    write(A[I]);
writeln
```

10.
```
const FirstNum = 661;
      LastNum = 753;
type Grade = 1 . . 10;
     Distribution = array[Grade] of integer; {part a.}
     Age = 5 . . 13;
     Count = array[Age] of integer; {part b.}
     CheckAmount =
            array[FirstNum . . LastNum] of real; {part c.}
```
(There is more than one right answer to this question.)

11.
```
type WeekDay = (Mon, Tue, Wed, Thur, Fri, Sat, Sun);
     WorkDay = Mon . . Fri;
     WorkHours = array[WorkDay] of integer;
     PlayHour = array[WeekDay] of integer;
```

12. A := B

13. To start with the *if-then-else* statement is poor style. The preferable way to write it is:

```
Found := (N = A[I])
```

However, the real problem is that it often returns the wrong value. Try it with Last equal to 5 and with array elements:
2, 4, 6, 8, 10,
and with N set equal to 8. The code will decide to return true when it tests A[4] and finds its value is 8, but when it sees A[5] it changes its mind and incorrectly returns false as the final value. The code in Figure 9.10 shows the correct way to accomplish the task.

14.
```
procedure Reverse(var A: Label);
var B: Label;
begin{Reverse}
   for I := 0 to 100 do
      B[I] := A[100 - I];
   A := B
end; {Reverse}
```

(It is possible to do this without the local variable B, but that is significantly harder to do.)

15. Replace the function Imin by a function Imax that computes the index of the largest element instead of the index of the smallest element.

```
function Imax(var A: List; Start: Index; Last: Index): Index;
{Returns the index I such that A[I] is the largest of the values: A[Start], A[Start + 1], . . . . A[Last].}
var Max, I: integer;
begin{Imax}
  Imax := Start; {tentatively}
  Max := A[Start]; {maximum so far}
  for I := Start + 1 to Last do
    if A[I] > Max then
      begin{then}
        Max := A[I];
        Imax := I
        {Max is the largest of the values A[Start], . . . , A[I];
        the tentative value of Imax is x such that A[x] = Max}
      end {then}
end; {Imax}
```

16. Change the array type and type of the parameters of Exchange, and the type of the local variable Min in Imin, all to real.

```
type . . .
       List = array[Index] of real;
procedure Exchange(var X, Y: real);
var Temp: real;
function Imin(var A: List; Start, Last: Index): Index;
var Min: real;
       I: integer;
           . . .
```

17. The same type changes as in Exercise 16, but use the type char rather than the type real.

Chapter 10

1. The array is not a legal argument for a writeln statement so the only output should be an error message. (Some systems do allow this and would output the string a b b b b.)

2. The code for the procedure StringWrite is the same as that for the procedure String-Writeln except that the writeln is omitted.

3. ```
   const Last = 17;
           MaxLength = 20;
   type CharString = array[1 . . MaxLength] of char;
           Index = 1 . . Last;
           NameList = array[Index] of CharString;
           BirthList = array[Index] of integer;
           VaccinationList = array[Index] of boolean;
   ```

4. Change the value of MaxLength to 40.

5. The first three are allowed. Some systems will and some systems will not allow the read statement. The last statement is an error because the string 'Hi! ' is less than five characters long.

6. a. ```
      for I := 1 to 20 do
         writeln(S[I, 1])
      ```

b. *for* I := 1 *to* 50 *do*
    write(S[20, I])

c. *for* I := 1 *to* 20 *do*
    begin{*line I*}
      for J := 1 *to* 50 *do*
        write(S[I, J]);
      writeln
    end {*line I*}

Chapter 11

1. 5   A
  6   A

2. *type* Sam =
    record
      Field1: integer;
      Field2: real;
      Field3: char
    end;

3. *program* Exercise3(input, output);
  const Space = ' ';
  type Sam =
    record
      Field1: integer;
      Field2: real;
      Field3: char
    end;
  var X: Sam;
  begin{*Program*}
    writeln('Enter an integer: ');
    readln(X.Field1);
    writeln('Enter a real: ');
    readln(X.Field2);
    writeln('Enter a symbol: ');
    readln(X.Field3);
    writeln('The record contains: ');
    writeln(X.Field1, Space, X.Field2, Space, X.Field3)
  end. {*Program*}

4. *type* Student =
    record
      Name: *array*[1 .. 20] *of* char;
      QuizScores: *array*[1 .. 10] *of* 0 .. 10;
      MidTerm, FinalExam, FinalScore: 0 .. 100;
      Grade: 'A' .. 'F'
    end;

5. B[3]
  B[3].Price
  B[10].Name.Symbols[6]
  B[2].Name.Length

6. Parallel arrays:

```
type StockNum = 0 . . Max;
     StyleNum = 0 . . 50;
     SizeRange = 3 . . 14;
     Style = array[StockNum] of StyleNum;
     Count = array[StockNum, SizeRange] of integer;
     Price = array[StockNum] of real;
```

Array of records:

```
type StockNum = 0 . . Max;
     StyleNum = 0 . . 50;
     SizeRange = 3 . . 14;
     Shoe = record
               Style: StyleNum;
               Count: array[SizeRange] of integer;
               Price: real
            end;
     InStock = array[StockNum] of Shoe;
```

Max is some defined constants.

7. [1, 3, 7, 8, 9], [7, 8, 9], [8], [ ], [7], true, false, true, true, false, true

Chapter 12

1. The problem is a "boundary" problem. When I is equal to 100, the loop terminates without adding in the 100. The easiest way to fix it is to change the end of the repeat loop to:

```
until I > 100
```

2. The values of A and B, and C do not matter, but you need a collection of different values for X. You need one value of X that is greater than or equal to 5 and one that is less than 5. You also need one value greater than zero and one less than or equal to zero. For example, the following two values of X will do: 5, 0. Since some numbers satisfy more than two of the required cases, you do not need four test values. You should use other test values as well, but that is enough to fully exercise the code.

3. There are four paths, but one is impossible. One of many possible sets of values for X is: 5, 4, 0. The values of A and B, and C do not matter for testing all paths.

4. The program uses more storage than is needed for a clear program. There is no need to use an array. All that is needed is a single variable as shown below:

```
Sum := 0;
for I := 1 to 10 do
   begin
      read(Next);
      Sum := Sum + Next
   end;
Average := Sum/10
```

The variable Next is of type integer. It is also a good idea to declare 10 as a named constant.

Chapter 13

1. 5 63
  5 6

(Remember: the blank is a character.)

5. Four score and seven years ago,
  o
  t
  The End.

6. ab
  ghijkHi

7. *program* WriteTen(input, output, NewFile);
  var NewFile: text;
      I: integer;
  begin{Program}
    rewrite(NewFile);
    writeln('Writing to NewFile');
    for I := 1 *to* 10 *do*
      writeln(NewFile, I);
    writeln('Done writing to NewFile')
  end. *{Program}*

8. *program* ReadTen(input, output, NewFile);
  var NewFile: text;
      Number, Sum: integer;
  begin{Program}
    reset(NewFile);
    Sum := 0;
    while not eof(NewFile) *do*
      begin{while}
        readln(NewFile, Number);
        Sum := Sum + Number
      end; *{while}*
    writeln('The sum of the numbers');
    writeln('in NewFile is ', Sum)
  end. *{Program}*

Chapter 14

1. 6

2. This is an example of infinite recursion. There will be no legitimate output. However, the error message *stack overflow* is likely.

3. 24
The function is the factorial function, usually written *n!* and defined as $n! = n*(n-1) * (n-2)* \ldots *1$.

4. 3
(The function returns the value $\log_2(N)$, i.e., the logarithm to the base 2 of the number N, but you need not know that to see that the value returned is 3.).

5. `Hip Hip Hurray`

6. *function* Mystery(N: integer): integer;
    {Precondition: N >= 1}
    var Sum, I: integer;
    begin{Mystery}
        Sum := 0;
        for I := 1 *to* N *do*
            Sum := Sum + I;
        Mystery := Sum
    end; *{Mystery}*

7. *function* Rose(N: integer): integer;
    {Precondition: N >= 0}
    var Product, I: integer;
    begin{Rose}
        Product := 1;
        for I := 1 *to* N *do*
            Product := Product * I;
        Rose := Product
    end; *{Rose}*

8. *procedure* RecStar(N: integer);
    const Star = '*';
    {Writes N ''s to the screen. Precondition: N > 0.}*
    begin{RecStar}
        writeln(Star);
        if N > 1 *then*
                RecStar(N − 1)
    end; *{RecStar}*

You should also type up and run your procedure for this exercise.

Chapter 15

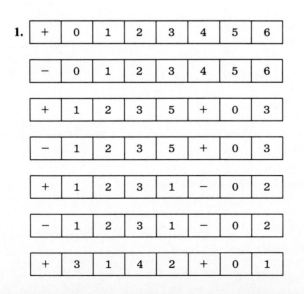

1.	+	0	1	2	3	4	5	6
	−	0	1	2	3	4	5	6
	+	1	2	3	5	+	0	3
	−	1	2	3	5	+	0	3
	+	1	2	3	1	−	0	2
	−	1	2	3	1	−	0	2
	+	3	1	4	2	+	0	1

2. In each case, the largest value of type `real` is: $+0.999E+999$, $+0.99E+9999$, $+0.99999E+9$

3. 7, 5, 4, 27, 22, 0.5, 0.25, 0.125, 0.625, 1.125, 5.625

4. Thirty-two bit machine:

$2^{31} - 1 = 0.2147836 \times 10^{10}$ *(approx.)*

Sixty-four bit machine:

$2^{63} - 1 = 0.9223372 \times 10^{19}$ *(approx.)*

5. 0.3000×10^3
$\underline{+0.00012345678 \times 10^3}$

$0.30012345678 \times 10^3$

After rounding it is stored as 0.3001×10^3. Hence, the output is:

$0.3001E+03$

6. X*Y*Z has value

```
(1.0E-90 * 1.0E-25) * 1.0E+25 =
(1.0E-115) * 1.0E+25
```

but the first number produces floating point underflow and so is rounded to zero (on our hypothetical computer). Hence, the final value is 0.0 * 1.0E+25 which is equal to 0.0. On the other hand, X*Z*Y has value

```
(1.0E-90 * 1.0E+25) * 1.0E-25 =
(1.0E-65) * 1.0E-25 = 1.0E-90 =
0.1000E-91
```

Thus, the output is:

```
0.0    0.1000E-91
```

(As this shows, rounding to zero can occasionally produce surprising results.)

Chapter 16

1.
```
const MaxLength = 20;
type Student =
        record
          Name: array[1 . . MaxLength] of char;
          Final: 0 . . 100;
          Grade: 'A' . . 'F'
        end;
      GradeBook = file of Student;
```

2.
```
program Writer(input, output, NumFile);
var NumFile: file of integer;
    I: integer;
begin
  rewrite(NumFile);
  for I := 1 to 10 do
    write(NumFile, I);
  writeln('End of Program')
end.
```

3. ```pascal
program Reader(input, output, NumFile);
var NumFile: file of integer;
    I: integer;
begin
  reset(NumFile);
  while not eof(NumFile) do
    begin
      read(NumFile, I);
      writeln(I)
    end;
  writeln('End of Program')
end.
```

4. ```pascal
program Searcher(input, output, NumFile);
var NumFile: file of integer;
    I, Key: integer;
    Found: boolean;
begin
  writeln('Enter integer to be searched for');
  readln(Key);
  reset(NumFile);
  Found := false;
  while (not eof(NumFile)) and (not Found) do
    begin
      read(NumFile, I);
      if I = Key then
          Found := true
    end;
  if Found then
    writeln(Key, ' Found in file.')
  else
    writeln(Key, ' Not found in file.')
end.
```

5. ```pascal
function Search(var F: PayRecords; N: integer): boolean;
{Returns true if PayRecords contains a record
with Number field equal to N; returns false otherwise.}
var Found: boolean;
    OneRecord: Employee;
begin{Search}
  reset(F);
  Found := false;
  while (not eof(F)) and (not Found) do
    begin{while}
      read(F, OneRecord);
      if OneRecord.Number = N then
          Found := true
    end; {while}
  Search := Found
end; {Search}
```
```

An alternative version using put and get (Optional) is given below:

```
function Search(var F: PayRecords; N: integer): boolean;
{Returns true if PayRecords contains a record
with Number field equal to N; returns false otherwise.}
var Found: boolean;
begin{Search}
  reset(F);
  Found := false;
  while (not eof(F)) and (not Found) do
    begin{while}
      if F↑.Number = N then
          Found := true;
      get(F)
    end;  {while}
  Search := Found
end;  {Search}
```

Chapter 17

1. 10 20
   20 20
   30 30
   40 40

2. 10 20
   20 20
   30 20
   30 40

3. It would not change at all.

4.

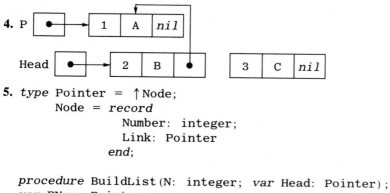

5. *type* Pointer = ↑Node;
         Node = *record*
                    Number: integer;
                    Link: Pointer
                end;

   procedure BuildList(N: integer; *var* Head: Pointer);
   var PNew: Pointer;
        I: integer;

```
begin{BuildList}
   Head := nil;
   for I := N downto 1 do
      begin{Insert I}
         new (PNew);
         PNew↑.Number := I;
         PNew↑.Link := Head;
         Head := PNew
      end   {Insert I}
end;  {BuildList}
```

6. ```
procedure ShowList(Head: Pointer);
var Next: Pointer;
begin{ShowList}
   Next := Head;
   while Next <> nil do
      begin{Process one node}
         writeln(Next↑.Number);
         Next := Next↑.Link
      end   {Process one node}
end; {ShowList}
```

7. Replace the lines

   ```
   Before↑.Link := PNew;
   PNew↑.Link := After
   ```

   with the lines:

   ```
   PNew↑.Link := Before↑.Link;
   Before↑.Link := PNew
   ```

   Notice that the order of the last two assignment statements is now critically important. Also notice that if Before is pointing to the last node in the list, then, with this change, the procedure correctly inserts a node at the end of the list.

8. There is no difference in the general form of the nodes. The difference is in the way they are used.

9. ```
type Pointer = ↑TreeNode;
        TreeNode = record
                      Data: integer;
                      Left, Right, Parent: Pointer
                   end;
```

Photo Credits

P. 6   Texas Instruments

P. 7   All photos: IBM Corporation

P. 42   Left: IBM Corporation. Right: Smithsonian Institution

P. 101   Trustees of the Science Museum, London.

P. 455   Left: Culver Pictures. Right: IBM Corporation. Bottom: IBM Corporation

INDEX

Reserved Words

and
array
begin
case
const
div
do
downto
else
end
file
for
forward
function
goto
if
in
label
mod
nil
not
of
or
packed
procedure
program
record
repeat
set
then
to
type
until
var
while
with

Precedence of Operators

Unless determined by parentheses,
operators are evaluated as follows:
First: *not*
Second: * / *div mod and*
Third: + − *or*
Fourth: <= = >= > < <> *in*
Operators in the same group are evaluated in their
left to right order in the expression.

Ordinal Types

integer, char, boolean,
any enumerated type, any subrange type.

Types that May Be Used for the Value Returned by a Function

All the ordinal types.
The type real.
Any pointer type.
No other types may be used.

Standard Identifiers

abs	ln	reset
arctan	maxint	rewrite
boolean	new	round
char	odd	sin
chr	ord	sqr
cos	output	sqrt
eof	pack	succ
eoln	page	text
exp	pred	true
false	put	trunc
get	read	unpack
input	readln	write
integer	real	writeln